Julius Caesar, William Duncan

Commentaries on the Discourse Concerning the Roman Art of War

and Life of Caius Julius Caesar

Julius Caesar, William Duncan

Commentaries on the Discourse Concerning the Roman Art of War and Life of Caius Julius Caesar

ISBN/EAN: 9783744774352

Printed in Europe, USA, Canada, Australia, Japan

Cover: Foto ©Thomas Meinert / pixelio.de

More available books at **www.hansebooks.com**

JULIUS CÆSAR.

Engraved by Welch from the

THE

COMMENTARIES OF CÆSAR,

TRANSLATED INTO ENGLISH:

TO WHICH IS PREFIXED,

A DISCOURSE CONCERNING THE ROMAN ART OF WAR,

BY WILLIAM DUNCAN,

PROFESSOR OF PHILOSOPHY IN THE UNIVERSITY OF ABERDEEN.

WITH A

LIFE OF CAIUS JULIUS CÆSAR,

BY

LEONARD SCHMITZ, LL.D., F.R.S.E.,

PRINCIPAL OF THE HIGH SCHOOL OF EDINBURGH, AUTHOR OF HISTORY OF GREECE, HISTORY OF ROME, ETC.

NEW YORK:

H. W. DERBY, 625 BROADWAY.

1861.

LIFE OF CAIUS JULIUS CÆSAR.

CAIUS JULIUS CÆSAR, the son of C. Julius Cæsar and Aurelia, was born B. C. 100, on the twelfth of Quintilis, afterward called Julius in honour of this Cæsar. His aunt Julia was the wife of Caius Marius. In his seventeenth year he married Cornelia, the daughter of Cinna, by whom he had a daughter, Julia. This connection with Marius and Cinna, the two great opponents of the dictator Sulla, exposed him to the resentment of the opposite faction. Sulla is said to have spared his life with great reluctance. He first served under M. Thermus in Asia, and distinguished himself at the capture of Mityléne (B. C. 80 or 79). In the following year he served under P. Servilius Isauricus in Cilicia. The news of Sulla's death brought him back to Rome, B. C. 78. After his unsuccessful impeachment of Dolabella for maladministration in his province, he retired to Rhodes, and for a time became the pupil of the rhetorician Molo, whose instruction Cicero had attended, probably a year or two before Cæsar's visit, B. C. 75.

About B. C. 69, being elected one of the military tribunes, he procured an enactment for the restoration of L. Cinna, his wife's brother, and of those partisans of M. Lepidus who after his death had joined Sertorius in Spain. The following year he was quæstor in Spain, and on his return to Rome, he was elected curule ædile for B. C. 65. The office of ædile gave Cæsar an opportunity of indulging his taste for magnificence and display, by which he secured the favour of the people. Cæsar, who was now five-and-thirty years of age, had enjoyed no opportunity of distinguishing himself in a military capacity; while Cn. Pompeius, who was only six years older, was spreading his name and the terror of the Roman arms throughout the East. By a judicious application of money among the poorer voters, and of personal influence among all classes, he obtained the Pontificatus Maximus (B. C. 63), or headship of the college of Pontifices, a place to which an official residence in the Sacra Via was attached. This union of civil and religious functions in the same person, at least in the higher and more profitable places, was part of the old Roman polity.

At the time of the debate on the conspiracy of Catiline (B. C. 63), Cæsar was prætor designatus (prætor elect for the following year), and accordingly spoke in his place in the senate. He was the only person who ventured to oppose the proposition for putting the conspirators to death: he recommended their property to be confiscated, and that they should be dispersed through the different municipia of Italy, and kept under a strict surveillance.

An affair which happened during his prætorship (B. C. 62) caused no little scandal at Rome. While the ceremonies in honour of the Bona Dea were performing in the house of Cæsar, at which women only could be present, the profligate P. Clodius, putting on a woman's dress, contrived to get admission to these mysterious rites. On the affair being discovered, Cæsar divorced his wife Pompeia, whom he had married after the death of Cornelia; and Clodius, after being brought to a public trial for an offence against religion, only escaped by bribing the jury. From motives of policy, Cæsar did not break with Clodius: he probably saw that he could make him a useful tool against Cicero.

The year 61 B. C. was spent by Cæsar in his province of Southern Spain, where he speedily restored order, and he hurried back to Rome before his successor came to canvass for the consulship. The aristocratical party saw that it was impossible to prevent **Cæsar's election**; their only chance was to give him a colleague who should be a **check upon him. Their** choice of Bibulus was singularly unfortunate. Bibulus, after unavailing **efforts to resist** the impetuosity of his colleague, shut himself up in his house, and Cæsar acted **as sole** consul, B. C. 59. He had contrived to render ineffectual all opposition on the part of his opponents. Pompeius was dissatisfied because the senate delayed about confirming all his measures in the Mithridatic war and during his command in Asia: Crassus, who was the richest man in the state, and second only to Pompey in influence with the senatorial faction, was not on good terms with Pompeius. If Cæsar gained over only one of these rivals, he made the other his enemy; he determined, therefore, to secure them both. He began by courting Pompeius, and succeeded in bringing about a reconciliation between him and Crassus. It was agreed **that** there should be a general understanding among the three as to the course of policy. To cement their alliance more closely, Cæsar gave Pompeius his daughter Julia in marriage. He himself also took a new wife on the occasion, Calpurnia, the daughter of L. Piso, whom he nominated one of the consuls for the ensuing year, B. C. 58. This union of Pompeius, Crassus, and Cæsar, destroyed the credit of Pompeius, threw disunion among the aristocrats, and put the whole power of the state into the hands of one vigorous and clear-sighted man.

One of the most important measures of Cæsar's consulship was an agrarian law for the division of some public lands in Campania among the poorer citizens, which was carried by intimidation. Clodius, the enemy of Cicero, was, through Cæsar's influence **and** the help of Pompeius, adopted into a plebeian family, and thus made capable of holding the office of tribune. Clodius, the next year, was elected a tribune, and drove Cicero into exile, B. C. 58.

The Roman consuls, on going out of office, received the government of a province for one year. Cæsar's opponents unwisely made another effort against him; they proposed to give him the superintendence of the roads and forests. Vatinius, one of his creatures, forthwith procured a law to be passed, by which he obtained for Cæsar the province of Gallia Cisalpina, or North Italy, and Illyricum, for five years; and the senate, fearing the people might grant still more, not only confirmed the measure, but added the province of Gallia Transalpina. "From this moment," remarks Schlosser " the history of Rome presents a striking parallel to the condition of the French repub**lic** during Bonaparte's first campaigns in Italy. In both cases we see a weak republican administration in the capital involved in continual broils, which the rival factions **are** more interested in fostering than **in** securing the tranquillity and peace of the **empire.** In both cases we find **a** province of the distracted republic occupied by a general **with** unlimited power—the uncontrolled master of a territory which, in extent and importance, is equal to a mighty kingdom—a man of superior understanding, desperate **resolves,** and, if circumstances rendered it necessary, of fearful cruelty—a man who, under the show of democratical opinions, behaved like a despot, governed a province at his pleasure, and established an absolute control over his soldiers by leading them to victory, bloodshed, and pillage."

The Gallic provinces at this **time subject to Rome, were Gallia Citerior,** or Cisalpine Gaul ; and Gallia Ulterior, or the southern part of Transalpine Gaul, also called emphatically Provincia, whose capital was Narbo, now Narbonne. The Provincia extended from the Mediterranean to the Cebenna mountains, and included the modern provinces of East Languedoc, Provence, and Dauphiné. On the north it joined the Allobroges, then lately subjected to Rome. When Cæsar, in his Commentaries, speaks of Gaul, which he divides into Aquitania, Celtica, and Belgica, he means the Gaul which was then independent, and which he conquered, exclusive of the Provincia already subject to Rome. Cæsar's campaigns in Gaul, which are the most eventful periods of his life, belong to the history of Rome. They comprise the time from the beginning of B. C. 58 to B. C. 51. During this period he stopped the Helvetii, who were emigrating from their native country, a part of modern Switzerland, with the intention of settling in the southern part of Gaul. He totally defeated Ariovistus, a powerful German chief, with immense slaughter. Some of the fugitives escaped across the Rhine in boats, and Ariovistus among them. The two sons of Ariovistus and one daughter were killed in the flight, and another daughter was taken prisoner.

The campaign of 57 B. C. was against the Belgic Gauls, a powerful race of German origin, who had been long settled in the country between the Rhine and the Séquana (Seine). The war was conducted with his usual vigour and success, though the resistance of some of the Belgic tribes, especialy the Nervii, was most desperate. In this campaign, Cæsar advanced north of the Axona, a branch of the Seine. Crassus, the son of Crassus with whom Cæsar had made a coalition, being detached by Cæsar across the Sequana into Western Gaul, received the submission of the Aulerci, Unelli, and Veneti, and other maritime people on the coasts of the Atlantic ; and, as the season was growing late, the army went into winter-quarters in the country of the Carnutes, Turones, and other parts of Central Gaul. Cæsar set off, according to his custom, for Cisalpine Gaul, where his friends flocked from Rome to congratulate him on his successes. The senate, on receiving from the victorious general the usual official letters, ordered fifteen days of public thanksgiving to the gods, a period never granted before for any other general.

His third campaign, 56 B. C., was against the Western Gauls, of whom the Veneti were a powerful commercial, seafaring people, who had numerous ships in which they traded with Britain and other countries. Having recovered from the alarm of Cæsar's conquests, they arrested the officers of Crassus, and refused to give them up until their own hostages were restored. All the neighbouring maritime tribes made common cause with the Veneti. Cæsar immediately ordered galleys to be constructed on the Ligeris, and sent also to collect ships on the coast of the Pictones and Sántones, who were friends with Rome. He directed the fleet to attack the Veneti by sea, while he marched against them by land. A great naval battle, which lasted all day, ended with the destruction of the fleet of the Veneti, to the number of above two hundred ships. Cæsar put to death all the senators or chief men of the Veneti, and sold the rest as slaves. After the defeat of the Veneti, he marched against the Morini and Menapii, and placed his troops for the winter among the Aulerci, Lexovii, &c.

The following year, 55 B. C., the campaign was carried on against the Germans upon the Mosa and the Rhine, and they were defeated with great slaughter, probably near Coblenz, at the junction of the Moselle and the Rhine. After this battle, Cæsar constructed a bridge over the Rhine in ten days, when he marched across and ravaged the country of the Sicambri. He recrossed the Rhine after spending eighteen days on German ground.

He next made his first expedition into Britain. In this year Cæsar's period of government was extended for five years by a senatus consultum.

The next year, 54 B. C., after making an excursion into Illyricum, he returned into Gaul, where he had ordered a fleet to assemble at Portius Itius for a second attempt upon Britain. On his return from Britain, owing to the bad harvest and scarcity of provisions, he dispersed his legions in various parts of the country for the winter, a measure which proved nearly fatal to the Roman arms. He himself remained in Belgic Gaul. The Eburones revolted and attacked the camp of Titurius Sabinus and L. Cotta, who had one legion and five cohorts with them. The Romans, against Cotta's opinion, made an effort to retire to the next Roman garrison, but they were attacked on their march and cut to pieces. The Eburones, under their king Ambiorix, next attacked the camp of Quintus Cicero, brother to the orator, who was stationed with one legion in the country of the Nervii. Quintus made a brave defence, and was finally relieved by Cæsar. The following year, 53 B. C., which was the sixth of his government, symptoms of general disaffection manifested themselves throughout Gaul. This was a year of desultory though destructive warfare. Cæsar crossed the Rhine again from the country of the Tréviri. This movement led to no result, and he withdrew his army. He then ravaged the country of the Eburones, and having put his legions to winter among the Treviri, Lingones, and Senones, repaired to Cisalpine Gaul. The disturbances at Rome, in consequence of the murder of P. Clodius, made him turn his attention toward that quarter. He raised troops in every part of the Cisalpine province. The Gauls now thought the time was come for one great effort while Cæsar was engaged in Italy. The Cárnutes massacred all the Romans whom they found in the town of Genabum. Vercingetorix, a young man of one of the first families of the Arverni, was placed at the head of a confederacy of the whole of Celtic Gaul. Cæsar, hearing the news, set off in the middle of winter for Gaul north of the Alps, and took Vellaunodunum, Genabum, and Noviodunum. He also took Avaricum, garrisoned by the Gauls, who made a courageous defence. But the great event of this campaign was the siege of Alesia, now a village called Saint Reine, and also Alise, near Flavigny, and Semur, in North Burgundy. For this celebrated siege we must refer to Cæsar's own account. Cæsar found himself besieged in his own lines, having to fight Vercingetorix who had retired within the town, and the confederates from without. Alesia finally surrendered, and Vercingetorix, several years later, walked before the triumphal car of the conqueror; after which he was put to death in prison. Cæsar's eighth and last campaign in Gaul (51 B. C.) is related by Hirtius, who has continued his 'Commentaries' by writing an eighth or supplementary book. During the winter, which followed this campaign, he endeavoured to conciliate the principal inhabitants of Gaul by rewards, and treated the people with kindness; and, by rendering the Roman yoke light, he pacified Gaul, exhausted by its long and unfortunate struggle. In the spring 50 B. C., he set off for North Italy, where he was received with great rejoicings. On his return to Belgic Gaul, he reviewed his troops, and soon after returned to the north of Italy, where the dissensions between him and the senate had begun which led to the civil war. This was the ninth and last year of Cæsar's government of the Gauls.

Cæsar's connection with Pompeius had dissolved by the death of Julia without any surviving offspring, and by the growing jealousy with which his success in Gaul and his popularity with his army had filled all the aristocratical party. His object now was to obtain the consulship a second time, and a special enactment had been already passed enabling him to stand for the consulship in his absence. But Pompeius prevailed upon the senate to require him to give up the command of the army and come to Rome in person to be a candidate. Cæsar, who was at Ravenna, in his province of Gallia Cisalpina, sent Curio to Rome with a letter expressed in strong terms, in which he proposed to give up his army and come to the city, if Pompeius would also give up the command of the troops which he had. The senate made a decree that Cæsar should give up his army by a certain day, or be considered an enemy to the state. The tribunes, M. Antonius and Q. Cassius, the friends of Cæsar, attempted to oppose the measure; but their opposition was treated with contempt, and thus they gained a good excuse for hurrying to Cæsar with the news. Upon receiving the intelligence, Cæsar crossed the Rubicon, a small stream which formed the southern limit of his province, and directed his march toward the south, B. C. 49. Rome was filled with confusion; councils were divided and hesitating; and Pompeius, who was the commander-in-chief on the side of the senate, was unprovided with troops to oppose the veterans of the Gallic wars. Domitius, who had thrown himself into Corfinium to defend the place, was given up to Cæsar by his soldiers, who joined the invading army. The alarm now became still greater, and Pompeius, with a large part of the senate and his forces, hurried to Brundisium, whence he succeeded in crossing the sea to Dyrrachium in Epirus. Cæsar, who had reached Brundisium before Pompeius left it, advanced to Rome, and took possession of the public money, which the other party in their hurry had left behind. His next movement was into Spain, where Afranius and Petreius, who were on the side of Pompeius, were at the head of eight legions. After reducing this important province, Cæsar on his return took the town of Massilia, the siege of which had been commenced on his march to Spain.

The title of "dictator" was assumed on his return to Rome, and he nominated himself and Servilius consuls for the following year, B. C. 48. The campaign of this year, which is described in the third book of the "Civil Wars," comprises the operations of Cæsar and Pompeius at Dyrrachium, and the subsequent defeat of Pompeius on the plain of Pharsálus, in Thessaly. After his defeat, Pompeius fled to Egypt, and on his landing, was treacherously murdered by Achillas, the commander of the troops of the young king Ptolemæus, and L. Septimius, a Roman, who had served under Pompeius in the war with the pirates.

Cæsar arrived in Egypt shortly after the death of Pompeius. The disputes in the royal family of Egypt and the interference of Cæsar brought on a contest between the Romans and the king's troops, which ended in a new settlement of the kingdom by the Roman general. Here he formed his intimacy with Cleopatra, the young queen of Egypt. Early in the year B. C. 47, he marched into Pontus, and defeated Phárnaces. He returned to Italy in the autumn, by way of Athens. At Brundisium he was met by Cicero, who was glad to make peace with him. On his return to Rome, he was named dictator for one year, and consul for the following year, with M. Lepidus. During the winter he crossed over into Africa, where the party of Pompey had rallied under Scipio; gained a complete victory at the battle of Thapsus, and was again at Rome in the autumn of B. C. 46. In B. C. 45, Cæsar was sole consul, and dictator for the third time. During the greater part of this year he was absent in Spain, where Cn. Pompeius, son of Pompeius the Great, had raised a large force. The great battle of Munda, in which thirty thousand are said to have fallen on the side of Pompeius, terminated the campaigns of Cæsar. Pompeius was taken after the battle, and his head was carried to Cæsar, who was then at Hispalis.

On his return to Rome, Cæsar was created consul for ten years and dictator for life. On the ides (15th) of March, B. C. 44, he was assassinated in the senate-house. After his death he was enrolled among the gods, under the appellation of ΔΙΥΟΣ ΙΥΛΙΥΣ, as appears from his medals.

The energy of Cæsar's character, his personal accomplishments and courage, his talents for war, and his capacity for civil affairs, render him one of the most remarkable men of any age. Though a lover of pleasure, and a man of licentious habits, he never neglected what was a matter of business. As a writer and an orator, he has received the highest praise from Cicero; and his "Commentaries," written in a plain, perspicuous style, are a model of their kind. His projects were vast and magnificent. He reformed the Roman calendar, under the direction of Sosigenes. He established public libraries, and gave to the learned Varro the care of collecting and arranging the books. The three books of the "Civil Wars" were written by Cæsar; but the single books on the Alexandrian, African, and Spanish wars, respectively, are generally attributed to another hand. The fragments of various other works of Cæsar's have been collected by his editors.

ADVERTISEMENT.

THE following translation of Cæsar's Commentaries was done from the celebrated edition of the late Dr. Clarke, printed for J. Tonson, in 1712. All possible care has been taken to render it exact, and to preserve the distinctness and perspicuity of expression for which the original is so justly famous. The reader will perceive that the very turn and manner of Cæsar have been copied with the utmost attention; and though the success may not always answer expectation, yet candour will induce him to make great allowances when he considers the inimitable beauty of the Latin, and the difficulty of expressing ancient manners and transactions in modern language. It was at first intended to accompany the translation with notes, explaining what was difficult and obscure in the Roman art of war. But, as a few loose, scattered remarks would have contributed little toward giving the reader a distinct idea of what was necessary to be known on this head, there is substituted in their place a discourse concerning the military customs of the ancients, in which all that is curious and most interesting relating to these matters is fully and copiously explained. Besides the ancient authors, Rollin, Folard, Orrery, Feuquiere, Machiavel, Montesquieu, and several other moderns, have been consulted, and all such passages selected as tended to throw light upon this branch of the Roman antiquities. As the author, by his situation in life, is necessarily a stranger to the practical part of war, he pretends not to offer anything of his own upon the subject. If he has collected with care from the writers before mentioned, and disposed the materials they furnished, in such a manner as sufficiently to display the proficiency and improvements of the ancients in military knowledge, he has compassed all he intended, and the reader will have no cause to complain. The ancient names of places are retained in the translation, as well to avoid giving too modern a turn to the author by a contrary practice, as because they are sufficiently familiar to an English ear, being constantly made use of by all historians who treat of those times in our language. But, as the following work may perhaps fall into the hands of persons little acquainted with ancient geography—and who would, therefore, be at a loss in comparing Cæsar's descriptions with the present face of the country— the reader will find at the end of the book a Geographical Index, in which the ancient names of places, as near as can be discovered with any certainty, are explained by the modern. It may be just proper to mention, that besides the seven books of the Gallic War, and the three of the Civil, written by Cæsar himself, the Supplements of A. Hirtius Pansa are likewise inserted in the following translation, consisting of one additional book to the Gallic War, and three books of the Alexandrian, African, and Spanish Wars.

A DISCOURSE

CONCERNING

THE ROMAN ART OF WAR.

A DISCOURSE

CONCERNING

THE ROMAN ART OF WAR.

CHAP I.

OF THE UNDERTAKING AND DECLARATION OF WAR.

I. The Romans, from small beginnings and an almost contemptible original, rose by degrees to be sovereigns of the world. If we inquire into the causes of this, we shall find, that nothing so much contributed to it, as the excellence of their military discipline. War is a profession of the greatest importance to society. The security of our lives, liberties, properties, and indeed of all that is dear and valuable among men, depends in a manner entirely on it. Good and wholesome laws may establish peace and unity within, and if executed with vigour, will prevent the inroads of vice and corruption; but are by no means sufficient to screen a state from powerful neighbours, or secure it against the assaults of the ambitious and aspiring. Hence in the most peaceful times, it has ever been esteemed a maxim of sound policy, to cultivate the science of arms with the same application, as when we are threatened with war and invasions. For however little we may ourselves be disposed to disturb the tranquillity of the nations around us, yet the experience of all ages makes it abundantly evident, that the most powerful and prevailing argument to keep those quiet, from whom we have reason to apprehend any danger, is by letting them see that we are prepared to receive them, and capable of making them repent of their rashness, should they unjustly seek a pretence of falling upon us. In all wise states, therefore, the profession of a soldier has ever been held in honour: nor do we read any part of ancient history with greater pleasure, than that by which we learn, how free nations have defended themselves against the attempts of encroaching tyrants, and when roused to a thorough exertion of their strength, overthrown in the end that very power, which once threatened to crush them. It is not indeed to be denied, that the military virtues of a free people, have not always been confined to self-defence, and the avenging themselves of their enemies. Ambition, and a consciousness of superiority, have sometimes prompted even these to aspire at universal dominion. This is remarkably exemplified in the history of the Roman commonwealth, from whose constitution, and love of liberty, one would naturally expect a very different spirit. Who more likely to become the great patrons and defenders of the common rights and privileges of mankind than a people, whose prevailing passion was an abhorrence of slavery; and who, in a long series of struggles with the nations around them, were never weary of fighting in defence of that liberty, which is the birthright and inheritance of every reasonable creature? And yet we find, that no sooner were they secure of their own freedom, than a thirst of rule took possession of their minds, and they forcibly imposed that yoke upon others, which they had disdained to submit to themselves. The superiority of their military discipline enabled them by degrees to accomplish this unjust design. Trained up in a continued succession of wars, and equally attentive to their own victories and defeats, they were daily impro-

3

ing themselves in the art of conquest, and attained at length to so great a mastery in it, that no nation was able to withstand their attacks. It cannot therefore but be an agreeable, as well as useful inquiry, to trace out the military customs of a people so renowned for their knowledge in the art of war. And as it is my design, to present the public with a new translation of the Commentaries of Cæsar, who was confessedly the greatest general Rome ever produced, I imagine a discourse of this nature may not be improperly prefixed to that work.

II. Let us then take a view of the conduct of the Romans, from their first engaging in a war, through all the different branches of its management, until they at last bring it to a appy period. This will naturally lead us to consider the ceremonies attending the declaration of war; the manner of levying troops, and forming a Roman army; the precautions used in marches and encampments; their order of battle, conduct in sieges, and the machines and other contrivances made use of in the attack and defence of places. Under these several heads may be comprehended every thing that is material and important upon this subject. It is not, however, my design, to enter into grammatical niceties, or a minute detail of particular criticisms, but only to give a general idea of the military customs of the Romans, intermixed with such remarks as may serve to lay open the policy of their first contrivance, and show their natural tendency to that superiority and universal dominion, which they at length procured the commonwealth.

III. The ceremonies relating to the declaration of war were instituted by Numa Pompilius, the second king of Rome. Romulus, the founder of that colony, was, during the whole course of his reign, engaged in perpetual contests with his neighbours. The necessity he was under, at his first setting out, of procuring wives for his subjects, by the rape of the Sabine virgins, exasperated all the nations round about, and begot no small jealousy of the new colony, which seemed to be founded on maxims of violence and injustice. We are not therefore to wonder, if this drew on him a series of wars, which continued almost without intermission to the end of his life. Thus the Romans, who were originally in a great measure a band of fugitives and outlaws, improving their natural fierceness by having their arms constantly in their hands, gradually grew to be a

brave and warlike people. Numa, who succeeded Romulus, being a prince of a pacific temper, set himself to check this martial ardour, and form them to religion, and a respect for the gods. In order to stifle that impetuous desire of war, which he found so prevalent among them, he established certain ceremonies, which were always to precede the commencing of hostilities, and committed them to the care of a college of heralds, called Feciales. The chief or head of this society had the name of Pater Patratus; and it was his peculiar office to make peace, or denounce war. Livy, indeed, seems to consider him as a temporary minister: for, in his account of the treaty concluded with the Albans, before the triple combat of the Horatii and Curiatii, he makes one of the Feciales choose a Pater Patratus, on purpose to perform that ceremony. But as I have no design to enter into a controversy of this nature, little important in itself, and not easy to be decided, I shall content myself with observing, that the officer here mentioned, whether constant or temporary, was one who had a father and son both alive. Hence this title of Pater Patratus, which may be interpreted to imply a more perfect kind of father, as they seem to have imagined him to be, whose own father was still living, after he himself had been a father for some time. Such a one, it was believed, would be an equitable and moderate judge in affairs of this kind, and not over forward to plunge his country into a war, in which so many lives that must be dear to him, would unavoidably be exposed to hazard.

IV. And indeed the ceremonies themselves, as instituted by Numa, seem peculiarly calculated to render the Romans cautious and circumspect, in a matter of so great importance. For before they entered upon a war with any state, the college of heralds were to commission the Pater Patratus, to go and demand satisfaction in the name of the Roman people. Accordingly this officer, clothed in the habit of his order, set forward for the enemy's country; and entering the frontiers, proclaimed aloud the cause of his arrival, calling all the gods to witness that he came to demand satisfaction, and imprecate the divine vengeance on himself and country, if he said any thing contrary to truth. When he came to the chief city of the enemy, he again repeated the same declaration, adding fresh oaths and imprecations, and withal desired satisfaction. If his demands were granted, he returned immediately to Rome, and all thoughts of war were laid aside. But if they required time to consider, he gave them ten days, and then came again to hear their resolution. This he did, in some cases, three times; but if, after thirty days, nothing was done towards an accommodation, he called gods and men to witness the refusal, and expressly denounced, that the Romans would now think themselves sufficiently authorized to take such measures as the case required, in order to do themselves justice. Upon his return to Rome, he repaired to the senate, attended by the whole college of heralds; having there made a report of his embassy, declared the legality of the war. The affair was then debated among the Fathers: and if the majority of voices were for war, the same officer was sent back to the enemy's frontiers, where, in presence of at least three persons, he pronounced the usual declaration, throwing a spear at the same time into their territories, in token of defiance.

V. These institutions continued long in force at Rome, even during the times of the commonwealth; and it must be owned, were admirably well contrived to answer Numa's great design, of habituating the Romans to peace, and blunting the edge of their martial fury. For as a certain space of time was necessarily to intervene, between the injury received and the commencing of hostilities: this left room for reason and reflection, and gave them an opportunity of weighing maturely all the consequences of the step they were about to take. The imprecations too to be denounced by the herald against himself and country, if he advanced any thing contrary to truth, would naturally make them very cautious in their demands, and extremely attentive to the equity and justice of them. Add to all this, the great probability of adjusting matters amicably, and obtaining a reasonable satisfaction, which cannot by any means be expected, where the parties fly immediately to arms, and by mutual acts of hostility exasperate one another. One would think, that a state under the check of so many restraints against oppression, could not easily break out into violent or unjust wars. Accordingly we find, not only the ancient historians, but even many modern writers of fame and reputation, extolling the modera-

tion and disinterestedness of the Romans; their faith in treaties; steady adherence to their allies; and care to have equity on their side in all their undertakings. It is, however, methinks, a sufficiently obvious reflection that a people, who by degrees accomplished the conquest of the universe, and forced all nations to submit to their dominion, must in many instances have been the aggressors. For although in the first beginnings of their state, they were perhaps often unjustly attacked by their neighbours, out of envy and jealousy; yet it is certain, that their power at last became so very formidable, that no nation was willing to enter the lists with them. We find them, notwithstanding, still pushing on their conquests, still engaged in new wars, and extending the limits of their empire. Now both reason and experience tell us, that in a controversy between states of unequal strength, the weaker will submit to many insults and hardships, rather than draw upon themselves a war which they foresee must end in the subversion of their liberties. And indeed if we examine narrowly into the conduct of the Romans, we shall find, that their reputation of justice is owing rather to an exact observance of certain outward forms, and the partiality of their historians, than any steady adherence to the principles of equity. For as their power and dominion increased, and they became conscious of their superiority, they readily gave way to the dictates of ambition, and were never at a loss in contriving some ground of quarrel with those nations, whom, in their plan of universal conquest, they had resolved to bring next under subjection. But as all their attempts of this kind were preceded by complaints of injuries received, pretended grievances, and formal declarations of war; this gave a colour of justice to their undertakings, and effectually deceived the people; who, convinced that they had equity on their side, followed their generals with an assured confidence, imagining themselves under the immediate protection of the gods. Add to this, that the historians, partly misled by the same notions, partly through a national and almost unavoidable partiality, have vied with one another in extolling the equity and moderation of the Romans, and varnishing over such parts of their behaviour, as seemed most liable to exception. The merit of these writers, and the veneration paid them by suc

2

reading ages, have given a kind of sanction and authority to their opinions. It looks like presumption to contradict authors of so established a reputation; and being accustomed to admire them from our infancy, we are easily led to believe, that we cannot do better than blindly give in to their sentiments. It is only upon this principle I am able to excuse some late writers of great name, who, in treating of the Roman commonwealth, have not scrupled to adopt the prejudices of the ancient historians, and represent that people as patterns of equity and justice in all their proceedings.

VI. As nothing is of greater importance in history, than to form a right judgment of events and their causes, and penetrate into the real character of states and nations, I shall take some pains to set this matter in a true light; and to that end shall lay before the reader a short view of the transactions between the Romans and Carthaginians. It is well known, that these last were characterized by the Romans, as a faithless and perfidious people, regardless of oaths, and whom no ties or treaties could blind. They even went so far as to make *Punic faith* serve only as another expression for *insincerity*. Who would imagine, after such a representation of things, that in all the Punic wars the Romans were the aggressors; and that, in the two last especially, they forced the Carthaginians into them by the most flagrant acts of injustice? But let truth and an impartial account of facts determine. The occasion of the first Punic war was as follows. A body of Campanian soldiers, known in history by the name of Mamertines, and who had served under Agathocles, tyrant of Syracuse, upon the death of that prince retired to Messina; where, being received as friends, they treacherously massacred one part of the inhabitants, expelled the rest, and seizing upon the lands, houses, and even wives of those unfortunate men, remained sole masters of that important city. Some time after this, the people of Rhegium, to screen themselves from the insults of the Carthaginians, whose fleets appeared frequently off their coast, applied to the Roman senate for a garrison. A legion of four thousand men, raised in Campania, and commanded by Decius Jubellius, was appointed to that service. At first they behaved suitably to the intention of those who employed them: but at length, tempted by the wealth of the place, emboldened by the example of

the Mamertines, and strengthened by their aid, they acted the same perfidious and cruel part towards the Rhegians, which the other had acted towards the people of Messina.

VII. As these two cities were parted only by the narrow strait which separates Italy from Sicily, and were not insensible of the odium they had brought upon themselves by their treachery, they entered into a strict confederacy mutually to support each other in their usurpations. This alliance subsisted for some time. But at length the Romans, having disengaged themselves from the many wars, in which they were entangled, turned their thoughts towards the punishment of their perfidious legion. Rhegium was invested, and after an obstinate resistance taken by assault. All that remained alive of the garrison, amounting to about three hundred, were carried to Rome, beaten with rods, and then publicly beheaded in the Forum. The destruction of this confederate city produced a mighty change in the affairs of the Mamertines. While aided by their friends at Rhegium, they had not only lived fearless of danger, but had often made inroads into the territories of the Carthaginians and Syracusans, putting many of their towns and villages under contribution. The case was now greatly altered; for being attacked by Hiero, prætor of Syracuse, they were overthrown in battle, and their army almost totally cut off. Humbled and reduced by so terrible a blow, they thought themselves no longer in a condition to defend Messina; and differing in opinion about what measures to pursue, one party surrendered **the citadel** to the Carthaginians, whilst another **sent ambassadors to** implore the protection of the **Romans.**

VIII. The affair **was debated in the senate;** where, being considered in all its lights, it gave no small perplexity to the Fathers. On the one hand they thought it dishonourable, and altogether unworthy of the Roman virtue, to undertake the defence of traitors, whose perfidy was exactly the same with that of the Rhegians, which they had lately punished with so exemplary a severity. But then again it was of the utmost consequence to stop the progress of the Carthaginians; who, not satisfied with their conquests in Africa and Spain, had also made themselves masters of Sardinia, and the adjacent isles on the coast of Italy; and would certainly get all Sicily into their hands, if they should be suffered to posses themselves of Messina. From thence, into Italy, the passage was very short: and it was in some measure to invite an enemy to come over, to leave him that entrance open. These reasons, though strong, could not prevail with the senate to declare in favour of the Mamertines; and accordingly motives of honour and justice prevailed over those of interest and policy. But the people were not so scrupulous. In an assembly held on this subject, it was resolved that the Mamertines should be assisted; and Appius Claudius, one of the consuls, was ordered to conduct an army into Sicily for that purpose. Appius, to learn the true state of things, went over in person to Messina, and conducted himself so happily, as by some means to persuade the Carthaginian officer to evacuate the citadel. This so highly offended the people of Carthage, that they condemned their officer to be crucified as a traitor and a coward. At the same time they invested the place by sea and land, and entering into an alliance with Hiero the new king of Syracuse, were joined by his troops. Meanwhile Appius, having by an artful stratagem eluded the vigilance of the Carthaginian admiral, crossed the strait with all his forces, and attacking the Syracusans and Carthaginians one after another, compelled them to abandon the siege.

IX. Such was the beginning of the first Punic war, in which I think it evidently appears, that the Romans were the aggressors. For they undertook the defence of a traitorous and perfidious set of men, against a people with whom they were in alliance and amity. I deny not that reasons of state, and the maxims of policy, plead strongly in their behalf on this occasion. It was certainly not their interest to suffer the Carthaginians to become too powerful, or get entire possession of an island that lay so contiguous to Italy. But if we examine their conduct by the rules of strict justice, it will be found no easy matter to vindicate it. And in fact we have seen, that the senate absolutely declared against aiding the Mamertines, as inconsistent with honour, and the dignity of the Roman name. Whether they acted sincerely upon this occasion, or only to save appearances, is not my business to determine. It is enough that the thing itself serves to justify the Carthaginians, and exempt them from the charge of having been the first aggressors in this war. Nor indeed do the Roman writers throw the blame of it upon them,

but generally allow, that jealousy, and an apprehension of each other's growing power, embroiled the two states upon the present occasion.

X. But let us now pass to the second Punic war. Here it is that the charge of insincerity seems to lie heaviest against the Carthaginians. The Romans, exasperated by the losses they had received, gave a free vent to their hatred, and spared no endeavours to blacken their adversaries, and lay the whole blame of the war upon them. And indeed they have contrived to give a specious colour to this accusation, by representing the taking of Saguntum as the cause of the quarrel. For to consider only the first appearance of this step; Hannibal, contrary, as they pretend, to the express tenor of treaties and without any formal declaration of war, falls upon a city in alliance with the Romans. But as Polybius has very judiciously observed, the taking of Saguntum is to be looked upon as the beginning, not the cause of the war: and if we trace matters to their source, we shall find that the Carthaginians were provoked to this step, by a series of the most unjustifiable injuries on the side of the Romans. Soon after the conclusion of the peace of Sicily, the mercenaries who had served in the armies of Carthage revolting, brought that state to the very brink of destruction. The Sardinians, taking advantage of these troubles, shook off the Carthaginian yoke, and expelled all their garrisons out of the island. Things continued for some time in this situation, until at length the Carthaginians, having quelled the rebellion in Africa, prepared to recover possession of Sardinia. The Romans, who during all the foregoing troubles of Carthage had behaved with great justice and moderation, now seeing that people like to regain their former strength, pretended a jealousy of the new preparations, and declared war against them. The Carthaginians, unable at that time to enter the lists with so powerful an adversary, were forced to submit to a second treaty; by which they gave up Sardinia to the Romans, and obliged themselves to an additional payment of twelve hundred talents.

XI. This injustice of the Romans may be considered as the first and principal cause of the second Punic war. For Hamilcar, surnamed Barcha, highly exasperated on account of a treaty, which necessity alone had compelled the Carthaginians to submit to, resolved to break with Rome the first favourable opportunity; and accordingly directed all his views to the success of that enterprise. How deeply he resented the injury of which we speak, appears by his making Hannibal swear upon the altar, at the age of nine years, that he would ever be an irreconcilable enemy to the Romans. During his command in Spain he brought the greatest part of that country under the power of the Carthaginians; but falling in battle before he had completed the conquest of it, Asdrubal his son-in-law succeeded him, and continued the war with success. This alarmed the Romans, who thinking it a necessary piece of policy to check the growing power of a rival state, obliged Asdrubal to enter into a new treaty, in which it was stipulated, that he should attempt no conquest beyond the Iberus. How this may appear to others I cannot say, but to me it carries the idea of a fresh insult, as the Romans hereby claimed a manifest superiority over the Carthaginians, and assumed the power of setting bounds to their empire: a point upon which they were always so very nice themselves, that no excuse can be offered for their disregarding it in their conduct towards others.

XII. Hannibal succeeded Asdrubal in the command of the army; and having in a very short time completed the reduction of Spain, began to think seriously of avenging the many wrongs done his country by the Romans. To that end he contrived a pretence of quarrel with the Saguntines, that by attacking their city, he might give occasion to a rupture between the two states. For though Saguntum lay on this side the Iberus, and therefore was within the plan of conquest permitted to the Carthaginians by the Romans; yet these last, as if repenting of the concession they had made to their adversaries, concluded an alliance with the Saguntines soon after the signing of the treaty with Asdrubal. Now as by an article of that treaty, neither state was to make war upon the allies of the other, the Romans pretended that Saguntum, though on this side the Iberus, could not be attacked without violating the peace. On the other hand the Carthaginians maintained, that the very alliance with the Saguntines was a violation of the treaty, as being no other than a mean artifice to wrest the power of making war upon the Saguntines out of their hands, after it had been expressly conceded to them by that article, which permitted

the conquest of all the nations of Spain on this side the Iberus. I think it needless to enter into a discussion of this nice point, because the taking of Saguntum ought to be considered rather as the beginning of the quarrel, than the cause of the war. The Carthaginians were determined upon hostilities; and it appears by the above deduction, that the Romans, by a continued series of insults and provocations, had given them but too just ground to come to that extremity. Polybius himself, a great admirer of the Romans, and who endeavours on all occasions to represent their conduct in the most favourable light, though he blames the attempt upon Saguntum as an infraction of the treaty, is yet forced to acknowledge thus much. "It would be a great mistake," says that judicious historian, " to consider the taking of Saguntum by Hannibal as the real cause of the second Punic war. It was the beginning, but not the cause of it. The regret of the Carthaginians for the loss of Sicily; the violence and injustice of the Romans, in seizing Sardinia, and imposing a new tribute; and lastly, the success of the Carthaginian armies in Spain, which inspired that state with courage and alarmed their adversaries; these were the real causes of the rupture. If we consider only the siege of Saguntum, we cannot avoid throwing the whole blame upon the Carthaginians, whose attack of that city was a manifest violation of the treaty with Asdrubal. For though the Saguntines were not in alliance with Rome at the time of the conclusion of that treaty, it is evident the Romans did not thereby divest themselves of the liberty of making new alliances. In this view of things, therefore, the Carthaginians would be altogether inexcusable. But if we go back to the times when Sardinia was forcibly seized, and a new tribute imposed, it must be confessed," adds the historian, " that the conduct of the Romans in these two points cannot be justified."

XIII. Thus we see that Polybius throws the whole blame of the second Punic war upon the Romans; and I believe every thinking man will be of the same opinion; which ought to make us cautious of giving too easy credit to the representations of their historians, when they charge their enemies with infidelity and breach of faith, and bestow such magnificent eulogiums of justice and moderation upon their own commonwealth. For allowing the Carthaginians to have been the first in breaking the peace, it may with reason be asked, whether the notorious injustice of the Romans, previously committed, did not justify them in no longer observing a treaty concluded in all the forms; and whether it was not a legitimate reason for entering into a war. I cannot however but observe, that Polybius seems to be a little too severe in his censure of the Carthaginians for attacking Saguntum. It will surely admit of debate, whether the article relating to the allies of both states could be extended any farther than to the alliance actually subsisting at the time of the signing of the treaty. If we extend it to all alliances whatsoever, either made or to be made, this seems mutually to invest them with a power of prohibiting each other from engaging in any war: because either of them contracting an alliance with that people against whom war was intended, rendered them thereby sacred and inviolable. But allowing the reflection of Polybius to be just, that the two states by that treaty did not absolutely divest themselves of the liberty of making new alliances: it seems yet pretty evident that the Romans did so, in respect of all the nations lying on this side the Iberus. For by giving up to the Carthaginians the entire conquest of those countries, they plainly bound themselves not to come under any engagement inconsistent with that article. The alliance therefore with the Saguntines, as it tended to divest the Carthaginians of a power expressly conceded to them by the treaty, ought to be considered as a direct violation of it; and the Romans might with equal justice have contracted amity with all the other nations of Spain yet unsubdued, and thereby utterly deprived the Carthaginians of the power of making war in that country.

XIV. But it is now time to take a view of the causes that gave rise to the third Punic war; in which, I believe, it will be abundantly manifest, that the Romans proceeded without the least appearance of justice. Among the conditions of the peace granted by Scipio to the Carthaginians, there was one which imported, that they should not make war without the consent of the Romans. Masinissa, king of Numidia, taking advantage of this article, made daily encroachments upon their territories and dispossessed them of several towns and districts. He was himself in great favour with the Romans, on account of the many services

he had done them in the second Punic war; and being no stranger to their hatred and jealousy of the Carthaginians, imagined they would not be displeased at his attempts to weaken the power of a rival state. The event showed that he was not mistaken in his judgment. The Carthaginians not daring to do themselves justice, applied to the Romans for redress. But all their solicitations were to no purpose. Commissioners indeed set out for Africa, to examine the pretensions of the parties, and bring matters to an issue. These finding Masinissa already possessed of the territories in question, chose rather to leave the affair undecided than either oblige the king to abandon his conquests, or declare expressly against the Carthaginians. The same conduct was observed in two following deputations: whence it was generally believed, that the commissioners acted in a manner by order of the senate, and had received private instructions to favour Masinissa, who, by this delay, had an opportunity of establishing himself in his usurpations.

XV. It was upon occasion of the last of these deputations that the elder Cato, who was one of the commissioners, observing the flourishing condition of Carthage, and its great power and riches, notwithstanding the many losses it had sustained, could not help considering it as a very dangerous rival to his country. Accordingly at his return, he declared in the senate, that Rome could never be safe, so long as Carthage should subsist. Nay, so deeply had this apprehension rooted itself in his mind, that in order to keep alive in his countrymen a sense of their danger, he never spoke upon public affairs, but he always concluded his opinion with this sentence, Carthage must be destroyed.—And indeed the Romans, naturally averse to that city, and mindful of the many calamities they had suffered from it, were easily persuaded to come into this design. Nor was it long before an opportunity offered itself.

The Carthaginians, exasperated to the last degree by the continual encroachments of Masinissa, and seeing no hopes of redress from the senate, had recourse to arms. A battle was fought, in which they were defeated, their camp taken, and their whole army cut to pieces. The Romans resolving to take advantage of this blow, and on the pretence furnished by the quarrel with Masinissa, declared war in form. All the endeavours of the Carthaginians to mollify them were without effect. They even

2*

C

made an absolute surrender of their city and territories; and, in obedience to the orders of the senate, sent three hundred of their principal nobility as hostages, and delivered up without fraud all their arms. But these acts of submission were enjoined, only in the view of weakening, and rendering them incapable of resistance. For the Romans still peremptorily demanding that they should abandon their city and give it up to be demolished, compelled them at last to arm in their own defence.

XVI. I thought it necessary to be thus particular in my account of the wars between these two states, because they best serve to show what credit is due to the pompous accounts we meet with in historians, of the sincerity and inviolable justice of the Romans. For here, if any where, we may expect to find samples of that equity and moderation. Here we may look for a conduct altogether clear and void of reproach. It is certain that the Romans always valued themselves in a particular manner upon their good faith, and exact observance of treaties with the Carthaginians. This evidently appears by the advantageous testimony Cæsar gives of his countrymen in this respect, in that famous speech of his in Sallust, upon occasion of the conspiracy of Catiline. "Bellis Punicis omnibus, cum sæpe Carthaginienses, et in pace, et per inducias, multa nefanda facinora fecissent; nunquam ipsi per occasionem talia fecere; magis quod se dignum foret, quam quod in illis jure fieri posset, quærebant." "Although in all the Punic wars, the Carthaginians, both in peace, and during truces, were guilty of many abuses and violations of their engagements; the Romans, how inviting soever the opportunity might be, could yet never be prevailed upon to retaliate the like usage. They were more attentive to their own glory, than to the revenge they might have justly taken on such perfidious enemies." We find likewise a great many reflections to the same purpose sprinkled up and down the writings of Cicero; from all which it is easy to judge, how irreproachable they thought their conduct on this head, and what a pattern of justice and moderation. But if, notwithstanding all these favourable representations, it still appears so very liable to exceptions, how much less can it be justified with regard to other states? And, indeed, were I to enter into a particular detail, I could easily evince, that it was no other than a continued train of insults and provocations designedly calculated to exasperate such states as were most obnoxious, and force them to have recourse to arms. It will doubtless appear wonderful to the reader, how, amidst such a series of oppressive conduct, the Romans still found means to preserve, in some measure, the reputation of justice and equity. But this, as we have before intimated, was chiefly owing to their observance of certain outward forms. They never failed to contrive some ground of complaint against those nations they intended to attack; to send deputies to demand satisfaction; and to make formal declaration of war by a herald, previous to the commencing of hostilities. It must indeed be owned, that it required no small art and policy, so to involve and entangle themselves with all the nations of the then known world, that they could at pleasure find some specious pretence of quarrel, when their interest required them to break with any state. This gave a colour of justice to all their undertakings, inspired their armies with assurance and confidence, inviolably attached to them their old friends, and procured them new allies at pleasure. And as it seems to have been one of their master-strokes in politics, and the principal engine by which they pushed on their conquests, it may not be amiss to give the reader some little insight into their artful conduct in this respect, that he may the better comprehend the motives and tendency of it.

XVII. Although I cannot bring myself to think, with some modern writers, of pretended depth and penetration, that Numa Pompilius had a political view in the several religious regulations he established at Rome; yet I am ready enough to allow, that many of his institutions were afterwards, by the prudent management of the senate, converted into maxims of state, and rendered very serviceable in the administration of the government. Of this nature particularly were the ceremonies relating to the declaration of war. Nothing is of greater consequence to an ambitious republic, which aims at universal dominion, and a gradual subjection of all nations, than to prevent such a general confederacy against her, as might not only put a stop to her conquests, but even threaten her in her turn with destruction. This the senate effected by their singular address and conduct, in the several wars in which they were engaged. For they always found means to colour them over with such a specious pretence of justice, as gave no umbrage to the neighbouring states, nor begot any jealousy of a power which seemed to have nothing in view but the redressing of its own wrongs, or those of other nations in alliance with it. That strong bent towards religion, and the worship of the gods, which Numa introduced among the people, and which the senate carefully cherished for many generations, helped greatly to forward this **persuasion.** Men were not apt to distrust a religious republic, where virtue was held in honour, and **vice** of every kind discountenanced. **Let me** add, that in the early ages of this state, this **was more than** mere pretence. They were **really** distinguished by their probity, **by a steady adherence** to justice, and **a faithful observance** of treaties. Most of their wars were defensive, or undertaken for the sake of their allies. And though in after times, in proportion as their power increased, they gave way to the dictates of ambition and became less scrupulous in their conduct; yet as they never departed from those outward observances, by which the appearance of justice is maintained, and took care to signalize themselves from time to time, by such particular instances of moderation, as could not fail to make a deep impression; their reputation for equity and good faith continued still the same.

XVIII. Observe, I beseech you, the different sentiments entertained of the Romans and Carthaginians, at the time of the rupture between **the** two states. The Romans, though **they had** gradually subjected all the nations **of** Italy, and raised themselves to a very formidable pitch of greatness, were yet so far from being considered as an ambitious republic, against whom it was necessary for other states to be upon their guard, that the fame of their virtue **and justice** seems at this time to have **been at** the highest; insomuch that foreign nations, instead of dreading their power, courted their alliance and amity. It was otherwise with the Carthaginians. They had been less careful to conceal their ambition, or cover their breach of treaties under a pretence of injuries. Hence their designs became suspected, all their actions were viewed in their worst light, and the general prejudice against them was so strong, that every thing laid to their charge by their enemies found a ready belief. By this means it happened, that though in the interval between the first and second Punic wars, the Romans acted without the least regard to justice and the faith of treaties, yet very little notice was taken of the complaints of the Carthaginians: and when, in consequence of repeated insults and provocations, they were at last obliged to have recourse to arms, the whole blame of the war, though so manifestly flowing from the injurious behaviour of the Romans, was nevertheless charged upon **the perfidy of** the Carthaginians.

XIX. After the entire conquest of Italy, and the reduction of the greatest part of Sicily in **the first** Punic war, it required a more refined policy in the Romans, to extend the limits of their empire, and at the same time keep up the reputation of their integrity. They were not immediately surrounded with those nations, which it was their interest to attack; and therefore could not easily provoke them to such acts of hostility, as might justify a declaration of war. And should they upon slight pretences transport an army out of their own territories, to fall upon a distant prince, their design of conquest would be visible, and beget a general alarm. Besides, their power was become so very formidable, that foreign states did not care to contend with them, and therefore industriously avoided giving them any just ground of complaint. In this situation they took upon themselves the title of patrons and protectors of all nations, and by contracting alliances with weaker states, found means to fall upon the stronger at pleasure, without seeming themselves to have any particular interest in the quarrel. It was upon this principle that they attached themselves to the Saguntines and Ætolians, which afterwards furnished them with such a plausible colour for the Carthaginian and Macedonian wars. **To** know the full reach and value of this policy, we need only reflect, that though the second Punic war was unexceptionably just on **the part** of the Carthaginians; yet the Romans, by diverting the attention of the public from the usurpation of Sardinia, and fixing it upon the fate of Saguntum, threw the whole odium of that war upon their adversaries, whilst themselves were considered as a humane generous people, actuated merely by a concern for their allies.

XX. And here it is particularly deserving of our notice, that amongst the many wars in which they were engaged, after the conclusion of that with Hannibal, we hardly meet with any that can be deemed personal. It was always, at least in appearance, to support the cause of some of their allies, or prevent their being crushed by a powerful neighbour. One would be apt to think, that they had it not so much in view to aggrandize themselves, as to prevent the growth of any dangerous power, from which weaker states might be exposed to suffer. Upon the conclusion of the first Macedonian war, they proclaimed liberty to all the states of Greece. This action, so magnificent in appearance, was in reality a refined stroke of policy. The Greeks were a warlike people, well disciplined, and capable of bringing great armies into the field. Had they suspected the Romans of a design upon their liberties, and united in their own defence, they must have been invincible. But this seeming grant of freedom effectually lulled them asleep, and by the artful conduct of the Romans, gave birth to infinite divisions among them; which ending commonly in an appeal to Rome, furnished the senate with frequent opportunities of taking part in their quarrels. Thus they insensibly grew to be rulers and dictators over them, and by slow imperceptible steps accomplished their subjection.

XXI. Their ambassadors to foreign princes, and such as had not yet felt the weight of their power, commonly delivered themselves in such a haughty magisterial way, as could not fail to draw upon them some indignity or ill treatment, and thereby furnish a sure pretence of war, when the interest of the commonwealth rendered such a step necessary. If a people at any time had given them umbrage, and afterwards repenting of their rashness, surrendered up the principal offenders; they would often refuse to punish them, choosing rather to consider the whole nation as guilty, and reserve to themselves an useful vengeance. When they saw two nations engaged in war, although they were not in alliance, nor had any contest with either of them, they would nevertheless appear upon the stage of action, and affected always to side with the weakest. It was an ancient custom, says Dionysius of Halicarnassus, for the Romans to grant succour to all who came to implore it. If princes of the same blood were at variance for the crown, they seldom failed to make themselves parties in the dispute; and if one of them was a minor, declared in his favour, proclaiming themselves his guardians, in quality of protectors of the world. When subjects, oppressed and tyrannised over by their sovereigns, were provoked to renounce their allegiance, they immediately indulged them the title of ally, declaring themselves the professed enemies of tyranny and lawless power.

XXII. These were the arts and policies, by which the Romans so entangled themselves with all nations, that they could with pleasure engage in a war with any state, and colour it over with such an appearance of justice, as not only prevented any general confederacy against them, but even warmly engaged their allies in the support of their usurpations. Nor were they less politic in the choice of their wars, and in the manner of conducting and bringing them to a period. For as their power was very formidable, and they had contrived to draw many nations over to their interest; whatever state took up arms against them, found it impossible to make any long resistance, and was in the end forced to accept of such conditions of peace as they thought fit to propose. For this reason war was seldom declared against them, but themselves always made it, at a season, with a people, and in such a manner as best suited their interest. If they were opposed by several enemies at the same time, they granted a truce to the weakest, who thought themselves happy in obtaining it, considering it as a great advantage, that their ruin was at least suspended. They never engaged in far-distant wars, till they had first made an alliance with some power contiguous to the enemy they invaded, who might unite his troops to the army they sent; and as this was never considerable with regard to numbers, they always had another in that province which lay nearest the enemy, and a third, in Rome, ever ready to march at a minute's warning. In this manner they hazarded but a small part of their forces at once, and found it easy to repair any loss they might sustain, whilst their enemy was often ruined by a single battle. It was this consideration that inspired Hannibal with the resolution of attacking them in Italy itself, the centre of their dominions. He was sensible that a blow struck there, must effectually weaken them; whereas distant defeats, so long as the capital remained unmolested, and was at liberty to send a fresh supply of troops to recruit the army, were, properly speaking, little other than so many lessons of prudence to their generals, who soon found themselves in a condition to renew the war with greater forces, and more circumspection. Accordingly we find, that when the same Hannibal afterwards offered his service to Antiochus, in his intended war against the Romans, there was no principle he inculcated more earnestly, than the necessity of sending an army into Italy, and cutting them off from those continual resources, by which, in any other method of attack, they found themselves invincible.

XXXIII. But nothing gives us a greater idea of the address and policy of this people, than the manner in which they terminated their wars, when they had at last brought them to the point they desired. They sent the garrisons out of the strong holds; had the horses and elephants delivered up to them; and if their enemies were powerful at sea, obliged them to burn their ships, and sometimes remove higher up in the country. If the prince they had overcome was possessed of numerous armies, and surrounded with warlike nations, one of the articles of the treaty was, that he should not make war with any of the allies of the Romans, but submit his differences to arbitration. And as they never refused their alliance to any people who bordered on a powerful prince, this condition inserted in a treaty of peace, cut him off from all opportunities of making war, or employing his troops, and thereby deprived him of a military power for the time to come. Nay, they even bereaved their very allies of this force. The instant any contest broke out amongst them, they sent ambassadors who obliged them to conclude a peace. It was in this manner they terminated the wars between Attalus and Prusias; and whoever is in the least acquainted with their history, must be sensible, that they all along adhered strictly to this policy. The result was, that they alone were possessed of warlike and veteran armies, whilst those of other nations degenerated into a raw unpractised rabble. When any state composed too formidable a body, from its situation or union, they never failed to divide it. The republic of Achaia was formed by an association of free cities. The senate declared, that every city should be governed by its own laws, independent on the general authority. Macedonia was surrounded with inaccessible mountains. The senate divided it into four

parts; declared those free; prohibited them every kind of alliance among themselves by marriage; carried off all the nobles into Italy; and by that means reduced this power to nothing.

XXIV. These customs of the Romans were not certain particular incidents which happened by chance; but so many invariable principles, from which, in a long course of years, they never deviated. The maxims they put in practice against the greatest monarchs, were exactly the same with those they had employed in their infant state, against the little cities which stood round them. They made Eumenes and Masinissa contribute to the subjection of Philip and Antiochus, as they had before employed the Latins and Hernici to subdue the Volscians and the Tuscans. They obliged the Carthaginians and the kings of Asia to surrender their fleets to them, in like manner as they had forced the citizens of Antium to give up their little vessels. And indeed it is surprising to consider, that during the course of that long and mighty prosperity which attended the Roman arms, and in which it is so usual for mankind to forget themselves the senate continued to act all along with the same depth of judgment, and the same steady views to the public interest. They were not dazzled by their good fortune, nor moved to precipitate their enterprises before the proper season. Observe, I entreat you, the wisdom and policy of their conduct. After the defeat of Antiochus, they were possessed of Africa, Asia, and Greece, without having a single city in those countries, that could be called immediately their own. They seemed to conquer with no other view but to bestow. But then they obtained so complete a sovereignty, that whenever they engaged in war with any prince, they oppressed him, as it were, with the weight of the whole universe. The time proper for seizing upon the conquered countries was not yet come. Had the Romans kept the cities they took from Philip, the Greeks would have seen at once into their designs. Had they, after the second Punic war, or that with Antiochus, possessed themselves of lands in Africa and Asia, they could never have preserved conquests so slightly established. It was the interest of the senate to wait till all nations were accustomed to obey as free and as confederate, and to let them blend and lose themselves insensibly in the Roman commonwealth before they should attempt reducing them to the condition of subjects. After overcoming a nation, they contented themselves with weakening it, and imposing such conditions as consumed it insensibly. If it recovered, they depressed it still more, and it became subject, without a possibility of dating the era of its subjection. This was indeed a slow way of conquering, but founded in the deepest policy. Rome, by steady adherence to these maxims, gradually increased in strength; and having at length got the better of all opposition, securely took possession of the sovereignty of the universe.

CHAP. II.

OF THE MANNER OF LEVYING TROOPS, AND FORMING A ROMAN ARMY.

I. The levies, during the times of the commonwealth, to which period we chiefly confine ourselves, were commonly made by the consuls. Every year they issued out an edict, commanding all who had reached the military age, to appear in the field of Mars, or in the capital. Two legions composed a consular army; and as there were two consuls, it was usual to raise four legions yearly. The age for serving in the army was from seventeen to forty-five. None but citizens were admitted; and all of that rank within the age prescribed by law, were obliged to be present on the day prefixed, under pain of a fine. To fail in this respect was long criminal during the commonwealth. The people being assembled, the consuls began, by nominating the military tribunes, twenty-four in number, six to every legion. Of these, fourteen were chosen out of the body of the knights, and the rest from among the people. The first were required to have served at least five years, and the others ten. They were divided to the four legions in this manner. Of the fourteen youngest tribunes, four were assigned to the first legion, three to the second, four to the third, and three to the last. Of the ten eldest, two to the first and third legions, and three to the second and last.

II. The four and twenty tribunes thus chosen and appointed, every tribe was called out by lot, and ordered to divide into its proper centuries. Four men, as much alike in all circumstances as could be found, being presented out of the century on whom the lot fell, the tribunes of the first legion chose one, then the tribunes of the second legion another, the tribunes of the third legion a third, and the remaining person fell to the tribunes of the fourth. After this four more were drawn out. And now the right of choosing first belonged to the tribunes of the second legion; in the next four to the tribunes of the third legion; then to the tribunes of the fourth legion; and so continually, those always choosing last in every turn, who chose first the time before. From this manner of choosing the soldiers, one by one, the several large bodies into which they were formed, obtained the name of legions, from the Latin word *legere*, to choose; and the levy itself was called *delectus*, choice. No soldier was admitted under the height of five Roman feet and ten inches, except in an extreme want of troops, which would not allow of choosing. It is observed, that the men of the first cohorts of each legion were not under six feet high, which amounts to five feet ten inches of our measure, the Roman foot making eleven inches and six hundred and four decimal parts of an inch English.

III. The horse were chosen out of the body of the *Equites*, into which order, after the institution of the *Census* by Servius Tullius, all were admitted who were worth four hundred *sestertia*. They had a horse and ring given them at the public charge, and formed a third and middle order between the senate and the people. They are known in history under the name of Roman knights, and were obliged to appear on horseback, as often as the state had occasion for their service. Thus there was always a sufficient number of cavalry in readiness, and it belonged to the censors to review them, and furnish what was necessary to complete the legions. It is indeed hard to conceive, that all the Roman horse in the army should be knights; and therefore many learned men are of opinion, that, after the siege of Veii, there were two sorts of cavalry in the Roman armies: one, whom the public supplied with horses, and who were said to serve *equo publico*; the other, who furnished themselves, and served *equo privato*. The former they allow to have been of the order of knights, the latter not. But Gravius has abundantly demonstrated, by the course of history, that from the beginning of the Roman state, till the time of Marius, no other horse entered the legions out the true and proper knights, except in the midst of public confusion, when order and discipline were neglected. After that period, the military affairs being new modelled, the knights thought not fit to expose themselves abroad in the legions, as they had formerly done, but generally kept at home to enjoy their estates, and to have a hand in the transactions of the city, leaving their places in the army to be supplied by foreign horse. Or if they ever made campaigns themselves, they held some post of honour and command. Hence, under the emperors, a man might be a knight and have the honour of a public horse, without ever engaging in the public cause, or so much as touching arms: which consideration made some princes lay aside the custom of allowing the knights a horse, and leave them only the gold ring to distinguish their order, as Pliny the elder affirms to have been done in his time.

IV. When the levies were completed, the tribunes of every legion obliged the soldiers, one by one, to take the military oath. The form in this case was, to choose out a soldier, who repeated the oath aloud. By this oath he engaged to hazard his life for the commonwealth, to obey his general, and not to quit the army without leave. In pronouncing it he held up his right hand, raising the thumb of it upright; after which all the soldiers of each legion declared that they swore the same thing, but without repeating the form. This was not a mere ceremony, but a very solemn act of religion, and so essential to the military state, that no man was deemed a soldier nor allowed to strike or kill an enemy, if he had not taken the customary oath. We have a remarkable example of this in the behaviour of Cato the Censor. A legion, in which the son of that illustrious senator served, being dismissed by the consul who commanded in Macedonia, young Cato chose to continue with the army. His father, thereupon, wrote immediately to the consul, to desire, if he thought fit to suffer his son to remain in the service, that he would make him take a new oath, because being discharged from the former, he had no longer any right to join in battle against the enemy. We find, likewise, that among the Greeks the military oath was accounted inseparable from the state of a soldier. And Xenophon in his history of Cyrus the Great, informs us, that that prince exceedingly applauded the action of an officer, who having raised his arm to strike an enemy, upon hearing the retreat sounded, stopped short, regarding that signal as an order to proceed no farther.

V. After administering the military oath, the next care of the tribunes was to form the troops into legions. The exact number of soldiers in such a battalion was not always the same. Romulus fixed it at three thousand foot, and three hundred horse. It afterwards rose to four, five, and six thousand. Under the consuls it was commonly four thousand two hundred foot, and three hundred horse. This was the number in the time of Polybius, and here I shall fix it. In order thoroughly to comprehend the nature of the legion, so famous in history, we must begin with observing that the whole infantry of which it was composed, was divided into four orders, *Velites, Hastati, Principes,* and *Triarii.* The Velites were young, active soldiers, and formed the light-armed troops of the Roman commonwealth: They had their name *à volando,* or *à velocitate,* from their swiftness and expedition. They were not divided into companies, nor had any fixed post assigned them in a day of battle, but hovered in loose order before the army, or were disposed among the cavalry and heavy-armed troops, as occasion required. The Hastati were so called, because they used in ancient times to fight with spears, which were afterwards laid aside as incommodious. These were taken out in the next age to the Velites, and formed the first line in a day of battle. The Principes were generally men of middle age, in the prime and vigour of life, whence probably they took their name. Their post in an engagement was the second line. The Triarii were old soldiers of distinguished valour, who had served long and acquired great experience. They had their name from their post in the field of battle, forming the third line or reserve. They are likewise sometimes called Pilani, from their weapon the Pilum.

VI. These several divisions formed twelve hundred men a piece in the three first orders, and six hundred in the last, amounting in all to four thousand two hundred, the entire infantry of a legion. Each body, the Velites excepted, was subdivided into ten parts or maniples, consisting of a hundred and twenty in the Hastati and Principes, and of sixty in the Triarii. Every maniple made two centuries or companies. Anciently, and at its first institution by Romulus, the century had a hundred men, from which it took its name. But afterwards, it consisted only of sixty in the *hastati* and *principes*, and of thirty in the *triarii*. Three maniples, one of the *hastati*, another of the *principes*, and a third of the *triarii*, composed a cohort. Every legion, therefore, consisted of ten cohorts, besides the twelve hundred *velites*, who, as we have already observed, were divided into distinct companies. The number of legions kept on foot was different according to the different exigencies of the state. During the commonwealth, four legions were usually levied every year, and divided between the two consuls. But in case of necessity, the number was augmented, and we sometimes meet with eighteen in Livy.

VII. We have observed that every maniple was divided into two centuries or companies. Over each of these presided an officer, called a centurion. To determine the point of priority between them, they were created at two different elections. Those of the first election, as the most honourable, always took the precedency of their fellows, and therefore commanded the right hand orders, as the others did the left. He who commanded the first century of the first maniple of the *triarii*, called also *pilani*, was the most considerable of all the centurions, and had a place in the counsel of war with the consul and principal officers. He bore the name of *primipilus*, or *primipili centurio ;* and was called likewise *primipilus prior*, to distinguish him from the centurion who commanded the second century of the same maniple, who had the title of *primipilus posterior*. This distinction of *prior* and *posterior* had place also in all the other maniples. The centurion who commanded the first century of the second maniple of the *triarii* was called *secundi pili centurio ;* and so on to the tenth, who was called *decimi pili centurio*. The same order was observed among the *hastati* and *principes*. The first centurion of the *principes* was called *primus princeps*, or *primi principis centurio*. The second, *secundus princeps*, &c. and so on to the last. So likewise among the *hastati*, *primus hastatus*, or *primi hastati centurio*, *secundus hastatus*, &c. through all the different orders. As it belonged to the military

tribunes to appoint the centurions, so these last chose *vexillarii*, or ensigns, two to every maniple. They had likewise officers under them, called *succenturiones*, or *optiones*, and who were in the nature of our lieutenants. Polybius mentions them under the name of *tergiductores*, their post being in the rear of the company.

VIII. The cavalry required to a legion was three hundred. They were divided into ten *turmæ*, or troops, thirty to a troop. Every troop consisted of three *decuriæ*, or bodies of ten men. Over each of these was a captain, called *decuria*. He that was first elected commanded the whole troop, and had the title of *præfectus*. The decurions had every one his *optio*, or deputy, under him, who, in like manner as in the foot, were called *tergiductores*. These squadrons often occur in history under the name of *alæ*, because they always formed the wings of the legion. At the time the Romans warred against the lesser nations of Italy, their horse was incomparably superior to that of their enemies, for which reason they were composed of none but the most considerable among the citizens, being, as we have observed, selected wholly out of the order of the knights. When they alighted, no infantry was more formidable, and they very often turned the scale of victory. It must be owned, however, that their cavalry were but few, in proportion to their foot; and though they served well enough for their Italian wars, yet they became fully sensible of this inconvenience when they had to do with Hannibal. It was chiefly by the superiority of his cavalry, and his manner of using it, that he gained so many victories over them. Accordingly, they applied themselves seriously to the improvement of this part of their strength, not only by intermixing platoons of foot with their cavalry and training them particularly to that service, but likewise by taking foreign horse into their pay, Numidians, Gauls, and Germans.

IX. Besides the troops already mentioned, there were always in the Roman armies a number of soldiers, of a more eminent degree, known by the title of *evocati*. They were such as had served out the legal time, and been distinguished by particular marks of favour, as a reward of their valour. It was usual for the consuls, especially in important wars, to invite a great number of these into the service, by circular letters despatched for that purpose. The reputation of a general was what chiefly induced them to grant their attendance, and therefore it was considered as a particular mark of honour. In the field they usually guarded the chief standard, being excused from all the military drudgery of standing on the watch, labouring in the works, or other servile employments. They had likewise the privilege of using the *vitis* or rod, which was the badge of the centurion's office, and indeed were in all respects rather superior to the centurions. It was very common, when any general of an established reputation, and who had long distinguished himself in the service of his country, was appointed to the management of a difficult war, to see great numbers of these flock to his standard, and offer themselves anew to dangers and fatigues, in hopes of gaining fresh laurels, under the auspices of a commander who had often in their youth led them to honour and victory. Thus it happened to Paulus Æmilius, when he was charged with the conduct of the Macedonian war. And thus also to the younger Scipio Africanus, when, after a series of disgraces before Numantia, the Romans cast their eyes upon him, as alone capable of restoring the reputation of their arms.

X. But to return to the legions. The officers next in dignity to the centurions were the military tribunes, of whom we have already given some account. They owed their name and institution to Romulus, who having divided the whole body of the citizens into three tribes, appointed an officer over each, with the title of tribune. The number afterwards increased to six in every legion. During the infancy of the commonwealth they were nominated by the consuls; and afterwards, partly by the consuls, partly by the people. Their business was to decide all controversies in the army; to give the word to the watch; to see that the soldiers observed discipline, obeyed orders, and did their duty; and to take care of the works and camp. None could attain this dignity, who had not served in the army five years; and of the twenty-four that were annually chosen, ten at least must have served ten years. Care was also taken to distribute them in such a manner, that in each legion the most experienced were united with those who were younger, in order to instruct and form them for commanding. By this means the legions were always provided with able officers, which could not fail of having an excellent effect upon the troops, as it naturally tended to inspire them with valour, and beget an esteem and confidence in their commanders. During the campaign, which lasted six months, they commanded the legion by turns, two at a time, for two months together. The order in which they were to command was decided by lot.

XI. The troops we have hitherto been describing, may properly be termed the natural forces of the republic, as consisting wholly of her own citizens. They were indeed the original armies of Rome, and all along constituted her main strength. But this political commonwealth, when she began to extend her dominion over Italy, instead of reducing the vanquished nations to slavery, indulged them the title of allies, and the free enjoyment of their own laws, upon condition of supplying her in her wars with a certain proportion of men. These were called the allied troops, and as to number, were equal to the natural forces in foot, and double in horse. The manner of levying them was this. The consuls, while they were employed in completing the legions at Rome, gave notice to the allied states what number of forces they would have occasion for, and appointed a time and place of rendezvous. The states accordingly convened their men, and choosing out the desired number, gave them an oath, and assigned them a commander-in-chief, and a paymaster-general. When they arrived in the camp, they were divided into two great bodies, termed *alæ*, or *cornua*, from their position in the army. For the Romans always reserved the centre to themselves, placing the confederates, half on the right, and half on the left wings. And because they were more numerous than the natural forces, care was taken farther to separate them, by selecting a third part of the horse, and a fifth of the foot, and posting them near the consul's person, under the name of *extraordinarii*. It is not certainly known how the smaller bodies of the confederate forces were commanded. Most probably the Romans marshalled them according to their own discipline, and assigned them officers of the same nature with those of the legions. This seems to follow from the manner in which they fought, it appearing evidently by the course of history, that, both as to their arms and order of battle, they differed in nothing from the troops of the republic. We are assured, however, that the two *alæ*, or great divisions of the allies, had each a prefect appointed them by the Roman consul, who governed in the same manner as the legionary tribunes. In aftertimes, all the states of Italy were admitted to share the freedom of the city, and their forces incorporated with those of the republic. From this period, therefore, the name of the allies ceased, and in their stead the auxiliary troops were procured. These were sent by foreign states and princes, at the desire of the Roman senate, or generals, and were allowed a set pay from the republic; whereas the allies received no consideration for their service, but a distribution of corn.

XII. Over these armies of the Roman people, the two consuls presided, who were the standing generals of the republic. They were created yearly, and in the field possessed an unlimited authority: the senate reserving to themselves only the power of making peace, and decreeing war, unless upon extraordinary occasions. The annual change of generals was doubtless in some cases an obstacle to the advancement of affairs; but the danger of infringing on the public liberty, by continuing the same man longer in the command of all the forces of the state, obliged them to overlook this inconvenience, from the apprehension of a much greater. The necessity of affairs, the distance of places, and other reasons, reduced the Romans at length to continue their generals in the command for several years together, under the name of proconsuls or propraetors. And as these generals had often a great extent of country to defend, and were obliged to employ different bodies of troops in different places, they found it necessary to have officers under them, of a more extensive authority than the military tribunes. This gave rise to the institution of the Legati, who commanded in chief under the general, and managed all affairs by his permission. We find them sometimes at the head of one legion, sometimes of three or four, and sometimes of only part of a legion. Their office was accounted very honourable, insomuch that the greatest men of the state, and even such as had been consuls and dictators, did not disdain to accept of it. The great Fabius, as is well known, was his son's lieutenant; and Scipio Africanus served in the same capacity under the consul his brother. The number was according to the general's pleasure, on whom alone the choice depended;

and it appears, that they commanded under him, and received his orders, as lieutenant-generals in our armies serve under the generalissimo. In the absence of the consul, or proconsul, they had the honour of using the fasces, and were intrusted with the same charge as the officer whom they represented.

XIII. Having thus sufficiently explained how the armies of the Roman people were formed, and the different degrees of rank and military service that prevailed in them, it is time to consider a little more particularly wherein their strength consisted, and to what they were indebted for that superiority, which rendered them victorious over the troops of all other nations. The first thing that offers itself to our observation here is, the nature and form of the legion; whose contrivance was so admirable, that Vegetius thinks nothing less than a god could inspire the idea of it. The soldiers of which it was composed, were armed with weapons of a heavier and stronger kind than those of other nations, as we shall have occasion to show more at large in the next chapter. But because some things must be done in war, which a heavy body is not able to execute, it was therefore made to include within itself a band of light forces, which might issue from it in order to provoke the enemy to battle, or draw back into it in case of necessity. It was likewise strengthened with cavalry, and with spearmen and slingers, to pursue those who fled, and complete the victory. The troops were all of different experience and standing in the service, and so mixed **together in the cohorts that no party** of Roman forces **was without a sufficient** number of veterans, **to give** life and vigour to its operations. The number of men in a legion seems likewise to have been the effect of a wise policy. For those amounting to four thousand five hundred, formed a considerable body of troops, animated by one and the same spirit, and who, from their mutual relation among themselves, would take a near interest in each other's preservation. They were in effect men of the same regiment, and had all that zeal and concern for one another, which is usual among those lesser divisions of our troops.

XIV. The Marquis de Feuquire, in his Memoirs, observes, that the regiments of which modern armies consist, are not sufficient-

.y strong in the number of men. He thinks it might do well to form them of several battalions; because such a multitude of different bodies, without any immediate tie among themselves, seems directly contrary to that union and subordination, which constitutes the great beauty of military discipline. It is certain that troops always exert themselves more in behalf of those of the same regiment, than where the party for which they are engaged belong to a different division. This the Romans were fully sensible of, and had an eye to it particularly in the constitution of their legion. It was doubtless of great advantage to them in a day of battle, that their lines were made up of a few large bodies, linked together by the strongest military ties, and nearly interested in each other's preservation. Nor did the number of men in these bodies render them unwieldy or unmanageable; because being judiciously disposed into cohorts, they could be commanded with the same ease, and were no less nimble in their operations, than if they had formed so many independent battalions. And here it is worthy of notice, that in drawing up the army, the troops were so disposed, as tended wonderfully to their mutual support and encouragement. For as the Romans commonly fought in three lines, so in every one of these lines, the soldiers were always so posted, as to be sustained by others of the same legion. This was owing to the manner of forming the lines, not by entire legions, but by the different military orders that composed the legions. The Hastati were placed in the first line, the Principes in the second, and the Triarii in the third. By this means the Hastati of every legion were supported by the Principes of the same legion, and these again by the Triarii. What spirit and confidence this must add to the troops, and how effectually in would tend to preserve them from slaughter, when any particular line was broken, will be evident upon the least reflection. It is found by experience, that soldiers never fight better, nor exert a greater share of courage, than when they know themselves to be well supported; and if at last they are obliged to give way, yet still the retreat is managed with less terror and confusion. The Romans, in case of a repulse, retired through the intervals of the lines behind them; and these consisting of men of the same legion, advanced imme-

diately to their relief, and doubtless would do every thing in their power to preserve their fellows. This kept up the spirits of those that fled, prevented their throwing away their arms, and encouraged them to rally and renew the charge.

XV. There was also another advantage in the constitution of the legion, arising from the several military orders of which it was composed, with their division into maniples and companies. For these being very numerous, and differing in point of rank and superiority, opened a large field for preferment, and thereby excited an incredible ardour and emulation among the troops. A private soldier, after passing through the different military orders, came to be a centurion among the Hastati; and rising from one maniple to another, was at length promoted into the rank of the Principes. Thence, by a like gradation, he reached the order of the Triarii; and in time attained the dignity of Primipilus. Nor was he even obliged to stop here. For as military merit was every thing at Rome, it seldom failed to raise those who possessed it, in any eminent degree, to the first dignities of the state. The manner too in which promotions were made, seems wonderfully calculated for the advancement of true bravery. Every higher order of officers created those next below them, and so in train continually, through all the different steps of the service. As therefore the persons on whom the choice depended, had the best opportunities of knowing the merits of the several competitors, and were likely to be determined by that alone, in a matter that so nearly concerned their own honour and safety, it is natural to suppose, that every one would endeavour to recommend himself by such qualifications, as rendered him truly worthy of the place to which he aspired. This progressive choice of officers, which established so just a subordination in the army, and gave a great ascendant to the principal commanders, contributed more than any thing to the perfection of military discipline. It is worth while to observe how gradually the Romans proceeded herein. The people, or state, elected the two consuls; the consuls chose the military tribunes; the military tribunes, the centurions; and the centurions, their vexillarii and tergiductors. This method opened the fairest prospect to valour, and tended to beget that spirit among the troops, which is of all others the happiest that can be raised in an army, an emulation to surpass each other in deserving honours.

XVI. What we have hitherto said regards chiefly the form and structure of the legion. Let us now consider the quality of the troops of which it was composed. None but citizens were admitted into this body, and of all these the tribunes had their choice, from seventeen to forty-five years of age. We are to observe, however, that it was not every citizen whom they judged worthy of this honour. By the institution of the *Census*, the whole Roman people were divided into distinct classes, founded on a valuation of their estates. Those of the sixth and lowest class, consisting of the poorer citizens, useful only by stocking the commonwealth with children, were not allowed to serve in the army. The Romans were for having soldiers, whose real interest in the preservation of the state, would prompt them to act with zeal in its defence. They had every one their portion of land, and for the most part lived in the country, to improve and cultivate it with their own hands. Thus accustomed to the toil of husbandry, to endure sun, rain, and hail, to handle heavy instruments, dig trenches, and carry burdens; when they entered the service they only changed their arms and tools, and came with bodies inured to labour, and seasoned to all the fatigues of the field. Besides, as war was the proper profession of this people, and what they were all obliged to engage in, as soon as they reached the age for bearing arms, military exercises made an essential part of their education. They were trained up in them from their infancy, and had a space of ground within the city, called the Campus Martius, where, as if actually in the field, they formed themselves to all the branches of the service. After their fatigues they plunged into the Tiber, to accustom themselves to swimming, and cleanse away **the dust** and sweat. Hence the Romans were **never** obliged, on any sudden emergency, to **commit** the honour and safety of the state to a raw undisciplined multitude. They had always a sufficient number of men in readiness, trained and habituated to war, for the forming and recruiting their armies.

XVII. In reading the history of ancient commonwealths, we can hardly forbear fancying, that we peruse the annals of a set of men altogether different from ourselves. The prodigious fortune to which the Romans attained, seems incredible to us. We are amazed to see that republic, from an obscure inconsiderable village, rising insensibly to power, extending her dominion over Italy, and at last rendering herself mistress of the universe : to behold her citizens, even those of weight and authority in the administration, serving as private men in her armies ; and to find that soldiers, who in our days are the dregs of every nation, were in that commonwealth made up of the very same people, who, at home, in times of peace, created magistrates, enacted laws, and obliged the senate itself to submit to their decisions. Nor is it less a matter of wonder when we consider the number and greatness of her armies. It is evident, by experience, with respect to modern times, than a European prince, who has a million of subjects, cannot, without destroying himself, keep up and maintain above ten thousand men. But when we look into the affairs of ancient states, especially those of Sparta, Athens, and Rome, the case appears to be quite otherwise. We there find, that this proportion between the soldiers and the rest of the people, which is now as one to a hundred, could not in them be less than as one to eight. Rome was yet confined within very narrow bounds, when the Latins having refused to succour her with the troops which had been stipulated, **ten legions** were presently raised in the city **alone.** And if we examine the histories **of Athens and Sparta, we shall** there meet with **instances no less surprising,** of powerful and **numerous armies, when com-**pared with the **extent of their territories.**

XVIII. **To account, in some measure, for** so **wonderful a revolution in the course of** human affairs, it behoves us to call to mind, that the founders of ancient commonwealths had taken care to make an equal distribution of lands, and that the several portions were allotted to individuals, upon condition of serving the state in her wars. This circumstance alone raised a nation to power, gave strength to its armies, and made it a well regulated society. By this it became equally the interest of every member of the commonwealth, **and** that a very great interest too, to exert **him**self in defence of his country. Romulus, after assigning one part of the Roman territory to the expenses of religious worship, and another to the uses of the state, divided the renumber into thirty portions, to answer to the thirty Curiæ. Under the commonwealth, in proportion as the public domain increased, it was the constant practice of the senate, for several ages, to allot part of the conquered lands to the use of the poor citizens, and share it equally among them. This was what at first enabled Rome to soar above its humble condition; and the people were strongly sensible of it, even in their corrupted state. We find them constantly struggling for an agrarian law, and contriving means to check the artifices of those who endeavoured to elude it. The avowed patrons of liberty considered this law as the main bulwark of the state, and were ever sounding in the ears of the senate, the mischiefs to which they exposed themselves by the violation of it. Tell me, would Tiberius Gracchus say to the nobles, which is the most valuable character, that of a citizen, or of a perpetual slave? Who is most useful, a soldier, or a man entirely unfit for war? Will you, merely for the sake of enjoying a few more acres of land than your fellow-citizens, quite lay aside the hopes of conquering the rest of the world, or be exposed to see yourselves dispossessed, by the enemy, of those very lands which you refuse us?

XIX. And in fact we find, that in proportion as the Romans deviated from this great and original principle of government, affairs began to wear the very same face, under which they appear in our days. The avarice of some, and the lavish profuseness of others, occasioned the land to become the property of a few. Immediately arts were introduced, to supply the reciprocal wants of the rich and poor; by which means but very few soldiers or citizens were to be seen. For the revenues of the lands, that had before been employed to support the latter, were now wholly bestowed on slaves and artificers, who administered to the luxury of the new proprietors. But it was impossible that people of this cast should be good soldiers, they being cowardly and abject, already corrupted by the luxury of cities, and often by the very art they professed. Besides, as they might reap the fruits of their industry in every clime, and could not properly call any country their own, they had no sufficient tie to bind them to its defence. Nor was this revolution peculiar to the republic of Rome. Sparta before her had experienced the like vicissitude. Lycurgus left no less

than thirty thousand citizens behind him, who in the time of Agis and Cleomenes were reduced to seven hundred, scarce an eighth part of whom was possessed of lands. The rest were no more than a cowardly populace. These two kings undertook to revive the ancient laws on this occasion, and from that time Lacedemonia recovered its former power, and again became formidable to all the states of Greece. Had Tiberius and Caius Gracchus equally succeeded in their design of reforming the Roman commonwealth, the loss of liberty, and all the miseries consequent upon it, might have been prevented. But their untimely fate discouraging others from engaging in the same cause, Rome soon after, instead of being defended by, became a prey to, her own legions. Nor ought we to wonder, if men who had no property in the state, and might hope more from its overthrow than preservation, were easily induced to conspire its ruin.

XX. But the equal distribution of lands, was not that alone which gave strength to the armies of Rome. There were other circumstances, peculiar to the times and constitution of that republic, which contributed not a little to its grandeur. The trade of a soldier was not then, as in our days, a slavery for life, attended with infinite fatigue, and scarce any profit. As the art of exactly fortifying places was little known, and less practised, national quarrels were decided by battle, and one gained, often put an end to the war. Hence the service was, properly speaking, little more than so many summer campaigns. The armies were renewed yearly, and for several ages never kept the field during the winter. A battle commonly was attended with the conquest of an entire province or kingdom; and the pillage got in over-running the enemy's country, was often not only sufficient to enrich the conquerors, but sometimes even served to aggrandize their posterity. At the close of the campaign, the soldiers were dismissed, every one to his own home, to look after his domestic affairs, and cultivate his inheritance. Thus there were many inducements to a military life: the short duration of the service, the prospect of wealth and affluence, to which it often conducted; the necessity of defending their own possessions; and the hope of acquiring new ones from the enemy. For as we have already observed, it was the constant practice of the senate, for several ages to assign part of the cónquered lands to the use of the poor citizens; either dividing it among those who had no patrimony of their own, or granting an additional allowance to such whose inheritance was but scanty. In our times the condition of a soldier is very different. National quarrels are not now decided by battles, but most commonly by sieges, which spins out the war to an immoderate length, and occasions an infinite loss of men. Towns are seldom taken by storm, or abandoned to be plundered, but given up by capitulation, and the inhabitants left in the quiet possession of their properties. A country exposed to pillage redeems itself by contributions, no part of which comes into the hands of the private men, whose pay at the same time is so small, that the meanest occupation yields a far greater income. Thus the miseries of hunger, heat, and cold, which are inseparable from a military life, the certainty of blows, and the uncertainty of plunder, render the usual parts of war full of sufferings and dangers, and of little or no profit to the soldiers.

XXI. Indeed in the latter times of the commonwealth, war began to partake of those inconveniences, with which it is attended in the present age. But then the encouragements they had to face the dangers of the service, and the high honours to which it paved the way, made all difficulties vanish and disappear. For as the Romans devoted themselves entirely to the profession of arms, and considered it as the only study worthy their care, they omitted no methods to recommend and place it in esteem. Innumerable rewards and distinctions were invented, suited to the different stations of men, and the several kinds of valour in which they might render themselves conspicuous. Magistracies and dignities were almost always conferred, according to the reputation of the candidate for bravery in war. And at the same time that military merit never failed to promote the person in whom it was lodged, no one was capable of civil employment in the commonwealth, who had not served in the army at least ten years. We are not therefore to wonder, that amidst so many incentives, which rendered the life of a soldier not only honourable, but in some measure necessary, multitudes flocked to the service and strove with emulation to be admitted into the legions. Interest and ambition are the two ruling principles of human life; and as

both conspired to urge the Romans to war, it was easy for them to find armies, and to increase and multiply them at pleasure. But in our days, none of those motives operate upon the minds of men. The condition of a common soldier is of all others the most despicable; and even with regard to officers of the first rank, long service is so far from being a recommendation to state-preferment, that they are on that very account, in the judgment of many, the less fit for civil employments.

XXII. But what chiefly contributed to the strength and greatness of the Roman armies, was the custom established by Romulus, of incorporating the vanquished nations, and admitting them to the privileges of citizens. Without this it would have been impossible for Rome to raise herself to that height of grandeur, to which in time she attained. The spirit of her citizens, the bravery of her troops, and the admirable discipline of her armies, might have enabled her to subject the nations around her, and extend her sway over a considerable part of Italy; but in proportion as she advanced in conquest, she would have become sensible of her own weakness; and the difficulty of maintaining herself in her new territories, when they grew large enough to employ the whole natural forces of the commonwealth, would have either made her drop all thoughts of farther empire, or forced her to **have recourse to** mercenary troops, which have **always in** the end proved the ruin of those states, who were imprudent enough to venture upon **so dangerous** an **expedient**. This **is** remarkably exemplified in the history of Athens, Sparta, and Carthage. The two first **of these** cities acquired considerable dominion and authority in Greece, and for some time maintained themselves in the possession of that power, to which their valour, and abilities in war had raised them. But as the number of citizens in either state seldom exceeded thirty thousand, and they were unacquainted with the policy of incorporating the vanquished nations, it was impossible for them to enlarge their territories in any extensive degree. For great conquests require great armies to maintain them, which cities so constituted as Athens and Sparta, were not able to furnish. Accordingly we find, that when ambition prompted them to undertakings beyond their strength, they were so far from being able to increase their dominions, that their very conquests proved their ruin, and they sunk under the weight of their own greatness. For the countries they had brought under subjection, not considering themselves as part of the state, but rather as tributaries and slaves, were glad of an opportunity of shaking off the yoke; and therefore seldom failed to revolt, when they saw them engaged in any difficult war. By this means they were not only deprived of a considerable part of the revenues, at a time when they stood most in need of money and supplies; but obliged likewise to divide their forces, which was a great check upon their designs, and in the end so weakened them, that they were no longer able to maintain themselves in that grandeur and reputation they had acquired.

XXIII. The case of Carthage was indeed somewhat different. That commonwealth, by its riches and commerce, was able to set great armies on foot, and make extensive conquests. But as the genius of the citizens was turned more to traffic than war, and as they never admitted the conquered nations to the privileges of natural subjects, they were under a necessity of employing mercenary troops, both for enlarging their territories, and holding the vanquished countries in obedience. Hence the many shocks and convulsions to which that state was liable. For as her armies had no other tie to the republic, but that of their pay, they were easily induced to throw off their allegiance, when any more advantageous prospect offered itself. Their revolt more than once brought Carthage to the very brink of destruction. Instead of contributing to secure the tranquillity of the tributary countries, they often spirited them up to rebellion; and, which is indeed a necessary consequence of employing mercenary troops, upon any sudden reverse of fortune, they were ever ready to abandon the service. Thus the Carthaginians, though absolute masters at sea, possessed of immense territories, and able to set on foot numerous armies, were in reality rather a rich than a powerful republic. They were successful indeed for a time against a number of barbarous states and nations, without discipline or experience in war; but when they came to enter the lists with a brave and a military people, their undertakings almost always miscarried. Witness

their many attempts upon Syracuse, the extremity to which they were reduced by Agathocles; and the ease with which they were in a manner totally driven out of Sicily, by Pyrrhus. Indeed in their first and second war with the Romans, they make a very considerable figure in history, whether we regard the greatness of their victories, or the strength of their armies. But the merit of that seems rather owing to the abilities of their generals, than to the intrinsic power of the commonwealth itself. Accordingly, in the third Punic war, when they had neither a Hamilcar, nor a Hannibal at the head of their troops, they in a very short time fell a prey to their enemies.

XXIV. But now the Romans, by the admirable policy of incorporating the vanquished nations, avoided all the inconveniences to which the above-mentioned cities were liable, and built their greatness upon a sure foundation. The forces of the state increased with their territories, insomuch that it is amazing to consider, in how short a time, from small beginnings, they rose to an incredible multitude of citizens. The conquered provinces were so far from being an incumbrance upon them, by exhausting their strength in guards and garrisons, that, on the contrary, they became real parts of the commonwealth, and contributed greatly to her power, by augmenting her revenues, and adding to the number of her subjects. Thus, in proportion as Rome grew in greatness, and stood in need of mighty armies to support the weight of her enterprises, she found within herself an inexhaustible stock of men and riches, and without having recourse to mercenary troops, could furnish more than sufficient to answer all the demands of the state. Polybius, when he comes to speak of the war with the Italic Gauls, takes occasion to describe the mighty preparations made by the Romans, to oppose that formidable enemy. We there find, that the forces of the commonwealth, at that time, amounted to about seven hundred thousand foot, and seventy thousand horse. Compare this account with the histories of Athens and Sparta, and it will soon appear, what a disadvantage these two states lay under, for want of such an institution as that of Romulus. For as they never admitted the vanquished nations to the right of citizens, but always reduced them to the condition of tributaries, the multitude of their conquests served only to enlarge their territories, without adding to the number of their natural subjects. Hence even in the most flourishing period of their greatness, they could seldom bring into the field above thirty thousand men. Rome, on the other hand, by a contrary policy, increased daily in the multitude of her citizens, and in time was enabled to furnish out armies, adequate to the conquest of the universe.

CHAP. III.

OF THE ARMS AND DISCIPLINE OF THE ROMANS.

I. It is generally allowed among the writers upon the art of war, that as in many other things, so particularly in their arms, the Romans excelled all other nations. I shall not here confine myself to the usual distinction into offensive and defensive, but rather describe them according to the several military orders of which the legions were composed. By the *velites* we are to understand all the light-armed troops of the commonwealth, of whatever rank and denomination. They were equipped with bows, slings, javelins, a Spanish sword, a buckler, and a helmet. The bow is of very remote antiquity, and has been used by almost all nations. Crete in particular was famous for its excellent archers. It does not seem to have been much regarded by the Romans in the earliest times of the republic, and when it was afterwards introduced, was confined chiefly to the auxiliary troops. We find, however, in the description of battles, frequent mention made of the *sagittarii*; and it appears, that they sometimes contributed not a little to the victory. The sling was also an instrument of war much used by many nations. The Baleareans especially, who inhabited the islands now called Majorca and Minorca, are beyond all others celebrated for their expertness at this weapon. They were so attentive in exercising their youth in the use of it, that they did not give them their food in a morning till they hit a mark. These Baleareans were much employed in the armies of the Carthaginians and Romans, and greatly contributed to the gaining of victories. Livy mentions some cities of Achaia, particularly Egium, Patræ, and Dymæ, whose inhabitants were still more dextrous at the sling than the Baleareans.

They threw stones farther, and with greater force and certainty, never failing to hit what part of the face they pleased. Their slings discharged stones with so much force, that neither buckler nor head-piece could resist their impetuosity. Instead of stones, they sometimes charged the sling with balls of lead, which it carried much farther, and with greater impetuosity. The javelin, or *hasta*, was the proper missive weapon of the *velites*. It was a kind of dart not unlike an arrow, the wood of which was generally three feet long, and one inch thick. The point was four inches long, and tapered to so fine an end, that it bent at the first stroke in such a manner, as to be useless to the enemy. Every man carried seven of them to battle. The Spanish sword was for a close encounter. The Romans judged this weapon the fittest for execution, as having both edge and point. It was short, of excellent temper, and in shape not unlike a Turkish scimitar, only sharper at the point. Livy tells us, that though it was principally intended for stabbing, it would yet serve likewise to cut off arms, legs, and heads at a blow. The buckler or *parma*, was of a round form, about three feet in diameter, and made of wood, covered with leather. The helmet, called *galea*, or *galerus*, was a light casque for the head, generally made of the skin of some wild beasts, to appear the more terrible.

II. The arms of the *hastati*, *principes*, and *triarii*, were in a great measure the same; for which reason we shall not divide them in our description, but speak of them altogether. Those most deserving our notice are the sword, the *scutum*, the *pilum*, the *galea*, and the *lorica*. The sword was the same as that of the *velites*, and therefore requires not any particular description here. It was usual with the Romans to wear it on the right side, that they might be the more at liberty to manage their shields. In ancient monuments however we sometimes meet with it on the left. The *scutum* was a buckler of wood, oblong, and bending inward like a half cylinder. Its parts were joined together with little plates of iron, and the whole was covered with a bull's hide. An iron ring went round it without, to keep off blows; and another within, to hinder it from taking any damage by lying on the ground. In the middle was an iron boss, or *umbo*, jutting out, very serviceable to glance off stones and darts, and sometimes to press violently upon the enemy, and drive all before them. It appears that these bucklers were large enough to cover almost the whole body. Polybius makes them four feet long, and two and a half broad. And in Livy we meet with soldiers who stood on the guard, sometimes sleeping with their head laid on their shield, having fixed the other part of it on the earth. Some make the *scutum* the same with the *clypeus*: but this is evidently a mistake; since in the institution of the *census*, by Servius Tullius, we find the *clypeus* given to those of the first class, and the *scutum* to those of the second. In fact, the *scutum* was long and square, and came at last to be the only shield of the heavy-armed troops. The *clypeus* was of a smaller size, and quite round, belonging more properly to other nations, though for some time used by the Romans.

III. The *pilum* was a missive weapon, which in a charge they darted at the enemy. It was commonly four-square, but sometimes round; composed of a piece of wood about three cubits long, and a slip of iron of the same length, hooked and jagged at the end. They took abundance of care in joining the two parts together, and did it so artificially, that it would sooner break in the iron itself, than in the joint. Every man had two of these *pila*, which they discharged at the enemy before they came to close fight. When they had neither time nor room they threw it upon the ground, and charged the enemy sword in hand. Marius, in the Cimbrian war, contrived these *pila* after a new fashion. For whereas before the head was fastened to the wood with two iron pins, he suffered one of them to remain as it was, and pulling out the other, put a weak wooden peg in its place. By this means, when it stuck in the enemy's shield it did not stand outright as formerly: but the wooden peg breaking, the javelin hung down, and sticking fast by its crooked point, drew after it the shield. Next to the *pilum* we mentioned the *galea*. This was a head-piece, or morion, coming down to the shoulders. It was either of iron or brass, open before, and leaving the face uncovered. Some of them were so contrived, that they might be let down, on occasion, to cover the face. Upon the top was the *crista*, or crest, in adorning of which the soldiers took great pride. In the time of Polybius they wore plumes of feathers, dyed of various colours, to render them beautiful to their friends, and terrible to their enemies.

The officers in particular were extremely curious and splendid in their crests, which were usually worked in gold and silver, and so contrived as to represent animals of various kinds, lions, leopards, tigers, and griffins. If we might speak of those of foreign commanders, the crest of king Pyrrhus, as very singular, would deserve our notice. It was made, according to Plutarch's description, of two goats' horns. Alexander the Great, as he is represented on ancient medals, wore a crest of the same nature.

IV. We come now to the *lorica*, which was a defensive armour for the body, as the *galea* was for the head and neck. In our language it is called the cuirass, and was generally made of leather, covered with plates of iron in the form of scales, or iron rings twisted within one another in the form of chains. These are what we call coats of mail, in Latin, *lorica hamis conserta*, or *hamata*. Sometimes the cuirass consisted of thongs, with which the soldier was girt from the arm-pits to the waist, and whence probably it took the name of *lorica*, from *lorum*, a thong or strap of leather. We find likewise that it was oftentimes a sort of linen cassock, made with many folds, which resisted, or very much broke the force of blows. Amongst the Greeks this piece of armour had the name of *thorax*, and was made either of iron or brass, in two pieces, which were fastened upon the sides by buckles. Alexander left the cuirass only the two pieces which covered the breast, that the fear of being wounded on the back, which had no defence, might prevent the soldiers from flying. Some of these cuirasses were of so hard a metal, as to be absolutely proof against weapons. Zoilus, an excellent artist in this way, offered two of them to Demetrius Poliorcetes. To show the excellency of them, he caused a dart to be discharged from a *catapulta*, at the distance of only twenty-six paces; which, though it struck the cuirass with the utmost violence, yet made no impression, and scarce left the least mark behind it. After all it must be owned, that the *thorax* of the Greeks was much less capable of motion, agility, and force; whereas the girts of leather, successively covering each other, left the Roman soldier entire liberty of action, and fitting him like a vest, defended him against darts. The poorer soldiers, who were rated under a thousand drachms, instead of the *lorica*, wore a

E.

pectorale, or breastplate of thin brass, about twelve inches square; and this, with what has been already described, and greaves and gauntlets upon their legs and arms, which were common likewise to the rest, rendered them completely armed.

V. What we have hitherto said regards only the foot. It is now time to speak of the cavalry, who at first were but very indifferently armed, either for offence or defence. They used only a round shield, with a helmet on their head, and a couple of javelins in their hand, great part of the body being left without defence. But as soon as they found the many inconveniences to which they were hereby exposed, they began to arm themselves like the Grecian horse, or much in the manner of their own foot, only their shield was a little shorter and squarer, and their lance or javelin thicker, with spikes at each end, that if one miscarried, the other might be serviceable. It is remarkable, and what indeed we are hardly able to comprehend, that amongst the ancients, the horse had neither stirrups nor saddle. Education, exercise, and habit, had accustomed them not to want those aids, and even not to perceive that there was any occasion for them. There were some horsemen such as the Numidians, who did not know so much as the use of bridles to guide their horses: and who, notwithstanding, by their voice only, or the use of the heel or spur, made them advance, fall back, stop, turn to the right or left; in a word, perform all the evolutions of the best disciplined cavalry. Sometimes, having two horses, they leaped from one to the other, even in the heat of battle, to ease the first when fatigued. These Numidians, as well as the Parthians, were never more terrible than when they seemed to fly through fear and cowardice. For then, facing suddenly about, they discharged their darts or arrows upon the enemy, and often put them to flight with great slaughter. The Romans were more than once surprised by these unexpected attacks, and on some occasions suffered considerably. But they at last found out a method of securing themselves, by holding their targets over their heads, and forming what historians call the *testudo*. It was to this invention that Marc Antony owed the preservation of his army, when miscarrying in his expedition against the Parthians, he found himself obliged to retreat into Syria before a great body of their horse.

VI. These were the arms with which the Romans conquered the world: and I believe it will be readily owned, that they were admirably well calculated both for defending themselves, and offending their enemies. Polybius, in more places than one, gives them the advantage in this respect over all other nations, and expressly affirms, that the many victories they obtained over the Gauls was owing entirely to the superiority of their arms. It is true the cutting swords of that people terrified them greatly at first, and was the cause of a fatal overthrow. But they soon learnt from experience what a contemptible weapon that was, when employed in close fight against troops substantially armed for defence: for the Gauls, to give force and vigour to their blows, were obliged to avoid too near an approach to the enemy, that they might have room to wield their swords. Their first ranks therefore only could do execution, because the Romans, knowing their safety to lie in close fight, advanced continually under cover of their shields, and crowded upon them in such manner, that they left them not sufficient space for the free use of their weapons. It is besides observed, that the swords of the Gauls were of so ill a temper, as after two or three strokes to stand bent in their hands, and thereby become wholly useless to them, if they had not time to straighten them on the ground with their feet. This was not to be expected in the heat of fight against an enemy that pressed so hard; so that the Romans closing in with them, stabbed them in the face and breast with their pointed swords, and made terrible **slaughter**. The Chevalier Fohard is astonished, that under all these disadvantages, **his** countrymen should obtain so many victories over the Romans. He can hardly forbear fancying, that, had they so far improved by their defeats, as to change the fashion of their weapons, and arm themselves after the manner of their adversaries, we should not have heard so much of the boasted exploits and conquests of that people. Be that as it will, it is certain the Gauls wanted neither bravery, nor military conduct, and, if we except the single article of their arms, showed themselves on many occasions no way inferior to the Romans.

VII. But let us now compare their arms with those of the Greeks. Here, it must be owned, the advantage does not appear so manifest. Many are rather of opinion, that the

Greeks excelled the Romans in this respect. The Earl of Orrery particularly, in his Treatise of the Art of War, wonders much that the Romans, who borrowed most of their weapons, whether offensive or defensive, from the Greeks, did not also follow their example in furnishing some of their infantry with long pikes, which he observes are the best offensive arms, either to charge or defend, and of excellent use against horse. It is well known that the Macedonian phalanx, to which Philip and Alexander were indebted for most of their victories, fought always with this weapon. One would therefore be apt to think, that an experience so much in its favour, could not have failed of recommending it powerfully to the Romans. And yet it is certain, that after making trial of it for some time, they laid it aside as incommodious, ordering the *hastati*, who at first were equipped with it, and thence took their name, to arm themselves after the fashion of the rest of the legionary foot. This could not arise from any scrupulous attachment to their own customs, or dislike of foreign manners; because no people were ever less tenacious in this respect, or showed a greater readiness to adopt the institutions of other nations, when they saw any real benefit likely to accrue from them. The principal reason seems to have been, that they found the use of the weapon incompatible with that of the shield. For as it necessarily required to be managed with both hands, those who fought with it were obliged to lay aside the buckler; which piece of armour appeared to the Romans of greater consequence than the pike, because this last was in some measure supplied by the sword and javelin. If we might judge of things by the event, the Romans reasoned very justly on this occasion; since without the assistance of the pike, they not only gained greater and more numerous victories than the Macedonian phalanx, but even beat that very phalanx itself, so formidable by the use of this weapon. As this is a very curious and interesting subject, and capable of furnishing many useful reflections in relation to the ancient art of war, it will not, I believe, be disagreeable to the reader, if we enlarge a little upon it.

VIII. The Macedonian phalanx was a body of sixteen thousand men, armed with pikes, four and twenty feet long, which historians describe under the name of *sarissæ*. This corps was generally divided into ten battalions, each consisting of sixteen hundred men, a hundred in front, and sixteen deep. To form some idea of their strength and order of battle, we need only reflect upon what passed a few centuries ago in Europe, when Italy was a continual theatre of war, by reason of the different pretensions of France, Spain, and the Emperor. The battalions of Switzerland were then in great reputation, and generally looked upon as the best infantry in the world, chiefly on account of the many victories they had gained by the pike. They were forced at first to have recourse to this weapon, in order to secure themselves against the ambition of the German princes, who were daily making attempts upon their liberty. For these princes being rich, and able to bring into the field a numerous cavalry, the Switzers, whose whole strength, on the contrary, lay in their foot, saw themselves under a necessity of contriving arms, that might defend them against the enemy's horse. None appeared so proper for this purpose as the pike; and so successful were they, by the perfection they attained to in the use of it, and their admirable orders and discipline, that with fifteen or twenty thousand foot, they would often venture to attack a vast body of horse, and generally came off victorious. From that time the pike became famous, and was introduced into all the armies of Europe. We find that they usually had one half of their infantry shot, and the other half pikes; and it is particularly deserving of our notice, that for several ages, the chief dependence of the general in a day of battle seems to have been upon the pikes. By degrees the musket began to prevail over the pike; yet gained ground so very slowly, that it is not much above half a century, since we find one third of the infantry still pikes.

IX. But though the pike was found to be of admirable service in engagements with horse, experience constantly made it appear, that it was by no means sufficient against a resolute and well-armed infantry. For as this weapon required to be managed with both hands, and therefore necessarily excluded the use of the target, those who carried it were left altogether without defence, if, in the course of an engagement, the enemy should chance to get within their pikes. Hence the generals who were acquainted with this weakness in the Swiss battalions, and could bring their troops to press th charge vigorously, seldom failed of defeating them with great slaughter. We have a remarkable example of it in the case of Count Carmignola, general to Philip Viconti, Duke of Milan. That brave officer being sent against a body of eighteen thousand Switzers, with only six thousand horse, and a few foot, advanced boldly to the encounter; but though the attack was resolute and well conducted, he was repulsed with considerable loss. Carmignola quickly perceived the advantage which the enemy had in their foot over his horse. As he was a man of determined courage, and rather roused than dispirited by the check he had lately received, he soon rallied his men, and led them on again to the charge. When he came within a certain distance, he ordered his cavalry to dismount; and engaging the Switzers smartly in that posture, put them all to the rout, and most of them to the sword. Only three thousand were left, who, finding themselves past remedy, threw down their arms. It will be proper to take notice on this occasion, that the cavalry led by Carmignola were all men at arms, and therefore completely provided both for offence and defence. Now such a body of troops was well enough able to deal with the Switzers, if they but once got close up with them, and came to use their swords. For then the enemy being without defensive arms, and deriving no assistance from their pikes, whose very length rendered them unserviceable, were exposed to unavoidable slaughter. Considering, therefore, the advantages and disadvantages on both sides, it will appear, that they who have no defensive arms are without remedy, if the enemy charges but home, and passes their pikes. This cannot miss to happen in an engagement with resolute troops: because battles always advancing, and the parties on each side pressing on perpetually, they must of necessity come so near at last, as to reach one another with their swords; and though some few perhaps may be killed or tumbled down by the pikes, yet those that are behind, still pressing on, are sufficient to carry the victory.

X. From these reasons it will be easy to conceive, why Carmignola overcame, with so great a slaughter of the Switzers, and so little of his own army. Nor is this example singular in its kind. We meet with many others

in history, all tending to demonstrate, that an infantry, armed with swords and bucklers, have great advantages over the pike. When Gonsalva was besieged in Barletta by the French, a detachment of Spanish foot was sent out of Sicily, and landed in the kingdom of Naples, with orders to march to his relief. Monsieur d'Aubigny had notice of their approach, and went to meet them with his men at arms and a body of about four thousand Switzers. These last pressed upon them with their pikes, and at first put them into some disorder; but the Spaniards, by the help of their bucklers, and the agility of their bodies, having at length got under the pikes of the Switzers and so near that they could come at them with their swords, defeated them with great slaughter, and very little loss on their own side. Every one knows what terrible havoc was made of the Switzers, at the battle of Ravenna, and all upon the same account, the Spanish foot having got to them with their swords: nay, it is certain they must have been all cut to pieces, had they not been happily rescued by the French horse, and yet the Spaniards, drawing themselves into close order, bravely sustained the assaults of the cavalry, and retired without loss. It appears therefore, that though the pike be excellent against horse, it is yet insufficient in an encounter with foot; whereas an army judiciously armed for offence and defence, at the same time that it can very well deal with cavalry, is likewise an overmatch for a body of pikes.

XI. And hence it was that the Macedonian phalanx, which seems to have been just such an order of battle as the battalions of Switzerland, experienced likewise the same fate, when it came to encounter the warlike and well-armed troops of the Romans. Historians ascribe the defeat of it to several causes; the advantageous disposition of the Roman troops, who fought in separate bodies, yet so drawn up that they could unite and join upon occasion: the artful conduct of the generals, in drawing it into rugged and uneven places, where it could not preserve itself entire, but became disjointed and broken: the opportunity this gave of charging it in the openings and void spaces, whereby it was totally disunited, and being attacked in front and rear, fell an easy prey to its enemies. These things doubtless contributed in part to the overthrow of which we speak ; but the principal defect of the phalanx lay in its disadvantageous armour and order of battle. In reality, the pikes of the two first ranks only were serviceable in an engagement ; those of the rest scarce availed any thing. The men of the third rank could not see what passed in the front, nor had any command of their long pikes, which were entangled and locked up between the files, without a possibility of moving them to the right or left. Hence the Romans found no great difficulty in surmounting an obstacle, formidable indeed in appearance, but at bottom very trifling. They had only to gain upon the pikes of the two first ranks, that they might join the enemy, and fight hand to hand. This they were enabled to do by the help of their large bucklers, with which they bore up the pikes of the Macedonians, and forcing their way under, reached them with their swords. All resistance then was at an end. The phalanx, unprovided for defence, and rather embarrassed than aided by their pikes, could no longer stand the furious charge of the Romans, who made dreadful havoc with their pointed swords. We find at the battle of Pydna, where Paulus Æmilius gained so complete a victory over Perseus, that no less than twenty thousand Macedonians were slain with the loss of only one hundred men on the side of the Romans. This agrees so exactly with what we have above related of the Switzers, that it is impossible not to ascribe it to the same cause, namely, the insufficiency of the pike, when opposed to an infantry armed with swords and bucklers.

XII. We come now to speak of the military discipline of the Romans, to which, no less than to their arms, they were indebted for their many victories and conquests. If we compare this with other nations, we do not find that they surpassed the Gauls in number or boldness, the Germans in stature, the Spaniards in strength of body, the Africans in stratagem, or the Greeks in learning and the arts of civil life. Nay, it is evident from history, that they were inferior in all these respects. But as to what regards the use and exercise of arms, the choice of soldiers, and the training them up in all the duties of war ; here indeed lay their chief excellence, and by this they were enabled to baffle all the advantages of their enemies, whether derived from nature or education. We have already observed, that

none were admitted into the legions till they had reached their seventeenth year. But though this was the age for entering the service, it was not then that they began to learn. For as war was the darling study of the Romans, they habituated their youth to it from their infancy, and carefully instructed them in all its branches, having set apart the Field of Mars for this purpose, which was a kind of military school within the city. We are not however to imagine, that they looked upon this early institution as sufficient, or were less assiduous in exercising their men, after they were admitted into the service. They knew that constant practice alone makes troops expert, and brings them to the habit of applying their knowledge with readiness upon all occasions. Hence not only among the young soldiers, but even among those of oldest standing in the army, the military exercises were continued without intermission. These exercises had a threefold tendency : to inure the men to labour, and render them robust and active : to instruct them in the use of their arms, and lastly, to teach them the necessary evolutions, and how to preserve their ranks and orders, in marches, battles, and encampments.

XIII. As to the first, the Romans took great pains to form their youth to be nimble in running, active to leap, strong to throw the bar and to wrestle, which are all necessary qualifications in a soldier. For running and nimbleness fit them to get possession of a place before the enemy, to fall upon them on a sudden in their quarters, and to pursue them with more execution in a rout ; activity enables them with greater ease to avoid blows, leap a ditch, or climb a bank ; and strength makes them carry their arms better, strike better, and endure the shock better. Swimming was likewise considered as an essential part of a military education. Armies are not sure of bridges wherever they come, nor are boats always to be had ; so that if men cannot swim, they will necessarily be deprived of several conveniences, and lose many fair opportunities of action. One principal reason why the Romans made choice of the *Campus Martius* to exercise their youth in was, its nearness to the Tiber, into which they plunged after their fatigues, to accustom themselves to swimming, and cleanse away the dust and sweat. But of all their exercises of this kind, none was pursued with greater attention, than

4

the inuring the troops to the military pace; that is, to walk twenty miles, and sometimes four and twenty, in five hours. This habituated the soldiers to a certain stated and regular progress in their marches, taught them to keep close together, and prevented their exposing themselves scattered and dispersed to the enemy. They were obliged likewise on these occasions, to carry burdens of threescore pound weight, which not only accustomed them to bear fatigue, but was found serviceable in many other respects. For whether it might be necessary in an expedition to take along with them several days' provisions, or to carry a certain quantity of water through a desert and sandy country, or to provide a number of stakes for the execution of any particular enterprise; against all these exigencies they had prepared themselves by the practice of which we speak: and hence great dangers were many times avoided, and great victories many times obtained.

XIV. The second particular we mentioned in the Roman exercises was, the instructing the men in the use of their arms. Here also we meet with many proofs of the industry and sagacity of that people. They set up a great post about six feet high, suitable to the stature of a man, and fastened it so strongly, that no blows might be able to batter or shake it. Thus the soldiers were wont to assail with all the instruments of war, as if it had been indeed a real enemy. Sometimes they would aim their blows at the head, sometimes strike it on the face, then on the sides, legs, before and behind, now retreating, and then advancing again; during all which they were taught to proceed with so much caution, that in directing their weapon against their adversary, they should not meanwhile lay themselves open to wounds. By this contrivance they learned how to place their blows aright, and became dextrous and nimble, both at defending themselves, and offending their enemies. They were instructed rather to thrust than to cut with their swords; because thrusts are more mortal, harder to be defended, and he that makes them is not so easily discovered, and is readier to double his thrust than his blow. We must not here forget, that in these exercises they made use of helmets, shields, and swords, double the weight of common weapons. This made them ready and alert in battle, which they found so far from being attended with any unforeseen encumbrances, that it was rather an ease from the fatigue of ordinary duty. Nor let any one wonder that the Romans were so extremely attentive to these little things, since, according to the manner of fighting then used, in which the troops encountered hand to hand, every small advantage was of great importance. They were besides sensible, that experience in this kind makes men bold and courageous; for no one fears to do that which he thinks he understands. A soldier who had often made trial of himself in these imaginary combats, grew impatient to come to action in good earnest, that he might the better judge of his own proficiency, and have an opportunity of putting that in practice, which he had so well learned in theory. Hence battles were not what they dreaded, but what they desired; and generals often found it more difficult to restrain their men from fighting, and check the ardour of their courage, where prudence obliged them to decline the onset, than to prevail upon them to face the enemy, when they judged it necessary to come to an engagement.

XV. But it is not sufficient to inure men to labour, to make them strong, swift, and expert at the use of their weapons; they must learn likewise to keep their ranks well, to obey orders, and follow the directions and signals of their commanders. This was the third branch of the Roman exercises, about which they were no less solicitous than about the other two. I shall not here enter into a minute detail of the common evolutions, the opening and closing of the files, doubling their ranks, turning to the right, and left, marchings, wheelings, &c. because they differed but a little from the practice of the present age. Their manner of forming too in order of battle, their conduct in an attack or repulse, with the general disposition of their marches, will come in more properly under other heads of this discourse. Let it suffice for the present to observe, that they exercised their men without intermission in all these different branches of the service, and by the force of constant habit brought them to that degree of expertness, that they could practise without hurry and confusion in the heat of fight, what they had been so thoroughly trained to in the field. Above all, it was their particular care to accustom the troops to rally and recover their order readily when broken. To this end, besides distinguishing the several companies by peculiar ensigns, every man had his fixed and invariable post in the battalion, and was taught, by long practice, to know, in a manner habitually, the number of his file, his place in that file, his right and left-hand man, where he belonged to the front rank, and both these and his file-leader, where he belonged to the other ranks. Nay, so very curious were the Romans in this point, that to imprint these things the deeper upon the minds of the soldiers, they caused them to be engraven in great characters upon their helmets and bucklers.

XVI. Nor were they less careful in training up the cavalry, whom they taught particularly to ride well, and sit fast when they came to a charge. To this end they had horses of wood, upon which they were exercised, vaulting upon them, sometimes with their arms, and sometimes without, very neatly and exactly, without any assistance; so that, upon a signal from their captain, they were immediately on horseback, and upon another signal, as soon upon the ground. As they fought in squadrons, like the cavalry of our time, their evolutions were much the same with those in use at present, allowing only the difference of armour; and among the horse, as well as the foot, were carried on without intermission. Indeed, there is nothing more admirable in the whole Roman discipline than the continual exercise to which the troops were kept, either within or without the camp; insomuch that they were never idle, and had scarce any respite from duty. The now raised soldiers performed their exercises regularly twice a day, and the old ones once: for it was not, in the opinion of this people, length of service that constituted warlike and veteran troops, but the uninterrupted habit and practice of arms; nor did they consider an unexercised soldier, after what number of campaigns you will, as any other than a novice in the profession. Accordingly, they were constant and indefatigable in training their men to all the different operations of the field. They obliged them to make hasty marches of a considerable length, laden with their arms and several palisades, and that often in steep and craggy countries. They habituated them always to keep their ranks, even in the midst of disorder and confusion, and never to lose

sight of their standards. They made them charge each other in mock battles, of which the officers, generals, and even the consul himself were witnesses, and in which they thought it for their glory to share in person. When they had no enemy in the field, the troops were employed in considerable works, as well to keep them in exercise, as for the public utility. Such in particular were the highways, called for that reason *viæ militares*, which still subsist, and are the fruits of that wise and salutary custom.

XVII. How much the Romans relied upon this manner of training and employing their troops, appears evidently from the conduct of their senate and generals, during a course of several ages; for in all their difficulties and straits, this was that to which they had immediate recourse, as their surest refuge, and the only means by which they could hope to extricate themselves. Did they think themselves exposed to any danger, or were they desirous to repair some loss? It was a constant practice among them to invigorate and give new life to their military discipline. Are they engaged in a war with the Latines, a people no less martial than themselves? Manlius reflects upon the best method of strengthening the command in the field, and puts to death his own son, for conquering without his orders. Are they defeated before Numantia? Scipio Æmilianus immediately removes the several blandishments which had enervated them. Have the Roman legions passed under the yoke in Numidia? Metellus wipes away the ignominy the instant he has obliged them to resume their ancient institutions. Marius, that he may be enabled to vanquish the Cimbri and the Teutones, begins by diverting the course of rivers; and Sylla employs in such hard labour his soldiers, who were terrified at the war which was carrying on against Mithridates, that they sue for battle to put an end to their hardships. Publius Nasica made the Romans build a fleet of ships at a time when they had no occasion for such a force. In a word, industry, diligence, and a perseverance in all kind of military toils, was the very characteristic of this people; they dreaded idleness more than an enemy.

XVIII. These men thus inured were generally healthy and vigorous. We do not find, by historians, that the Roman armies, which waged war in so great a variety of climates, fell often a prey to diseases; whereas, in the present age, we daily see armies, without once engaging, perish and melt away, if I may use the expression, in a single campaign. Nor can I forbear taking notice, that the dexterity and address the soldiers attained, by means of their continual exercises, served not only to render them skilful and active in the duties of the field, but inspired them likewise with boldness and intrepidity. In the battles fought in our age, every single soldier has very little security and confidence, except in the multitude; but among the Romans, every individual, more robust and of greater experience in war, as well as more inured to the fatigues of it than his enemy, relied upon himself only. He was naturally endued with courage, or, in other words, with that virtue which a sensibility of our own strength inspires. To the same admirable discipline too were they indebted for a certain haughtiness and opinion of superiority, which made them rank themselves above the troops of all other nations, and despise the service of any foreign prince or state, compared with that of their country. Desertions are very common among us, for this reason, because the soldiers are the dregs of every nation, and not one of them possesses, or thinks himself possessed of a certain advantage, which renders his condition preferable to that of his adversaries. But among the Romans they were less frequent, it being scarce possible that soldiers, raised from among a people naturally so imperious and aspiring, and so sure of commanding over others, should demean themselves to such a degree as to cease to be Romans. We may likewise observe, as a necessary consequence of their being so carefully trained, that it was next to impossible in a battle, how unfortunate soever, but some troops must rally in one part or other of it, or the enemy be defeated in some quarter of the field, either of which was often sufficient to secure the victory. And indeed we find every-where in history, that whenever the Romans happened to be overpowered in the beginning, whether by numbers or the fierceness of the onset, they seldom failed at last to wrest the victory out of the enemy's hands.

XIX. There are still many other particulars that might be mentioned to the advantage of the Roman discipline: their strict regulations with regard to all the different branches of the service; their admirable policy in making motives of honour and shame operate strongly upon the troops; their steady adherence to the received maxims of war, so as never, on any occasion, to abate of the rigour of military severity, where the soldiers were found to have neglected their duty, abandoned their post, thrown away their arms, or surrendered themselves to the enemy. History abounds with examples of this kind. As their armies were for the most part but small, the commander had a better opportunity of knowing the several individuals, and could more easily perceive the various faults and misdemeanors committed by the soldiery, against which care was taken to provide immediately. Nor were they so tenacious of their own customs as not to pay a due attention to those of other nations, which they adopted without hesitation, wherever they appeared attended with any real benefit. In their war with Pyrrhus, they improved themselves in the knowledge of posts and encampments: in that with Hannibal, they learned the true use of cavalry, and how to apply address and stratagem in the conduct of a campaign. If any nation boasted, either from nature or its institution, any peculiar advantage, the Romans immediately made use of it. They employed their utmost endeavours to procure horses from Numidia, bowmen from Crete, slingers from the Balearean Isles, and ships from the Rhodians: so that it may with justice be said of them, that no nation in the world ever prepared for war with so much wisdom, and carried it on with so much intrepidity.

XX. Thus have we endeavoured to give some account of the arms and discipline of the Romans, and to point out their excellency over those of other nations. How much they were indebted to them for their grandeur and successes, appears evidently from this: that so long as their armies adhered strictly to these primitive institutions, they were invincible; but in proportion as they deviated from them, became like other men. When they began to look upon their armour as too weighty and cumbersome, and their discipline as attended with too many restraints, and of course to relax in these two important articles, they gradually sunk into a level with the troops of their enemies, and at last so totally degenerated, that we find not in their behaviour the least traces of their original bravery. I know it is a maxim of long standing, that money is the sinews of war. How far this may suit the constitution of the present age, I will not pretend to say; but it seems by no means to agree with antiquity. I am sure the whole current of history is against it. Had this been the case, Cyrus could never have prevailed against Crœsus, nor the Greeks against the Persians, nor the Romans against the Carthaginians. It is true money is requisite for the carrying on of a war, but not principally, and in the first place. Good soldiers and good discipline are of infinitely greater avail. Where these are, it will be easy to find money; but money is not always sufficient to procure them. Had not the Romans done more in their wars with their iron than their gold, the treasure of the whole world would not have been sufficient for them, considering their great enterprises abroad, and their no less difficulties at home. But having good and well disciplined troops, they were never in want of money; for those who were afraid of their armies, strove with emulation to supply them. Nay, it is remarkable, that their most celebrated victories, and those which required the greatest exertion of strength, were gained during the period of their poverty. It was then that they subdued the Samnites, forced Pyrrhus to quit Italy, and cut in pieces the mighty armies of the Carthaginians. After they became possessed of the treasures of the universe, they had, for the most part, only weak and effeminate nations to deal with, and were so far from increasing in real power, that by the concurrent testimony of all historians, they are to be considered from that time as upon the decline. Livy, in that famous question relating to the Greeks and Romans, where he endeavours to determine what would have been the event, had Alexander the Great turned his arms against Italy, observes, that in war there are three things fundamentally necessary; good soldiers, good officers, and good fortune: and then arguing whether Alexander or the Romans were more considerable in these three points, concludes without the least mention of money. It is well known that the Spartans, so long as they adhered to their primitive institutions and poverty, were the most powerful people of all Greece, and never proved unsuccessful in their wars, till they became possessed of great riches and revenues. I conclude therefore, that it was by the bravery of their troops, the advantage

of their arms, and the excellence of their discipline, that the Romans rendered themselves victorious over all nations: and, accordingly, we find, that when they ceased to have the superiority in these, the revenues of the whole world were not sufficient to defend them.

CHAP. IV.

OF THE SPIRIT AND BRAVERY OF THE ROMAN TROOPS.

I. ALTHOUGH military discipline, and the continual exercise of arms, naturally conduce to make a people bold, daring, and intrepid; yet there is something so peculiar in the spirit and character of the Romans, that I flatter myself it will not be unacceptable to the reader, to offer a few reflections on this subject, and give some insight into those institutions and maxims of conduct, which chiefly contributed to exalt their courage, and animate their bravery. Two things here naturally present themselves to our consideration. First, the admirable principles upon which the commonwealth was founded. Secondly, the succession of great men that for several ages prevailed in it, and who supported, invigorated, and, from time to time, gave new life to these principles. Among the principles of the Roman polity, none seems to have taken deeper root, than the fear of the gods, and a veneration for religion. This perhaps, at first sight, may not be thought so immediately to concern a martial people; but if we examine the effect of it upon their armies, and the many valuable purposes it was made to serve in war, we shall have reason to conclude that, of all their institutions, not one contributed more to the grandeur of the state. For hence in particular it was, that the military oath was held so sacred among the troops, and became an inviolable bond of fidelity and subjection. The soldiers, however displeased and enraged, did not dare to quit their generals so long as this tie was supposed to remain in force: nay, so very tender and scrupulous were they, that even in their greatest impatience to be discharged, they would yet never admit of any interpretation, that carried in it the least strain or appearance of deceit. We have a remarkable example of this, in their behaviour to Quinctus Cincinnatus, after the defeat of Appius Herdonius. That Sabine had seized the Capitol, with four thousand men. The danger was imminent, and required speedy redress; but the Tribunes, who were then pushing the Terentian law, in order to force the senate to a compliance, opposed the levies. The people however, partly by promises, partly by remonstrating on the danger of the city, were at length prevailed upon to take an oath of fidelity to the consuls; and marching against Herdonius, soon recovered possession of the Capitol. Publius Valerius, to whom the charge of the attack fell, chancing to be slain, Quinctius Cincinnatus was immediately chosen in his room; who, to keep the troops employed, and leave them no room to think of their law *Terentilla*, ordered them out upon an expedition against the Volsci, alleging, that the oath that they had taken to the late consul obliged them to follow him. The tribunes, to evade the engagement, pretended that the oath bound them only to the person of Valerius, and so was buried with him in his tomb. But the people, more sincere, and plain-hearted, could not resolve to shelter themselves under so frivolous a distinction, and therefore prepared every man to take arms, though very unwillingly. "Nondum (says Livy) hæc, quæ nunc tenet seculum, negligentia deum venerat, nec interpretando sibi quisque jusjurandum, et leges aptas faciebat." "That neglect of the gods, which so much dishonours the present age, was not known in those days, nor had men learned the pernicious art of interpreting the laws of religion according to their own purposes."

II. I could produce many instances of the like nature, all tending to show, how serviceable religion was, to the governing of armies, the uniting of the people, and the keeping them in due subjection to their officers and magistrates; insomuch that should it fall into dispute, whether Rome was more indebted to Romulus or Numa, I am clearly of opinion that Numa would have the preference. For where religion is once fixed, military discipline may be easily introduced: but where religion is wanting, discipline is not brought in without great difficulty; and never can be carried to perfection. If we inquire into the nature of the religion professed by the Romans, we find that it ran much upon the answers of oracles, divinations, soothsayings, sacrifices, and innumerable other ceremonies, that argue more of

superstition, than any just knowledge of the deity. But absurd as this religion may appear, it had nevertheless a wonderful influence upon the minds of men, and was often made use of with success, to inspire courage in battles and dangers. It is well known that all their military expeditions were preceded by the auguries and auspices: and according to the omens that offered on these occasions, did the people judge of the issue. Hence their wisest and best generals, by a strict regard to these observances, and accommodating the ceremonies of religion to their own designs, generally found means to give a favourable turn to the omens; which greatly contributed to exalt the courage of their troops, and made them face the enemy with confidence. On the contrary, it is observed, that where the usual forms were neglected, and generals affected to act in contempt of the auspices, they seldom succeeded in their designs. This may well enough be accounted for, without allowing any real influence to these ceremonies, or supposing that the flight and chirping of birds could in the least affect future events. Nothing in truth can be more trifling, than the pretended presages of which we speak; but as they were firmly believed by the bulk of the army, where at any time they appeared unfavourable, it could not fail of casting a great damp upon the spirits of the soldiers. And yet this does not seem to me to have been the principal cause of those miscarriages, that were usually observed to **follow a neglect of the** auspices. The ignorance **and incapacity of the** generals will much better **account for them**; nor need we a stronger proof **of** this incapacity, than the contempt with which they affected to treat religion. War is necessarily attended with so much uncertainty, and requires such a multitude of different attentions, that a prudent general will be far from neglecting any advantages, which he sees may be drawn from the established prejudices of those under his command; much less will he turn those very prejudices to his own hurt, by an ill-judged contempt; and the general who is so indiscreet as to act in this manner, plainly discovers himself unfit for the conduct of any great enterprise. I know it is asserted by some, that religion checks the natural fierceness and obstinacy of men, and renders them poor-spirited and abject; but whoever talks in this manner, shows himself little conversant in the history of mankind. Consider the Romans in the best times of the republic, the English under Queen Elizabeth and Oliver Cromwell, the French in the age of Henry the Fourth, the United Provinces in that of Philip the Second, and the Swedes under Gustavus Vasa, and then tell me, whether the most flourishing and formidable periods of nations, be not those when a spirit of religion has strongly taken possession of the minds of the people.

III. Next to a veneration for religion, love of their country was the prevailing characteristic of the Romans. This virtue naturally rouses men to great designs, and begets vigour and perseverance in the execution of them; and as it had taken a deeper root among the people of whom we speak, than in any other nation mentioned in history, no wonder we here meet with so many instances of magnanimity, public spirit, fortitude, and all the virtues that tend to form a race of heroes. It is certain that the constitution of the Roman commonwealth was peculiarly fitted to nourish this spirit. The people had many ties and obligations to the state, many endearing connections to inspire the love of it. They chose the senators, by whose counsels the republic was governed, the magistrates, by whom justice was administered, and the generals who conducted and terminated their wars; so that the public successes were in a manner their own work. Hence the principle of which we speak became so strong in them, that they were ready to sacrifice every other consideration to it, whether of interest or ambition. No hazards, no sufferings appeared great where their country stood in need of their assistance. We find, even in the disputes between the different orders of the state, where the passions of men are wont most strongly to be engaged, and where particular animosities are but too apt to get the better of reason, that the consideration of the public safety was always sufficient to calm their resentments, and bring them to temper and moderation. How violent soever the contest might be, however much the parties appeared exasperated against one another, they were yet sure to unite, when any danger from without threatened the commonwealth. This is evident through the whole course of the Roman history, and requires not to be illustrated by particular examples. I shall therefore only add, that a principle so powerful and universally diffused, as

it could not fail of having many desirable effects upon the people, so did it in a particular manner tend to render them brave and resolute; for courage being of indispensable necessity to the defence of our country, wherever the love of that predominates, there we are sure to find the other likewise.

IV. But if the Romans are remarkable for the love they bore the country, they are no less so when we consider how passionately fond they were of liberty. This spirit subsisted from the very foundation of the state. Though Rome was at first governed by kings, these kings were far from being absolute; for besides the authority enjoyed by the senate, the people too had a considerable share in the administration, since to their assemblies were committed the creation of magistrates, the enacting of laws, and the resolving upon peace or war. Indeed, under Tarquin the Proud, the government degenerated into a real tyranny; but this, instead of extinguishing served only to rouse the love of liberty; and the behaviour of Brutus, who puts his own sons to death, for attempting to establish the royal authority, made so strong an impression upon the minds of the people, that they henceforward considered slavery as the greatest of evils, and bent all their thoughts to the preserving and enlarging the freedom they had acquired. I need not here say how much liberty tends to ennoble the mind, and how necessary it is to the prosperity and greatness of a state. It is well known that Athens, so long as it continued under the tyranny of Pisistratus and his descendants, made scarce any figure in Greece: and whereas, soon after their expulsion, it rose to so astonishing a pitch of grandeur, as not only to baffle all the efforts of the Persians, but even to render itself formidable to that mighty empire. And if we look into the history of the Roman commonwealth, we find, that in proportion as liberty increased, and the people got from under the dominion of the nobles, they became inspired with a more elevated courage, a more unwearied fortitude, and pushed their conquests with greater rapidity. Nay, in the very infancy of their freedom, when Tarquin was endeavouring to recover his lost authority, they gave manifest indications of that spirit, for which they are so justly admired by succeeding ages. It is upon this occasion that we read of the astonishing valour of Horatius Cocles, the intrepid firmness of Scævola, and the masculine boldness of Clelia; insomuch that Porsenna, king of the Clusians, who had undertaken the reinstating of Tarquin, admiring their bravery, would not any longer disturb them in the enjoyment of a liberty to which their merit gave them so just a title, and which he found them so resolutely bent to defend.

V. And here I cannot but observe, that this passionate desire of freedom gave rise to a peculiar circumstance in the Roman constitution, which, though seemingly inconsistent with the prosperity of the state, was yet in reality one of the principal causes of its grandeur, as it more than any thing contributed to exalt the character of the people, and produce among them the most finished models in every species of merit. What I mean is, those continual dissensions between the nobles and commons, of which we meet with so frequent mention in the early ages of the commonwealth. Two bodies at Rome divided the whole authority: the senate and the people. A mutual jealousy, founded on the one side upon a desire of governing, on the other, upon that of keeping themselves free and independent, raised between them contentions and quarrels, which ended not but with the republic itself. These contests, though attended with many inconveniences, procured notwithstanding a considerable advantage to the state, in forming a number of persons of distinguished merit, and perpetuating a succession of them in the commonwealth. The patricians, who were obstinately bent to keep to themselves alone the commands, the honours, the magistracies, as they could not obtain them but by the suffrages of the plebeians, were obliged to use their utmost endeavours to prove themselves worthy by superior qualities, by real and repeated services, by illustrious actions of which their adversaries themselves were witnesses, and to which they could not refuse their esteem and applause. This necessity of depending on the judgment of the people for admission to posts, obliged the young patricians to acquire all the merit capable of gaining the suffrages of the judges, who examined them rigorously, and were not inclined to have a remiss indulgence for the candidates, as well out of love to the honour and welfare of the state, as out of an hereditary jealousy of the patrician order. The plebeians on their side, in as-

piring to the highest dignities of the state, were forced to prepare themselves so as to convince their brethren, that they had all the qualities necessary to fill them with honour. Proofs were to be given of a distinguished valour, of a wise and prudent conduct, of a capacity to discharge all the functions of government, and to pass with reputation through the several offices, which led by degrees to the highest. It was needful to have no only the military virtues, and ability to conduct an army; but the talent of haranguing the senate and people, of reporting the great affairs of state, of answering foreign ambassadors, and entering with them into the nicest and most important negotiations. By all these obligations, imposed by ambition on the plebeians, to qualify them for the posts to which they aspired, they were under the necessity of making proof of an accomplished merit, at least equal to that of the patricians.

VI. These were some of the advantages arising from the sharp contests between the senate and the people, from whence resulted a lively emulation between the two orders, and a happy necessity of displaying talents, which perhaps by a continual concord and peace would have lain dormant and fruitless: just as, if I may use the comparison, from a steel struck with a flint, sparks of fire fly out, which without that violence would remain for ever concealed. This is not all. It was by means of these contests that the public liberty was improved and settled, without which the commonwealth would never have become great and flourishing. By the revolution which expelled Tarquin the Proud, the commons of Rome were delivered from a tyrant, but not from tyranny. The patricians still hold them under subjection; and though, while their fears of Tarquin's return were alive and strong, they behaved with great lenity and moderation, yet no sooner were they informed of that prince's death, than the weight of oppression was renewed, and fell as heavy upon the people as ever. The Valerian law, to permit appeals from the sentence of the magistrates to the people assembled, was not sufficient to protect the plebeians from injustice and cruelty. They found it necessary to have magistrates of their own body, to screen them from the tyranny of the great, and therefore extorted from the senate a consent to the establishment of the tribunitian power. The institution of the *Comitia Tributa*, and the practice of bringing into judgment, before those assemblies, the most exalted of the nobles, upon accusations of treason against the people, was another bulwark against the overflowings of ambition. The publication of the laws of the twelve tables, gave some check to the abuse of that prerogative, which the patricians tenaciously kept, of being the sole judges in civil causes; and on many other occasions we find, that the commons, urged by oppression to fury, exerted their natural strength in such a manner as proclaimed them sovereign masters of the administration, and gradually extended their privileges.

VII. But the commonwealth of Rome was never truly a free state, till after the publication of the Licinian laws, those laws which, in their consequences, made merit alone the ordinary scale whereby to ascend to the highest offices; and which, by admitting the plebeians to a reasonable share of what was purchased with their blood, delivered them from that servile subjection to the wealthy nobles in which their indigence had so long detained them. From this period, the Roman people, when they made laws, or elected magistrates for the execution of them, were generally speaking, free from all undue influence; not overawed, as before, by the rich and the great, nor constrained by any force, but that of reason and natural justice, in the most absolute subjection to which is the most perfect freedom. No citizen who had showed superior talents and **virtue,** stood excluded, on account of the low **degree of** his birth, from the dignities of the **state; and** hence proceeded an emulation **among the** individuals to surpass each other in deserving honours. Indeed the haughty patricians, as, when vanquished by the plebeians, they had given ground with an angry reluctance, and retired fighting, so they afterwards, from time to time, showed a strong disposition to renew their unrighteous sovereignty: but their efforts were faint and ineffectual; and at length acquiescing in what they could not undo, there ensued domestic peace and union, and an established liberty. Union at home gave new strength to the state, and liberty seems to have inspired the people with a nobler spirit, a more exalted courage, and a greater ardour to enlarge the bounds of their empire. For, whereas, before,

during the space of four hundred years, they had not pushed their conquests beyond a few leagues round the city; we find that from that period, in the course of seventy years, they, by a series of victories, made themselves masters of all Italy. And though destitute of naval strength and naval skill, their next enterprise was against a rival republic beyond the continent; a republic that with greater riches, and more ample territories than theirs, had possession of the absolute dominion of the sea. The boldness of **the undertaking, and** the amazing constancy with which they supported it, in spite of the most terrible adversities, are not to be paralleled in the history of any other nation; but the Roman legions were, at that time, legions of free citizens, whose predominant passion was glory, and who placed the highest glory in facing every danger, and surmounting every difficulty, to preserve their liberty, and extend their empire.

VIII. The love of glory is indeed a natural consequence of liberty, and if to this we join that remarkable disregard of wealth, which prevailed for so many ages among this people, we shall have reason to conclude, that these likewise contributed not a little, towards forming in them that firm and intrepid bravery, which makes a distinguishing part of their character. For the love of glory pushes men on to great actions, and a disregard of wealth prevents their being biassed by mean sordid views, or shaken by the low considerations of self-interest. It is certain that glory was the main spring of all those noble and illustrious undertakings, which have rendered the Romans so famous. By this motive, the republic, after liberty prevailed, made an incredible **pro**gress in a short time. The frequent examples of patriotism, and of an inviolable attachment to the public good of which Rome was witness in those critical times, **and** which she rewarded in so eminent a manner, kindled, not only in the patricians, but likewise among the plebeians, that noble fire of emulation and glory, which dares all things, and influenced all along the whole nation. Greedy of praise, they reckoned money as nothing, and valued it only to disperse it. They were content with moderate fortunes, says Sallust, but desired glory without measure. Accordingly we **find,** that for four hundred years after the building of Rome, the city was in very great poverty: and of this the probable cause seems to be, that poverty was no impediment to preferment. Virtue was the only thing required in the election of magistrates, and the distribution of offices; and wherever it was found, let the person, or family, be ever so poor, he was sure to be advanced. Quinctius Cincinnatus was taken from the plough, and raised to the office of dictator, though his estate did not exceed four acres of land. Fabricius and Atilius Regulus are likewise examples of this kind; and indeed the Roman history everywhere abounds with them.

IX. The thirst of glory usually produces that of dominion. It appears noble to be masters, to command others, to compose laws, to be feared and obeyed. This passion, natural to mankind, was more strong and active in the Romans, than in any other people. One would think, at seeing the air of authority that they very early assume, that they already believed themselves destined to become one day lords of the universe. Nay, it appears from many indications in their history, that this notion subsisted from the foundation of the state. The answers and interpretations of the augurs frequently glanced this way. A head was found in digging for the foundations of the Capitol. This was given out to imply the eternity of their empire, and that the city to which that temple belonged, was to become the head of the universe. We see likewise in the speech of Coriolanus to the deputies of the senate, upon occasion of his investing Rome with an army of Volscians, that the conceit of universal dominion not only strongly prevailed in his time, but was carefully cherished among the people. Nor was it without reason that the senate contrived to raise and propagate this persuasion, as it tended wonderfully to exalt the courage of the citizens, and not only animated them in the pursuit of conquest, but kept them firm and steady under the severest strokes of adversity. Thus at the same time that poverty and a disregard of wealth rendered them modest, the love of glory and dominion inspired them with magnanimity. When put into command, and placed at the head of armies, kings appeared but little before them; nor was any danger, difficulty, or opposition able to dismay them: but when their commissions expired, and they returned to a private station, none so frugal, none so humble, none so laborious, so obedient to the magistrates, or respectful to their superiors as

they; insomuch that one would think it impossible the same minds should be capable of such strange alterations.

X. From these distinguishing characteristics of the Roman people, it will be easy to perceive, how courage and a sense of honour came to be so prevalent in their armies. And here I cannot but observe, that the military rewards were wonderfully calculated to promote this spirit; since without being considerable for their intrinsic value, they were extremely coveted by the troops, because glory, so precious to that warlike people, was annexed to them. A very small crown of gold, and generally a crown of laurel or oak-leaves, became inestimable to the soldiers, who knew not any marks more excellent than those of virtue; nor any distinction more noble than that which flows from glorious actions. These monuments of renown were to them real patents of nobility, and descended to their posterity as a precious inheritance. They were, besides, sure titles to rise to places of honour and advantage, which were granted only to merit, and not procured by intrigue and cabal. We have already had occasion to take notice of the large field there lay for promotion in the Roman armies, and that such as distinguished themselves by their valour had reason to hope for every thing. What an agreeable prospect for an inferior officer, to behold at a distance the chief dignities of the state and army, as so many rewards to which he could aspire!

XI. And indeed, if **any thing** be capable of inspiring man with **bravery, and a** martial ardour, to pass **through a succession of** different honours, and **to be entitled to** a number of military rewards, which were all considered as so many standing monuments of renown, seems to bid fairest for it. I cannot better represent the effect this had upon the troops, than by the following relation, from which the reader may form some idea of what a Roman soldier was. When the war against Perseus, the last king of Macedonia, was resolved upon at Rome, amongst the other measures taken for the success of it, the senate decreed, that the consul charged with that expedition, should raise as many centurions and veteran soldiers as he pleased, out of those who did not exceed fifty years of age. Twenty-three centurions who had been *Primipili*, refused to take arms, unless the same rank was granted them, which they had in preceding campaigns. As it was impossible to gratify them all, and they persisted obstinately in their refusal, the affair was brought before the people. After Popilius, who had been consul two years before, had pleaded the cause of the centurions, and the consul his own, one of the centurions, who had appealed to the people, having obtained permission to speak, expressed himself to this effect.

XII. "I am called Spurius Ligustinus of the Crustumine tribe, descended from the Sabines. My father left me a small field and cottage, where I was born, brought up, and now live. As soon as I was at age to marry, he gave me his brother's daughter to wife. She brought me no portion but liberty, chastity, and a fruitfulness sufficient for the richest houses. We have six sons, and two daughters, both married. Of my sons four have taken the robe of manhood, the other two are still infants. I began to bear arms in the consulship of P. Sulpicius and C. Aurelius, and served two years as a private soldier in the army sent into Macedonia against King Philip. The third year, T. Quintius Flamininus, to reward me for my services, made me captain of a century in the tenth maniple of the *Hastati.* I served afterwards as a volunteer in Spain under Cato ; and that general, who is so excellent a judge of merit, made me first centurion of the first maniple of the *Hastati.* In the war against the Ætolians and King Antiochus, I rose to the same rank amongst the *Principes.* I afterwards made several campaigns, and in a very few years have been four times *Primipilus:* I have been four and thirty times rewarded by the generals, have received six civic crowns, have served two and twenty campaigns, and am above fifty years old. Though I had not completed the number of years required by the law, and my age did not discharge me, substituting four of my children in my place, I should deserve to be exempt from the necessity of serving. But by all I have said, I only intend to show the justice of my cause. For the rest, as long as those who levy the troops shall judge me capable of bearing arms, I shall not refuse the service. The tribunes may rank me as they please ; that is their business : mine is to act, that none be ranked above me for valour ; as all the generals under whom I have had the honour to serve, and all my comrades can witness for me, I have hitherto never failed to do. For you, centu-

rions, notwithstanding your appeal ; as even during your youth you have never done any thing contrary to the authority of the magistrates and senate, in my opinion, it would become your age, to show yourselves submissive to the senate and consuls, and to think every station honourable, that gives you opportunity to serve the republic."

XIII. It is easy to discern in this speech, the spirit and magnanimity of a true Roman ; and particularly a certain boldness and confidence, derived from a sense of his many services, and the rewards and honours with which they had been attended. And if this be so conspicuous in the inferior officers, what may we not expect in those of a more eminent degree ? If civic and mural crowns, collars, chains, bracelets, and such like, were sufficient to rouse these sentiments of heroism among the lower order of troops, what would not the prospect of a triumph effect in the mind of the general ? This honour was granted only to dictators, consuls, and prætors. After the general had distributed a part of the spoils to the soldiers, and performed some other ceremonies, the procession began, and entered the city through the triumphal port, to ascend to the capitol. At the head of it were the players upon musical instruments, who made the air resound with their harmony. They were followed by the beasts that were to be sacrificed, adorned with fillets, and flowers, many of them having their horns gilt. After them came the whole booty, and all the spoils, either displayed upon carriages, or borne upon the shoulders of young men in magnificent habits. The names of the nations conquered were written in great characters, and the cities that had been taken represented. Sometimes they added to the pomp extraordinary animals, brought from the countries subjected, as bears, panthers, lions, and elephants. But what most attracted the attention and curiosity of the spectators, were the illustrious captives, who walked in chains before the victor's chariot ; great officers of state, generals of armies, princes, kings, with their wives and children. The consul followed upon a magnificent chariot, drawn by four horses, and robed with the august habit of triumph, his head encircled with a crown of laurel, holding also a branch of the same tree in his hand, and sometimes accompanied with his young children sitting by him. Behind the chariot marched the whole army, the cavalry first, then the infantry. All the soldiers were crowned with laurel, and those who had received particular crowns, and other marks of honour, did not fail to show them on so great a solemnity. They emulated each other in celebrating the praises of their general, and sometimes threw in expressions, sufficiently offensive, of raillery and satire against him, which savoured of the military freedom; but the joy of the ceremony entirely blunted their edge, and abated their bitterness. When the procession arrived at the capitol, the consul, immediately upon his entering the temple, made this very remarkable prayer to the god: —" Filled with gratitude and with joy, I return you thanks, O most good and most great Jupiter, and you queen Juno, and all the other gods, the guardians and inhabitants of this citadel, that to this day and hour you have vouchsafed, by my hands, to preserve and guide the Roman republic happily. Continue always, I implore you, to preserve, guide, protect, and favour it in all things." This prayer was followed by sacrificing the victims, and a magnificent feast, given in the capitol, sometimes by the public, and sometimes by the person himself who triumphed. It must be allowed, that this was a glorious day for a general of an army; and it is not surprising that all possible endeavours should be used to deserve so grateful a distinction, and so splendid an honour. Rome had not any thing more majestic and magnificent than this pompous ceremony, which seemed to raise the person in favour of whom it was granted, above the condition of mortals.

XIV. The Romans, in war, knew how to make use of punishments, as well as rewards. The steadiness of a dictator, with respect to his general of horse, who could not be saved from death but by the entreaties and urgent prayers of all the people; the inexorable severity of the consul Manlius to his own son, whom he unmercifully put to death, though victorious, for fighting contrary to his orders; these examples made a terrible impression of fear upon the people, which became for ever the firm bond of military discipline. Wherefore never was it observed in any nation so inviolably as among the Romans, nor did any thing contribute so much to render them victorious over all their enemies. How should they have been otherwise than victorious with

troops formed as we have seen, and above all guided in their operations by principles the most proper to make conquerors? One of which was, not to know any other end of wa. but victory, and for its sake to surmount, by an indefatigable perseverance, all the obstacles and all the dangers by which it can be retarded. The greatest misfortunes, the most desperate losses, were incapable of daunting their courage, or making them accept a base and dishonourable peace. To grant nothing by compulsion, was a fundamental law of the Roman policy, from which the senate never departed; and in the most melancholy junctures, weak counsels, instead of prevailing, were not so much as heard. As far back as Coriolanus, the senate declared, that no agreement could be made with the Volsci, so long as they remained on the Roman territory. They proceeded in the same manner with Pyrrhus. After the bloody battle of Cannæ, wherein above fifty thousand of the Romans lay dead on the field, it was resolved no proposal of peace should be listened to. The consul Varro, who had been the occasion of the defeat, was received at Rome as if he had been victorious, because in so great a misfortune he had not despaired of the Roman affairs. Thus, instead of disheartening the people by an unseasonable instance of severity, these generous senators taught them, by their example, to bear up against ill fortune, and assume in adversity the haughtiness with which others are inspired by prosperity.

XV. One thing, indeed, has been generally considered, as tending greatly to obstruct the conquests of the Roman people: I mean the two limited space of the consulship, which often afforded not the general time to finish a war he had begun, a good part of the year being sometimes spent in preparations. This inconvenience was afterwards remedied, as far as possible, by prolonging the command to the general, as proconsul, and sometimes continuing him in the consulship itself. But this was practised sparingly in the wiser ages of the republic: the danger of infringing the public liberty, making the frequent change of generals appear necessary to the safety of the state. If the generals had been long continued at the head of the armies, they might have been able to usurp all the authority, and become masters of the government, as happened under Cæsar, in the latter end of the commonwealth. We are likewise to call to mind, that these annual commands were well enough suited to the earlier times of Rome, when wars seldom lasted above one campaign; and though perhaps they might not be without their inconveniences afterwards, yet they had this one manifest advantage attending them, that thereby a number of great generals was formed in the state, and the Romans were not often reduced to the necessity of placing all their hopes in the abilities of a single person. For this quick circulation of authority, by raising many in their turns to the highest offices of the republic, excited an incredible emulation among individuals, to qualify themselves for the conduct of armies; and at the same time furnished them with frequent opportunities of acquiring experience in supreme command, which is one of the most requisite accomplishments in a great general.

XVI. Thus every thing at Rome led to great conquests: the constitution of the government; the admirable political principles on which it was founded; the nature of the troops; the ability of the generals; and above all, the steadiness of the senate, in attachment to the ancient maxims of the state. This last particular leads me to the second thing I mentioned, as the cause of that noble spirit which we so much admire in the Roman armies, namely, the succession of great men that for several ages prevailed in the commonwealth, and who supported, invigorated, and from time to time gave new life to the fundamental principles of the constitution. Happy is the state that is blessed with this privilege! and it was the good fortune of the Romans to enjoy it in a supreme degree. It were endless to recount all the names that history furnishes on this subject; I shall therefore content myself with mentioning only two, Manlius Torquatus and Valerius Corvinus; the one famed for his severity, the other for his clemency. Manlius commanded with rigour, excused his soldiers from no labour, and never remitted any punishment. Valerius, on the other side, used them with as much gentleness and familiarity. Manlius, to support the vigour of military discipline, executed his own son. Valerius acted upon principles so different, that he is said never to have offended any man. Yet, in this great diversity of conduct, the effects were the same, both as to the enemy, the commonwealth, and themselves: for none of their soldiers ever declined fighting, none of them rebelled, none so much as disputed their orders, though the discipline of Manlius was so severe, that afterwards all excessive and arbitrary commands were from him called *Manliana imperia*. If Manlius be considered as he is represented by historians, we find him to have been very valiant, pious to his father and country, and submissive to his superiors. This appears by his defence of his father, at the hazard of his own life, against a tribune who accused him; by his readiness to offer himself in single combat with a Gaul, where he thought the honour of his country concerned; and by his first applying to the consul for leave, before he would accept the challenge. Now when a man of this constitution arrives at command, he desires that all men may be as punctual as himself; and being naturally brave he commands brave things, and when they are once commanded, requires that they be executed exactly; this being a certain rule, that where great things are commanded, strict obedience must be exacted; in which case mildness and gentleness will not always prevail. But where a man has not this greatness and magnificence of mind, he is by no means to command extraordinary things, and may therefore safely exercise the virtue of clemency; with which ordinary punishments are compatible enough, because they are not imputed to the prince, but to the laws and customs of the place. Manlius then was a severe man, and kept up the Roman discipline exactly; prompted first by his own nature, and then by a strong desire to have that obeyed, which his own inclination had constrained him to command. Valerius Corvinus, on the other hand, might exercise his gentleness without inconvenience, because he commanded nothing extraordinary, or contrary to the customs of the Romans at that time: for, as those customs were good, and not very troublesome to observe, he was seldom necessitated to punish offenders, because there were but few of that sort; and where they were, their punishment was imputed to the laws, and not to his cruelty. Hence, Valerius had an opportunity, by his gentleness, to gain both affection and authority in the army, which was the cause, that the soldiers, being equally obedient to the one as the other, though their tempers and discipline were so very different, they could yet do the same things, and their actions have the same effects. I shall only add, that could a state be so happy, as to have always persons succeeding one another within a reasonable time, who, however different in inclination and temper, would yet by their examples renew the laws, restrain vice, and remove every thing that tended to its ruin or corruption, that state must be immortal.

XVII. In thus ascribing the bravery and successes of the Romans, to the excellent principles of their constitution, and the great men by whom these principles were supported, I do no more than follow the opinion of their own writers upon this subject. Sallust tells us, "that after much reading and reflection upon the causes of the growth and grandeur of the Romans, he found reason to conclude, that the distinguished virtue of a few citizens had effected all that mighty run of prosperity." Cicero too, in his reflection upon that verse of the poet Ennius,

Moribus antiquis res stat Romana, virisque,

makes the same observation. "It is," says he, "the union of these two advantages, which has produced all the grandeur of Rome: on the one hand, the good manners, the wise political principles established from the beginning: on the other, a succession of great men, formed upon these principles, and employed by a state in the administration of affairs. Before our times, that happy union was always the same, and these two advantages ever existed together; otherwise a republic so powerful and extensive as ours could not have subsisted so long with honour, nor so constantly kept up its reputation amongst all nations." I omit the complaints Cicero subjoins to the degeneracy of the age in which he lived, and of the total decay of ancient manners. Every one knows, that these soon after occasioned the ruin of the republic. Meanwhile it may not be improper to observe that these two advantages were not only the chief causes of the Roman greatness, but likewise produced that slow and gradual increase of power, so necessary to lay a solid foundation of strength, and support the weight of their many and extensive conquests.

XVIII. For there never was an empire, either more flourishing, or more extensive than the Roman. From the Euphrates and Tanais, to Hercules' pillars, and the Atlantic ocean, all the lands and all the seas, were under their obedience. It is astonishing to consider, that the nations which at present make kingdoms so considerable, all Gaul, all Spain, almost the whole island of Great Britain, Illyria, to the Danube, Germany, to the Elbe, Africa to the frightful and impassable deserts, Greece, Thrace, Syria, Egypt, all the kingdoms of Asia Minor, and those between the Euxine and Caspian seas, with many others, became Roman provinces, almost all before the end of the republic. I have often wondered to observe in historians a certain affectation of ascribing the successes of the Romans to fortune, as if that, rather than valour and wisdom, had been the occasion of their prosperity. To me it evidently appears, through the whole course of their history, that the unusual pitch of grandeur to which they arrived, was the necessary result of the talents and accomplishments of which they were possessed, whether they are considered with regard to moral virtues, or to a political government, or to martial merit and the art of war. For as Livy observes, in the preface to his history, there never was a republic more religious, or more abounding in good examples, or where avarice and luxury gained ground so late, or where simplicity and poverty were so much and so long held in honour. All the debates and transactions of the senate, show, to a demonstration, how much wisdom of counsel, love of the public, steadiness to the maxims of the state, lenity and moderation with **regard** to the conquered **nations**, prevailed in that **august** assembly. **Courage, boldness, intrepidity** in the midst of the **greatest** dangers, an **invincible** patience in **the** hardest labours, an inexorable firmness **to maintain** the military discipline in its utmost **rigour, a** settled resolution to conquer or **die, a greatness** of soul, and **a** constancy, proof against all misfortunes, have at all times constituted the character of the Romans, and rendered them in the end victorious over all other nations. Cyrus and Alexander, it is true, founded great empires; but the qualities proper for the execution of such a design, being confined to the persons of these two illustrious conquerors, and not inherited by their descendants, the grandeur to which they gave a beginning, did not support itself long with any reputation. It was very different with the Romans. Their empire was no, founded, nor raised to the state of grandeur it attained by the rare endowments, or rapid conquests, of a single person. The Roman people themselves, the body of the state, formed that empire by slow degrees, and at several times. The great men that helped, each in their time, to establish, enlarge, and preserve it, had all different characters, though in the main they followed all the same principles; and hence the empire itself was both more extensive, and of longer duration, than any that had ever gone before it.

CHAP. V.

OF MARCHES.

I. What we have hitherto seen, relating to the raising of troops, their divisions, and subdivisions, armour, discipline, and exercises, is in a manner only the mechanism of war. There are other still more important cares, which constitute what is called the higher detail of the service, and depend more immediately upon the general's ability and experience. To him it belongs to settle the general disposition of marches; to encamp the troops advantageously; to draw them up in order of battle, provide against the exigencies of the field; pursue with caution, or retreat with judgment; and lastly, in conducting an attack or defence, to put in practice all the arts, stratagems, and address, that long experience in the service, and a consummate knowledge of all the parts of war, are jointly able to suggest. I shall offer some reflections upon the practice of the Roman generals in all these great points of military conduct, and begin with that which follows immediately after the rendezvous of the troops, I mean, the marching of an army. This subject naturally divides itself into three branches; the general order of marches in advancing against an enemy; the knowledge and choice of posts; and lastly, the disposition and conduct of a retreat. We shall speak of each in order.

II. The marching against an enemy supposes many preliminary cares in the general, and many previous steps taken, in order to his own safety, and the success of his designs. I shall suppose the plan of the war settled, as likewise the manner of acting, and measures concerted accordingly. Yet still it is incumbent upon a wise commander, before he puts his troops in motion, to provide every thing necessary for their accommodation and subsistence; to acquire an exact knowledge of the country through which he marches; to inform himself of the number and quality of the enemy's forces; to penetrate, if possible, into his designs; to study the character of the generals employed against him; and, by a wise foresight, to be prepared for all the events and contingencies that may happen in the course of a campaign. Now though these things come not so properly under fixed rules, but depend in a great measure upon the ability and prudence of the commander in chief; yet we find every where in history, that the Romans had many regulations about them, and always treated them with particular attention. To begin with the care of provisions, which is of principal account in an army, it appears to have been the constant practice, to furnish the soldiers with a certain proportion of corn, which they were obliged to carry along with them in their marches. This, on extraordinary occasions, amounted to four bushels, or a month's allowance, and seldom was less than what might serve for fifteen or twenty days. They chose rather to give them corn than bread, because it was lighter, and might therefore be carried with greater ease. Indeed this put them to the trouble of grinding and baking it themselves; but then they were used to it, and could upon occasion make it into I know not what variety of dishes. Besides the common bread, they made a kind of soft boiled food of it, very agreeable to the troops: they mingled it with milk, roots, and herbs, and made pancakes of it upon a small plate laid over the fire, or upon hot ashes, as was anciently the manner of regaling guests, and is still practised throughout the east, where these kind of thin cakes are much preferred to our best bread. Their drink was answerable to this diet, being no more than a mixture of vinegar and water. It was called *posca*, could at all times be easily procured, and was particularly serviceable to quench the thirst immediately.

III. I have heard it observed, that nothing gives greater difficulty to military men, in the reading of ancient history, than the article of provisions. Cato's maxim, that the war feeds the war, holds goods in plentiful countries, and with regard to small armies:

yet still it is more generally true, that the war does not furnish provisions upon command, or at a fixed time. They must be provided both for the present and the future. We do not however find, that either the Greeks or Romans had the precaution to provide magazines of forage, to lay up provisions, to have a commissary-general of stores, or to be followed by a great number of carriages. But then we are to consider, that in the wars of the Greeks against each other, their troops were little numerous, and accustomed to a sober life; that they did not remove far from their own country, and almost always returned regularly every winter; so that it is plain, it was not difficult for them to have provisions in abundance, especially the Athenians, who were masters at sea. The same may be said of the Romans. The care of subsisting the troops was infinitely less weighty with them, than it is at present with most of the nations of Europe. Their armies were much less numerous, and they had a much smaller number of cavalry. A consular army consisted of near seventeen thousand foot, to which they had not above eighteen hundred horse. In our days, to seventeen thousand foot, we have often more than six thousand horse. What a vast difference must this make in the consumption of forage and provisions! Let me add, that the sober manner of life in the army, confined to mere necessaries, spared them an infinite multitude of servants, horses, and baggage, which now exhaust our magazines, starve our armies, retard the execution of enterprises, and often render them impracticable. Nor was this the manner of living only of the soldiers, but likewise of the officers and generals. Not only consuls and dictators in the early ages of the commonwealth, but even emperors themselves; Trajan, Adrian, Pescennius, Severus, Paobus, Julian, and many others, not only lived without luxury, but contented themselves with boiled flour or beans, a piece of cheese or bacon, and made it their glory to level themselves, in this respect, with the meanest of the soldiers. It is easy to conceive how much this must contribute to diminish the train of an army, to support the taste of frugality and simplicity amongst the troops, and banish all luxury and idle show from the camp.

IV. But though the care of provisions was less burdensome to the ancients, we find that both it, and all other accommodations proper for the march of an army, were not less attended to by their generals. Xenophon, who was himself a soldier, and whose writings abounds with maxims of war, is frequent in his reflections upon this article. One of the principal instructions he makes Cambyses king of Persia give his son Cyrus, who afterwards became so glorious, was not to embark in any expedition, till he had first informed himself, whether subsistence were provided for the troops. In his account of the behaviour of the same Cyrus, after his arrival in the camp of his uncle Cyaxares, he enters into an immense detail, with respect to all the necessaries of an army. That prince was to march fifteen days, through countries that had been destroyed, and in which there were neither provisions nor forage. He ordered enough of both for twenty days to be carried, and that the soldiers, instead of loading themselves with baggage, should exchange that burden for an equal one of provisions, without troubling themselves about beds and coverlets for sleeping, the want of which their fatigues would supply. They were accustomed to drink wine; and as a sudden and total disuse of it might be attended with ill consequences, he ordered them to carry a certain quantity with them, and to use themselves by degrees to do without it, and be contented with water. He advised them also to carry salt provisions along with them, hand-mills for grinding corn, and medicines for the sick; to put into every carriage a sickle and a mattock, and upon every beast of burden an axe and a scythe; and to take care to provide themselves with a thousand other necessaries. He carried also along with him, smiths, shoemakers, and other workmen, with all manner of tools used in their trades. For the rest, he declared publicly that whoever would charge himself with the care of sending provisions to the camp, should be honoured and rewarded by himself and his friends; and even supplied with money for that service, provided they would give security, and engage to follow the army.

V. The reader will here be pleased to observe, that as I am now entered upon the higher detail of war, I shall not so entirely confine myself to the Romans, as not from time to time to mention the practices of other nations, where they any way tend to illustrate the point in hand. For as the Roman writers upon this subject are but few, and have not entered very circumstantially into matters, we are often at a loss with regard to some of the most important parts of their discipline. This however we may be certain of, that as they excelled particularly in the art of war, and readily adopted the improvements of other nations, the more we know of the progress and attainments of the ancients in this respect, the better we shall be able to judge of the uncommon proficiency of the Romans. We have already seen some of their wise precautions with regard to the subsistence and accommodation of the troops; for which they provided no less by fixed and general regulations, than Cyrus does in the particular instance recorded by Xenophon. I shall only add, that history abounds with examples of this prudent care and foresight in their generals. Paulus Æmilius would not set out for Macedonia, till he had fully settled every thing relating to provisions. Cæsar, in all his wars, was extremely attentive to the safety of his convoys, and the keeping up a free communication with those countries whence he received his supplies. We find that he regularly distributed corn to the army, and always took care, before the time for a new distribution arrived, to have it brought to the camp by means of his allies: or if he chanced to be disappointed here, so contrived his march, as to pass by some great town, where he could readily be furnished with whatever he stood in need of.

VI. But besides the care of provisions, it is further incumbent upon a wise general, to acquaint himself thoroughly with the nature of the country through which he is to march. I take it for granted that the Romans omitted none of the usual and obvious methods for this purpose: that they furnished themselves with guides; interrogated the natives; and, where such were to be had, procured exact maps of the country, delineating the towns, their number and distance, the roads and mountains, the rivers, the fords; and the nature and qualities of them all. But what particularly deserves our notice in the Roman policy; they scarce ever entered into a war with any distant state, till they had first contracted an alliance with some contiguous power, who might unite his forces to theirs in the intended invasion. This practice was attended with numberless advantages. They had hereby timely notice of the enemy's designs; they were made acquainted with the number and quality of his forces: and when they approached with their army, were not only plentifully supplied with all kind of military stores, but joined by a considerable body of troops perfectly acquainted with the country, and able to inform them where they might make their impression with greatest probability of success. Thus when they invaded Philip king of Macedonia, they took care to secure the friendship of the Ætolians, whose troops were of unspeakable service to them in that war. In their expedition against Antiochus they made use of the same policy, having previously contracted amity with several of the petty princes and states of Asia Minor. Every one knows what use Cæsar made of the pretended alliance with the Æduans; and that it was one of the principal engines by which he completed the reduction of Gaul. Indeed nothing can fall out more fortunately for an army, about to invade a country to which they are strangers, than to act in conjunction with troops contiguous to the territories they attack: because as by this means they make war with all the advantage of natives, they are not only the better enabled to guard against ambuscades and surprises, but can in their turn make use of all those stratagems and favourable opportunities of action, which the particular nature of the country furnishes. Whoever therefore considers the artful conduct of the Romans in this respect, will find himself necessitated to own, that designs concerted with so much wisdom and foresight merited all the success with which they were for the most part attended.

VII. These preliminary cares settled, it is now time to put the troops in motion. The Romans were very exact in the order of their marches. In the morning, at the first sounding of the trumpet, every one took down his tent, and began to make up his baggage; at the second sounding, every one loaded his baggage; and at the third, the legions moved out of their quarters, and put themselves in the form and order they were that day to march in. But none were to take down their tents, till the consul and military tribunes had first taken down theirs; whether for the greater respect, or because their tents and baggage being larger than the rest, it was necessary they should be the first at work, that their

5*

baggage might be in a readiness to march at the third sound of the trumpet, as well as that of the private soldier. For commanders, who give rules to all the rest, ought to be very exact in observing them themselves; since, if they break their own orders, they encourage others to do the like; example always operating more strongly than precept. Hence that constant care in the Roman generals, to be themselves patterns to the troops, with regard to all the duties of the service; nor do we meet with any thing in their whole discipline, more truly deserving of imitation, or better calculated to promote submission and obedience in the army. For when soldiers find the general keeps strictly to the rules he gives, they are the more careful to observe them likewise; concluding, that as he therein grants no indulgence to himself, he certainly will not do it to others: nay, they implicitly believe such orders good and necessary, because he that gave them is so punctual an observer of them.

VIII. As to the particular form and disposition of the Roman march, we meet with very little on that subject in ancient authors. In the general it appears, that whether they marched in a friend's or enemy's country, whether they believed the enemy near or far off, they proceeded with the same care and circumspection: and this certainly was a very wise policy. For a general may be mistaken in his intelligence or intelligencers; nay, may think those friends, who want but an advantageous opportunity of declaring themselves foes: so that all imaginable caution ought to be observed, in all times, and in all places. To which let me add, that were there nothing else as a motive to it, but the keeping up exactly the military discipline, yet for that reason singly, it ought constantly to be done. The method followed most commonly by the Romans in their marches seems to have been this. They had always some troops of horse scouting abroad, in order to discover the roads. After them followed the right wing, with all its carriages immediately in the rear. Then came a legion, with its carriages; after that another; and so a third, a fourth, &c. in order. Last of all came the left wing and its baggage, with a party of horse in their rear. If, during the march, the army happened to be assaulted in the front or in the rear, they caused all their carriages to withdraw to the right wing or the left, as they found it convenient, and most agreeable to the nature of the place; and then, when they were cleared and disencumbered of their baggage, all of them unanimously made head against the enemy. If they were assaulted in the flank, they drew their carriages on that side where they were like to be most safe, and then addressed themselves to the fight.

IX. This, I say, was the most common order of their marches: for as to any fixed and standing rule, none could possibly be established; because the form must vary, according to the country you are in, and the enemy you have to do with. Julius Cæsar, when he marched against the Nervians, so long as he thought the enemy at a distance, proceeded exactly according to the disposition here described. But upon a nearer approach, he changed it entirely. For then all the cavalry were sent before. After them followed six legions, without baggage; and last of all, the carriages, guarded by two new raised legions. This was an excellent method, as he was sure the enemy could only attempt him in the van; but might be of ill consequence, where the rear of the army was liable to be attacked. One thing the Romans particularly attended to, and that was, that the troops did not straggle or march unequally, some too fast, others too slow, which **very** much weakens an army, and exposes it to great disorder. Hence their care, in training up their men, to inure them to the military pace: that is, to the **walking over a certain** stated piece of ground **within a fixed and** limited time. This, **as we have already** observed, amounted to twenty **miles in five** hours, which made the **usual** day's march of a Roman army. To accustom the soldiers to it, three times a month, the foot as well as horse were obliged to take this march. Upon extraordinary occasions they were wont to march four and twenty miles in the same space of time. By an exact calculation of what Cæsar relates of a sudden march, which he made at the time he besieged Gergovia, we find that in four and twenty hours he marched fifty miles. This he did with the utmost expedition. In reducing it to less than half, **it** makes the usual rate of an extraordinary day's march.

X. It is remarkable with regard to modern wars, that they not only impoverish the princes that are overcome, but even the conquerors themselves: for as one loses his country, so the other loses his money. In ancient times the case was otherwise; it appearing that the conqueror always enriched himself by the war. The reason of this difference seems to be, that in our times no public account is taken of the plunder; or indeed rather, that the barbarous custom of pillaging the conquered countries, is not now so much practised as formerly. Amongst the Romans, all the spoil was delivered in and appropriated to the public, which afterwards distributed it as it saw cause. To this purpose they had their questors, in whose hands all the pillage and taxes were deposited, of which the general disposed as he thought good, for the payment of his soldiers, the curing of the wounded or sick, and discharging the other necessities of the army. It is true the consul had power to give the plunder of a town to his soldiers, and he frequently did it; but that liberty never bred any disorder. For when a town was taken, or an army defeated, all the spoil was brought into a public space, and distributed man by man, according to every one's merit. This custom made the soldiers more intent upon victory than plunder. The practice of the Roman legions was, to break and disorder an enemy, but not to pursue; for they never went out of their ranks upon any occasion whatever. Only the horse, the light armed troops, and what other soldiers were not of the legions, followed the chase. But had the plunder of the field belonged to whoever could catch it, it would have been neither reasonable nor possible to have kept the legions to their ranks, or to have exposed them to so many dangers. Hence it was, that upon a victory, the public was always enriched. For when a consul entered in triumph, he brought with him great riches into the treasury of Rome; consisting of taxes, contributions, ransoms, and plunder. The Romans had likewise another custom well contrived for the preservation of discipline; and that was, to deposit a third part of every soldier's pay, with the ensigns of their respective companies, who never restored it, till the war was at an end. This served two very excellent purposes; first every soldier had a stock of his own, which without this precaution would have been squandered away, as they were most of them young and profuse. Secondly,

knowing their stocks to be in their ensign's hands, they were the more careful to defend and keep by him, whether in the camp, in the field of battle, or upon a march. This custom contributed much to their valour, and is necessary to be observed by any general, who would reduce his soldiers to the discipline of the Romans.

XI. Among the various orders of the Roman marches, one particularly deserves our notice, which is frequently mentioned by historians, and which they term forming the army *itineri et prœlio*. It was, when the line of march was so contrived, as to correspond exactly with the line of battle; or, to express myself a little more clearly, when the columns of horse and foot were disposed in such a manner, that, upon the sudden appearance of an enemy, they could fall immediately into an order proper for fighting. There is not perhaps any thing in the science of arms more subtle and useful than this, and the Romans seem to have made it their particular study. I do not at present recollect in any of their historians, a minute and circumstantial account of a march of this kind, where the disposition of the columns is exactly marked, and the manner in which they formed in order of battle, upon the approach of the enemy. What most readily occurs to my memory, is the fine march of Hamilcar against Spendius, which has been so judiciously explained by the Chevalier Folard, in his admirable comment upon Polybius. As the whole art of War furnishes nothing more complete in its kind, whether we regard the boldness of the attempt, or the well concerted motions by which it was accomplished, I am satisfied I shall do the reader a particular pleasure, in laying a full and distinct account of it before him.

XII. Upon the conclusion of the first Punic war, the Carthaginian mercenaries revolting, chose Matho and Spendius for their leaders. Hanno was sent against them with an army; but receiving a considerable check, the rebels blocked up Carthage on every side, and possessed themselves of all the passes leading to the peninsula on which it stood. In this exigence, the Carthaginians had recourse to Hamilcar, the father of Hannibal, who had given eminent proof of his abilities when he commanded their armies in Sicily. Accordingly he took the field with ten thousand men, and seventy elephants; but was for some time at a loss how to meet with the enemy upon equal ground. For besides the other places of advantage which the mercenaries had seized, Hanno had suffered them to get possession of the only bridge by which the river Bagradas was passable to those who were to travel from Carthage into the continent. This river had not many fords, and the few it had were so well watched, that it was not easy for even a single man to get over without being seen. As for the bridge itself, the enemy guarded it with the utmost care, and had built a town close by it, for the more commodious lodgings of the troops that were appointed to that service. Hamilcar having in vain tried all means possible to force a passage, at length bethought himself of an expedient to gain one by stealth. He had observed, that upon blowing of certain winds, the mouth of the Bagradas used to be choked up with sand and gravel, which formed a kind of bar across, and rendered it fordable. Remaining therefore in his camp between the sea and the mountains, he waited the opportunity of these winds; which no sooner arrived, than marching suddenly in the night, he passed the stream unperceived, and the next morning appeared in the plain, to the great astonishment both of the Carthaginians and the enemy.

XIII. Hamilcar by this step put all to the hazard. Had he failed in his attempt against Spendius, his whole army must inevitably have been destroyed; for a retreat was now become impossible. But neither was the danger less great to his country by continuing inactive; and therefore he wisely considered, that in such an extremity it was better to try some way where fortune and his own ability in war offered a prospect of success, than by a timorous diffident conduct expose himself to the same ruin, without a single effort to evade it. He was now upon the other side the Bagradas. The plains were favourable to him, because he had a considerable body of horse. The river itself too was of no small advantage, as it served to secure his baggage, and cover one of his flanks. Spendius was advancing to meet him at the head of ten thousand men. Besides these he understood that a detachment of fifteen thousand was marching with all diligence from Utica; and as it was their

business to come upon his flank and rear rather than to join Spendius, he made no doubt of their proceeding accordingly. Upon these considerations he regulated his order of battle, and the disposition of his march. To make head against Spendius, he placed his elephants in the first line, and immediately behind them his cavalry, intermixed with platoons of light armed foot. The heavy-armed infantry formed the third line, in order to oppose the detachment he expected upon his rear, from Utica. By this disposition he was enabled to make head on all sides. For as he made no doubt but his first line of elephants, of which Spendius was totally unprovided, would be sufficient to break the body he commanded; and that the cavalry, aided by the light armed foot, falling in immediately, would serve to complete the rout: so his third line, consisting of the flower of his African infantry, he thought himself strong enough likewise to deal with the rebels from Utica.

XIV. Each of these lines marched in four columns, the columns of cavalry following immediately behind the elephants, and those of the infantry immediately behind the cavalry. The distance between the columns was equal to the space they were to occupy in the line of battle. By this disposition, upon the first appearance of the enemy, the army could form in an instant. For the columns being commanded to halt, and wheel at once into their place in the line, were in order of battle presently. Hamilcar continuing his march, perceived, as the enemy approached, that the detachment from Utica, instead of coming in upon his rear, had actually joined Spendius, and formed a second line of foot behind that he commanded. As he had foreseen that this might happen, his order of march was contrived to furnish a speedy remedy. It now became necessary to change his whole disposition, and oppose a strong front of infantry to the enemy, with the elephants at the head of all, according to the usual custom. To that end the columns were ordered to halt, and the elephants forming in front, the cavalry meanwhile fell back between intervals of the foot, ranging themselves in two divisions behind the two extremities of the line of infantry, which was formed in an instant by the wheeling of the columns. The rebels deceived by th s artful motion, and mistaking the retreat of the cavalry for a real flight, advanced briskly to the attack, broke through the elephants, and charged the Carthaginian foot. Meanwhile the cavalry, which, as we have already observed, had ranged itself in two columns behind the two wings of the infantry, wheeling to the right and left from the rear, appeared all on a sudden in the same line with the foot, covering the flanks of the Carthaginian army, and considerably overwinging the enemy. The rebels, astonished at this extraordinary motion, quickly fell into disorder, and at last betook themselves to flight. Hamilcar pursued them with his horse and elephants; and following them quite to the town and bridge, easily got possession of that important pass.

XV. From this recital it appears, to what a degree of perfection the ancients had arrived in the science of marches, which is a capital article in the grand operations of war. And though the instance here given be of an African commander, and therefore does not so immediately regard the Roman people, yet if we consider, that these last are allowed to have excelled all nations in the knowledge of arms, and that they often regulated their marches upon this plan, it seems reasonable to believe, that had their historians entered into particular details of this kind, we should have met with many examples of military conduct in their generals, no less surprising than that now before us. Indeed, as it frequently happens in war, that the enemy, though not actually in sight, is yet hourly expected, this way of ordering an army seems very necessary; and the general who excels in it, and is at the same time sufficiently on his guard against surprises, will seldom or ever be worsted. I have often admired, in reading Cæsar's Commentaries, the consummate prudence and circumspection of that great man, especially in relation to surprises. Though he was the ablest general of his time, and commanded the finest army that perhaps ever appeared in the world, yet he always proceeded with the utmost caution, and was extremely careful of believing any thing too easily, that was not reasonably to be supposed. If a great number of the enemy was beaten and pursued by a few of his men, if a few of them attacked a greater party of his, if they ran unexpectedly, and without any visible cause, on these occasions he was always very much upon his guard, and

never fancied his enemy so weak, as not to understand his own business. It seems in the general a good rule, the weaker and more careless an enemy appears to be, the more to apprehend and dread him. In cases of this kind, an experienced commander will comport himself in two different manners. He will fear the enemy in his own thoughts, and order his affairs accordingly; but in his words and outward behaviour, he will affect to despise him. This last way gives courage to the soldiers, and makes them confident of victory. The other keeps the general upon his guard, and renders him less liable to be circumvented; for to march through an enemy's country is more dangerous, and requires a greater address and foresight than to fight a pitched battle.

XVI. We proceed now to the second particular mentioned on the head of marches, namely, the knowledge and choice of posts. As this will again fall under our notice in the next chapter, concerning encampments, we need say the less of it here. It has however a strict and necessary connexion with the marching of an army. For whether we are to retreat or advance, or which way so ever our route lies, it often happens, that the safety of the army depends upon seizing some advantageous posts that command the country through which we march. The Romans applied themselves with particular attention to this part of war, and we meet with several very early traces of it in their history. Livy relates an example of this kind in the person of Publius Decius, who being a military tribune in the army which the consul Cornelius commanded against the Samnites, and finding the consul and army falling by accident into a vale, where they might have been encompassed and cut off by the enemy: "Do you see, (said he to Cornelius,) that eminence which commands the enemy's camp? There lies our hope. It is a post that may serve to extricate us out of our present danger, if we are careful only to seize it quickly, and avail ourselves of the blindness of the Samnites, who have neglected it." The historian had before informed us, that Decius observed a hill over the enemy's camp, not easily to be ascended by those who were completely armed, but to those lightly armed, accessible enough. The consul ordered him to take possession of it with three thousand men. He obeyed the order, secured the Roman army, and designing to

H

march away in the night, and save both himself and his party, addressed himself in these words to some of his companions : " Follow me, fellow-soldiers, that whilst we have yet light, we may explore where the enemy keeps his guards, and which way we may make our retreat." Accordingly he went out in person upon this design, and habited like a soldier, that the enemy might not know his rank in the army, took an exact view of the ground, and the situation of their camp. Whoever attentively considers this relation, will find how useful and necessary it is for a commander to be acquainted with the nature of coasts and countries, and that not only in a general, but in an exquisite and more particular way. Had not Decius understood those things very well, he could not so suddenly have discerned the advantage of that hill, and of what importance it would be to the preservation of the Roman army. Neither could he have judged, at that distance, whether it was accessible or not : and when he had possessed himself of it, and was to draw off afterwards, as the enemy environed him on every side, he could never have found out the best way for his retreat, nor have guessed so well where the enemy kept his guards. Fabius Maximus is another example of a consummate knowledge this way. He commanded the Roman army six months against Hannibal, and by a series of well-concerted motions, and a judicious choice of posts, conducted himself so happily, that during all that time he never suffered any considerable disaster, nor could be compelled to fight against his will, though the artful Carthaginian left no stratagem untried, to draw him to an engagement, or entangle him in an ambuscade. But of all the Roman generals, none seems to have been a greater master in this part of war than Julius Cæsar. We meet with many instances of it in his Commentaries, particularly in that famous campaign in Spain, where by a happy choice of posts, and an exquisite address in improving the advantages the nature of the country afforded, he compelled a veteran army to surrender themselves prisoners of war, without striking a blow.

XVII. The third and last particular we mentioned in relation to marches, was the disposition and conduct of a retreat. This is, without dispute, the nicest point in the whole business of war. For besides all the attentions requisite in ordinary marches, you are under the disadvantage of being continually pressed by an enemy, commonly superior in force, and flushed with success. The finest retreat we meet with in ancient history, is that of the ten thousand Greeks under the conduct of Xenophon, who has left us a particular account of that famous expedition. We there see that the hollow square, which was invented purposely for a retreat, is very incommodious when the enemy is directly in your rear. Xenophon says so in express terms, and that the Greeks were obliged to discontinue that order, and march in two columns, with a body of reserve of six hundred men, who were not confined to the space between the columns, so as to complete the figure of the square, but formed sometimes the van, sometimes the rear, filed off by the two flanks where the columns were obliged to approach, or posted themselves in the interval when they extended to the right and left ; in a word, without being tied down to any fixed post, ran wherever their assistance was wanted. What surprises most in this retreat is, that upon a computation of the way made by the troops, which Xenophon regularly sets down, we find their day's marches one with another, to fall but little short of twenty-four miles. Our armies seldom advance half the way, even when they have no enemy upon their hands, nor any of those other disadvantages the Greeks laboured under. We find likewise in the Roman history, several examples of well-conducted retreats, in which their generals have happily extricated themselves out of dangers that seemed to threaten their armies with unavoidable destruction. Quintus Lutatius having the Cambri upon his heels, and being arrived at a river ; that the enemy might give him time to pass, pretended a resolution to fight them, pitched his camp, intrenched himself, set up his standard, and set out parties of horse to provide forage. The Cambri believing he meant to encamp there, came and encamped by him, and divided themselves into several parties, to go in quest of provisions. Lutatius having notice of this, seized the opportunity so favourable to his design, and throwing bridges over the river, passed it before the enemy could have time to disturb him. Lucius Minucius a Roman consul was in Liguria with an army, and shut up by the enemy between two mountains, insomuch that he could not disengage himself. Being sensible of the danger he was in, he sent certain

Numidians which he had in his army, upon small ill-conditioned horses, towards the places where the enemy had their guard. At first sight they put themselves into a posture to defend the passes: but when they observed the Numidians in ill order, and ill-mounted in respect of themselves, they began to despise them, and to be more remiss in their guard; which was no sooner perceived by the Numidians, than clapping spurs to their horses, and charging them suddenly, they passed on in spite of all opposition, and by the mischief and devastation they made every where in the country, constrained the enemy to give free passage to the whole army. I shall mention only one instance more, and that is the retreat of Marc Antony, when he was pursued into Syria by a great body of Parthian horse. He observed that every morning by break of day they were upon his back as soon as he moved, and continued skirmishing and molesting him quite through the march. In order to deceive them, and obtain some respite, he resolved not to remove before noon; which the Parthians observing, concluded he could not stir that day, and returned to their posts, insomuch that he had an opportunity of marching all the rest of the day without interruption. But this was only a temporary expedient, calculated for present relief; and therefore to screen himself from the arrows of the Parthians, with which the army was greatly incommoded, he made use of the following device, practised often by the Romans on other occasions. He ordered the soldiers, when the enemy came near them, to cast themselves into the figure of the testudo, so that their targets should close altogether above their heads, and defend them from the missive weapons discharged at them. In this case the first rank stood upright on their feet, and the rest stooped lower and lower by degrees, till the last rank kneeled down upon their knees; so that every rank covering with their targets the heads of all in the rank before them, they represented a tortoise-shell, or a sort of pent-house. By this contrivance he made good his retreat, and arrived in Syria, without considerable loss.

XVIII. Before I conclude this chapter, it will naturally be expected I should explain what was the practice and discipline of the Romans, when they had finished the day's march, and were arrived near the place of encampment. In this case the military tribunes

and centurions appointed for that service advanced before all the rest diligently to view and consider the situation of the place. When they had chosen the ground, they began by marking the general's quarter with a white flag or streamer, and distinctly set out its boundaries. Then the quarters of the several tribunes were appointed, and afterwards those of the legions, all with distinct flags of several colours. Every legion, as well of the allies as of the Romans, had their portion of ground assigned and marked out, for drawing the line round the camp, which was set about immediately, part of the troops continuing meanwhile under arms, to defend those that were at work upon the intrenchment, in case of any sudden surprise. All this was finished in a very short space, the Romans being remarkably expert in it by constant practice; for they never altered the figure of their camp, nor omitted to fortify it in all the forms, though but for one night's continuance. But this naturally leads me to the subject of the next chapter.

CHAP. VI.

OF ENCAMPMENTS.

I. ONE of the most necessary and beneficial parts of the military art is, to know how to encamp well, and to practise it constantly. No wonder therefore that the Romans, among whom military discipline was carried to such a degree of perfection, and who exacted the most rigorous submission to all the laws and rules of it, were particularly attentive to this article. And indeed the armies of that people, though still in the territory of Rome, and though they had only one night to pass in a place, encamped nevertheless in all the forms, with no other difference than that the camp was less fortified there, perhaps, than in the enemy's country. It was always of a square form, contrary to the custom of the Greeks, who made theirs round. The ditch and rampart, which consisted of four equal sides, was equally distributed to be raised by the two Roman legions, and the two legions of the allies who perfected it without intermission. If the enemy were near, part of the troops continued under arms, whilst the rest were employed in throwing up the intrenchments. They began by digging trenches of greater or less depth according to the occasion. They were at least eight feet broad by six deep: but we often find them twelve feet in breadth, sometimes more, to fifteen or twenty. Of the earth dug out of the trenches, and thrown up on the side of the camp, they formed the rampart, and to make it the firmer, mingled it with turf cut in a certain size and form. Sometimes they drove double rows of stakes into the earth, leaving so much of the length above ground, as the height of the work was to be of; and then interweaving them with twigs, in the manner of basket-work, filled the space between with the earth rising out of the ditch. This was an expeditious and safe way of forming the line, and appears to have been always practised, when they encamped in places where these materials were to be found. Upon the brow of the rampart the palisades were planted. Polybius, speaking of the order given by Q. Flaminius to his troops, to cut stakes against there should be occasion for them, offers several very curious remarks upon this subject ; and as that judicious historian, who was himself an expert warrior, seems to lay great stress upon the conduct of the Romans in this point, I shall beg leave to lay some of his observations before the reader.

II. This custom, says Polybius, which is easy to put in practice amongst the Romans, passes for impossible with the Greeks. They can hardly support their own weight upon their marches, whilst the Romans, notwithstanding the buckler which hangs at their shoulders, and the javelins, which they carry in their hands, load themselves also with stakes or palisades, which are very different from those of the Greeks. With the latter those are best, which have many strong branches about the trunk. The Romans, on the contrary, leave but three or four at most upon it, and that only on one side. In this manner a man can carry two or three bound together, and much more use may be made of them. Those of the Greeks are more easily pulled up. If the stake be fixed by itself; as its branches are strong, and in great number, two or three soldiers will easily pull it away, and thereby make an opening for the enemy, without reckoning that the neighbouring stakes will be loosened, because their branches are too short to be interwoven with each other. But this is not the case with the Romans. The branches of their palisades are so strongly inserted into

each other, that it is hard to distinguish the stake they belong to; and it is as little practicable to thrust the hand through these branches to pull up the palisades; because, being well fastened and twisted together, they leave no opening, and are carefully sharpened at their ends. Even though they could be taken hold of, it would not be easy to pull them out of the ground, and that for two reasons. The first is, because they are driven in so deep, that they cannot be moved: and the second, because their branches are interwoven with each other in such a manner, that one cannot be stirred without several more. Two or three men might unite their strength in vain to draw one of them out, which however if they effected, by drawing a great while to and fro until it was loose, the opening it would leave would be almost imperceptible. These stakes therefore have three advantages. They are every where to be had ; they are easy to carry ; and are a secure barrier to a camp, because very difficult to break through. In my opinion, adds the historian, there is nothing practised by the Romans in war, more worthy of being imitated.

III. The form and distribution of the several parts of the Roman camp, admits of great difficulties, and has occasioned many disputes amongst the learned. The following description is taken chiefly from Polybius, who of all the ancients is the most full and explicit upon this article. He speaks of a consular army, which in his time consisted of two Roman legions, and two legions of the allies. A Roman legion contained four thousand two hundred foot, and three hundred horse. A legion of the allies was equal to the number of infantry, and generally double in cavalry. Altogether therefore, Romans, and allies, they made eighteen thousand six hundred men. After the place for the camp was marked out, which was always chosen for its convenience in respect to water and forage, a part of it was allotted for the general's tent, called otherwise the prætorium, because the ancient Latins styled all their commanders prætores. The ground pitched upon for this purpose was generally higher than the rest of the camp, that he might with the greater ease see all that passed, and despatch the necessary orders. A flag was planted upon it, and round that a square space marked out in such a manner that the four sides were a hundred feet distant from the flag, and the ground occupied by the consul about four acres. Near this tent were erected the altar, on which the sacrifices were offered, and the tribunal for dispensing justice. The two Roman legions had each six tribunes, which made twelve in all. Their tents were placed in a right line parallel to the front of the prætorium, at the distance of fifty feet. In the space of fifty feet were the horses, beasts of burden, and the whole equipage of the tribunes. Their tents were pitched in such a manner, that they had the prætorium in the rear, and in the front all the rest of the camp. The tents of the tribunes, at equal distance from each other, took up the whole breadth of the ground upon which the two Roman legions were encamped.

IV. Between the tents of the legions and tribunes, a space of a hundred feet in breadth was left, which formed a large street, called principia, that ran across the whole camp, and divided it into two parts, the upper and lower. Beyond this street, were placed the tents of the legions. The space which they occupied was divided in the midst, into two equal parts, by a street of fifty feet broad, which extended the whole length of the camp. On each side of this street, in so many several lines, were the quarters of the horse, the triarii, the principes, and the hastati. The velites had no distinct quarters, but were variously mingled with the rest of the foot, four hundred and eighty of them being joined to the hastati, a like number to the principes, and two hundred and forty to the triarii. To form a distinct idea of the Roman camp, we must call to mind that the cavalry of each legion was divided into ten troops, thirty men to a troop; and that the triarii, principes, and hastati, were likewise severally divided into ten maniples, of a hundred and twenty men each, except those of the triarii, which consisted only of half that number. In conformity to this distribution, the lines on which these several bodies encamped, were each divided into ten squares, extending length-wise from the tents of the tribunes. These squares were a hundred feet every way, except in the lines of the triarii, where, because of the smaller number of troops, they were only fifty feet broad by a hundred long, and may therefore more properly be termed half squares. Across the middle of these lodgments, between the fifth and sixth squares, ran a street of fifty feet broad, cutting

the line at right angles, and extending from one side of the camp to the other. It was called quintana, because it opened beyond the fifth maniple.

V. The order and disposition of the several lines was as follows. On each side of the middle-street, that ran according to the length of the camp, the cavalry of the two legions were quartered facing each other, and separated by the whole breadth of the street. As there were ten squares on each side, and every square lodged thirty horse, the twenty together contained just six hundred, which made the entire cavalry of two legions. Adjoining to the cavalry the triarii were quartered, a maniple behind a troop of horse, both in the same form. They joined as to the ground, but faced differently, the triarii turning their backs upon the horse. And here, as we have already observed, because the triarii were less in number than the other troops, the ground assigned to each maniple was only half as broad as long. Fronting the triarii on each side, was a street of fifty feet broad, running parallel to that between the quarters of the horse. On the opposite side of the street was the line of the lodgments belonging to the principes. Behind the principes the hastati were quartered, joining as to the ground, but fronting the other way.

VI. Thus far we have described the quarters of the two Roman legions. It remains that we dispose of the allies. Their infantry equalled that of the Romans, and their cavalry was twice the number. In removing for the extraordinarii a fifth part of the foot, or sixteen hundred and eighty men, and a third of the horse, or four hundred men, there remained in the whole seven thousand five hundred and twenty men, horse and foot, to quarter. These were disposed upon the two wings of the legions, being separated from the hastati on each side, by a street of fifty feet. The cavalry were directly opposite to the hastati upon a breadth of a hundred and thirty-three feet, and something more. Behind them, and on the same line, the infantry were encamped upon a breadth of two hundred feet. The præfecti were lodged at the sides of the tribunes, over against their respective wings. At the head of every troop and maniple, were the tents of the captains of horse and centurions. On the right side of the prætorium stood the quæstorium, assigned to the quæstor, or treasurer of the army, and hard by the forum. This last served not only for the sale of commodities, but also for the meeting of councils and giving audience to ambassadors. On the other side of the prætorium were lodged the legati, or lieutenant-generals. On the right and left, still in the same line with the prætorium, and directly behind the præfects of the allies, were the quarters of the extraordinary cavalry, evocatorum, and of the other volunteer Roman horse, selectorum. All this cavalry faced on one side towards the forum and place of the quæstor, and on the other towards the lodgments of the legati. They not only encamped near the consul's person, but commonly attended him upon marches, that they might be at hand to execute his orders. The extraordinary and volunteer Roman foot adjoined to the horse last spoken of, forming the extremities of the line towards the two sides of the camp. Above this line was a street of a hundred feet broad, extending the whole breadth of the camp, and beyond that the quarters of the extraordinary horse of the allies, facing the prætorium, treasury, and the tents of the legati. The extraordinary foot of the allies were directly behind their horse, fronting the intrenchment and upper extremity of the camp. The void spaces that remained on both sides were allotted to strangers and allies, who came later than the rest.

VII. Between the ramparts and the tents, there was an open place or street of two hundred feet in breadth, which was continued all along the four equal sides of the camp. This interval was of very great use, either for the entrance or departure of the legions. For each body of troops advanced into that space by the street before it, so that marching thither different ways, they were in no danger of crowding and breaking each other's ranks. Besides which, the cattle, and whatever was taken from the enemy was placed there, where a guard was kept during the night. Another considerable advantage of it was, that in the attacks by night, neither fire nor dart could do any great execution in the camp; the soldiers being at so great a distance, and under cover of their tents. But the principal intention of it seems to have been, for the drawing up of the troops who were to defend the line, and to leave sufficient room for the cavalry to scour it. My Lord Orrery, however, is of opinion, that it was rather too narrow to answer both these services. If it was only designed for the

foot, they lost the benefit of their horse, which experience teaches us to be of singular use on such occasions. For whatever foot storm a line, must enter it in great confusion and disorder, and can very hardly indeed resist small squadrons of horse, who are ready to receive them, and charge them all along the inside of the line. For these reasons he considers the narrowness of this space as a defect in the Roman method of encamping, and thinks that a breadth of three hundred feet at least ought to have been allowed for the defence and scouring of the line. It is probable the Romans would have done so, had they not found the other sufficient; and we have this to say in their favour, that though their camps were frequently attacked, we meet with but few instances in history of their being forced.

VIII. The gates were only four in number, one to each side. Livy says so in express terms. "Ad quator portas exercitum instruxit, ut, signo dato, ex omnibus portubus eruptionem facerent." "He drew up his men facing the four gates, that upon a signal given, the army might sally from all the several gates at once." These are afterwards called by the same author, the extraordinary, the right principal, the left principal, and the quæstorian. They have also other names, about which it is not a little difficult to reconcile authors. It is believed that the extraordinary gate **was so called, because near** the place where the **extraordinary troops** encamped; **and that it was the same as the** prætorian, which **took its name from its** nearness to the **prætorium. The gate** opposite to this, **at the other extremity of the** camp, was called Porta Decumana, **because** near the ten maniples of each legion; and without doubt is the same with the quæstorian, mentioned by Livy in the place above cited. As to the right and left principals, they had their name from being on the right and left of the camp, fronting the street called principia. I shall conclude this description of the Roman camp with observing, that when a consular army consisted of more than four legions, they were lodged still in the same order, only the figure of the camp was a long square in proportion to the additional forces which were to be contained in it. When both the consular armies were united, they took up the ground of two such perfect squares.

IX. A wonderful order was observed night

and day throughout the camp, in respect to the watchword, sentinels and guards; and it was in this its security and quiet consisted. To render the guard more regular and less fatiguing, the night was divided into four parts or watches, and the day into four stations. There seems to have been assigned one company of foot, and one troop of horse to each of the four gates every day. The Roman discipline was extremely strict in this particular, punishing with an exemplary severity such as deserted their post, or abandoned their corps of guard. Polybius takes notice of the excellent effects of this discipline, upon occasion of the siege of Agrigentum in Sicily, during the first Punic war. The Roman guards had dispersed themselves a little too far in quest of forage. The Carthaginians laying hold of the opportunity, made a vigorous sally from the town, and had well nigh forced the camp; when the soldiers, sensible of the extreme penalty they had incurred by neglecting their duty, resolved to repair the fault by some remarkable behaviour; and accordingly rallying together, they not only sustained the shock of the enemy, to whom they were far inferior in number, but in the end made so great a slaughter among them, as compelled them to retreat into the town, though they were upon the very point of carrying the Roman lines. The night guards were four out of every manipulus, who continued on duty three hours, and were then relieved by those next in turn. To keep the soldiers alert they had the *circuitio vigilum*, or patrols, performed commonly four times in the night by some of the horse. Upon extraordinary occasions, the tribunes and lieutenant-generals, and sometimes the general himself, made these circuits in person, and took a strict view of the watch in every part of the camp.

X. What we have hitherto said, regards only the plan, disposition, and well ordering of the Roman camp. But there are many other particulars to be taken into consideration, in encamping an army to advantage: the choice of the ground; the convenience of provision and forage; the security of convoys; and the precautions needful to prevent surprise, or the being taken at a disadvantage. We cannot however here enter into a particular detail of the Roman practice, with relation to these several articles; because not being

subject to any fixed and invariable rules, they depend in a manner entirely upon the prudence and discretion of the general, who must therein be guided by the nature of the country, the posture of the enemy, and his own strength. Two things in particular they were more than ordinarily attentive to; health, and safety. The first they endeavoured to secure, by avoiding all morasses and fenny places, or where the wind was cold and unwholesome; which unwholesomeness they did not so much compute from the situation of the place as from the appearance and complexion of the inhabitants. Exercise contributes greatly to health, and therefore the Romans took care to keep their troops always employed, either in casting up new works round the camp, or in hunting after provision and forage, or in performing those several exercises, that tend to render the body robust and active. It is observed in our days, that the immoderate labour soldiers are obliged to undergo, destroys our armies: and yet it was by incredible labour that the Romans preserved themselves. The reason of the difference I take to be this: their fatigues were continual and without respite: whereas our men were perpetually shifting from the extremes of labour to the extremes of idleness, than which nothing can be more destructive. Who could believe, that there was nothing, even to cleanliness, of which particular care was not taken in the Roman camp. As the great street situated in the front of the prætorium was much frequented by the officers and soldiers, who passed through it to receive and carry orders, and upon their other occasions; a number of men were appointed to sweep and clean it every day in winter, and to water it in summer to prevent the dust.

XI. But besides health, safety was likewise another important consideration with the Romans. To this end, in choosing a place of encampment, they always had a particular eye for the convenience of water, provisions, and forage. We see evidently in Cæsar's Commentaries, that there was nothing about which he was more solicitous, than the contriving his marches in such manner, as to have his camp seated near some navigable river, and a country behind him, whence he could be easily, and at a reasonable rate, supplied with every thing necessary for the subsistence of his army. Other inconveniences may find a remedy in time, but hunger, the longer it lasts the more infallibly it destroys. And hence it was, that where the above-mentioned advantages could not be obtained, the Romans made it their first care, after fortifying their camp, to lay in such a quantity of all necessary stores, as might be sufficient for the time of their continuance in it. Nor were they less attentive to the strength of their camp, and the precautions necessary for its defence. This is a part of the *art of war* in which they incontestably excelled all nations. Constant practice made them expert in it; for they never quartered their troops in towns and open villages, but always in standing camps, which were carefully intrenched and fortified, in proportion to the danger to which they fancied themselves exposed. And here we may observe, that whereas the Greeks chose always to encamp where there was some river, or wood, or bank, or other natural rampart to defend them; the Romans, on the contrary, stood not so much on the strength of situation, as on their own ways of fortifying. Hence the Grecian camps were often without intrenchments, and varied in their form, according to the nature of the place: but among the Romans one constant method was inviolably observed, nor would they ever lodge in a camp, that was not surrounded with a ditch and a rampart.

XII. The practice of intrenched and fortified camps was attended with many solid and desirable advantages. The army was hereby kept safe, and freed from the danger of having any of its quarters beat up, by surprise or a sudden attack. It was eased of the trouble of keeping many and great guards, since a few serves the turn of all, when all are at hand in case of an attempt. It could never be compelled to fight against its will, than which no greater misfortune can befall an army. In fine, as the success of arms is uncertain, it had always a secure retreat in case of the worst. These things considered, it will not appear wonderful, that the Romans were so strict in this article, and considered the custom of fortifying camps regularly, as one of the most essential parts of military discipline. In the war with the Gauls, the commanders of the Roman army were reproached with having omitted this wise precaution, and the loss of the battle of Allia was in part attributed to it. Hence it was, that to avoid the like misfortune for the time to come, it became in a manner an established law amongst them, never, to hazard a battle until they had finished their camp. Paulus Æmilius, in the second Macedonian war, suspended and arrested the ardour of his whole army to attack Perseus, for no other reason, but because they had not formed their camp. The fortified camp, in case of a disaster, put a stop to the enemy's victory, received the troops that retired in safety, enabled them to renew the battle with more success, and prevented their being entirely routed; whereas without the refuge of a camp, an army, though composed of good troops, was exposed to a final defeat, and to being inevitably cut in pieces. I may add to all these advantages that an intrenched camp, by reason of the open air, the healthiness of its situation, which always must be minded, and the cleanliness which may and ought to be kept in it, is exceedingly less subject to infection and sickness, than villages and strong towns; insomuch that some great captains have concluded, an army would be likelier preserved, and kept sound and untainted three months in a well seated and regulated camp, than three weeks in the ordinary villages and country towns.

XIII. I have the longer and more particularly insisted on the practice of intrenched camps, because it appears evident from history, that the Romans owed as many of their victories to their ability in this part of war, as to their other excellent military discipline and valour. It would be almost endless to enumerate, what kingdoms and provinces they kept in obedience by their standing camps; and how often they warded off dangers, and brought their wars to a fortunate issue by the same proceeding. For having first wearied out their enemies by safe and beneficial delays, they would, on some great advantage, give them battle and defeat them; which artful method of making war they neither could have effected, nor rationally attempted, but by their thoroughly knowing how to encamp advantageously, by constantly practising it, and by a timely providing of food and forage. Vegetius observes, that one of the principal causes of the ruin of the Roman empire was, that they had lost the art of fortifying their camp: by which negligence they were easily overwhelmed by the barbarian horse. And indeed when, under the emperors, they had ascertained the limits of their dominion, resolving to extend their conquest no farther, but to rest satisfied with maintaining the possession of what they had acquired: it is well known, that they effectually accomplished this design by means of the standing camps, which they kept upon the Euphrates, the Danube, and the Rhine. And so long as this method was followed, the bordering nations found it impossible to break through the Roman barriers, or hurt the tranquillity of their empire. But when, in process of time the military discipline began to decline, and the art of encamping, in particular, was lost, or grew into disuse; the Romans, by abandoning the banks of these several rivers, opened a free passage to the barbarians, who, meeting now with no resistance, poured in upon them like a torrent, and easily overwhelmed a feeble race of men, whom luxury, and an undisturbed peace of many ages, had rendered utterly unfit for war.

XIV. And here, as it falls so naturally in my way, and has a strict connexion with my subject, I cannot forbear observing, that in the last age, the French, who had many excellent commanders, if not the most in any one nation, and to whom the *art of war* owes much of its present improvement, began to revive, and with great benefit to themselves, this almost obsolete part of it. For when the Prince of Orange, the Imperialists under the Count de Souches, and the Flemish forces were united; the Prince of Conde, one of the greatest captains that any age has produced, being sent to oppose them, would not give them battle, but encamped himself advantageously on the French frontiers, so that they were justly afraid to enter them, and leave him at their backs. By this management he kept them long at bay, and when he found his opportunity, gave them, at Seneff, so considerable a blow, that the French, from having been on the defensive, became afterwards the assaulters, and closed that campaign with taking some of the enemy's towns. The Marshal de Turenne also, who was sent general to the war in Germany, and who in the military art had hardly a superior, having there to do with Count de Montecuculi, one of the greatest captains of his time, would still, by intrenched camps, when the Germans were the strongest, preserve himself and army, spin out the war, and cover those territories and places he had won while he himself had been the most powerful.

6*

XV. And here it is particularly worthy of notice, that when, upon the Marshal de Turenne's death, the French king sent the Prince of Conde to command in his stead, he also, by intrenched encampments, weathered that storm; which in itself was so threatening, not only by the sudden loss of so great a captain, but also by the Germans being led by the Count de Montecuculi, and the Duke of Lorraine, two persons as considerable as the very forces they headed. I say, it particularly deserves our observation, that two such justly celebrated commanders as the Prince of Conde and Monsieur Turenne, should observe the very same methods in managing the same war; whereas, usually, when one general succeeds another, in heading the same army, and ordering the same war; the last comer judges it a kind of diminution to his own skill, to tread in the very paths of his predecessor. But as the Prince of Conde observed a quite different conduct on this occasion, we may thence naturally gather the three following particulars. *First,* that he judged himself so justly secure in his own reputation, that it could receive no diminution by his following the steps of the dead general, more especially as he had done the like before, and successfully, in Flanders. *Secondly,* that a wise and great captain will rather, by imitating his predecessor, confirm that course to be the best which he knows to be so in itself, than try new methods of war, whereby out of a mere hope to do the like thing by a different way, he may hazard his reputation, his army, and the country he is to cover and protect. *Thirdly,* what two such generals have practised, all circumstances considered, amounts to little less than a demonstration, that by camps intrenched and well posted, a country may be best secured, an invading enemy best resisted, and in time, all advantages being judiciously taken, defeated, or made to retire.

XVI. These examples, ancient and modern, sufficiently evince the benefit of **this** practice, and with what judgment the Romans made it an essential part of their military discipline. I shall only add, as **an** indisputable argument in its favour, that **the great** Cæsar himself has given his sanction to **it,** by constantly following it in his wars with the Gauls. He had to do with a brave and warlike nation, passionately fond of liberty, and therefore extremely averse to the Roman yoke. To keep them in awe,

I

he established standing camps in different parts of the country, where the soldiers were quartered in large bodies, and surrounded with strong intrenchments. This he thought the likeliest method to prevent insurrections, or suppress them speedily when they should happen, as the troops would be always in readiness to march, and in condition to act. It was likewise the best security against treachery and surprise. Accordingly we find, that all the efforts of the Gauls to recover their liberty were without effect, the Roman camps standing as so many bulwarks, against which, though they made frequent attacks, they were yet never able to prevail.

CHAP. VII.

OF BATTLES.

I. Having raised our troops, armed and disciplined them, put them upon the march, and lodged them in a camp, it is now time to draw them out into the field, that we may see how they acquitted themselves on a day of battle. It is in this view military merit appears in all its extent. To know whether a general were worthy of that name, the Romans examined the conduct he observed on this critical occasion. They did not expect success from the number of troops, which is often a disadvantage, but from his prudence and valour, the cause and assurance of victory. They considered him as the soul of his army, that directs all its motions, whose dictates every thing obeys, and upon whose good or bad conduct the issue of the battle depends. The first consideration, and that which demands the greatest force of judgment, is, to examine whether it be proper or not to come to an engagement, and to balance exactly the advantages with the disadvantages. The blind temerity of Varro, notwithstanding his colleague's remonstrances, and the advice of Fabius, drew upon the republic the unfortunate battle of Cannæ; whereas a delay of a few weeks would probably have ruined Hannibal for ever. Perseus, on the contrary, let slip the occasion of fighting the Romans, in not taking the advantage of the ardour of his army, and attacking them instantly after the defeat of their horse, which had thrown their troops into disorder and consternation. Cæsar had been lost after the battle of Dyrrhachium, if Pompey had known how to improve his advantage. Great enterprises have their decisive moments. The important point lies, in wisely resolving what to choose, and in seizing the present occasion which never returns when once neglected.

II. But not to insist any longer upon this, which rests entirely in the breast of the general; we shall suppose the resolution to fight taken, and proceed to examine what precautions the Romans made use of, in order to secure the victory. These may in general be reduced to two. First, the inspiring their troops with courage and confidence. Secondly, the ranging them judiciously in order of battle. To inspire their troops with confidence, they began by consulting the gods, and endeavouring to incline them in their favour. They consulted them either by the flight or singing of birds, by the inspection of the entrails of the victims, by the manner in which the sacred chickens pecked their corn, and by things of the like nature. They laboured to render them propitious by sacrifices, vows, and prayers. Many of the generals, especially in the earlier times, discharged these duties with great solemnity and sentiments of religion; and would never hazard an engagement, until by some favourable omens they had brought the troops to believe that the gods were on their side. Paulus Æmilius, before he gave Perseus battle, sacrificed twenty oxen successively to Hercules, without finding any favourable sign in all those victims. It was not until the one-and-twentieth, that he believed he saw something which promised him the victory. This attention to religion was highly necessary among a people strongly addicted to superstition, and over whom the omens of which we speak, however trifling in themselves, had yet a powerful influence. Hence the generals who neglected this precaution, had often but too just cause to repent of their folly: as it tended greatly to dispirit the troops, and begot an ill opinion of their conduct; insomuch that we seldom find them successful in their undertakings. The wisest and best commanders chose always to comply with the prejudices of the vulgar; and even where they despised these ceremonies in their hearts, affected yet a greater veneration for them in public.

III. After having paid these duties to the gods, they applied themselves to men, and the general exhorted his soldiers. It seems to have been an established custom with all nations among the ancients, to harangue their troops before a battle; nor can we deny that the custom was very reasonable in itself, and might contribute greatly to the victory. When an army is upon the point of engaging an enemy, what can be more proper, than to oppose the fear of a seemingly approaching death with the most powerful reasons, and such as, if not capable of totally extinguishing it, may yet in some measure allay and overcome it. Such reasons are the love of our country, the obligation to defend it at the price of our blood, the remembrance of past victories, the necessity of supporting the glory of our nation, the injustice of a violent and cruel enemy, the dangers to which the fathers, mothers, wives, and children of the soldiers are exposed; these motives, I say, and many of the like nature, represented from the mouth of a general, beloved and respected by his troops, may make a very strong impression upon their minds. Not, as Cyrus, in Xenophon, observes, that such discourses can in an instant change the disposition of the soldiers, and from timorous and abject as they might be, make them immediately bold and intrepid: but they awaken, they rouse the courage nature had before given them, and add a new force and vivacity to it. To judge rightly of this custom of haranguing the troops, as constantly practised among the Romans, we must go back to the ages wherein they lived, and consider their manners with particular attention. Their armies were composed of the same citizens, to whom in the city, and in time of peace, it was customary to communicate all the affairs of the state. The general did no more in the camp, or in the field of battle, than he would have been obliged to do in the rostrum or tribunal of harangues. He did his troops honour, and attracted their confidence and affection in imparting to them his designs, motives and measures. Add to this, that the sight of the generals, officers, and soldiers assembled, communicated a reciprocal courage and ardour to them all. Every one piqued himself at that time upon the goodness of his aspect and appearance, and obliged his neighbour to do the same. The fear of some was abated or entirely banished by the valour of others. The disposition of particular persons became that of the whole body, and gave affairs their aspect.

IV. Let me observe here, that there were many occasions, besides battles, when it was necessary to excite the good will and zeal of the soldier; if, for instance, a difficult and hasty march was to be made, to extricate the army out of a dangerous situation, or obtain one more commodious; if courage, patience, and constancy were required for supporting famine, and other distresses, painful to nature: if some difficult, dangerous, but very important enterprise was to be undertaken; if it was necessary to console, encourage, and re-animate the troops after a defeat; if a hazardous retreat was to be made in view of the enemy, in a country he was master of: in fine, if only a generous effort was wanting to terminate a war, or some important undertaking. Upon these and the like occasions, the generals never failed to speak in public to the army, in order to sound their dispositions by their acclamations more or less strong; to inform them of their reasons for such and such conduct, and conciliate them to it; to dispel the false reports, which exaggerated difficulties, and discouraged them: to let them see the remedies preparing for the distresses they were under, and the success to be expected from them; to explain the precautions it was necessary to take, and the motives for taking them. It was the general's interest to flatter the soldier, in making him the confidant of his designs, fears, and expedients, in order to engage him to share in them, and act in concert, and from the same motives with himself. The general in the midst of soldiers, who, as well as himself, were all not only members of the state, but had a share in the authority of the government, was considered as a father in the midst of his family.

V. It may not be easy to conceive how he could make himself heard by the troops: but if we call to mind, that the armies of the Roman people were not very numerous, that difficulty will in a great measure vanish. Besides, I pretend not to say that the generals were heard distinctly, or in any other manner than the orators in the public assemblies. All people did not hear: yet the whole people were informed, the whole people deliberated and decided; and none of them complained of not having heard. It sufficed that the most ancient, the most considerable, the principals of companies and quarters were present at the harangue, of which they afterwards gave an account to the rest. On the column of Trajan, the emperor is seen haranguing the troops from a tribunal of turf, raised higher than the soldiers' heads, with the principal officers around him upon the platform, and the multitude forming a circle at a distance. The great men at Rome accustomed themselves from their youth to speak upon occasion with a strong and clear voice; and as these harangues were made in the camp to the soldiers quiet and unarmed, it is not easy to conceive in how little room a great number of them could stand upright, when they pressed close to each other. I insist the longer upon this, because many blame the historians of antiquity, for the supposititious harangues, as they call them, which they have inserted in their works. It must indeed be owned, that the discourses made by generals on the occasions of which we speak, were not always exactly the same as historians have repeated them. For the most authors, writing in the time when the art of eloquence was highly in esteem, have endeavoured, in adorning and enlarging the harangues they record, to leave proofs to posterity, that they were not less excellent orators than historians. But the fact itself, that generals frequently spoke in public to their troops, is evident beyond dispute. Cæsar, whose Commentaries are a plain and naked relation of what he himself performed at the head of his army, furnishes many examples of this kind. When he marched against Ariovistus, a sudden consternation seizing the soldiers, which was like to be attended with very disagreeable effects, he assembled them, reprehended them in a long and severe speech, and thereby put a stop to the growing evil. In like manner, upon occasion of a considerable check received before Gergovia, owing to the too forward valour of the troops, and their neglect of his injunctions, he judged it necessary to call them together, expostulate with them upon their ill-timed bravery, and fortify them against any damp their late disaster might have thrown upon their spirits. I could easily produce other instances of the same kind, but these are abundantly sufficient to evince the point in question.

VI. When the armies were numerous, and upon the point of giving battle, the ancients had a very simple and natural way of haranguing the men. The general on horseback rode through the ranks, and spoke something to the several bodies of troops, in order to animate them. Where he had to do

with different nations, as very often happened, he addressed those of his own language in person, and made known his views and designs to the rest by interpreters. Hannibal acted in this manner at the battle of Zama in Africa. He thought incumbent on him to exhort his troops: and as every thing was different among them, language, customs, laws, arms, habits, and interests, so he made use of different motives to animate them. To the auxiliary troops he proposed an immediate reward, and an augmentation of their pay out of the booty that should be taken. He inflamed the peculiar and natural hatred of the Gauls against the Romans. As for the Ligurians, who inhabited a mountainous and barren country, he set before them the fertile valleys of Italy, as the fruit of their victory. He represented to the Moors and Numidians, the cruel and violent government of Masinissa, to which they would be subjected, if overcome. In this manner he animated these different nations, by the different views of hope and fear. As to the Carthaginians, he omitted nothing that might excite their valour, and addressed himself to them in the warmest and most pathetic terms. He put them in mind of their country, their household gods, the tombs of their ancestors, the terror and consternation of their fathers and mothers, their wives and children; in fine, that the fate of Carthage depended upon that battle, the event of which would either ruin and reduce her into perpetual slavery, or render her mistress of the universe, **every thing being extreme which she had either to hope or fear**. This is a very fine discourse; but how did he make these different nations understand it? Livy informs us: he spoke to the Carthaginians himself, and ordered the commanders of each nation to repeat to their respective troops what he had said. In this manner the general sometimes assembled the officers of his army, and after having explained what he desired the troops might be told, he sent them back to their several brigades or companies, in order to report what they had heard, and animate them for the battle. Arrian observes this particular of Alexander the Great, before the famous battle of Arbela.

VII. After inspiring the troops with resolution and confidence, and disposing them to act courageously against the enemy, the next care of the general was, to range them judiciously in order of battle. The manner of drawing up the infantry in three lines, continued long in use among the Romans, and with uniformity enough. The *hastati* were placed in the front, in thick and firm ranks; the *principes* behind them, but not altogether so close; and after them the *triarii*, in so wide and loose an order, that upon occasion, they could receive both the *principes* and *hastati* into their body, in any distress. The *velites*, and in latter times, the bowmen, and slingers, were not drawn up in this regular manner, but disposed of either before the front of the *hastati*, or scattered up and down among the void spaces of the same *hastati*, or sometimes placed in two bodies in the wings; but wherever they were fixed, these light soldiers began the combat, skirmishing in flying parties with the first troops of the enemy. If they prevailed, which very seldom happened, they prosecuted the victory; but upon a repulse, they fell back by the flanks of the army, and rallied again in the rear. When they were retired, the *hastati* advanced against the enemy; and in case they found themselves overpowered, retiring softly towards the *principes*, fell into the intervals of their ranks, and, together with them, renewed the fight. But if the *principes* and *hastati*, thus joined, were too weak to sustain the fury of the battle, they all fell back into the wider intervals of the *triarii*, and then altogether being united into a firm mass, they made another effort, much more impetuous than any before. If this assault proved ineffectual, the day was entirely lost as to the foot, there being no farther reserves. This way of marshalling the foot, was exactly like the order of trees, which gardeners call the *quincunx*; as appears from the beautiful comparison between them in Virgil's second Georgic. And as the reason of that position of the trees is not only for beauty and figure, but that every particular tree may have room to spread its roots and boughs, without entangling and hindering the rest; so in this ranking of the men, the army was not only set out to the best advantage, and made the greatest show, but every particular soldier had free room to use his weapons, and to withdraw himself between the void spaces behind him, without occasioning any confusion or disturbance.

VIII. The stratagem of rallying thus three times, has been reckoned almost the whole art and secret of the Roman discipline; and it was almost impossible it should prove unsuccessful, if duly observed. For fortune, in every engagement, must have failed them three several times, before they could be routed; and the enemy must have had the strength and resolution to overcome them in three several encounters, for the decision of one battle; whereas most other nations, and even the Grecians themselves, drawing up their whole army as it were in one front, trusted themselves and fortunes to the success of a single charge. The Roman cavalry was posted at the two corners of the army, like the wings on a body; and fought sometimes on foot, sometimes on horseback, as occasion required, in the same manner as our dragoons. The confederate, or auxiliary forces, composed the two points of the battle, and covered the whole body of the Romans. As to the stations of the commanders, the general commonly took up his post near the middle of the army, between the *principes* and the *triarii*, as the fittest place to give orders equally to all the troops. The *legati* and tribunes were usually posted by him; unless the former were ordered to command the wings, or the others some particular part of the army. The centurion stood every man at the head of his century, to lead them up; though sometimes, out of courage and honour, they exposed themselves in the van of the army, or were placed there for particular reasons by the general: as Sallust reports of Catiline, that he posted all his choice centurions, with the *evocati*, and the flower of the common soldiers, in the front of the battle. But the *primipili*, or chief centurions, had the honour to stand with the tribunes near the general's person. The common soldiers were placed in several ranks, at the discretion of the centurions, according to their age, strength, and experience, every man having three feet square allowed him to manage his arms in; and it was religiously observed in their discipline, never to abandon their ranks, or break their order upon any account.

IX. But besides the common methods of drawing up a Roman army, which are sufficiently explained by every historian of any note; there were several other very singular methods of forming their battle into odd shapes, according to the nature of the body they were to oppose. Of this kind was the *cuneus*, when the army was ranged in the figure of a wedge, the most proper to pierce and break the order of the enemy. This was otherwise called *caput porcinum*, which it in some measure resembled. And here I beg leave to observe, that this last name seems to confirm the conjecture of the Chevalier Folard, who maintains that the *cuneus* was no other than the *column*, or a battalion drawn up with a small front and great depth. The triangular order he looks upon as childish and absurd, and such as never was nor could be practised with success, because of the extreme weakness of the angles. The authors, however, who give that form to the *cuneus*, have invented another order of battle in opposition to it, which they term the *forfex*. This was when the army was drawn up in the figure of a pair of shears, as it were on purpose to receive the *cuneus*, in case the enemy should make use of that disposition. For while he endeavoured to open, and as it were to cleave their squadrons with his wedge, by keeping their troops extended like the shears, and receiving him in the middle, they not only hindered the damage designed to their own men, but commonly cut the adverse body in pieces. The *globus* was when the soldiers cast themselves into a circular order, upon an apprehension of being surrounded. Cæsar, in the fifth book of his Commentaries, speaks of this disposition as very proper in cases of danger and extremity. The *turris* represented an oblong square, after the fashion of a tower, with very few men in a file, and the ranks extended to a great length. This seems of very ancient original, as being mentioned in Homer. The last order I shall take notice of is the *serra* or saw; when the first companies in the front of the army, beginning the engagement, sometimes proceeded, and sometimes drew back; so that by the help of a large fancy, one might find some resemblance between them and the teeth of that instrument.

X. It was usual enough among the Romans, to raise great cries, and to strike their swords against their bucklers, as they advanced to charge an enemy. This noise, joined to that of the trumpets, was very proper to suppress in them, by a kind of stupefaction, all fear of danger, and to inspire them with a courage and boldness, that had no view but victory, and defied death. But though such shoutings were allowed, nay, even encouraged as useful, going towards the enemy, yet a deep silence was observed by the soldiery, when they were about to engage, that the orders of the officers, and the words of command, might be clearly heard, and punctually obeyed. It is observed that the Greeks went always silently to battle, alleging for it, that they had more to do than to say to their enemies. But the shoutings of which we speak, is in reality a kind of doing, as it stirs up the men, and often damps the enemy. The troops marched sometimes softly and coolly to the charge, and sometimes, when they approached the enemy, they sprung forward with impetuosity as fast as they could move. Great men have been divided in opinion upon these different methods of attacking. It seems however to be generally agreed, that where two armies engage in a plain field, a commander ought never to allow, much less order, his men to receive the charge, but still to meet the enemy in giving it. Pompey in the decisive battle of Pharsalia, by the advice of Triarius, commanded his soldiers to receive Cæsar's assault, and to undergo the shock of his army, without removing from the place whereon they stood, as by this means Cæsar's men would be disordered in their advance, and Pompey's by not moving, keep their order. But Cæsar himself observes upon it, that according to his judgment, the advice was against all reason; because there is a certain keenness and alacrity of **spirit naturally planted in every man, who is inflamed with a desire to fight, and therefore no commander should repress or restrain it, but rather increase and set it forward. The event justified Cæsar's opinion, and showed that it was well-grounded.**

XI. Hitherto we have contented ourselves with general observations: but as it is impossible from these alone, to give any tolerable idea of the address and ability of a commander in a day of battle, because his conduct must vary according to circumstances; I shall now beg leave to lay before the reader, an account of some celebrated actions of antiquity, taken from the descriptions of such historians, as being themselves military men, have traced them with the utmost exactness, and distinctly explained the reasons of the several steps taken. The first instance of this kind that we meet with in history, is the famous battle of Thymbra, between Cræsus and Cyrus, which transferred the empire of Asia from the Assyrians of Babylon to the Medes and Persians. Though this action does not so immediately and strictly regard the subject we are upon, as having no relation to the Roman history, I shall yet give a particular description of it here, not only because it is the first pitched battle, of which we have any full and circumstantial account, but because Cyrus being looked upon as one of the greatest captains of antiquity, those of the profession may be glad to trace him in all his steps, through this important engagement; and the rather, as what we shall present them with on this subject, is taken from Xenophon, one of the greatest commanders, as well as finest writers, of the age in which he lived.

XII. In Cyrus's army the companies of foot consisted of a hundred men each, exclusive of the captain. Each company was subdivided into four parts, which consisted severally of four and twenty men, not including the person who commanded the platoon. Each of these subdivisions was again divided into two files, consisting, in consequence, of twelve men. Every ten companies had a particular superior officer to command them, who sufficiently answers to what we call a colonel. Over ten of these again was another superior commander, whom we shall term a brigadier. When Cyrus came at the head of the thirty thousand Persians, who had been sent to the aid of his uncle Cyaxares, he made a considerable change in the arms of his troops. Until then, two thirds of them made use only of javelins and bows, and therefore could not fight but at a distance from the enemy. Instead of these, Cyrus armed the greatest part of them with cuirasses, bucklers, and swords or battle-axes, and left only a few of his soldiers in light armour. The Persians did not know at that time what it was to fight on horseback. Cyrus, who was convinced that nothing was of so great importance towards the gaining of a battle as cavalry, was sensible of the great inconvenience he laboured under in that respect, and therefore took wise and early precautions to remedy that evil. He succeeded in his design, and by little and little formed a body of Persian cavalry, which amounted to ten thousand men, and were the best troops in his army.

XIII. Xenophon has not acquainted us with the precise number of troops on both sides, but as this may be in some sort collected by putting together certain scattered passages of our author, we shall endeavour to fix it in the best manner we can. Cyrus's army amounted in the whole to a hundred and ninety-six thousand men, horse and foot. Of those there were seventy thousand natural born Persians, viz. ten thousand cuirassiers of horse, twenty thousand cuirassiers of foot, twenty thousand pikemen, and twenty thousand light-armed soldiers. The rest of the army, to the number of one hundred and twenty-six thousand men, consisted of a hundred thousand Median, **Armenian, and Arabian foot, and** twenty-six thousand horse of the same nations. Besides these troops, Cyrus had three hundred chariots of war, armed with scythes, each chariot drawn by four horses abreast, covered with trappings that were shot-proof; as were also the horses of the Persian cuirassiers. He had likewise ordered a great number of chariots to be made of a larger size, upon each of which was placed a tower of about eighteen or twenty feet high, in which were lodged twenty archers. Each chariot was drawn upon wheels by sixteen oxen yoked in abreast. There was moreover a considerable number of camels, upon each of which were two Arabian archers, back to back; so that one looked towards the head, and the other towards the tail of the camel.

XIV. Crœsus's army was above twice as numerous as that of Cyrus, amounting in all to four hundred and twenty thousand men, of which sixty thousand were cavalry. The troops consisted chiefly of Babylonians, Lydians, Phrygians, Cappadocians, of the nations about the Hellespont, and of Egyptians, to the number of three **hundred and** sixty thousand men. The Egyptians **alone** made a body of one hundred **and** twenty thousand. They had bucklers that covered them from head to foot, very long pikes, and short swords, but very broad. The rest of the army was made up of Cyprians, Cilicians, Lycaonians, Paphlagonians, Thracians, and Ionians. The army in **order** of battle was ranged in one line, the infantry in the centre, and the cavalry on the two wings. All the troops, both foot and horse, were thirty men deep; but the Egyptians, who, as we have taken notice, were a hundred and twenty thousand in number, and who were the principal strength of Crœsus's infantry, in the centre of which they were posted, were divided into twelve large bodies or square battalions, of ten thousand men each, which had a hundred men in front, and as many in depth, with an interval or space between every battalion, that they might act and fight independent of, and without interfering with one another. Crœsus would gladly have persuaded them to range themselves in less depth, that he might make the wider front. For the armies being in an immense plain, which gave room for extending their wings to right and left, he was in hopes by this means of surrounding and hemming in the enemy. But he could not prevail with the Egyptians to change the order of battle to which they had been accustomed. His army, as it was thus drawn out into one line, took up near forty stadia, or five miles in length.

XV. Araspes, who under pretence of discontent had retired to Crœsus's army, and had received particular orders from Cyrus, to observe well the manner of that general's ranging his troops, returned to the Persian camp the day before the battle. Cyrus in drawing up his army, governed himself by the disposition of the enemy, of which that young Median Nobleman had given him an exact account. The Persian troops had been generally used to engage four and twenty men deep, but Cyrus thought fit to change that disposition. It was necessary for him to form as wide a front as possible, without too much weakening his phalanx, to prevent his army's being inclosed and hemmed in. His infantry was excellent, and most advantageously armed with cuirasses, partizans, battle-axes, and swords; and provided they could join the enemy in close fight, there was but little reason to believe the Lydian phalanx, that were only armed with light bucklers and javelins, could support the charge. Cyrus therefore thinned the files of his infantry one half, and ranged them only twelve men deep. The cavalry was drawn out on the two wings, the right commanded by Chrysantes and the left by Hystaspes. The whole front of the army took up but thirty-two stadia, or four miles in extent, and consequently was at each end near four stadia, or half a mile short of the enemy's front. Behind the first line, at a little distance, Cyrus placed the spear men, and behind them the archers. Both the one and the other were covered by the soldiers in their front, over whose heads they could fling their javelins, and shoot their arrows at the enemy.

XVI. Behind all these he formed another line, to serve for the rear, which consisted of the flower of his army. Their business was to have their eyes upon those that were placed before them, to encourage those that did their duty, to sustain and threaten those that gave way, and even to kill those as traitors that persisted openly in flying; by that means to keep the cowards in awe, and make them have as great a terror of the troops in the rear as they could possibly have of the enemy. Behind the army were placed those moving towers which I have already described. These formed a line equal and parallel to that of the army, and did not only serve to annoy the enemy by the perpetual discharges of the archers that were in them, but might likewise be looked upon as a kind of moveable forts or redoubts, under which the Persian troops might rally, in case they were broken and pushed by the enemy. Just behind these towers were two other lines, which also were parallel and equal to the front of the army: the one was formed of the baggage, and the other of the chariots which carried the women, and such other persons as were unfit for service. To close all these lines, and to secure them from the insults of the enemy, Cyrus placed in the rear of all two thousand infantry, two thousand horse, and the troop of camels, which was pretty numerous. Cyrus's design in forming two lines of the baggage was, not only to make his army appear the more numerous, but likewise to oblige the enemy, in case they were resolved to surround him, as he knew they intended, to make the longer circuit, and consequently to weaken their line, by stretching it out so far. We have still the Persian chariots of war, armed with scythes, to speak of. These were divided into three bodies of a hundred each. One of these bodies, commanded by Abradatas, king of Susiana, was placed in the front of the battle, and the other two upon the flanks of the army.

XVII. When the two armies were in sight of each other, and the enemy had observed how much the front of theirs exceeded that of Cyrus, they made the centre of their army halt whilst the two wings advanced projecting to the right and left, with the design to inclose Cyrus's army, and begin their attack on every side at the same time. This movement did not at all alarm Cyrus, because he expected it; but observing that many of his officers, and even Abradates himself, discovered some uneasy apprehensions; these troops disturb you, says he: believe me they will be the first routed, and to you Abradates I give that as a signal, for falling upon the enemy with your chariots. When the two detached bodies of the Lydians were sufficiently extended, Croesus gave the signal to his main body to march up directly to the front of the Persian army, whilst the two wings that were wheeling round upon their flanks, advanced on each side; so that Cyrus's army was inclosed on three sides; and, as Xenophon expresses it, looked like a small square drawn within a great one. In an instant, on the first signal Cyrus gave, his troops faced about on every side, keeping a profound silence in expectation of the event. The prince himself, at the head of some horse, briskly followed by a body of foot, fell upon the forces that were marching to attack his right flank, and put them in great disorder. The chariots then driving furiously upon the Lydians, completed the defeat. In the same moment the troops of the left flank, knowing by the noise that Cyrus had begun the battle on the right, advanced to the enemy; and immediately the squadron of camels was made to advance likewise, as Cyrus had ordered. The enemy's cavalry did not expect this, and their horses at a distance, as soon as they were sensible of the approach of those animals, whose smell they cannot endure, began to snort and prance, to run foul upon and overturn one another, throwing their riders, and treading them under their feet. Whilst they were in this confusion, a small body of horse, commanded by Artageses, pushed them very warmly to prevent their rallying; and the chariots armed with the scythes falling furiously upon them, they were entirely routed, with a dreadful slaughter.

XVIII. This being the signal which Cyrus had given Abradates for attacking the front of the enemy's army, he drove like lightning upon them with all his chariots. Their first rank was not able to stand so violent a charge, but gave way and were dispersed. Having broken and overthrown them, Abradates came up to the Egyptian battalions, which being covered with their bucklers,

and marching in such close order that the chariots had not room to pierce amongst them, gave him much more trouble, and would not have been broken had it not been for the violence of the horses, that trode upon them. It was a most dreadful spectacle to see the heaps of men and horses, overturned chariots, broken arms, and all the direful effects of the sharp scythes, which cut every thing in pieces that came in their way. But Abradates' chariot having the misfortune to be overturned, he and his men were killed, after they had signalized their valour in a very extraordinary manner. The Egyptians then, marching forward in close order and covered with their bucklers, obliged the Persian infantry to give way, and drove them beyond their fourth line, as far as to their machines. There the Egyptians met with a fresh storm of arrows and javelins, that were poured upon their heads from the rolling towers: and the battalions of the Persian rear-guard advancing sword in hand, hindered their archers and spearmen from retreating any farther, and obliged them to return to their charge.

XIX. Cyrus in the meantime having put both the horse and foot to flight on the left of the Egyptians, did not amuse himself in pursuing the runaways, but pushing on directly to the centre, had the mortification to find his Persian troops had been forced to give way; and rightly judging that the only means to prevent the Egyptians from gaining farther ground would be to attack them behind, he did so, and fell upon their rear. The cavalry came up at the same time, and the enemy was pushed with great fury. The Egyptians being attacked on all sides, faced about every way, and defended themselves with wonderful bravery. Cyrus himself was in great danger; his horse, which a soldier stabbed under the belly, sinking under him, he fell in the midst of his enemies. Here was an opportunity, says Xenophon, of seeing how important it is for a commander to have the affection of his soldiers. Officers and men, equally alarmed at the danger in which they saw their leader, ran headlong into the thick forest of pikes to rescue and save him. He quickly remounted another horse, and the battle became more bloody than ever. At length Cyrus admiring the valour of the Egyptians, and being concerned to see such brave men perish, offers them honourable conditions, if they would surrender, letting them know at the same time that all their allies had abandoned them. The Egyptians accepted the conditions, after which the Persians meeting with no farther opposition, a total rout of the enemy ensued.

XX. It is allowed that Cyrus's victory was chiefly owing to his Persian cavalry, which was a new establishment, and entirely the fruit of that prince's care and activity in forming his people, and perfecting them in a part of the military art, of which till his time they had been utterly ignorant. The chariots armed with scythes did good service, and the use of them was ever after retained among the Persians. The camels too were not unserviceable in the battle, though Xenophon makes no great account of them, and observes, that in his time they made no other use of them, than for carrying the baggage. I shall not undertake here to enlarge upon Cyrus's merit. It is sufficient to observe, that in this affair we see all the qualities of a great general shine out in him. Before the battle, an admirable sagacity and foresight in discovering and disconcerting the enemy's measures; an infinite exactness in the detail of affairs, in taking care that his army should be provided with every thing necessary, and all his orders punctually obeyed at the time prefixed; a wonderful application to gain the hearts of his soldiers, and to inspire them with confidence and ardour. In the heat of action, what a spirit and activity! what a presence of mind in giving orders as occasion requires! what courage and intrepidity, and at the same time what humanity towards the enemy, whose valour he respects, and whose blood he is unwilling to shed! I have met with but one objection to the manner in which he drew up his troops in order of battle, namely, no troops to cover his flanks, to sustain his armed chariots, and to oppose the two bodies of troops which Crœsus had detached to fall upon the flanks of his army. But it is very possible that such a circumstance might escape Xenophon in describing the battle; though it must be owned, that the fall of Abradates, which was immediately followed by the attack of the Persian infantry, hardly leaves room for such a conjecture.

XXI. I shall now present the reader with the description of two battles in which the Romans were concerned, those of Cannæ and Zama, distinguished by the importance of their consequences, and the abilities of the generals

who commanded in them. Hannibal having defeated the Romans in three successive engagements, and desirous of bringing them to another general action, that by one decisive blow he might put an end to the war, removed his camp to the neighbourhood of Cannæ, an open champaign country, and fit for cavalry to act in, in which he was greatly superior to the enemy. The Romans, headed by the consuls Paulus Æmilius and Varro, followed him thither, where after some disputes Paulus was obliged to give way to the obstinacy of his colleague, who was resolutely bent upon fighting. The two armies were very unequal as to number. There was in that of the Romans, including the allies, four-score thousand foot, and something more than six thousand horse; and in that of the Carthaginians, forty thousand foot, all well disciplined and inured to war, and ten thousand horse. Varro at day-break, having made the troops of the great camp pass the Aufidus, drew them up immediately in battle, after having joined them with those of the little camp. The whole infantry were upon one line, closer and of greater depth than usual. The cavalry was upon the two wings; that of the Romans on the right, defended by the Aufidus; and that of the allies on the left wing. The light-armed troops were advanced in the front of the battle to some distance. Paulus Æmilius commanded the right wing of the Romans, Varro the left, and Servilius Geminus the consul of the preceding year, was in the centre.

XXII. Hannibal immediately drew up his army in one line. **He posted his Spanish and Gallic cavalry on the left, sustained by the Aufidus, to oppose the Roman horse; and upon the same line, half his heavy-armed African infantry: then the Spanish and Gallic infantry, which properly formed the centre; on their right, the other half of the African infantry; and lastly the Numidian horse, who composed the right wing. The light-armed troops were in the front, facing those of the Romans. Asdrubal had the left, Hanno the right; Hannibal, having his brother with him, reserved the command of the centre to himself. The African troops might have been taken for a body of Romans, so much did they resemble them by their arms, which they had gained in the battles of Trebia and Thrasymenus, and which they now employed against those who had suffered them to be taken from them.

The Spaniards and Gauls had shields of the same form; but their swords were very different. Those of the former were equally proper for cutting and thrusting, whereas those of the Gauls cut only with the edge, and at a certain distance. The soldiers of those two nations, especially the Gauls, had a dreadful aspect, in consequence of their extraordinary stature. The latter were naked from their belts upwards. The Spaniards wore linen habits, the extreme whiteness of which exalted by a border of a purple colour, made a surprisingly splendid appearance. Hannibal, who knew how to take his advantages as a great captain, forgot nothing that could conduce to the victory. A wind peculiar to that region, called in the country vulturnus, blew always at a certain period. He took care to draw up in such a manner, that his army, facing the north, had it in their backs, and the enemy fronting the south, had it in their faces; so that he was not in the least incommoded with it, whereas the Romans, whose eyes it filled with dust, scarce saw before them. From hence we may judge how far Hannibal carried his attention, which nothing seems to escape.

XXIII. The two armies marched against each other, and began the charge. After that of the light-armed soldiers on both sides, which was only a prelude, the action began by the two wings of the cavalry on the side of the Aufidus. Hannibal's left wing, which was an old corps, to whose valour he was principally indebted for his successes, attacked that of the Romans with so much force and violence, that they had never experienced the like. This charge was not made in the usual manner of attacks of cavalry, by sometimes falling back, and sometimes returning to the assault; but in fighting man to man, and very near, because they had not room enough to extend themselves, being pent up on one side of the river, and on the other by the infantry. The shock was furious, and equally sustained on both sides; and whilst it was still doubtful to which side the victory would incline, the Roman horse, according to a custom usual enough in their corps, and which was sometimes successful, but was now very ill applied, dismounted and fought on foot. When Hannibal was informed of this, he cried out: I am as well pleased with them in that posture, as I should be to have them all delivered up to me to be bound hand and foot. Accor-

dingly, after having defended themselves with the utmost valour, most of them fell upon the spot. Asdrubal pursued those that fled, and made a great slaughter of them.

XXIV. Whilst the horse was thus engaged, the infantry of both armies advanced also against each other. The battle began at first in the centre. As soon as Hannibal perceived that his left wing began to have the advantage, he made the Gauls and Spaniards move that were in the main body, and whom he commanded in person. In proportion as he advanced, he rounded his front in form of a half moon, with its convex side towards the enemy. At first the opposite centre of the Romans charged them. After some resistance the Spaniards and Gauls began to give way, and to lose ground. The rest of the Roman infantry also moved on in order to take them in flank. They fell back according to the orders they had received, continuing to fight, and regained the ground where they had at first been drawn up in battle. The Romans, seeing that the Spaniards and Gauls continued to retreat, continued also to pursue them. Hannibal, well pleased to see every thing succeed according to his design, and perceiving the moment was come for acting with all his forces, gave orders, that his Africans should wheel to the right and left upon the Romans. These two bodies, which were fresh, well armed, and in good order, having wheeled about suddenly, towards the space or hollow, into which the Romans had thrown themselves in disorder and confusion, charged them on both sides with vigour, without giving them time to look about them, or leaving them ground to form themselves.

XXV. In the mean time the Numidian cavalry on the right wing was engaged also with the enemy opposite to them, namely, the cavalry of the allies of the Romans. Though they did not distinguish themselves in this battle, and the advantage was equal on both sides, they were however very useful: for they found the enemies which they had in their front sufficient employment, to prevent them from having time to assist their own people. But when the left wing, where Asdrubal commanded, had routed, as we have said, the whole horse of the right wing of the Romans, and had joined the Numidians, the cavalry of the allies did not wait to be attacked ly them, but fled with the utmost precipitation. It is said, that Asdrubal then did a thing, which no less shows his prudence, than it contributed to the success of the battle. As the Numidians were very numerous, and never did their duty better than when an enemy fled, he ordered them to pursue the Romans to prevent their rallying, and led on the Spanish and Gallic horse to the charge, to support the African infantry. Accordingly he fell upon the Roman foot in the rear, which being attacked at the same time in the flanks, and surrounded on all sides, was entirely cut to pieces, after having acted prodigies of valour.

XXVI. The battle of Zama, between Hannibal and Scipio, is one of the most memorable recorded in history; the disposition on both sides being the masterpiece of two of the greatest generals that ever the world produced. Scipio drew up his troops in the following manner:—He posted the *hastati* in the front line, leaving intervals between the cohorts. In the second line he placed the *principes*, with their cohorts not behind the spaces of the first line, as was the custom of the Romans, but behind the cohorts of that front line, in order to leave openings for the elephants of the enemy, which were very numerous. The triarii formed the third line, in the same order, and served as a body of reserve. He placed Lælius on the left wing, with the Italian cavalry, and Masinissa on the right, with his Numidians. In the spaces of the first line he placed the light-armed soldiers, and ordered them to begin the battle in such a manner, that if they could not sustain the charge of the elephants, they should retire; such of them as were most speedy, behind the whole army, through the spaces that divided it in right lines; and those who should find themselves too much pressed, through the spaces between the lines on the right and left, in order to leave those animals a passage, in which they would be exposed to the darts discharged upon them on all sides. As to Hannibal, in order to give the enemy more terror, he placed in the front his fourscore elephants, a number which he never had before in any battle. In the first line he posted the auxiliary troops of the Ligurians and Gauls, with the Baleareans and Moors, who amounted in all to twelve thousand men. The second line, in which the principal force of the army consist-

ed, was composed of Africans and Carthaginians. He posted the troops he had brought with him from Italy in the third line, and placed them above a stadium from the second line. The Numidian cavalry were upon the left wing, and the Carthaginian upon the right.

XXVII. Every thing being ready for the battle, and the Numidian cavalry on both sides having long skirmished, Hannibal gave orders for the elephants to move against the enemy. The Romans immediately made the trumpets sound, and at the same time raised such great cries, that the elephants which advanced against the right of the Romans, turned back, and put the Moors and Numidians that formed Hannibal's left into disorder. Masinissa seeing their confusion, easily put them entirely to the rout. The rest of the elephants advanced between the two armies into the plain, and fell upon the light armed Romans, a great number of whom they crushed to death, notwithstanding the continual shower of darts discharged upon them from all sides. At length being terrified, some of them ran through the spaces Scipio had prudently left, and others in their flight returned upon their own right wing, pursued by the Roman horse, who with their spears drove them quite out of the field of battle. Lælius took this instant for charging the Carthaginian cavalry, who turned about and fled full speed. He pursued them warmly, whilst Masinissa did the same on his side.

XXVIII. The army of the Carthaginians was uncovered on the right and left by its cavalry. The **infantry then** on both sides advanced slowly and in good order, except that which Hannibal **had** brought from Italy, **which formed the third** line, and continued in its first post. When they were near each other, the Romans raising great cries, according to their custom, and striking their swords upon their shields, charged the enemy with vigour. On the sides of the Carthaginians, the body of foreign troops that formed the front line, also raised great cries, but confused, and dissonant from each other, because they were of different nations. As they could use neither swords nor javelins, but fought hand to hand, the strangers at first had some advantage over the Romans by their agility and boldness, and wounded a great number. However, the latter having the superiority by their good order, and the nature of their arms, gained ground, supported by the second line, who followed, and incessantly encouraged them to fight with valour; whereas the strangers being neither followed nor assisted by the Carthaginians, whose inaction on the contrary intimidated them, lost courage, gave way, and believing themselves openly abandoned by their own troops, fell, in retiring, upon their second line, and attacked it in order to open themselves a passage. The latter found themselves obliged to defend their lives courageously: so that the Carthaginians attacked by the strangers, contrary to their expectation, saw they had two enemies to fight, their own troops and the Romans. Quite out of their senses, and in a manner transported with fury, they made a great slaughter of both, and put the hastati into disorder. Those who commanded the principes having made their troops advance, rallied them without difficulty. The greatest part of the strangers and Carthaginians fell in this place, partly cut in pieces by one another, and partly by the Romans. Hannibal would not suffer those that fled to mingle with those who remained, lest full of terror as they were, and covered with wounds, they might induce disorder among those who had received no blow hitherto: he even ordered the front rank to present their pikes, which obliged them to retire along the wings into the plain.

XXIX. The space between the two armies being then covered with blood, and with the dead, Scipio was in perplexity enough; for he did not know how to make his troops move in good order, over that confused heap of arms and dead bodies, still bleeding and lying upon each other. He ordered the wounded men to be carried behind the army; the retreat to be sounded for the *hastati*, who were pursuing the enemy; posted them opposite to the centre of the Carthaginians in expectation of a new charge; and made the *principes* and *triarii* advance on both wings. When they were upon the same front with the *hastati*, a new battle began between the two armies. The infantry alternately gave way, and returned to the charge with great courage and vigour. As number, resolution, and arms were equal on both sides, and they fought with such obstinacy that they fell in their posts rather than gave way, the fate of the battle was long doubtful, and it could not be conjectured which side would remain masters of the field. Things being in this state, Læ-

lius and Masinissa, after having pursued the enemy's cavalry a considerable time, returned very opportunely for attacking the infantry in the rear. This last charge decided the victory. A great number of the Carthaginians were killed upon the field of battle, where they were surrounded on all sides. Many of them having dispersed in the plains round about, were cut off by the Roman cavalry that occupied all the country. The Carthaginians left above twenty thousand dead upon the spot, as well of their own citizens as allies. Almost as many were taken, with a hundred and thirty ensigns and standards, and eleven elephants. Hannibal escaped with a small number of horse to Adrumetum, after having tried, both before and during the battle, all possible means for obtaining the victory. The Romans lost only fifteen hundred men.

XXX. Having thus given an account of some of the most memorable battles of antiquity, explained the conduct of the generals, and laid open the reasons of that conduct; I shall conclude this chapter with a few general remarks, tending still further to illustrate this great branch of war, and which in some measure offer themselves in consequence of what has been already said. The first is, that though most nations had a certain fixed and particular form of giving battle, yet they never adhered to it so closely, as not to vary when circumstances required it. The drawing up an army to the very best advantage, is doubtless a great furtherance to the gaining of the victory. But the doing so depends much, not only on the wisdom and skill of the general, the nature of the ground, and the quality of his own forces, but also on those of his enemies, and on the disposition of him who commands them. Hence the greatest captains of older times, whose military knowledge and practice the moderns so justly value, always acted herein according to their own judgment, without confining themselves to any standing rules. We have seen that Cyrus being to fight against Crœsus in a large plain, where he found the enemy taking measures to surround him, drew up his men but twelve deep in file, whereas formerly the file was twenty-four deep. By this means he augmented the front of his army double, prevented his being too much over-winged by Crœsus, and won the victory. It is observable

THE ROMAN

too of Scipio at the battle of Zama, that he placed the battalions of his several lines directly behind one another, and not facing the intervals of the lines before them, as was the common custom. His design in this was, to give free issue to the elephants, whose shock might otherwise have disordered his men, and rendered them incapable of making any resistance. Cæsar, at the battle of Pharsalia against Pompey, quite altered the manner of the Roman embattling. For having found that Pompey exceedingly out-numbered him in horse, he covered one of his flanks with a little river, and drew all his cavalry to the other flank; among the squadrons whereof he placed bodies of his best infantry, and there began the battle. By this means having all his horse in one wing, and those accompanied with select legionary foot, he soon routed that half of Pompey's horse which opposed all his, and then falling into the flanks and rear of his enemy, gained the victory.

XXXI. The drawing up the army in several lines, as the nature of the ground, and the number of the forces would allow, is what was most peculiar to the Roman discipline, and has been found so consonant to reason and experience, that it is established as a standing maxim of war at this day. In effect these lines are so many armies; and the second line being entire, though the first should be broken, often recovers the day; especially if the second line be at so just a distance from the first, as not to be disordered by it when overthrown; and also so near, that some battalions of the second line can come up timely enough to redress any beginnings of a breach in the first, without too much discomposing itself. It has likewise been often observed, that whoever in a battle keeps together a body of men, that are not led to fight until all the enemy's squadrons have fought, rarely misses to carry away the victory; and that he who has the last reserves, is the likeliest in the end to have the honour of the day. One signal illustration of this truth among many I shall instance. At the battle of Dreux in France, where the constable Montmorency, and Francis Duke of Guise, the greatest captains of that age, commanded the royalists; and Lewis, Prince of Conde, and the Admiral Chatillon the protestants; the two last defeated all the forces they saw, took the constable prisoner, passed over the bellies of the Switzers, who made al-

most a miraculous resistance, and concluded they had therefore won the victory. In the meanwhile the Duke of Guise, who led the left wing of the French king's army, either by design, as his enemies said, or as an act of high conduct, so covered his troops with the village of Blainville, and the trees and shrubs about it, that he was not so much as seen by the protestants: nor moved from thence, until the constable was taken prisoner, the Marshal de St. André killed, and all those forces which were considered by the Protestants as the whole army of the royalists, entirely routed, and so confusedly flying, that he was in no danger of having his squadrons disordered by the runaways of his own party. But then advancing with his troops, which were entire, he soon turned the fortune of the day, took the Prince of Conde prisoner, and overthrew all that opposed him. For it is a tedious and difficult, if not an impossible task, to put into good order again an army that has newly fought, so as to bring it suddenly to renew the charge; some being busied about the pillage and prisoners they had taken, or are pursuing; others being loth to return to new dangers; and all in effect being so heated and disordered, that they do not, or will not hear the commands of their superiors.

XXXII. One thing among the Romans particularly deserves our notice, and that is, that though they strove with incredible emulation to obtain the first posts in the army, yet that ambition once gratified, they did not disdain to accept of inferior offices after the higher, and to serve under those over whom they had commanded. It is amazing to consider what a multitude of consular senators fell in the battle of Cannæ. We have seen that Fabius, who had been thrice consul, and dictator, served as lieutenant under his own son; and that the great Scipio accepted the same character from his brother. Nor are these to be considered as instances singular in their kind, for it was in reality the common practice. Hence it was always in the power of a Roman general, to have expert, vigilant, and valiant commanders, at the head of those several larger divisions, of which an army is usually composed in a day of battle: men of judgment, authority, and presence of mind, to remedy all disorders, and to improve all advantages in the critical moments, than which there is nothing of greater importance in general engagements, as the least delay or remissness is but too often irreparable. I believe it will readily be allowed, that the most able and consummate general, neither is nor can be of himself sufficient to redress all disorders, and lay hold of all advantages in an instant, when armies are once engaged. The utmost he can do is, to choose well the field of battle, to draw up his army according thereto to most advantage, to give his general orders with prudence and foresight, and to give the best orders wherever he is in person; but he cannot be everywhere, nor send his orders timely enough to every place to have them successfully obeyed. And therefore it is indisputably necessary, that he have under him expert chief officers, at the head of **all the great** divisions of the army, **who may supply what** is impossible for him **singly to command.** For he can be well obeyed to the time he sends his troops to the charge; after that, those **only** who lead them, and are with them, can actuate **them according** to the general orders, or as the occasion requires; which those under him must have the judgment to lay hold of as it were in the twinkling of an eye, so short are the moments to acquire the victory!

XXXIII. The placing the best men in the wings of an army, is very ancient, and seldom has been omitted, but to the loss of those who were guilty of such an omission. The reason is, that the troops on the wings are not wedged in, as the troops in the main battle are; but **are at** liberty to take all advantages, which accident, the good conduct of the commander in chief, or the ill conduct of the enemy, throw in their way: nor can a general so much as rationally hope to fall into the flank **and rear** of his enemy, but by attacking one of his wings; because he cannot over-wing him, but only by falling upon one of his outward flanks. Hence an able commander chooses always to begin the battle on that side where he judges himself the strongest, and the enemy the weakest; advancing with those troops as expeditiously as he can, whilst the rest of the army moves as slowly as they may. For if this first impression be successful, he may fall into the flank and part of the rear of the enemy, while the residue of the whole army is marching to attack them in front: but then the motion of the army must be quicker, as soon as ever they see that the advanced wing is successful. Such was the conduct of Epaminondas, at the famous battle of Leuctra and Mantinea. Such too was the method followed by Julius Cæsar, when he fought against Ariovistus and the Germans. Hannibal, so justly celebrated for his skill in drawing up an army, at the famous battle of Cannæ, placed, as we have seen, all his best men in his two wings, and his worst men in the centre; whereby, when the Romans came to the charge, who had placed their choicest men in their main battle, they soon pierced into the body of Hannibal's army, which was the very thing he designed they should do; for then with his two wings, in which were the flower of all his troops, he immediately wheeled upon the Romans, **and totally defeated** them.

XXXIV. After the battle was fought, and the victory apparently won, the great danger was, as it still is, to pursue with too **much** ardour, without regard to what **passed in the** rest of the army. Hence that custom so inviolably observed among the Romans, of never suffering the legions to follow the chace, or break their ranks upon any occasion whatever. Only the horse, the light-armed men, and what soldiers were not of the legions, were sent upon this service; and the pursuit was conducted with so much caution, that a certain number of squadrons always followed in good order, ready to fall upon and break the enemy anew, should they rally and face about. How many victories seemingly won, have in an instant been lost, for want of care in these two particulars of such high concernment, which therefore ought never to be omitted. It is certain that nothing more encourages flying enemies to rally, and fight again, than the seeing a disorderly pursuit of them. For in such a pursuit, all the advantages of the prevailing party immediately vanish, **if the** chased do but turn about; such an **evidence** of restored valour, too often daunting **those** who are to oppose it; nor can any thing more deter the flying party from such **a** step, than to see several bodies in good order following close behind them, and ready **to** make them repent of their confidence, should they venture upon any further **opposition.** And though brave officers will **not cease** pressing, promising, and even threatening their men that fly, to face about; yet the private soldier, who sees those bodies ready to fall on, concludes it is safer to run than to resist, and therefore is too often deaf to all oratory or menaces of that nature: for when once terror has seized the minds of the troops, they hear no counsels but those which their own fears suggest.

CHAP. VIII.

OF THE ATTACK AND DEFENCE OF PLACES.

I. WHAT we have to offer upon this subject falls naturally under three general heads. First, The manner of fortifying towns in use among the ancients. Secondly, The machines of war employed by them in sieges. Thirdly, The nature and conduct of an attack and defence. As to the first, how far soever we look back into antiquity, we find amongst the Greeks and Romans, cities fortified in a regular manner, with their fosses, curtains, and towers. Vitruvius, in treating of the construction of places of war in his time, says, that the towers ought to project beyond the walls, in order that when the enemy approaches, the defenders upon the right and left may take them in flank: that they ought to be round, and faced with many stones, because such as are square, are soon beat down by the machines of war and battering rams, which easily break their angles: and that near the towers the wall should be cut within-side the breadth of the towers, and the ways broke in this manner only be joined and continued by beams laid upon the two extremities, without being made fast with iron; that in case the enemy should make himself master of any part of the wall, the besieged might remove this wooden bridge, and thereby prevent his passage to the other parts of the wall, and into the towers. The best towns of the ancients were situated upon eminences. They inclosed them sometimes within two or three walls and ditches. Berosus cited by Josephus, informs us that Nebuchadnezzar fortified Babylon with a triple inclosure of brick walls, of a surprising strength and height. Polybius, speaking of Syringa, the capital of Hyrcania, which Antiochus besieged, says, that city was surrounded with three ditches, each forty-five feet broad, and twenty-two deep. Upon each side of these was a double intrenchment, and behind all, a strong wall. The city of Jerusalem, says Josephus, was surrounded by a triple wall, except on the sides of the valleys, where there was but one, because they were inaccessible. To these they had added many other works, one of which, continues the historian, had it been completed, would have rendered the city impregnable. The stones of which it was built, were thirty feet long by fifteen broad, which made it so strong, that it was in a manner impossible to sap or shake it with machines. The whole was flanked with towers from space to space of extraordinary solidity, and built with wonderful art.

II. The ancients did not generally support their walls on the inside with earth, in the manner of the talus or slope, which made the attacks more dangerous. For though the enemy had gained some footing upon them, he could not assure himself of taking the city. It was necessary to get down, and to make use of the ladder by which he had mounted; and that descent exposed the soldier to very great danger. Vitruvius however observes, that there is nothing renders a rampart so strong, as when the walls both of the curtain and towers are supported by earth. For then neither rams, mines, nor any other machines can shake them. The places of war of the ancients were not always fortified with stone walls. They were sometimes inclosed within good ramparts of earth, of great firmness and solidity. The manner of coating them with turf was not unknown to them, nor the art of supporting the earth with strong fascines, made fast by stakes, and of arming the top of the rampart with a ruff or fraise of palisades, and the foot of the parapet, or *pas de souris* with another. They often planted palisades also in the ditch, to defend themselves against sudden attacks. They made walls also with beams crossed over one another, with spaces between them in manner of a chequer, the void parts of which they filled up with earth and stones. Such almost were the walls of the city of Bourges, which Cæsar, in the seventh book of his wars with the Gauls, describes as follows. The walls of Bourges, and almost all those of the country, were made of pieces of wood forty feet in length, laid along the earth, at the distance of two feet from each other, and crossed over by others of equal length and at equal distance, with their ends to the front of the wall. The spaces on the inside were filled up with earth and fascines, and on the outside with solid stones. He adds, that the work by this disposition was agreeable to the eye, and very strong; because the wood was of great force against the ram, and the stones against fire: besides which, the thickness of the wall, which was generally forty feet, or the length of the beams, made it next to impossible either to make a breach in it, or throw it down in any manner.

III. What I shall say in the sequel, when I come to explain the manner of attacking and defending places, will show more distinctly what kind of fortifications those of the ancients were. It is pretended that the moderns excel them very much in this point. But as the method of attack and defence is entirely different, no just comparison can be made. The use of muskets, bombs, cannons, and other fire-arms since the invention of gunpowder, has occasioned many alterations in the way of conducting sieges, the duration of which has been very much abridged of late. But these changes are not so considerable as many imagine, and have added nothing either to the merit or capacity of generals. The moderns have imagined nothing that the ancients could use, and have not used. We have borrowed from them the breadth and depth of fosses, the thickness of walls, the towers to flank the curtains, the palisades, the intrenchments within the ramparts, and towers, the advantage of many flanks, in multiplying of which consists the chief improvement of modern fortification, and which fire-arms make the more easy to execute. These are the remarks of men of ability and judgment, who to a profound knowledge of the manner in which the ancients made war, unite a perfect experience of the modern practice of it.

IV. But let us now proceed to the machines made use of by the ancients in their sieges. The principal of these were, the tortoise, the catapulta, the balista, the ram, and moving towers. The tortoise was a machine composed of very strong and solid timber-work. The height of it, to the uppermost beam, which sustained the roof, was twelve feet. The base was square, and each of its fronts twenty-five feet. It was covered with a kind of quilted mattress made of raw hides, and prepared with different drugs, to prevent its being set on fire by combustibles. This heavy machine was supported upon four wheels, and had the name of tortoise from its serving as a very strong covering and defence, against the enormous weight thrown down on it: those under it being safe in the same manner as a tortoise under her shell. It was used both to fill up the ditch, and for sapping. For the filling up

of the ditch, it was necessary to join several of them together in a line, and very near one another. Diodorus Siculus, speaking of the siege of Halicarnassus by Alexander the Great, says, that he first caused three tortoises to approach, in order to fill up the ditch, and that afterwards he planted his rams upon the space filled up, to batter the wall. This machine is often mentioned by authors. There were, without doubt, tortoises of different forms and sizes. Some indeed are of opinion, that because of its enormous weight, it could not be moved from place to place on wheels, but was pushed forwards on rollers. Under these rollers the way was laid with strong planks, to facilitate its motion, and prevent its sinking into the ground, from whence it would have been very difficult to have removed it. The ancients have observed, that the roof had a thicker covering of hides, hurdles, sea-weed, &c. than the sides, as it was exposed to much greater shocks from the weight thrown upon it by the besieged. It had a door in front, which was drawn up by a chain as far as was necessary, and covered the soldiers at work in filling up the ditch.

V. The musculus, though very little understood by modern authors, who have represented it variously, was undoubtedly a kind of tortoise, very low, and with a sharp roof. Such was that of Cæsar at the siege of Marseilles. It was sixty feet in length, and was moved forward to the walls upon rollers, where it was fixed over the part of the ditch filled up. The tower of brick which he built there, communicated with this musculus and the trenches Cæsar says the planks of the roofs were covered with bricks and mortar, over which hides were laid to prevent the mortar from dissolving by the water which the besieged might pour down upon it; and to secure it from stones and fire, it was again covered over with thick quilted mattresses properly prepared. All this was hone under mantles, after which it was thrust forward on a sudden from the tower to the walls. Besides this, there was another kind of musculus, that was used for levelling the ground, and laying the planks on which the tortoises and moving towers were to advance to the ditch. They were like this, of greater length than breadth, and equal in breadth to the way they were to level. There were several other machines intended to cover the soldiers, called *crates, plutei, vineæ*, which

L.

I shall not undertake to describe here, to avoid prolixity. They may be comprised in general under the name of mantles or sheds.

VI. The catapulta and balista were intended for discharging darts, arrows, and stones. They were of different sizes, and consequently produced more or less effect. Some were used in battles, and might be called field-pieces: others were employed in sieges, which was the use most commonly made of them. The balistæ must have been the heaviest and most difficult to carry, because there was always a greater number of catapultæ in the armies. Livy, in his description of the siege of Carthage, says, that there were a hundred and twenty great, and more than two hundred small catapultæ taken, with thirty-three great balistæ, and fifty-two small ones. Josephus mentions the same difference amongst the Romans, who had three hundred catapultæ, and forty balistæ, at the siege of Jerusalem. These machines had a force which it is not easy to comprehend, but which all good authors attest. Vegetius says, that the balistæ discharged darts with so much rapidity and violence, that nothing could resist their force. Athenios tells us, that Agesistratus made one of little more than two feet in length, which shot darts almost five hundred paces. These machines were not unlike our cross-bows. There were others of much greater force, which threw stones of three hundred weight, upwards of a hundred and twenty-five paces. We find surprising effects of them in Josephus. The darts of the catapultæ, he tells us, destroyed abundance of people. The stones from the balistæ beat down the battlements, and broke the angles of the towers; nor was there any phalanx so deep, but one of these stones would sweep a whole file of it from one end to the other. Folard, in his Commentary upon Polybius, says their force was very near equal to that of artillery.

VII. The ram was composed of a large long beam, armed at one end with iron in the form of a ram's head, and of the same bigness with the beam. This piece of wood was suspended by chains in *æquilibrio*, in order to be set in motion with the greater ease. A hundred men, more or less, worked it by main strength, to strike it against a wall or rampart, in order to beat them down after having shaken them by repeated blows. Care was taken to clothe this beam with wet leather, to prevent its be-

ing set on fire. It was slung under a kind of moving tortoise or gallery, which covered more than half of it, in order to shelter those who worked the ram from the stones and darts of the besieged. The effects of this machine were prodigious. As it was one of those that did most hurt, many methods were contrived to render it useless. Fire was darted upon the roof that covered, and the timber that supported it, in order to burn them with the ram. To deaden its blows, sacks of wool were let down against the place at which it was levelled. A machine was also made use of against it, called the wolf, by way of opposition to the ram, with which they endeavoured to grapple it, in order to draw it to themselves, or break it. Josephus relates a surprising action of a Jew, who at the siege of Jotophat, threw a stone of uncommon size upon the head of the ram with such violence, that he loosened it from the beam, and made it fall down. He leaped afterwards from the top of the wall to the bottom, took the head from the midst of the enemy, and carried it back with him. He received five arrows in his body; and notwithstanding those wounds boldly kept his post, till, through loss of blood and strength, he fell from the wall, and the ram's head with him, with which he would never part.

VIII. The moving towers were made of an assemblage of beams and strong planks, not unlike a house. To secure them against the fires thrown by the besieged, they were covered with raw hides, or with pieces of cloth made of hair. Their height was in proportion to their base. They were sometimes thirty feet square, and sometimes forty or fifty. They were higher than the walls or even towers of the city. They were supported upon several wheels according to mechanic principles, by the means of which the machine was easily made to move, how great soever it might be. The town was in great danger, if this tower could approach the walls; for it had stairs from one story to another, and included different methods of attack. At bottom it had a ram to batter the wall, and on the middle story a draw-bridge, made of two beams with rails of basket work, which let down easily upon the wall of the city, when within reach of it. The besiegers passed upon this bridge to make themselves masters of the wall. Upon the higher stories were soldiers armed with partizans and missive weapons, who kept a perpetual discharge upon the works. When affairs were in this posture, a place seldom held out long: for what could those hope who had nothing to confide in but the height of their ramparts, when they saw others suddenly appear which commanded them? The people of Namur demanded to capitulate, when Cæsar's tower, of which they had made a jest whilst at a distance, was seen to move towards them very fast. They believed this a prodigy, says Cæsar, and were astonished that men of our size should think of carrying so vast and heavy a machine to their walls. Their deputies observed, that the Romans were doubtless assisted by the gods in their wars, since they could make machines of so enormous a size advance so swiftly. It is indeed no wonder they were surprised, as they had neither seen nor heard of any such thing before, and as this tower seemed to advance by enchantment and of itself, the mechanic powers that moved it being imperceptible to those of the place. These towers were sometimes surrounded with corridors or galleries at each story, to prevent their being set on fire; and indeed nothing better could have been invented for this purpose, as the galleries were filled with troops armed with missive weapons, who made their discharges from behind the parapets, if we may so term them, and were always ready to pull out the darts of fire, and extinguish all other combustibles thrown against the tower: so that it was impossible for the fire to make the least progress, the remedy being always at hand. These corridors were built upon beams that projected five or six feet beyond the tower, several of which kind are still to be seen upon Trajan's column.

IX. Having thus described the principal machines made use of by the ancients in sieges, I now proceed to the attack and defence of places, which I shall treat in as brief a manner as possible, confining myself to the most essential parts. When cities were extremely strong and populous, they were surrounded with an intrenchment on the side next the town, and another on that towards the country. These were called lines of circumvallation and contravallation. The besiegers pitched their camp between these two lines. Those of contravallation were against the besieged city, the others against attempts from without. When it was foreseen that the siege would be of long duration, it was often changed into a blockade, and then the two lines in question were solid walls of strong masonry, flanked with towers at proper distances. There is a remarkable example of this at the siege of Platæa by the Lacedæmonians and Thebans, of which Thucydides has left us a very particular account. The two surrounding lines were composed of two walls sixteen feet distant, and the soldiers lay in that space, which was divided into quarters: so that it might have been taken for only one wall with high towers from distance to distance. These towers occupied the whole interval, in order to enable the besiegers to defend themselves, at the same time against those within and those without. The quarters of the soldiers could not be gone round without crossing the towers, and the top of the wall was skirted with a parapet of osier. There was a ditch on each side, the earth of which had been used to make bricks for the wall. In this manner Thucydides describes these two surrounding walls, which were of no great circumference, the city being very small. This siege, or rather blockade, was very famous among the ancients, and the more on account of the surprising escape of the garrison, notwithstanding all these fortifications. For this purpose they applied ladders to the inward wall. After they had got upon the platform, and seized the two adjoining towers, they drew up the ladders, and let them down on the other side of the outward wall, by which they descended to the bottom, drawing up in line of battle as fast as they came down. In this manner, by the favour of a dark night, they got safe to Athens.

X. The camp of the Roman army before Numantia, took up a much greater extent of ground. That city was four and twenty stadia in circumference, that is to say a league. Scipio, when he invested it, caused a line of circumvallation to be drawn, which inclosed more than twice the ground the city stood upon. When this work was finished, another line was thrown up against the besieged, at a reasonable distance from the first, composed of a rampart of eight feet thick by ten high, which was strengthened with strong palisades. The whole was flanked with towers of a hundred feet from each other. It is not easy to comprehend in what manner the Romans completed these immense works; a line of circumvallation of more than two leagues in compass! but nothing is more certain than the fact. He also erected four posts on the banks of the river Duæra, contiguous to the lines: and contrived a stoccado or chain of floating beams, pierced through cross-wise with long stakes pointed with iron, to prevent barks from entering, and divers from getting any intelligence of what was doing in the camp.

XI. Cæsar's circumvallation before Alexia, was formed of fascines instead of turf, with its parapet and fraise made of large stakes, whose branches were cut in points, and burnt at the ends, like stag's horns. They seemed like wings at the foot of the parapet, or like the oars of a galley inclining downwards. Of the same nature are the fraises of the moderns, that are far from being so well imagined, and are smooth-pointed palisades, bending downwards to prevent scaling. The moderns fix them in the same manner at the bottom of the parapet, where they form a kind of cincture very agreeable to the eye. The battlements mentioned by Cæsar were like the modern embrazures for cannon. Here the archers were placed. Upon the parapet of the towers, field balistæ were planted to flank the works. Towers were not always of wood, but sometimes of earth covered with turf, or strengthened with fascines. They were much higher than the rest of the intrenchment, and sometimes had towers of wood raised upon them for battering the places that commanded the camp. Some authors have believed, that these intrenchments and works of the ancients in the field, were perpendicular; but that opinion is very absurd. These had a platform with its talus, or slope, and sometimes banquettes, in the form of steps for ascending; besides which, at the towers, they were ways made to go up. All this was indispensably necessary in Cæsar's lines, as they were very high, to prevent the earth from falling away.

XII. Thus much for the two lines of circumvallation. We proceed now to the ground inclosed between the two fosses, which is far the most curious part of this celebrated blockade, and will be best explained in Cæsar's own words. "As the soldiers were employed at the same time to fetch wood and provisions from a considerable distance, and to work at the fortifications, and the enemy often sallied at several gates to interrupt them; Cæsar

found it necessary to make some addition to his lines, that they might not require so many men to guard them. He therefore took trees of no great height, or large branches, which he caused to be made sharp at the ends, and running a trench of five feet deep before the lines, he ordered them to be put into it, and made fast at bottom, so that they could not be pulled up. This trench was again filled up in a such a manner that nothing but the tops of the branches appeared, of which the points must have run into those who should have endeavoured to pass them. As there were five rows of them interwoven in a manner with each other, they were unavoidable. In the front of these he caused pits of three feet deep to be dug, in the form of the quincunx. In those pits he fixed strong stakes, burnt and sharpened at the top, which rose only four inches above the level of the ground, into which they were planted three feet deeper than the pits for the sake of firmness. The pits were covered over with bushes to deceive the enemy. There were eight rows of them, at the distance of three feet from each other. In the front of all he sowed the whole space between the pits and the advanced ditch, with crows-feet of an extraordinary size, which the soldiers called spurs." The other line, to prevent succours from without, was entirely the same with this.

XIII. Though trenches, oblique lines, mines, and other the like inventions, seem neither often nor clearly expressed in authors, we can hardly suppose with reason, that they were not in use amongst the Greeks and Romans. Is it probable, that with the ancients, whose generals, among their other excellent qualities, had in an imminent degree that of taking great care to spare the blood and lives of their soldiers, approaches were made in besieging without any precautions against the machines of the besieged, whose ramparts were so well provided, and defence so bloody? Though there were no mention of this in any of the historians, who might possibly in the description of sieges omit this circumstance, as well known to all the world; we should not conclude that such able generals either did not know, or neglected things, on the one side so important, and on the other so easy; and which must naturally have entered the thoughts of every man, ever so little versed in attacking places. But several historians speak of them; of which one shall suffice for all the rest: this is Polybius, where he relates the siege of the city Echinna by Philip. He concludes the description of it with these words: "To cover from the arrows of the besieged, as well those that went from the camp to the works, as those who returned from the works to the camp, trenches were drawn from the camp to the tortoises, and those trenches covered at top." Long before Philip, Demetrius Poliorcetes, had used the same method at the siege of Rhodes. Diodorus **Siculus** tells us, that famous warrior caused tortoises, and galleries cut in the earth, **or covered mines, to** be made, for communi-**cation with the batteries** of rams; and ordered **a trench, with blinds over** head, to **cover** and **secure the troops, in** going and coming from the towers and tortoises. The seamen and marines were appointed for this service: the work was four stadia **in length,** that is to say, five hundred paces.

XIV. But though their approaches were not entirely like those of the moderns, nor so deep in the earth, the fire from our works being of a quite different nature from that of the *catapultæ* and *balistæ*, though surprisingly violent, yet it is certain from the above accounts, and others that might be produced in great number, that they went under cover from their camp to their batteries, and used more or less precaution, according to the strength and valour of the besieged, and the number of their machines, by which they regulated the form of their approaches or trenches. These were of two sorts. The first were composed of a blind of hurdles or strong fascines, placed on the side of each other, without any space between them; so that they formed a kind of wall of five or six feet high, with loop-holes cut from space to space, between the fascines or through the hurdles. To support this blind, it is supposed they planted forked pieces of wood in the ground, upon which long poles were laid cross-wise, with the fascines or hurdles made fast to them. The other kind of approaches was very different from the former, and consisted of several trenches or galleries of communication covered at top, drawn in a right line from the camp to the works, or to the parallels, not much unlike ours. The galleries of communication were cut ten or twelve feet broad in the earth. The workmen threw up

the earth on both sides, which they supported with fascines, and covered the space with hurdles and earth laid upon poles and rafters. The whole length of these galleries in the earth, they cut loop-poles through the sides and issues to go out at. On the sides of those covered trenches or communications were esplanades, or places of arms which extended the whole front of the attack. These places were spacious, and capable of containing a **great body** of troops in order **of battle; for** here they were posted to support their towers, tortoises, batteries of rams, balistas, and cata-**pultas,** against the sallies of the besieged.

XV. The first parallel trench, **next the** body of the place, was drawn along the side of the fosse, and served as a communication to the battering towers and tortoises of the besiegers. This sort of communications to the moving towers were sometimes covered at top by a blind of hurdles and fascines; because as they ran along the side of the counterscarp, they were exposed to the downright discharges of the towers and ramparts of the besieged. Loop-holes were cut in the sides of them, through which the besiegers battered without intermission the works. These covered lines served besides for filling up the fosses, and had passages of communication with the battering tortoises cut in them, which tortoises were pushed forward upon the part of the fosse filled. When the walls of a place were not high, these trenches were not covered with blinds, either at top or in front, but only with a parapet of the earth dug out of them, like those of the moderns. At some distance from this parallel another was cut behind it, which left a space between them of the nature of our esplanades or places of arms. Here the batteries of balistas and catapultas were erected, which differed only from ours in being higher. There was sometimes a third upon the same parallel line. These places of arms contained all the troops that guarded the works. The lines communicated by the galleries or trenches covered at top.

XVI. It is certain therefore the use of trenches was well known to the ancients, without which they could have formed no siege. The trenches are often mentioned in authors by the Latin word *aggeres*, which does not always signify cavaliers or platforms. The cavaliers were mounts of earth, on which machines were planted, and were thrown up a

8

the following manner. The work was begun at a small distance from that side of the fosse next the country. It was carried on under the cover of mantles, or moving sheds, of considerable height, behind which the soldiers worked in security from the machine of the besieged. This sort of mantles or galleries were not always composed of hurdles and fascines, but of raw hides, mattresses, or of a curtain made of strong cables, the whole suspended between very high masts fixed in the ground, which broke the force of whatever was discharged against it. The work was continued to the height of these suspended curtains, which were raised in proportion with it. At the same time the void spaces of the platform were filled up with stones, earth, and other materials; whilst some were employed in levelling and beating down the earth, to make it firm, and capable of sustaining the weight of the towers and machines to be planted upon it. From these towers and batteries of ballistas and catapultas, a hail of stones, arrows, and large darts were discharged upon the ramparts and works of the besieged.

XVII. The terrace which Alexander the Great caused to be raised against the rock of Coriænæ was very surprising. That rock, which was supposed impregnable, was two thousand five hundred paces high, and seven or eight hundred round. It was excessively steep on all sides, having only one path hewn out of the rock, by which no more than one man could ascend without difficulty. It was besides surrounded with a deep abyss, which served instead of a fosse, and which it was necessary to fill up, in order to approach it. All these difficulties were not capable of discouraging Alexander, to whose valour and fortune nothing appeared impossible. He began therefore by ordering the high fir-trees, that surrounded the place in great numbers, to be cut down, in order to use them as stairs to descend into the fosse. His troops worked night and day in filling it up. Though the whole army were employed in their turns at this work, they could do no more than thirty feet a day, and something less a night, so difficult was the work. When it was more advanced, and began to come nearer the due height, they drove piles into both sides of the fosse at proper distances from each other, with beams laid across, in order to support the weight to be laid on it. They then formed a kind of floor

or bridge of wicker and fascines, which they covered with earth to equal the height of the side of the fosse, so that the army could advance on a way even with the rock. Till then the barbarians had derided the undertaking, believing it utterly impracticable: but when they saw themselves exposed to the darts of the enemy, who worked upon their terrace behind the mantles, they began to lose courage, demanded to capitulate, and soon after surrendered the rock to Alexander.

XVIII. The filling up of the fosses was not always so difficult as in this instance, but never failed to require great precautions and labour. The soldiers worked under cover in the tortoises, and other the like machines. The fosses were filled up with stones, the trunks of trees, and fascines, the whole mingled with earth. It was necessary that these works should be of great solidity, to bear the prodigious weight of the machines planted upon them, which would have made them fall in, if this kind of causeway had been composed only of fascines. If the fosses were full of water, they began by drawing it off, either entirely or in part, by different drains which they cut for that purpose.

XIX. Whilst the works were carrying on, the besieged were not idle. They ran many mines under the fosse to the part of it filled up, in order to carry off the earth, which they handed from man to man into the city. This hindered the work from advancing, the besieged carrying off as fast as the besiegers laid on. They used also another more effectual stratagem, which was to cut large cavities underneath the works of the enemy. After having removed some of the earth without its being discovered, they supported the rest with props or large beams, which they smeared over with grease and other combustibles. They then filled up the void space between the props with dry wood, and such things as would soonest burn, and set them on fire. Hence, when the props gave way, the whole fell into a kind of gulf, with the tortoises, battering rams, and the men employed in working them.

XX. The besiegers used the same artifice to make the walls of places fall down. When Darius besieged Chalcedon, the walls were so strong, and the place so well provided of all necessaries, that the inhabitants were in no pain about the siege. The king did not make any approaches to the walls, nor lay waste the country; he lay still, as if he expected a considerable reinforcement. But whilst the people of Chalcedon had no other thought than that of guarding their walls, he opened, at the distance of three quarters of a league from the city, a mine, which the Persians carried on as far as the market-place. They judged themselves directly under it, from the roots of the olive-trees which they knew grew there. They then opened their mine, and entering by that passage, took the place, whilst the besieged were still employed in keeping guard upon the walls. In the same manner, A. Servilius the dictator took the city Fidenæ, having caused several false attacks to be made on different sides, whilst a mine carried on as far as the citadel, opened him a passage there for his troops. Another dictator, the celebrated Camillus, could not terminate the long siege of Veii but by this stratagem. He undertook to run a mine as far as the citadel of that place; and that the work might not be discontinued, nor the troops discouraged by the length of it, he divided them into six brigades, who relieved each other every six hours. The work being carried on night and day, it extended at length to the citadel, and the city was taken. At the siege of Athens, by Sylla, it is astonishing to consider the mines and countermines used on both sides. The miners were not long before they met and fought furiously under ground. The Romans having cut their way as far as the wall, sapped a great part of it, and supported it in a manner in the air on props of wood, to which they set fire without loss of time. The wall fell suddenly into the fosse with an incredible noise and ruins, and all that were upon it perished.

XXI. The mines from the camp to the inside of a place were long used before the invention of sapping, and consisted at first in only running the mine from the camp to the wall, and from thence a considerable way into the place, underneath some large temple, or other great building little frequented in the night. When they came thither they cut a large space, which they propped up with large timbers. They then opened a passage of the whole breadth of this space, for entering the place in great numbers, whilst the soldiers advanced into it through the mine, with the utmost diligence. The other kind of mines for sapping the foundation of a wall, were opened very near the camp to avoid being discovered, and were carried under the fosse to the foot of the wall, when they were enlarged to the right and left foundations. This latter part was made very large, to receive the great number of workmen, and long in proportion to the extent of the wall to be thrown down. This being done, they began to sap at bottom, and as the stones were pulled out, and the work advanced, they propped the superstructure with timbers four feet high, which were fixed under the bottom stones of the foundation. As soon as the work was finished, they laid faggots and other combustibles between the props; and after they had set them on fire they quitted that part of the mine, and repassed the fosse, to avoid being stifled with the smoke; besides which, there was reason to fear, that the wall in falling would break into the mine, and bury all under in its ruins.

XXII. The ancients used several methods to defend themselves against the enemy after the breach was made. Sometimes, but not so frequently, they made use of trees cut down, which they extended along the whole front of the breach very near each other, in order that the branches might mingle together; they tied the trunks very firmly to one another, so that it was impossible to separate these trees, which formed an impenetrable fence, behind which a multitude of soldiers were posted, armed with pikes and long partizans. Sometimes the breaches were made so suddenly, either by saps above, or under ground, or by the violent blows of the rams, that the besieged often found their works laid open when they least thought of it. They had recourse on such occasions to a very simple refuge, in order to gain time to look about them, and to intrench behind the breach. They threw down upon the ruins of the wall a prodigious quantity of dry wood, and other combustible matter, to which they set fire. This occasioned so violent a flame, that it was impossible for the besiegers to pass through it, or approach the breach. The garrison of Haliartus in Bœotia thought of this remedy against the Romans.

XXIII. But the most useful method was to erect new walls behind the breaches, which are now called retirades, or retrenchments. These works generally were not parallel with the ruined walls, but described a kind of semicircle towards the place, of which the two ends joined the two sides of the wall that remained whole. They did not omit to cut a very large deep ditch before this work, in order that the besiegers might be under the necessity of attacking it with no less difficulty, and all the machines employed against the strongest walls. Sylla having beat down great part of the walls of the *piræum* with his battering rams, caused the breach to be immediately attacked, where so furious a battle ensued, that he was obliged to sound a retreat. The besieged, improving the opportunity this gave them, immediately ran a second wall behind the breach. Sylla perceiving it, made his machines advance to batter it, rightly judging, that being newly built, it could not resist their violence. The effect answered with no great difficulty, and he immediately ordered the assault to be given. The action was warm and vigorous, but he was at last repulsed with loss, and obliged to abandon his design. History abounds with examples of this kind.

XXIV. Having thus given some account of the fortifications of the ancients, described the principal machines made use of by them in their sieges, and explained their conduct in the Attack and Defence of Places; I might here, agreeably to what I have done in the chapter upon Battles, entertain the reader with a description of some of the most celebrated sieges of antiquity, in order to give him the juster idea of this part of war. But as this would too much swell the Discourse, and is besides rather curious than useful, because of the great changes that have been introduced by the invention of artillery and gunpowder, I shall content myself with referring to the historians themselves, where these sieges are related at large. Thucydides, Polybius, Livy, and Josephus furnish abundant examples of this kind. The most curious and remarkable are those of Platæa by the Lacedæmonians and Thebans; of Syracuse by the Athenians; of Lilybæum, Syracuse, Carthage, and Numantia by the Romans; but, above all, of Alesia by Julius Cæsar, and of Jerusalem by Titus Vespasian. These two last are so minutely and circumstantially described; the one by Cæsar, who formed and conducted it; the other by Josephus, who was an eye-witness of all that passed, that whoever peruses them attentively will meet with every thing that is worth knowing upon this subject, and be enabled to form a clear and comprehensive judgment of the high degree of perfection to which the ancients, and in particular the Romans, had carried this important branch of the Art of War.

CÆSAR'S COMMENTARIES

OF

HIS WARS IN GAUL.

———————

BOOK I.

THE ARGUMENT.

CÆSAR'S COMMENTARIES

OF

HIS WARS IN GAUL.

BOOK I.

I. The whole country of Gaul is divided into three parts: of which the Belgians inhabit one; the Aquitains another; and a people called in their own language Celts, in ours Gauls, the third. These all differ from each other in their language, customs, and laws. The Gauls are divided from the Aquitains by the river Garonne, and by the Marne and the Seine from the Belgians. Of all these nations the Belgians are the most warlike: as being farthest removed from the culture and refinements of the province, and but little resorted to by merchants, who furnish the means of luxury and voluptuousness. They are also situated next to the Germans, who inhabit beyond the Rhine, with whom they are continually engaged in war. For this reason likewise the Helvetians are distinguished by their bravery beyond the rest of the Gauls; because they are almost constantly at war with the Germans, either for the defence of their own territories, or acting themselves as the aggressors. One of these divisions, that which we have said was possessed by the Gauls, begins at the river Rhine, and is bounded by the Garonne, the Ocean, and the territories of the Belgians. It touches also, towards the Helvetians and Sequani, upon the river Rhine, extending itself northward. The country of the Belgians, commencing from the remotest confines of Gaul, stretches as far as the lower Rhine, running all the way between the north and east. Aquitain extends from the Garonne to the Pyrenean mountains, and that part of the ocean which borders upon Spain. Its situation is north-west.

II. Orgetorix was by far the richest and most illustrious of the Helvetians. This nobleman, in the consulship of M. Messala and M. Piso, prompted by an aspiring ambition, formed a confederacy of the principal men of the state; and persuaded the people to quit their country in a body, representing, " That as they surpassed all the nations around them in valour, it would be easy for them to gain the entire sovereignty of Gaul." He the sooner brought them into this design, because the Helvetians, by the nature of their situation, are every where confined within very narrow territories: on one side by the Rhine, a broad and deep river, which separates their country from that of the Germans; on the other by Mount Jura, a high ridge of hills, which runs between them and the Sequani; lastly, by the Lake Lemanus, and the river Rhone, which is the boundary on the side of the Roman province. By this means it happened, that they could not so easily enlarge their territories, or make conquests on the neighbouring states; which, to men of a warlike spirit, and fond of fighting, was abundant cause of discontent: for being a numerous people, and of great fame for their bravery, they thought themselves much too strained in a country, which was but two hundred and forty miles in length, and about one hundred and eighty in breadth.

III. Urged by these considerations, and still more by the authority and persuasions of Orgetorix, they resolved to provide every thing necessary for an expedition; to buy up a great number of wagons and carriage-horses o form large magazines of corn, that they might have sufficient to supply them in their march ; to establish peace and amity with the neighbouring states. They imagined two years would be sufficient for these preparations, and obliged themselves by a law to begin their march on the third. The whole management of this design was committed to Orgetorix, who undertook an embassy to the neighbouring states. On this occasion he persuaded Casticus, the son of Catamantales, of the nation of the Sequani, whose father had for many years enjoyed the sovereignty over that people, and been styled friend and ally by the senate of Rome, to possess himself of the supreme authority in his own country, which his father had held before him. He likewise persuaded Dumnorix the Æduan, the brother of Divitiacus, who was at that time the leading man in his own state, and greatly beloved by the people, to attempt the same among the Æduans : and the more to secure him to his interest, gave him his daughter in marriage. He told them, " That they might with the greatest facility accomplish their designs ; as he was himself assured of attaining the supreme authority in his own state, which was without dispute the most powerful and considerable of all Gaul ; and would then employ his whole interest and forces, to establish them in their respective sovereignties." Moved by these considerations, they reciprocally bound themselves by a solemn oath ; not doubting, when they had once attained the chief sway in their several states, with the united forces of three such powerful and mighty nations, to render themselves masters of all Gaul. The Helvetians having notice of this design, obliged Orgetorix, according to the custom of their country, to answer to the charge brought against him in chains : and had he been found guilty, the law condemned him to be burnt alive. On the day appointed for his trial, he assembled all his slaves and domestics, amounting to ten thousand men ; and all his clients and debtors, of which the number was very great : by their means he rescued himself out of the hands of his judges. While **the** people, provoked at this contempt of the laws, were preparing to support their authority by force, and the magistrates had assembled a great number of men for that purpose, Orgetorix died ; **nor** are the Hel-

vetians without suspicion of his having made away with himself.

IV. After his death, the Helvetians still continued to prosecute, with the same diligence, the design they had formed of quitting their country. When they had completed their preparations, they set fire to all their towns, to the number of twelve ; to their boroughs and villages, which amounted to four hundred ; and to their other private buildings. They likewise burnt all their corn, except what they had resolved to carry along with them ; that, having no hope of returning to their own country, they might be the more disposed to confront all dangers. Each man had orders to carry out with him provisions for three months. The Rauraci, Tulingians, and Latobrigians, neighbouring nations, being persuaded to follow the same counsel, likewise set fire to their towns and villages, and joined with them in the expedition. The Boians too, who had formerly inhabited beyond the Rhine, and passing over into Noricum, had settled in that country, and possessed themselves of Noreia, its capital city, were associated into the design.

V. There were only two ways by which they could march out of their own country. One through the territories of the Sequani, between Mount Jura and the Rhone, narrow and difficult, insomuch that in some places a single file of wagons could hardly pass. The impending mountain was besides very high and steep, so that a handful of men was sufficient to stop them. The other lay through our province, far easier and readier ; because the Rhone, which flows between the confines of the Helvetians and Allobrogians, a people lately subjected to the Romans, was in some places fordable ; and Geneva, a frontier town of the Allobrogians, adjoining to the territories of the Helvetians, had a bridge belonging to this last people. They therefore doubted not, either of persuading the Allobrogians, who as yet seemed to bear no great affection to the people of Rome, or at least of obliging them by force, to grant them a passage through their territories. Every thing being now ready for the expedition, they appointed a day for their general rendezvous on the banks of the Rhone. The day fixed on was the twenty-eighth of March, in the Consulship of L. Piso and A. Gabinius

VI. Cæsar having notice of these proceedings, and that it was the design of the Helvetians to attempt a passage through the province, hastened his departure from Rome; and posting by great journeys into farther Gaul, came to Geneva. He began with breaking down the bridge over the Rhone; and as there was at that time but one Roman legion in Transalpine Gaul, he ordered great evies to be made throughout the whole province. The Helvetians being informed of his arrival, deputed several noblemen of the first rank, with Numeius and Verodoctius at their head, to wait upon him in the name of the state, and represent, "That they meant not to offer the least injury to the Roman province; that necessity alone had determined them to the design of passing through it, because they had no other way by which to direct their march; that they therefore entreated they might have his permission for that purpose." But Cæsar, bearing in mind that L. Cassius the consul had been slain, and his army routed, and made to pass under the yoke, by the Helvetians, did not think proper to grant their request. Neither could he persuade himself, that men so ill affected to the people of Rome, if permitted to pass through the province, would abstain from acts of hostility and violence. However, that he might gain time, till the troops he had ordered to be raised could assemble, he told the ambassadors he would consider of their demand; and that if they returned by the nineteenth of April they should have his final answer. Meanwhile, with the legion he then had, and the soldiers that came in to him from all parts of the province, he ran a wall sixteen feet high, and nineteen miles in length, with a ditch from the lake Lemanus, into which the Rhone discharges itself, to mount Jura, which divides the territories of the Sequani from the Helvetians. This work finished, he raised redoubts from space to space, and manned them with troops, that if the enemy should attempt to force a passage, he might be in a condition to hinder them. When the day appointed came, and the ambassadors returned for an answer, he told them that he could not, consistent with the usage and behaviour of the people of Rome on the like occasions, grant any troops a passage through the province: and should they attempt it by force, he let them see he was prepared to oppose them.

VII. The Helvetians, driven from this hope, endeavoured to force the passage of the river; some with boats coupled together, or floats, which they had prepared in great numbers: others by the fords of the Rhone, where was the least depth of water; sometimes by day, but oftener in the night; but being repulsed by the strength of the works, the concourse of the troops, and the discharge of darts, they at last abandoned the attempt. There was still one way left, through the territories of the Sequani, by which, however, without the consent of the natives, they could not march, because of the narrowness of the pass. As they were not able to prevail by their own application, they sent ambassadors to Dumnorix the Æduan, that through his intercession they might obtain this favour of the Sequani. Dumnorix by his popularity and generosity had great influence with the Sequani, and was also well affected to the Helvetians, because from among them he had married the daughter of Orgetorix. Besides, urged by ambitious views, he was framing to himself schemes of power, and wanted to have as many states as possible bound to him by offices of kindness. He therefore charged himself with the negotiation, obtained for the Helvetians the liberty of passing through the territories of the Sequani, and engaged the two nations mutually to give hostages: the Sequani, not to molest the Helvetians in their march; and the Helvetians, to pass without offering any insult or injury to the country.

VIII. Cæsar soon had intelligence of their march, and that they now designed to pass through the country of the Sequani and Æduans into the territories of the Santones, which border upon those of the Tolosatians, a state that makes part of the Roman province. Should this happen, he foresaw many inconveniences likely to arise, from the neighbourhood of a warlike and disaffected people, in an open and plentiful country. For these reasons he gave the command of the new works he had raised to T. Labienus his lieutenant, and he himself hastened by great journeys into Italy. There he raised two legions, and drew three more, that were cantoned round Aquileia, out of their winter-quar ters: and with these five legions, took the nearest way over the Alps into farther Gaul. The Centrones, Graioceli, and Caturigians, seizing the higher ground, endeavoured to oppose his march; but having repulsed them in several encounters, he, in seven days after setting out from Ocelum, a city in the extreme confines of the nearer province, arrived among the Vocontians, whose territories lie within the farther province. Thence he led his army into the country of the Allobrogians; and crossing their territories, entered upon the lands of the Segusians. These are the first on the other side the Rhone, beyond the boundaries of the Roman province.

IX. The Helvetians had by this time marched their forces through the narrow pass of Mount Jura, and the territories of the Sequani; and were come into the country of the Æduans, plundering their lands. The Æduans, unable to defend themselves and possessions from the violence of their enemies, sent ambassadors to Cæsar to request aid. They told him, "That such at all times had been their merit with the people of Rome, that they might challenge greater regard, than to have their lands laid waste, their children led into captivity, and their towns assaulted and taken, almost in the very sight of a Roman army." At the same time also the Ambarri, friends and allies of the Æduans, sent to inform him, "That compelled to abandon the open country, they could hardly defend their towns from the rage of the enemy." The Allobrogians likewise, who had dwellings and possessions beyond the Rhone, fled to him for protection, and assured him, "That there was nothing left them but a naked and desolate country." Whereupon Cæsar, moved by these complaints and remonstrances, resolved not to wait till the fortunes of his allies should be consumed, and the Helvetians arrive in the territories of the Santones.

X. The river Arar flows into the Rhone, through the confines of the Æduans and Sequani, with a current incredibly smooth and gentle, insomuch that it is impossible to distinguish by the eye, which way its waters glide. The Helvetians were at this time employed in passing it on floats and a bridge of boats. When Cæsar was informed, by his spies, that three parts of their forces were got over the river, and that the fourth still remained on this side, he left the camp about midnight with three legions, and came up with the party of the enemy that had not yet passed. As he found them unprepared, and encumbered with their baggage, he attacked them immediately, and killed a great number on the spot. The rest fled and sheltered themselves in the nearest woods. This was called the Tigurine Canton, being one of the four into which the whole body of the Helvetians are divided. This very canton, in the memory of our fathers, marching out of their own territories, had vanquished and killed the Consul L. Cassius, and obliged his army to pass under the yoke. Thus, whether by chance or the direction of the immortal gods, that part of the Helvetian state which had brought so signal a calamity upon the Roman people, were the first to feel the weight of their resentment. In this Cæsar avenged not only the public, but likewise his own domestic injuries: because in the same battle with Cassius, was slain also L. Piso, his lieutenant, the grandfather of **L.** Piso, Cæsar's father-in-law.

XI. After this battle, that he might come up with the remaining forces of the Helvetians, he caused a bridge to be made across the Arar, and carried over his army. The Helvetians, dismayed at his sudden approach, as he had spent only one day in passing the river, which they had with the utmost difficulty accomplished in **twenty**, sent an embassy to him, at the head **of which was** Divico, **who** had been general **of the** Helvetians in the war against Cassius. **He addressed** Cæsar to this effect: "That **if the people of** Rome **were** disposed to conclude **a peace** with the Helvetians, they would **go** and settle in whatever country Cæsar should think fit to assign them; but if they persisted in the design of making war, he would do well to call to mind the ancient disgrace of the Roman people, and the valour of the Helvetic nation: that in having surprised one of the cantons, while the others, who had passed the river, could not return to succour it, there was no reason to be much elated on the advantage, nor to despise his enemies: that the Helvetians had learned of their ancestors, to depend more on courage than on cunning and ambushes; and it therefore imported him to beware, not to render the place where they were then posted, famous and memorable with posterity, by a new defeat of the Roman people, and the destruction of their army."

XII. To this Cæsar replied: "That he therefore the less doubted of the issue, as he well knew all the circumstances of the affair to which the Helvetians referred; and resented them the more strongly, as they had happened undeservedly to the Roman people; that had they been conscious of any injury on their side, it would have been easy for them to have kept upon their guard; but herein were they deceived, that neither did they know of any thing which might give them cause of fear, nor could they apprehend they had any thing to fear, without cause: that supposing him inclined to overlook old injuries, could they expect he would also forget their late insults, in attempting, against his will, to force a passage through the province, and laying waste the territories of the Æduans, Ambarri, and Allobrogians? That their boasting so insolently of their victory, and wondering that vengeance had been deferred so long, were a new set of provocations. But they ought to remember, that the immortal gods were sometimes wont to grant long impunity, and a great run of prosperity to men, whom they pursued with the punishment of their crimes, that by the sad reverse of their condition, vengeance might fall the heavier. Though these were just grounds of resentment, yet, if they would satisfy the Æduans and their allies for the ravages committed in their country, as likewise the Allobrogians, and give hostages for the performance of their promises, he was ready to conclude a peace with them." Divico replied, "That such were the institutions of the Helvetians, derived from their ancestors, that they had been accustomed to receive, not to give hostages; and that nobody knew it better than the Romans." Having returned this answer, he departed.

XIII. The next day they decamped. Cæsar did the same; and ordered all the cavalry, whom, to the number of four thousand, he had raised in the province, and drawn together from the Æduans and their allies, to go before, and observe the enemy's march. But pressing too close upon their rear, they were obliged to engage in a disadvantageous place, and lost a few men. The Helvetians, encouraged by this success, as having, with no more than five hundred horse, repulsed so great a multitude, began to face us more boldly, and sometimes to sally from their rear, and attack our van. Cæsar kept back his men from fighting; thinking it sufficient for the present, to straiten the enemy's forages, and prevent their ravaging and plundering the country. In this manner the armies marched for fifteen days together; insomuch that between our van, and the rear of the Helvetians, the distance did not exceed five or six miles.

XIV. In the meantime Cæsar daily pressed the Æduans for the corn which they had promised in the name of the public. For, by reason of the coldness of the climate, (Gaul, as we have said, lying considerably to the north,) he was so far from finding the corn ripe in the fields, that there was not even sufficient forage for the horses. Neither could he make use of those supplies which came to him by the way of the Arar, because the Helvetians had turned off from the river, and he was determined not to leave them. The Æduans put him off from day to day with fair speeches; sometimes pretending that it was bought up, and ready to be sent; sometimes, that it was actually on the way. But when he saw no end of these delays, and that the day approached for delivering out corn to the army, calling together their chiefs, of whom he had a great number in his camp; among the rest Divitiacus, and Liscus their supreme magistrate, who is styled Vergobret in the language of the country, and created yearly, with a power of life and death; he severely inveighed against them: "That at a time when corn was neither to be procured for money, nor had out of the fields, in so urgent a conjuncture, and while the enemy was so near, they had not taken care to supply him:" adding, "that as he had engaged in that war chiefly at their request, he had the greatest reason to complain of their abandoning him."

XV. Upon this, Liscus, moved by Cæsar's speech, thought proper to declare what he had hitherto concealed: "That there were some among them whose authority with the people was very great; and who, though but private men, had yet more power than the magistrates themselves. That these, by artful and seditious speeches, alarmed the multitude, and persuaded them to keep back their corn; insinuating, that if their own state could not obtain the sovereignty of Gaul, it would be better for them to obey the Helvetians, Gauls like themselves, than the Romans; there not being the least reason to question, but these last, after having subdued the Helvetians, would, along with the rest of Gaul, deprive the Æduans also of their liberty. That the very same men gave intelligence to the enemy of all the designs of the Romans, and whatsoever was transacted in their camp; his authority not being sufficient to restrain them. Nay, that though compelled by necessity, he had now made a discovery of the whole matter to Cæsar, he was not ignorant of the danger to which he exposed himself by such a conduct; and had, for that reason, chosen to be silent, as long as he thought it consistent with the safety of the state." Cæsar perceived that Dumnorix, the brother of Divitiacus, was pointed at by this speech. But as he was unwilling that these matters should be debated in the presence of so many witnesses, he speedily dismissed the council, retaining only Liscus. He then questioned him apart on what he had just said, and was answered with greater courage and freedom. He put the same questions to others also in private, who all confirmed the truth of what had been told him: That Dumnorix was a man of an enterprising spirit, fond of revolutions, and in great favour with the people, because of his liberality: that he had for many years farmed the customs, and other public revenues of the Æduans, at a very low price; no one daring to bid against him: that by this means he had considerably increased his estate, or I was enabled to extend his bounty to all about him; that he constantly kept a great number of horsemen in pay, who attended him wherever he went; that his interest was not confined merely to his own country, but extended likewise to the neighbouring states: that the better to support this interest, he had married his mother to a man of principal rank and authority among the Biturigians, had himself taken a wife from among the Helvetians, and matched his sister and the rest of his kindred into other the most powerful states; that he favoured and wished well to the Helvetians, on the score of that alliance, and personally hated Cæsar and the Romans, because by their arrival his power had been diminished, and Divitiacus his brother restored to his former credit and authority: that should the Romans be overthrown he was in great hopes of obtaining the sovereignty, by means of the Helvetians. On the contrary, should they prevail, he must not only give up these hopes, but even all expectation of retaining the influence he had already acquired." Cæsar like-

wise found, upon inquiry, that in the last engagement of the horse, Dumnorix, who commanded the Æduan cavalry, was the first that fled, and by that flight struck a terror into the rest of the troops.

XVI. These things appearing, and other undoubted circumstances concurring to heighten his suspicion; that he had procured for the Helvetians a passage through the territories of the Sequani; that he had effected an exchange of hostages between the two nations; that he had done all this not only without permission from him, or his own state, but even without their knowledge and participation; that he was accused by the chief magistrate of the Æduans: they seemed altogether a sufficient ground to Cæsar, why he should either himself take cognizance of the matter, or order the state to proceed against him. One thing, however, still kept him in suspense; the consideration of his brother Divitiacus, a man of singular probity, justice, and moderation; a faithful ally of the Roman people, and on the foot of friendship with Cæsar. That he might not therefore give offence to one for whom he had so great a value; before he took any further step in the affair, he sent for Divitiacus; and having removed the usual interpreters, addressed him by C. Valerius Procillus, a prince of the province of Gaul, his intimate friend, in whom he reposed the greatest confidence. He put him in mind of what had been said of Dumnorix in his own presence in the council of the Gauls, and repeated the fresh complaints made to himself against him in private. He urged, and even requested, that without offence to him, he might either proceed against him himself, or order the state to take the matter under consideration. Divitiacus, embracing Cæsar with many tears, begged him not to take any severe resolution against his brother. "He was sensible," he told him, "of the truth of all that was alleged, and had himself more reason to be dissatisfied than any man: that at a time when his authority was great, both at home and in the other provinces of Gaul, and his brother but little considered on account of his youth, he had used his interest to bring him into credit; that though Dumnorix had made use of that power acquired by his means to diminish his favour with the people, and even to urge on his ruin, he nevertheless still found himself swayed by his affection, and a regard for the esteem of the public: that should his brother meet with any rigorous treatment from Cæsar, while he himself possessed so large a share of his favour, all men would believe it done with his consent, and the minds of the Gauls be for ever alienated from him." Cæsar observing his concern, took him by the hand, comforted him, desired him to make an end of speaking, assured him, that such was his regard for him, he would for his sake overlook not only his own injuries, but even those of the republic. He then sent for Dumnorix, called him into his brother's presence, declared the subjects of complaint he had against him, mentioned what he himself knew, what was laid to his charge by the state, and admonished him for the future to avoid all cause of suspicion; adding, that ne would forgive what was past, for the sake of his brother Divitiacus. He appointed, however, some to have an eye over him, that he might be informed of his behaviour, and of those he conversed with.

XVII. The same day, having learned, by his scouts, that the enemy had posted themselves under a hill about eight miles from his camp, he sent out a party to view the ground, and examine the ascent of the hill. These reporting it to be extremely easy, he detached T. Labienus, his lieutenant, about midnight, with two legions, and the same guides who had examined the ground the day before; and having acquainted him with his design, ordered him to get possession of the top of the hill. He himself set out three hours after, with the rest of the army, by the same route the Helvetians had taken, and sent all the cavalry before. P. Considius, an officer of reputation, who had served in the army of L. Sylla, and afterwards that of M. Crassus, advanced with a small party, to get intelligence.

XVIII. At day-break when Labienus had got possession of the top of the hill, and Cæsar was within a mile and a half of the enemy's camp; while they in the meantime, as he afterwards learnt from his prisoners, knew nothing either of his, or Labienus's approach, Considius came galloping back, and assured Cæsar, that the summit of the mountain was possessed by the enemy, and that he had seen the Gallic arms and ensigns there. Cæsar retired to a neighbouring hill, and drew up his men in order of battle. Labienus, whose instructions were, not to engage the enemy till he saw the rest of the army approaching their camp, that the attack might be made on all sides at the same time, having gained the top of the hill, waited the arrival of our men, without stirring from his post. At length, when the day was far spent, Cæsar understood by his spies, that Labienus was in possession of the mountain, that the enemy had decamped, and that Considius, blinded by fear, had reported what he never saw. The rest of that day he followed the enemy at the usual distance, and encamped within three miles of them.

XIX. The day after, as the time drew near for delivering out corn to the army, and as he was not above eighteen miles from Bibracte, the capital of the Æduans, where he hoped to find sufficient supplies for the subsistence of his troops, he quitted the pursuit of the Helvetians, and directed his march thither. The enemy, being informed of this motion by some deserters, who had belonged to the troop of L. Emilius, an officer of horse among the Gauls, and either ascribing it to fear in the Romans, the rather, because they had not attacked them the day before, though possessed of the higher ground; or flattering themselves with the hopes of intercepting their provisions, all on a sudden changed their resolution, and instead of continuing their former march, began to pursue and harass our rear. Cæsar observing this, retired to a neighbouring hill, and sent his cavalry to sustain the charge of the enemy. In the meantime he drew up his four veteran legions in three lines towards the middle of the hill; in such a manner, that the two legions newly raised in Cisalpine Gaul, and all the auxiliaries, were posted above them; and the whole mountain was covered with his troops. He ordered all the baggage to be brought into one place, and committed it to the charge of those who stood on the upper part of the hill. The Helvetians following with all their forces, drew their carriages likewise into one place; and having repulsed our cavalry, and formed themselves into a phalanx, advanced in close order to attack our van.

XX. Cæsar having first sent away his own horse, and afterwards those of all his officers, that by making the danger equal, no hope might remain but in victory, encouraged his men, and began the charge. The Romans, who fought with the advantage of the higher ground, pouring their darts upon the enemy from above, easily broke their phalanx; and then fell upon them sword in hand. What greatly encumbered the Gauls in this fight, was, that their targets being many of them pierced and pinned together by the javelins of the Romans, they could neither draw out the javelins, because forked at the extremity, nor act with agility in the battle, because deprived in a manner of the use of their left arms: so that many, after long tossing their targets to and fro to no purpose to disengage them, chose rather to throw them away, and expose themselves without defence to the weapons of their enemies. At length, however, being overpowered with wounds, they began to give ground; and observing a mountain at about a mile's distance, gradually retreated thither. Having gained the mountain, and our men pursuing them, the Boians and Tulingians, who, to the number of fifteen thousand, covered their retreat, and served as a guard to their rear, falling upon the Romans in flank as they advanced, began to surround them. This being perceived by the Helvetians, who had retired to the mountain, they again returned upon us, and renewed the fight. The Romans facing about, charged the enemy in three bodies; their first and second line making head against those who had been forced to retreat, and their third sustaining the assault of the Boians and Tulingians. The battle was bloody, and continued for a long time doubtful; but the enemy being at last bliged to give way, one part withdrew towards the hill whither they had before retreated, and the rest sheltered themselves behind the carriages. During this whole action, though it lasted from one o'clock in the afternoon till evening, no man saw the back of an enemy. The fight was renewed with great obstinacy at the carriages, and continued till the night was far spent; for the Gauls making use of their carts by way of a rampart, darted their javelins upon us from above; and some thrusting their lances through the wheels of the wagons, wounded our men. After a long dispute, we at last got possession of their baggage and camp. A son and daughter of Orgetorix were found among the prisoners. Only a hundred and twenty thousand of the enemy survived this defeat; who, retreating all that night, and continuing their march without intermission, arrived on the fourth day in the territories of the Lingones. The Romans meanwhile made no attempt to pursue them; the care of their wounded, and

of burying their dead, obliging them to continue upon the spot three days. Cæsar sent letters and messengers to the Lingones, not to furnish them with corn or other necessaries, if they would avoid drawing upon themselves the same treatment with the fugitives; and after a repose of three days, set forward to pursue them with all his forces.

XXI. The Helvetians, compelled by an extreme want of all things, sent ambassadors to him to treat **about a surrender.** These meeting him on the way, and throwing themselves at his feet, in suppliant terms, and with many tears, begged for peace. Cæsar gave them no express answer at that time; only ordered the Helvetians to wait for him in the place where they then were, which they did accordingly. Upon his arrival, he demanded hostages, their arms, and the slaves who had deserted to their camp. As the execution of all this took up some time, about four thousand men of the canton called Urbigenus, either fearing punishment, should they deliver up their arms, or induced by the hopes of escaping, because in so great a multitude they fancied their flight might be concealed, nay, perhaps remain altogether unknown, stole out of the camp in the beginning of the night, and took the route of Germany and the Rhine. Cæsar being informed of it, despatched orders to those through whose territories they must pass, to stop and send them back wherever they should be found, if they meant to acquit themselves of favouring their escape. He was obeyed, and the fugitive Urbigenians were treated as enemies. All the rest, upon delivering the hostages that were required of them, their arms, and the deserters, were admitted to a surrender. The Helvetians, Tulingians and Latobrigians had orders to return to their own country, and rebuild the towns and villages they had burnt. And because having lost all their corn, they were utterly without the means of subsisting themselves, he gave it in charge to the Allobrogians to supply them. Cæsar's design in this was, that the lands deserted by the Helvetians might not be left vacant, lest the Germans beyond the Rhine, drawn by the goodness of the soil, should be tempted to seize them, and thereby become neighbours to the Allobrogians, and the Roman province in Gaul. The Boians, at the request of the Æduans, who esteemed them highly on account of their valour, were permitted to settle in their territories; where they assigned them lands, and by degrees admitted them to all the rights and privileges of natives. A roll was found in the Helvetian camp, written in Greek characters, and brought to Cæsar. It contained a list of all who had set out upon this expedition capable of bearing arms; likewise of the children, women, and old men. By this it appeared, that the number of the Helvetians was two hundred and sixty-three thousand; of the Tulingians, thirty-six thousand; of the Latobrigians, fourteen thousand; of the Rauraci, twenty-three thousand; of the Boians, **thirty-two** thousand; in all three hundred and sixty-eight thousand, of which ninety-two thousand were fit to bear arms. A review being made, by Cæsar's command, of those that returned to their own country, the number was found to be a hundred and ten thousand.

XXII. The war with the Helvetians being ended, ambassadors from all parts of Gaul, men of principal consideration in their several states, waited upon Cæsar to congratulate his success. They told him: "That though they were sensible the people of Rome, in the war against the Helvetians, meant chiefly **to** avenge the injuries formerly **received** from that nation, yet had the event of it been **highly** advantageous to all Gaul; because in a time of full prosperity, the Helvetians had left their territories with design to make war upon the **other** states; that having brought **them** under subjection, they might choose themselves a habitation at pleasure, and render all the rest of the country tributary." They requested, "That they might have his permission to hold, by a day prefixed, **a** general assembly of all the provinces of Gaul; there being some things they wanted to discuss and propose to him, which concerned the whole nation in common." Leave being granted accordingly, they fixed the day for the assembly, and bound themselves by an oath, not to discover their deliberations to any, unless named for that purpose by general consent.

XXIII. Upon the rising of the council, the same chiefs of the states as before, returned to Cæsar, and begged to be admitted to confer with him, in private, of matters that regarded their own and the common safety. Their desire being granted, they all threw themselves at his feet, and with tears represented: "That it was of no less importance to them to **have** their present deliberations kept secret, than to succeed in the request they were going to make; because, should any discovery happen, they were in danger of being exposed to the utmost cruelties." Divitiacus the Æduan spoke in the name of the rest. He told him: "That two factions divided all Gaul; one headed by the Æduans, the other by the Averni; that after a contention of many years between these for the superiority, the Averni and Sequani came at last to a resolution of calling in the Germans: that at first only fifteen thousand had crossed the Rhine; but being a wild and savage people, and greatly liking the customs, manners, and plenteous country of the Gauls, others soon followed: insomuch that at present there were not less than a hundred and twenty thousand of them in Gaul: that the Æduans, and their allies, had frequently tried their strength against them in battle; but by a succession of defeats had lost all their nobility, senate, and cavalry: that broken by these calamities and losses, though formerly they held the first sway in Gaul, both by their own valour, and the favour and friendship of the people of Rome, yet now they were reduced to the necessity of sending their principal noblemen as hostages to the Sequani, and of obliging themselves by an oath, neither to demand their hostages back, nor implore the assistance of the Roman people, nor refuse a perpetual submission to the dominion and authority of the Sequani: that he alone of all the Æduans had refused to take the oath, or give his children for hostages, and on that account had fled his country, and came to Rome to implore the assistance of the senate; as being the only man in the state, whom neither obligation of oath, nor the restraint of hostages, withheld from such a step: that after all it had fared worse with the victorious Sequani, than with the vanquished Æduans; because Ariovistus, king of the Germans, had seated himself in their territories, had seized a third of their lands, the most fertile in all Gaul, and now ordered them to give up another third in behalf of the Harudes, who passed the Rhine a few months before, with twenty-four thousand men, and wanted a settlement and habitations: that in a **few** years all the native Gauls would be driven from their territories, and all the Germans transplant themselves over the Rhine, the climate being far superior to that of their own country, and the way of living not admitting a comparison : that Ariovistus, ever since the defeat of the Gauls at Amagetobria, had behaved with unheard-of tyranny and haughtiness, demanding the children of the first nobility as hostages, and exercising all manner of cruelties upon them, if his orders were not implicitly followed in every thing : that he was a man of a savage, passionate, and imperious character, whose government was no longer to be borne ; and unless some resource was found in Cæsar and the people of Rome, the Gauls must all follow the example of the Helvetians, and like them abandon their country, in order to find some other habitation and settlement, remote from the Germans, wherever fortune should point it out to them ; that were these complaints and representations to come to the knowledge of Ariovistus, he made no doubt of his inflicting the severest punishments upon all the hostages in his hands: but that it would be easy for Cæsar, by his own authority, and that of the army he commanded ; by the fame of his late victory, and the terror of the Roman name ; to hinder any more Germans from passing the Rhine, and to defend Gaul from the insults of Ariovistus."

XXIV. When Divitiacus had made an end of speaking, all who were present, with many tears, began to implore Cæsar's aid. He observed that the Sequani alone did nothing of all this: but pensive, and with downcast looks, kept their eyes fixed upon the ground. Wondering what might be the cause, he questioned them upon it. Still they made him no answer, but continued silent, as before, with the same air of dejection. When he had interrogated them several times, without being able to obtain one word in return, Divitiacus the Æduan again resumed the discourse, and observed : " That the condition of the Sequani was so much more deplorable and wretched than that of the rest of the Gauls, as they alone durst not, even in secret, complain of their wrongs, or apply any where for redress ; and no less dreaded the cruelty of Ariovistus, when absent, than if actually present before their eyes: that other states had it still in their power to escape by flight; but the Sequani, who had received him into their territories,

and put him in possession of all their towns were exposed, upon discovery, to every kind of torment." Cæsar being made acquainted with those things, encouraged the Gauls, and promised to have a regard to their complaints. He told them: " That he was in great hopes Ariovistus, induced by his intercession, and the authority of the people of Rome, would put an end to his oppressions." Having returned this answer, he dismissed the assembly.

XXV. Many urgent reasons occurred upon this occasion to Cæsar, why he should consider seriously of the proposals of the Gauls, and redress the injuries of which they complained. He saw the Æduans, friends and allies of the people of Rome, held in subjection and servitude by the Germans, and compelled to give hostages to Ariovistus, and the Sequani ; which in the present flourishing state of the Roman affairs, seemed highly dishonourable both to himself and the commonwealth. He saw it likewise of dangerous consequence, to suffer the Germans by little and little to transport themselves over the Rhine, and settle in great multitudes in Gaul. For that fierce and savage people, having once possessed themselves of the whole country of Gaul, were but too likely, after the example of the Teutones and Cimbri, to break into the Roman province, and thence advance to Italy itself; more especially as the Rhone was the only boundary by which the Sequani were divided from the territories of the republic. It therefore appeared necessary to provide without delay against these evils; and the rather, because Ariovistus was become so insolent, and took so much upon him, that his conduct was no longer to be endured.

XXVI. For these reasons he thought proper to send ambassadors to Ariovistus, to desire he would appoint a place for an interview, that they might discourse together about some public affairs of the highest importance to them both. Ariovistus replied : " That if he had wanted any thing of Cæsar, he would himself have waited on him for that purpose ; and if Cæsar had any thing to desire of him, he must likewise come in person to demand it ; that for his own part, he could neither venture into these provinces of Gaul where Cæsar commanded without an army, nor bring an army into the field without great trouble and expense: that he besides wondered extremely.

what business, either Cæsar, or the people of Rome, could have in his division of Gaul, which belonged to him by right of conquest." This answer being reported to Cæsar, he again sent an embassy to him to this effect: "That since, notwithstanding the great obligations he lay under both to himself and the people of Rome, in having, during his consulship, been declared king and ally by the senate; he yet manifested so little acknowledgment to either, as even to refuse an interview, and decline treating of affairs that regarded the common interest; these were the particulars he required of him: First, not to bring any more Germans over the Rhine into Gaul. Secondly, to restore the hostages he had taken from the Æduans, and permit the Sequani likewise to do the same. Lastly, to forbear all injuries towards the Æduans, and neither make war upon them nor their allies. That his compliance with these conditions would establish a perpetual friendship and amity between him and the people of Rome. But if he refused conditions so just, as the senate had decreed in the consulship of M. Messala and M. Piso, that whoever had the charge of the province of Gaul, should, as far as was consistent with the interests of the commonwealth, defend the Æduans and the other allies of the people of Rome; he thought himself bound not to overlook their just complaints."

XXVII. To this Ariovistus replied: "That by the laws of war, the conqueror had a right to impose what terms he pleased upon the conquered: that in consequence of this, the people of Rome, did not govern the vanquished by the prescriptions of another, but according to their own pleasure: that if he did not intermeddle with the Roman conquests, but left them to the free enjoyment of their rights, no more ought they to concern themselves in what regarded him. That the Æduans having tried the fortune of war, had been overcome and rendered tributary, and it would be the highest injustice in Cæsar to offer at diminishing his just revenues: that he was resolved not to part with the hostages the Æduans had put into his hands; but would nevertheless engage, neither to make war upon them nor their allies, provided they observed the treaty he had made with them, and regularly paid the tribute agreed upon; if otherwise, the title of friends and allies of the people of Rome would be found to stand

them but in little stead: that as to Cæsar's menace of not overlooking the complaints of the Æduans, he would have him to know, no one had ever entered into a war with Ariovistus, but to his own destruction: that he might when he pleased bring it to a trial, and would, he doubted not, soon be made sensible what the invincible Germans, trained up from their infancy in the exercise of arms, and who for fourteen years together had never slept under a roof, were capable of achieving."

XXVIII. At the same time that Cæsar received this answer, ambassadors also arrived from the Æduans and Treviri. From the Æduans, to complain: "That the Harudes who had lately come over into Gaul, were plundering their territories; insomuch, that even by their submissions and hostages they were not able to obtain peace of Ariovistus." From the Treviri, to inform him: "That a hundred cantons of the Suevians, headed by two brothers, Nassua and Cimberius, were arrived upon the banks of the Rhine, with design to cross that river." Cæsar, deeply affected with this intelligence, determined to undertake the war without delay, lest this new band of Suevians, joining the old forces of Ariovistus, should enable him to make a greater resistance. Having therefore with all diligence provided for the subsistence of his army, he advanced towards him by great marches.

XXIX. The third day he was informed that Ariovistus approached with all his forces to take possession of Vesontia, the capital of the Sequani: and that he had already got three days' march beyond his own territories. Cæsar judged it by all means necessary to prevent him in this design, as the town itself was not only full of all sorts of warlike ammunition, but likewise strongly fortified by nature, and commodiously situated for carrying on the war. For the river Doux forming a circle round it, as if described with a pair of compasses, leaves only an interval of six hundred feet, which is also inaccessible by reason of a very high and steep mountain, whose roots are washed on each side by the river. This mountain is shut in with a wall, which, forming a citadel, joins it to the town. Hither Cæsar marched day and night without intermission; and having possessed himself of the place, put a garrison into it.

XXX. While he tarried here a few days,

to settle the order of his convoys and supplies, the curiosity of our men, and the talk of the Gauls, (who proclaimed on all occasions the prodigious stature of the Germans, their invincible courage, and great skill in arms; insomuch that in the frequent encounters with them they had found it impossible to withstand their very looks,) spread such a sudden terror through the whole army, that they were not a little disturbed by the apprehensions it occasioned. This fear first began amongst the military tribunes, the officers of the allies, and others that had voluntarily followed Cæsar from Rome; who being but little acquainted with military affairs, lamented the great danger to which they fancied themselves exposed. Some of these, upon various pretences, desired leave to return. Others, out of shame, and unwilling to incur the suspicion of cowardice, continued in the camp. But these last, incapable of putting on a cheerful countenance, and at times even unable to suppress their tears, skulked in their tents, either bemoaning their fate, or discoursing with their companions upon the common danger. Wills were made all over the camp, and the consternation began to seize even those of more experience, the veteran soldiers, the centurions, and the officers of the cavalry. Such among them as affected a greater show of resolution, said it was not the enemy they feared, but the narrow passes and vast forests that lay between them and Ariovistus, and the difficulty there would be in furnishing the army with provisions. Some even told Cæsar, that when he gave orders for marching, the army, attentive to nothing but their fears, would refuse to obey.

XXXI. Cæsar observing the general consternation, called a council of war; and having summoned all the centurions of the army to be present, inveighed against them with great severity; for presuming to inquire, or at all concern themselves, which way, or on what design they were to march. "Ariovistus," he told them, "during his consulship, had earnestly sought the alliance of the Roman people. Why, therefore, should any one imagine, he would so rashly and hastily depart from his engagements? That, on the contrary, he was himself firmly persuaded, that as soon as he came to know his demands, and the equal conditions he was about to propose to him, he would be very far from rejecting either his

friendship, or that of the people of Rome. But if urged on by madness and rage, he was resolved upon war, what, after all, had they to be afraid of? Or why should they distrust either their own bravery, or his care and conduct? That they were to deal with enemies of whom trial had been already made in the memory of their fathers, when, by the victory of C. Marius over the Teutones and Cimbri, the army itself acquired no less glory than the general who commanded it: that trial had likewise been lately made of them in Italy in the servile war, when they had also the advantage of being exercised in the Roman discipline; on which occasion it appeared, how much resolution and constancy were able to effect: since they had vanquished in the end those very enemies, armed and flushed with victory, whom at first they had without cause dreaded even unarmed. In fine, that they were the very same Germans, with whom the Helvetians had so often fought, not only in their own country, but in Germany itself, and for the most part came off victorious, though they had by no means been a match for our army: that if the defeat and flight of the Gauls gave uneasiness to any, these would readily find, upon inquiry, that Ariovistus confining himself many months to his camp and fastnesses, and declining a general action, had thereby tired out the Gauls with the length of the war; who despairing at last of a battle, and beginning to disperse, were thereupon attacked and routed, rather by conduct and craft, than the superior valour of the Germans. But though a stratagem of this kind might take with rude and uncultivated people, yet could not even the German himself hope that it would avail against a Roman army: that as to those who sheltered their cowardice under the pretence of narrow passes, and the difficulty of procuring provisions, he thought it argued no small presumption in them, either to betray such a distrust of their general's conduct, or offer to prescribe to him what he ought to do: that these things fell properly under his care: that the Sequani, Leuci, and Lingones were to furnish him with provisions: that the corn was now ripe in the fields; and that themselves would soon be judges as to what regarded the ways. That the report of the army's refusing to obey him, gave him not the least disturbance; because he very well knew, that no general had ever been so far slighted by his soldiers, whose ill success, avarice, or other crimes, had not justly drawn that misfortune upon him: that in all these respects he fancied himself secure, as the whole course of his life would witness for his integrity, and his good fortune had shown itself in the war against the Helvetians: that he was therefore resolved to execute without delay, what he otherwise intended to have put off a little longer; and would give orders for decamping the very next night, three hours before day, that he might as soon as possible know, whether honour and a sense of duty, or an ignominious cowardice had the ascendant in his army: nay, that should all the rest of the troops abandon him, he would, nevertheless, march with the tenth legion alone, of whose fidelity and courage he had no manner of doubt, and which would serve him for his Prætorian guard." Cæsar had always principally favoured this legion, and placed his chief confidence in it, on account of its valour.

XXXII. This speech made a wonderful change upon the minds of all, and begot an uncommon alacrity and eagerness for the war. The tenth legion in particular, returned him thanks, by their tribunes, for the favourable opinion he had expressed of them, and assured him of their readiness to follow him. Nor were the other legions less industrious, by their tribunes and principal centurions, to reconcile themselves to Cæsar; protesting they had never either doubted or feared, nor ever imagined that it belonged to them, but to the general, to direct in matters of war. Having accepted of their submission, and informed himself, by means of Divitiacus, in whom of all the Gauls he most confided, that by taking a circuit of above forty miles, he might avoid the narrow passes, and lead his army through an open country, he set forward three hours after midnight, as he had said; and after a march of seven days successively, understood by his scouts, that he was within four and twenty miles of Ariovistus's camp.

XXXIII. Ariovistus being informed of his arrival, sent ambassadors to acquaint him: "That he was now willing to accept of an interview, as they were now come nearer one another, and he believed it might be done without danger." Cæsar did not decline the proposal, imagining he was now disposed to listen to reason, since he offered that of his own accord, which he had before refused at his request: neither was he without hope, that in

regard of the benefits he had received, both from himself and the people of Rome, he would, upon knowing his demands, desist from his obstinacy. The fifth day after was appointed for the interview. Meantime, as ambassadors were continually passing and repassing, Ariovistus, under pretence that he was afraid of an ambuscade, demanded: "That Cæsar should bring no infantry with him to the conference: that they should both come attended by their cavalry only: that otherwise he could not resolve to give him a meeting." Cæsar, unwilling to drop the design of the interview, but neither caring to trust his safety to the Gauls, thought the best way was, to dismount all the Gallic cavalry, and give their horses to the soldiers of the tenth legion, who had the greatest share of his confidence; that, in case of danger, he might have a guard on which he could rely. This being done accordingly, one of the soldiers of that legion said pleasantly enough: "That Cæsar had done even more than he had promised; that he had only given them hopes of becoming his Prætorian guard; and now he had raised them to the rank of horse."

XXXIV. There was a large plain, and in the midst of it a rising ground of considerable height, equally distant from both camps. At this place, by appointment, the conference was held. Cæsar stationed the legionary soldiers, whom he had brought with him, on the horses of the Gauls, two hundred paces from the mount. Ariovistus did the same with the German cavalry. The conversation was on horseback, each being accompanied by ten friends, or principal officers, for so Ariovistus had desired. When they were come to the place, Cæsar began, by putting him in mind of the favours he had received both from himself and the people of Rome: "That he had been styled friend and ally by the senate; that very considerable presents had been sent him; that these honours, conferred by the Romans on very few, and only for signal services to the state, had yet been bestowed on him, not on account of any just claim on his side, but merely by the favour of Cæsar, and the bounty of the senate." He told him likewise, "of the just and ancient alliance between the Romans and the Æduans: of the many honourable decrees of the senate in their favour: that they had always held the first rank and authority in Gaul, even before their alliance with

Rome: that it was the constant maxim of the Roman people, not only to defend their friends and allies in the possession of their just rights, but likewise to study the enlargement of their honour, interest, and dignity; that it could never therefore be supposed they would submit to see them stripped of those privileges which had belonged to them before they were received into their friendship." In fine, he concluded with repeating the same demands which he had before made by his ambassadors: "That he would not make war upon the Æduans or their allies; that he would restore their hostages; that if he could not oblige any of the Germans to repass the Rhine, at least he would suffer no more of them to come into Gaul."

XXXV. Ariovistus spoke little to Cæsar's demands, but enlarged greatly on his own virtues: "That he had crossed the Rhine, not of his own motion, but invited and entreated by the Gauls themselves; that the great hopes and expectations they had given him had been his only inducement to quit his country and relations; that he had settlements in Gaul assigned by the Gauls themselves, hostages voluntarily sent, and a tribute in consequence of the rights of war, it being the constant practice of conquerors to impose that mark of subjection on those they had subdued: that he had not made war upon the Gauls, but the Gauls upon him; that though all their several states had united against him, and brought up their forces with design to crush him, he had yet found means to vanquish and disperse them in one battle; that if they were again resolved to try the fortune of war, he was ready and prepared to receive them, but if they rather chose peace, it was unjust in them to refuse a tribute which they had hitherto voluntarily paid; that the friendship of the people of Rome ought to be an honour and security to him, not a detriment, nor had he courted it in any other view; but if by their alliance he must submit to lose his tribute and his right over the people he had subdued, he was no less willing to give it up, than he had been ambitious to obtain it: that he had indeed brought over a multitude of Germans into Gaul, yet not with any design of disturbing the country, but merely for his own security, as appeared by his not coming but at the request of the natives, and his not attacking them, but defending himself: that his arrival in Gaul

was prior to that of the Romans, whose army had never till that time passed the boundaries of their own province. What could they mean by coming into a country that belonged to him? Or why should they concern themselves with a part of Gaul that was no less his property, than the province itself was that of the people of Rome? If it would not be allowable in him to make any attempt upon their possessions, neither could they without injustice, disturb him in the enjoyment of his rights. That as to the pretence of alliance between the Romans and Æduans, he was not a barbarian, nor so wholly a stranger to the affairs of the world as not to know, that neither had the Æduans assisted the Romans in the late war against the Allobrogians, nor received any assistance from them in their many conflicts with himself and the Sequani. That he ought to be jealous of Cæsar's pretended regard to the Æduans, and had but too much reason to suspect that the continuance of the Roman army in Gaul could be with no other design than that of oppressing him. That if he did not therefore depart, and withdraw his troops out of those parts, he would no longer look upon him as a friend, but an enemy. That he was well assured, should he even slay him in battle, he should do a pleasure to many of the nobles and great men at Rome, who had explained themselves to him by couriers, and whose favour and friendship he might procure by his death: but that if he would retire, and leave him in the undisturbed possession of Gaul, he would not only amply reward him, but engage, at his own cost and hazard, to put an end to any war Cæsar should think fit to undertake."

XXXVI. Many reasons were offered by Cæsar, in return to this speech, why he could not depart from his first demands: "That neither his own honour, nor that of the people of Rome, would suffer him to abandon allies, who had deserved so well of the commonwealth; that it no way appeared to him wherein Ariovistus had a juster claim to the possession of Gaul than the Romans: that the Averni and Ruteni had been subdued by Q. Fabius Maximus, who yet contented with their submission, had neither reduced their country into a province, nor subjected it to tribute: that if antiquity of title was to decide the Romans had an undoubted right to the sovereignty of Gaul: if, on the contrary, th licence of the senate was to take place, Gaul must remain free, and subject only to its own laws."

XXXVII. Whilst these things passed at the interview, Cæsar was informed that Ariovistus's cavalry were drawing nearer the mount, and had even assaulted the Romans with stones and darts. Cæsar immediately broke off the conference, retreated to his own men, and strictly charged them to forbear all acts of hostility towards the enemy. He did not fear the success of an action, with that chosen legion, against the German cavalry; but he was willing to maintain a conduct perfectly clear, and not give the enemy the least handle to assert, that they had been treacherously drawn into an ambuscade by a pretended conference. When it was known in the camp, with what haughtiness Ariovistus had behaved at the interview; that he had ordered the Romans to depart out of Gaul; that his cavalry had fallen upon Cæsar's guard; and that an end had thereby been put to the conference, a much greater alacrity and desire of fighting spread themselves through the whole army.

XXXVIII. Two days after, Ariovistus sent ambassadors to propose a renewal of the negotiation begun; and that he would either again appoint a day for a conference, or depute some one to bring the treaty to a conclusion. Cæsar saw no reason for granting a second interview; more especially when he considered that the time before, the Germans could not be restrained from falling upon our men. Neither was he inclined to send any of his principal officers; it seeming too great a venture, to expose them to the perfidy of these barbarians. He therefore cast his eye upon C. Valerius Procillus, the son of C. Valerius Caburus, a young man of great merit and politeness, whose father had been made free of the city by C. Valerius Flaccus. His singular integrity, and knowledge of the language of the Gauls, which Ariovistus, by reason of long stay in those parts, spoke readily, fitted him in a particular manner for this embassy: and as he was likewise one towards whom it would no way avail the Germans to use any treachery, he thought him less liable to an insult of that kind. M. Mettius was joined in commission with him, who was allied to Ariovistus by the rights of hospitality. Their instructions were, to hear the Germans' propo-

sals, and carry back a report of them to Cæsar. But no sooner were they arrived in Ariovistus's camp, than in presence of the whole army, calling out to know their business, and whether they were come as spies, he commanded them to be put in irons, without suffering them to make any reply.

XXXIX. The same day he came forward with all his forces, and lodged himself under a hill, about six miles from our camp. The day after he went two miles beyond it, to cut off Cæsar's communication with the Æduans and Sequani, from whom he received all his provisions. Cæsar, for five days continually, drew up his men in order of battle before the camp, that if Ariovistus had a mind, he might not be without an opportunity of coming to an engagement. The Germans kept all that time within their lines; only we had daily skirmishes with their cavalry, whose manner of fighting was this. They had about six thousand horse, who chose a like number out of the foot, each his man, and all remarkable for strength and agility. These continually accompanied them in battle, and served them as a rear-guard, to which, when hard pressed, they might retire; if the action became dangerous, they advanced to their relief: if any horseman was considerably wounded, and fell from his horse, they gathered round to defend him: if speed was required, either for a hasty pursuit, or sudden retreat, they were become so nimble and alert by continual exercise, that laying hold of the manes of their horses, they could run as fast as they.

XL. Cæsar finding that Ariovistus declined a battle, thought it necessary to provide for the freedom of his convoys. With this view he marked out a place for a camp, six hundred paces beyond that of the enemy, whither he marched with his whole army drawn up in three lines. The first and second lines had orders to continue under arms, and the third to employ themselves in fortifying the camp. Ariovistus sent sixteen thousand light-armed foot, and all his horse, to alarm our men, and hinder the work. But Cæsar remained firm to his first design, ordering the two lines that continued under arms to keep off the enemy, and the third to go on with the intrenchments. The work being finished, he left two legions there, with part of the auxiliaries, and carried back the other four to his former camp. The next day he assembled all his troops from

O

both camps, drew them up according to custom and offered the enemy battle ; but they still refusing to come to an engagement, he retired again about noon. Ariovistus then detached part of his forces to attack the lesser camp. A sharp conflict ensued, that lasted till night. At sun-set Ariovistus thought proper to sound a retreat, after many wounds given and received. Cæsar inquiring of the prisoners, why Ariovistus so obstinately refused an engagement, found, that it was the custom among the Germans, for the women to decide, by lots and divination, when it was proper to hazard a battle ; and that these had declared the army could not be victorious, if they fought before the new moon.

XLI. The day after, Cæsar having left a sufficient guard in his two camps, ranged all the auxiliary troops before the lesser camp, placing them directly in view of the enemy for the greater show, because the number of legionary soldiers was but inconsiderable, compared with that of the Germans. Then advancing at the head of all his forces in three lines, he marched quite up to the enemy's camp. Upon this the Germans, compelled by necessity, appeared before the intrenchments, and having distributed their troops by nations, and disposed them at equal distances one from another, the Harudes, Marcomani, Tribocci, Vangiones, Nemetes, Sedusians, and Suevians, encompassed the whole army with a line of carriages, to take away all hopes of safety by flight. The women mounted upon these carriages, weeping and tearing their hair, conjured the soldiers, as they advanced to battle, not to suffer them to become slaves to the Romans. Cæsar having appointed a lieutenant and questor to each legion, to serve as witnesses of every man's courage and behaviour, began the battle in person at the head of the right wing, observing the enemy to be weakest on that side. The signal being given, our men charged so briskly, and the enemy advanced so swiftly and suddenly to meet them, that the Romans not having time to throw their darts, betook themselves immediately to their swords : but the Germans quickly casting themselves into a phalanx, according to the custom of their country, sustained the shock with great firmness. Many of our soldiers leaped upon the phalanx, tore up the bucklers of the enemy with their hands, and wounded those that lay under them. Their left wing was soon routed and put to flight ; but on the right they had the

advantage, and were like to overpower the Romans by their number. Young Crassus, who commanded the cavalry, and was more at liberty than those immediately engaged in the fight, observing this, made the third line advance to support them. Upon this the battle was renewed, and the enemy every where put to the rout ; nor did they cease their flight till they had reached the banks of the Rhine, about fifty miles distant from the place of combat. There only a few escaped, some by swimming, others by boats. Of this last number was Ariovistus, who, embarking in a small vessel he found by the edge of the river, got safe to the other side : all the rest were cut to pieces in the pursuit, by our cavalry. Ariovistus had two wives, one a Suevian, whom he had brought with him from Germany : the other a Norican, sister to King Vocian, whom he had married in Gaul : both perished in this flight. Of his two daughters, one was killed, the other taken prisoner. C. Valerius Procillus, whom his keepers dragged after them in their flight, bound with a triple chain, fell in with Cæsar in person as he was pursuing the German cavalry. Nor was the victory itself more grateful to that general, than his good fortune in recovering out of the hands of the enemy, a man the most distinguished for his probity of the whole province of Gaul, his intimate and familiar friend ; and to find the joy and success of that day no way diminished or clouded by the loss of a person he so highly esteemed. Procillus told him, that lots had been thrice drawn in his own presence, to decide, whether he should be burnt alive upon the spot, or reserved for another time, and that the lot, three times favourable, had preserved his life. Mettius was likewise recovered and brought.

XLII. This battle being reported beyond the Rhine, the Suevians, who were advanced as far as the banks of that river, thought proper to return to their own country ; but re treating in disorder and confusion, they were attacked by the Ubians, a people bordering upon the Rhine, and many of them cut to pieces. Cæsar having in one campaign put an end to two very considerable wars, went into winter quarters somewhat sooner than the season of the year required. He distributed his army among the Sequani, left Labienus to command in his absence, and sent out himself for Cisalpine Gaul, to preside in the assembly of the states.

CÆSAR'S COMMENTARIES

OF

HIS WARS IN GAUL.

BOOK II.

THE ARGUMENT.

I. The confederacy of the Belgians against the people of Rome.—III. The Rhemi submit upon the approach of Cæsar.—IV. And inform him of the strength and designs of the confederates.—VI. Cæsar passes the Axona with his army.—VII. Bibrax, a town belonging to the Rhemi, assaulted by the Belgians.—VIII. Cæsar relieves it, and obliges the Belgians to retire.—IX. The armies drawn up on both sides, but without coming to an engagement.—XI. The Belgians, despairing of success, decamp and return home.—XII. Cæsar attacks their rear, and makes great slaughter.—XIII. He then marches against the Suessiones, and obliges them to submit.—XIV.—Advancing next into the country of the Bellovaci, he pardons them at the intercession of Divitiacus.—XVI.—The Ambiani surrender, but the Nervians stand on their defence.—XXIII. They are defeated, however, in a long and bloody engagement, and almost all cut off.—XXIX. Cæsar prepares to attack the Atuatici.—XXXI. They submit.—XXXIII.—But falling treacherously upon the Romans during the night.—XXXIV. Are many of them cut to pieces, and the rest sold for slaves.

CÆSAR'S COMMENTARIES

OF

HIS WARS IN GAUL.

BOOK II.

I. In the winter, while Cæsar was in hither Gaul, as we have intimated above, he was alarmed by frequent reports, which were also confirmed by letters from Labienus, that all the Belgians, who, as has been said, possessed one of the three divisions of Gaul, had joined in a league against the people of Rome, and ratified it by an exchange of hostages. The causes of this confederacy were: First, their fear lest the Romans, having subdued all the rest of Gaul, should next turn their arms against them; and then the persuasions and importunity of some among the Celtæ, many of whom, as they had greatly disliked the neighbourhood of the Germans in Gaul, so were they no less displeased to see a Roman army take up winter-quarters and grow habitual in the country; others, from a levity and inconstancy of temper, were fond of every project that tended to a revolution. In fine, some were influenced by ambitious views, it being usual in Gaul for such as were most powerful in their several states, and had men and money at command, to exercise a kind of sovereignty over their fellow-subjects, which they foresaw would be greatly checked by the authority and credit of the Romans in Gaul.

II. Cæsar, roused by these messages and reports, levied two new legions in hither Gaul, and early in the spring, sent Q. Pedius, his lieutenant, to conduct them over the Alps. Himself, as soon as there began to be forage in the fields, came to the army; he commissioned the Senones, and other Gauls who bordered on the Belgians, to inform themselves of the motions and designs of the confederates, and send him from time to time an exact account. They all agreed in their reports, that they were levying troops, and drawing their forces to a general rendezvous; whereupon, thinking he ought no longer to delay marching against them, and having settled the necessary supplies for his army, he decamped, and in fifteen days arrived on the confines of the Belgians.

III. As his approach was sudden, and much earlier than had been expected, the Rhemi, who, of all the Belgians, lay the nearest to Celtic Gaul, despatched Iccius and Autobrigius, the two principal men of their state, to represent to Cæsar: "That they put themselves and fortunes under the power and protection of the Romans, as having neither approved of the designs of the rest of the Belgians, nor had any share in their confederacy against the people of Rome: that on the contrary, they were ready to give hostages, to execute his commands, to receive him into their towns, and to furnish him with corn and other supplies for his army; that indeed, the rest of the Belgians were all in arms, and that the Germans on this side the Rhine had associated with them: nay, that so universal and prevalent was the infatuation, they had not even been able to draw off the Suessiones, a people united to them by the nearest ties of blood and friendship, who were subject to the same laws, lived under the same form of government, and acknowledged but one common magistrate."

IV. Cæsar inquiring of the ambassadors

what states had taken up arms, of what name and consideration, and what forces they could bring into the field, found that the Belgians were for the most part Germans originally, who having formerly crossed the Rhine, had been drawn by the fertility of the country to settle in those parts, after driving out the ancient inhabitants; that in the late eruption of the Teutones and Cimbri, when all the other provinces of Gaul were overrun, they alone had ventured to stand upon their defence, nor suffered the barbarians to set foot in their territories: whence it happened, that presuming on so well known an instance of their bravery, they laid claim to great authority, and challenged high military renown. As to their numbers, the Rhemi told him they could give him the most exact information. because in consequence of their affinity and neighbourhood, they had opportunities of knowing what quota of men each particular state had promised to furnish in the common council of Belgium. "That the Bellovaci held the most distinguished rank, as surpassing all the other states in prowess, authority, and number of forces; that they were able to muster a hundred thousand fighting men, and had promised out of that number sixty thousand chosen troops, in consideration of which they demanded the whole administration of the war. That next to them in dignity were the Suessiones, a people bordering upon their own territories, and possessed of a very large and fruitful country, over which, even of late years, Divitiacus had been king, one of the most powerful princes of all Gaul, and who, besides his dominions in those parts, reigned also over Britain; that their present sovereign was Galba, whose singular prudence and justice had procured him, by the consent of all the confederates, the supreme command in the war: that these had within their territories twelve fortified towns, and promised to bring into the field fifty thousand men: that the like number had been stipulated by the Nervians, who, inhabiting the remotest provinces of Gaul, were esteemed the most fierce and warlike of all the Belgian nations: that the Atrebatians were to furnish fifteen thousand, the Ambiani ten thousand, the Morini twenty-five thousand, the Menapians nine thousand, the Caletes ten thousand, the Velocassians and Veromanduans be like number; the Atuatici twenty-nine thousand; and the Condrusians, Eburones, sians, and Pæmani, all comprehended

under the common name of Germans, forty thousand.

V. Cæsar exhorting the men of Rheims to continue firm in their alliance, and promising amply to reward their fidelity, ordered the whole body of their senate to repair to his camp, and the sons of their principal nobility to be brought him as hostages, all which was accordingly performed by the day appointed. He then addressed himself to Divitiacus, the Æduan, representing, in the warmest manner, of what consequence it was to the common cause, to divide the forces of the enemy, that he might not be reduced to the necessity of encountering so great a multitude at once. This he told him, might easily be effected, if the Æduans would march their forces into the territories of the Bellovaci, to plunder and lay waste the country. With these instructions he dismissed them.

VI. Meantime, being informed by his scouts, and the people of Rheims, that all the forces of the Belgians were marching towards him in a body, and that they were even advanced within a few miles, he made all the haste he could to pass his army over the Axona, which divides the Rhemi from the rest of the Belgians, and encamped on the farther side of that river. By this situation he secured all behind him, covered one side of his camp with the river, and rendered the communication with the Rhemi, and those other states, whence he expected to be supplied with provisions, safe and easy. Adjoining to his camp was a bridge over the river; there he placed a strong guard, and left Q. Titurius Sabinus, his lieutenant, on the other side, with six cohorts. He then drew round his camp a ditch eighteen feet broad, strengthened with a rampart twelve feet high.

VII. The Belgians, in their march, fell furiously upon Bibrax, a town belonging to the Rhemi, about eight miles distant from Cæsar's camp. The inhabitants, with great difficulty, held out against that day's assault. The manner of storming a town is the same among the Belgians as among the Gauls; for having surrounded the walls with the whole body of their army, and by a continual discharge from their slings, cleared the ramparts, they approach the gates under covert of their bucklers, and undermine the walls. This was easy in the present case, because the multitude employed in throwing stones and darts was so great, that none of the garrison durst appear upon the walls. When night had put an end to the assault, Iccius, who then commanded in the town, a man of principal rank and authority among the Rhemi, and one of those who had come ambassadors to Cæsar to treat about a peace, despatched messengers to acquaint him, that unless he was speedily relieved, it would be impossible for him to hold out any longer.

VIII. Hereupon Cæsar, making use of those for guides who had come express to his camp from Iccius, detached about midnight a party of Cretan and Numidian archers, with some Balearean slingers, to the assistance of the garrison. Their arrival encouraged the besieged to stand upon their defence, and inspired them with hopes of repulsing the enemy, who now began to despair of success, when they heard that a reinforcement had entered the town. Wherefore, after a short stay before the place, having plundered all the country round about, and burnt the houses and villages wherever they came, they marched in a body towards Cæsar's camp, and posted themselves within two miles of his army, inclosing a space of more than eight thousand paces in circumference, as near as could be computed from the smoke and fires of their camp.

IX. Cæsar at first resolved to avoid coming to a battle, as well on account of the numbers of the enemy, as the high opinion entertained of their courage. He suffered the horse, however, to engage daily in small skirmishes, that he might the better judge of the valour of the Belgian troops, and the resolution and bravery of his own men. Finding that the Romans were nothing inferior to the enemy in courage, he resolved to wait for them before his camp; the ground being very commodious, and as it were formed by nature for the reception of an army. For the hill on which the camp stood, rising with an easy ascent from the plain, was but just of a sufficient breadth on the side facing the enemy to receive the several lines of the army, drawn up in order of battle. On the right hand and on the left the descent was steep, whereby the mountain swelling in front, but gradually abating its declivity as you advanced towards the bottom, came at last to a plain. Along each side of the hill Cæsar dug a trench of about four hundred paces in length, and built forts at the extremities, where he placed engines to repulse the enemy, should

they offer to attack him in flank, or endeavour, during the fight, to surround him with their numbers. These dispositions being made, and having left the two new levied legions in his camp, as a body of reserve in case of need, he drew up the other six in order of battle. The Belgians likewise drew up their troops, and stood fronting our army.

X. Between Cæsar and the enemy there was a small morass. The Belgians waited to see if we would pass it; our men, on the other hand, were ready in arms, that, should the enemy attempt to come over, they might fall upon them, and take advantage of their confusion. Meantime the cavalry on both sides engaged; but as neither army would hazard the passage of the morass, Cæsar, who had the better in the skirmish of the horse, led back his men to their camp. The Belgians marched directly towards the Axona, which, as we have said, lay behind our camp, and having found a ford, endeavoured to pass over part of their army. Their design was, if possible, to make themselves masters of the fort where Q. Titurius commanded, and break down the bridge, or, should they fail in that attempt, to ravage and lay waste the territories of the Rhemi, whence our army was supplied with provisions.

XI. Cæsar being informed of these things by Titurius, crossed the bridge with his cavalry, light-armed Numidians, archers, and slingers, and marched to attack the enemy. A very sharp conflict ensued; for the Romans falling upon them while they were yet passing the river, and by reason of their disorder unable to defend themselves, slew great numbers. The rest, who with undaunted courage advanced upon the bodies of their companions, were repulsed by the multitude of darts from our men; and the cavalry surrounding those that were already got over, put them **all to the** sword. The Belgians being thus disappointed, both in their design upon Bibrax, and the passage of the Axona, finding too that provisions began to be scarce, and that our army could not be drawn to fight them at a disadvantage, called a council of war. It was there judged most expedient to separate, and return every man to his own country, with a resolution, however, to assemble from all parts, in defence of that state whose territories should be first invaded by the Romans: for they concluded it much safer to carry on the war a home, where they might have provisions and every thing at command, than venture a battle within the confines of a foreign state. These reasons were at the same time backed by a still more powerful consideration: for the Bellovaci having intelligence that Divitiacus and the Æduans were advancing towards their territories, could not be restrained from marching directly homewards, to defend their own country.

XII. This resolution being taken; about the second watch of the night, they left their camp with great noise and tumult, regarding neither the order of their march, nor the due subordination of command, but each man pressing for the foremost rank, that he might get the sooner home, insomuch that their retreat had all the appearance of a precipitate flight. Cæsar, who had immediate notice of this from his spies, apprehending some stratagem, because he as yet knew nothing of the reason of their departure, would not stir out of his trenches. But early in the morning, upon more certain intelligence of their retreat, he detached all the cavalry, under Q. Pedius and L. Arunculeius Cotta, his lieutenants, to harass and retard them in their march. T. Labienus had orders to follow with three legions. These falling upon their rear, and pursuing them many miles, made a dreadful slaughter of the flying troops. Whilst the rear, upon finding themselves attacked, faced about, and valiantly sustained the charge of our men, the vanguard, as fancying themselves out of danger, were not to be restrained either by necessity or the voice of their commanders, but upon hearing the alarm behind them, broke their ranks, and betook themselves to flight. Thus the Romans, with little or no loss on their side, continued the slaughter all the remaining part of the day. About sunset, they gave over the pursuit, and, in obedience to the orders they had received, returned to their camp.

XIII. The next day, before the enemy had time to rally, or recover out of their consternation, Cæsar led his army into the territories of the Suessiones, which join to those of the Rhemi; and after a long march reached Noviodunum. He was in hopes of carrying the town by assault, because he understood it was destitute of a garrison; but as the ditch was broad, and the wall very high, the defendants, though few in number, withstood all his

efforts; wherefore, having fortified his camp, he began to provide engines, and get every thing in readiness for a siege. Meantime such of the Suessiones as had escaped the late slaughter, threw themselves during the night into the town. But Cæsar advancing his preparations with great expedition, and approaching under cover of his mantlets to the very walls, where he cast up a mount, and planted his battering towers, the Gauls, astonished at the greatness of the works, as having never seen nor heard of any such before, and at the despatch wherewith they were carried on, sent deputies to treat about a surrender, and by the mediation of the Rhemi, obtained conditions of peace.

XIV. Cæsar having received the principal men of their state as hostages, amongst whom were the two sons of Galba, their king; and obliged them to deliver up all their arms, admitted the Suessiones to a surrender, and led his army against the Bellovaci. These, retiring with their effects into Bratuspantium, their capital city, and understanding that Cæsar was advanced within five miles of the town, sent a deputation of all their old men, who came forth in venerable procession to meet him, signifying, by out-stretched hands, and in the most submissive terms, that they had put themselves under his power and protection, nor pretended to appear in arms against the people of Rome; and when he approached still nearer the city, and encamped within view of the walls, the women and children from the ramparts, with extended arms, according to the custom of their country, besought the Romans for peace.

XV. Hereupon Divitiacus, who, after the retreat of the Belgian army, had dismissed the Æduans and returned to Cæsar's camp, interposed in their behalf, representing: "That the Bellovaci had always lived in strict friendship and alliance with the Æduans that the artful insinuations of their chiefs, who misrepresented Cæsar, as one that had ensnaved the Æduan state, and held it under an ignominious tyranny and oppression, had alone induced them to forsake their ancient allies, and take up arms against the people of Rome: that the authors of this advice, seeing its pernicious effects, and the ruin they had brought upon their country, were retired into Britain: that not only the Bellovaci themselves, but the Æduans too, in their behalf, implored his clemency and forgiveness; that in granting their request, he would greatly enlarge the credit and authority of the Æduans among the Belgian states; which was of so much the greater moment, as in all their wars they were wont to have recourse to them for assistance." Cæsar, out of regard to Divitiacus and the Æduans, promised to grant them pardon and protection; but as they were possessed of very extensive territories, and surpassed in power and number of forces all the other Belgian states, he demanded six hundred hostages.

XVI. These being accordingly delivered, together with all their arms, Cæsar left their city, and advanced into the country of the Ambiani; who submitted immediately upon his approach. Adjoining to them were the Nervians; of whose manners and genius Cæsar inquiring, found; "That they suffered no resort of merchants into their cities, nor would allow of the importation of wine, or other commodities tending to luxury; as imagining that thereby the minds of men were enfeebled, and their martial fire and courage extinguished: that they were men of a warlike spirit; but altogether unacquainted with the refinements of life; that they continually inveighed against the rest of the Belgians, for ignominiously submitting to the Roman yoke, and abandoning the steady bravery of their ancestors. In fine, that they had openly declared their resolution, of neither sending ambassadors to Cæsar, nor accepting any terms of peace." Cæsar, after a march of three days across their territories, understood from some prisoners, "That he was now advanced within ten miles of the Sambre, on the other side of which the enemy had posted themselves, and there waited the coming up of the Romans; that they had been joined by the Atrebatians and Veromanduans, neighbouring nations, whom they had persuaded to take part in, and share the fortune of the war: that they expected also to be reinforced by the Atuatici, who were already on their march: and that all their women, and such as on account of their age were unfit to bear arms, had been conveyed to a place of safety, inaccessible by reason of the marshes that surrounded it."

XVII. Cæsar, upon this intelligence, sent his scouts and centurions before, to choose out a convenient place for his camp. Meantime, as many of the Belgians who had lately submitted, and also not a few Gauls, followed the Roman army, some of these, as was afterwards known from the prisoners, observing the order and disposition of our march, deserted in the night to the enemy, and informed them: "That the several legions were separated from one another, by a number of carriages posted between them: that they would therefore have a favourable opportunity, as soon as the first legion was arrived in the camp, and while the rest were yet a great way behind, of falling upon it encumbered with the baggage, and obtaining an easy victory; by which, and the plunder of the carriages, they would strike such a terror through the whole army, as must necessarily draw after it a total defeat." This advice was the more readily listened to, because of old, the Nervians, being very weak in horse, (nor even as yet have they greatly increased their strength this way, placing their whole confidence in their foot,) in order to secure themselves against the inroads of the cavalry of the neighbouring nations, had every where fortified the country with barricadoes of young trees; which being split in the middle, and bent down on both sides, the void spaces were so closely interwoven with brambles, thorns, and a multitude of boughs, issuing from the trees themselves, that they formed a fence not only impossible to be passed, but even to be seen through. As these, therefore, must greatly impede and perplex the march of the Roman army, they thought the advice given them by the Belgians was by no means to be neglected.

XVIII. The place chosen by our men for their camp was a hill, running with an even descent from the summit till it reached the banks of the Sambre. Directly opposite to this, on the farther side of the river, and at the distance of about two hundred paces, was another hill, of a like acclivity with the former, plain and open round the bottom, but covered on the top with woods, so thick that they hindered the prospect. Among these woods the enemy lay concealed, and only a few squadrons of horse appeared on the open ground by the river side, whose depth in that place did not exceed three feet.

XIX. Cæsar having sent the cavalry before, followed himself with the rest of the army. But the order and disposition of his march differed from the account given in to the ene-

10*

P

my by the Belgians. For knowing that the Nervians were near, he led up six legions, in front, ready equipped for battle, according to his usual custom. After them followed the baggage of the whole army; and then the two new legions, who closed the march, and served as guard to the carriages. Meantime the Roman cavalry, with the slingers and archers, having passed the river, engaged the enemy's horse; but as they retired from time to time into the woods, and again sallied upon our men, who durst not pursue them beyond the open ground; the six legions that formed the van, coming up during these successive rencounters, began to intrench themselves. When the first line of our carriages appeared within sight of those that lay concealed in the woods, which was the time previously concerted by the enemy for giving the onset, the Nervians, who stood ready drawn up within the thicket, and had mutually exhorted one another to a resolute behaviour, rushed suddenly forward with all their forces, and fell **furiously** upon our cavalry. These being easily repulsed and broken,' they ran down with incredible speed to the Sambre, insomuch, that at one and the same instant, they seemed to be in the woods, in the river, and charging our men on the other side. Nor were they less expeditious in mounting the hill, and attacking those who were employed in fortifying the camp.

XX. Now had Cæsar all the parts of a general upon his hands at once; to erect the standard, which was the signal for the men to fly to arms; **to** proclaim the battle by sound of trumpet; **to** draw off the soldiers from the works; to recall those that were gone to fetch materials for the rampart; to draw up the army in order of battle; to encourage his men; and give the word of onset: in most of which he was prevented by the shortness of the time, and the sudden assault of the enemy. In this emergency, two things chiefly contributed to the preservation of the Romans: one, the ability and experience of the soldiers, who, practised in former battles, knew their duty and what was expedient in the present conjuncture, no less than the officers themselves; the other, the orders given by Cæsar to his several lieutenants, not to quit the works, and the legions where they commanded, till the fortifications of the camp were finished. For these, upon seeing the danger, and sudden approach of the enemy, waited not for new instructions from the general, but gave forth such orders, as their own prudence and the present necessity suggested.

XXI. Cæsar, having made the necessary dispositions, ran to encourage his men; and, as chance ordered it, fell in with the tenth legion. When exhorting them in few words to exert **their** wonted bravery, and manfully **sustain the assault without** terror or dismay, as he saw the enemy **within** reach of dart, he gave the signal to engage. Hastening thence to another quarter of the **field,** he found the battle already begun. So **short was** the time allowed us to prepare ourselves, **and** such the resolution and impetuosity of the Nervians in rushing to the encounter, that neither could the officers find leisure to regulate the ensigns, nor the soldiers to put on their helmets, or uncase their targets. Each man, as he arrived from the works, joined himself to the first standard that came in his way, that he might not lose that time in looking for his own company, which was to be employed in fighting the enemy.

XXII. The army being drawn up, rather according to the nature of the place, the declivity of the hill, and the particular necessity of the time, than agreeable to order and the rules of war; as the legions were forced to engage separately, some in one place, some in another, and the view of the fight was every where interrupted by the thick hedges described above; it was not possible in these circumstances, to distinguish, with any certainty, where to send the necessary supplies; how to provide against **the** exigencies of the field; nor indeed for **one** man to have an eye to all **the occurrences that called** for notice and redress. In such **an** unequal situation of things, therefore, **much** room was left for the various events and interposition of fortune.

XXIII. The soldiers of the ninth and tenth legions, who were upon the left of the army, having cast their darts, advanced against the Atrebatians, with whom it was their fortune to engage. These now weary, breathless, and overpowered with wounds, were quickly driven from the higher ground quite back to the Sambre, where the Romans, still pressing them sword in hand, slew great numbers as they endeavoured to pass the river. Nor did our men decline pursuing them to the other side; but following too far, till they were drawn into a place of disadvantage, the enemy suddenly faced about, and renewed the charge; yet were a second time obliged to betake themselves to flight. So likewise, in another quarter of the field, the eleventh and eighth legions, having overthrown the Veromanduans, against whom they fought, drove them from the higher ground to the very banks of the river.

XXIV. As by this means the front and left side of the Roman camp lay in a manner quite exposed, for the twelfth legion, and not far from that, the seventh were posted in the right wing; the Nervians, headed by Boduognatus, **their king,** advanced thither in a close body, **and whilst one** party endeavoured to **surround the legions,** by taking them in flank, **the rest mounted the** hill, in order to get possession of the camp. At the same time our **cavalry, with** the light-armed infantry, who in the very beginning of the engagement had been repulsed and broken, as we have related above, returning to the camp, and meeting the enemy in front, again betook themselves to flight. The servants too of the army, who from the top of the hill had beheld our men victorious, and pursuing the enemy across the river, having sallied out for the sake of plunder, when they now looked back, and saw the Nervians in possession of the camp, fled with the utmost precipitation. This confusion was still more increased by the clamour and uproar of those that attended the carriages; insomuch **that** the panic spreading on all sides, each **man** thought of providing for his safety by **flight.** The cavalry of Treves, who were in **the highest** esteem among the Gauls for their **valour, and had been** sent by the state to reinforce Cæsar's army, alarmed by these several appearances, when they saw our camp filled with multitudes of the enemy, the legions overpowered, and in a manner quite surrounded; the horse, archers, slingers, and Numidians, routed, dispersed, and flying on all hands; imagining all was lost, returned to their own country, and reported, that the Romans were utterly overthrown, and their camp and baggage in possession of the enemy.

XXV. Cæsar, having encouraged the tenth legion, hastened to the right wing of the army. He there found his men overpowered by the enemy; the ensigns of the twelfth legion all crowded into one place, and the soldiers themselves standing so close together, that they had not room to use their arms; all the centurions of the fourth cohort slain, the standardbearer killed, and the standard taken; the centurions of the other cohorts almost all either killed or dangerously wounded; among these P. Sextius Baculus, the first centurion of the legion, a man of great courage, so weakened by the multitude of his wounds, that he was hardly able to support himself; the rest discouraged and avoiding the fight, and some even running away, because abandoned by the troops that were to sustain them; the enemy pressing vigorously in front from the lower ground, and at the same time flanking the legions on either side with great fury: in a word, things reduced to the last extremity, and no body of reserve to restore the battle. Whereupon, snatching a buckler from a soldier, who stood in the rear of the legion, for he himself was come thither without one, and pressing to the front of the battle, he called the centurions by name, encouraged the rest, and commanded the soldiers to advance the ensigns, and widen their ranks, that they might be the more at liberty to use their swords. His arrival inspiring the men with hope, and reviving their courage, as every one was ambitious of distinguishing himself in the presence of his general, and even in his greatest extremity, redoubled his efforts, the progress of the enemy was a little checked.

XXVI. Cæsar observing that the seventh legion, which fought at some distance from the other, was likewise very much pressed by the enemy, commanded the military tribunes to draw the two legions together by degrees, and joining them back to back oppose the enemy with a double front. This being done; as they were now in a condition to support each other, and no longer feared being **surrounded,** they began to make a more vigorous opposition, and fight with greater **courage.** Meantime the two new legions that **formed** the rear of our army, and had been appointed to guard the baggage; hearing of the battle, advanced with all possible speed, and were seen by the Nervians from the top of the hill; and T. Labienus, who had made himself master of the enemy's camp, observing from the higher ground how matters went on our side, detached the tenth legion to our assistance. These understanding, by the flight of our cavalry and servants, the distress we were in and the danger that threatened the camp, the legions, and the general, made all the haste they could to join us.

XXVII. The arrival of this detachment produced so great a change in our favour, that many of the soldiers, who before lay oppressed with wounds, now resuming courage, and supporting themselves with their shields, renewed the fight. Nay, the very servants of the camp, observing the consternation of the enemy, unarmed as they were, rushed amongst their armed battalions. The cavalry too, striving by extraordinary efforts of valour to wipe away the ignominy of their late flight, charged the enemy in all places where the void spaces between the legions suffered them to advance. Meantime the Nervians, though now reduced to the last extremity, exerted themselves with such determined courage, that their front ranks being cut off, those who stood behind mounted the bodies of the slain, and thence continued to maintain the fight; and when these too by their fall had raised a mountain of carcasses, such as remained ascending the pile, poured their javelins upon us as from a rampart, and even returned the darts thrown at them by our men. Fame therefore deceived not, in proclaiming so loudly the bravery of a people, who thus adventured to cross a very broad river, climb the steepest banks, and rush upon an enemy possessed of all the advantages of ground: difficulties, which, though seemingly insurmountable, appeared yet as nothing to men of their resolution and magnanimity.

XXVIII. The battle being ended, and the name and nation of the Nervians in a manner quite extinguished, the old men, who, with the women and children, as we have related above, had been conveyed into a place surrounded with bogs and marshes, hearing of this terrible overthrow, and judging that nothing would be able to stop the progress of the conquerors, or protect the conquered from their victorious arms, resolved, with the consent of all that survived the late disaster, to send ambassadors to Cæsar and surrender themselves. These, in reciting the calamities of their country, represented, that of six hundred senators, there remained only three; and that from sixty thousand fighting men, they were reduced to five hundred. Cæsar, as a proof of his compassion towards this brave and unfortunate people, readily took them under his protection, allowing them free and full possession of their towns and territories, and strictly commanding all the neighbouring nations to abstain from injuries and wrongs.

XXIX. The Atuatici, of whom mention has been made above, being upon their march with all their forces to join the Nervians, and hearing of their defeat, immediately returned home; when abandoning all their other towns and castles, they conveyed themselves and their riches into a place of great strength, which nature had fortified with uncommon care; for it was on every side surrounded with high rocks and precipices, having only one avenue of about two hundred feet broad, that approached the town with a gentle rising. Here they raised a double wall of prodigious height, whereon, as a further security, they laid great numbers of huge stones, and strong pointed beams. This people were descended from the Teutones and Cimbri, who, in their march towards the Alps and Italy, left their heavy baggage on this side the Rhine, with a detachment of six thousand men to guard it. These, after the final overthrow of their countrymen, being for many years harassed and persecuted by the neighbouring states, sometimes invading others, sometimes defending themselves, at last, with the consent of all the bordering nations, obtained peace, and chose this place for a habitation.

XXX. On the first arrival of the Roman army, they made frequent sallies from the town, and engaged our men in small skirmishes. But Cæsar having drawn a line of contravallation, twelve feet high, fifteen miles in circumference, and every where well fortified with redoubts, they kept themselves within their walls. When we had now finished our approaches, cast up a mount, and were preparing a tower of assault behind the works, they began at first to deride us from the battlements, and in reproachful language ask the meaning of that prodigious engine raised at such a distance! With what hands or strength, men of our size and make, (for the Gauls, who are for the most part very tall, despise the small stature of the Romans,) could hope to bring forward so unwieldy a machine against their walls!

XXXI. But when they saw it removed and approaching near the town, astonished at the new and unusual appearance, they sent ambassadors to Cæsar to sue for peace.

These being accordingly introduced, told him: "That they doubted not but the Romans were aided in their wars by the gods themselves, it seeming to them a more than human task to transport with such facility an engine of that amazing height, by which they were brought upon a level with their enemies, and enabled to engage them in close fight. That they therefore put themselves and fortune into his hands, requesting only, that if his clemency and goodness, of which they had heard so much from others, had determined him to spare the Atuatici, he would not deprive them of their arms: that the neighbouring nations were almost all their enemies, as envying their superior valour, nor would it be possible for them to defend themselves from their attacks, if their arms were taken away: in fine, that if such must be their fate, they would rather choose to undergo any fortune from the hands of the Romans, than expose themselves to be cruelly butchered by those over whom they had been wont to exercise dominion."

XXXII. To this Cæsar replied: "That in regard of his usual conduct on these occasions, rather than for any merit of theirs, he was willing to grant them terms of peace, provided they submitted before the battering-ram touched their walls; but that no surrender would be accepted unless they agreed to deliver up their arms: that he would take the same care of them as he had done before of the Nervians, and lay his express commands upon the neighbouring nations to abstain from all injuries towards a people who had put themselves under the protection of the Romans." The ambassadors returning with this answer to their countrymen, they accepted in appearance the conditions offered them by Cæsar, and threw so vast a quantity of arms into the ditch before the town, that the heap almost reached to the top of the wall. Nevertheless, as was afterwards known, they retained about a third part, and concealed them privately within the town. The gates being thrown open, they enjoyed peace for the remaining part of that day.

XXXIII. In the evening Cæsar ordered the gates to be shut, and the soldiers to quit the town, that no injury might be offered to the inhabitants during the night. Whereupon, the Atuatici, in consequence of a design they had before concerted, imagining that the Romans, after a surrender of the place, would either set no guard at all, or at least keep watch with less precaution; partly arming themselves with such weapons as they had privately retained, partly with targets made of bark or wicker, and covered over hastily with hides, made a furious sally about midnight with all their forces, and charged our works on that side where they seemed to be of easiest access.

XXXIV. The alarm being immediately given, by lighting fires, as Cæsar before commanded, the soldiers ran to the attack from the neighbouring forts. A very sharp conflict ensued, for the enemy now driven to despair, and having no hope but in their valour, fought with all possible bravery, though the Romans had the advantage of the ground, and poured their javelins upon them both from the towers and the top of the rampart. About four thousand were slain upon the spot, and the rest obliged to retire into the town. Next day the gates were forced, no one offering to make the least resistance, and the army having taken possession of the place, the inhabitants, to the number of fifty-three thousand, were sold for slaves.

XXXV. About the same time P. Crassus, whom Cæsar had sent with a legion against the Venetians, Unellians, Osismians, Curiosolitæ, Sesuvians, Aulerci, and Rhedones, maritime states inhabiting along the sea coast, despatched messengers to acquaint him, that all these nations had submitted to the dominion and authority of the Romans.

XXXVI. The campaign being ended, and all the provinces of Gaul subdued, such was the opinion conceived of this war amongst all the barbarians round about, that even the nations beyond the Rhine sent ambassadors to Cæsar, offering to give hostages, and submit to his commands. But he being then in haste to return to Italy and Illyricum, ordered them to attend him the next spring. Meantime, having disposed his army into winter quarters in the territories of the Andes, Turones and Carnutes, which states lay the nearest to the provinces that had been the seat of the war, he himself set out for Italy. The senate being informed of these successes by Cæsar's letters, decreed a thanksgiving of fifteen days; a number never allowed to any general before.

CÆSAR'S COMMENTARIES

OF

HIS WARS IN GAUL.

BOOK III.

111

THE ARGUMENT.

I. The Nantuates, Veragrians, and Seduni, fall unexpectedly upon Ser. Galba, Cæsar's lieutenant.—III. But are overthrown with great slaughter.—VI. Galba leads back his legion into the country of the Allobrogians. —VII. At the same time, the Venetians, and other states bordering upon the ocean, revolt.—IX. Cæsar prepares to attack them, not without great difficulty.—X. He divides his army, and distributes it into the several provinces of Gaul.—XII. The advantages of the Venetians, and the manner of their defence.—XIII. A description of their shipping, and its suitableness to the nature of the coast.—XIV. Cæsar finding it in vain to attack them by land, comes to a naval engagement with them, and gets the victory.—XVII. Meantime, Q. Titurius Sabinus, his lieutenant, by an artful stratagem, defeats the Unellians.—XXI. At the same time, P. Crassus, in Aquitain, having vanquished the Sotiates, obliges them to submit.—XXIV. Together with several other states of the same province.—XXIX. Cæsar attacks the Morini and Menapians with success; but the season being far advanced, he is obliged to send his army into winter quarters.

CÆSAR'S COMMENTARIES

OF

HIS WARS IN GAUL.

BOOK III.

I. CÆSAR, upon his departure for Italy, sent Sergius Galba with the twelfth legion, and part of the cavalry, against the Nantuates, Veragrians and Seduni, whose territories extended from the confines of the Allobrogians, the Lake Lemanus, and the river Rhone, all the way to the top of the Alps. His design in this expedition was to open a free passage over those mountains to the Roman merchants, who had hitherto travelled them with great danger, and subject to many grievous exactions. Galba, whose orders also were to put the legion into winter quarters in those parts, if he saw it necessary, after some successful encounters, and making himself master of several forts, was addressed by ambassadors from all nations round. Having settled the terms of peace, and received hostages for their fidelity, he resolved to quarter two cohorts among the Nantuates, and himself, with the other cohorts, to winter in a town of the Veragrians, called Octodurus. This town, which is situated in the midst of a valley, upon a plain of no great extent, is bounded on all sides by very high mountains. As it was divided into two parts by a river, he left one part to the Gauls, and assigned the other to his legion for their winter-quarters, commanding it to be fortified with a ditch and rampart.

II. After many days spent here, and that orders had been given, for the bringing in of corn to supply the camp, he was suddenly informed by his spies, that the Gauls had abandoned in the night that part of the city allotted to them, and that the impending mountains were covered with great multitudes of the Veragrians and Seduni. Many reasons conspired to induce the Gauls to this sudden resolution of renewing the war, and falling upon our men. First, the small number of the Roman troops, who were therefore despised by the enemy, as not amounting in all to one legion : two entire cohorts having been detached, and even of those that remained with Galba, many being gone out in quest of provisions ; and then their persuasion, that by reason of the inequality of the ground, where it would be easy for them to pour upon us from the top of the mountains, and overwhelm us with their darts, our men would not be able to stand the very first assault. Add to all this, their inward regret at seeing their children torn from them under the name of hostages, and that they firmly believed it to be the design of the Romans, in seizing the summits of the mountains, not only to open a free passage over the Alps, but to secure to themselves the perpetual possession of those parts, and annex them to the adjoining province.

III. Upon this intelligence, Galba, who had neither completed the fortifications of his camp, nor laid in sufficient stores of corn and other provisions, as little apprehending an insurrection of this kind, among a people that had submitted and given hostages, having speedily assembled a council of war, began to ask their advice in the present exigence. As the danger which threatened them was sudden and unexpected, and as they saw the mountains on every side covered with multi tudes of armed soldiers, insomuch that there was no room to hope, either for succours, or any convoys of provision, because the enemy were in possession of all the avenues to the camp; some believing the case to be altogether desperate, proposed to abandon the baggage, and attempt by a sally the recovery of their old quarters. But the greater number were for reserving this expedient to the last extremity, and in the meantime to wait the decision of fortune, and in the best manner they were able, defend the camp.

IV. After a short space, and even before there was sufficient time for the putting in execution what had been resolved on, the enemy, at a signal given, came rushing upon us from all parts, and began the assault by a shower of stones and darts. Our men at first made a brave and vigorous resistance, plying them with their javelins from the ramparts, whence not a single weapon was discharged in vain; and as any part of the camp appeared hard pressed for want of men to defend it, thither they ran, and made head against the assailants. But in this the Gauls had greatly the advantage, that when fatigued with the length of the fight, they found themselves under a necessity to retire, fresh men succeeded in their place, whereas on our side, by reason of the small number of troops, no resource of this kind was left; so that not only such as were wearied with fighting were yet obliged to continue in their posts, but we could not even permit the wounded to retire, or for a moment to abandon the charge.

V. The battle had now lasted upwards of six hours without intermission, insomuch, that the Romans not only found their strength greatly exhausted, but even began to be in want of weapons, wherewith to annoy the enemy. The Gauls, on the other hand, urged the combat with greater fury than ever, and meeting with but a faint resistance, fell to demolishing the rampart and filling up the ditch. All was giving way before them, when P. Sextius Baculus, a centurion of the first rank, the same, who, as we have related above, received so many wounds in the battle against the Nervians; as likewise C. Volusenus, a military tribune, one equally distinguished for his conduct and bravery, came to Galba, and represented: That the only refuge now left, was by a sudden sally, to put all upon the issue of a bold attack. Accordingly, Galba,

calling the centurions together, by them gave immediate notice to the soldiers to keep for some time only on the defensive, and having provided themselves with the weapons thrown at them by the enemy, and a little recovered their strength, upon a signal given, to sally out of the camp, and place all their hopes of safety in their valour. These orders were exactly followed: and the Romans rushing furiously upon the enemy from all parts, neither gave them time to comprehend the meaning of so unexpected an attack, nor to recover out of the confusion into which it had thrown them. Thus fortune changing sides, they every where surrounded and put to the sword the Gauls, who had so lately entertained hopes of mastering our camp. Of thirty thousand armed troops, which number, as it appeared afterwards, were present in this assault, more than ten thousand perished in the field. The rest fled in great terror and confusion, and were even forced to abandon the summits of the mountains. The Romans seeing the enemy entirely dispersed, and obliged every where to throw down their arms, quitted the pursuit, and retired within their intrenchments.

VI. After this battle, Galba, unwilling a second time to expose himself to the inconstancy of fortune, and besides, considering that he had met with an opposition he little expected, when he first resolved to winter in these parts; above all, finding himself in great want of corn and forage, the next day set fire to the town, and began his march back into the province. As there was no enemy in the field to disturb or oppose him in his retreat, he brought the legion safe into the country of the Nantuates, and thence into the territories of the Allobrogians, where he put them into winter quarters.

VII. The insurrection being thus entirely quelled, Cæsar, for many reasons, believed that Gaul was now restored to a state of tranquillity. The Belgians had been overcome, the Germans quelled, and the Seduni, and other inhabitants of the Alps, forced to submit. He therefore, in the beginning of winter, ventured upon a progress into Illyricum, from a desire he had to visit those nations, and acquaint himself with the country, when all on a sudden a new war broke out in Gaul. The occasion of it was as follows: the seventh legion, commanded by young Crassus, was quartered among the Andes, a people bordering upon the ocean. As there was great scarcity of corn in these parts, Crassus sent some officers of the cavalry and military tribunes to solicit a supply from the neighbouring states. Of this number were T. Terrasidius, sent to the Eusubians, M. Trebius Gallus, to the Curiosolitæ, and Q. Velanius, and T. Silius, to the Venetians.

VIII. This last state is by far the most powerful and considerable of all the nations inhabiting along the sea coast; and that not only on account of their vast shipping, wherewith they drive a mighty traffic to Britain, and their skill and experience in naval affairs, in which they greatly surpass the other maritime states; but because lying upon a large and open coast, against which the sea rages with great violence, and where the havens, being few in number, are all subject to their jurisdiction; they have most of the nations that trade in those seas tributaries to their state. Among them the revolt began, by detaining Silius and Velanius, as by this means they hoped to recover the hostages they had put into the hands of Crassus. The neighbouring states, moved by their authority and example, as the Gauls are in general very sudden and forward in their resolves, detained for the same reason Trebius and Terrasidius, and speedily despatching ambassadors from one to another, they, by their princes, entered into a confederacy of acting in all things with common consent, and alike exposing themselves to the same issue of fortune, earnestly soliciting at the same time the other provinces, rather to stand up in defence of that liberty they had received of their ancestors, than tamely submit to the ignominious yoke of the Romans. All the nations upon the sea coast coming readily into this alliance, they jointly sent ambassadors to Crassus, to acquaint him: "That if he expected to have his officers restored, he must first send them back their hostages."

IX. Cæsar having intelligence of these things from Crassus, and being then at a great distance from Gaul, ordered in the meantime, that a number of galleys should be built upon the Loire, a river which runs into the ocean; and that mariners, rowers, and pilots should be drawn together from the province. These orders being executed with great despatch, he himself, as soon as the season of the year permitted, came to the army. The Venetians, and other states in alliance with them, having no-

tice of his arrival, and reflecting at the same time upon the greatness of their crime, in detaining and loading with irons ambassadors, a name ever looked upon amongst all nations as sacred and inviolable, began to make preparations proportioned to the danger that threatened them, more especially to provide themselves with all kinds of warlike stores, and that with so much the greater alacrity and confidence, as the nature and situation of the country gave them good hopes of being able to defend themselves. They knew that the passes by land were every where cut asunder, by the many friths and arms of the ocean that run up in those parts; and that the approach by sea was not less difficult, on account of the small number of harbours and the little knowledge the Romans had of the coast. Neither did they imagine it possible for our army to continue long in that country, by reason of the great scarcity of corn; and should even all these expectations deceive them, they had still a mighty confidence in the strength and number of their shipping. The Romans, they were sensible, had but a very inconsiderable fleet; and were besides perfect strangers to the ports, islands, and shallows of the coast, where the chief weight of the war was like to fall. At the time they foresaw that our pilots, accustomed only to the navigation of the Mediterranean, a sea bounded and shut in on all sides by the continent, must needs find themselves greatly at a loss, when they came to enter the vast and open spaces of the wide Atlantic ocean. In consequence of these reflections, and the resolutions formed upon them, they set about fortifying their towns, and conveying all their corn into places of strength, ordering as many ships as could be got together to rendezvous in the Venetian ports; it appearing, that Cæsar intended to begin the war by attacking that state. They likewise brought over to their alliance the Osismians, Lexovians, Nannetes, Ambiani, Merini, Diablintes, and Menapians, and despatched ambassadors into Britain, which lies over against their coast, to solicit assistance from thence.

X. All these difficulties before mentioned attended the prosecution of this war: but Cæsar was urged by many considerations to undertake and carry it on with vigour: the insult offered to the commonwealth in detaining the Roman knights; a revolt and insurrection after submission, and hostages given ; the confederacy of so many states : above all his fear, lest by neglecting to oppose these first commotions, he should give encouragement to the other provinces of Gaul to follow the example. Reflecting, therefore, upon the genius and temper of the Gauls, fond of revolutions, and ever forward and ready to engage in new wars, and considering at the same time, that it was the natural bent and disposition of mankind to aspire after liberty, and abhor the yoke of servitude, he determined, before the infection should spread wider, to divide his army, and distribute it into the several provinces of Gaul.

XI. Pursuant to this design, T. Labienus, his lieutenant, was sent with the cavalry to Treves, whose territory extends along the banks of the Rhine. To him he gave it in charge, to take a progress to Rheims, and the other Belgian states, in order to retain them in obedience, as likewise to oppose the Germans, should they attempt by force the passage of the river ; a report then prevailing, that they had been invited over by the Belgians. P. Crassus, with twelve legionary cohorts, and a great body of horse, had orders to march into Aquitain, to prevent the arrival of any supplies from that quarter, and the junction of the forces of so many powerful nations. Q. Titurius Sabinus, at the head of three legions, entered the country of the Unellians, Curiosolitæ, and Lexovians, to find employment for the troops that had been drawn together in those parts. To young Brutus he gave the command of the fleet, and of all the vessels from Gaul, which he had ordered to be fitted out by the Santones, Pictones and other provinces that continued in obedience, strongly recommending to him at the same time, to use the greatest despatch, and sail with all expedition for the Venetian coast. He himself, at the head of the land army, set out upon his march thither.

XII. The situation of most of the towns in those parts is such, that standing upon the edges of promontories, or upon points of land that run out into the sea, there is no approaching them with an army at high water, which happens always twice in twelve hours. Neither is it possible for a fleet to draw near ; because, upon the recess of the tide, the ships would be in danger of being dashed against the shallows and banks of sand. Both these

reasons therefore concurred to secure their towns from assault ; and if at any time, by the greatness of the works carried on against them, and huge artificial mounts, that served to prevent the ingress of the sea, and were raised to a height nearly equalling their walls, they saw themselves reduced to an extremity, then, by bringing up their ships, of which they had always a great number in readiness, they easily found means to carry off their effects, and withdraw into the nearest towns, where they again defended themselves by the same advantages of situation as before. In this manner did they elude all Cæsar's attempts during a great part of the summer, and that with so much the more success, because our fleet was kept back by tempests, and found the navigation extremely dangerous in that vast and boundless ocean, where the tides are great, and the havens both few in number, and at a considerable distance one from another.

XIII. For the Venetian ships were built and fitted out in this manner : Their bottoms were somewhat flatter than ours, the better to adapt themselves to the shallows, and sustain without danger the regress of the tides. Their prows were very high and erect, as likewise their sterns, to bear the hugeness of the billows, and the violence of tempests. The body of the vessel was entirely of oak, to stand the shocks and assaults of that tempestuous ocean. The benches of the rowers were made of strong beams of about a foot in breadth, and fastened with iron nails an inch thick. Instead of cables, they secured their anchors with chains of iron ; and made use of skins, and a sort of pliant leather, by way of sails, either because they wanted canvass, and were ignorant of the art of making sail-cloth, or which is more probable, because they imagined that canvass sails were not so proper to bear the violence of tempests, the rage and fury of the winds, and to govern ships of that bulk and burthen. Between our fleet, and vessels of such a make, the nature of the encounter was this ; that in agility, and a ready command of oars, we had indeed the advantage, but in other respects, regarding the situation of the coast, and the assaults of storms, all things ran very much in their favour ; for neither could our ships injure them with our beaks, so great was their strength and firmness ; nor could we easily throw in our darts, because of their height above us; which also was the reason, that we found it extremely difficult to grapple the enemy, and bring them to close fight. Add to all this, that when the sea began to rage, and they were forced to submit to the pleasure of the winds, they could both weather the storm better, and more securely trust themselves among the shallows, as fearing nothing from the rocks and cliffs upon the recess of the tide. The Romans, on the other hand, had reason to be under a continual dread of these and such like accidents.

XIV. Cæsar having taken many of their towns, and finding that he only fatigued his army to no purpose, because he could neither prevent the retreat of the enemy, nor force their garrisons to a surrender, resolved to wait the arrival of his fleet; which being accordingly come up, was no sooner descried by the Venetians, than about two hundred and twenty of their best ships, well equipped for service, and furnished with all kind of weapons, stood out to sea, and drew up in order of battle, against us. Neither Brutus, who commanded the fleet, nor the centurions and military tribunes who had the charge of particular vessels, knew what course to take, or in what manner to conduct the fight; for they were no strangers to the strength and firmness of the Venetian shipping, which rendered them proof against our beaks; and when they had even raised turrets upon the decks, yet being still overtopped by the lofty sterns of the enemy, the Romans could not with any advantage throw in their darts; whereas those sent by the Gauls, coming from above, descended with great violence on our men. In this exigence, a particular kind of instrument, used by the mariners, proved of signal service, in giving a favourable issue to the combat. They had provided themselves with long poles, armed at one end with long scythes, not unlike those made use of in attacking the walls of towns. With these they laid hold of the enemy's tackle, and drawing off the galley by the extreme force of oars, cut asunder the ropes that fastened the sail-yards to the mast. These giving way, the sail-yards necessarily came down; insomuch, that as all the hopes and expectations of the Gauls depended entirely on their sails and rigging, by depriving them of this resource, we at the same time rendered their vessels wholly unserviceable. The rest

depended altogether upon the valour of the troops, in which the Romans had greatly the advantage; and the rather, because they fought within view of Cæsar and the whole army, so that not a single act of bravery could pass unobserved; for all the adjoining hills and eminences which afforded a near prospect of the sea, were covered with our men.

XV. The enemy's sail yards being, as we have said, cut down, and many of their ships singly surrounded by two or three of ours at a time, the Romans used their utmost endeavours to board them; which the Venetians observing, and that we had already made ourselves masters of a great part of their fleet, as they could fall upon no expedient to prevent so great a misfortune, they began to think of providing for their safety by flight. Accordingly they tacked about, in order to have the advantage of the wind, when all of a sudden so dead a calm ensued, that not a vessel could stir out of its place: nor could any thing have fallen out more opportunely towards putting at once a final period to the war; for the Romans attacking their ships one after another, took them with ease, insomuch, that of all that vast number that came out against us, but a very few, under favour of the night, escaped to land, after a conflict that continued from nine in the morning till sun-set.

XVI. This battle put an end to the war with the Venetians, and all the nations upon the sea coast. For as the entire body of their youth, and all those also of more advanced age, who were capable of serving their country by their credit and counsels, were present in the action, and as they had likewise drawn together their whole naval strength; such as survived this defeat, having neither any place of refuge whereunto to retire, nor means left of defending their towns, surrendered themselves and their all to Cæsar's mercy. But he thought it necessary to proceed against them with the greater severity, that he might impress upon the mind of the Gauls for the future, a more inviolable regard to the sacred character of ambassadors. Having therefore caused all their senators to be put to death, he ordered the rest to be sold for slaves.

XVII. During these transactions against the Venetians, Q. Titurius Sabinus entered the territories of the Unellians, at the head of the troops put under his command by Cæsar, Viridovix was invested with the supreme au-

11*

thority in these parts, and had been appointed general in chief by all the states concerned in the revolt: out of which he had drawn together a very numerous and powerful army. Nay, but a very few days before, the Aulerci, Eburovices, and Lexovians, having massacred their senate, because they refused to engage in the war, had shut their gates against the Romans, and joined themselves to Viridovix. Besides all this, he had very much strengthened his army by the great numbers that flocked to him from all parts of Gaul; men of desperate fortunes, or accustomed to live by robbery, whom the hopes of plunder, and love of war had drawn off from the daily labours of their calling and the cares of agriculture.

XVIII. Sabinus kept close within his camp, which was situated in a manner every way advantageous, while Viridovix, who had posted himself at the distance of about two miles, daily drew out his men, and offered him battle. This behaviour of the Roman general not only drew upon him the contempt of the enemy, but occasioned also some murmuring among his own troops, and filled the Gauls with so high a conceit of his fear, that they even adventured to come up to his very trenches. The reason of his acting in this manner was, that he thought it not justifiable in a lieutenant, in the absence of the commander in chief, to hazard a battle with so superior an army, unless upon terms of evident advantage.

XIX. Having confirmed them in this belief, that his reserve was the effect of fear, he made choice of a certain Gaul from among the auxiliaries, a man of address, and every way qualified for carrying on his design. Him he persuaded, by great rewards, and still greater promises, to go over to the enemy, instructing him at the same time in the part he was to act. This Gaul, coming to their camp as a deserter, laid before them the fear of the Romans, and the extremities to which Cæsar was reduced in the war against the Venetians; nor did he fail to insinuate, that there was great reason to believe Sabinus intended the next night privately to draw off his army, and march to Cæsar's assistance. No sooner was this heard by the Gauls, than they all cried out with one voice, that they ought not to lose so fair an occasion of success, but to go and attack the Roman camp. Many reasons concurred to fix them in this resolution. The reserve of Sabinus for some days past; the in-

telligence from the deserter, confirming their belief of his fear; the want of provisions, of which they had taken no great care to lay in a sufficient stock; the hopes conceived from the Venetian war; and, in fine, that readiness with which men are apt to believe what falls in with their expectations and wishes. Urged by these considerations, they would not suffer Viridovix and the rest of the general officers to dismiss the council before they had obtained their consent for the taking up of arms, and falling upon the Roman camp. The proposal being at last agreed to, they provided themselves with fascines and hurdles, to fill up the ditch, and joyfully began their march, as to a certain victory.

XX. The Roman camp stood upon an eminence, which rose with a gentle ascent, for the space of about a mile. Hither the Gauls advanced with so much haste, in order to come upon our troops unprepared, that by that time they were arrived, they had run themselves quite out of breath. Sabinus having encouraged his men, whom he saw eager to engage, gave the word of onset. As the enemy were very much encumbered with the loads of fascines they had brought to fill up the ditch, he ordered a sudden sally from the two several gates of the camp, and so well did it succeed, by reason of the advantage of the ground, the inexperience and weariness of the Gauls, the bravery of the Roman troops, and their ability acquired in former battles, that the enemy could not sustain the very first charge of our men, but immediately betook themselves to flight. The Romans, who were fresh and vigorous, pursuing them under all these disadvantages, put great numbers to the sword, and the rest being followed by the cavalry, very few escaped the slaughter. Thus at one and the same time, Sabinus had an account of the defeat of the Venetians by sea, and Cæsar of the victory obtained by Sabinus at land. All the several states in those parts readily submitted to Titurius: for as the Gauls are very prompt and forward to undertake a war, so are they of a disposition that easily relents, and gives way to the strokes of adversity.

XXI. Much about the same time P. Crassus arrived in Aquitain, a country, which as we have before observed, for extent of territory, and number of inhabitants, is deservedly counted a third part of Gaul. This general understanding that he was to conduct a war

in those parts, where but a few years before
L. Valerius Præconinus had been slain, and
his army put to the rout, and whence L.
Manilius, the proconsul, had been driven with
the loss of his baggage, soon became sensible
that he must act with more than ordinary circumspection and vigour. Having therefore
made provision of corn, assembled his auxiliary troops and cavalry, and strengthened his
army with a choice body of volunteers, drawn
together by name from Toulouse, Carcaso, and
Narbonne, which states make up that part of
the Roman province that lies the nearest to
Aquitain, he advanced with all his forces into
the territories of the Sotiates. These, upon
the first notice of his arrival, having levied a
great army, and attacking him in his march
with the whole body of their cavalry, in which
their chief strength consisted, were nevertheless repulsed and pursued by our men. But all
on a sudden their infantry appearing in a valley, where they had been designedly placed in
ambush, fell furiously upon the Romans, disordered with the pursuit, and renewed the fight.

XXII. The battle was long and obstinate.
For the Sotiates, proud of their former victories, imagined that the fate of all Aquitain
depended singly on their bravery. The Romans, on the other hand, were ambitious of
showing what they could achieve under a
young leader, in the absence of their general,
and unsupported by the rest of the legions.
At length, however, the enemy, overpowered
with wounds, betook themselves to flight, and
a great slaughter ensuing, Crassus marched
immediately and invested their capital, where
meeting with a brave resistance, he was forced
to make his approaches by towers and mantelets. The enemy sometimes sallying out,
sometimes carrying on their mines to our very
works, (in which kind of service the Aquitains
are particularly skilful, as inhabiting a country
that abounds in veins of copper,) when they
saw that the diligence of the Romans enabled
them to surmount all these difficulties, sent
ambassadors to Crassus, and requested they
might be admitted to a surrender: which being accordingly agreed to, they, in obedience
to his desire, delivered up their arms.

XXIII. But while the Romans were wholly
intent upon the execution of the treaty, Adiatomus, who commanded in chief, endeavoured
to escape on the other side of the town, with
a body of six hundred sworn friends, who,

in the language of the country, are called Sol-
durians. Their condition and manner of life
is this: To live in a perfect community of
goods with those to whom they have engaged
themselves in friendship; if any misfortune
befalls them, to share in it, or make away with
themselves; nor is there a single instance of
any one upon record, who, upon the death of
him to whom he had vowed a friendship, refused to submit to the same fate. Adiatomus,
as we have said, endeavouring to make his
escape with his body of friends, and the alarm
being given on that side of the works, the
soldiers immediately ran to arms, when a furious combat ensued, in which he was at last
repulsed, and driven back into the town. He
obtained, however, from Crassus, the same
conditions of surrender as had been granted to
the rest of the inhabitants.

XXIV. Crassus having received their arms
and hostages, led his troops into the territories
of the Vocatians and Tarusatians. But now,
the Gauls, roused by the unexpected progress
of the Romans, who had in a few days after
their arrival made themselves masters of a
town strongly fortified both by art and nature,
began to send ambassadors into all parts, to
join in a mutual league, to ratify their engagements by an exchange of hostages, and to levy
troops. Ambassadors were likewise despatched
to all the states of hither Spain that bordered
upon Aquitain, to solicit a supply of troops
and leaders: upon whose arrival, they immediately took the field with great confidence,
and a numerous and well appointed army.
None were suffered to command but such as
had served under Sertorius, and were therefore accounted men of consummate ability
and experience in the art of war. These, according to the custom of the Romans, made it
their study to choose a camp to advantage, to
secure themselves by lines and intrenchments,
and to intercept our convoys. Crassus, perceiving their design, as his own army was not
strong enough to admit of sending out detachments, and as the Gauls could upon all occasions employ numerous parties, possess themselves of the passes, and at the same time have
a sufficient number of troops to guard the
camp, by which means he foresaw he must
soon be reduced to great straits for want of
provisions, while the enemy would be every
day growing more powerful, he, for all these
reasons, resolved not to delay coming to an

engagement. Having laid his design before a council of war, and finding them unanimous in their approbation of it, he appointed the next day for the engagement.

XXV. Early in the morning he drew all his forces out of the camp, and disposing them in two lines, with the auxiliary troops in the centre, stood expecting what resolution the enemy would take. But the Gauls, though they believed they might safely hazard a battle, on account of their numbers, their former renown in war, and the handful of men they were to oppose; yet thought it would be still better, by seizing the passes, and intercepting our convoys, to secure the victory without expense of blood: and should the want of provisions at length force the Romans to think of a retreat, they might then fall upon them, embarrassed in their march, encumbered with their baggage, and dejected by their misfortunes. This resolution being approved by all their leaders, they kept within their camp, though our men appeared before them in order of battle.

XXVI. Crassus, perceiving their design, and that this delay served rather to abate the courage of the enemy, and add fresh spirits to his own men, among whom a universal cry arose, that he ought no longer to put off the engagement, but march directly to their camp; having encouraged his troops, he resolved to give way to their present ardour, and accordingly led them to the assault. There some were employed in filling up the ditch, others in driving the enemy with their darts from the works; while the auxiliaries, in whom Crassus had no great confidence, yet that they might appear to have some share at least in the engagement, were appointed to carry stones and darts to them that fought, and to supply materials for raising the mount. At the same time the enemy fought with great constancy and resolution, and made no small havoc with their darts, which came upon us from above. During this warmth of opposition, the cavalry, having taken a compass round the camp, came and told Crassus that the intrenchments were not fortified with the same care in all parts, and that it would be easy to force an entrance by the postern gate.

XXVII. Crassus, having exhorted the officers of the cavalry to encourage their men by great rewards and promises, instructed

them in the part they were to act. They, in consequence of the orders they had received, drawing out four cohorts, which, having been left to guard the camp, were quite fresh and fit for action, and fetching with them a large compass, that they might not be seen from the enemy's camp; while the eyes and minds of all were intent upon the combat, fell suddenly upon that part of the intrenchments of which we have spoken above; and having forced their way through, were actually got within the camp before they were so much as seen by the enemy, or any apprehension entertained of what they were about. Upon this, a great uproar being heard on that side, our men redoubled their efforts, and, as always happens to troops animated with the hopes of victory, began to push the Gauls with greater fury than ever. The enemy, thus surrounded on all sides, and without hopes of retrieving their affairs, endeavoured to make their escape over the rampart, and save themselves by flight. But being pursued by the cavalry, who soon came up with them in these open and level plains; of fifty thousand men that had been drawn together out of Spain and Aquitain, scarce a fourth part escaped; nor did the horse return to the camp until very late in the evening, after they had quite tired themselves with the slaughter.

XXVIII. Upon the report of this defeat, the greatest part of Aquitain immediately submitted to Crassus, and of their own accord sent him hostages. Of this number were the Tarbelli, Bigerriones, Preciani, Vocates, Tarusates, Elusates, Garites, Ausci, Garumni, Siburzates, and Cocasates. Only a few nations, and those the most remote, relying on the season of the year, because the winter was at hand, neglected to take this step.

XXIX. Much about the same time Cæsar, though the summer was now almost spent, yet because all the rest of Gaul being subdued, the Morini and Menapians were still in arms, and had not sent ambassadors to treat about a peace, resolved to lead his army against them, hoping he should soon be able to put an end to that war. Their manner of opposing him was very different from that of the other Gauls. For, understanding that the most powerful nations, when it came to a battle, had always been overthrown and put to rout; and inhabiting themselves in a country that abounded in woods and marshes, they retired thither with all their effects. Cæsar coming to the entrance of the wood, began to intrench himself: and although no enemy in the meantime appeared, yet no sooner had our men dispersed themselves in order to set about fortifying the camp, than on a sudden they came pouring upon us from all parts of the wood, and charged with great briskness. The Romans immediately flew to their arms, and drove them back with considerable slaughter; but adventuring a little too far into the wood lost some men.

XXX. Cæsar spent the remaining days in cutting down the wood; and to screen his men from any sudden and unexpected attack, ordered the trees that had been felled to be placed on each side the army, that they might serve as a barricade against the attempts of the enemy. Having with incredible despatch advanced a great way into the wood in a few days, insomuch that all their cattle and baggage fell into our hands, they themselves retired into the thicker and more covered spaces of the forest. The season growing bad, we were forced to intermit the work: and the rains soon became so violent and continual that the soldiers could no longer endure to lie in their tents. Wherefore Cæsar, having laid waste their lands, and set fire to their towns and houses, led back his army, and disposed it into winter quarters among the Aulerci, Lexovians, and other states, whom he had last subdued.

CÆSAR'S COMMENTARIES

OF

HIS WARS IN GAUL.

BOOK IV.

THE ARGUMENT.

I. The Usipetes and Tenchtheri, German nations expelled by the Suevians, come over into Gaul.—II. The manners and way of life of the Suevians.—III. And of the Ubians.—IV. The Usipetes and Tenchtheri drive the Menapians from their habitations.—V. Cæsar, knowing the wavering and unsettled temper of the Gauls, repairs early in the spring to the army.—VI. Embassy of the Germans to Cæsar, and his answer.—IX. An action between the cavalry, in which the Germans have the advantage.—X. But are afterwards driven from their camp with great slaughter.—XIII. And pursued by Cæsar, who makes a bridge over the Rhine for that purpose.—XVI. Cæsar lays waste the territories of the Sigambri.—XVII. And having freed the Ubians from the servitude under which they lived, returns into Gaul.—XVIII. He then passes over into Britain.—XXII. And lands his army with great difficulty, the natives making a vigorous opposition.—XXIV. They are defeated at length, and send ambassadors to sue for peace.—XXVI. Cæsar's fleet almost entirely ruined by a storm, which induces the Britons to revolt.—XXIX. Their way of fighting from their chariots.—XXX. which disconcerts the Romans at first.—XXXI. But being again put to flight, they obtain peace.—XXXII. After which Cæsar returns into Gaul.—XXXIII. And marching against the Morini, whom the hope of plunder tempted to fall upon some of his detached parties, obliges them to submit.

CÆSAR'S COMMENTARIES

HIS WARS IN GAUL.

BOOK IV.

I. The following winter, being that in which Cn. Pompey and M. Crassus were consuls, the Usipetes and Tenchtheri, German nations, passed the Rhine in a great body, not far from its mouth. The cause of their taking this step was, that being much exposed to the hostilities of the Suevians, they had for many years been harassed with continual wars, and hindered from cultivating their lands.

II. The Suevians are by far the most warlike and considerable of all the German nations. They are said to be composed of a hundred cantons, each of which sends yearly into the field a thousand armed men. The rest, who continue in their several districts, employ themselves in cultivating their lands, that they may furnish a sufficient supply both for themselves and for the army. These again take up arms the following campaign, and are succeeded in the care of the lands by the troops that served the year before. Thus they live in the continual exercise both of agriculture and war. They allow of no such thing as property, or private possession in the distribution of their lands; their residence, for the sake of tillage, being confined to a single year. Corn is not much in use among them, because they prefer a milk or flesh diet, and are greatly addicted to hunting. Thus the quality of their food, their perpetual exercise, and free unconfined manner of life, (because being from their childhood fettered by no rules of duty or education, they acknowledge no law but will and pleasure,) contribute to make them strong, and of an extraordinary stature. They have likewise accustomed themselves, though inhabiting a climate naturally very cold, to bathe in their rivers, and clothe themselves only with skins, which, as they are very small, leave great part of their body quite uncovered. Merchants indeed resort to them, but rather to purchase their spoils taken in war, than import any goods into the country; for even beasts of carriage, in which the Gauls take so much delight, that they are ready to purchase them at any price, are yet very little valued by the Germans, when brought among them. And though those of their own country are both small and very ill shaped, yet by daily exercise they make them capable of all kinds of service. Their cavalry often dismount in time of action, to fight on foot; and their horses are so trained, that they stir not from the place where they are left, but wait the return of their riders, who betake themselves to them again in case of necessity. Nothing is more dishonourable, in their account, or more opposite to their customs, than the use of horse-furniture; and therefore, however few themselves, they scruple not to attack any number of their enemies whom they see so equipped. They suffer no wine to be imported into their territories, as imagining that it both enervates the mind, and unfits the body for exercise and labour. It is accounted much to the honour of the nation, to have the country for a great way round them waste and uninhabited; for by this they think is intimated, that the united force of many states has been found insufficient to withstand their single valour. And hence it is, that on one side, the country is said to lie desolate for the space of six hundred miles.

III. On the other side they are bounded by the Ubians, heretofore a flourishing and potent people, and somewhat more civilized than the other German nations; because inhabiting along the banks of the Rhine, they are much resorted to by merchants; and have besides, by bordering upon the states of Gaul, given into many of their customs. The Suevians having tried the strength of this people in many wars, and finding them too numerous and potent to be driven out of their territories, prevailed yet so far as to impose a tribute upon them, and very much reduce and weaken their power.

IV. The Usipetes and Tenchtheri, of whom we have spoken above, were likewise engaged in this quarrel; and after withstanding the power of the Suevians for many years, were nevertheless at length driven from their territories. Having wandered over many regions of Germany during the space of three years, they arrived at last upon the banks of the Rhine, towards those parts inhabited by the Menapians, who had houses, lands, and villages on both sides of the river. But alarmed at the approach of so prodigious a multitude, they abandoned all their habitations beyond the Rhine; and having disposed their troops on this side the river, set themselves to oppose the passage of the Germans. These having tried every expedient; and finding they could neither force the passage, because of their want of shipping; nor steal over privately by reason of the guards kept by the Menapians, counterfeited a retreat into their own country, and after three days' march, suddenly turned back; when their cavalry, recovering all this ground in the space of one night, easily overpowered the Menapians, little expecting or prepared for such a visit; for having been apprized by their scouts of the departure of the Germans, they had returned, fearless of danger, to their habitations beyond the Rhine. These being all put to the sword, and their shipping seized before the Menapians on this side had intelligence of their approach, they passed the river; and seizing all their towns and houses, supported themselves the rest of the winter with the provisions there found.

V. Cæsar being informed of these things, and dreading the levity of the Gauls, who are very changeable in their counsels, and fond of novelties; determined to trust nothing to their resolves. For it is the custom of that people to stop travellers even against their will, and inquire of them what they have heard or know relating to any affair; and in their towns, upon the arrival of a foreign merchant, they gather round him in crowds, and oblige him to tell what country he comes from, and how things stood at his departure. Moved by these reports, they often enter upon the most important deliberations, and concert measures they soon have cause to repent, as being founded wholly on vain rumours, and answers feigned for the most part designedly to please them. Cæsar, who was aware of this custom, fearing the war, if neglected, might become formidable, made all the haste he could to join the army. Upon his arrival he found, that things were fallen out exactly as he had foreseen. Some of the states of Gaul had sent ambassadors to the Germans, inviting them to leave the banks of the Rhine, and assuring them that all their demands should be readily complied with. The Germans, allured by these hopes, were already extending their incursions on all sides, and had penetrated into the territories of the Eburones and Condrusians, both which nations are under the protection of the Treviri. Cæsar having assembled the chiefs of the Gauls, dissembled his knowledge of their secret designs; and endeavouring rather to win them over, and confirm them in their alliance with the people of Rome, demanded a certain **number of** cavalry of them, and prepared **to march against the Germans.**

VI. Having provided **himself with corn, and** drawn together **a select body of horse, he be-**gan his march **towards** those **parts where he** understood **the** Germans then were. **When he** was come within a few days' journey of their camp, ambassadors arrived from them, who addressed him to this effect:—" That the Germans had no design of being the first to begin a war with the people of Rome; but neither, if they were attacked, would they decline having recourse to arms: that it was the custom of their nation, handed down to them by their ancestors, rather to oppose the efforts of their enemies, than expect relief from remonstrances; but thus far they were however willing to own, that it was against their inclination they were come into those parts, having been driven from their habitations; that if the Romans were disposed to accept of their friendship, they might become very useful and serviceable allies, and would rest satisfied either with such lands as they should think proper to assign them, or in the quiet possession of those they had already obtained by force of arms; that they yielded in valour to the Suevians alone, for whom the immortal gods themselves were not an equal match; but knew of no other nation under heaven able to resist the efforts of their bravery." Cæsar made such a reply as best suited his present views, but the conclusion of his speech was to this purpose :—" That he could enter into no treaty of friendship with them so long as they continued in Gaul; that men who had been unable to defend their own territories were not likely to gain countries by force from others; that there were no uncultivated lands in Gaul, sufficient to satisfy so great a multitude, without invading the properties of others; but that, if they pleased, they might incorporate themselves with the Ubians, whose ambassadors were then in his camp, to complain of the injuries of the Suevians, and request his aid against their encroachments; this he promised to obtain for them of the Ubians." The ambassadors replied, they would report this to their countrymen, and in three days return with an answer; requesting in the meantime, that he would not advance with his army. But this Cæsar refused, as knowing, that a few days before they had sent a great body of cavalry over the Meuse, to forage and plunder in the territories of the Ambivariti. He therefore concluded, that they only waited the return of this party, and with that view were for interposing delays.

VII. The Meuse rises in the mountains of Vause, in the territories of the Lingones, and receiving a certain branch of the Rhine, called the Vahal, forms with it the island of the Batavians, about fourscore miles below which it discharges itself into the sea. The Rhine itself takes its rise in the territories of the Lepontians, who inhabit the Alps; and after a long and rapid course through the country of the Nantuates, Helvetians, Sequani, Mediomatrici, Treboci, and Treviri, divides itself, as it approaches nearer the sea, into several channels, and forming a great number of very large islands, inhabited for the most part by fierce and savage nations, some of whom are reported to feed only on fish and the eggs of birds, it at last discharges itself into the ocean by many different mouths.

VIII. Cæsar being now only twelve miles distant from the enemy, was met upon his way by the ambassadors on the day appointed. They were very earnest in their requests that he would advance no farther; but not being able to prevail, entreated, that he would send to the cavalry, who made the advance-guard, to restrain them from beginning the fight; and in the meantime permit them to send ambassadors to the Ubians; from whose senate and magistrates, if they could obtain the conditions offered them by Cæsar, under the sanction of a solemn oath, they declared themselves ready to accept them; requiring only that he would allow them the space of three days to bring matters to a final issue. But Cæsar, imagining all these proffers to have no other tendency than the delay of a few days, until their cavalry should arrive, told them, nevertheless, that he would advance that day only four miles farther, for the sake of water; but desired their chiefs to attend him the day after, that he might know their demands. Meantime he sent orders to the officers of the cavalry, who were gone before, not to attack the enemy; and in case they should be attacked themselves, only to maintain their ground until he should come up with the rest of the army.

IX. But the enemy, upon seeing our horse advance, whose number amounted to five thousand, whereas they themselves did not exceed eight hundred, by reason of the absence of those who had been sent to forage beyond the Meuse yet falling suddenly upon the Romans, wh: had no apprehension of their design, because they knew their ambassadors had been with Cæsar a little before, and obtained a day's truce, they easily put them into disorder. And when our men, recovering a little, began to make resistance, they, according to custom, dismounted, and stabbing our horses under the belly, and by that means overthrowing many of the riders, in a very short time put the rest to flight; and so great was the consternation, that they continued driving them before them, until at last they came within sight of the army. In this skirmish we lost seventy four men, and among them Piso of Aquitain, a man of distinguished valour and illustrious descent, whose grandfather had been sovereign magistrate in his own state, and been honoured by the senate of Rome with the title of friend. This brave officer, seeing his brother surround ed by the enemy, ran to his assistance, and rescued him; but his own horse being wounded, and he overthrown, the enemy fell upon him, against whom nevertheless he made a brave resistance; till at last, surrounded on all sides, he fell overpowered with wounds. Which his brother perceiving, who was by this time out of danger, and had got to a considerable distance, setting spurs to his horse, he rushed among the thickest of the enemy, and was slain.

X. After this battle, Cæsar resolved neither to give audience to their ambassadors, nor admit them to terms of peace, seeing they had treacherously applied for a truce, and afterwards of their own accord broken it. He likewise considered, that it would be downright madness to delay coming to an action until their army should be augmented, and their cavalry join them; and the more so, because he was perfectly well acquainted with the levity of the Gauls, among whom they had already acquired a considerable reputation by this successful attack, and to whom it therefore behoved him by no means to allow time to enter into measures against him. Upon all these accounts he determined to come to an engagement with the enemy as soon as possible, and communicated his design to his quæstor and lieutenants. A very lucky accident fell out to bring about Cæsar's purpose; for the day after, in the morning, the Germans, persisting in their treachery and dissimulation, came in great numbers to the camp: all their nobility and princes making part of their embassy. Their design was, as they pretended, to vindicate themselves in regard to what had happened the day before; because, contrary to engagements made and come under at their own request, they had fallen upon our men; but their real motive was to obtain if possible another insidious truce. Cæsar, overjoyed to have them thus in his power, ordered them to be secured, and immediately drew his forces out of the camp. The cavalry, whom he supposed terrified with the late engagement, were commanded to follow in the rear.

XI. Having drawn up his army in three lines, and made a very expeditious march of eight miles, he appeared before the enemy's camp before they had the least apprehension of his design. All things conspiring to throw them into a sudden consternation, which was not a little increased by our unexpected ap-

pearance, and the absence of their own officers; and hardly any time left them either to take counsel, or fly to arms, they were utterly at a loss what course to take, whether to draw out their forces and oppose the enemy, or content themselves with defending the camp, or in fine to seek for safety in flight. As this fear was evident from the tumult and uproar we perceived among them, our soldiers, instigated by the remembrance of their treacherous behaviour the day before, broke into the camp. Such as could first provide themselves with arms made a show of resistance, and for some time maintained the fight amidst the baggage and carriages. But the women and children (for the Germans had brought all their families and effects with them over the Rhine) betook themselves to flight on all sides. Cæsar sent the cavalry in pursuit of them.

XII. The Germans hearing the noise behind them, and seeing their wives and children put to the sword, threw down their arms, abandoned their ensigns, and fled out of the camp. Being arrived at the confluence of the Rhine and the Mouse, and finding it impossible to continue their flight any farther; after a dreadful slaughter of those that pretended to make resistance, the rest threw themselves into the river; where, what with fear, weariness, and the force of the current, they almost all perished. Thus our army, without the loss of a man, and with very few wounded, returned to their camp, having put an end to this formidable war, in which the number of the **enemy** amounted to four hundred and thirty thousand. **Cæsar** offered those whom he had detained in his camp liberty to depart; but they, dreading the resentment of the Gauls, whose lands they had laid waste, chose rather to continue with him, and obtained his consent for that purpose.

XIII. The war with the Germans being ended, Cæsar for many reasons resolved to carry his army over the Rhine. But what chiefly swayed with him was, that as he found the Germans were easily prevailed upon to transport their forces into Gaul, he thought it might be of no small service to alarm them upon their own account, by letting them see, that the Romans wanted neither ability nor resolution to pass the Rhine with an army. Add to all this, that the cavalry of the Usipetes and Tenchtheri, who as we have related above, had passed the Meuse for the sake of forage and plunder, and by that means escaped the disaster of the late fight, upon hearing of the defeat of their countrymen, had repassed the Rhine, retired into the territories of the Sicambrians, and joined their forces to theirs. And upon Cæsar's sending deputies to require, that these troops, which had presumed to make war upon him and the Gauls, might be delivered up, he had received for answer;—"That the Rhine was the boundary of the Roman empire; that if he thought it unjustifiable in the Germans to pass over into Gaul without his leave, upon what pretence could he claim any power or authority beyond the Rhine?"

XIV. But the Ubians, who alone of all the nations beyond the Rhine had sent ambassadors to Cæsar, entered into an alliance with him, and given him hostages, earnestly entreated him to come over to their assistance, they being very hard pressed by the Suevians: Or, if the affairs of the commonwealth would not allow of his being there in person, that he would only order his army to cross the Rhine, which would both be sufficient for their present support, and also secure them for the time to come. Because such was the reputation and opinion conceived of a Roman army, even amongst the remote German nations, from their defeating Ariovistus, and the success of the last battle, that their friendship and name would alone be a sufficient defence. They promised likewise a great number of ships for the transporting of the army."

XV. Cæsar, for all these reasons abovementioned, determined to cross the Rhine. But to make use of shipping appeared to him neither safe, nor suitable to the dignity of the Roman name. Wherefore, although he understood that the making of a bridge would be attended with very great difficulties, on account of the breadth, depth, and rapidity of the river, yet was he of opinion, that in this manner alone ought he to carry over his army, or lay aside the design altogether. The form therefore and contrivance of the bridge was thus:—two beams, each a foot and a half thick, sharpened a little toward the lower end, and of a length proportioned to the depth of the river, were joined together at the distance of about two feet. These were sunk into the river by engines, and afterwards strongly driven with rammers, not perpendicularly, but inclined according to the direction of the stream. Directly opposite to these, at the distance of forty feet lower down, were placed two other beams joined together like the former, but sloping against the current of the river. These stakes were kept firm by a large beam, extended from one to the other, and which being two feet in thickness, exactly filled the interval of the two stakes, and was strongly fastened at either end with iron nails, so contrived, that the violence of the stream served only to bind the work faster together. This being continued through the whole breadth of the river, he ordered planks to be laid across, which for the greater convenience of passing, were further covered with hurdles. Towards the lower part of the stream other stakes were sunk in the form of buttresses, which supported the bridge against the violence of the current; and above, at some distance, there were others; that if trunks of trees or vessels should be sent down the river by the enemy, to destroy the work, the shock might be broken by these defences, and the bridge thereby secured from damage.

XVI. The bridge being finished within ten days from the time they began to fetch the materials, Cæsar led over his army; and leaving a strong guard on each side of the river, marched directly into the territories of the Sicambri. Meantime ambassadors arriving from several states to desire peace, and court his alliance, he gave them a very favourable reception, and appointed them to send hostages. The Sicambri, when they understood that the bridge was begun, by advice of the Usipetes and Tenchtheri, who had taken shelter among them, resolved upon a retreat, and having abandoned their territories, and carried off all their effects, withdrew into the neighbouring woods and deserts.

XVII. Cæsar, after a short stay in their country, having burned all their houses and villages, and cut down their corn, marched into the territories of the Ubians. As he had promised these last his assistance against the attempts of the Suevians, he understood from them that the Suevians, being informed by their spies, of the bridge built upon the Rhine, had, according to their custom, called a council, and despatched orders into all parts for the people to forsake their towns, and convey their wives, children, and effects into the woods, commanding, at the same time, that all such as were able to bear arms should meet at the place of general rendezvous, which they had appointed towards the middle of the country, resolving there to wait the arrival of the Romans, and give them battle. Cæsar, upon this intelligence, having accomplished all he intended in carrying his army over the Rhine, by spreading a universal terror among the Germans, taking vengeance of the Sicambri, and setting the Ubians at liberty, after a stay of only eighteen days beyond the Rhine, thinking he had done enough both for his own reputation and the service of the republic, led back his army into Gaul, and broke the bridge.

XVIII. Though but a small part of the summer now remained, for in those regions, Gaul, stretching very much to the north, the winters begin early, Cæsar, nevertheless, resolved to pass over into Britain, having certain intelligence, that in all his wars with the Gauls, the enemies of the commonwealth had ever received assistance from thence. He indeed foresaw, that the season of the year would not permit him to finish the war; yet he thought it would be of no small advantage, if he should but take a view of the island, learn the nature of the inhabitants, and acquaint himself with the coast, harbours, and landing-places, to all which the Gauls were perfect strangers: for almost none but merchants resort to that island, nor have even any knowledge of the country except the sea coast, and the parts opposite to Gaul. Having therefore called together the merchants from all parts, they could neither inform him of the largeness of the island, nor what or how powerful the nations were that inhabited it, nor of their customs, art of war, or the harbours fit to receive large ships. For these reasons, before he embarked himself, he thought proper to send C. Volusenus with a galley, to get some knowledge of these things, commanding him, as soon as he had informed himself in what he wanted to know, to return with all expedition. He himself marched with his whole army into the territories of the Morini, because thence was the nearest passage into Britain. Here he ordered a great many ships from the neighbouring ports to attend him, and the fleet he had made use of the year before in the Venetian war.

XIX. Meanwhile the Britons, having notice of his design, by the merchants that resorted to their island, ambassadors from many of their states came *: Cæsar, with an offer of hosta-ges, and submission to the authority of the people of Rome. To these he gave a favourable audience, and exhorted them to continue in the same mind, sent them back into their own country. Along with them he despatched Comius, whom he had constituted king of the Atrebatians, a man in whose virtue, wisdom and fidelity he greatly confided, and whose authority in the island was very considerable. To him he gave it in charge, to visit as many states as he could, and persuade them to enter into an alliance with the Romans, letting them know at the same time that Cæsar designed as soon as possible to come over in person to their island. Volusenus having taken a view of the country, as far as was possible for one who had resolved not to quit his ship, or trust himself in the hands of the barbarians, returned on the fifth day and acquainted Cæsar with his discoveries.

XX. While Cæsar continued in those parts, for the sake of getting ready his fleet, deputies arrived from almost all the cantons of the Morini, to excuse their late war with the people of Rome, as proceeding wholly from a national fierceness, and their ignorance of the Roman customs, promising likewise an entire submission for the future. This fell out very opportunely for Cæsar, who was unwilling to leave any enemies behind him, nor would the season of the year have even allowed him to engage in a war; besides, he judged it by no means proper so far to entangle himself in these trivial affairs, as to be obliged to postpone the expedition into Britain. He therefore ordered them to send him a great number of hostages, and upon their being delivered, received them into his alliance. Having got together about **eighty transports**, which **he thought would be sufficient for the carrying** over two legions, he distributed **the galleys** he had over and above to the questor, lieutenants, and officers of the cavalry. There were, besides, eighteen transports detained by contrary winds at a port about eight miles off, which he appointed to carry over the cavalry. The rest of the army, under the command of Q. Titurius Sabinus, and L. Aruncu16ius Cotta, were sent against the Menapians, and those cantons of the Morini which had not submitted. P. Sulpicius Rufus had the charge of the harbour where he embarked, with a strong garrison to maintain it.

XXI. Things being in this manner settled.

and the wind springing up fair, he weighed anchor about one in the morning, ordering the cavalry to embark at the other port, and follow him. But as these orders were executed but slowly, he himself, about ten in the morning, reached the coast of Britain, where he saw all the cliffs covered with the enemy's forces. The nature of the place was such, that the sea being bounded by steep mountains, the enemy might easily launch their javelins upon us from above. Not thinking this therefore a convenient landing-place, he resolved to lie by till three in the afternoon, and wait the arrival of the rest of his fleet. Meanwhile, having called the lieutenants and military tribunes together, he informed them of what he had learned from Volusenus, instructed them in the part they were to act, and particularly exhorted them to do every thing with readiness, and at a signal given agreeable to the rules of military discipline, which in sea affairs especially required expedition and despatch, because of all others the most changeable and uncertain. Having dismissed them, and finding both the wind and tide favourable, he made the signal for weighing anchor, and after sailing about eight miles farther stopped over against a plain and open shore.

XXII. But the barbarians perceiving our design, sent their cavalry and chariots before, which they frequently make use of in battle, and following with the rest of their forces, endeavoured to oppose our landing: and indeed we found the difficulty very great on many accounts; for our ships being large, required a great depth of water; and the soldiers, who were wholly unacquainted with the places, and had their hands embarrassed and loaden with a weight of armour, were at the same time to leap from the ships, stand breast high amidst the waves, and encounter the enemy, while they, fighting upon dry ground, or advancing only a little way into the water, having the free use of all their limbs, and in places which they perfectly knew, could boldly cast their darts, and spur on their horses, well inured to that kind of service. All these circumstances serving to spread a terror among our men, who were wholly strangers to this way of fighting, they pushed not the enemy with the same vigour and spirit as was usual for them in combats upon dry ground.

XXIII. Cæsar observing this, ordered some galleys, a kind of shipping less common with the barbarians, and more easily governed and put in motion, to advance a little from the transports towards the shore, in order to set upon the enemy in flank, and by means of their engines, slings, and arrows, drive them to some distance. This proved of considerable service to our men, for what with the surprise occasioned by the make of our galleys, the motion of our oars, and the playing of the engines, the enemy were forced to halt, and in a little time began to give back. But our men still demurring to leap into the sea, chiefly because of the depth of the water in those parts; the standard-bearer of the tenth legion, having first invoked the gods for success, cried out aloud: " Follow me, fellow-soldiers, unless you will betray the Roman eagle into the hands of the enemy; for my part, I am resolved to discharge my duty to Cæsar and the commonwealth." Upon this he jumped into the sea, and advanced with the eagle against the enemy: whereat, our men exhorting one another to prevent so signal a disgrace, all that were in the ship followed him, which being perceived by those in the nearest vessels, they also did the like, and boldly approached the enemy.

XXIV. The battle was obstinate on both sides; but our men, as being neither able to keep their ranks, nor get firm footing, nor follow their respective standards, because leaping promiscuously from their ships, every one joined the first ensign he met, were thereby thrown into great confusion. The enemy, on the other hand, being well acquainted with the shallows, when they saw our men advancing singly from the ships, spurred on their horses, and attacked them in that perplexity. In one place great numbers would gather round a handful of the Romans; others falling upon them in flank, galled them mightily with their darts, which Cæsar observing, ordered some small boats to be manned, and ply about with recruits. By this means the foremost ranks of our men having got firm footing, were followed by all the rest, when falling upon the enemy briskly, they were soon put to the rout. But as the cavalry were not yet arrived, we could not pursue or advance far into the island, which was the only thing wanting to render the victory complete.

XXV. The enemy being thus vanquished in battle, no sooner got together after their defeat, than they despatched ambassadors to

Cæsar to sue for peace, offering hostages, and an entire submission to his commands. Along with these ambassadors came Comius, the Atrebatian, whom Cæsar, as we have related above, had sent before him into Britain. The natives seized him as soon as he landed, and though he was charged with a commission from Cæsar, threw him into irons. But upon their late defeat, they thought proper to send him back, throwing the blame of what had happened upon the multitude, and begged of Cæsar to excuse a fault proceeding from ignorance. Cæsar, after some complaints of their behaviour, in that having of their own accord sent ambassadors to the continent to sue for peace, they had yet without any reason begun a war against him, told them at last he would forgive their fault, and ordered them to send a certain number of hostages. Part were sent immediately, and the rest, as living at some distance, they promised to deliver in a few days. Meantime they disbanded their troops, and the several chiefs came to Cæsar's camp, to manage their own concerns, and those of the states to which they belonged.

XXVI. A peace being thus concluded four days after Cæsar's arrival in Britain, the eighteen transports appointed to carry the cavalry, of whom we have spoken above, put to sea with a gentle gale. But when they had so near approached the coast as to be even within view of the camp, so violent a storm all on a sudden arose, that being unable to hold on their course, some were obliged to return to the port whence they set out, and others driven to the lower end of the island, westward, not without great danger; there they cast anchor, but the waves rising very high, so as to fill the ships with water, they were again in the night obliged to stand out to sea, and make for the continent of Gaul. That very night it happened to be full moon, when the tides upon the sea coast always rise highest, a thing at that time wholly unknown to the Romans. Thus at the one and the same time, the galleys which Cæsar made use of to transport his men, and which he had ordered to be drawn up on the strand, were filled with the tide, and the tempest fell furiously upon the transports that lay at anchor in the road: nor was it possible for our men to attempt any thing for their preservation. Many of the ships being dashed to pieces, and the rest having lost their anchors, tackle, and rigging, which rendered

them altogether unfit for sailing, a general consternation spread itself through the camp, for there were no other ships to carry back the troops, nor any materials to repair those that had been disabled by the tempest. And as it had been all along Cæsar's design to winter in Gaul, he was wholly without corn to subsist the troops in those parts.

XXVII. All this being known to the British chiefs, who after the battle had repaired to Cæsar's camp, to perform the conditions of the treaty, they began to hold conferences among themselves, and as they plainly saw that the Romans were destitute both of cavalry, shipping, and corn, and easily judged, from the smallness of the camp, that the number of their troops was but inconsiderable; in which notion they were the more confirmed, because Cæsar having brought over the legions without baggage, had occasion to inclose but a small spot of ground; they thought this a convenient opportunity for taking up arms, and, by intercepting the Roman convoys, to protract the affair till winter; being confidently persuaded, that by defeating these troops, or cutting off their return, they should effectually put a stop to all future attempts upon Britain. Having therefore entered into a joint confederacy, they by degrees left the camp, and began to draw the islanders together: but Cæsar, though he was not yet apprized of their design, yet guessing in part at their intentions, by the disaster which had befallen his fleet, and the delays formed in relation to the hostages, determined to provide against all events. He therefore had corn daily brought into his camp, and ordered the timber of the ships that had been most damaged to be made use of in repairing the rest, sending to Gaul for what other materials he wanted. As the soldiers were indefatigable in this service, his fleet was soon in a condition to sail, having lost only twelve ships.

XXVIII. During these transactions, the seventh legion being sent out to forage, according to custom, as part were employed in cutting down the corn, and part in carrying it to the camp, without suspicion of attack, news were brought to Cæsar, that a greater cloud of dust than ordinary was seen on that side where the legion was. Cæsar, suspecting how matters went, marched with the cohorts that were upon guard, ordering two others to succeed in their room, and all the soldiers in the camp to arm and follow him as soon as possible. When he was advanced a little way from the camp, he saw his men overpowered by the enemy, and with great difficulty able to sustain the fight, being driven into a small compass, and exposed on every side to the darts of their adversaries. For as the harvest was gathered in every where else, and only one field left, the enemy, suspecting that our men would come thither to forage, had hid themselves during the night in the woods, and waiting till our men had quitted their arms, and dispersed themselves to fall a reaping, they suddenly attacked them, killed some, put the rest into disorder, and began to surround them with their horses and chariots.

XXIX. Their way of fighting with their chariots is this: first, they drive their chariots on all sides, and throw their darts, insomuch, that by the very terror of the horses, and noise of the wheels, they often break the ranks of the enemy. When they have forced their way into the midst of the cavalry, they quit their chariots, and fight on foot: meantime the drivers retire a little from the combat, and place themselves in such a manner as to favour the retreat of their countrymen, should they be overpowered by the enemy. Thus in action they perform the part both of nimble horsemen, and stable infantry; and by continual exercise and use have arrived at that expertness, that in the most steep and difficult places they can stop their horses upon a full stretch, turn them which way they please, run along the pole, rest on the harness, and throw themselves back into their chariots with incredible dexterity.

XXX. Our men being astonished and confounded with this new way of fighting, Cæsar came very timely to their relief; for upon his approach the enemy made a stand, and the Romans began to recover from their fear. This satisfied Cæsar for the present, who not thinking it a proper season to provoke the enemy, and bring on a general engagement, stood facing them for some time, and then led back the legions to the camp. The continual rains that followed for some days after, both kept the Romans within their intrenchments, and withheld the enemy from attacking us. Meantime the Britons despatched messengers into all parts, to make known to their countrymen the small number of the Roman troops, and the favourable opportunity they had of

making immense spoils, and freeing their country for ever from all future invasions, by storming the enemy's camp. Having by this means got together a great body of infantry and cavalry, they drew towards our intrenchments.

XXXI. Cæsar, though he foresaw that the enemy, if beaten, would in the same manner as before escape the danger by flight; yet having got about thirty horse, whom Comius, the Atrebatian, had brought over with him from Gaul, he drew up the legions in order of battle before the camp; and falling upon the Britons, who were not able to sustain the shock of our men, soon put them to flight. The Romans pursuing them as long as their strength would permit, made a terrible slaughter, and setting fire to their houses and villages a great way round, returned to the camp.

XXXII. The same day ambassadors came from the enemy to Cæsar, to sue for peace. Cæsar doubled the number of hostages he had before imposed upon them, and ordered them to be sent over to him into Gaul, because the equinox coming on, and his ships being leaky, he thought it not prudent to put off his return till winter. A fair wind offering, he set sail a little after midnight, and arrived safe in Gaul. Two of his transports not being able to reach the same port with the rest, were driven into a haven a little lower in the country.

XXXIII. In these two vessels were about three hundred soldiers, who having landed, and being upon their march to the camp, the Morini, who had submitted to Cæsar upon his setting out for Britain, drawn by the hopes of plunder, surrounded them at first with only a few men, and ordered them to lay down their arms under pain of being put to the sword. But they, casting themselves into an orb, stood upon their defence, when all on a sudden six thousand more of the enemy appeared, roused by the noise of the combatants. Cæsar having notice of what passed, sent all his cavalry to the assistance of the Romans: meanwhile our men withstood all the attacks of the enemy, and bravely maintained the fight for upwards of six hours, having slain great numbers of the Morini, while on their side only a few were wounded; but no sooner did our cavalry appear, than the enemy, throwing down their arms, betook themselves to flight, and were almost all slain in the pursuit.

XXXIV. The day after, Cæsar sent T

Labienus with the legions returned out of Britain, against the rebellious Morini, who being deprived, by the drought, of the benefit of their marshes, which had served them for shelter the year before, almost all fell into his power. Meantime, Q. Titurius, and L. Cotta, who had been sent against the Menapians, having laid waste their territories with fire and sword, and plundered their habitations, returned to Cæsar, not being able to come up with the Menapians themselves, who had retired into impenetrable forests. Cæsar quartered all his troops among the Belgians. Only two of the British states sent hostages into Gaul, the rest neglecting to perform the conditions of the treaty. For these successes a thanksgiving of twenty days was decreed by the senate.

CÆSAR'S COMMENTARIES

OF

HIS WARS IN GAUL

———

BOOK V.

THE ARGUMENT.

CÆSAR'S COMMENTARIES

OF

HIS WARS IN GAUL.

BOOK V.

I. In the consulship of Lucius Domitius, and Appius Claudius, Cæsar leaving his winter quarters to go into Italy, as was his yearly custom, gave orders to his lieutenants, who had the charge of the legions, to build as many ships as possible during the winter, and to repair such as were old. He prescribed the form and manner of building, ordering them to be somewhat lower than was usual in the Mediterranean, for the convenience of embarking and landing his men, which he judged the more necessary, as he had observed, that by reason of the frequent returns of the tide, there was less depth of water upon the British coast. He likewise commanded them to be built broader than ordinary, that they might receive the greater number of horses and carriages, and to be contrived for lightness and expedition, to which the lowness of their decks greatly contributed. He sent to Spain for the materials necessary in building and equipping them; and having finished the diet of Cisalpine Gaul, set out for Illyricum, upon advice, that the Pirustæ were laying waste the province by their incursions. When he arrived there, he ordered the several states to furnish their contingents, and appointed a place of general rendezvous. The report of this no sooner spread among the Pirustæ, than they sent ambassadors to inform him, that nothing had been done against the province by public authority, and that they were ready to make what satisfaction he required. Cæsar, pleased with their submission, ordered them to bring him hostages, and named the day by which they were to be delivered, threatening them with a fierce war in case of disobedience. These being accordingly brought by the day prefixed, he appointed arbitrators between the contending states, to estimate the damages, and determine what reparation was to be made.

II. Having despatched these affairs, and held a general diet of the province, he returned again into Cisalpine Gaul, and thence went to the army. Upon his arrival, he visited all the quarters of the legions, and found, that by the singular diligence of the soldiers, notwithstanding the greatest scarcity of materials, no less than six hundred transports, such as we have described above, and twenty-eight galleys, were in such forwardness, that in a few days they would be ready to be launched. Having praised his soldiers, and those whom he had set over the works, he gave them what further instructions he thought necessary, and ordered the whole fleet to rendezvous at port Itius, whence he knew lay the most commodious passage to Britain, it being there not above thirty miles distant from the continent. Leaving what soldiers he thought necessary for this purpose, he advanced at the head of four legions, without baggage, and eight hundred horse, into the country of the Treviri, because they neither appeared at the general diets of Gaul, nor submitted to the orders of the commonwealth; and were, besides, reported to be soliciting the Germans beyond the Rhine.

III. This state is by far the most powerful of all Gaul in horse; they have likewise a very strong and numerous infantry; and as we have before observed, bordered upon the

Rhine. Two of their principal men, Indutio-marus and Cingetorix, were at this time competitors for the supreme authority. Cingetorix, as soon as he heard of the arrival of Cæsar and the legions, came to him, and assured him, that he and all his party would continue firm to their duty, and never abandon the interest of the Romans: at the same time, he informed him of all that had passed among the Treviri. But Indutiomarus drawing together great numbers of horse and foot, and securing such as were unable to bear arms, in the forest of Arden, which extends from the Rhine quite across the country of Treves, to the territories of the Rhemi, resolved to try the fortune of war. But soon after, as several of the leading men of the state, partly out of attachment to Cingetorix, partly terrified by the approach of the Roman army, came to Cæsar to solicit in their own behalf, since they found themselves incapable of effectually serving their country, Indutiomarus fearing a universal defection, sent likewise ambassadors to him to acquaint him, "That he had chosen to stay at home, and forbear coming to the Roman camp, with no other view but to keep the state in its duty, lest, in the absence of the nobility, the people might have been drawn into some rash step: that the whole country was now at his command, and he ready, with Cæsar's permission, to attend him in person, and put his own concerns, as well as those of the state, under his protection." Though Cæsar well understood the reason of his present submission, and by what considerations he had been deterred from the prosecution of his first design, yet unwilling to waste the whole summer in the country of Treves, when every thing was in readiness for his expedition into Britain, he ordered Indutiomarus to attend him with two hundred hostages. These being accordingly brought, and among them the son, and all the nearest relations of Indutiomarus, whom he had specified by name, Cæsar encouraged and exhorted him to continue firm in his duty. Nevertheless, assembling all the principal men of Treves, he reconciled them one after another to Cingetorix, as well on account of his singular merit, as because he thought it of the greatest importance to establish thoroughly the authority of a man, of whose steady and inviolable attachment he had such convincing proof. Indutiomarus highly resented this pro-

ceeding, which tended so much to the diminution of his power; and as he had all along been an enemy to the Romans, this new affront provoked him still more.

IV. These affairs being settled, Cæsar arrived with his legions at the port of Itius. There he found, that about forty of his ships, built in the country of the Belgians, having been attacked by a storm, and disabled from continuing their voyage, had been obliged to put back. The rest were all equipped and rigged, ready to obey the first signal. All the cavalry of Gaul, about four thousand in number, and the prime nobility of the several states, met him likewise, by order, at this place. His design was, to leave only a few of these nobles behind him in Gaul, on whose fidelity he could rely, and to take the rest with him to Britain as hostages, the better to prevent any commotions during his absence.

V. Dumnorix, the Æduan, of whom we have spoken above, was one of those that attended him on this occasion. Him in particular he resolved to carry along with him, as he knew him to be a lover of novelties, ambitious, enterprising, and of great interest and authority among the Gauls. Besides all this, he had publicly said in an assembly of the Æduans, that Cæsar had invested him with the sovereignty of their state; which resolution, though by no means pleasing to the Æduans, they yet durst not send ambassadors to Cæsar, either to oppose or get reversed; nor was Cæsar otherwise informed of the matter, but by those whom he had placed about Dumnorix, to have an eye over his conduct. Dumnorix, at first, earnestly petitioned to be left in Gaul, sometimes pretending he was unused to sailing, and afraid of the sea, sometimes urging religious engagements, which required him to stay at home. But finding all his endeavours to no purpose, he began to solicit the chiefs of the Gauls, discoursing them apart, and advising them not to leave the continent. The more to awaken their fears, he told them: "That Cæsar had his particular reasons for carrying with him all the nobility of Gaul; because not daring to despatch them in their own country, he was in hopes of finding a favourable opportunity to execute his cruel purpose in Britain." He therefore exhorted them to join in a mutual alliance, and oblige themselves by a solemn oath, to pursue with common consent such measures as should appear necessary for the preservation of Gaul.

VI. Though Cæsar was fully informed of these practices, yet in consideration of his singular regard for the Æduans, he contented himself with endeavouring to check and traverse his designs, determined, notwithstanding, to continue inflexible, and at all hazards prevent any misfortune to himself and the commonwealth, from a spirit, which he found every day growing more hardy and intrepid. Being therefore detained in this place about five and twenty days, during which the north-west wind, very common on that coast, hindered him from sailing, he studied by the ways of gentleness and persuasion, to keep Dumnorix in his duty, without neglecting however to watch all his motions. At last, the wind springing up fair, he ordered the horse and foot to embark. As this universally engaged the attention of the camp, Dumnorix unknown to Cæsar, drew off the Æduan cavalry, and began his march homeward. Cæsar being informed of it, immediately put a stop to the embarkation, and postponing every other consideration, ordered out a strong party of horse to pursue and bring him back. If he made resistance, or refused to obey, they had orders to kill him; for he judged, that a man who slighted his personal authority, would not pay any great regard to his commands in his absence. When they had overtaken him, he refused to return, and defending himself sword in hand, implored the assistance of his followers, often calling out, that he was free, and the subject of a free state. The Romans, according to the orders they had received, surrounded and slew him, upon which all the Æduan cavalry returned to Cæsar.

VII. This affair concluded, and Labienus being left in Gaul with three legions, and two thousand horse to defend the port, provide corn, have an eye upon the transactions of the continent, and take measures accordingly, Cæsar weighed anchor about sun-set with five legions, and the same number of horse he had left with Labienus, and advancing with a gentle south wind, continued his course till midnight, when he found himself becalmed; but the tide still driving him on, at day-break he saw Britain on his left. When again following the return of the tide, he rowed with all his might, to reach that part of the island which he had marked out the summer before, as most convenient for landing; and on this occasion the diligence of the soldiers cannot be enough commended, who, labouring incessantly on the oar, urged the transports and ships of burden so swiftly, that they equalled the course of the galleys. The whole fleet reached the coast of Britain about noon; nor did any enemy appear in view. But as Cæsar afterwards understood from the prisoners, though a great army of Britons had repaired to the coast, yet terrified by the vast number of ships, which, together with those of the last year's expedition, and such as had been fitted out by particular persons for their own use, amounted to upwards of eight hundred, they retired hastily from the shore, and hid themselves behind the mountains.

VIII. Cæsar having landed his army, and chosen a proper place for his camp, as soon as he understood from the prisoners where the enemy's forces lay, leaving ten cohorts upon the coast, together with three hundred horse, to guard the fleet, he set out about midnight in quest of the enemy, being under the less concern for his ships, because he had left them at anchor upon a smooth and open shore, under the charge of Q. Atrius. After a march of twelve hours, during the night, he came within sight of the enemy, who, having posted themselves behind a river, with their cavalry and chariots, attacked us from the higher ground, in order to oppose our passage; but being repulsed by our horse, they retreated towards the woods, into a place strongly fenced both by nature and art, and which, in all probability, had been fortified before on occasion of some domestic war; for all the avenues were secured by strong barricadoes of felled trees. They never sallied out of the wood but in small parties, thinking it enough to defend the entrance against our men. But the soldiers of the seventh legion advancing under cover of their shields, and having cast up a mount, forced the intrenchments with little loss, and obliged the enemy to abandon the wood. Cæsar forbid all pursuit, both because he was unacquainted with the nature of the country, and the day being far spent, he resolved to employ the rest of it in fortifying the camp.

IX. Early the next morning he divided his troops, both horse and foot, into three bodies, and sent them out in pursuit of the enemy. They were advanced but a little way, and just come within sight of the rear of the Britons, when a party of horse from Atrius came to Cæsar, and informed him, "That a dreadful storm arising the night before, had fallen violently upon the fleet, and driven almost all the ships ashore; that neither anchors nor cables, nor all the address of the mariners and pilots, had been able to resist the fury of the tempest, which had done unspeakable damage to the fleet, by reason of the ships running foul of one another." Cæsar, upon this intelligence, recalls his legions and cavalry, commanding them to give over their pursuit. He himself returns to his ships, and finds every thing according to the reports and letters he had received, forty of them being entirely destroyed, and the rest so damaged, that they were hardly repairable. He therefore set all the carpenters of the army to work, and wrote for others to Gaul, ordering Labienus at the same time, with the legions under his command, to build what ships he could. He thought it likewise safest, though a work of great labour and difficulty, to draw all his ships on shore, and inclose them within the fortifications of his camp. Ten days were spent in the service, during which the soldiers had no intermission of fatigue, not even in the night. The ships being in this manner secured, and the camp strongly fortified, he left the same troops to guard it as before, and returned to the place where he had quitted the pursuit of the enemy. Upon his arrival he found the forces of the Britons considerably increased. The chief command and administration of the war, was, by common consent, conferred upon Cassibelanus, whose territories were divided from the maritime states by the Thames, a river eighty miles distant from the sea. This prince had hitherto been engaged in almost continual wars with his neighbours; but the terror of our arrival making the Britons unite among themselves, they intrusted him with the whole conduct of the war.

X. The inland parts of Britain are inhabited by those, whom fame reports to be the natives of the soil. The sea coast is peopled with the Belgians, drawn thither by the love of war and plunder. These last, passing over from different parts and settling in the country, still retain the names of the several states whence they are descended. The island is

well peopled, full of houses, built after the manner of the Gauls, and abounds in cattle. They use brass money, and iron rings of a certain weight. The provinces remote from the sea produce tin, and those upon the coast iron; but the latter in no great quantity. Their brass is all imported. All kinds of wood grow here the same as in Gaul, except the fir and beech-tree. They think it unlawful to feed upon hares, pullets, or geese; yet they breed them up for their diversion and pleasure. The climate is more temperate than in Gaul, and the cold less intense. The island is triangular, one of its sides facing Gaul. The extremity towards Kent, whence is the nearest passage to Gaul, lies eastward: the other stretches south-west. This side extends about five hundred miles. Another side looks towards Spain, westward. Over against this lies Ireland, an island esteemed not above half as large as Britain, and separated from it by an interval equal to that between Britain and Gaul. In this interval lies the isle of Mona, besides several other lesser islands, of which some write, that in the time of the winter solstice, they have night for thirty days together. We could make out nothing of this upon inquiry, only discovered by means of our hour-glasses, that the nights were shorter than in Gaul. The length of this side is computed at seven hundred miles. The last side faces the north-east, and is fronted by no part of the continent, only towards one of its extremities it seems to eye chiefly **the German coast. It** is thought to extend **in length about eight** hundred miles. **Thus the whole island takes** in a circuit of two thousand miles. The inhabitants of Kent, which lies wholly on the sea coast, are **the** most civilized of all **the** Britons, and differ but little in **their manner** from the Gauls. The greater part of those within the country never sow their lands, but live on flesh and milk, and go clad in skins. All the Britons in general paint themselves with woad, which gives a bluish cast to the skin, and makes them look dreadful in battle. They are long haired; and shave all the rest of the body except the head and upper lip. Ten or twelve of them live together, having their wives in common, especially brothers, or parents and children amongst themselves; but the issue is always ascribed to him who first espoused the mother.

XI. The enemy's horse, supported by their

chariots, vigorously charged our cavalry on their march, yet we everywhere had the better, and drove them to their own woods and hills; but after making great slaughter, venturing to continue the pursuit too far, we lost some men. Some time after, sallying unexpectedly from the woods, and falling suddenly upon our men while employed in fortifying their camp, a sharp conflict ensued between them and the advanced guard. Cæsar sent two cohorts to their assistance, whom the Britons charging in separate parties, so surprised with their new manner of fighting, that they broke through, routed them, and returned without loss. Q. Laberius Durus, a military tribune, was slain on this occasion; but some fresh cohorts coming up, the Britons were at last repulsed.

XII. By this action which happened within view of the camp, and of which the whole army were spectators, it evidently appeared, that our heavy armed legions, who could neither pursue those that retired, nor durst venture to forsake their standards, were by no means a fit match for such an enemy: nor could even the cavalry engage without great danger, it being usual for the Britons to counterfeit a retreat, until they had drawn them a considerable way from the legions, when suddenly quitting their chariots, they charged them on foot, and by this unequal manner of fighting, made it alike dangerous to pursue or retire. Add to all this, that they never fought in a body, but in small parties, and with considerable intervals between. They had likewise their detachments so placed, as easily to protect their flying troops, and send fresh supplies where needful.

XIII. The next day they stationed themselves among the hills, at a distance from our camp, and appeared only in small bodies, nor seemed so forward to skirmish with our cavalry as the day before. But about noon, Cæsar ordering out three legions to forage, with all the cavalry, under the command of C. Trebonius, his lieutenant, they fell suddenly upon the foragers on all sides, and even attacked the legions and standards. Our men vigorously returning the charge, repulsed them, and the cavalry finding themselves supported by the foot, continued the pursuit till they had utterly broken them; insomuch, that great numbers being slain, they could neither find an opportunity to rally, descend from their chariots, or face about to make resistance. After this defeat

the auxiliary troops, which had come in from all parts, returned severally to their own homes; nor did the enemy, from this time, appear any more against us with their whole forces.

XIV. Cæsar perceiving their design, marched towards the Thames, to penetrate into the kingdom of Cassibelanus. This river is fordable only in one place, and that not without great difficulty. When he arrived, he saw the enemy drawn up in great numbers on the other side. They had likewise secured the banks with sharp stakes, and driven many of the same kind into the bottom of the river, yet so as to be covered by the water. Cæsar having intelligence of this, from the prisoners and deserters, sent the cavalry before, ordering the legions to follow close after, which they did with so much expedition and briskness, though nothing but their heads were above the water, that the enemy, unable to sustain their charge, quitted the banks, and betook themselves to flight.

XV. Cassibelanus, as we have before intimated, finding himself unable to keep the field, disbanded all his other forces; and retaining only four thousand chariots, watched our motions, always keeping at some distance from us, and sheltering himself in woods and inaccessible places, whither he had likewise made such of the inhabitants, with their cattle, retire, as lay upon our route: and if at any time our cavalry ventured upon a freer excursion into the fields, to plunder and lay waste the country; as he was perfectly acquainted with all the roads and defiles, he would sally from the woods with some of the chariots, and fall upon our men, dispersed and in disorder. These frequent alarms obliged us to be much upon our guard; nor would Cæsar suffer the cavalry to remove to any distance from the legions, or to pillage and destroy the country, unless where the foot was at hand to sustain them.

XVI. Meantime the Trinobantes, one of the most powerful states in those parts, send ambassadors to Cæsar. Of this state was Mandubratius, who had fled for protection to Cæsar in Gaul, that he might avoid the fate of his father Imanuentius, whom Cassibelanus had put to death. The ambassadors promised obedience and submission in the name of the province: and withal entreated him to defend Mandubratius against the violence of Cassibelanus, and restore him to the government of their state. Cæsar ordered them to deliver forty hostages, and furnish his army with corn;

13*

sending back at the same time Mandubratius. They yielded to his demands without delay, sent the appointed number of hostages, and supplied him with corn.

XVII. The protection granted to the Trinobantes, securing them from the insults of the soldiers; the Cenimagni, Segontiaci, Ancalites, Bibroci, and Cassi send ambassadors to Cæsar, and submit. From them he had intelligence, that he was not far from the capital of Cassibelanus, which was situated amidst woods and marshes, and whither great numbers of men and cattle were retired. A town among the Britons is nothing more than a thick wood, fortified with a ditch and rampart, to serve as a place of retreat against the incursions of their enemies. Thither he marched with his legions; and though the place appeared to be extremely strong, both by art and nature, he nevertheless resolved to attack it in two several quarters. The enemy, after a short stand, were obliged at last to give way, and retire by another part of the wood. Vast numbers of cattle were found in the place; and many of the Britons were either made prisoners, or lost their lives in the pursuit.

XVIII. While these things passed beyond the Thames, Cassibelanus despatched messengers to Kent, which, as we have before observed, was situated along the sea coast. This country was then under the government of four kings, Cingetorix, Carnilius, Taximagulus, and Segonax. who had orders to draw all their forces together, and fall suddenly upon the naval camp of the Romans. But our men sallying upon them as they approached, made great slaughter of their troops, took Cingetorix, one of their leaders, prisoner, and returned safe to the camp. Cassibelanus, upon the news of this battle, discouraged by so many losses, the devastation of his territories, and above all, the revolt of the provinces, sent ambassadors to Cæsar to sue for peace, by the mediation of Comius of Arras.

XIX. Cæsar designing to pass the winter in Gaul because of the frequent commotions in that country; and reflecting that but a small part of the summer remained, during which it would be easy to protract the war: demanded hostages, and appointed the yearly tribute which Britain was to pay to the Romans. At the same time he strictly charged Cassibelanus to offer no injury to Mandubratius or the Trinobantes. Having received the hostages,

he led his troops back to the sea-side, where he found his fleet repaired. Orders were immediately given to launch it; and because the number of prisoners was exceeding great, and several ships had been destroyed by the tempest, he resolved to carry over his men at two embarkations. Happily it so fell out, notwithstanding the great number of ships, and their frequent passing and repassing, that not one perished either this or the preceding year, which had any soldiers on board: whereas those sent empty to him from the continent, as well the ships concerned in the first embarkation, as others built afterwards by Labienus, to the number of sixty, were almost all driven back or lost. Cæsar having waited for them a considerable time to no purpose, and fearing to lose the proper season for sailing, as the time of the equinox drew near, chose to stow his men on board the few ships he had; and taking the opportunity of an extraordinary calm, set sail about ten at night, and by daybreak brought his whole fleet safe to the continent of Gaul.

XX. Having laid up his fleet, and held a general assembly of the Gauls at Samarobriva; as the crop had been very indifferent this year, by reason of the great droughts, he was obliged to quarter his legions otherwise than in former winters, and canton them one by one in the several provinces of Gaul. One legion he quartered on the Morini, under the command of C. Fabius: another among the Nervians, under Q. Cicero; a third with the Æduans, under L. Roscius; and a fourth in the country of the Rhemi, on the borders of the Treviri, under Labienus. Three were sent into Belgium, over whom he appointed three commanders; M. Crassus, his quæstor, L. Munatius Plancus, and C. Trebonius. The eighth and last, which Cæsar had newly raised on the other side of the Po, was sent, together with five cohorts, among the Eburones, between the Rhine and the Meuse, where Ambiorix and Cativulcus reigned. At the head of this body were two commanders, Q. Titurius Sabinus, and L. Aruncuieius Cotta. By this distribution of his legions, he thought he had found an easy remedy against the scarcity of corn; and yet they all lay within the compass of a hundred miles, except that under L. Roscius, for which he was in no pain, as being quartered in a very quiet and friendly country. He resolved however not to leave Gaul till he had received advice from all his lieutenants, and was assured that their quarters were esta-.lished, fortified, and secured.

XXI. Among the Carnutes lived Tasgetius, a man of distinguished birth, and whose ancestors had been possessed of the sovereignty in that state. Cæsar had restored him to the dignity of his forefathers, in consideration of his virtue and affection to him, and the many signal services he had done him in all his wars. It was now the third year of his reign, when his enemies, many of whom were of his own state, conspiring against him, openly assassinated him. The affair was laid before Cæsar; who fearing lest the great number concerned in the plot might draw the state into a revolt, ordered L. Plancus, with a legion from Belgium, to march speedily into the country of the Carnutes, fix his winter quarters, in that province, and seizing all who had been concerned in the murder of Tasgetius, send them prisoners to him. Meantime he was informed by his lieutenants and questors to whom he had committed the care of the legions, that they were severally arrived at their appointed quarters, and had fortified themselves in them.

XXII. About fifteen days after the arrival of the legions in their winter quarters, a sudden insurrection and revolt broke out among the Eburones, by the secret practice of Ambiorix and Cativulcus. These two princes had been to meet Sabinus and Cotta on their frontiers, and in a friendly manner had supplied them with corn; but now, instigated by Indutiomarus of Treves, they excited their people to take up arms: and having surprised some soldiers that were gone to cut wood, came with a great body of troops to attack the Roman camp. Our men immediately flew to arms, ascended the ramparts, and sending out a detachment of Spanish horse, put their cavalry to rout. Upon this, despairing of success, they drew off their men from the attack; and, according to their custom, demanded a conference; pretending they had something to say, which concerned the common interest, and might serve to put an end to their present differences.

XXIII. Accordingly C. Arpinius, a Roman knight, the friend of Q. Titurius, and Q. Junius of Spain, who had frequently before been sent by Cæsar to Ambiorix, were deputed to treat. Ambiorix addressed them in words to this effect: "That he had in no sort forgot the many obligations he lay under to Cæsar, who had freed him from the tribute he had been wont to pay the Atuatici; and who had restored him his son and nephew, whom that people, after receiving them as hostages, had treated as slaves: that the hostilities he had just committed were not the effect of his own private animosity to the Romans, but in consequence of a resolution of the state; where the government was of such a nature that the people had as much power over him, as he over the people: that even the state itself had been in a manner forced into this war, by a sudden confederacy of all Gaul: that he could appeal to his own weakness for the truth of what he said, being not so very unskilled in affairs as to imagine, that the forces of the Eburones were a match for the power of the Romans; that it was a project formed by all the states of Gaul in common, who had agreed to storm in one day, the very day on which he spoke, all the quarters of the Roman army; so that no one might be able to succour another: that it was not easy for Gauls to resist the importunity of those of their own nation, especially in a proposal to act in concert for the recovery of their liberty; but that, after having performed what the common voice of his country demanded, he thought he might now listen to that of gratitude: that he found himself compelled by his attachment to Cæsar, and by his friendship for Sabinus, to give notice of the extreme danger to which the legion was exposed: that a great body of Germans had actually passed the Rhine, and would be there in two days at furthest: that Sabinus and Cotta were to consider, whether it would not be proper to retire with their troops, before the neighbouring states could be apprized of their design; and go and join Labienus, or Cicero, who were neither of them distant much **above** fifty miles. That as far as regarded himself, he engaged by all that was **sacred** to secure their retreat through his territories; and undertook it the more readily, as he **should** thereby not only discharge his duty **to his** country, in delivering it from the inconvenience of wintering the Romans, but at the same time manifest his gratitude to Cæsar." Having made this speech, he withdrew.

XXIV. Arpinius and Junius reported what they had heard to the lieutenants; who, alarmed at the suddenness of the thing, thought the information not to be neglected, though it came from an enemy: nor were they a little moved by this consideration, that it appeared to them altogether incredible, that the Eburones, a weak and inconsiderable state, should of their own accord presume to take up arms against the Romans. They therefore laid the matter before a council of war, where a warm debate arose. L. Arunculeius, with a great number of military tribunes, and centurions of the first rank, were against undertaking any thing hastily, or quitting their winter quarters, before they had received orders to that purpose from Cæsar. They alleged: "That having strongly fortified their camp, they were able to defend themselves, even against all the forces of the Germans: that the late attempt of the Gauls was a sufficient proof of this, whom they had not only withstood with courage, but repulsed with loss: that they had provisions in abundance, and might therefore securely wait the arrival of relief from Cæsar and the neighbouring legions: in fine, that nothing could be more dishonourable, or argued greater want of judgment, than in affairs of the highest moment, to take measures upon the information of an enemy." Titurius, on the other hand, exclaimed; "That it would be then too late to think of retiring, when the enemy, in greater numbers, and strengthened by the accession of the Germans, should come up against them; or when the quarters next them should have received some signal check: that the time for deliberation was short: that Cæsar, he made no question, was gone into Italy, it not being likely that either the Carnotes would have formed the design of assassinating Tasgetius, or the Eburones in so contemptuous a manner assaulted the Roman camp, had they not been assured of his departure: that the information of an enemy weighed not with him, but the real circumstance of things. The Rhine was not far off. The Germans were much exasperated by the death of Ariovistus, and their late frequent defeats. Gaul burned with impatience to throw off the Roman yoke, avenge the many losses they had sustained, and recover their former glory in war, of which now scarce a shadow remained. In short, who could imagine that Ambiorix, without a certainty of being supported, would have embarked in so dangerous an enterprise? That his opinion was in all respects safe; because, if no such confederacy had been formed, they had nothing to apprehend in marching to the

nearest legion; if, on the contrary, all Gaul and Germany were united, expedition alone could save them from destruction: whereas, by following the advice of Cotta, and those who were against a retreat, though the danger perhaps might not prove immediate, yet were they sure in the end of perishing by famine." The dispute continued for some time; Cotta, and the principal officers, strongly opposing the march of the troops. At last Sabinus raising his voice, that he might be heard by the soldiers without: "Be it so then, (says he,) since you seem so resolved: I am not he among you who is most afraid of death. But, if any misfortune happens, those who hear me will know whom to blame. In two days, did not you oppose it, we might easily reach the quarters next us; and there, in conjunction with our fellow-soldiers, confront the common danger; whereas, by keeping the troops separate and at a distance, you reduce them to the necessity of perishing by sword or famine."

XXV. The council was then going to rise: but the officers, surrounding their generals, conjured them not to put all to hazard by their dissension and obstinacy. They told them, "That whatever resolution was taken, whether to go or stay, the danger was by no means great, provided they acted with union among themselves; but their disagreement threatened the troops with inevitable destruction." The debate continued till midnight: when at length Cotta, vanquished by importunity, yielded to the opinion of Sabinus. Orders were given for marching by break of day. The remainder of the night was none of it employed in sleep; each man being taken up in choosing what things to carry along with him, and what of his winter necessaries to leave behind. In short, they did every thing to make their stay more dangerous; and by their fatigue and want of rest, incapacitate themselves for a vigorous defence upon their march. At day-break they left their camp, not like men acting by the advice of an enemy, but as if Ambiorix had been their particular friend; marching in a very extended column, and followed by a great train of baggage.

XXVI. The enemy judging from the hurry and motion in the camp, that the Romans intended to leave it, placed themselves in ambuscade in two bodies in a wood; where, well sheltered and covered from view, they waited, at about two miles distance, their arrival; and when he greatest part of the army had entered a large valley, suddenly appearing on both sides of it, they attacked them at the same time in front and rear, and obliged them to fight in a place of great disadvantage.

XXVII. Then at length Titurius, like one who had neglected all the necessary precautions, unable to hide his concern, ran up and down among the troops, and began to dispose them in order of battle, but with an air so timid and disconcerted, that it appeared he had no hopes of success; as happens for the most part to those who leave all to the last moment of execution. But Cotta, who had foreseen that this might happen, and had therefore opposed the departure of the troops, omitted nothing in his power for the common safety; calling to and encouraging the men like an able general, and at the same time fighting with the bravery of a common soldier; and, because the great length of the column rendered it difficult for the lieutenants to remedy all disorders, and repair expeditiously enough to the places where their presence was necessary, orders were given to quit the defence of the baggage, and form into an orb. This disposition, though not improper in these circumstances, was nevertheless attended with very unhappy consequences; for being considered as the effect of terror and despair, it discouraged our men, and augmented the confidence of the enemy. Besides, as unavoidably happens on such occasions, many of the soldiers quitting their ensigns, hastened to fetch from the baggage what they had most of value, and filled all parts with uproar and lamentation.

XXVIII. The Gauls meanwhile conducted themselves with great prudence: their officers proclaimed through the ranks "That not a man should stir from his post; that the booty was theirs, and every thing belonging to the Romans must certainly fall into their hands; but that all depended upon securing the victory." Our men were not inferior to the enemy, either in valour, number, or way of fighting. Though they had neither general, nor fortune on their side, they hoped still by their bravery to surmount all difficulties; and whenever any of the cohorts sallied out, so as to join the enemy, hand to hand, a considerable slaughter of the Gauls ensued. This being perceived by Ambiorix, he ordered his men to cast their darts at a distance, to avoid

a close fight, retire before the Romans whenever they advanced, and pursue them as they returned to their standards: in which way of fighting they were become so expert, by the lightness of their arms, and daily exercise, that it was impossible to do them any hurt. These orders were exactly followed; insomuch that when any cohort left the orb, and came forward to attack the enemy, they retreated and dispersed in a moment: meanwhile it uncovered its own flanks, and exposed them to the darts on either side. The danger was still greater when they returned; for then not only the troops that stood next them, but those who had retired before them, surrounded and charged them on all hands. If, on the contrary, they chose to continue in their post, neither could their valour any thing avail them, nor was it possible for men standing so close together, to avoid the darts of so great a multitude. And yet, notwithstanding all these disadvantages, and the many wounds they had received, they still maintained their ground; and though much of the day was now spent, the fight having continued from sun-rise till two in the afternoon, they did nothing in all that time unworthy the dignity of the Roman name. At length T. Balventius, who the year before had been made first centurion of a legion, a man of distinguished courage, and great authority among the troops, had both his thighs pierced with a dart. Q. Lucanius, an officer of the same rank, endeavouring to rescue his son, whom he saw surrounded by the enemy, was killed after a brave resistance. And L. Cotta, the lieutenant, encouraging the several cohorts and companies, received a blow on the mouth from a sling.

XXIX. So many misfortunes quite dispirited Titurius; who perceiving Ambiorix at a distance animating his troops, sent Cn. Pompey, his interpreter, to beg quarters for himself and his soldiers. Ambiorix replied, "That he was ready to grant him a conference if he desired it. That he hoped to prevail with the multitude to spare the Romans; and that as to Sabinus himself, he gave his word no hurt should be done him." Sabinus communicated this answer to Cotta, proposing that they should leave the battle, and go and confer with Ambiorix, from whom he was in hopes of obtaining quarter both for themselves and their men. Cotta absolutely refused to treat with an armed enemy, and persisted in

U

that resolution. Sabinus ordered the military tribunes and principal centurions that were about his person to follow him, and when he drew near to Ambiorix, being commanded to lay down his arms, obeyed; charging those that were with him to do the same. Meanwhile, as they were treating about the conditions, Ambiorix spinning out the deliberations on purpose, he was by degrees surrounded and slain. Then the Gauls, according to their custom, raising a shout, and calling out victory, charged our troops with great fury, and put them into disorder. L. Cotta, fighting manfully, was slain, with the greatest part of the soldiers. The rest retreated to the camp they had quitted in the morning; of whom L. Petrosidius, the standard-bearer, finding himself sore pressed by the enemy, threw the eagle within the intrenchments, and was killed fighting bravely before the camp. Those that remained, with much ado, sustained the attack till night; but finding themselves without hope, they killed one another to the last man. A few who escaped out of the fight, got by different ways to Labienus's camp, and brought him the news of this sad event.

XXX. Ambiorix, elated with this victory, marched immediately at the head o his cavalry into the country of the Atuatici, which bordered upon his territories; and travelling day and night without intermission, left orders for the infantry to follow him. Having informed them of his success and roused them to arms, he the next day arrived among the Nervians, and urged them not to lose the favourable opportunity of freeing themselves for ever from the yoke of slavery, and avenging the injuries they had received from the Romans. He told them, "That two of their lieutenants had been slain, and a great part of their army cut to pieces: that it would be an easy matter suddenly to attack and destroy the legion quartered in their country under Cicero: and that he was himself ready to assist them in the enterprise." By this speech he easily drew in the Nervians.

XXXI. Accordingly, having forthwith despatched messengers to the Centrones, Grudii, Levaci, Pleumosians, and Gorduni, who are all subject to their state, they assembled what forces they could, and came unexpectedly upon Cicero's quarters, who as yet had heard nothing of the fate of Titurius. Here likewise it unavoidably fell out, that the soldiers sent to cut wood for firing and the fortifications of the camp, were intercepted by the sudden arrival of their cavalry. Having put all these to the sword, the Eburones, Atuatici, and Nervians, with their allies and tributaries, amounting to a formidable army, came and attacked the camp. Our men immediately flew to arms, ascended the rampart, and with great difficulty sustained the day's assault; for the enemy placed all their hopes in despatch, and firmly believed that if they came off conquerors on this occasion, they could not fail of victory every where else.

XXXII. Cicero's first care was to write to Cæsar, promising the messengers great rewards if they carried his letters safe. But as all the ways were beset by the enemy's troops, his couriers were continually intercepted. Meanwhile of the materials brought for fortifying the camp a hundred and twenty towers were built, during the night, with incredible despatch, and the works about the rampart completed. Next day the enemy, with a much greater force than before, attacked the camp, filled the ditch, but were again repulsed by our men. This continued for several days together. The night was wholly employed in repairing the breaches made by day, insomuch that neither the sick nor wounded were permitted to rest. Whatever might be of use to resist the next day's assault, was prepared with great diligence during the night. Stakes were hardened in the fire, palisades planted in great numbers, towers raised upon all parts of the rampart, **and the whole** strengthened with a parapet and **battlements.** Cicero himself, though much **out of order,** would **take no** rest, even during the night; so that the soldiers were obliged to force him from time to time to take some repose.

XXXIII. Meantime such of **the** Nervian chiefs and leaders, as had any intimacy or friendship with Cicero, desired a conference. This being agreed to, they addressed him in the same strain as Ambiorix had before used towards Sabinus: "That all Gaul was in arms: that the Germans had passed the Rhine: that Cæsar and the rest of the troops were besieged in their winter quarters." They told him likewise of the fate of Sabinus; and, to gain credit, produced Ambiorix; adding, "That it was in vain to expect relief from those who were themselves in the utmost distress: that they meant not however any injury to Cicero and the people of Rome, but merely to prevent their wintering in the country, and establishing that practice into a custom: that he was therefore at liberty to leave his quarters without molestation and retire in safety where he pleased." To this Cicero only answered: "That it was not usual with the people of Rome to accept conditions from an armed enemy: but if they would lay down their arms, he promised to interpose his mediation, and permit them to send ambassadors to Cæsar, from whose justice they might reasonably expect redress."

XXXIV. The Nervians, driven from this hope, surrounded the camp with a line, whose rampart was eleven feet high, and ditch fifteen feet deep. They had learned something of this in former wars with Cæsar, and the prisoners they had made gave the further instructions. But being unprovided of the tools necessary in this kind of service, they were obliged to cut the turf with their swords, dig up the earth with their hands, and carry it in their cloaks. And hence it will be easy to form some judgment of their number; for in less than three hours they completed a line of fifteen miles in circuit. The following days were employed in raising towers, proportioned to the height of our rampart, and in preparing scythes, and wooden galleries, in which they were again assisted by the prisoners.

XXXV. On the seventh day of the attack, a very high wind arising, they began to throw red hot balls of clay, and burning javelins upon the barracks of the Romans, which, after the manner of the Gauls, were thatched with straw. These soon took fire, and the flames were in a moment spread by the wind into all parts of the camp. The enemy falling on with a mighty shout, as if already secured of victory, advanced their towers and galleries, and prepared to scale the rampart. But such was the constancy and presence of mind of the soldiers, that though the flames surrounded them on every side, and they were oppressed with the multitude of the enemy's darts; though they saw their huts, their baggage, and their whole fortunes in a blaze; yet not only did they continue firm in their posts, but scarce a man offered so much as to look behind him; so intent were they on fighting and repelling the enemy. This was much the hardest day for our troops: but had nevertheless this fortunate issue, that far the greatest number of the en-

emy were on that day wounded or slain; for as they had crowded close up to the rampart, those behind prevented the front ranks from retiring. The flames abating by degrees, and the enemy having brought forward one of their towers to the very foot of the rampart, the centurions of the third cohort drew off their men a little, beckoning to the Gauls, and challenging them to enter: but as not a man would run the hazard, they attacked them on all sides with stones, drove them from the tower, and set it on fire.

XXXVI. In this legion were two centurions of distinguished valour, T. Pulfio, and L. Varenus, who stood fair for being raised to the first rank of their order. These were perpetually disputing with one another the pre-eminence in courage, and at every year's promotion contended with great eagerness for precedence. In the heat of the attack before the rampart, Pulfio addressing Varenus, "What hinders you now, (says he,) or what more glorious opportunity would you desire of signalizing your bravery? This, this is the day for determining the controversy between us." At these words he sallied out of the camp, and rushed amidst the thickest of the Gauls. Nor did Varenus decline the challenge; but thinking his honour at stake, followed at some distance. Pulfio darted his javelin at the enemy, and transfixed a Gaul that was coming forward to engage him: who falling dead of the wound, the multitude advanced to cover him with their shields, and all poured their darts upon Pulfio, giving him no time to retire. A javelin pierced his shield, and stuck fast in his belt. This accident entangling his right hand, prevented him drawing his sword, and gave the enemy time to surround him. Varenus, his rival, flew to his assistance, and endeavoured to rescue him. Immediately the multitude quitting Pulfio, as fancying the dart had despatched him, all turned upon Varenus. He met them with his sword drawn, charged them hand to hand, and having laid one dead at his feet, drove back the rest; but, pursuing with too much eagerness, stept into a hole, and fell down. Pulfio in his turn hastened to extricate him; and both together, after having slain a multitude of the Gauls and acquired infinite applause, retired unhurt within the intrenchments. Thus fortune gave such a turn to the dispute, that each owed his life to his adversary; nor was it possible to decide, to which of them the prize of valour was due.

XXXVII. As the defence every day became more difficult and hazardous, chiefly by the great multitude of killed and wounded, which considerably lessened the number of defendants, Cicero sent letter upon letter to inform Cæsar of his danger. Many of these couriers failing into the enemy's hands, were tortured to death within view of our soldiers. There was at that time in the Roman camp a Nervian of distinction, by name Vertico, who in the beginning of the siege had fled to Cicero, and given ample proofs of his fidelity. This man, by the hopes of liberty, and a promise of great rewards, engaged one of his slaves to carry a letter to Cæsar. Having concealed it in his javelin, and passed through the camp of the Gauls without suspicion, as being himself of that nation, he arrived safe at Cæsar's quarters, who by this means was informed of the danger of Cicero and the legion.

XXXVIII. Cæsar, receiving the letter about five in the afternoon, immediately despatched a messenger to M. Crassus, who was quartered among the Bellovaci, twenty-five miles off, ordering him to draw out his legion at midnight, and march with all the expedition he could to join him. Crassus, according to his orders, came along with the courier. He sent likewise to C. Fabius, directing him to lead his legion into the country of the Atrebatians, which lay in the way to Cicero. He wrote to Labienus, if it could be done with safety, to meet him upon the frontiers of the Nervians. He himself in the meantime assembled about four hundred horse from the nearest garrisons, resolving not to wait for the rest of the army, which lay at too great a distance.

XXXIX. At nine in the morning he had notice from his scouts of the arrival of Crassus. That day he marched twenty miles, leaving Crassus with a legion at Samarobriva, where he had deposited the baggage, hostages, public papers, and had all the provisions which had been laid up for the winter. Fabius, in consequence of his instructions, having made all the haste he could, met him with his legion. Labienus, who had been informed of the death of Sabinus, and the destruction of the troops under his command, and who saw all the forces of Treves advancing against him, fearing lest, if he should quit his quarters,

the enemy might construe it as a flight, and that it would be impossible for him to sustain their attack, especially as they were flushed with their late success, wrote to Cæsar informing him of the danger that would attend the quitting his camp, of the disaster that happened among the Eburones; and that all the forces of the Treviri, both horse and foot, were encamped within three miles of him.

XL. Cæsar approving his reasons, though he thereby found himself reduced from three to two legions, was yet sensible that all depended upon expedition. He makes forced marches; and reaching the territories of the Nervians, learned from some prisoners the state of the siege and the danger the legion was in. Immediately he engages a Gaulish horseman, by the promise of great rewards, to carry a letter to Cicero. It was wrote in Greek characters, that if it fell into the enemy's hands, it might not be intelligible to them. The messenger had orders, in case he found it impracticable to penetrate himself into the Roman camp, to tie the letter to a javelin, and throw it in. In this letter Cæsar sent Cicero word that he was already on the march to relieve him, and would be up very soon: exhorting him in the meantime, to defend himself with his wonted bravery. The Gaul, dreading a discovery, threw the letter into the camp as had been ordered; but the javelin by accident sticking in a tower, remained there two days unperceived. On the third, a soldier saw it, took it down, and brought it to Cicero, who immediately read it in full assembly, and diffused the common joy through the whole camp. On the same time they perceived the smoke of the villages fired by Cæsar in his march, which put the arrival of the succours beyond all doubt.

XLI. The Gauls having notice of it also by their scouts, thought proper to quit the siege; and go to meet Cæsar. Their army consisted of about sixty thousand men. Cicero, now at liberty, applied again to Vertico for the slave spoken of above; and having admonished him to use the utmost diligence and circumspection, despatched him with a letter to Cæsar, informing him that the enemy had raised the siege, and were advancing against him with all their forces. Cæsar received the letter about midnight, communicated the contents to his army, and exhorted them to meet the enemy with courage. Next day he de camped early, and after a march of about four miles, discovered the Gauls on the other side of a large valley, with a river in front. It was dangerous to engage so great a force upon unequal ground. Knowing therefore that the siege of Cicero's camp was raised, and having no longer any reason to be in a hurry, he encamped in the most convenient spot he could find, and completed his intrenchments. His army consisting of no more than seven thousand men, without baggage, required at best but a very small camp; yet he purposely contracted it as much as possible, to inspire the enemy with the greater contempt of him. Meantime, sending out scouts on all sides, he endeavoured to find where he might cross the valley with most safety.

XLII. The rest of the day passed in slight skirmishes between the cavalry near the brook; but the main body of the army on both sides kept within their lines: the Gauls, in expectation of more forces, which were not yet come up; Cæsar, that by pretending fear, he might draw the enemy on this side the valley, and engage them before his camp; or, if that could not be effected, that having discovered the passes, he might be enabled to cross the valley and rivulet with less danger. Early next morning the enemy's cavalry coming up to our camp, charged our horse; who by Cæsar's orders, purposely gave ground, and retired behind the works. At the same time he caused the ramparts to be raised higher, the gates to be barricaded, and cautioned the soldiers in the execution of these orders, to run up and down tumultuously, and affect an air of timidity and concern. The enemy, invited by all these appearances, crossed the valley, and drew up in a very disadvantageous post. Our men meanwhile retiring from the rampart, they approached still nearer, cast their darts on all sides within the trenches, and sent heralds round the camp to proclaim, that if any of the Gauls or Romans had a mind to come over to them, they should be at liberty to do so till nine o'clock, after which no quarter would be granted. Nay, so far did they carry their contempt, that thinking they could not break in by the gates, (which to deceive them, were stopped up with single rows of turf,) some began to scale the rampart, others to fill up the ditch. But then, Cæsar, sallying by all the gates at once, and charging them briskly with his cavalry, put them so precipitately to flight, that not a man offered to make the least resistance. Great numbers of them were slain, and the rest obliged to throw down their arms.

XLIII. Not caring to pursue them far, on account of the woods and marshes that lay in his way; and finding that considerable execution had been done upon the spot, he the same day joined Cicero with all his forces; where, beholding the towers, galleries, and other works of the Gauls, he could not help being struck with admiration. He then reviewed Cicero's legion, and found that not a tenth man had escaped without wounds, which gave him a just idea of the greatness of the danger to which they had been exposed, and of the vigorous defence they had made. He bestowed great commendations on the legion, and its commander; and addressed himself to the military tribunes by name; of whose valour Cicero made honourable mention. He learned particularly from the prisoners all the circumstances of the unhappy affair of Sabinus and Cotta: and calling the soldiers together next day, gave them an account of the whole transaction, comforted them, confirmed their courage, and told them, that a disaster occasioned by the imprudence and rashness of the lieutenant, ought to give them the less disturbance; as by the favour of the immortal gods, and their valour, vengeance had followed so suddenly, that neither had the joy of the enemy for the victory continued any time, nor their grief for the loss remained long without allay.

XLIV. Meantime the report of Cæsar's victory flew with incredible speed, through the country of the Rhemi, to Labienus. For though he lay at the distance of fifty miles from Cicero's camp, whither Cæsar did not arrive till past three in the afternoon, yet before midnight a shout was raised at the gates of his camp; by which the Rhemi signified to him Cæsar's victory, and their own congratulation on that success. The report of this being carried to the Treviri, Indutiomarus, who the next day had determined to attack Labienus's camp, made off in the night, and retired with all his forces into his own country. Cæsar sent back Fabius with his legion to his former quarters, resolving to winter himself near Samarobriva, with three legions, distributed in three different cantonments; and

14

as all Gaul was in motion, to continue with the army in person. For the defeat and death of Sabinus spreading every where, almost all the states of Gaul were meditating a revolt; and with this view sent messengers and deputies into all parts, to concert measures, and contrive where to begin the war. Nay, they held assemblies by night in desert places; insomuch, that during the whole winter, scarce a day passed, but Cæsar had intelligence of some new resolves or insurrections of the Gauls. Among the rest, L. Roscius, his lieutenant, who commanded the thirteenth legion, sent him word that great numbers of Gauls from the several states of Armorica, had assembled to attack him, and advanced within eight miles of his camp; but upon hearing of Cæsar's victory, had separated so hastily, that their retreat had all the appearance of a flight.

XLV. But Cæsar summoning the principal noblemen of every state to attend him; partly by menaces, making them sensible he was no stranger to their designs; partly by exhortations, found means to keep the greatest part of Gaul in its duty. The Senones, however, a potent state, and of great authority among the Gauls, formed the design of publicly assassinating Cavarinus, whom Cæsar had given them for a king; whose brother, Moritasgus, had held the sovereignty at Cæsar's arrival in Gaul, and whose ancestors had long been in possession of the same dignity. But he having intelligence of the plot, thought proper to fly; whereupon, pursuing him to the very frontiers, they drove him from his palace and throne: and sending ambassadors to Cæsar to justify their conduct, upon his ordering their whole senate to repair to him, they refused to submit. So powerful was this example amongst the barbarians, that some at last were found of courage enough to begin the war; and so great a change did it produce in the inclinations of all, that except the Æduans and Rhemi, who had been always particularly distinguished and favoured by Cæsar; the first, on account of their ancient and inviolable fidelity to the people of Rome; the last, for their late services in the Gallic war; scarce was there a single state in all Gaul that did not incur suspicion. Nor is this, in truth, so much to be wondered at; as for many other reasons, so particularly for this: that a people famed above all nations for their military virtues,

could not with patience bear to see themselves so far stripped of their former renown, as to be forced to submit to the yoke of the Romans.

XLVI. Indutiomarus and the Treviri ceased not, during the whole winter, to send ambassadors over the Rhine; soliciting the German states; offering them money; and urging, that a great part of our army having already been cut off, much the least considerable remained. But no part of that country could be persuaded to come into their designs: because having twice before tried their fortune with the Romans, in the war with Ariovistus, and in the defeat of the Tenchtheri, they were resolved, they told them, to run no more hazards. Indutiomarus, disappointed of this hope, was no less active in drawing forces together, soliciting recruits from the neighbouring states, providing horses, and encouraging even outlaws and convicts, by the promise of great rewards, to engage in his service. And so great an authority had he by this means acquired in Gaul, that ambassadors flocked from all parts, some publicly, others in a private manner, to request his protection and friendship.

XLVII. Finding himself thus voluntarily applied to; on one side, by the Senones and Carnutes, impelled by a consciousness of the guilt they had incurred; on the other, by the Nervians and Atuatici, who were preparing for a war with the Romans; and that if he once took the field, forces would not be wanting; he called an assembly of the states in arms. This, according to the custom of the Gauls, implies an actual commencement of war; and, by a standing law, obliges all their youth to appear at the diet, in arms; in which they are so extremely strict, that whosoever has the misfortune to come last, is put to death in sight of the multitude, with all manner of torments. In this assembly, Cingetorix, the head of the opposite faction, and son-in-law of Indutiomarus, who, as we have related above, had declared for Cæsar, and still continued firm to him, was proclaimed a public enemy, and his estate confiscated. After which Indutiomarus acquainted the council, that the Senones, Carnutes, and several other states of Gaul had solicited his assistance; that he accordingly intended to join his forces with theirs, taking his route through the territories of the Rhemi, and giving up their lands to be plundered; but that before he began his march, he was desirous of mastering the camp of Labienus. To that end he gave the necessary directions.

XLVIII. Labienus, whose camp, both **by** the nature of the ground, and the fortifications he had added, **was extremely** strong, feared nothing, **either for himself or** the legion; but nevertheless was intent how he might give the enemy some considerable blow. Having there been informed by Cingetorix and his adherents, of the speech made by Indutiomarus in the council of Gaul, he sent deputies to the neighbouring states, solicited cavalry from all parts, and appointed them a day of rendezvous. Meantime Indutiomarus, with all his cavalry, appeared almost every day within sight of the camp; one while to examine its situation; another, to intimidate Labienus, or invite him **to a** conference. On these occasions, it was **usual for** the enemy to cast their darts over the rampart. Labienus kept his men within the works, and used all the methods he could think of to make the Gauls believe he was afraid of them.

XLIX. Indutiomarus approaching the trenches every day with greater contempt than before, Labienus received into his camp, by night, all the cavalry he had sent for from the neighbouring states; and was so careful to restrain his men within their lines, by guards planted at all the outlets, that it was impossible for the Treviri to get intelligence of the reinforcement he had received. Meantime Indutiomarus, according to custom, came up to the camp, and continued there the greater part of the day. The cavalry discharged their darts over the rampart, and in opprobrious language challenged our men to fight. The Romans making no answer, they retired towards night, but dispersed and without order. Then Labienus, ordering a sudden sally with all the cavalry, strictly cautioned and charged his **men, that** as soon as they had put the Gauls **to flight, (which** happened according to his **expectation,) they** should all single out Indutiomarus, nor offer to wound **a man** of the enemy, till they saw him slain: for he was unwilling that any delay, occasioned by the slaughter of the rest, should give him an opportunity to escape. He promised great rewards to the man that should kill him; and sent the cohorts after to sustain the horse. The design succeeded; for as all were intent upon Indutiomarus alone, he was overtaken and slain in passing a river, and his head brought back to the camp. Our cavalry, in their return, put all to the sword that came in their way. Upon the news of this defeat, the forces of the Eburones and Nervians returned home, and Gaul was somewhat quieter **the** rest of the winter.

CÆSAR'S COMMENTARIES

OF

HIS WARS IN GAUL.

BOOK VI

THE ARGUMENT.

CÆSAR'S COMMENTARIES

OF

HIS WARS IN GAUL.

BOOK VI.

1. CÆSAR, for many reasons, expecting greater commotions in Gaul, ordered his lieutenants, M. Silanus, C. Antistus Reginus, and T. Sextius, to levy troops. At the same time, he desired of Cn. Pompey, the proconsul, that since he was himself detained by public affairs at Rome, he would set on foot the legion he had enlisted in Cisalpine Gaul, during his consulship, and send it to him ; for he considered it as of the utmost importance towards securing a proper respect from the Gauls for the time to come, to give them such an idea of the power of Italy, as might convince them that it was not only able speedily to repair any losses sustained, but even to bring a greater force into the field. Friendship and the good of the commonwealth equally determined Pompey to yield to this request ; and the levies being completed with great diligence by the lieutenants, three new legions were formed and brought into Gaul before the end of winter. Thus having doubled the number of cohorts lost under Titurius, he soon made the enemy sensible both by his expedition and the strength of the reinforcement, of what they had to apprehend from the power and discipline of the Romans.

II. Indutiomarus being slain, as we have related above, the Treviri conferred the command on his relations. They persisted likewise in soliciting the Germans, and making them offers of money. But not being able to prevail with those that lay nearest them, they applied to some of the more remote states ; and finding them inclined to treat, entered into a solemn engagement with them, giving hostages for the security of the money stipulated,

and associating Ambiorix into the confederacy. Cæsar, informed of these things, and finding that he was threatened with war on all sides ; that the Nervians, Atuatici, and Menapians, with all the Germans on this side the Rhine, were actually in arms ; that the Senones refused to attend him according to orders, and were tampering with the Carnutes and other neighbouring states ; and that the Treviri were soliciting the Germans by frequent embassies ; he judged it would be necessary to open the campaign early. Accordingly, without waiting till the winter was at an end, he drew together the four nearest legions, and fell unexpectedly into the territories of the Nervians, before they could either assemble in a body, or find means to save themselves by flight. Having carried off a great number of men and cattle, enriched his soldiers with the booty, and laid waste the country, he compelled them to submit and give hostages ; and then led back his legions to their winter-quarters.

III. Early in the spring, having summoned a general assembly of Gaul, pursuant to his design ; as all the other states but the Senones, Carnutes, and Treviri, appeared, looking upon this as the beginning of a revolt, and willing to postpone every thing else, he adjourned the diet to Paris. This city was upon the borders of the Senones, and had been united with them about an age before ; but was thought to have no share in their present revolt. Having declared the adjournment to the assembly, he the same day set out with his legions against the Senones, and by great

168

marches reached their territories. Acco, who was at the head of the confederacy, hearing of his approach, ordered the multitude to shelter themselves in the towns; but before that could be done, the Romans appeared. This obliged them to change their measures, and send deputies to Cæsar, to implore forgiveness. They were seconded by the Æduans, the old and faithful allies of the Romans, at whose request Cæsar readily pardoned them; and the rather, because the summer being now come, he had no mind to spend the season for action in proceeding formally against the guilty. He ordered them to send a hundred hostages, whom he committed to the custody of the Æduans. The Carnutes too, at the intercession of the Rhemi, under whose protection they were, having sent deputies and hostages, obtained the same conditions. Cæsar then went to the assembly of the states, put an end to the diet, and ordered the Gauls to provide him cavalry.

IV. Tranquillity being restored in these parts, Cæsar turned all his thoughts to the management of the war with Ambiorix and the Treviri. He ordered Cavarinus to attend him with the cavalry of the Senones, to prevent any new commotions in his absence, either in consequence of the resentment of that prince, or the hatred he had incurred of the state. And having thus settled all things to his mind, as he knew Ambiorix was determined not to hazard a battle, he set himself to watch his other designs.

V. The Menapians, whose territories border upon those of the Eburones, are secured by woods and morasses on every side; and were the only people of Gaul, who had not sent ambassadors to Cæsar to desire a peace. He knew Ambiorix was in good intelligence with them; and that by means of the Treviri, he had also entered into an alliance with the Germans. He therefore thought it best to deprive him of these resources, before he attacked him in person; lest despairing of being able to defend himself, he should either retire among the Menapians, or throw himself into the arms of the Germans beyond the Rhine. This resolution being taken, he sent the baggage of the whole army to Labienus, in the country of the Treviri, ordered him a reinforcement of two legions, and marched himself against the Menapians with five legions, who carried nothing with them but their arms.

That nation trusting to their situation, instead of assembling forces, retreated to their woods and morasses, and carried all their effects along with them. Cæsar divided his forces with C. Fabius his lieutenant, and M. Crassus his questor, and having speedily finished his bridges, entered their country in three bodies, set all their houses and villages on fire, and carried off such numbers of men and cattle, that the Menapians were at last constrained to sue for peace. He granted it on condition they sent him hostages, and engaged not to admit Ambiorix, or any one from him, into their territories; threatening to treat them as enemies if they did. These things settled, he left Comius of Arras there, with a body of horse, to keep them in awe, and set out himself against the Treviri.

VI. Whilst Cæsar was thus employed, the Treviri, having drawn together a great number of horse and foot, were preparing to attack the legion, which had wintered in their territories, under Labienus. They were now advanced within two days' march of the lieutenant's camp, when they learned that he had received a reinforcement of two legions from Cæsar. Upon this, encamping at about fifteen miles' distance, they resolved to wait for the auxiliaries they expected from Germany. Labienus, having intelligence of their design, and hoping their rashness might furnish him with an opportunity of fighting, left the baggage under a guard of five cohorts; and with the twenty-five remaining, and all his cavalry, marched towards the enemy, and pitched his camp about a mile from them.

VII. Between Labienus and the enemy was a river, with steep banks, and difficult to pass. And indeed neither was Labienus himself minded to try the passage, nor did he expect the enemy would offer at such an attempt. The hope of being joined by the auxiliaries grew stronger in the camp of the Gauls every day. Labienus declared publicly in a council of war, "That as the Germans were said to be upon the march, he was determined not to expose himself and the army to danger, but would decamp early next morning." This was soon carried to the enemy; for as our cavalry consisted mostly of Gauls, it was natural for some of them to favour their countrymen. Labienus, assembling the military tribunes and principal centurions during the night, laid before them his real design; and the better to betray the enemy into a suspicion of his being afraid, gave orders for decamping with more noise and tumult than was usual in a Roman army. By this means his march had all the appearance of a flight; and the enemy, whose camp was so very near, had notice of it before daybreak from their spies.

VIII. Scarce had our rear got without the trenches, when the Gauls encouraging one another not to lose a fair prey, or stay in expectation of the Germans, at a time the Romans were retreating in such a panic: and considering it as an indignity, with so great a superiority of forces, to forbear attacking a handful of men already put to flight and encumbered with their baggage, resolved to pass the river, and engage the Romans, notwithstanding the disadvantage of the ground. Labienus, who had foreseen this, that he might draw them all over the river, continued the feint of his march, and went on quietly. Then sending the baggage a little before, and ordering it to be placed upon a rising ground:— "Behold, fellow-soldiers," says he, "the opportunity you so much desired: you have the enemy at a disadvantage, and in a place where they cannot sustain the onset: show only under my command the valour you have so often manifested to our general; think him present and that he sees and observes you." At the same time he ordered them to face about, and form in line of battle; and detaching a few troops of horse to guard the baggage, drew up the rest on the two wings. Our men gave a sudden shout, and threw their javelins. The enemy, contrary to their expectation, seeing those whom they imagined put to flight, marching against them with displayed banners, could not sustain the very first shock; but betaking themselves immediately to flight, took refuge in the nearest woods. Labienus pursuing with his cavalry, put many of the enemy to the sword, and took a great number of prisoners; insomuch that within a few days the whole state was obliged to submit: for the Germans, who were coming to their assistance, upon hearing of their defeat, returned home. The relations of Indutiomarus, who had been the authors of the revolt, chose likewise to retire with them, and abandon their country. Cingetorix, who had always continued faithful to the Romans, was thereupon invested with the supreme authority.

IX. Cæsar after his arrival in Treves, from among the Menapians, resolved for two reasons to pass the Rhine: one, because the Germans had assisted the Treviri against the Romans; the other to deprive Ambiorix of a retreat into those parts. In consequence of this resolution, he set about making a bridge on the river, but somewhat higher up than before. As the form and manner was known, the soldiers, by their extraordinary diligence, finished the work in a few days. Leaving a strong guard on the side of Treves, to prevent any sudden insurrection in that country, he carried over the rest of his army. The Ubians, who had before submitted and given hostages sent ambassadors to him to vindicate their conduct, and assure him, that they had neither sent troops to the assistance of the Treviri, nor in any instance departed from their engagements. They urged and requested that he would spare their territories, and not, out of a general hatred to the Germans, involve the innocent in the punishment of the guilty. If he desired more hostages they told him they were ready to send them. Cæsar finding, upon inquiry, that the supplies had been sent by the Suevians, accepted the submission of the Ubians; and preparing to march against the Suevians, informed himself of the ways and accesses to their country.

X. A few days after, he had intelligence from the Ubians, that the Suevians were drawing their forces to a general rendezvous, and had sent orders to all the nations under their jurisdiction, to furnish their contingents of horse and foot. Upon this, having furnished himself with provisions, and chosen a proper place for his camp, he ordered the Ubians to retire into their towns, with their cattle and effects; hoping that so unskilful and barbarous an enemy might easily be drawn, by the want of provisions, to fight in a place of disadvantage. He further enjoined the Ubians to send spies into all parts, to learn the designs and motions of the Suevians. They readily complied; and in a few days brought him back word, "That the Suevians, upon certain information of the arrival of the Roman army, had retired to the remotest part of the country, with all their own forces, and those of their allies: that there they had resolved to wait the coming up of the Romans, at the entrance of a forest of immense extent, called Bacenis, which reached a great way into the country, and served as a barrier between the Cherusci and Suevians, to prevent their mutual incursions."

XI. On this occasion it may not be improper to say somewhat of the manners of the Gauls and Germans, and the difference of customs between these two nations. A spirit of faction prevails throughout Gaul, and that not only in their several states, districts, and villages, but almost in every private family. The men of greatest esteem and consideration among them, are commonly at the head of these factions, and give what turn they think proper to all public deliberations and counsels. This custom is of long standing, and seems designed to secure those of lower rank from the oppression of the powerful: for the leaders always take care to protect those of their party, otherwise they would soon lose all their authority. This equally obtains through the whole continent of Gaul, the provinces being in general divided into two factions.

XII. When Cæsar arrived in the country, the Æduans were at the head of one faction, and the Sequani of the other. These last being the weaker, because the Æduans had long borne the greatest sway, and had a number of considerable states in their dependence, they united with Ariovistus and the Germans, whom by great presents and promises they drew over the Rhine to their assistance. This alliance made them so powerful, that having worsted their adversaries in several battles, and killed almost all their nobility, they forced the states dependent upon the Æduans to have recourse to them for protection; obliged the Æduans themselves to give the children of their principal nobility as hostages, swear publicly not to attempt any thing against the Sequani, and resign up to their possession a part of their territories; and by this means rendered themselves in a manner sovereigns of all Gaul. Divitiacus, in this necessity, applied to the senate of Rome for relief, but without effect. Cæsar's arrival soon changed the face of affairs. The Æduan hostages were sent back, their former clients restored, and new ones procured them by Cæsar's interest; it appearing, that such as were under their protection, enjoyed a more equal and milder lot: by all which, their fortune and authority being considerably enlarged, the Sequani were obliged to resign the sovereignty. The Rhemi succeeded in their place; and, as they were known to be in the same degree of favour with

Cæsar, such as could not get over their old animosity to the Æduans, put themselves under their protection. The Rhemi were extremely attentive to the interests of their clients, and thereby both preserved their old authority, and that which they had newly acquired. Such therefore was the then situation of Gaul, that the Æduans possessing indisputably the first rank, the Rhemi were next in consideration and dignity.

XIII. Over all Gaul, there are only two orders of men, in any degree of honour and esteem: for the common people are little better than slaves, attempt nothing of themselves, and have no share in the public deliberations. As they are generally oppressed with debt, heavy tributes, or the exactions of their superiors, they make themselves vassals to the great, who exercise over them the same jurisdiction as masters do over slaves. The two orders of men, with whom, as we have said, all authority and distinctions are lodged, are the Druids and nobles. The Druids preside in matters of religion, have the care of public and private sacrifices, and interpret the will of the gods. They have the direction and education of the youth, by whom they are held in great honour. In almost all controversies, whether public or private, the decision is left to them: and if any crime is committed, any murder perpetrated; if any dispute arises touching an inheritance, or the limits of adjoining estates; in all such cases, they are the supreme judges. **They** decree rewards and punishments; and **if** any one refuses to submit to their sentence, **whether** magistrate or **private** man, they **interdict him** the sacrifices. This is the greatest punishment that can be inflicted among the Gauls; because such as **are under** this prohibition, are considered as impious and wicked: all men shun them, and decline their conversation and fellowship, lest they should suffer from the contagion of their misfortunes. They can neither have recourse to the law for justice, nor are capable of any public office. The Druids are all under one chief, who possesses the supreme authority in that body. Upon his death, if any one remarkably excels the rest, he succeeds; but if there are several candidates of equal merit, the affair is determined by plurality of suffrages. Sometimes they even have recourse to arms before the election can be brought to an issue. Once a yea they assemble at a consecrated place in the terr-tories of the Carnutes, whose country is supposed to be in the middle of Gaul. Hither such as have any suits depending, flock from all parts, and submit implicitly to their decrees. Their institution is supposed to come originally from Britain, whence it passed into Gaul; and even at this day, such as are desirous of being perfect in it, travel thither for instruction. The Druids never go to war, are exempted from taxes and military service, and enjoy all manner of immunities. These mighty encouragements induce multitudes of their own accord to follow that profession; and many are sent by their parents and relations. They are taught to repeat a great number of verses by heart, and often spend twenty years upon this institution; for it is deemed unlawful to commit their statutes to writing; though in other matters, whether public or private, they make use of Greek characters. They seem to me to follow this method for two reasons: to hide their mysteries from the knowledge of the vulgar; and to exercise the memory of their scholars, which would be apt to lie neglected, had they letters to trust to, as we find is often the case. It is one of their principal maxims that the soul never dies, but after death passes from one body to another; which, they think, contributes greatly to exalt men's courage, by disarming death of its terrors. They teach likewise many things relating to the stars and their motions, the magnitude of the world and our earth, the nature of things, and the power and prerogatives of the immortal gods.

XIV. The other order of men is the nobles, whose whole study and occupation is war. Before Cæsar's arrival in Gaul, they were almost every year at war either offensive or defensive; and they judge of the power and quality of their nobles, by the vassals, and the number of men he keeps in his pay; for they are the only marks of grandeur they make any account of.

XV. The whole nation of the Gauls is extremely addicted to superstition; whence, in threatening distempers and the imminent dangers of war, they make no scruple to sacrifice men, or engage themselves by vow to such sacrifices; in which they make use of the ministry of the Druids: for it is a prevalent opinion among them, that nothing but the life of man can atone for the life of man; insomuch that they have established even public sacrifices of this kind. Some prepare huge Colossuses, of osier twigs, into which they put men alive, and setting fire to them, those within expire amidst the flames. They prefer for victims such as have been convicted of theft, robbery, or other crimes; believing them the most acceptable to the gods: but when real criminals are wanting, the innocent are often made to suffer. Mercury is the chief deity with them; of him they have many images, account him the inventor of all arts, their guide and conductor in their journeys, and the patron of merchandise and gain. Next to him are Apollo and Mars, and Jupiter, and Minerva. Their notions in regard to him are pretty much the same with those of other nations. Apollo is their god of physic; Minerva of works and manufactures; Jove holds the empire of heaven; and Mars presides in war. To this last, when they resolve upon a battle, they commonly devote the spoil. If they prove victorious, they offer up all the cattle taken, and set apart the rest of the plunder in a place appointed for that purpose: and it is common in many provinces, to see these monuments of offerings piled up in consecrated places. Nay, it rarely happens that any one shows so great a disregard of religion, as either to conceal the plunder, or pillage the public oblations; and the severest punishments are inflicted upon such offenders.

XVI. The Gauls fancy themselves to be descended from the god Pluto; which, it seems, is an established tradition among the Druids. For this reason they compute the time by nights, not by days; and in the observance of birth days, new moons, and the beginning of the year, always commence the celebration from the preceding night. In one custom they differ from almost all other nations; that they never suffer their children to come openly into their presence, until they are of age to bear arms; for the appearance of a son in public with his father, before he has reached the age of manhood, is accounted dishonourable.

XVII. Whatever fortune the woman brings, the husband is obliged to equal it with his own estate. This whole sum, with its annual product, is left untouched, and falls always to the share of the survivor. The men have power of life and death over their wives and children; and when any father of a family of illustrious rank dies, his relations assemble, and upon the least ground of suspicion, put even his wives to the torture like slaves. If they are found guilty, iron and fire are employed to torment and destroy them. Their funerals are magnificent and sumptuous, according to their quality. Every thing that was dear to the deceased, even animals, are thrown into the pile : and formerly, such of their slaves and clients as they loved most, sacrificed themselves at the funeral of their lord.

XVIII. In their best regulated states, they have a law, that whoever hears any thing relating to the public, whether by rumour or otherwise, shall give immediate notice to the magistrate, without imparting it to any one else ; for the nature of the people is such, that rash and inexperienced men, alarmed by false reports, are often hurried to the greatest extremities, and take upon them to determine in matters of the greatest consequence. The magistrates stifle things improper to be known, and only communicate to the multitude what they think needful for the service of the commonwealth ; nor do the laws permit to speak of state affairs, except in public council.

XIX. The Germans differ widely in their manners from the Gauls : for neither have they Druids to preside in religious affairs, nor do they trouble themselves about sacrifices. They acknowledge no gods but those that are objects of sight, and by whose power they are apparently benefited ; the sun, the moon, fire. Of others they know nothing, not even by report. Their whole life is addicted to hunting and war ; and from their infancy they are inured to fatigue and hardships. They esteem those most, who continue longest strangers to women ; as imagining nothing contributes so much to stature, strength and vigour of body : but to have any commerce of this kind before the age of twenty is accounted in the highest degree ignominious. Nor is it possible to conceal an irregularity this way ; because they bathe promiscuously in rivers, and are clothed in skins, or short mantles of fur, which leave the greatest part of their bodies naked.

XX. Agriculture is little regarded among them, as they live mostly on milk, cheese, and the flesh of animals. Nor has any man lands of his own, or distinguished by fixed boundaries. The magistrates, and those in authority, portion out yearly to every canton and family, such a quantity of land, and in what part of the country they think proper ; and the year following remove them to some other spot.

Many reasons are assigned for this practice ; lest seduced by habit and continuance, they should learn to prefer tillage to war ; lest a desire of enlarging their possessions should gain ground, and prompt the stronger to expel the weaker ; lest they should become curious in their buildings, in order to guard against the extremes of heat and cold ; lest avarice should get footing amongst them, whence spring factions and discords : in fine, to preserve contentment and equanimity among the people, when they find their possessions nothing inferior to those of the most powerful.

XXI. It is accounted honourable for estates to have the country all around them lie waste and depopulated : for they think it an argument of valour to expel their neighbours, and suffer none to settle near them ; at the same time that they are themselves all the safer, as having nothing to apprehend from sudden incursions. When a state is engaged in war, either offensive or defensive, they make choice of magistrates to preside in it, whom they arm with a power of life and death. In time of peace there are no public magistrates ; but the chiefs of the several provinces and clans administer justice, and decide differences within their respective limits. Robbery has nothing infamous in it, when committed without the territories of the state to which they belong : they even pretend that it serves to exercise their youth and prevent the growth of sloth. When any of their princes in this case offers himself publicly in council as a leader, such as approve of the expedition rise up, profess themselves ready to follow him, and are applauded by the whole multitude. They who go back from their engagement are looked upon as traitors and deserters, and lose all esteem and credit for the time to come. The laws of hospitality are held inviolable among them. All that fly to them for refuge, on whatever account, are sure of protection and defence ; their houses are open to receive them, and they plentifully supply their wants.

XXII. Formerly the Gauls exceeded the Germans in bravery, often made war upon them, and as they abounded in people beyond what the country could maintain, sent severe colonies over the Rhine. Accordingly the more fertile places of Germany, in the neighbourhood of the Hercynian forest, (which I find mentioned by Eratosthenes, and other Greek writers, under the name of Orcinia,) fell to the share of the Volcæ, who settled in those parts, and have ever since kept possession. They are in the highest reputation for justice and bravery, and no less remarkable than the Germans for poverty, abstinence, and patience of fatigue, conforming exactly to their customs, both in habit and way of living. But the neighbourhood of the Roman province, and an acquaintance with traffic, has introduced luxury and abundance among the Gauls, whence becoming by little and little an unequal match for the Germans, and being worsted in many battles, they no longer pretend to compare with them in valour.

XXIII. The Hercynian forest, of which we have been just speaking, is about nine days' journey in breadth; for as the Germans are ignorant of the use of measures, there is no other way of computing it. It begins from the confines of the Helvetians, Nemetes, and Rauraci; and following directly the course of the Danube, extends to the territories of the Anartes and Dacians. Thence turning from the river to the left, it runs through a multitude of different regions; and though there are many in the country, who have advanced six days' journey into this forest, yet no one pretends to have reached the extremity of it, or discovered how far it extends. Many different species of animals, unknown in other countries, harbour here; the most remarkable of which, and that best deserve to be mentioned, are these.

XXIV. There is a bull that nearly resembles a stag, with only one horn rising from the middle of his forehead, taller and straighter than those of our cattle, and which at top divides into many large branches. The males and females are shaped alike, and have horns the same in size.

XXV. Here are likewise a kind of wild asses, shaped and spotted like goats, but of a larger size; without horns, or joints in their legs, that never lie down to sleep, nor can raise themselves, if by any accident they are overthrown. They lean against trees, which serve to support them when they sleep. Hence the huntsmen, after having discovered their haunts, either loosen the roots of the trees, or saw them almost quite off; so that when the animal, according to custom, reclines against them, they immediately give way, and both fall down together.

XXVI. A third species of animals are the uri, nearly equalling the elephant in bulk; but in colour, shape, and kind, resembling a bull. They are of uncommon strength and swiftness, and spare neither man nor beast that comes in their way. They are taken and slain by means of pits dug on purpose. This way of hunting is frequent among the youth, and serves to inure them to fatigue. They who kill the greatest number, and produce their horns in public, as a proof, are in high reputation with their countrymen. It is found impossible to tame them, or conquer their fierceness, though taken ever so young. Their horns, both in largeness, figure, and kind, differ much from those of our bulls. The natives preserve them with great care, tip their edges with silver, and use them instead of cups on their most solemn festivals.

XXVII. Cæsar understanding from the Ubian scouts, that the Suevians were retired into their woods; and fearing the want of provisions, because, as we have already observed, the Germans are but little addicted to agriculture, resolved not to advance any further. But to keep the enemy still under some awe of his return, and prevent their sending succours to Gaul, having repassed the Rhine, he only broke down about two hundred feet of his bridge, on the German side; and to secure the rest, built at the extremity a tower of four stories, where he left a garrison of twelve cohorts, and strengthened the place with all manner of works. Young C. Volcatius Tullus had the charge of the fort and garrison. He himself, as soon as the corn began to be ripe, marched against Ambiorix; taking his way through the forest of Arden, which is much the largest in all Gaul, and reaches from the banks of the Rhine, and the confines of Treves, quite to the Nervians, through a space of more than five hundred miles. L. Minucius Basilus was sent before, with all the cavalry, in hopes that the quickness of his march, and the opportunity of some lucky conjuncture, might enable him to do something considerable. He had orders to light no fires in his camp, the better to conceal his approach from the enemy; and Cæsar assured him, that he would follow with all expedition. Basilus exactly followed his instructions; and coming suddenly and unexpectedly upon the Gauls, surprised great numbers of them in the field. Being informed by them, of the place whither Ambiorix had retired, with a few cavalry, he marched directly against him.

XXVIII. But as fortune has a considerable share in all human concerns, so particularly in those of war. For as it was a very extraordinary chance, that he should thus come upon Ambiorix unprepared, and surprise him with his personal arrival, before he had the least notice of it from fame or report; so was it an equal effect of fortune, that the Gaul himself, after having lost his arms, horses, and chariots, should yet find means to escape. This was principally owing to the situation of his house, which was surrounded with a wood; it being customary among the Gauls, in order to avoid the seats, to build in the neighbourhood of woods and rivers. By this means his attendants and friends possessing themselves of a defile, sustained for a time the attack of our cavalry; during which, one of his servants having provided him with a horse, he escaped into the woods. Thus fortune remarkably played her part, both in bringing him into the danger and delivering him out of it.

XXIX. Ambiorix, after his escape, made no attempt to draw his forces together; nor is it known whether he acted in this manner out of choice, as not thinking it safe to hazard a battle; or because he thought he should not have sufficient time, being surprised by the sudden arrival of the cavalry, and believing that all the rest of the army followed. Despatching, therefore, messengers privately through the country, he counselled every one to provide for his own safety; upon which some took refuge in the forest of Arden, and some in the adjoining morasses. Those who lived upon the sea-coast, hid themselves in the islands formed by the tide at high water; and many abandoning their country altogether, trusted themselves and their all to the faith of foreigners. Cativulcus, who, jointly with Ambiorix, was king of the Eburones, and had associated with him in all his designs, being of a very advanced age, and unable to bear the fatigues of war or flight, after many imprecations against Ambiorix, who had been the prime contriver of the revolt, poisoned himself with an extract of yew, a tree very common in Gaul and Germany. The Segni and Condrusi, originally German nations, whose territories lay between those of Treves and the Eburones, sent ambassadors to Cæsar, to entreat "That he would not consider them as enemies, nor look upon all the Germans on this side the Rhine as equally obnoxious: that they had harboured no thoughts of war, nor been any ways aiding to Ambiorix." Cæsar finding it to be so by the answers of the prisoners, ordered them to deliver up such of the Eburones as had fled to them for refuge; and promised, upon that condition, not to molest their territories.

XXX. Then dividing his army into three bodies, he sent all the baggage to Atuatuca, a castle situated almost in the heart of the country of the Eburones, where Titurius and Arunculeius had been quartered during the winter. This place he chose, as for other reasons, so likewise because the fortifications, raised the year before, were still entire, which would lessen the labour of his soldiers. He left the fourteenth legion to guard the baggage, being one of the three lately levied in Italy, and brought thence into Gaul. Q. Tullius Cicero had the charge both of the legion and fort, which was further strengthened with an additional guard of two hundred horse. The army being thus divided, he sent T. Labienus, with three legions, towards the sea coast, and the provinces that border upon the Menapians; C. Trebonius, with a like number of legions, to lay waste the country adjoining to the Atuatici; and resolved to march himself with the other three towards the Scheld, which flows into the Meuse, and to the extremities of the forest of Arden, whither he was informed Ambiorix had retired with a few horse. He promised, at his departure, to return in seven days; the legion he had left in garrison being provided with corn only for that time: and exhorted Labienus and Trebonius, if they found it consistent with the public advantage, to return likewise with their legions within the same space; that joining counsel together, and taking their measures from the conduct of the enemy, they might resolve where next to carry the war.

XXXI. There was, as we have already observed, no formed body of troops, no garrison, no fortified town to defend by arms; but a multitude dispersed on all sides. Wherever a cave, or a thicket, or a morass offered them shelter, thither they retired. These places were well known to the natives; and great care and caution was required on our part not for the security of the whole army, (which had no danger to fear whilst in a body, from enemies dispersed and full of terror;) but for the preservation of each individual. And yet even this regarded not a little the whole army: for the desire of plunder drew many of the men to a great distance; and the woods, full of defiles and hidden ways, hindered them from keeping together in a body. If Cæsar meant to terminate the war altogether, and extirpate this race of perfidious men, the soldiers must be divided into small parties, and detached on all sides. If, on the contrary, he kept his men together, as the rules of war and the Roman discipline required, the enemy were sheltered by their situation, nor wanted boldness to form ambuscades, and cut off stragglers. Amidst these difficulties, all possible precautions were taken; and although the soldiers were eagerly bent upon revenge, yet Cæsar chose rather not to push the enemy too far, than expose his men to danger. He therefore sent messengers to the neighbouring states, inviting them all by the hopes of plunder, to join the destruction of the Eburones; choosing rather to expose the lives of the Gauls in the woods, than of the legionary soldiers; and hoping, by the multitude employed against them, totally to extirpate the name and memory of a state, whose revolt had rendered them so obnoxious. Accordingly great numbers flocked suddenly thither from all parts.

XXXII. Thus were the Eburones attacked on all sides; and the havoc continued till the seventh day, which Cæsar had appointed for returning to his camp and baggage. It then evidently appeared what influence fortune has over war, and how many accidents spring from her interposition. The enemy being dispersed and full of terror, as we have related above, there remained no body of troops in the field, to give any the least ground of fear. A report spread among the Germans beyond the Rhine, that the territories of the Eburones were given up to plunder, and all without distinction invited to share the spoil. The Sicambri, who inhabit upon the Rhine, and had afforded a retreat to the Usipetes and Tenchtheri, as mentioned above, assembled immediately a body of two thousand horse, passed the river in barks about thirty miles below Cæsar's bridge and fort, and advanced directly towards the territories of the Eburones. Many of those

that fled, and had dispersed themselves up and down the country, fell into their hands, as likewise abundance of cattle, of which the barbarians are extremely covetous. Allured by this success, they advanced farther. Neither woods nor morasses proved any obstacles to men, trained up from their infancy to wars and incursions. Inquiring of the prisoners concerning Cæsar, they understood that he was a great way off, and had left the country with his whole army. One in particular addressing them: "Why, says he, do you lose time in pursuit of so slight and trifling a booty, when fortune offers one of so much greater value? In three hours you may reach Atustuca, where the Romans have deposited all their wealth. The garrison is hardly sufficient to line the rampart, much less to sally out of their intrenchments." Urged by this hope, they left their present booty in a place of safety, and marched directly to Atustuca, being conducted by the captive who had given them the information.

XXXIII. Cicero, who hitherto had kept his soldiers strictly within the camp, according to Cæsar's orders, nor suffered so much as a servant to straggle beyond the lines; seeing the seventh day arrive, began to despair of Cæsar's return, who, as he had heard, marched farther into the country, and had sent him no notice of his route. Wherefore, tired with the continual murmurs of the soldiers, who complained of his patience, and told him they were kept like men besieged; and not suspecting that any accident could befall him, within the small extent of three miles, especially as the enemy, opposed by nine legions, and a very numerous cavalry, were in a manner totally dispersed and cut off; he sent out five cohorts to forage in an adjoining field, separated from the camp only by a single hill. A great many sick men had been left behind by Cæsar, of whom about three hundred, that were now pretty well recovered, joined the detachment. These were followed by almost all the servants of the camp, together with a vast number of carts and carriage-horses.

XXXIV. In that very instant, as fortune would have it, the German cavalry arrived; and without discontinuing their course, endeavoured to force an immediate entrance by the Decuman gate. As their march had been covered by a wood, they were not discovered till they were just upon the camp; insomuch that the sutlers, who kept their booths under the rampart, had not time to retire within the intrenchments. Our men were so surprised at this sudden and unexpected attack, that the cohort upon guard could scarce sustain the first onset. The enemy spread themselves on all sides to find a place of entrance. The Romans with difficulty defended the gates; the rampart securing them every where else. The whole camp was in an uproar, every one inquiring of another the cause of the confusion; nor could they determine which way to advance the standards, or where to post themselves. Some reported the camp was already taken; others, that the Germans, having destroyed Cæsar and his army, were come victorious, to storm their trenches. The greater number, full of imaginary fears, when they considered the place in which they were encamped, called to mind the fate of Cotta and Titurius, who perished in that very fort. This universal consternation being perceived by the barbarians, confirmed them in the belief of what the prisoners had told them, that there was scarce any garrison within to defend the camp. They renewed their endeavours to force the intrenchments, and mutually exhorted one another, not to let so fair a prize escape out of their hands.

XXXV. Among the sick in garrison was P. Sextius Baculus, a centurion of the first rank, of whom mention has been made in former battles, and who had not tasted food for five days. This officer, anxious for his own safety, and that of the legion, rushed unarmed out of his tent. He saw the enemy at hand, and the danger extreme. Snatching the first arms that offered, he posted himself in the gate of the camp. The centurions of the cohort upon guard followed the example, and for a while sustained the enemy's charge. Sextius expired under a number of wounds, and was with difficulty carried off by the soldiers. This short delay give the rest time to resume their courage; so far at least, as to mount the rampart, and make a show of defending themselves.

XXXVI. Meantime our foragers returning, heard the noise at the camp. The cavalry advancing before, were soon apprized of the danger. Here was no fortification to shelter the frighted troops. The new levies, inexperienced in matters of war, fixed their eyes upon the tribunes and centurions, waiting their orders. Not a man was found so hardy and resolute as not to be disturbed by so unexpected an accident. The Germans perceiving our ensigns at a distance, gave over the attack of the camp, imagining at first that it was Cæsar and the legions, which the prisoners had informed them were marched farther into the country. But soon observing how few they were, they surrounded and fell upon them on all sides.

XXXVII. The servants of the camp fled to the nearest rising ground; whence being immediately driven, they threw themselves amongst the ranks of the cohorts, and thereby increased their terror. Some were for drawing up in form of a wedge, and forcing their way through the enemy: for as the camp was so very near, they imagined, that if some fell, the rest at least must escape. Others were for retiring to an eminence, and all sharing there the same fate. The veteran soldiers, who had marched but with the detachment, could by no means relish this proposal: wherefore mutually encouraging one another, and being led by C. Trebonius, a Roman knight, under whose command they were, they broke through the midst of the enemy, and all to a man arrived safe in the camp. The servants and cavalry following them, and seconding their retreat were likewise, by their bravery, preserved. But the troops who had retired to the hill, being inexperienced in military affairs, could neither persist in the resolution they had taken of defending themselves from the higher ground, nor imitate that brisk and vigorous effort which they saw had been so serviceable to their companions: but endeavouring to gain the camp, quitted the advantage of their situation. The centurions, some of whom had been selected from veteran legions, and on account of their bravery promoted to higher stations among the new levies, fought resolutely to maintain the glory they had acquired, and endeavoured to sell their lives as dear as they could. Their valour obliging the enemy to fall back a little, part of the troops, contrary to expectation, reached the camp. The rest were surrounded and cut to pieces by the barbarians.

XXXVIII. The Germans, despairing to carry the camp, as they saw our men now prepared to defend the works, repassed the Rhine with the booty they had deposited in the woods

But so great was the terror of the Romans even after their retreat, that C. Volusenus arriving in the camp the same night with the cavalry, could not persuade them that Cæsar and the army were safe. For the fear had taken so thorough a possession of their minds, that, as if bereft of understanding, they persisted in believing the infantry was wholly destroyed, and that the cavalry alone had escaped: it seeming to them altogether incredible, that the Germans would have dared to attack the camp, had no misfortune befallen the Roman army. But Cæsar's arrival soon put an end to their fears.

XXXIX. Upon his return, being informed of what had happened, he only complained of the sending out the cohorts to forage: observing, " That in war nothing ought to be left to fortune, whose power appeared evidently in the sudden arrival of the enemy, and much more in their coming up unperceived to the very gates of the camp." But nothing in this whole affair appeared to him more wonderful, than that the Germans, having crossed the Rhine with design to plunder the territories of Ambiorix, should, by falling upon the Roman camp, do him a most acceptable service.

XL. Cæsar marched a second time to harass the enemy, and having drawn a great number of troops together from the neighbouring states, sent them into all parts upon this service. All the houses and villages were set on fire; the plunder was universal; the vast number of men and horses not only destroyed great quantities of corn, but the rains and advanced seasons made havoc of all that was left; insomuch that if any of the enemy escaped for the present, it seemed yet likely, that after the retreat of the army, they must perish by famine. As the cavalry were divided into many parties, they often came to places where the prisoners not only informed them they had seen Ambiorix flying, but that he could even yet be scarce out of view. The hope of coming up with him made them leave nothing unattempted, as imagining they would thereby gain the highest favour with Cæsar, whose good fortune wanted only this to render it complete. But all their endeavours were fruitless; for he still found means to hide himself in the woods and morasses; whence removing privately in the night, he escaped into other regions, accompanied with only four horsemen, in whom alone he durst confide.

XLI. Cæsar, having destroyed the whole country, led back his army into the territories of the Rhemi, with the loss of only two cohorts. There he summoned a general assembly of Gaul, to examine into the affair of the Senones and Carnutes: and having passed a severe sentence against Acco, the contriver of the revolt, ordered him to be executed on the spot. Some fearing a like fate, fled; whom having banished by a decree of the diet, he quartered two legions in Treves, two among the Lingones, and the remaining six at Agendicum, in the country of the Senones. And having provided the army with corn, he went, pursuant to his design, into Italy, to hold the assemblies of Cisalpine Gaul.

CÆSAR'S COMMENTARIES

OF

HIS WARS IN GAUL.

————

BOOK VII.

THE ARGUMENT.

CÆSAR'S COMMENTARIES

HIS WARS IN GAUL.

BOOK VII.

I. CÆSAR having quieted the commotions in Gaul, went, as he designed, into Italy, to preside in the assembly of the states. There he was informed of the death of P. Clodius: and understanding further, that the senate had passed a decree, ordering all the youth of Italy to take up arms, he resolved to levy troops over the whole province. The report of this soon spread into farther Gaul: and the Gauls themselves, forward to encourage such rumours, added of their own accord what the case seemed to require:—" That Cæsar was detained by a domestic sedition, and could not, while these disorders continued, come to head the army." Animated by this opportunity, they, who before lamented their subjection to the Romans, now began with more freedom and boldness to enter upon measures of war. The leading men of the nation, concerting private meetings among themselves, in woods and remote places, complained of the death of Acco; remonstrated that such might one time or other be their own fate; and after bemoaning the common fortune of their country, endeavoured by all manner of promises and rewards, to draw over some to begin the war, and with the hazard of their own lives, pave the way to the liberty of Gaul. But chiefly they thought it incumbent upon them, before their secret conferences should be discovered, to cut off Cæsar's return to the army. This appeared abundantly easy; because neither would the legions, in the absence of their general, dare to quit their winter quarters; nor was it possible for the general to join the legions, without a body of troops

to guard him. In fine, they concluded it was better to die bravely in the field, than not recover their former glory in war, and the liberty they had received from their ancestors.

II. Such were the debates in the private councils of the Gauls: when the Carnutes, declaring their readiness to submit to any danger for the common safety, offered to be the first in taking up arms against the Romans. And because the present giving of hostages might endanger a too early discovery of their designs, they proposed, that the other states should bind themselves by a solemn oath, in presence of the military ensigns, which is the most sacred obligation among the Gauls, not to abandon them during the course of the war. This offer of the Carnutes was received with universal applause, the oath required was taken by all present: and the time for action being fixed, the assembly separated.

III. When the appointed day came, the Carnutes, headed by Cotuatus and Conetodunus, men of desperate resolution, flew, upon a signal given, to Genabum; massacred the Roman citizens settled there on account of trade; among the rest, C. Fusius Cotta, a Roman knight of eminence, whom Cæsar had appointed to superintend the care of provisions; and plundered their effects. The fame of this soon spread into all the provinces of Gaul. For when any thing singular and extraordinary happens, they publish it from place to place by outcries, which being successively repeated by men stationed on purpose, are carried with incredible expedition over the whole country. And thus it was on the present oczasion. For what had been done at Genabum about sun-rise, was known before nine at night in the territories of the Averni, a distance of one hundred and sixty miles.

VI. Fired by this example, Vercingetorix, the son of Celtillus, of the nation of the Averni, a young nobleman of great power and interest, whose father had presided over Celtic Gaul, and for aiming at the sovereignty been put to death by his countrymen, calling his clients and followers together, easily persuaded them to a revolt. His design being discovered, the people immediately flew to arms; and Gobannitio his uncle, with the other principal men of the state, dreading the consequences of so rash an enterprise, united all their authority against him, and expelled him the city Gergovia. Yet still he adhered to his former resolution, and assembling all the outlaws and fugitives he could find, engaged them in his service. Having by this means got together a body of troops, he brought all to whom he applied himself to fall in with his views; pressed them to take up arms for the common liberty; and finding his forces greatly increased, quickly drove those out of the territories of Auvergne, who had so lately expelled him the city Gergovia. Upon this he was saluted king by his followers: and despatching ambassadors into all parts, exhorted them to continue firm to the confederacy. The Senones, Parisians, Pictones, Cadurci, Turones, Aulerci, Lemovices, Andes, and all the other nations bordering upon the ocean, readily came into the alliance, and with unanimous consent declared him generalissimo of the league. Armed with this authority, he demanded hostages of the several states; ordered them to furnish a certain number of men immediately; appointed what quantity of arms each was to prepare, with the time by which they must be in readiness; and, above all, applied himself to have on foot a numerous cavalry. To the most extreme diligence, he joined an extreme rigour of command; and by the severity of his punishments, obliged the irresolute to declare themselves: for in great faults the criminals, after having been tortured, were burned alive; and for lighter offences, ordering the ears of the guilty to be cut off, or one of their eyes put out, he sent them, thus mutilated, home, to serve as an example to the rest, and by the rigour of their sufferings to keep others in awe.

V. Having, by the terror of these punishments, speedily assembled an army, he sent Luterius of Quercy, a bold and enterprising man, with part of the forces, against the Rutheni, and marched himself into the territories of the Biturigians. The Biturigians, upon his arrival, despatched ambassadors to the Æduans, under whose protection they were, to demand succours against the enemy. The Æduans, by advice of the lieutenants Cæsar had left with the army, ordered a supply of horse and foot to the assistance of the Biturigians. This body of troops, advancing to the banks of the Loire, which divides the Biturigians from the Æduans, halted there a few days; and not daring to pass that river, returned again to their own country. The reason of this conduct, according to the report made to our lieutenants, was an apprehension of treachery from the Biturigians: for that people, as they pretended, had formed the design of surrounding them beyond the Loire, on one side with their own troops, on the other with those of Auvergne. Whether this was the real cause of their return, or whether they acted perfidiously in the affair, is what we have not been able to learn with certainty, and therefore cannot venture to affirm. The Biturigians, on their departure, immediately joined the forces of the Averni.

VI. These things being reported to Cæsar, in Italy; as the troubles in Rome were in a great measure quieted by the care and vigilance of Pompey, he set out immediately for Transalpine Gaul. Upon his arrival there, he found it extremely difficult to resolve after what manner to rejoin the army. For should he order the legions to repair to the province, he foresaw they would be attacked on their march in his absence: and should he himself proceed to the quarters of the legions, he was not without apprehensions of danger, even from those states that seemingly continued faithful to the Romans.

VII. In the meantime, Luterius of Quercy, who had been sent into the territories of the Rutheni, brought over that state to the alliance of the Averni; advancing thence among the Nitobrigians and Gabali, he received hostages from both nations, and having got together a numerous body of troops, drew towards Narbonne, to attack the Roman province on that side. Cæsar being informed of his design, thought it first and principally incumbent upon him, to provide for the security of the province. With this view he flew to Narbonne; confirmed the wavering and timorous; placed garrisons in the towns of the Rutheni subject to the Romans; also in those of the Volscians, Tolosatians, and other states bordering upon the enemy: and having thus taken effectual measures against Luterius, ordered part of the provincial forces, with the recruits he had brought from Italy, to rendezvous upon the frontiers of the Helvians, whose territories adjoin to those of the Averni.

VIII. These dispositions being made, and Luterius checked and forced to retire, because he did not think it advisable to venture among the Roman garrisons, Cæsar advanced into the country of the Helvians. Although the mountains of the Sevennes, which separate the Helvians from Auvergne, by the great depth of the snow in that extreme rigorous season, threatened to obstruct his march; yet having cleared away the snow, which lay to the depth of six feet, and, with infinite labour to the soldiers, opened a passage over the mountains, he at length reached the confines of the Averni. As they were altogether unprepared, regarding the Sevennes as an impenetrable barrier, impassable at that season even to single men, he ordered the cavalry to spread themselves on all sides, and strike as universal a terror into the enemy as possible. Fame and messengers from the state soon informed Vercingetorix of the disaster befallen his country. All the Averni gathered round him in a body, and with looks full of dismay, conjured him to regard their fortunes, and not abandon them to the ravages of the Roman army; more especially, as he now saw the whole war pointed against them. Vercingetorix, moved by their entreaties, put his army upon the march, and quitting the territories of the Biturigians, drew towards Auvergne.

IX. This Cæsar had foreseen; and after a stay of two days in those parts, set out under pretence of fetching a reinforcement. He left young Brutus to command in his absence; charged him to disperse the cavalry as wide as he could; and promised to return, if possible, within three days. Then deceiving the Romans themselves, that he might the better impose upon the Gauls, he posted by great journeys to Vienne. There he found the new levied cavalry whom he had sent thither some time before; and travelling day and night without intermission, through the country of

the Æduans, to prevent, by his expedition any designs they might form against him, he at length reached the confines of the Lingones where two of his legions wintered. Thence sending immediately to the rest, he drew them altogether into a body, before the Averni could be apprized of his arrival.

X. Vercingetorix, upon notice of this, led back his army into the territories of the Biturigians; and marching thence, resolved to invest Gergovia, a town belonging to the Boii, where they had been settled by Cæsar after the defeat of the Helvetians, and made subject to the Æduan state. This step greatly perplexed the Roman general: if he continued encamped with his legion in one place during the rest of the winter, and abandoned the subjects of the Æduans to the attempts of the enemy, he had reason to apprehend that the Gauls, seeing him afford no protection to his friends, would universally give in to a revolt; if, on the contrary, he took the field early, he risked the want of provision and forage, by the great difficulty of procuring convoys. Resolving however, at all hazards, not to submit to an affront, that must for ever alienate the hearts of his allies, he pressingly enjoined the Æduans to be very careful in supplying him with provisions: and despatching messengers to the Boii, to inform them of his approach, exhorted them to continue firm to their duty, and sustain with courage the assaults of the enemy. Meanwhile leaving two legions and the baggage of the whole army at Agendicum, he set out upon his march to their relief.

XI. Arriving the next day before Vellaunodunum, a city of the Senones, that he might leave no enemy behind him capable of obstructing his convoys, he resolved to besiege it, and in two days completed his circumvallation. On the third, deputies came from the town to treat about a surrender; when, ordering them to deliver up their arms, horses, and six hundred hostages, he left C. Trebonius, one of his lieutenants, to cause the articles to be put in execution; and continuing his march with all diligence, advanced towards Genabum. The Carnutes, to whom this city belonged, were drawing troops together for its defence; imagining that the siege of Vellaunodunum, of which they had just then received intelligence, would be a work of some time. Cæsar reached the place in two days, encamped before it, and finding it began to be late, deferred the assault till next morning. Meanwhile he gave the necessary orders to his men; and because the town had a bridge over the Loire, by which the inhabitants might endeavour to escape in the night, he obliged two legions to continue under arms. A little before midnight, the Genabians, as he had foreseen, stole silently out of the city, and began to pass the river. Notice being given of this by his spies, he set fire to the gates, introduced the legions whom he had kept in readiness for that purpose, and took possession of the place. Very few of the enemy escaped on this occasion; because the narrowness of the bridge and passages obstructed the flight of the multitude. Cæsar ordered the town to be plundered and burnt, distributing the spoil among the soldiers: and crossing the Loire with his whole army, advanced into the territories of the Biturigians.

XII. Vercingetorix, upon notice of his approach, quitted the siege of Gergovia, and marched directly to meet him. Cæsar, meanwhile, had sat down before Noviodunum, a city of the Biturigians, that lay upon his route. The inhabitants sending deputies to the camp, to implore forgiveness and safety, that he might the sooner accomplish his designs, in which expedition had hitherto availed him so much, he ordered them to deliver up their arms, horses, and a certain number of hostages. Part of the hostages had been already sent; the other articles of the treaty were upon the point of execution; and even some centurions and soldiers had entered the place, to search for arms and horses, when the enemy's cavalry, who were a little advanced before the rest of the army, appeared at a distance. Immediately the besieged, upon this prospect of relief setting up a shout, flew to arms, shut the gates, and manned the walls. The centurions in the town, judging from the noise among the Gauls, that they had some new project in view, posted themselves, with their swords drawn, at the gates; and getting all their men together, retreated without loss to the camp. Cæsar ordering the cavalry to advance, fell upon the enemy's horse; and finding his troops hard pressed, sustained them with some squadrons of Germans, whom, to the number of about four hundred, he had all along retained in his service. The Gauls, unable to stand their charge, at length betook themselves to flight, and were driven, with great slaughter,

to the main body of their army. Upon this the people of Noviodunum, terrified anew by the defeat of their friends, seized all who had been instrumental in breaking the capitulation, sent them prisoners to Cæsar's camp, and delivered up the town. These affairs despatched, Cæsar directed his march towards Avaricum. As this was the strongest and most considerable city of the Biturigians, and situate in the finest part of the country, he easily persuaded himself, that by the reduction of it, he should bring the whole nation under subjection.

XIII. Vercingetorix, after so many successive losses, at Vellaunodunum, Genabum, Noviodunum, calling a general council of his followers, represented: "That it was necessary to resolve upon a very different plan of war, from that which hitherto had been pursued; and above all things make it their endeavour to intercept the Roman convoys and foragers: that this was both a sure and practicable scheme, as they themselves abounded in horse, and the season of the year greatly favoured the design: that the ground as yet affording no produce, the enemy must unavoidably disperse themselves in the villages for subsistence, and give them daily opportunities of cutting them off by means of their cavalry. That where life and liberty were at stake, property and private possession ought to be neglected: that therefore the best resolution they could take was, to set all their houses and villages on fire, from the territories of the Boii, to wherever the Romans might extend their quarters for the sake of forage: that they themselves had no reason to apprehend scarcity, as they would be plentifully supplied by those states, whose territories should become the seat of the war; whereas the enemy must be either reduced to the necessity of starving, or making distant and dangerous excursions from their camp; that it equally answered the purpose of the Gauls, to cut the Roman army to pieces, or seize upon their baggage and convoys; because, without these last, it would be impossible for them to carry on the war: that they ought to set fire even to the towns themselves, which were not strong enough by art or nature, to be perfectly secure against all danger; as by this means they would neither become places of retreat to their own men, to screen them from military service; nor contribute to the support of the Romans by the supplies and plunder they might furnish. In fine, that though these things were indeed grievous and terrible, they ought yet to esteem it **still** more terrible and grievous, to see their wives and children dragged into captivity, and themselves exposed to slaughter, which was the unavoidable lot of the vanquished."

XIV. This proposal being approved by all, upwards of twenty cities of the Biturigians were burnt in one day. The like was done in other states. Nothing but conflagrations were to be seen over the whole country. And **though** the natives bore this desolation with extreme regret, they nevertheless consoled themselves with the hope, that an approaching and certain victory would soon enable them to recover their losses. A debate arising in council about Avaricum, whether it would be proper to defend or set it on fire, the Biturigians, falling prostrate at the feet of the rest of the Gauls, implored : "That they might not be obliged to burn, with their own hands, one of the finest cities of all Gaul, which was both the ornament and security of their state ; more especially as the town itself, almost wholly surrounded by a river and morass, and affording but one very narrow approach, was, from the nature of its situation, capable of an easy defence." Their request prevailed. Vercingetorix, though he at first opposed, afterwards coming into the design ; partly moved by the entreaties of the Biturigians, partly by the compassion of the multitude. A chosen garrison was immediately put into the place.

XV. Vercingetorix followed Cæsar by easy marches, and chose for his camp a place surrounded with woods and marshes, about fifteen miles distant from Avaricum. There he had hourly intelligence by his scouts, of all that passed before the town ; and sent his orders from time to time to the garrison. Meanwhile he strictly watched our convoys and foragers ; set upon our dispersed parties, who were obliged to fetch provisions from a great distance ; and, in spite of all endeavours to prevent it, by choosing such times and routes, as were most likely to deceive his vigilance, very much incommoded them by his attacks.

XVI. Cæsar encamping on that side of the town, where the intermission of the river and morass formed, as we have said, a narrow approach ; began to raise a mount, bring for-

ward his battering engines, and prepare two towers of assault ; without troubling himself about lines of circumvallation, which the nature of the ground rendered impossible. Meanwhile he was continually soliciting the Æduans and Boii for corn : but received no great supplies from either ; partly occasioned by the negligence of the Æduans, who were not hearty in the affair ; partly by the want of ability in the Boii, who possessing only a small and inconsiderable territory, soon consumed all the produce of their own lands. But though the army laboured under the greatest scarcity of corn, through the inability of the Boii, the want of inclination in the Æduans, **and the** universal devastation of the country ; though they were even for many days altogether without bread, and had nothing to appease their extreme hunger, but the cattle brought from distant villages ; yet not an expression was heard over the whole camp, unworthy the majesty of the Roman name, or the glory they had acquired by former victories. Nay, when Cæsar visited the different quarters of the legions in person, and offered to raise the siege, if they found the famine insupportable, they all with one voice requested him not to do it, adding : "That during the many years they had served under him, they never yet had met with any check or undertaken aught in which they had not succeeded : that they could not but look upon it as inglorious, to relinquish a siege they had once begun ; and had rather undergo the greatest hardships, than not revenge the blood of the Roman citizens, perfidiously massacred by the Gauls, at Genabum." The same they said to the centurions and military tribunes, entreating them to report their sentiments to Cæsar.

XVII. And now the towers began to approach the wall ; when Cæsar was informed by some prisoners, that Vercingetorix having consumed all the forage round him, had removed his camp nearer to Avaricum, and was gone himself at the head of the cavalry, and the light-armed troops accustomed to fight in their intervals, to form an ambuscade for the Romans in a place where it was supposed they would come next day to forage. Upon this intelligence, setting out about midnight in great silence, he arrived next morning at the enemy's camp. But they, having had timely notice of his approach by their scouts, instantly conveyed their baggage and carriages into a thick wood, and drew up in order of battle upon an open hill. Cæsar then ordered all the baggage to be brought together into one place, and the soldiers to prepare for an engagement.

XVIII. The hill itself where the enemy stood rising all the way with an easy ascent, was almost wholly surrounded by a morass, difficult and dangerous to be passed though not above fifty feet over. Here the Gauls, confiding in the strength of their post, and having broke down all the bridges over the morass, appeared with an air of resolution. They had formed themselves into different bodies, according to their several states; and planting select detachments at all the avenues and fords, waited with determined courage, that if the Romans should attempt to force their way through, they might fall upon them from the higher ground, while entangled in the mud. To attend only to the nearness of the two armies, they seemed as if ready to fight us on even terms; but, when the advantage of their situation was considered, all this ostentation of bravery was easily discerned to be mere show and pretence. Nevertheless, the Romans, full of indignation, that the enemy should dare to face them with so small a space between, loudly demanded to be led to battle. Cæsar checked their ardour for the present, and endeavoured to make them sensible, that in attacking an army so strongly posted, the victory must cost extremely dear, and be attended with the loss of many brave men. To this he told them he was the more averse, because, finding them prepared to face every kind of danger for his glory, he thought he could not be too tender of the lives of those who merited so highly at his hands. Having by this speech consoled the soldiers, he led them back the same day to their camp, and applied himself wholly to the carrying on of the siege.

XIX. Vercingetorix, upon his return to the camp, was accused by the army of treason. The removal of his quarters nearer to those of the enemy; his departure at the head of all the cavalry; his leaving so many troops without a commander in chief; and the opportune and speedy arrival of the Romans during his absence: all these, they said, could not easily happen by chance, or without design; and give great reason to believe, that he had rather **owe** the sovereignty of Gaul to Cæsar's grant, than to the favour and free choice of his countrymen. To this charge he replied; "That the removal of his camp was occasioned by the want of forage, and done at their own express desire: that he had lodged himself nearer to the Romans, on account of the advantage of the ground, which secured him against all attacks; that cavalry were by no means wanted in a morass, but might have been extremely serviceable in the place to which he had carried them; that he purposely forebore naming a commander in chief at his departure, lest the impatience of the multitude should have forced him upon a battle; to which he perceived they were all strongly inclined, through a certain weakness and effeminacy of mind, that rendered them incapable of long fatigue; that whether accident or intelligence brought the Romans to their camp, they ought to thank, in the one case, fortune, in the other, the informer, for giving them an opportunity of discovering from the higher ground the inconsiderable number, and despising the feeble efforts of the enemy; who, not daring to hazard an engagement, ignominiously retreated to their camp; that for his part, he scorned treacherously to hold an authority of Cæsar which he hoped soon to merit by a victory, already in a manner assured, both to himself and the rest of the Gauls: that he was willing even to resign the command, if they thought the honour done to him by that distinction too great for the advantages procured by his conduct. And," added he, "to convince you of the truth and sincerity of my words, hear the Roman soldiers themselves." He then produced some slaves, whom **he had made prisoners a few days before in foraging, and by severity and hard usage brought to his purpose.** These, according to the lesson taught them beforehand, declared: "That they were legionary soldiers; that urged by hunger, they had privately stolen out of the camp, to search for corn and cattle in the fields: that the whole army laboured under the like scarcity, and was reduced to so weak a condition, as no longer to be capable of supporting fatigue: that the general had therefore resolved, if the town held out three days longer, to draw off his men from the siege." "Such (said Vercingetorix) are the services you receive from the man whom you have not scrupled to charge with treason. To him it is owing, that without drawing a sword, you see a powerful and victorious army almost wholly destroyed by famine; and effectua-

care taken, that, when necessity compels them to seek refuge in a shameful flight, no state shall receive them into its territories."

XX. The whole multitude set up a shout; and striking, as their manner was, their lances against their swords, to denote their approbation of the speaker, declared Vercingetorix a consummate general, whose fidelity ought not to be questioned, and whose conduct deserved the highest praises. They decreed that ten thousand men, chosen out of all the troops, should be sent to reinforce the garrison of Avaricum; it seeming too hazardous to rely upon the Biturigians alone for the defence of a place, whose preservation, they imagined, would necessarily give them the superiority in the war.

XXI. And indeed, though the siege was carried on by our men with incredible bravery, yet were all their efforts in a great measure rendered ineffectual, by the address and contrivances of the Gauls. For they are a people of singular ingenuity, extremely quick of apprehension, and very happy in imitating what they see practised. They not only turned aside our hooks with ropes, and after having seized them, drew them into the town with engines; but likewise set themselves to undermine the mount: in which they the more succeeded, because the country abounding with iron mines, they are perfectly skilled in that whole art. At the same time they raised towers on all parts of the wall, covered them carefully with raw hides; and continuing their sallies day and night, either set fire to the mount, or fell upon the workmen. In proportion as our towers increased in height, by the continual addition to the mount, in like manner did they advance their towers upon their walls, by raising one story perpetually over another; and counterworking our mines with the utmost diligence, they either filled them up with great stones, or poured melted pitch into them, or repulsed the miners with long stakes, burnt and sharpened at the end; all which very much retarded the approaches, and kept us at a distance from the place.

XXII. The fortified towns among the Gauls have their walls mostly built in the following manner:—Long massy beams of wood are placed upon the ground, at the equal distance of two feet one from another, and so as to constitute by their length the thickness of the wall. These being again crossed over by others, which serve to bind them together, have their intervals on the inside filled up with earth, and on the outside with large stones. The first course thus completed and firmly joined, a second is laid over it; which allowing the same openings between the beams, rests them not immediately upon those of the order below, but disposes them artfully above their intervals, and connects them, as before, with interjacent earth and stones. In this manner the work is carried on to a proper height, and pleases the eye by its uniform variety, the alternate courses of stones and beams running in even lines, according to their several orders. Nor is it less adapted to security and defence. For the stones are proof against fire, and the whole mass is impenetrable to the ram; because being strongly bound together by continual beams, to a depth of forty feet, it can neither be disjointed nor thrown down.

XXIII. Such were the obstacles we met with in the siege. But the soldiers, though obliged to struggle during the whole time, with cold, dirt, and perpetual rains; yet by dint of labour, overcame all difficulties, and at the end of twenty-five days, had raised a mount three hundred and thirty feet broad, and eighty feet high. When it was brought almost close to the walls, Cæsar, according to custom, attending the works, and encouraging the soldiers to labour without intermission, a little before midnight it was observed to smoke, the enemy having undermined and fired it. At the same time they raised a mighty shout, and sallying vigorously by two several gates, attacked the works on both sides. Some threw lighted torches and dry wood from the walls upon the mount, others pitch and all sorts of combustibles; so that it was hard to determine on which side to make head against the enemy, or where first to apply redress. But as Cæsar kept always two legions upon guard in the trenches, besides great numbers employed in the works, who relieved one another by turns; his troops were soon in a condition, some to oppose those that sallied from the town, others to draw off the towers, and make openings in the mount; whilst the whole multitude ran to extinguish the flames.

XXIV. The fight continued with great obstinacy during the remaining part of the night; the enemy still entertained hopes of victory; and persisted with the more firmness, as they saw the mantles that covered the towers burnt down, and the Romans unable to rescue them for want of shelter. At the same time fresh troops were continually sent to supply the place of those that were fatigued; the besieged believing, that the safety of Gaul entirely depended upon the issue of that critical moment. And here I cannot forbear mentioning a remarkable instance of intrepidity, to which I was myself a witness on this occasion. A certain Gaul, posted before the gate of the city, threw into the fire balls of pitch and tallow, to feed it. This man being exposed to the discharge of a Roman battery, was struck through the side with a dart, and expired. Another striding over his body, immediately took his place. He also was killed in the same manner. A third succeeded: to the third a fourth, nor was this dangerous post left vacant till the fire of the mount being extinguished, and the enemy repulsed on all sides, an end was put to the conflict.

XXX. The Gauls having tried all methods of defence, and finding that none of them succeeded, consulted next day about leaving the town, in concert with, and even by the order of Vercingetorix. This they hoped easily to effect in the night, as that general's camp was not far off, and the morass between them and the Romans would serve to cover their retreat. Night came, and the besieged were preparing to put their design in execution; when suddenly the women running out into the street, and casting themselves at their husbands' feet, conjured them with many tears, not to abandon to the fury of an enraged enemy, them and their common children, whom nature and weakness rendered incapable of flight. But finding their entreaties ineffectual, (for in extreme danger fear often excludes compassion,) they began to set up a loud cry, and inform the Romans of the intended flight. This alarmed the garrison, who, apprehending the passages would be seized by our horse, desisted from their resolution.

XXVI. Next day Cæsar brought forward the tower, and gave the necessary directions about the works. A heavy rain chancing just then to fall, he thought it a favourable opportunity for effecting his design; as he observed the wall to be less strictly guarded. Wherefore ordering the soldiers to abate a little of their vigour, and having instructed them in what manner to proceed, he exhorted the legions, who advanced under cover of the machines, to seize at last the fruits of a victory acquired by so many toils. Then promising rewards to those who should first scale the town, he gave the signal of attack. The Romans rushed suddenly upon the enemy from all parts, and in a moment possessed themselves of the walls.

XXVII. The Gauls terrified at this new manner of assault, and driven from their towers and battlements, drew up trianglewise in the squares and open places, that on whatever side our men should come to attack them, they might face in order of battle. But, observing that we still kept upon the walls, and were endeavouring to get possession of their whole circuit, they began to fear they should have no outlet to escape by; and throwing down their arms, ran tumultuously to the farthest part of the town. There many fell within the city, the narrowness of the gates obstructing their flight; others were slain by the cavalry without the walls, nor did any one for the present think of plunder. The Romans, eager to revenge the massacre at Genabum, and exasperated by the obstinate defence of the place, spared neither old men, women, nor children; insomuch that of all that multitude, amounting to about forty thousand, scarce eight hundred, who had quitted the town on the first alarm, escaped safe to Vercingetorix's camp. They arrived there late in the night, and were received in great silence; for Vercingetorix, fearing lest their entrance in a body, and the compassion it would naturally raise among the troops, might occasion some tumult in the camp, had sent out his friends, and the principal noblemen of each province, to meet them by the way, and conduct them separately to the quarters of their several states.

XXVIII. Next day having called a council, he consoled and exhorted the troops, not to be too much disheartened, or cast down by their late misfortune: " That the Romans had not overcome by bravery, or in the field; but by their address and skill in sieges, with which part of war the Gauls were less acquainted: that it was deceiving themselves to hope for success in every measure they might think to pursue: that himself, as they all knew, had never advised the defence of Avaricum, and could not but impute the present disaster to the imprudence of the Biturigians, and the too easy compliance of the rest: that he hoped, however, soon to compensate it by superior advantages, as he was using his utmost endeavours to bring over the other states which had hitherto refused their concurrence, and to join one general confederacy of all Gaul, against whose united strength, not the whole earth would be able to prevail: that he had even in a great measure effected his design, and in the meantime only required of them, for the sake of the common safety, that they would set about fortifying their camp, the better to secure them from the sudden attacks of the enemy." This speech was not unpleasing to the Gauls: and the rather, as notwithstanding so great a blow, Vercingetorix seemed to have lost nothing of his courage: neither withdrawing from public view, nor shunning the sight of the multitude. They even began to entertain a higher opinion of his prudence and foresight, as from the first he had advised the burning of Avaricum, and at last sent orders to abandon it. And thus, bad success, which usually sinks the reputation of a commander served only to augment his credit, and give him greater authority among the troops. At the same time they were full of hopes, from the assurances he had given them, of seeing the other states accede to the alliance. And now, for the first time, the Gauls set about fortifying their camp; being so humbled by their late misfortune, that though naturally impatient of fatigue, they resolved to refuse no labour imposed upon them by their general.

XXIX. Nor was Vercingetorix less active on his side to bring over the other provinces of Gaul to the confederacy, endeavouring to gain the leading men in each by presents and promises. For this purpose he made choice of fit agents, who by their address, or particular ties of friendship, were most likely to influence those to whom they were sent. He provided arms and clothing for the troops that had escaped from Avaricum: and to repair the loss sustained by the taking of that place, gave orders to the several states, to furnish a certain number of men, and send them to the camp by a day prefixed. At the same time he commanded all the archers, of which

there were great numbers in Gaul, to be sought out and brought to the army. By these measures he soon replaced the men whom he lost at the siege of Avaricum. Meanwhile Theutomatus, the son of Ollovico, and king of the Nitobrigians, whose father had been styled friend and ally by the senate of Rome, came and joined him with a great body of horse, which he had raised in his own territories, and in the province of Aquitain.

XXX. Cæsar finding great plenty of corn and other provisions at Avaricum, stayed there several days to refresh his men, after the fatigue and scarcity they had so lately undergone. Winter was now drawing towards a period; and, as the season itself invited him to take the field, he resolved to march against the enemy, either to draw them out of the woods and marshes, or besiege them in their fastnesses. While he was full of these thoughts, deputies arrived from the Æduans, to beg his interposition and authority, for settling the differences of their state. "Every thing there," they told him, "threatened an intestine war. For whereas it had all along been the custom to be governed by a single magistrate, who possessed the supreme power for the space of one year; they had now two disputing for that title, each pretending his election was according to law: that the one was Convictolitanis, an illustrious and popular young nobleman; the other Cotus, of an ancient family, great authority, and powerful relations, whose brother Videllacus had exercised the same office the year before: that the whole state was in arms, the senate divided, and each party backed by their clients among the people; nor had they any other hopes of escaping a civil war, but in his care and timely endeavours to put an end to the controversy."

XXXI. Although Cæsar was sensible it would greatly prejudice his affairs, to quit the pursuit of the war, and the enemy; yet reflecting on the mischiefs that often arise from divisions, and desirous if possible to prevent so powerful a state, in strict amity with the people of Rome, and which he had always in a particular manner cherished and befriended, from having recourse to the method of violence and arms, which might drive the party that least confided in his friendship, to seek the assistance of Vercingetorix; he resolved to make it his first care, to put a stop to the progress of these disorders. And because, by the constitution of the Æduans, it was not lawful for the supreme magistrate to pass beyond the limits of the state; that he might not seem to detract from their privileges, he resolved to go in person thither, and summoned the senate and two candidates to meet him at Decise. The assembly was very numerous; when finding upon inquiry, that Cotus had been declared chief magistrate by his own brother, in presence of only a few electors privately called together, without regard to time or place, and even contrary to the express laws of the state, which forbid two of the same family, while yet both alive, either to hold the supreme dignity, or so much as sit together in the senate; he obliged him to resign in favour of Convictolitanis, who, upon the expiration of the office of the preceding magistrate, had been elected, in all the forms, by the priests.

XXXII. This sentence being passed; and having exhorted the Æduans to lay aside their quarrels and divisions, and apply themselves solely to the business of the present war; to expect with confidence the full recompense of their services, as soon as the reduction of Gaul was completed; and to send him immediately all their cavalry, with ten thousand foot, to form a chain of posts for the security of his convoys; he divided his army into two parts. Four legions, under the conduct of Labienus, were sent against the Senones and Parisians. Six, headed by himself in person, marched along the banks of the Allier, towards the territories of the Averni, with design to invest Gergovia. Part of the cavalry followed the route of Labienus; part remained with Cæsar. Vercingetorix having notice of this, broke down all the bridges upon the Allier, and began his march on the other side of the river.

XXXIII. As both armies were continually in view, encamped almost over against each other, and the enemy's scouts so stationed, that it was impossible for the Romans to make a bridge for carrying over their forces; Cæsar began to be uneasy lest he should be hindered the greatest part of the summer by the river; because the Allier is seldom fordable till towards autumn. To prevent this inconvenience, he encamped in a place full of woods, over against one of those bridges which Vercingetorix had caused to be broken

down; and remaining there privately next day, with a good body of troops, formed by draughting every fourth cohort, that the number of legions might still appear complete; he sent forward the rest of the army with all the baggage as usual, ordering them to march as far as they could. When by the time of the day, he judged they might be arrived at the place of their encampment, he set about rebuilding the bridge, making use of the old piles, whose lower part the enemy had left standing. Having soon completed the work, marched over the troops he had with him, and chosen a proper place for his camp, he recalled the rest of the forces. Vercingetorix, upon intelligence of this, advanced before by long marches, that he might not be obliged to fight against his will.

XXXIV. Cæsar, after five days' march, came before Gergovia, where he had a slight engagement with the enemy's horse; and, having taken a view of the place, which he found situated upon a very high mountain, all whose approaches were extremely difficult, he not only despaired of reducing it by storm, but resolved even to forbear investing it until he had secured the necessary supplies for his army. Vercingetorix meanwhile was encamped near the town upon the hill, where he had disposed the forces of the several states around him, in different divisions, separated from one another by moderate intervals. As his army possessed all the summits of the mountain, whence there was any prospect into the plains below, they made a very formidable appearance. Every morning by day-break, the chiefs of each state, who composed his council, assembled in his tent, to advise with him, or receive his orders: nor did he suffer a single day to pass without detaching some cavalry, intermixed with archers, to skirmish with the Romans, that he might make trial of the spirit and courage of his men. There was a rising ground, that joined to the foot of the mountain on which the town stood, excellently well fortified by nature, as being very steep on all sides, and of extreme difficult access. This hill, though of such importance to the enemy, that by our getting possession of it, we could in a great measure deprive them of water and forage, was yet but very indifferently guarded. Cæsar therefore leaving his camp about midnight, before any assistance could arrive from the town, dislodged the enemy, seized the hill and having placed two legions upon it to defend it, drew a double ditch, twelve feet deep, from the greater to the lesser camp, that the soldiers might pass and repass in safety, even single and without a guard.

XXXV. While things were in this posture before Gergovia, Convictolitanis the Æduan, to whom, as we have related above, Cæsar had adjudged the supreme magistracy, being strongly solicited by the Averni, and at length gained over by their money, addressed himself to some young nobleman, the chief of whom were Litavicus and his brothers, of the most distinguished family of the province. **With these he shared the** reward he had received, **and exhorted them** to consider: "That **they were subjects of a free state, and born to command: that liberty and victory** were retarded by the Æduans alone, whose authority restrained the other states, and whose concurrence in the common cause would take from the Romans all possibility of supporting themselves in Gaul: that though he was himself under some obligation to Cæsar, at least so far as a just and equitable decision deserved that name, he thought he owed still more to his country, and could see no reason why the Æduans should rather have recourse to the Roman general, in what regarded their laws and customs, than the Romans in the like case to the Æduans." The representations of the magistrate, and the rewards he bestowed, soon prevailed; they even offered to become the chief conductors of the enterprise; and **nothing** was wanting but to consult of pro**per means** for accomplishing the design, as it **was easily** foreseen that the state would not be induced without great difficulty to engage in so dangerous a war. At last it was agreed, that Litavicus should have the command of the ten thousand foot appointed to join Cæsar; that he should begin his march; that his brothers should be sent before to the Roman camp; and that the rest of the project should be then executed, according to a plan previously concerted among them.

XXXVI. Litavicus having received the command of the army; when he was within about thirty miles of Gergovia, suddenly called the troops together, and addressing them with tears: "Whither, fellow-soldiers," said he, "are we going? All our cavalry, all our **nobility** are slain. Eporedorix and Virdumarus, men of the first quality in the state, being accused by the Romans of treason, are put to death without trial. Learn these things of those who have escaped this general massacre; for as to me, overwhelmed as I am with grief for the loss of my brothers and kinsmen, I have neither strength nor voice to utter our calamities." He then produced some whom he had beforehand instructed for that purpose, and who joining in the same story, told the multitude, "That the greatest part of the Æduan cavalry had been put to the sword, under pretence of holding intelligence with the Averni; and that themselves had escaped only in the crowd, by withdrawing during the general slaughter." Upon this the whole army called aloud to Litavicus, entreating him to provide for their safety. "As if," said he, "there was room for counsel; or any choice left, but that of marching directly to Gergovia, and joining the Averni. **Can we** doubt, after so black an instance **of Roman** perfidy, but that they are already on their way to complete the massacre? **Let us** therefore, if aught of spirit or courage remains in our breasts, revenge the death of our countrymen, so undeservedly slain, and put these inhuman spoilers to the sword." He then presented some Roman citizens, who had taken the opportunity of their march, for conducting a large convoy of corn and provisions to the camp. Instantly the convoy was plundered, the Romans themselves put to death with the most cruel torments, and messengers despatched through all the territories of the Æduans, to spread the same forgery of the massacre of their cavalry and princes, and thereby rouse them to a like vengeance.

XXXVII. Eporedorix the Æduan, a young nobleman of distinguished birth, and great interest in the state; as likewise Virdumarus, of equal age and authority, though **not** so well descended; whom Cæsar, **upon the** recommendation of Divitiacus, had raised from a low condition to the highest dignities; were both at this time in the Roman camp, having come along with the cavalry, at Cæsar's express desire. Between these two was a competition for greatness; and in the late dispute about the magistracy, the one had declared warmly for Convictolitanis, the other for Cotus. Eporedorix getting notice of Litavicus's design, came about midnight to Cæsar's tent, discovered the whole plot, and entreated him to obviate the mischievous counsels of a few young noblemen, and not suffer the state to fall off from the alliance of the Romans, which he foresaw must happen, should so many thousand men once join the enemy. For it was by no means probable, that either their own relations would neglect their safety, or the state itself make light of so great a part of its forces.

XXXVIII. This piece of intelligence gave Cæsar extreme concern, because he had always manifested a particular regard to the Æduans. He therefore drew out immediately four legions without baggage, together with all the cavalry; and because the affair seemed to depend wholly upon despatch, would not even take time to contract his camp, but left C. Fabius, his lieutenant, with two legions, to defend it against the enemy. Finding that Litavicus's brothers, whom he ordered to be seized, had some time before gone over to Vercingetorix, he began his march, exhorting the soldiers to bear the fatigue cheerfully in so pressing a conjuncture. They followed with great alacrity, and advancing about five and twenty miles from Gergovia, came at last within sight of the Æduans. Cæsar immediately detached the cavalry against them, to retard and stop their march: but with strict charge to abstain from bloodshed. He ordered Eporedorix and Virdumarus, whom they believed slain, to ride up and down among the squadrons, and call to their countrymen. As they were soon known, and Litavicus's forgery thereby discovered, the Æduans stretched out their hands, made signs of submission, and throwing down their arms, began to beg their lives. Litavicus with his clients, who, by the customs of the Gauls, cannot without infamy abandon their patrons, even in the greatest extremities of fortune, escaped safe to Gergovia.

XXXIX. Cæsar having despatched messengers to the Æduans, to inform them that his lenity and regard for their state, had prevailed with him to spare troops, whom by the right of war he might have put to the sword; after allowing the army three hours' rest during the night, marched back to Gergovia. About half way he was met by a party of horse, sent by Fabius, to give him notice of the danger that threatened his camp. They told him, "That the enemy had attacked it with all their forces, and by sending continual supplies of fresh men, were like in the end to overpower the Romans, whose fatigue admitted of no relaxation, because the vast extent of ground they

had to defend, obliged them to be perpetually upon the rampart: that the multitude of arrows and darts discharged by the Gauls, had wounded many of the soldiers, notwithstanding the protection received from the engines, which yet had been of good service in beating off the assailants: that Fabius, upon the retreat of the enemy, had closed up all the gates of the camp but two, carried a breastwork quite round the rampart, and made preparation for sustaining a like assault the next day." Cæsar informed of these things, hastened his march with all diligence, and seconded by the usual ardour of the troops, arrived in the camp before sun-rise.

XL. While these things passed at Gergovia, the Æduans, upon receipt of the first despatches from Litavicus, staid not for confirmation of the report; but prompted, partly by avarice, partly by revenge, and many by a native rashness, to which the Gauls in general are extremely addicted, being ready to catch up every flying rumour as a certain truth, flew immediately to arms, plundered the Roman citizens of their effects, slaughtered their persons, or dragged them into servitude. Convictolitanis fomented to the utmost this fury, which had already taken but too fast hold of the multitude; that by plunging them into some desperate act of violence, he might render a retreat the more difficult and shameful. At his instigation, they obliged M. Aristius, a military tribune, who was upon his way to join the army, to quit Cabillonum, promising not to molest him in his journey. The same they did by several Roman merchants, who stopped there on account of traffic; and attacking them treacherously on the road, stripped them of their baggage, invested day and night those that made resistance; and many being killed on both sides, drew together a great number of men to effect their design. Meanwhile coming to understand, that all their troops were in Cæsar's power: they ran to Aristius, assured him that nothing had been done by public authority, ordered informations to be brought against those who had been concerned in pillaging the Romans, confiscated the estates of Litavicus and his brothers, and sent ambassadors to Cæsar to excuse what happened. All this they did with a view to the recovery of their troops: but conscious of guilt; loth to part with the plunder, in which great numbers had shared; and dreading the punishment so gross an outrage deserved; they began privately to concert measures of war, and by their ambassadors solicited other states to join them. Though Cæsar was not ignorant of these practices, he spoke with the greatest mildness to the Æduan deputies, assuring them of the continuance of his favour, and that he would not consider as the crime of the whole nation, what was owing only to the imprudence and levity of the multitude. Apprehending, however, a universal revolt of Gaul, and that he might be surrounded by the forces of all the states at once, he began to think of retiring to Gergovia, and drawing his whole army again into a body; yet in such a manner, that a retreat occasioned by the fear of an insurrection, might not carry with it the appearance of a flight.

XLI. While he was full of these thoughts, an opportunity seemed to offer of acting against the enemy with success. For coming into the lesser camp, to take a view of the works, he observed a hill, that for some days before was scarce to be seen for the multitudes that covered it, now quite naked and destitute of troops. Wondering what might be the cause, he inquired of the deserters, who flocked daily in great numbers to the Roman camp. They all agreed with our scouts, that the back of the hill was almost an even ground, but narrow and woody in that part, where the passage lay to the other side of the town: that the enemy were mightily afraid of losing this post, because the Romans, who had already possessed themselves of one hill, by seizing the other likewise, would in a manner quite surround them; and being masters of all the outlets, might entirely cut off their forage: that Vercingetorix had therefore drawn all his forces on that side, with design to fortify the passage.

XLII. Cæsar, upon this intelligence, despatched some squadrons of cavalry thither about midnight, ordering them to ride up and down the place, with as much noise as possible. At day-break he drew a great number of mules and carriage horses out of the camp, sent away their usual harness, and furnishing the grooms and wagoners with helmets, that they might resemble horsemen, commanded them to march quite round the hill. With these he joined a few cavalry, who, for the greater show, were to expatiate a little more freely; and the whole detachment had orders to move towards the same parts, taking a very large circuit. All these dispositions were seen

from the town, which commanded a full view of the Roman camp, though the distance was too great to distinguish objects with certainty. At the same time Cæsar, the more effectually to deceive the enemy, detached a legion towards the same eminence, and when it was advanced a little way, stationed it at the foot of the hill, affecting to conceal it in the woods. This increased the jealousy of the Gauls, to such a degree, that they immediately carried all their forces thither to defend the post. Cæsar seeing their intrenchments abandoned, made his soldiers cover the military ensigns and standards, and file off in small parties from the greater to the lesser camp, that they might not be perceived from the town. He then opened his design to his lieutenants, whom he had appointed to command the several legions, counselling them above all things to moderate the ardour of the soldiers, that the hope of plunder, or desire of fighting, might not carry them too far. He represented particularly the disadvantage of the ground, against which there was no security but in despatch; and told them, that it was not a regular attack, but a sudden onset, to be pursued no farther than opportunity served. These precautions taken, he gave the signal to engage, and at the same time detached the Æduans by another ascent, to charge the enemy on the right.

XLIII. The wall of the town, had no breaks or hollows intervened, was about twelve hundred paces distant from the plain below, measuring in a direct line from the foot of the mountain. The circuit the troops were obliged to take, to moderate the steepness of the ascent, added still to this space upon the march. Half way up the hill, as near as the nature of the ground would allow, the Gauls had run a wall of large stones six feet high, the better to defend themselves against our attacks. All between this and the plain was left quite void of troops by the enemy; but the upper part of the hill, to the very walls of the town, was crowded with the camps of their several states. The signal being given, the Romans immediately mounted the hill, scaled the outward wall, and possessed themselves of three of the enemy's camps. Such too was the expedition wherewith they carried them, that coming suddenly upon Theutomatus king of the Nitobrigians, as he was reposing himself in his tent about noon, he very narrowly escaped being taken; for he was obliged to fly away half naked, and **had** his horse wounded under him.

XLIV. Cæsar having succeeded as far as his design required, ordered a retreat to be sounded ; and the tenth legion, which fought near his person, obeyed. The other legions, at hearing the signal, because separated from the general by a large valley, were yet commanded to halt by the lieutenants and military tribunes, according to the instructions given by Cæsar in the beginning. But elated with the hopes of a speedy **victory, the flight of the** enemy, and the remembrance of former successes, they thought nothing impracticable to their valour, nor desisted from the pursuit, till they had reached the very walls and gates of the town. Upon this a great cry arising from all parts, those that were farthest from the place of assault, terrified by the noise and tumult, and imagining the enemy already within the gates, quitted the town with precipitation. **The women throwing their** money and clothes from the walls, with naked breasts and extended arms, conjured the Romans to spare their lives, and not, as at Avaricum, sacrifice all to their resentment, without distinction of age or sex. Some being let down by their hands from the wall, delivered themselves up **to our soldiers.** L. Fabius, a centurion of the eighth legion, was that day heard to say, that he had not yet forgot the plunder of Avaricum, and was resolved no man should enter the place before him. Accordingly, having, with the assistance of three of his company, got upon the town wall, he helped them one after another to do the like.

XLV. Meanwhile the troops, who, as we have related above, were gone to defend the post on the other side of the town ; incited by the cries of the combatants, and the continual accounts brought that the enemy had entered the place ; sending all the cavalry before to stop the progress of the Romans, advanced in mighty crowds to the attack. In proportion as they arrived, they drew up under the wall, and augmented the number of those who fought on their side. As they soon became formidable by their multitude, the women, who a little before had implored the compassion of the Romans, now began to encourage their own troops, showing their dishevelled hair, and producing their children, according to the custom of the Gauls. The contest was by no means equal, either in respect of numbers, or

of the ground : and the Romans, already fatigued with the march and length of the combat, were little able to sustain the attack of fresh and vigorous troops.

XLVI. Cæsar, observing the disadvantage of the ground, and the continual increase of the enemy's troops, began to be apprehensive about the event ; and sending T. Sextius, his lieutenant, whom he had left to guard the **lesser camp, ordered him to bring** forth the cohorts with **all expedition, and post** them at the foot **of the hill, upon the** enemy's right ; that if our men **should give way,** he might deter the Gauls from **pursuing them.** He himself advancing **a** little with **the** tenth legion, waited the issue of the combat.

XLVII. While **the conflict was maintained** with the utmost vigour on both sides ; **the** enemy trusting to their post and numbers, the Romans to their courage ; suddenly the Æduans, whom Cæsar had sent by another ascent on the right, to make a diversion, appeared on the flank of our men. As they were armed after the manner of the Gauls, this sight greatly terrified the Romans ; and though they extended their right arms in token of peace, yet still our men fancied it a stratagem to deceive them. At the same time L. Fabius the centurion, and those who had got upon the wall with him, being surrounded and slain, **were** thrown down by the enemy from the battlements. M. Petreius, a centurion of the same legion, who had endeavoured to force the gates, finding himself overpowered by the enemy, and despairing of safety because he was already covered with wounds, turning to his soldiers that had followed him, said ; " As I find it impossible to preserve both myself and you, I will at least do my best to further your escape, whom I have brought into this danger through too eager a desire of glory. Take advantage therefore of the present opportunity." Then throwing himself upon the enemy, he killed two, drove the rest from the gate, and seeing his men run to his assistance : " In vain," says he, " do you endeavour to preserve my life. My blood and strength forsake me. Go therefore, while you may, and rejoin your legion." Continuing still to fight, he expired soon after, preserving his followers with the loss of his own life.

XLVIII. Our **men** thus pressed on all sides, were at length driven from the place, with the loss of forty-six centurions ; but the tenth legion, which had been posted a little more advantageously to cover their retreat, checked the impetuous pursuit of the Gauls: being sustained by the cohorts of the thirteenth legion, who had quitted the lesser camp under Sextius, and possessed themselves of an eminence. The legions having gained the plain, immediately halted, and faced about towards the enemy; but Vercingetorix drawing off his troops from the foot of the hill, retired within his intrenchments. The Romans lost that day about seven hundred men.

XLIX. Cæsar assembling the army next day, severely blamed the temerity and avarice of the soldiers; "That they had taken upon themselves to judge how far they were to proceed, and what they **were** to undertake; regarding neither the signal **to** retreat, nor the orders of their officers. He explained the disadvantage of the ground, and reminded them of his own conduct at the siege of Avaricum, when having surprised the enemy without a general, and without cavalry, he had rather chosen to give up a certain victory, than by attacking them in a difficult post, hazard an inconsiderable loss: that as much as he admired the astonishing courage of men, whom neither the intrenchments of several camps, nor the height of the mountain, nor the walls of the town should check; so much did he blame the licentiousness and arrogance of soldiers, who thought they knew more than their general, and could see better than him the way to conquest: that he looked upon obe**dience** and moderation in the pursuit of **booty**, as virtues no less essential to a good **soldier**, than valour and magnanimity."

L. Having made this speech, and in the end exhorted his soldiers not to be discouraged by their late misfortune, nor ascribe that to the bravery of the enemy, which was entirely owing to the disadvantage of the ground: as he still persisted in his design of retiring, he drew out his legions, and formed them in order of battle upon the plain. But Vercingetorix not thinking proper to descend; after a small and successful skirmish between the cavalry, Cæsar returned again to his camp. The like he did **the** following day: when thinking he had **done** enough to confirm the courage of his own men, and abate the pride of the Gauls, he decamped towards the territories of the Ædu**ans. As the** enemy made no attempt to pur-

sue him, he arrived the third day on the banks of the Allier, and having repaired the bridge, passed over with his whole army.

LI. Here he was informed by Eporedorix and Virdumarus, that Litavicus was gone with all the cavalry to solicit the Æduans; and it would be therefore necessary for themselves to set out, in order to prevent his designs, and confirm the state in their attachment to the Romans. Though Cæsar was by this time abundantly convinced of the perfidy of the Æduans, and plainly foresaw that their **depar**ture would only hasten their revolt, he **yet did** not think proper to detain them, that he might give no ground of offence, nor betray any suspicion of distrust. At parting, he briefly enumerated the services he had done the Æduans: "How low and depressed he had found them, shut up in their towns, deprived of their lands, without troops, tributaries to their enemies, and obliged to submit to the ignominious demand of hostages: to what power and greatness they were now raised by his favour, so as, not only to have recovered their former consideration in Gaul, but even to exceed in dignity and lustre all that appeared most flourishing in the ancient annals of their state." With this charge he dismissed them.

LII. Noviodunum was a town belonging to the Æduans, advantageously situated upon the banks of the Loire. Here Cæsar had lodged all the hostages of Gaul, his provisions, his military chest, and great part of his own and his army's baggage. Hither also he had sent many horses, brought up in Italy and Spain for the service of the war. When Eporedorix and Virdumarus arrived at this place, and were informed of the disposition of the state: "That Litavicus had been received with great marks of favour at Bibracte, the capital city of the province; that Convictolitanis, the chief magistrate, and almost all the senate were gone thither to meet him: that ambassadors had been publicly sent to Vercingetorix, to conclude a treaty of peace and alliance;" they thought the present favourable opportunity was by no means to be neglected. Having therefore put the garrison of Noviodunum, with all the Romans found in the place to the sword; they divided the money and horses between them, ordered the hostages to be conducted to Bibracte; and not thinking themselves strong enough to defend the town set it on fire, that it might not be of any ser vice to the Romans. All the corn they could, in so short a time, they carried away in barks; and burnt the rest, or threw it into the river. Then drawing together the forces of the neighbouring parts they lined the banks of the Loire with troops: and to strike greater terror, began to scour the country with their cavalry; hoping to cut off Cæsar's convoys, and oblige him, through want of provisions, to return into the Roman province. This appeared the easier, as the Loire was considerably swelled by the melting of the snow, and gave little room to think that it could be any where forded.

LIII. Upon advice of these proceedings, Cæsar thought it necessary to use despatch; and if he must build a bridge, endeavour to come to an action with the enemy, before they had drawn more forces together. For he did not even then think it necessary to return to the Roman province; not only as the retreat itself would be inglorious, and the mountains of the Sevennes, and the badness of the ways, were almost insuperable obstacles; but chiefly, because he was extremely desirous to rejoin Labienus, and the legions under his command. Wherefore marching day and night with the utmost diligence, contrary to all men's expectation, he arrived upon the banks of the Loire; and his cavalry very opportunely finding a ford, which however took the soldiers up to the shoulders, he placed the horse higher up to break the force of the stream, and carried over his army without loss; the enemy being so terrified by his boldness, that they forsook the banks. As he found a great deal of corn and cattle in the fields, the army was plentifully supplied, and he directed his march towards the country of the Senones.

LIV. Whilst Cæsar was thus employed, Labienus leaving the levies which had lately arrived from Italy, at Agendicum, to guard the baggage, marched with four legions to Lutetia, a city of the Parisians, situated in an island of the Seine. Upon notice of his approach, the enemy drew a great army together from the neighbouring states. The chief command was given to Camulogenus, an Aulercian, who though in a very advanced age, was yet urged to accept of that honour, on account of his singular knowledge in the art of war. This general observing there was a large morass, whose waters ran into the Seine, and obstructed all the passages round about, encamped there, to hinder the Romans from passing the river.

Labienus at first endeavoured to force a passage, filling up the morass with hurdles and mould, to give firm footing to the army. But finding the attempt too difficult, he privately quitted his camp about midnight, and returned towards Melodunum. This city belongs to the Senones, and is also situated in an island of the Seine, as we before said of Lutetia. He found there about fifty boats, which he speedily drew together, and manned them with his soldiers. The inhabitants terrified at this new manner of attack, and being too few to defend the place because the greater part of them had joined the army of Camulogenus, yielded upon the first summons. Having repaired the bridge which the enemy had cut down some days before, he crossed the Seine there; and following the course of the river, marched back towards Lutetia. The enemy having intelligence of this, by those who escaped from Melodunum, set fire to Lutetia, broke down its bridges, and covering themselves with the morass, encamped on the opposite bank of the Seine, over against Labienus.

LV. It was now known that Cæsar had departed from Gergovia. The revolt of the Æduans, and the universal insurrection of Gaul, were every where spread abroad by the voice of fame. The Gauls on all occasions gave out, that Cæsar finding his march obstructed by the Loire, and being reduced to great straits for want of corn, had been forced to take the route of the Roman province. At the same time the Bellovaci, naturally prone to throw off the yoke, upon hearing of the defection of the Æduans, began to raise forces, and openly prepare for war. Labienus perceiving so great a change in the posture of affairs, soon saw the necessity of pursuing other measures; and that it was not now his business to make conquests, or give the enemy battle, but to secure his retreat to Agendicum. On the one side he was pressed by the Bellovaci, reputed the most warlike people of all Gaul; on the other by Camulogenus, with a numerous and well appointed army. Add to all this, the baggage of the troops, and the detachment appointed to guard it, were separated from the legions by a great river. So many difficulties surrounding him at once, he saw no way to extricate himself but by his valour and presence of mind.

LVI. Accordingly in the evening he called a council of war; and having exhorted the officers to execute his orders with vigour and despatch, distributed the fifty boats he had brought from Melodunum to as many Roman knights, commanding them to fall down the river about nine at night, without noise, four miles below Lutetia, and there wait his coming. Five cohorts, such as appeared least fit for service, were left to guard the camp. The other five of the same legion, with all the baggage, had orders to march up the river at midnight, with much tumult and bustle, which was further increased by means of some small barks sent the same way, that made a mighty noise with their oars. He himself setting out soon after, with three legions, advanced silently to the boats that waited for him. There he surprised the enemy's scouts, who were stationed along the river, and had been prevented by a sudden storm from discerning his approach. The whole army was quickly carried over by the care and diligence of the Roman knights, to whom that affair had been given in charge. Almost at the same instant the enemy had notice, that an unusual tumult was heard in the Roman camp; that a strong detachment had marched up the river, on which side likewise a great noise of oars was heard; and that a little below they were passing the river in boats. This intelligence made the Gauls conclude, that the legions, alarmed at the revolt of the Æduans, were endeavouring to cross the Seine in three different places, for which reason they likewise divided their army into three bodies. For leaving one party to guard the passage over against our camp, and detaching another towards Metiosedum, with orders to advance to the place where the boats had stopped, they marched with the rest of their forces against Labienus. By day-break our troops had passed the river, and the enemy's army appeared in view. Labienus exhorting his men to remember their wonted bravery, the many victories they had gained, and even to fancy themselves in the immediate presence of Cæsar, under whose conduct they had so often been successful, gave the signal of battle. At the very first charge, the seventh legion, which formed the right wing of the Roman army, broke the enemy's left and put it to rout. But the right wing of the Gauls, which was engaged with the twelfth legion, and where Camulogenus was present in person to encourage his men, though the first ranks were destroyed by the Roman javelins, still maintained its ground with the utmost bravery, and seemed determined to conquer. The dispute was long and dubious; when the tribunes of the seventh legion, having notice how matters went, faced about, and attacked the enemy's rear. Even then not a man offered to fly; but at last being surrounded on all sides, they were cut to pieces with their general. The party left behind to watch our camp, hearing the noise of the battle, flew to the assistance of their countrymen, and posted themselves on a hill: but not being able to sustain the assault of the victorious Romans, they soon mingled with the rest of the fugitives, and were cut to pieces by the cavalry, those only excepted who sheltered themselves in the woods and mountains. After this victory, Labienus retreated to Agendicum, where he had left the baggage of the whole army; and from thence, with all his forces, went and joined Cæsar.

LVII. The revolt of the Æduans gave new strength to the confederacy. Deputies were immediately despatched into all parts. Interest, money, and authority were employed in their turns, to procure the concurrence of the states that still continued quiet. The hostages seized at Noviodunum, enabled the Æduans to compel such as were refractory. They sent to require of Vercingetorix, that he would come and concert with them measures for carrying on the war; and in particular insisted on being at the head of the league. But this demand meeting with opposition, a general assembly of Gaul was held at Bibracte, whither the deputies of all the confederated nations repaired, and after taking the affair into consideration, confirmed Vercingetorix in the title of generalissimo. The Rhemi, Lingones, and Treviri were not present at this assembly; the two first, because they had resolved to continue faithful to the Romans; and the Treviri on account of their great distance, and the employment found them by the Germans; which was the reason that they took no part at all in this war, nor lent their assistance to either side. The Æduans were greatly mortified at seeing themselves excluded from the chief command: they complained of this change in their fortune, and began to regret the loss of Cæsar's favour. But as they were already too far engaged in the revolt, they durst not think of detaching themselves from the confederacy. It was not however without reluctance, that Eporedorix and Virdumarus, two young noblemen of the greatest hopes, consented to take orders from Vercingetorix.

LVIII. As he was now invested with the supreme command, he enjoined the several states to send hostages, appointed a day for that purpose, and ordered all the cavalry, to the number of fifteen thousand, to assemble with the utmost expedition. He said, " He was sufficiently provided with infantry, as he had no mind to refer the decision of the war to fortune, or hazard an uncertain engagement; but abounding in horse, judged it the easier and safer way, to intercept the Roman convoys and foragers: that in the meantime they must resolve to destroy their corn, set fire to their houses, and patiently submit to a present and private loss, which was to be rewarded with liberty and perpetual empire." Having thus settled the plan of the war, he commanded the Æduans and Segusians, who border upon the Roman province, to raise ten thousand foot: to these he joined eight hundred horse, and put them under the conduct of Eporedorix's brother, with orders to attack the Allobrogians. At the same time he commissioned the Gabali, and the nearest cantons of Auvergne, to make an irruption into the territories of the Helvians: and the Rutheni and Cadurci, into those of the Volcæ Arecomici. He neglected not, however, by messengers and private emissaries, to sound the disposition of the Allobrogians, whose minds he hoped were not yet thoroughly reconciled to the Roman yoke; endeavouring to gain the leading men by presents, and the state by an offer of the sovereignty of the Roman province.

LIX. To oppose all these attacks, two and twenty cohorts were drawn together, which L. Cæsar, lieutenant-general, levied in the province; and with them prepared to make head on all sides. The Helvians venturing to come to an engagement with the enemy, were defeated, and forced to shelter themselves in their walled towns, after having lost C. Valerius Donatorus, the son of Cabaras, a man of principal rank in their state,

and several other persons of distinction. The Allobrogians placing detachments at proper distances along the banks of the Rhone, guarded all the accesses to their country with great diligence and care. Cæsar, as he found the enemy superior in cavalry, and that his communication with Italy and the province was cut off, so as to deprive him of all hopes of succour from that quarter, had recourse to the German nations beyond the Rhine, which he had subdued in the preceding campaigns, and obtained from them a supply of horse, with some light-armed foot, accustomed to fight amongst them. Upon their arrival, perceiving that they were but indifferently mounted, he took the horses from the military tribunes, centurions, Roman Knights, and volunteers, and distributed them among the Germans.

LX. Whilst these things passed, the enemy's forces from Auvergne, and the cavalry of all the confederate states of Gaul, met at the general rendezvous, and formed a very numerous army. Cæsar marching through the frontiers of the Lingones, into the country of the Sequani, to be the nearer at hand to succour the Roman province; Vercingetorix lodged himself at about ten miles distance, in three several camps: and having assembled the officers of the cavalry, told them; " That the season of victory was at length arrived, when they saw the Romans obliged to abandon Gaul, and seek a retreat in the province: that this indeed served to secure liberty for the present, but was insufficient to future ease and tranquillity, as they would doubtless return with greater forces than before, and persist in the design of making war. It was therefore best to attack them now, while they marched encumbered with their baggage. If the infantry faced about, in order to assist the horse, they would thereby be enabled to advance; but, if, as was more likely, they abandoned the baggage, to provide for their own safety, they would be deprived of every convenience, and return covered with ignominy and reproach: for as to the enemy's cavalry, it was not once to be imagined, that any of them would so much as stir from the body of the army. That to encourage them the more, and strike the greater terror into the enemy, he was resolved to have the whole army under arms before the camp." These words were followed by the acclamations of all the cavalry, who proposed taking an oath never to return to their homes, nor visit their parents, wives, and children, if they did not twice pierce through the Roman army from one end to another.

LXI. The proposal being approved, and the oath administered to all, Vercingetorix next day divided his cavalry into three bodies; two of which appeared upon the flanks of the Roman army, while the third began to charge and harass it in front. Notice of this being given to Cæsar, he also formed his horse in three divisions, ordering them to advance against the enemy. They made head on all sides at once, the infantry meanwhile continuing quietly under arms, with the baggage placed in the centre. Wherever the Romans gave way, or appeared hard pressed by the enemy, thither Cæsar sent detachments from the legions; which both checked the progress of the Gauls, and confirmed the courage of our men, as they thus saw themselves sure of being supported. At last the Germans on the right, having seized an eminence, drove the enemy before them, and pursued them with great slaughter as far as the river, where Vercingetorix was posted with the infantry. The rest of the Gauls perceiving the defeat of their countrymen, and apprehensive of being surrounded, betook themselves likewise to flight. A dreadful slaughter ensued on all sides. Three Æduan noblemen of the first distinction were brought prisoners to Cæsar; Cotus, general of the cavalry, who, the year before, had been competitor with Convictolitanis for the supreme magistracy; Cavarillus, who, after Litavicus's revolt, had been appointed to command the infantry: and Eporedorix, who was generalissimo of the Æduan troops in the war against the Sequani, before Cæsar's arrival in Gaul.

LXII. Vercingetorix, upon this total rout of the Gaulish cavalry, drew off his troops, whom he had formed in order of battle before the camp, and immediately retreated towards Alesia, a town belonging to the Mandubii, ordering the baggage to follow him with all expedition. Cæsar leaving his on a neighbouring hill, under a guard of two legions, pursued the enemy as far as day would permit, cut three thousand of their rear to pieces, and arrived on the morrow before Alesia. After examining the situation of the town; as he saw the enemy much daunted by the de-

feat of their cavalry, which was the part of their strength in which they chiefly confided, he exhorted his soldiers not to be discouraged at the labour they must undergo, and resolved to invest the place.

LXIII. The city of Alesia was situated on the top of a very high hill, so as not to be taken without a formal siege. The bottom of the hill was washed on the two sides by two rivers. Before the town was a plain, extending about three miles in length; but every where else a ridge of hills, whose summits were nearly upon a level, ran round the place at a moderate distance. Under the walls, on the side facing the east, lay all the forces of the Gauls encamped; who filled that whole space, and were defended by a ditch, and a rampart six feet high. The line of contravallation begun by the Romans, took in a circuit of eleven miles. The camp was conveniently situated, and strengthened with three and twenty redoubts, in which sentinels were placed by day, to give notice of any sudden irruption, and a strong guard by night to defend them in case of assault.

LXIV. Whilst the Romans were employed in those works, Vercingetorix ventured on another engagement of the horse, in the plain between the hills, which, we have said, extended about three miles in length. The contest was sharply maintained on both sides; but our men at length beginning to give ground, Cæsar detached the Germans to their assistance, and drew up the legions in order of battle before the camp, that he might be ready to oppose any sudden irruption of the enemy's infantry. The sight of the legions revived the courage of our men: the enemy were put to flight; and crowding upon one another in their retreat, so obstructed the gates of the camp, that it became in a manner impossible to enter. The Germans pursued them to their intrenchments, where a very great slaughter ensued. Some quitting their horses endeavour to pass the ditch, and get over the rampart. Cæsar, perceiving their disorder, ordered the legions, whom he had drawn out before the camp, to advance a little. This motion no less alarmed the Gauls within the rampart; who believing the whole body of the Roman army was coming to attack them, sounded to arms. Some in their fright fled into the town; upon which, Vercingetorix, fearing the camp would be abandoned, or dered the gates to be shut. At length the Germans, having slain great numbers of the enemy, and taken a multitude of horse, returned from the pursuit.

LXV. Vercingetorix, before our line was completed, resolved to dismiss his cavalry by night. At parting he enjoined them, "To repair severally to their respective states, and assemble all the men capable of bearing arms. He set forth the many services he had done them, and conjured them not to neglect his safety, or abandon to the cruelty of the enemy, one who had deserved so well of the common liberty. He told them, that if they were remiss in the execution of his orders, no less than eighty thousand chosen men must perish with him: that by computation, he had scarce corn for thirty days: and that even with the utmost economy it could be made to hold out but a very little longer." After giving these instructions, he dismissed them quietly about nine at night, on the side where the Roman line was not yet finished. He then ordered the people of the town to bring in all their corn, threatening them with death in case of disobedience. As there was a great number of cattle in the place, which had been driven thither by the Mandubians, he distributed them to the soldiers, man by man, resolving to deliver out the corn sparingly and by measure. At the same time he made all his forces enter the town: and having thus settled the plan of his defence, waited for the expected succours.

LXVI. Cæsar having notice of these things from the prisoners and deserters, constructed his lines in the following manner. He made a ditch twenty feet wide, with perpendicular sides, giving it the same breadth at the bottom as at top. All the other works were four hundred feet farther off the town than this ditch. As his lines included so great a space, and therefore could not be alike guarded in all parts, he judged this precaution necessary, to secure them against sudden sallies by night, and screen the workmen from the enemy's darts by day. Observing this distance, he made two other ditches, fifteen feet broad, and as many deep; and filled the innermost, which lay in a low and level ground, with water from the river. Behind these was a rampart of twelve feet high, strengthened with a parapet and battlements: and to prevent the enemy from getting over, a frieze ran along

the foot of the parapet, made of long stakes, with their branches cut in points, and burnt at the end like a stag's horn. The whole work was flanked with redoubts, eighty feet distant one from another.

LXVII. But as the soldiers were employed at the same time to fetch wood and provisions, and to work at the fortifications, which considerably lessened the number of troops left to defend the camp, many of them being at a distance on these services; and as the Gauls, besides, often sallied at several gates, with design to interrupt the works; for all these reasons, Cæsar judged it necessary to make some addition to his lines, that they might not require so many men to guard them. He therefore took trees of no great height, or large branches, which he caused to be made sharp at the ends; and running a trench of five feet deep before the lines, he ordered them to be put into it, and made fast at bottom, so that they could not be pulled up. This trench was again filled up in such a manner, that nothing but the branches of the head appeared, of which the points must have run into those who should have endeavoured to pass them. As there were five rows of them, interwoven in a manner with each other, they were unavoidable. The soldiers called them cippi. In the front of these he caused pits of three feet deep to be dug in form of the quincunx, and something narrower at bottom than at top. In these pits he fixed strong stakes, about the thickness of a man's thigh, burnt and sharpened at the top, which rose only four inches above the level of the ground, into which they were planted three feet deeper than the pits, for the sake of firmness. The pits were covered over with bushes to deceive the enemy. There were eight rows of them, at the distance of three feet from each other. They were called lilies, from the resemblance they bore to that flower. In the front of all, he sowed the whole space between the pits and the advanced ditch with crows-feet of an extraordinary size, which the soldiers called spurs.

LXVIII. These works completed, he drew another line, of fourteen miles in compass, constructed in the same manner as the former, and carried through the most even places he could find, to serve as a barrier against the enemy without; that if the Gauls should attack the camp in his absence, they might not be able to surround it with the multitude of their troops, or charge with equal vigour in all parts. At the same time to prevent the danger his men might be exposed to, by being sent in quest of provisions and forage, he took care to lay in a sufficient stock of both for thirty days.

LXIX. Whilst these things passed before Alesia, a general council being held of the principal noblemen of Gaul, it was not thought proper to assemble all that were able to bear arms, as Vercingetorix desired, but to order each nation to furnish a contingent; lest the confusion inseparable from so great a multitude, should bring on a scarcity of provisions, or render the observance of military discipline impracticable. The Æduans, with their vassals the Segusians, Ambivareti, Aulerci, Brannovices, and Brannovii, were rated at thirty-five thousand. A like number was demanded from the Averni, in conjunction with their dependants, the Cadurci, Gabali, and Velauni. The Senones, Sequani, and Biturigians, Santones, Rutherni, and Carnutes, were ordered each to furnish twelve thousand; the Bellovaci, ten thousand; the Lemovices, the same number; the Pictones, Turoni, Parisians, and Suessiones, each eight thousand; the Ambiani, Mediomatrici, Petrocorians, Nervians, Morini, Nitobrigians, and Aulerci Cenomani, each five thousand; the Atrebatians, four thousand; the Bellocasians, Lexovians, and Aulerci Eburovices, each three thousand; the Rauraci and Boii, thirty thousand; the maritime and Armorican states, of which number are the Curiosolites, Rhedones, Caletes, Osismians, Lemovices, Venetians, and Unellians, each six thousand. The Bellovaci alone refused to furnish the troops required, pretending it was their design to wage an independent war with the Romans, without being subject to the control of any one: however, at the request of Comius, for whom they had a great respect, they sent a body of two thousand men.

LXX. This Comius, as we have related above, had been singularly faithful and serviceable to Cæsar, in his Britannic expedition; in consideration of which, his state had been exempted from all tribute, restored to the full enjoyment of its laws and privileges, and even enlarged, by having the country of the Morini added to its territories. But such was the present unanimity of the Gauls, in the design of vindicating their liberty, and recovering their wonted reputation in war, that neither benefits received, nor the strictest ties of friendship,

could make any impression upon their minds; but all with one consent flew to arms, and contributed largely to the support of the war. The country of the Æduans was the general rendezvous of the army, which amounted to eight thousand horse, and two hundred and forty thousand foot. Four commanders in chief were appointed; Comius of Arras, Virdumarus and Eporedorix the Æduans, and Vergasillaunus of Auvergne, cousin-german to Vercingetorix. To these were added a select number of officers, chosen from among the several states, to serve by way of a council of war. The whole army advanced towards Alesia, full of courage and confidence, and satisfied that the Romans would not sustain the very sight of so prodigious a multitude; especially in an encounter attended with so much hazard, where they must be exposed to a vigorous sally from the town, at the same time that they saw themselves surrounded with such numbers of horse and foot.

LXXI. Meanwhile the troops shut up in Alesia, having consumed all their provisions, finding the day appointed for the arrival of succours expired, and knowing nothing of what was transacted among the Æduans, summoned a council of war, to debate upon what was requisite in the present exigence. Various opinions were proposed: some advised a surrender; others were for sallying while yet their strength would permit: among the rest, Critognatus, a man of the first rank and authority in Auvergne, addressed the assembly in a speech, which for its singular and detestable inhumanity, deserves a particular mention in this place. "I shall not," says he, "take notice of the opinion of those who endeavour to shelter an ignominious servitude, under the plausible name of a surrender; such should neither be reckoned Gauls, nor suffered to come to this council. Let me rather apply myself to them who propose a general sally: for here, as all of you seem to think, we meet with something worthy of our ancient virtue. And yet I am not afraid to say, that it is at the bottom weakness, and not courage, that inspires such thoughts, and renders us unable to support want a few days. It is easier to find those who will voluntarily rush on death, than such as can patiently endure pain. I shall not however, be against this proposal, which I confess has something generous in it, if only our own lives were at stake. But in this deliberation, we must keep all Gaul in view, whom we have called to our assistance. How would it dispirit our relations and friends, to see eighty thousand of their countrymen slaughtered in one place, and be obliged to fight in the midst of their dead bodies! Deprive not then of your assistance those, who, to save you, have exposed themselves to the greatest dangers; nor through an inconsiderate temerity, and mistaken valour, destroy at once all the expectations of Gaul, and plunge her into perpetual servitude. If the expected succours are not arrived exactly at the appointed time, ought you therefore to suspect the fidelity and constancy of your countrymen? And can you think that it is for amusement only, that the Romans labour on those lines towards the country? Though you hear not from your friends, because all communication is hindered; yet you may learn the approach of the succours from your enemies themselves; who, through fear of them work day and night, without ceasing, on those fortifications. What then should I propose? What but to do as our ancestors did in the war with the Teutones and Cimbri, much less interesting than that we are now engaged in. Compelled to shut themselves up in their towns, and reduced to a distress equal to that we now experience, rather than surrender to their enemies, they chose to sacrifice to their subsistence the bodies of those whom age incapacitated for war. Had we no such precedent to follow, yet still I should esteem it glorious, in so noble a cause as that of liberty, to institute and give one to posterity. For where had we ever a war upon our hands like that we are now engaged in? The Cimbri, after laying waste Gaul, and spreading desolation through the whole country, withdrew however their forces at length, and repaired to other regions, leaving us the full enjoyment of our laws, customs, lands, and liberties. But the Romans, instigated by envy, and jealous of a people so renowned and powerful in war, aim and intend nothing less than to establish themselves in our cities and territories, and reduce us to perpetual servitude. This has ever been the object of all their wars. If you are unacquainted with what passes in different countries, cast your eyes upon the adjoining Gaul, which, reduced into the form of a province, stripped of its laws and privileges, and subjected to the arbitrary sway of the conqueror, groans under an endless

yoke of slavery." When all had delivered their opinions, a resolution was taken, that such as by age or sickness were unfit for war, should be obliged to quit the town, and every expedient be tried, rather than give into the proposal of Critognatus: but if necessity urged, and relief was long deferred, they determined upon submitting to his advice preferably to peace or a surrender. The Mandubii, to whom the city belonged, were driven thence with their wives and children. When they came to the Roman lines, they with tears petitioned to be received as slaves, and saved from perishing miserably by famine. But Cæsar having planted guards along the rampart, refused to admit them into his camp.

LXXII. Meanwhile Comius, and the other general officers, on whom the chief command had been conferred, arrived before Alesia with all their forces, and encamped on a hill without the town, not above five hundred paces from the Roman lines. The next day they drew out their cavalry, and covered the whole plain under the hill, which, as we have already said, extended three miles in length. The infantry were stationed at some distance on the heights, yet so as to lie concealed from the view of the Romans. As Alesia commanded a full prospect of the plain below, the succours were soon discovered by the besieged, who assembling in crowds, congratulated each other; and testified a universal joy. Immediately they came forth with all their forces, posted themselves before the town, and having filled up the nearest ditch with earth and fascines, prepared for a vigorous sally, and every thing else that might happen.

LXXIII. Cæsar, having disposed his whole army on both sides the works, that in case of need, every soldier might know his post, and be ready to maintain it, ordered the cavalry to sally out upon the enemy, and begin the charge. The camp, running along a ridge of a rising ground, commanded a view of the plain on all sides; and the soldiers, to a man, with deep attention, waited the issue of the combat. The Gauls had interspersed among the cavalry some archers and light-armed troops, to sustain them in case of need, and check the impetuosity of our horse. Several of the Romans being wounded by these at the first charge, were obliged to quit the battle. The Gauls now believing they had the advantage, and seeing our men overpowered by numbers, set up a universal shout, as well within as without the place, to give new life to their troops. As the action passed in the view of both armies, who were, of course, witnesses to the valour or cowardice of the combatants, the desire of applause, or fear of ignominy, spurred on each side to exert their utmost bravery. After a conflict that lasted from noon till near sun-set, victory all the while continuing doubtful, the Germans, in close order, charged furiously the enemy on one side, and forced them to give ground. Their flight leaving the archers exposed, they were all surrounded and cut to pieces. The success was equal in other parts of the field, where our men pursuing the runaways to their camp, gave them no time to rally. The troops who had quitted Alesia, despairing now almost of victory, turned disconsolate to the town.

LXXIV. After the interval of a day, which was wholly spent in providing a great number of fascines, scaling ladders, and iron hooks; the Gauls issuing from their camp at midnight, in great silence, attacked the Roman lines, on the side of the plain. They began with setting up a sudden shout, to advertise the besieged of their arrival; threw their fascines into the ditch; endeavoured by a discharge of stones, darts and arrows, to drive our men from the rampart; and practised every thing necessary to render the storm successful. At the same time Vercingetorix, hearing their cries, sounded to arms, and led forth his men to the attack. The Romans, whose posts had been allotted them some days before, flew to the works, and with slings, darts, bullets, and engines, prepared on purpose, struck a terror into the assailants. As the parties could not see one another by reason of the darkness, many wounds were received on both sides, and a great number of darts discharged from the engines. But M. Antonius and C. Trebonius, who commanded on the one side that was most pressed by the enemy, took care to draw out parties from the more distant redoubts, and send them where their assistance was chiefly wanted.

LXXV. While the Gauls kept at a distance from our lines, they did great execution by the multitude of their darts; but in proportion as they approached, they either entangled themselves unawares among the caltrops, or tumbling into the wells, were wounded by the pointed stakes, or were pierced by the darts discharged from the towers and rampart. After many wounds given and received; finding, when day appeared, that they had not forced any part of the lines, and fearing to be taken in flank by some troops that were sallying from the redoubts on the eminence, they retreated to their camp. Meanwhile the besieged, after much time spent in preparing for a sally, and filling up the advanced ditch, finding that their countrymen were retired, before they could so much as approach the works, returned into the town without effecting any thing.

LXXVI. The Gauls thus twice repulsed with great loss, consult what new measure they are to pursue: and advising with those who knew the ground, learned from them the strength and situation of the upper camp. North of the town was a hill of too great a compass to be taken into the circumvallation; insomuch that the Romans had been obliged to post themselves on its ascent, in a very disadvantageous situation, because their camp was commanded by its summit. C. Antistius Reginus, and C. Caninius Rebilus, lieutenant-generals, guarded this quarter with two legions. The enemy's generals, after informing themselves of the nature of the country by their scouts, selected five and fifty thousand of their best troops, concerted privately among themselves the plan and manner of acting, appointed the time for the assault about noon, and assigned the command of the detachment to Vergasillaunus of Auvergne, one of the four principal leaders, and a near relation of Vercingetorix. Vergasillaunus leaving his camp in the evening, finished his march by day-break; and concealing his troops behind a hill, ordered his soldiers to refresh themselves after the fatigue. As soon as it was noon, he approached the quarters of the two legions. At the same time the cavalry advanced into the plain, and the whole army drew out before the camp.

LXXVII. Vercingetorix observing these motions from the citadel of Alesia, led forth his troops; carrying along with him the fascines, long poles, covered galleries, hooks, and other instruments he had prepared for the assault. The fight was maintained on all sides at once; nor did the Gauls leave any thing unattempted, but flocked continually to those parts of the works which appeared to be the weakest. The Roman forces having so many works to guard, were dispersed in different places, and scarce sufficed for the defence of them all. What mostly contributed to disturb them was, the cries of the combatants behind, which informed them that their safety depended on the valour of others. For such is the constitution of the human mind, as always to aggrandize absent objects, and magnify the danger that is out of sight.

LXXVIII. Cæsar chose a post from whence he could see every thing, and then sent reinforcements where necessary. Both parties called to mind, that now was the time for making the greatest effort. The Gauls had no hopes of safety, but in forcing the Roman lines. Our men again were sensible, that if they came off victorious on this occasion, all their labours would be at an end. The chief stress of the battle lay at the higher fortifications, where Vergasillaunus charged with his detachment; because the small eminence, which commanded the declivity of the hill, gave the enemy great advantage. Some were employed in throwing darts; others advanced to the attack, under cover of their shields; fresh men still succeeding in the room of those that were fatigued. The earth they threw up against our lines not only enabled them to ascend the rampart, but entirely frustrated the design of the works the Romans had made in the ground. In fine, our men had neither strength nor weapon left to make resistance.

LXXIX. Cæsar observing the danger they were in, sent Labienus, with six cohorts, to their assistance; ordering him if he found himself unable to defend the works, to sally out upon the enemy; yet this only in case of extremity. He himself went in person to the rest of the troops, exhorting them to bear up courageously under their present fatigue, and representing, that the fruit of all their former victories depended upon the issue of that critical day and hour. The troops within the place, despairing to force the intrenchments on the side of the plain, because of the great strength of the works, attacked them in the more steep and difficult places, whither they brought all the instruments prepared for the assault. They soon drove our men from the towers, by a discharge of darts, levelled the way with earth and fascines, and began to cut down the rampart and breastwork with their hooks.

LXXX. Cæsar first sent young Brutus, with six cohorts; after him, C. Fabius lieutenant-general, with seven more; and, last of all, as the dispute grew very warm, marched himself in person at the head of the whole detachment. Having, by this means, restored the battle, and forced the enemy to retire, he hastened to the side where Labienus was engaged. He drew four cohorts from the nearest fort, ordered part of the cavalry to follow him, and charged the rest to take a circuit round the outward works, and fall upon the enemy's rear. Labienus finding that neither the rampart nor ditch were sufficient to stop the progress of the enemy, drew together about thirty-nine cohorts from the nearest forts, and sent to inform Cæsar of his design. Cæsar immediately quickened his march, that he might be present at the action.

LXXXI. His arrival being known from the colour of his garments, by which he used to distinguish himself in the day of battle; and the troops and cohorts he had ordered to follow him, appearing; all which were easily discerned from the higher ground; the enemy began the charge. A mighty shout was raised on both sides, which being catched by those on the rampart, was carried quite round the lines. Our men, having cast their darts, fell upon the Gauls sword in hand. At the same time the cavalry appeared unexpectedly in their rear; fresh cohorts flocked continually to our assistance: the enemy took flight, and, in their retreat, were encountered by our horse: a dreadful slaughter ensued. Sedulius, chief and general of the Lemovices, was slain on the spot; Vergasillaunus of Auvergne, was made prisoner in the pursuit; seventy-four colours were taken, and brought to Cæsar; and, out of so great a multitude, very few regained the Gaulish camp. The rout and slaughter being observed from the town, the besieged, despairing of success, drew off their troops from the attack. Instantly, upon the report of this disaster, the Gauls abandoned their camp; and had not our troops been wearied out by the continual fatigue of the day, and the frequent reinforcements they were obliged to furnish, the enemy's whole army might have been exterminated. At midnight Cæsar detached the cavalry to pursue them, who, falling in with their rear, slew some, and took a great number of prisoners. The rest escaped to their several habitations.

LXXXII. Next day, Vercingetorix assembling a council, represented to the besieged: " That he had undertaken that war

COMMENTARIES. 193

not from a motive of private interest, but to recover the common liberty of Gaul: and that since there was a necessity of yielding to fortune, he was willing to become a victim for their safety, whether they should think proper to appease the anger of the conqueror by his death or to deliver him up alive." A deputation immediately waited on Cæsar to receive his orders. He insisted on the surrender of their arms, and the delivering up of all their chiefs. Having accordingly seated himself at the head of his lines, before the camp, their leaders were brought, Vercingetorix delivered up, and their arms thrown into the ditch. Reserving the Æduans and Averni, as a means to recover those two potent nations, he divided the rest of the prisoners among his soldiers, giving to each one.

LXXXIII. These affairs despatched, he marched into the territories of the Æduans, where he received the submission of their state. There he was addressed by the ambassadors of the Averni, who promised an entire obedience to his commands. He exacted a great number of hostages; sent his legions into winter quarters; and restored about twenty thousand captives to the Æduans and Averni. T. Labienus, with two legions and the cavalry, was quartered among the Sequani jointly with M. Sempronius Rutilus. C. Fabius, and L. Minutius Basilus, were ordered, with two legions, into the country of the Rhemi, to defend it against the attempts of the Bellovaci, their neighbours. C. Antistius Reginus had his station assigned him among the Ambivareti; T. Sextius among the Biturigians; and C. Caninius Rebilus among the Rutheni; each with one legion. Q. Tullius Cicero, and P. Sulpicius, were placed at Cabillo and Matisco upon the Arar, in the country of the Æduans, to have the care of provisions. He himself resolved to winter at Bibracte. The senate being informed of these things by Cæsar's letters, a procession of twenty days was decreed.

PANSA'S CONTINUATION

OF

CÆSAR'S COMMENTARIES

OF HIS

WARS IN GAUL.

———

BOOK VIII.

THE ARGUMENT.

Pansa's Preface.—I. The Gauls form a resolution to renew the war.—II. Cæsar falls unexpectedly upon the Biturigians, and compels them to submit.—IV. He afterwards disperses the Carnutes by the terror of his arms.—V. The Bellovaci prepare for war.—VI. Their designs.—VII. Cæsar endeavours to draw them to an engagement, by inspiring them with a contempt of his small numbers.—VIII. But as they carefully avoid a battle, he resolves to fortify his camp.—XI. The Bellovaci intercept the Roman foragers.—XII. Daily skirmishes within view of the two camps.—XIII.—The Bellovaci artfully counterfeit a retreat.—XVI. And falling upon the Romans from an ambuscade, after an obstinate fight, are entirely dispersed.—XVII. The Bellovaci and other states submit.—XX. Cæsar divides his army.—XXI. Caninius and Fabius relieve Duracius, besieged by Dumnacus in Limo.—XXIV. Caninius pursues Drapes and Luterius.—XXV. Fabius obliges the Carnutes and other states to submit.—XXVI. Drapes and Luterius possess themselves of Uxellodunum.—XXVII. Caninius invests the town.—XXVIII. Intercepts a convoy escorted by Luterius.—XXIX. Attacks and carries the camp of Drapes.—XXX. And joining the forces under Fabius, returns to the siege of Uxellodunum.—XXXI. Cæsar repairs to the camp of Caninius.—XXXIII. And depriving the besieged of water, compels the town to surrender.—XXXVII. He sends his army into winter quarters.—XXXVIII. Comius defeated in an engagement of horse, surrenders to Antony.—XLI. The year following, Gaul being in perfect quiet, Cæsar goes into Italy.—XLII. Where he is received with the highest demonstrations of respect.—XLIII. He returns to the army, **where he learns the designs** formed against him at Rome.—XLVI. And thereupon sets out again for **Italy.**

A CONTINUATION

OF

CÆSAR'S COMMENTARIES

OF

HIS WARS IN GAUL.

BY A. HIRTIUS PANSA.

BOOK VIII.

In consequence of your repeated importunities, Balbus, I have at last been prevailed with to engage in a very delicate work; fearing lest my daily refusals should be construed rather to flow from idleness, than any sense of the difficulty of the undertaking. I therefore here present you with a continuation of Cæsar's Commentaries of his Wars in Gaul, though not in any respect to be compared with what he himself wrote on the same subject, nor with the Memoirs of the civil war, which he likewise left behind him imperfect, and which I have in the same manner carried down from the transactions at Alexandria, to the end, I will not say of our civil dissensions, which are like to have no end, but of Cæsar's life. I would have all who read these pieces, know with how much reluctance I engaged in this design; that I may be the more easily acquitted of the charge of arrogance and folly, for presuming to insert my writings among those of Cæsar. It is universally agreed, that the most elaborate compositions of others, fall far short of the elegance of these Commentaries. He indeed intended them only as memoirs for future historians; but they are every where in such high esteem, as serves rather to discourage other writers, than furnish them for the attempt. This circumstance the more commands our admiration, because while the rest of the world can judge only of the beauty and correctness of the work, we besides know with what ease and despatch it was composed. Cæsar not only possessed the talent of writing in the highest perfection, but was likewise best able to unfold the reasons of those military operations of which he was himself the contriver and director. On the contrary, it was my misfortune to be present neither in the Alexandrian nor African wars; and though I had many of the particulars relating to both from his own mouth, yet we give a very different attention to things, when we hear them only through an admiration of their novelty and greatness, and when with a view of transmitting them to posterity. But I forbear any further apologies, lest in enumerating the reasons why my work ought not to be compared with that of Cæsar, I fall under the suspicion of flattering myself, that in the judgment of some, it may not seem altogether unworthy of that honour. Adieu.

I. Gaul being wholly reduced, Cæsar was desirous that his troops might enjoy some repose during the winter, especially after so long and fatiguing a campaign, in which there had been no intermission from the toils of war; but he soon understood, that several states were meditating a revolt, and contriving all at once to take up arms. The cause assigned for this conduct was not improbable; for though the Gauls were by this time fully sensible, that it was impossible for them to resist the Roman army entire, by any forces they could bring into the field; yet still they thought, that if many states revolted together, and set on foot as many different wars, the Romans would have neither time nor troops to subdue them all; and that though some among them must be sufferers, their lot would be the more supportable, as the delay occasioned by that diversion, might procure the liberty of the whole nation.

II. Cæsar, to stifle this opinion in its birth, left M. Antony the questor to command in his winter quarters; and setting out the last of December from Bibracte, with a guard of cavalry, went to the camp of the thirteenth legion, which he had placed among the Biturigians, not far from the territories of the Æduans. To this he joined the eleventh legion, whose quarters lay nearest; and leaving two cohorts to guard the baggage, marched with the rest of the army into the most fertile parts of the country of the Biturigians; who having large territories, and abounding in towns, had not been awed by the presence of a single legion, from forming confederacies, and preparing for war.

III. Cæsar by his sudden and unexpected arrival, as was natural to suppose, found them unprepared and dispersed up and down the fields; insomuch that they were easily surprised by the horse, before they could retreat into their towns. For he had expressly forbid setting fire to the houses, the usual sign of an invasion, that he might neither alarm the enemy by the conflagration, nor expose himself to the want of corn and forage, if he should advance far into the country. Having made many thousands of the Biturigians prisoners, such as could escape the first coming of the Romans, fled in great terror to the neighbouring states, relying either upon private friendship, or the ties of a mutual confederacy. But all was to no purpose: for Cæsar, by great marches, soon reached their places of retreat, and making every province anxious for its own safety, left them no time to think of giving shelter to others. This diligence confirmed the well-affected in their duty, and obliged the wavering to hearken to conditions of peace. The like offers were made to the Biturigians; who seeing that Cæsar's clemency left the way still open to his friendship, and that the neighbouring states, upon delivery of hostages, had been pardoned and received into protection, resolved to follow the example. Cæsar, to recompense the fatigue

and labour of his soldiers, who, in the winter season, through difficult ways, and during the most intense colds, had followed him with incredible patience and constancy; promised a reward of two hundred sesterces to every private man, and two thousand to every centurion: and having sent back the legions to their winter quarters, returned again to Bibracte, after an absence of forty days.

IV. Whilst he was there employed in the distribution of justice, ambassadors arrived from the Biturigians, to implore his assistance against the Carnutes, who were laying waste their country. Upon this intelligence, though he had not rested above eighteen days, he immediately sent for the sixth and fourteenth legions, which he had quartered along the Arar, for the convenience of provisions, as has been related in the foregoing book. With these two legions he marched against the Carnutes; who hearing of his approach, and dreading the same calamities which others had been made to suffer, abandoned their towns and villages, consisting mostly of little cottages run up in haste, to defend them from the cold, (for most of their cities had been destroyed in the late war,) and fled different ways. Cæsar unwilling to expose his soldiers to the severity of the storms, which commonly rage with the greatest violence at that season, fixed his camp at Genabum; and lodged his men, partly in the huts lately built by the Gauls, partly in the old houses, whose walls were still standing, and which he ordered to be thatched with straw, that they might afford the better shelter to the troops. But he sent the cavalry and the auxiliary foot into all parts where he understood the enemy were retired; nor without success; for they commonly returned loaden with spoil. The Carnutes, distressed by the difficulty of the season, the sense of their danger, (because being driven from their habitations, they durst not continue long in any place for fear of our parties,) and finding no protection in the woods against the extreme severity of the weather; were at length dispersed on all sides with great loss, and scattered among the neighbouring states.

V. Cæsar thinking it sufficient in that difficult season, to have dispersed the troops that began to assemble, and prevented their rekindling the war; and being likewise well assured, as far as human prudence could determine, that it would be impossible for them, during the ensuing summer, to raise up any very dangerous war; left C. Trebonius, with the two legions he had brought along with him, to winter at Genabum. Meanwhile, understanding by frequent embassies from the Rhemi, that the Bellovaci, the most distinguished for bravery of all the Belgian and Gallic nations, with some of the neighbouring states, under the conduct of Correus, general of the Bellovaci, and Comius the Atrebatian, were raising an army, and drawing their forces to a general rendezvous with design to invade the territories of the Suessiones, a people subject to the jurisdiction of the Rhemi; he thought that both honour and interest required him to undertake the defence of allies, who had deserved so well of the commonwealth. He therefore drew the eleventh legion again out of its winter quarters; wrote to C. Fabius, to march the two legions under his command into the country of the Suessiones, and ordered Labienus to send one of those he was charged with. Thus, as far as the convenience of winter quarters, and the nature of the war would allow, he employed the legions alternately in expedition, giving himself, meanwhile, no intermission from fatigue.

VI. With these forces he marched against the Bellovaci, and encamping within their territories, dispersed his cavalry on all sides to make prisoners, from whom he might learn the enemy's designs. The horse, in consequence of this commission, brought him back word, that the lands and houses were in a manner quite abandoned, and that the few prisoners they had found, after a most diligent search, were not left to cultivate the ground, but to serve as spies. Cæsar inquiring of these, whither the Bellovaci were retired, and what might be their designs, found: " That all of them capable of bearing arms, had assembled in one place, and been joined by the Ambians, Aulerci, Caletes, Vellocasians, and Atrebatians: that they had chosen for their camp, a rising ground, surrounded with a difficult morass, and disposed of their baggage in remote woods: that a great many of their chiefs were concerned in the war, but the principal authority rested in Correus, because he was known to bear an implacable hatred to the Roman name; that a few days before, Comius had left the camp to solicit aid of the Germans, who were their nearest neighbours, and abounded in troops: that it had been resolved

among the Bellovaci, with consent of all the generals, and at the earnest desire of the people, if Cæsar came at the head of only three legions, as was reported, to offer him battle; lest they should be afterwards obliged to fight upon harder and more unequal terms, when he had got his whole army together: but if he brought greater forces along with him, to continue within their camp, intercept his corn and convoys, and cut off his forage; which in that season of the year was extremely scarce, and very much dispersed."

VII. These things being confirmed by the testimony of all the prisoners, Cæsar, who found their designs full of prudence, and remote from the usual temerity of barbarians, resolved by all manner of ways to draw them into a contempt of his numbers, that he might the more easily bring them to an engagement. He had with him the seventh, eighth, and ninth legions, all veterans of approved valour; and though the eleventh was not of equal standing, nor had attained the same reputation of bravery, they were yet chosen youth of great hopes, who had served under him eight campaigns. Calling therefore the army together, he laid before them the advices he had received, and exhorted the soldiers to preserve their wonted courage. At the same time, to draw the enemy to an engagement, by an appearance of only three legions, he so contrived the order of his march, that disposing the seventh, eighth, and ninth legions, in front; the baggage, which, as in a hasty expedition, was but moderate, behind them; and the eleventh legion in the rear of all; no more troops were in view, than what the Gauls themselves had determined to hazard an action against. The army, thus drawn up, formed a kind of square, and arrived before the enemy's camp much sooner than expected.

VIII. When the Gauls perceived the legions advancing suddenly against them in order of battle, with a steady pace, they altered the resolution which had been reported to Cæsar; and either fearing the success of the battle, surprised at so sudden an approach, or willing to know our further designs, drew up before their camp, without descending from the higher ground. Cæsar though desirous to come to an engagement, yet surprised at the multitude of the enemy, and reflecting on the advantage of their situation; as being separated from him by a valley, still more con siderable for its depth than breadth; contented himself for the present to encamp directly over against them. He threw up a rampart twelve feet high, strengthened by a proportionable breast-work; and secured it by two ditches, each fifteen feet deep, with perpendicular sides. He likewise raised several turrets of three stories, and joined them to each other by galleries, having little parapets of osier before, that the works might be defended by a double range of soldiers; one of which fighting from the galleries, and secured by their height, would, with more boldness and advantage, launch their darts against the enemy; the other, though nearer danger, and planted upon the rampart itself, were yet screened by the galleries from the impending darts. All the entrances to the camp were secured by strong gates, over which he placed very high towers.

IX. He had a twofold design in these fortifications: one, by the greatness of the works, to make the enemy believe him afraid, and thereby increase their presumption and confidence; the other to enable him to defend his camp with a few troops, when it was necessary to go far in quest of corn and forage. Meantime there happened frequent skirmishes between the two camps, carried on for the most part with arrows at a distance, by reason of a morass that separated the combatants; sometimes indeed the auxiliary Gauls and Germans crossed the morass, and pursued the enemy: sometimes again the enemy having the advantage, passed in their turn, and drove back our men. And as we daily sent our parties to forage, who were obliged to disperse, and scatter themselves from house to house over the whole country, it now and then fell out, as was unavoidable in these circumstances, that our foragers were surprised and cut to pieces by their detachments. These losses, though very inconsiderable to us, as being mostly confined to some carriages and servants, yet strangely swelled the hopes of the barbarians; and the more, as Comius, who had gone to fetch the German auxiliaries, was now returned with a body of horse. And though the number was not great, they not making in all above five hundred, the enemy were nevertheless mightily encouraged by this supply.

X. Cæsar, after a stay of many days, finding that the enemy still kept within their camp, which was advantageously situated with a mo-

rass in front; and considering, at the same time, that he could neither force the intrenchments without great loss, nor inclose them with works with so small an army, wrote to Trebonius, to send, with all diligence, for the thirteenth legion, which was quartered among the Biturigians, under the care of T. Sextius; and with that, and the two legions under his own command, make what haste he could to join him. Meanwhile he detached the cavalry of Rheims, of the Lingones, and the other provinces of Gaul, of which he had great numbers in his camp, to guard by turns the foragers, and protect them from the sudden incursions of the enemy.

XI. This was done every day; but custom, by degrees, relaxing their diligence, as frequently happens in things of long continuance; the Bellovaci, who had observed the daily stations of our horse, placed a chosen body of foot in ambush in a wood, and sent their cavalry thither next day, to draw our men into the snare, and then attack them, surrounded on every side. This ill fortune fell upon the cavalry of Rheims, whose turn it was that day to guard the foragers: for these, suddenly discovering the enemy's cavalry, and despising their small numbers, pursued with such eagerness, that they were at length surprised and surrounded by the foot. This threw them into confusion, and obliged them to retreat hastily with the loss of Vertiscus their general, and the chief man of their state: who, though so far advanced in years that he could hardly sit on horseback, yet, according to the custom of the Gauls, would neither decline the command on account of his age, nor suffer them to fight without him. The enemy were animated and encouraged by this success and the death of the chief and general of the Rhemi: our men on the other hand, were cautioned by their loss, carefully to examine the ground before they took their posts, and pursue a retreating enemy with more reserve.

XII. Meanwhile the daily skirmishes between the two camps, at the fords and passes of the morass, still continued. In one of these, the Germans, whom Cæsar had brought from beyond the Rhine, that they might fight intermingled with the cavalry, boldly passing the morass in a body, put all that made resistance to the sword, and pursued the rest with great vigour. Fear not only seized those who fought hand to hand, or were wounded at a distance; but even the more remote parties, who were posted to sustain the others, shamefully betook themselves to flight; and, being driven from height to height, ceased not to continue the route, until they had reached their very camp; nay, some, quite confounded by their fear, fled a great way beyond it. Their danger spread so universal a terror among the troops, that it appeared hard to say, whether they were more apt to be elated by a trifling advantage, or depressed by an inconsiderable loss.

XIII. After a stay of many days in this camp; upon information that C. Trebonius was approaching with the legions, the generals of the Bellovaci, fearing a siege like that of Alesia, sent away by night all whom age or infirmities rendered unfit for service; and along with them the baggage of the whole army. But before this confused and numerous train could be put in order, (for the Gauls even in their sudden expeditions, are always attended with a vast number of carriages,) daylight appeared; and the enemy were obliged to draw up before their camp, to hinder the Romans from disturbing the march of their baggage. Cæsar did not think proper to attack them in so advantageous a post, nor was he willing to remove his legions to such a distance, as might give them an opportunity of retreating without danger. Observing therefore that the two camps were divided by a very dangerous morass, the difficulty of passing which might greatly retard the pursuit, and that beyond the morass there was an eminence, which in a manner commanded the enemy's camp, and was separated from it only by a small valley, he laid bridges over the morass, passed his legions, and quickly gained the summit of the hill, which was secured on each side by the steepness of the ascent. Thence he marched his legions, in order of battle, to the extremest ridge, and posted them in a place where his engines could play upon the enemy's battalions.

XIV. The Gauls, confiding in the strength of their post, resolved not to decline a battle if the Romans should attack them on the hill; and not daring to make their troops file off, for fear of being charged when separated and in disorder, continued in the same posture. Cæsar perceiving their obstinacy, kept twenty cohorts already drawn up; and marking out a camp in the place where he then stood, ordered it to be fortified immedi-

ately. The works being finished, he drew up his legions before the rampart, and assigned the cavalry their several posts, where they were to wait, with their horses ready bridled. The Bellovaci seeing the Romans prepared for the pursuit, and finding it impossible to pass the night, or continue longer in that place without provisions, fell upon the following stratagem to secure their retreat. They collected and placed at the head of their line all the fascines in the camp, of which the number was very great, (for, as has been already observed, the Gauls commonly sit upon these, when drawn up in order of battle,) and towards night, upon a signal given, set fire to them all at once. The flame blazing out on a sudden, with great violence, covered their forces from the view of the Romans; and the Gauls laying hold of that opportunity retreated with the utmost diligence.

XV. Though Cæsar could not perceive the enemy's departure, because of the flames, yet suspecting that this was only a contrivance to cover their flight, he made the legions advance, and detached the cavalry to pursue them. Meanwhile, apprehending an ambuscade, and that the enemy might perhaps continue in the same post, to draw our men into a place of disadvantage, he took care to follow slowly with the foot. The cavalry not daring to enter that thick column of flame and smoke, or if any had the courage to adventure it, being unable to discern the very heads of their horses, thought proper to retire for fear of a surprise, and left the Bellovaci at full liberty to escape. Thus by a flight, which equally spoke their fear and address, they retreated ten miles without loss, and encamped in a place of great advantage. Thence, by frequent ambuscades of horse and foot, they often attacked and cut to pieces the Roman foragers.

XVI. Cæsar having received many losses of this kind, understood at last by a certain prisoner, that Correus, general of the Bellovaci, had chosen six thousand of his best foot, and a thousand horse, to form an ambuscade in a place abounding in corn and grass, and where it was therefore presumed the Romans would come to forage. Upon this intelligence, he drew out a greater number of legionaries than usual; sent the cavalry, who formed the ordinary guard of the foragers, before; intermixed them with platoons of light-armed foot, and advanced himself as near as possible with the legions. The enemy, who lay in ambush, having chosen for the place of action a plain of about a mile every way, and environed on all sides with thick woods, or a very deep river, which enclosed it as in a toil, disposed their forces all around. Our men who knew their design, and advanced armed and resolved for battle, because the legions were behind to sustain them, entered the plain troop by troop. Upon their arrival, Correus thinking that now was the proper time for action, appeared first with a few of his men, and fell upon the nearest squadrons. Our men resolutely sustained the attack, nor flocked together in crowds, as frequently happens among the cavalry on occasion of sudden surprise, when the very number of combatants throws all into confusion. The squadrons fighting thus in good order, and preserving a proper distance, to prevent their being taken in flank; suddenly the rest of the Gauls broke from the woods, and advanced to the aid of those who fought under Correus. The contest was carried on with great heat, and continued for a long time with equal advantage on both sides: when at last the foot advancing slowly in order of battle from the woods, obliged our men to give way. Upon this the light-armed infantry, who, as we have observed, had been sent before the legions, marched up speedily to their assistance; and placing themselves in the intervals of the squadrons, continued the fight. The contest again became equal. At length, as was natural in an encounter of this kind, those who had sustained the first charge of the ambuscade, began for this very reason to have the superiority, because the enemy had gained no advantage over them. Meanwhile the legions approached, and both sides had notice at the same time that Cæsar was advancing with his forces in order of battle. Our troops, animated by this hope, redoubled their efforts; lest by pushing the enemy too slowly, the legions should have time to come in for a share of the victory. The enemy, on the contrary, lost courage, and fled different ways. But in vain: for the very difficulties of the ground, by which they hoped to have ensnared the Romans, served now to entangle themselves. Being at last vanquished and repulsed, with the loss of the best part of their men, they fled in great terror whither chance directed; some towards the woods, some towards the river. The Romans urged the pursuit with great keenness, and put many

to the sword. Meanwhile Correus, whose resolution no misfortune could abate, would neither quit the fight, and retire to the woods, nor accept of any offers of quarter from our men; but fighting on to the last with invincible courage, and wounding many of the victorious troops, constrained them at length to transfix him with their javelins.

XVII. After this action, Cæsar coming up just as the battle was ended, and naturally supposing that the enemy, upon intelligence of so considerable a defeat, would immediately abandon their camp, which was not above eight miles distant from the place of slaughter; though he saw his march obstructed by the river, he passed it notwithstanding, and advanced with his forces against them. But the Bellovaci, and the other states in their alliance, hearing of their disaster by some of the runaways, who though wounded, found means to escape under cover of the woods; and finding that every thing was against them, their general slain, their cavalry and the flower of their infantry destroyed, and the Romans doubtless upon the march to attack them; speedily assembling a council by sound of trumpet, demanded, with great cries, that ambassadors and hostages might be sent to Cæsar.

XVIII. This proposal being approved by all, Comius the Atrebatian fled to the Germans, whose assistance he had obtained in the war. The rest immediately despatched ambassadors to Cæsar, and requested; "That he would regard their present sufferings as a sufficient punishment for their revolt; since they were such, as his humanity and clemency would never have suffered him to inflict upon them, had he compelled them to submit entire, and without fighting; that their power was utterly broken by the late defeat of their cavalry; that several thousand of their best infantry were destroyed, scarcely enough being left to bring them news of the disaster; that yet in so great a calamity, it was no small advantage to the Bellovaci, that Correus, the author of the war, who had stirred up the multitude to revolt, was killed: because while he lived, the headstrong populace would always have had more authority in the state than the senate." Their ambassadors having ended their speech, Cæsar put them in mind; "That the year before, the Bellovaci had, in conjunction with the other states of Gaul, taken up arms against the Romans; that, of all the confederates, they had persisted with the greatest obstinacy in their revolt nor been induced by the submission of the rest to hearken to reason; that nothing was easier than to lay the blame of their misconduct upon the dead; but they would find it difficult to make him believe, that a single man could have so much influence, as, in spite of the opposition of the nobility and senate, and the efforts of all good men, to stir up and support a war, by the mere authority of the multitude; that, however, he would be satisfied for the present with the punishment they had brought upon themselves."

XIX. Next night the deputies returned with Cæsar's answer, and hostages were immediately sent to the Roman camp. The deputies of the other states, who only waited the event of this treaty, immediately flocked to Cæsar, gave hostages, and submitted to his commands. Comius alone would not hear of treating, from a particular distrust of the Romans. For the year before, while Cæsar was employed in the affairs of Cisalpine Gaul, Labienus understanding that Comius was soliciting several states to rebel, and join in a confederacy against the Romans, thought it might be allowed him to use perfidy towards the perfidious. And because he expected to be refused, should he send for him to the camp; that he might not by an unsuccessful attempt put him upon his guard, he employed C. Volusenus Quadratus to kill him, under pretence of an interview; furnishing him with some chosen centurions for that purpose. When the interview began, and Volusenus, by way of signal, had taken Comius by the hand; one of the centurions, as if surprised at a step so unusual, attempted to kill him, but Comius's friends hastily interposing, he was prevented; however, the first blow wounded him severely on the head. Both sides immediately drew, not so much with a design to engage, as to retire; our men because they believed Comius mortally wounded; the Gauls, because discovering the intended treachery, they apprehended the danger to be greater than as yet appeared. From that time Comius determined never to be in the same place with any Roman.

XX. Cæsar having thus subdued the most warlike nations of Gaul, and finding no state disposed to take up arms, or make resistance, but that only some few had left their towns and possessions, to avoid present subjection,

resolved to divide his army into several bodies. M. Antony the questor, with the eleventh legion, had orders to continue with him. C. Fabius was sent, at the head of twenty-five cohorts, into the remotest parts of Gaul; because he understood some states were in arms on that side, whom C. Caninius Rebilus, his lieutenant, who commanded in those provinces, was scarcely strong enough to oppose with only two legions. He then sent for T. Labienus, and ordered the twelfth legion, which he commanded, into Gallia Togata, to protect the Roman colonies there, that they might not suffer by the incursions of the barbarians, as had happened the year before to the Tergestini, whose territories had been plundered by a sudden and unexpected invasion. He himself marched to ravage and lay waste the territories of Ambiorix; for finding it impossible to lay hold on that perfidious Gaul, whose fear prompted him to fly continually before him, he thought it behoved him, in regard to his own dignity, so effectually to ruin the country, by destroying his towns, cattle, and subjects, as might render him odious to his followers, if any still remained, and deprive him of all hope of being restored to his possessions. Having spread his legions and auxiliaries over the whole country of Ambiorix, destroyed all with fire and sword, and either killed or made prisoners an infinite number of people, he despatched Labienus, with two legions, against the Treviri; whose country, bordering upon Germany, and exercised in continual wars, differed little from the temper and fierceness of that nation; nor ever submitted to his commands, unless enforced by the presence of an army.

XXI. Meantime C. Caninius, lieutenant-general, understanding by letters and messengers from Duracius, who had always continued faithful to the Romans, even in the defection of many of his own state, that great numbers of the enemy were assembled in the territories of the Pictones; marched towards the town of Limo. Upon his arrival there, having certain information from some prisoners, that Duracius was shut up and besieged in Limo, by a great army of Gauls, under the conduct of Dumnacus, general of the Andes, as he was not strong enough to attack the enemy, he encamped in a place of great advantage. Dumnacus, hearing of his approach, turned all his forces against the legions, and resolved to invest the Roman camp. But after many days spent in the attack, and the loss of a great number of men, without any impression made upon the intrenchments, he returned again to the siege of Limo.

XXII. At the same time, C, Fabius, having brought over many states to their duty, and confirmed their submission by receiving hostages, upon intelligence sent him by Caninius, of the posture of affairs among the Pictones, marched immediately to the assistance of Duracius. Dumnacus hearing of his arrival, and concluding himself lost, should he at the same time be obliged to make head against an enemy without, and sustain the efforts of the townsmen within, suddenly decamped with all his forces, resolving not to stop till he had got on the other side of the Loire, which, by reason of its largeness, could not be passed without a bridge. Fabius, though he had neither as yet come within sight of the enemy, nor joined forces with Caninius; yet instructed by those who were well acquainted with the country, easily conjectured the route the Gauls would take. Wherefore directing his march towards the same bridge, he ordered the cavalry to keep before the legions; yet so, that without too much fatiguing their horses, they might return and encamp with them again at night. The cavalry followed the enemy as directed; came up with their rear; and attacking them flying, dismayed and encumbered with their baggage, killed great numbers, gained a considerable booty, and returned in triumph to the camp.

XXIII. The night following, Fabius sent the cavalry before, with orders to engage the enemy, and keep the whole army employed, till he himself should come up with the legions. Q. Atius Varus, a prudent and experienced officer, who had the charge of the detachment, desirous to execute the commands of his general with success, exhorted his men; and coming up with the enemy, disposed some squadrons in the most convenient places, and engaged the Gauls with the rest. The enemy's cavalry made a resolute stand, being supported by their foot, who halting in a body, advanced to the assistance of their own men. The conflict was sharp on both sides. For the Romans, despising enemies whom they had overcome the day before, and remembering that the legions were coming up to join them;

partly ashamed to give way, partly eager to bring the battle to a speedy issue by their own valour alone, fought with great bravery against the enemy's foot. And the Gauls, who had no apprehension of the approach of more forces, because none other had appeared the day before, fancied they had now a favourable opportunity of cutting off our cavalry. As the fight continued with great obstinacy for a considerable time, Dumnacus advanced with the foot, in battle array, to sustain the horse; when suddenly the legions, marching in close order, appeared within view of the enemy. This sight discomposed the Gallic squadrons, and producing a universal confusion through the whole army, which spread even to the baggage and carriages, they with great uproar and tumult betook themselves to a precipitate flight. But our horse, who a little before had fought against an enemy who vigorously opposed them, now elated with the joy of victory, surrounded them with great cries, and urged the slaughter as far as the strength of their horses to pursue, and the vigour of their right hands to destroy, were able to bear them out. Upwards of twelve thousand perished on this occasion, partly in the battle, partly in the pursuit; and the whole baggage was taken.

XXIV. After this rout, Drapes, of the nation of the Senones, (who upon the first revolt of Gaul had drawn together a band of desperate men, invited slaves to join him by the hopes of liberty, assembled all the fugitives he could find, received even public robbers into his service, and with that profligate crew intercepted the Roman convoys and baggage,) having rallied about five thousand runaways, directed his march towards the province; being joined by Luterius of Quercy, who as we have seen in the foregoing book, had attempted an invasion on that side at the first breaking out of the war. Caninius, having notice of this design, marched in pursuit of them with two legions, to prevent any alarm in those parts, and hinder the province from falling a prey to the ravages of a desperate and needy crew.

XXV. Fabius, with the rest of his army, marched against the Carnutes, and other states, whose forces had served under Dumnacus, in the late action : for he made no doubt of finding them humbled by so great a blow and was unwilling, by any delay, to give Dumnacus an opportunity of rousing them to a continuance of the war. In this expedition, Fabius had all the success he could desire; the several states submitting immediately upon his approach. For the Carnutes, who though often harassed, had never yet made mention of peace, now surrendered, and gave hostages; and the other states, inhabiting the more remote parts of Gaul, bordering upon the ocean, and known by the name of Armorica, influenced by their authority, and the arrival of Fabius and his legions, readily accepted the terms he offered them. Dumnacus, expelled his territories, and forced to wander and hide himself in lurking holes, at length escaped into the farthest parts of Gaul.

XXVI. But Drapes and Luterius, understanding that Caninius was in pursuit of them with the legions; and sensible that having an army at their heels, they could not, without certain destruction, make an irruption into the province, nor safely indulge themselves in the liberty of plundering and ravaging the country; halted in the territories of the Cadurci. As Luterius, during his prosperity, had borne considerable sway in the state, been always in great reputation with the multitude, as the author of new and enterprising counsels: he seized upon Uxellodunum, a town strongly fortified by nature, which had formerly been under his patronage; and prevailed with the inhabitants to join his and Drapes's forces.

XXVII. Caninius soon arrived before the place, which he found surrounded on every side with steep rocks, so very difficult of access, that it was hardly possible for armed troops to ascend them even where there were no opposers. But knowing that there was a vast quantity of baggage in the town, which could not be conveyed away so privately as to escape the legions, much less the cavalry, he divided his army into three bodies; and encamping on three remarkable eminences, resolved gradually, and as the number of his troops would allow, to carry a line of circumvallation quite round the town, which the garrison perceiving, began to dread the fate of their countrymen at Alesia, especially Luterius, who had been present at that formidable siege, and therefore advised them to lay in store of corn. Accordingly, they resolved with unanimous consent to leave part of the forces to defend the town, and march out with the rest to fetch

provisions. This resolution being taken, the following night, Luterius and Drapes, leaving two thousand men in the place, marched at the head of all the rest. These, in a few days, drew together a vast quantity of corn in the territories of the Cadurci, who partly stood inclined to assist them in their present exigence, partly were unable to hinder their carrying it off. Sometimes they attacked our posts by night, which made Caninius delay the circumvallation of the town, fearing he would not be able to defend the line, or man it sufficiently in all parts.

XXVIII. Luterius and Drapes having got a great quantity of corn, took up their quarters about ten miles from the town, that they might convey it thither by degrees. Each chose his particular part: Drapes stayed behind with part of the army to guard the camp; Luterius set forward with the convoy. Having disposed parties along the road for the greater security, he began his march towards the town about four in the morning, by narrow ways, through the woods. But our sentinels hearing a noise, and intelligence being brought by the scouts of what was doing, Caninius speedily drew some cohorts together from the nearest posts, and fell upon the convoy about day-break; who, surprised at so unexpected an attack, retreated towards their guard. Our men perceiving this, fell with redoubled fury upon the escort, giving quarter to none. Luterius escaped with a few followers, but returned not to the camp.

XXIX. Caninius having succeeded in this action, understood from the prisoners that Drapes was encamped about ten miles off, with the rest of the army. This being confirmed from many hands; as he supposed it would be easy to overwhelm them, after the terror occasioned by the defeat of one of their leaders, he thought it very fortunate that none of the fugitives had retreated towards the camp, to inform Drapes of the disaster. As there was therefore no hazard in the attempt, he ordered all the cavalry, with the German infantry, who were of remarkable swiftness, to advance before; and having distributed one legion into his three camps, followed them with the other, without baggage. As he drew near the enemy he was informed by his scouts, whom he had sent before, that the Gauls, according to custom, had pitched their camp at the foot of a mountain by the river-side, and that the Ger man foot, and cavalry, coming suddenly and unexpectedly upon them, had begun the fight. Upon this intelligence, he brought forward the legion in order of battle, and giving the signal of onset, soon possessed himself of the higher ground. The Germans, and cavalry, encouraged by the ensigns of the legions, redoubled their efforts. The cohorts threw themselves in crowds upon the enemy, and having either slain or made them all prisoners, obtained a considerable booty. Drapes himself was taken in the battle.

XXX. Caninius, after so fortunate an action, in which scarce any of his soldiers had been wounded, returned to the siege of Uxellodunum. Having got rid of the enemy without, who had obliged him to augment his garrisons, and postpone the works about the place, he now resumed them with great diligence, and was the next day joined by Fabius and his forces, who undertook one side of the town.

XXXI. Meantime Cæsar, leaving M. Antony the questor, with fifteen chariots, in the country of the Bellovaci, to prevent any new insurrections among the Belgians; marched himself into other states, to enjoin hostages, and allay their fears. When he arrived among the Carnutes, by whom the war was first begun, as Cæsar has mentioned in the preceding book; observing that they in a particular manner dreaded his resentment, from a consciousness of their guilt; that he might the sooner free them from their fears, he desired them to deliver up to justice Guturvatus, the prime mover and incendiary of that war; who, though he hid himself even from his own countrymen, yet being diligently sought after by a whole people, was soon brought to Cæsar's camp. Cæsar, contrary to his natural clemency, was constrained to give him up to punishment by his soldiers, who imputed to Guturvatus all the losses they had sustained, and all the dangers they had been exposed to during the war. Accordingly he was scourged and beheaded.

XXXII. Here he was informed, by frequent advices from Caninius, of the defeat of Drapes and Luterius, and the resolution taken by the garrison of Uxellodunum. Though he despised them on account of the smallness of their number, he yet thought their obstinacy deserved the severest chastisement: that Gaul might not run into a persuasion, that not strength, but constancy, had been wanting, to enable them to resist the Romans; which might perhaps induce other states, who had the advantage of strong towns, to assert their liberty; it being universally known in Gaul, that only one year of his government remained; during which, if they could hold but out, they had no further danger to apprehend. Leaving therefore the two legions he had then with him to the care of Q. Calenus his lieutenant, with orders to follow him by easy marches; he himself, at the head of all the cavalry, hastened to Uxellodunum, to forward the siege begun by Caninius.

XXXIII. He arrived before the town, unexpected either by his own troops, or those of the enemy; saw the circumvallation completed; and that there was no quitting the siege without dishonour; but understanding from the deserters, that the place was well stored with provisions, he resolved, if possible, to cut off their water. Uxellodunum stood upon a steep rock, surrounded almost on every side by a very deep valley, through which ran a river. There was no possible way of turning the course of this stream; because it flowed by the foot of the rock in so low a channel, that ditches could not be sunk deep enough to receive it. But the descent was so difficult and steep, that the townsmen, in coming to and returning from it, lay greatly exposed to our troops, who might wound and kill them at pleasure. This being known to Cæsar, he posted his archers and slingers, with some engines, over against the places of easiest access, and thereby hindered their approach to the river. This obliged the whole multitude to water at one place, close under the walls of the town, whence issued a very plentiful fountain on the side where the river intermitted its circuit, and left an opening of about three hundred feet. The whole army were desirous to deprive the besieged of this resource; but Cæsar alone discovered the means of affecting it. He brought forward his galleries, and began a terrace over against the mountain, with much danger to the soldiers, incredible fatigue, and a continued series of fighting. For the garrison rushing furiously upon us from the higher ground, charged without danger, and wounded great numbers of our men, as they advanced obstinately to the combat; yet without deterring them from bringing forward their machines, and by their works and assiduity surmounting the difficulties of the ground. At the same time they carried on their mines, from the terrace and galleries, quite to the fountain; a kind of work in which they proceeded without danger or suspicion. A terrace was raised sixty feet high, and a tower of ten stories placed upon it; not indeed to equal the height of the walls, for which no works were sufficient; but to command the top of the spring. From this tower we were continually playing our engines upon all the accesses to the fountain, which made it extremely dangerous to water at the place; insomuch that not only cattle and beasts of carriage, but great numbers of people perished by thirst.

XXXIV. The enemy, terrified at this disaster, filled several barrels with tallow, pitch, and dry wood; and having set them on fire, rolled them down upon the works. At the same time they charged the Romans with great fury, that the anxiety and danger of the battle might hinder them from extinguishing the flames. The conflagration soon became general; for whatever was rolled down from above, being stopped by the machines and terrace, communicated the flame to that part. But our soldiers, though engaged in a dangerous kind of fight, because of the inequality of the ground, yet bore all with great firmness and resolution. For the action was in a conspicuous place, within view of our army, and great shouts were raised on both sides. Thus every one was the more ardent to signalize himself, and brave the flames and darts of the enemy, as his bravery would be better known, and have the testimony of many witnesses.

XXXV. Cæsar seeing many of his soldiers wounded, ordered the cohorts to ascend the mountain on all sides, and, as if preparing to scale the walls, raise a mighty shout. This alarmed the inhabitants, who not knowing what passed in other parts, recalled their troops from the attack, and disposed them along the walls. Thus our men, being relieved from the battle, soon found means to extinguish or put a stop to the flames. But as the besieged still continued to defend themselves with great obstinacy, and notwithstanding the loss of the greatest part of their number by thirst; persisted in their first resolution; Cæsar at last contrived to drain or avert the spring by mines. Upon this the fountain suddenly becoming dry, so effectually deprived the besieged of all hopes of safety, that they imagined it an event brought about, not by human counsels, but by the will of the gods; and therefore, compelled by necessity, immediately surrendered themselves.

XXXVI. Cæsar conscious that his clemency was known to all, and no way fearing that his severity on this occasion would be imputed to any cruelty of nature; as he perceived there would be no end of the war, if other states, in different parts of Gaul, should, in like manner, form the design of a revolt; resolved, by a signal example of punishment, to deter them from all such projects. He therefore cut off the hands of all whom he found in arms; granting them their lives, that their punishment might be the more conspicuous. Drapes who, as we have said, had been made prisoner by Caninius; either out of indignation at finding himself a captive, or dreading a severe fate, put an end to his life, by abstaining from food. At the same time, Luterius, who had escaped out of the battle, falling into the hands of Epasnactus of Auvergne, (for, by continually moving from place to place, he was obliged to confide in many, because he could stay no where long without danger, and knew the little reason he had to expect favour from Cæsar,) was, by him, a great favourer of the Roman people, delivered, without hesitation, bound, to Cæsar.

XXXVII. In the meantime Labienus engaged the cavalry of the Treviri with success: and having killed a considerable number on the spot, as likewise many Germans, who were always ready to join against the Romans, made the greatest part of their chiefs prisoners; and, among the rest, Surus the Æduan, a nobleman of distinguished birth and valour, and the only one of that nation, who had continued until then in arms. Upon notice of this victory, Cæsar, who saw his affairs in a flourishing condition in Gaul, and that his last campaigns had completed the subjection of the whole country; resolved upon a journey to Aquitain, where he had never yet been in person, though P. Crassus had in part reduced it to his obedience. He therefore set out for that country with two legions, designing to spend there the rest of the campaign. This expedition was attended with the desired success: for all the states of Aquitain sent ambassadors to him, and delivered hostages. He then went with a guard of cavalry to Nar bonne, and distributed his army into winter quarters, under the care of his lieutenants. M. Antony, C. Trebonius, P. Vatinius, and Q. Tullius, were quartered in Belgium, with four legions. Two were sent into the country of the Ædusns, whom he knew to be the most powerful people in Gaul; two into that of the Turones, bordering upon the Carnutes, to hold the maritime states in awe: and the remaining two were stationed among the Lemovices, not far from Auvergne, that none of the provinces of Gaul might be destitute of troops. He remained some days at Narbonne, held all the usual assemblies of the province, decided the differences subsisting among the people, recompensed those who had distinguished themselves by their faithful services; (for he had a wonderful faculty of discerning how men stood affected in the general revolt of Gaul, which he had been able to sustain, merely by the fidelity and assistance of the province;) and having despatched all these affairs, repaired to the legions in Belgium, and took up his winter quarters at Nemetocenna.

XXXVIII. Here he was informed that Comius of Arras had had an engagement with his cavalry. For, after the arrival of Antony in his winter quarters, as the Atrebatians, awed by his presence, continued in their duty to Cæsar; Comius, who, ever since the wound above-mentioned, had kept a watchful eye upon all the motions of his countrymen, that, in case of war, he might be ready to offer them his counsel and assistance; finding that the state now submitted quietly to the Romans, applied his troops to support himself and his followers by plunder; and often carried off the convoys that were going to the Roman winter quarters.

XXXIX. Among those who commanded under Antony, in his winter quarters, was C. Volusenus Quadratus, an officer of the first rank among the horse. Him Antony sent in pursuit of the enemy's cavalry. Volusenus, to his natural bravery, which he possessed in an eminent degree, added a particular hatred of Comius, which induced him the more readily to accept of this commission. Accordingly, having planted his ambuscades, he found means frequently to engage the enemy, and always came off victorious. At last, a very warm dispute ensuing; and Volusenus, through an eager desire of making Comius prisoner, urging the chase with only a few at-

tendants, while Comius, by a hasty retreat, drew him a considerable way from his party suddenly, the latter, invoking the assistance of his followers, called upon them to revenge the wound he had treacherously received from the Romans; and turning short upon our detachment, advanced without precaution towards Volusenus. All his cavalry did the same, and soon put our small party to flight. Comius, clapping spurs to his horse, ran furiously against Quadratus, and drove his lance through his thigh. Our men, seeing their commander wounded, instantly faced about, and forced the enemy to give ground. In this last attack, the Gauls, after a considerable slaughter, were entirely routed by the vigorous charge of our cavalry. Some were trodden to death in the pursuit, others made prisoners; but Comius escaped by the swiftness of his horse. Volusenus being dangerously wounded, almost beyond hope of recovery, was carried back to the camp. Comius, either satisfied with the revenge he had taken, or apprehensive he must at least be ruined, as he continually lost some of his men, sent a deputation to Antony, offering to retire wherever he should order him, to submit to whatever should be imposed on him, and to give hostages for the performance of these conditions; he only requested, that so much regard might be shown to his just fears, as not to have it insisted on that he should appear before any Roman. Antony, conscious that his apprehensions were but too well grounded, excused him, took hostages, and granted him peace.

Cæsar, I know, assigns a distinct book to each of his several campaigns. But I have not judged it necessary to pursue this method; because the ensuing year, under the consulship of L. Paulus, and C. Marcellus, furnishes nothing memorable transacted in Gaul. However, that none may be ignorant where Cæsar and his army were during this time, I have subjoined a short account to the present commentary.

XL. Cæsar, during the time of his winter quarters in Belgium, made it his whole study to ingratiate himself with the Gauls, and deprive them of all pretence or colour for a revolt. For there was nothing he more earnestly desired, than to leave Gaul peaceably disposed at his departure; lest, when he was about to withdraw his army, any sparks of rebellion should remain, which would infallibly rekindle into a war, were the Roman troops once removed. Wherefore, by treating the several states with respect, liberally rewarding their chiefs, and abstaining from the imposition of new burdens, he easily prevailed with the Gauls, wearied and exhausted by long unsuccessful wars, to embrace the ease and quiet attendant on their present submission.

XLI. The winter being over, contrary to his custom, he posted, by long journeys, into Italy, to visit the municipal towns and colonies of Cisalpine Gaul, and engage their interest in favour of M. Antony, his questor, who was then a candidate for the priesthood. He the more warmly interested himself in this affair, not only as it was in behalf of a man united to him by the strictest ties of friendship, but as it likewise gave him an opportunity of opposing a small faction, who aimed to diminish Cæsar's credit, by repulsing Antony. Although he heard upon the road, before he reached Italy, that Antony had been made augur, he still thought it incumbent upon him to visit the municipal towns and colonies of the province; in order to thank them for the zeal they had shown in behalf of his friend, and to recommend them his own petition for the consulship of the ensuing year. For his enemies every where boasted, that L. Lentulus and C. Marcellus had been chosen consuls, in the view of despoiling him of all his honours and dignities; and that Sergius Galba had been excluded, though much the strongest in the number of votes, because of his known intimacy with Cæsar, and having served under him as lieutenant.

XLII. He was received every where with incredible honours, and the warmest testimonies of the people's affection. For this was the first time he had appeared among them since the total reduction of Gaul. Nothing was omitted that could contribute to the ornament of the gates, ways, and places through which he was to pass. The people, with their children, came out to meet him; sacrifices were offered in all parts; tables, richly spread, were placed in the public squares and temples: and so great was the magnificence displayed by the rich, such the eagerness of the poor to express their satisfaction, that every thing wore the face of a most splendid triumph.

XLIII. Cæsar, having visited the several provinces of Cisalpine Gaul, returned, in all haste, to the army at Nemetocenna; and ordering the legions to quit their winter quarters, and rendezvous in the territories of the Treviri, went thither and reviewed them in person. He gave the government of Cisalpine Gaul to Labienus, the better to reconcile him to his demand of the consulship; and marched the army from place to place, that by the motion and change of air, he might prevent any sickness getting among the troops. Although he often heard, that Labienus was strongly solicited by his enemies; and was, for certain, informed, that some were labouring, by means of the senate's authority, to deprive him of part of his army; yet neither did he credit any reports to Labienus's disadvantage, nor could be induced to set himself in opposition to the authority of the senate. For he made no doubt of obtaining his demand by the free suffrages of the fathers; and the rather, because C. Curio, tribune of the people, having undertaken the defence of Cæsar's cause and dignity, had often proposed in the senate; "That if Cæsar's army gave umbrage to any, as Pompey was no less formidable to the true friends of liberty, both should be ordered to dismiss their troops, and return to a private condition, which would entirely free the commonwealth from all apprehensions of danger." Nor did he only propose this, but even began to put it to the vote. But the consuls and Pompey's friends interposed, which hindered the senate from coming to any resolution.

XLIV. This was an authentic testimony from the whole senate, and agreeable to what had passed on a former occasion. For when Marcellus who strove to render himself considerable by opposing Cæsar, had proposed, the year before, contrary to the law of Pompey and Crassus, to recall Cæsar before his commission was expired, the overture was rejected by a very full house. But this, instead of discouraging Cæsar's enemies, only pushed them on to new attempts; that they might, at length, bring the senate into their measures.

XLV. A *Senatus Consultum* soon after passed, that one legion from Pompey, and another from Cæsar, should be sent to the Parthian war. But it was visibly their design to take both legions from Cæsar alone. For Pompey offered the first legion for that service, which he had lent some time before to Cæsar, having raised it in his province. But Cæsar, though now fully satisfied of the ill designs of his enemies, readily sent back Pom pey's legion; and in compliance with the decree of the senate, ordered the fifteenth, one of his own number, which was then in hither Gaul, to be delivered to their commissioners; and sent the thirteenth into Italy to replace it, and supply the garrison whence it had been drawn. He then put his army into winter quarters. C. Trebonius, with four legions, was ordered into the country of the Belgians; and C. Fabius, with the like number, was placed among the Æduans. For thus he thought Gaul was most likely to be kept in subjection; if the Belgæ, the most renowned fo: their valour, and the Æduans, the most considerable for their authority, we e awed by the presence of two armies.

XLVI. After this he returned into Italy, where he understood, that the two legions he had sent, in conformity to the decree of the senate, to be employed in the Parthian war, had been delivered, by the Consul Marcellus, to Pompey, and were by him still detained in Italy. Although by this it was abundantly evident, that they were preparing fo take up arms against him, he yet resolved to suffer any thing, while any hope remained of adjusting their differences by the methods of peace rather than those of violence and war.

CÆSAR'S COMMENTARIES

OF

THE CIVIL WAR.

BOOK I.

THE ARGUMENT.

Different opinions in the senate in relation to Cæsar's letter.—III. The origin and causes of the opposition formed against him.—IV. The senate's severe decree, and flight of Cæsar's friends.—V. War against Cæsar resolved on.—VI. Cæsar harangues his troops.—VII. Pompey sends proposals of peace.—VIII. Cæsar's answer.—IX. Pompey sends proposals a second time.—X. Which not pleasing Cæsar, he prepares for war.—XI. Cæsar makes himself master of Iguvium and Auximum.—XII. Which so alarms his enemies at Rome, that they hastily quit the city, and retire to Capua.—XIII. Cæsar by his expedition, obliges many of the towns in Italy to submit.—XXIII. Pompey, after the reduction of Corfinium by Cæsar, withdraws with his troops to Brundusium.—XXIV. Cæsar besieges him there.—XXVI. He escapes by sea, after which the town surrender.—XXVIII. Cæsar cannot pursue him for want of a fleet.—XXIX. Valerius and Curio, partisans of Cæsar, drive Cotta from Sardinia, and Cato from Sicily. Varus compels Tubero to desist from his design upon Africa.—XXX. Cæsar's speech to the senate.—XXXI. Which producing no effect, he sets out for Transalpine Gaul.—XXXII. The people of Marseilles shut their gates against Cæsar.—XXXIV. Who commands Brutus and Trebonius to besiege the place.—XXXV. Fabius sent before into Spain.—XXXIX. Cæsar follows, and comes up with Afranius and Petreius at Lerida.—XLI. A skirmish, with almost equal advantage on both sides.—XLVI. A sudden storm having broke down his bridges, Cæsar is shut up between two rivers.—XLVIII. And reduced to great straits for want of provisions.—LI. He extricates himself at length, and surprises the enemy's foragers.—LII. Brutus defeats the people of Marseilles in a sea-fight.—LIII. Cæsar obtains the superiority near Lerida.—LIV. Many states declare for him.—LV. Afranius and Petreius remove towards Celtiberia.—LVI. Cæsar pursues them with his cavalry.—LVII. Then drawing out the legions, continues to urge them in their retreat.—LXIV. He cuts off their provisions.—LXVI. Afranius and Petreius's men talk with Cæsar's about a surrender.—LXVII. Petreius interrupts the conference.—LXVIII. And obliges the soldiers to take an oath of fidelity to their generals.—LXX. Who, finding both their provisions and forage intercepted, resolve to return to Lerida.—LXXI. Cæsar follows, and greatly molests them in their march.—LXXIII. At length, water, forage, and every thing failing them, they are forced to sue for peace, and accept of Cæsar's terms.

THE SUPPLEMENT

OF

DIONYSIUS VOSSIUS TO CÆSAR'S FIRST BOOK

OF

THE CIVIL WAR.

I THINK it needless to say any thing here, in opposition to those who pretend, that the following Commentaries, concerning the Civil War, were not penned by Cæsar himself. We have not only the express testimony of Suetonius to the contrary, but the very style sufficiently declares, that Cæsar alone could be the author of the work. There is room however to suspect, from the abrupt manner in which the subject is introduced, that the beginning of this first book is wanting: for history takes notice of several previous facts, of which no mention is made here. I have therefore collected out of Plutarch, Appian, and Dion, as much as was necessary to connect this and the former Commentary, and fancy it will not be disagreeable to the reader, to offer it here by way of Preface.

Gaul being wholly reduced, Cæsar, upon his arrival in Lombardy, thought proper, for many reasons, to send deputies to Rome, to demand the consulship, and a prolongation of his command. Pompey, who, though averse to Cæsar's interest, had not yet openly declared against him, neither furthered nor opposed his request. But the consuls Marcellus and Lentulus, who had already joined the party of his enemies, resolved by every method in their power to frustrate the design. Marcellus scrupled not to add other injuries to that of which we speak. For Cæsar had lately planted a colony at Novocomum in Cisalpine Gaul; and Marcellus, not satisfied with stripping the inhabitants of the privilege of Roman citizens, seized one of their chief magistrates at Rome, ordered him to be scourged, and then dismissed him to carry his complaints to Cæsar, an ignominy from which all free citizens were expressly exempted by the laws. While affairs were in this train, C. Curio, tribune of the people, came to Cæsar in Gaul. This nobleman, after many attempts in behalf of the commonwealth, and to promote Cæsar's interest; finding at length all his endeavours without effect, fled from Rome, to avoid the malice of his enemies, and informed Cæsar of all that was transacted against him. Cæsar received him with great marks of respect, as well on account of his rank in the commonwealth, as the many services he had done himself and the state; and thanked him for the signal zeal he had shown in his cause. But Curio advised him, since his enemies were now openly preparing for war, to draw his army together without delay, and rescue the commonwealth from the tyranny of an aspiring faction. Cæsar, though fully satisfied of the truth of Curio's report, resolved to sacrifice all other considerations to the public tranquillity, that no man might justly charge him with being the author of a civil war. He therefore only petitioned by his friends, that the government of Cisalpine Gaul and Illyricum, with the command of two legions, might be continued to him, in all which his principal aim was, by the equity of his demands, to induce his enemies to grant peace to the commonwealth. These offers appeared so reasonable, that even Pompey himself knew not how to oppose them. But the consuls still continuing inflexible, Cæsar wrote a letter to the senate, wherein, after briefly enumerating his exploits and services, he requested them not to deprive him of the benefit of the people's favour, who had permitted him to sue for the consulship in his absence. He protested his readiness, if such was the resolution of the senate and people of Rome, to dismiss his army, provided Pompey did the same : but could by no means resolve, so long as he continued in command and authority, to divest himself of troops, and lay himself open to the injuries of his enemies. Curio was commissioned to carry this letter, who travelling with incredible despatch, reached Rome in three days (a distance of a hundred and sixty miles,) before the beginning of January, and ere the consuls could get any thing determined relating to Cæsar's command. Curio, upon his arrival, refused to part with the letter, resolving not to deliver it but in full senate, and when the tribunes of the people were present : for he was apprehensive, should he do otherwise, that the consuls would suppress it.

CÆSAR'S COMMENTARIES

OF

THE CIVIL WAR.

BOOK I.

I. Cæsar's letter being delivered to the consuls, the tribunes, with much difficulty, procured it a reading in the senate; but could by no means prevail to have his demands brought under deliberation. The consuls proposed to debate upon the state of the republic. "Lentulus promised to stand by the senate and the people, if they would deliver their sentiments with freedom and courage; but if they regarded Cæsar, and affected to court his friendship, as had been the practice for some time past, he knew, he told them, what he had to do, and was determined to disclaim their authority; not doubting but he would find a ready admittance to the favour and protection of Cæsar." Scipio spoke much to the same purpose: "That Pompey was firmly bent not to abandon the republic, if he found the senators ready to support him; but if they cooled, or were remiss in their resolves, it would be in vain for them to expect his aid, if they saw cause afterwards to apply for it." This speech of Scipio, as the senate was held in the city, and Pompey resided in the suburbs, was considered as coming from Pompey's own mouth. Some were for following milder counsels, of which number was M. Marcellus, who gave it as his opinion: "That it was not proper to enter upon the present deliberation, till troops were raised over all Italy, and an army got ready, under whose protection the senate might proceed with freedom and safety in their debates." "Callidius was for sending Pompey to his government, to take away all occasion of discord; because Cæsar had reason to fear, as two of his legions had

been taken from him, that Pompey retained them in the neighbourhood of Rome, with a view to employ them against him." M. Rufus nearly agreed with Callidius. But they were all severely reprimanded by the consul Lentulus, who expressly refused to put Callidius's motion to the vote. Marcellus, awed by the consul's reprimand, retracted what he had said. Thus the clamours of Lentulus, the dread of an army at the gates of Rome, and the menaces of Pompey's friends, forced the greater part of the senate, though with the utmost reluctance and dislike, into a compliance with Scipio's motion: "That Cæsar should be ordered to disband his army before a certain day then fixed; and that in case of disobedience, he should be declared an enemy to the republic." M. Antonius and Q. Cassius, tribunes of the people, opposed their negative to this decree. Immediately a debate arose, upon the validity of their interposition. Many severe speeches were made against them; and the more warm and passionate any one appeared, the more was he applauded by Cæsar's enemies.

II. In the evening the senate rose; and Pompey sending for all those of his party, commended the forward; confirmed them in their resolutions; reproved and animated the more moderate. Multitudes of veterans who had formerly served under him, flocked to him from all parts, allured by the expectation of rewards and dignities. A great number of officers belonging to the two legions lately returned by Cæsar, had likewise orders to attend him. Rome was filled with troops. Curio

215

assembled the tribunes to support the decree of the people. On the other hand, all the friends of the consuls, all the partizans of Pompey, and of such as bore any ancient grudge to Cæsar, repaired to the senate : by whose concourse and votes the weaker sort were terrified, the irresolute confirmed, and the greater part deprived of the liberty of speaking their mind freely. L. Piso the censor, and L. Roscius the pretor, offered to go and acquaint Cæsar with the state of affairs, demanding only six days for that purpose. Some were for sending deputies to him, to inform him of the senate's disposition.

III. But all these proposals were rejected, because the consul, Scipio, and Cato, declared against them. Cato was incited by the remembrance of an old quarrel, and the disappointment he had sustained in standing candidate for the pretorship with Cæsar. Lentulus was oppressed with debt, and flattered himself with the command of armies, the government of provinces, and the largesses of the kings for whom he should procure the title of allies and friends of the Roman people. He was besides wont to boast, among those of his own party, that he doubted not of becoming a second Sylla, in whom the whole authority of the commonwealth should centre. Scipio entertained the same hope of commands and governments, which he expected to share with his son-in-law Pompey ; added to this his dread of a prosecution ; his vanity and self-conceit ; and the flatteries and applauses of his friends, who at that time bore a considerable sway in the commonwealth and courts of justice. Pompey himself, instigated by Cæsar's enemies, and not able to endure an equal dignity, was now entirely alienated from him, and had joined with their common adversaries, most of whom Cæsar had contracted during his affinity with Pompey. Beside, the fraudulent step he had taken, in detaining, for the purposes of his own ambition, the two legions destined to serve in Asia and Syria, determined him to use all his endeavours to bring on a civil war.

IV. Thus nothing but tumult and violence was to be seen in the public debates. Cæsar's friends had no time given them to inform him of what passed. Even the tribunes themselves were not exempt from danger, nor durst they have recourse to that right of intercession, which Sylla had left them, as the last bulwark of liberty ; insomuch that the seventh day after entering upon their office, they saw themselves obliged to provide for their safety ; whereas in former times, the most turbulent and seditious tribunes never began to apprehend themselves in danger, till towards the eighth month of their administration. Recourse was had to that rigid and ultimate decree which was never used but in the greatest extremities, when the city was threatened with ruin and conflagration : "That the consuls, the pretors, the tribunes of the people, and the proconsuls that were near Rome, should take care that the commonwealth received no detriment." This decree passed the seventh of January ; so that during the first five days in which it was permitted the senate to assemble, after Lentulus's entrance upon the consulship, (for two days are always appropriated to the holding of the comitia,) the most severe and rigorous resolutions were taken, both in relation to Cæsar's government, and the tribunes of the people, men of eminent worth and dignity. The tribunes immediately quitted the city, and fled to Cæsar who was then at Ravenna, waiting an answer to his late demands, whose equity he hoped would dispose all parties to entertain thoughts of peace.

V. The following days the senate assembled without the city, where Pompey confirmed everything he had before intimated by the mouth of Scipio. He applauded the resolution and courage of the senators, acquainted them with the state of his forces, that he had ten legions already in arms, and was besides well informed, that Cæsar's troops were by no means satisfied with their general ; nay, had even refused to support and follow him. It was then proposed in the senate, that troops should be raised over all Italy ; that Faustus Sylla should be sent proprætor into Mauritania ; that Pompey should be supplied with money out of the public treasury, and that king Juba should be declared friend and ally of the people of Rome : but Marcellus opposed the last of these ; and Philippus, tribune of the people, would not agree to the propretorship of Sylla. The other motions were approved by the senate. The affair of the provinces was next decided ; two of which were consular, the rest pretorian. Syria fell to the share of Scipio, and Gaul fell to L.

Domitius. Philippus and Marcellus were set aside, through the private views of the prevailing party. The rest of the provinces were assigned to men of pretorian rank; who waited not to have their nomination confirmed by the people, as had been the custom in former years, but after taking the usual oath, departed for their several commands in a military habit. The consuls left the city, a thing unheard of till that time, and lictors were seen walking before private men in the forum and capitol, contrary to the express practice of former ages. Troops were levied over all Italy, arms enjoined, money demanded of the colonies and free towns, and even taken from the very temples; in fine, neither divine nor human rights were regarded.

VI. Cæsar having intelligence of these proceedings, addressed himself to his troops; "He took notice of the many injuries he had received on all occasions from his enemies, who had alienated Pompey from him, by filling him with an envy and jealousy of his reputation, though he had done every thing in his power to promote his glory, and favour his advancement to the highest dignities. He complained of the new precedent introduced into the commonwealth, in checking, and hindering by arms, the opposition of the tribunes, which of late years had been restored to its wonted force. That Sylla, who had almost annihilated the tribuneship, had yet left it the liberty of opposition; whereas Pompey who valued himself upon the re-establishment of that office, deprived it now of a privilege it had always enjoyed. That the decree enjoining the magistrates to provide for the safety of the commonwealth, which implied an order to the Roman people to repair to arms, was never wont to be used but on occasion of dangerous laws, seditious measures pursued by the tribunes, or a general secession of the people, when they possessed themselves of the temples and places of strength; crimes, which in former ages had been expiated by the fate of Saturninus and the Gracchi. That at present nothing of this kind had been attempted, nor so much as thought of; no law promulged, no endeavour used to seduce the people, no appearance of revolt or disaffection. He therefore conjured them to defend against the malice of his enemies, the honour and reputation of a general, under whom they had served nine years with so much advantage to the commonwealth,

gained so many battles, and subdued all Gaul and Germany." The soldiers of the thirteenth legion, who were present, and whom he had sent for in the beginning of the troubles, (the rest not being yet arrived,) cried out, that they were determined to maintain the honour of their general, and to revenge the wrongs done to the tribunes.

VII. Being assured of the good will of the soldiers, he marched with that legion to Rimini, where he was met by the tribunes of the people, who had fled to him for protection. He ordered the other legions to quit their winter quarters, and follow him with all expedition. While he was at Rimini, young L. Cæsar, whose father was one of his lieutenants, came to him; and after acquainting him with the occasion of his journey, added, that he had a private message to him from Pompey, "who was desirous of clearing himself to Cæsar, that he might not interpret those actions as designed to affront him, which had no other aim but the good of the commonwealth: that it had been his constant maxim, to prefer the interest of the republic to any private engagement: that it was worthy of Cæsar, to sacrifice his passion and resentment to the same noble motive; and not prejudice the commonwealth, by pushing too far his revenge against his private enemies." He added something more to the same purpose, mingled with excuses for Pompey. The pretor Roscius joined likewise in the negotiation, declaring he was commissioned so to do.

VIII. Though all this tended little to redress the injuries of which Cæsar complained, yet considering these as proper persons by whom to transmit his thoughts, he begged of them, that as they had not scrupled to bring Pompey's demands to him, they would likewise carry back his proposals to Pompey; that, if possible, so small a labour might put an end to mighty differences, and deliver all Italy from the fear of a civil war. He told them "That the interest of the commonwealth had always been dearer to him than life; but he could not help grieving at the malice of his enemies, who had frustrated the good intentions of the Roman people in his favour, by cutting off six months from his command, and obliging him to return to Rome to sue for the consulship, though a law had been made dispensing with his personal attendance: that he had yet, for the sake of the commonwealth,

2 F

patiently submitted to this assault upon his honour; that even his proposal of disbanding the armies on both sides, which he had made by a letter to the senate, had been rejected: that new levies were making over all Italy: that two legions, which had been taken from him, **under pretence of the** Parthian war, were still **retained in the** service of his enemies: **that the whole state** was in arms. What could all this aim at but his destruction? That, nevertheless, he was ready to agree to any proposal, and expose himself to any danger, for the sake of his country. Let Pompey go to his government: let all the armies be disbanded: let every body throughout Italy lay down their arms: let every thing that participates of terror and force be removed: let the elections of magistrates be made with perfect freedom; and let the republic be administered by the authority of the senate and people. And **the** better **to settle all these** articles, **and** corroborate them **with the** sanction of **an oath,** let either Pompey himself draw nearer, or suffer Cæsar to approach him; as all their differences may be most easily terminated by a conference."

IX. **Roscius** and L. Cæsar, having received this answer, departed for Capua, where they found Pompey and the consuls, and laid before them Cæsar's proposals. After deliberating upon the affair, they sent a reply, in writing, by the same messengers, the purport of which was: "That Cæsar should quit Rimini, return to Gaul, and disband his army; which conditions performed, Pompey would go into Spain. In the meantime, till Cæsar gave the security for the performance of what he had promised, neither Pompey nor the consuls would discontinue the levies."

X. It was, by no means, a fair proposal, that Cæsar should be obliged to quit Rimini and return to Gaul, while Pompey held provinces and legions that were none of his: that he should dismiss his army, whilst the other was levying troops: and, that only a general promise of going into Spain should be given, without fixing a day for his departure; by **which** evasion, was he to be found in Italy, **even at the** expiration of Cæsar's consulship, he could not yet be charged with breach of faith. His forbearing too to appoint a time for a conference, and declining to approach nearer, gave little reason to hope for a peace. He therefore sent Antony **to** Arretium, with five cohorts; remained himself at Rimini, with two, where he resolved to levy troops; and seizing Pisaurum, Fanum, and Ancona, left a cohort in each for a garrison.

XI. Meantime being informed that Thermus, the praetor had entered Iguvium, with five cohorts, and was endeavouring to fortify the town; as he knew the inhabitants to be well inclined to **his** interest, **he** detached Curio thither, with three cohorts, drawn from Pisaurum and Rimini. Upon this, Thermus, who could not **confide in the** townsmen, retired with his cohorts, and **quitted the place:** but his troops abandoning him in his march, **returned** severally to their **own homes.** Curio was received into the place with great demonstrations of joy: which being reported to Cæsar, as he found he had the good will of the colonies and free towns, he drew the cohorts of the thirteenth legion out of garrison, and marched to Auximum, which Attius held with a body of troops, and whence he had despatched senators to levy forces over all Picenum. Cæsar's arrival being known, the chief citizens of Auximum went in a body to Attius Varus, and told him: "That it did not belong to them to determine on which side justice lay; but that neither they, nor the other municipal towns, could endure to see their gates shut against Cæsar, who by his great actions had deserved so well of the commonwealth: that therefore he would do well to consult his own safety and reputation." Attius, moved by this speech, drew off his garrison and fled. But some of Cæsar's first ranks pursuing him, obliged him to stop; and a battle ensuing, he was deserted by his men. Some of the troops returned home; the rest went over to Cæsar, and brought along with them L. Pupius, first centurion of the legion, who had formerly held the same rank in Pompey's army. Cæsar commended Attius's soldiers; dismissed Pupius, returned thanks to the inhabitants of Auximum; and promised to retain always a grateful remembrance of their attachment.

XII. These things being reported at Rome, the consternation was so great over the whole city, that when the consul Lentulus came to the treasury, to deliver out the money to Pompey, in consequence of the decree of the senate, he scarce waited the opening of the inner door, but precipitately left the place, upon a false rumour, that Cæsar was approaching, and some of his cavalry already in view. He was soon followed by his colleague Marcellus, and the greater part of the magistrates. Pompey had left the town the day before, and was upon his way to Apulia, where he had quartered the legions he had received from Cæsar. The levies were discontinued within the city, and no place appeared secure on this side Capua. Here, at last, they took courage and rallied, and began to renew their levies in the colonies round about, which had been sent thither by the Julian law. Lentulus summoned into the forum the gladiators whom Cæsar had ordered to be trained up there, gave them their liberty, furnished them with horses, and commanded them to follow him. But being afterwards admonished by his friends that this step was universally condemned, he dispersed them into the neighbouring town of Campania, to keep garrison there.

XIII. Cæsar meanwhile leaving Auximum, traversed the whole country of Picenum; where he was joyfully received in all parts by the inhabitants, who furnished his army with every thing necessary. Even Cingulum itself, a town founded by Labienus, and built at his own expense, sent deputies to him, with an offer of their submission and services. He demanded a certain number of soldiers, which were sent immediately. Meantime the twelfth legion joined him; and with these two he marched to Asculum, a town of Picenum. Here Lentulus Spinther commanded with ten cohorts; who, hearing of Cæsar's approach, quitted the place with his troops, who almost all deserted him upon the march. Being left with only a few, he fell in with Vibullius Rufus, whom Pompey had sent into Picenum to encourage his followers in those parts. Vibullius understanding from him the state of affairs in Picenum, dismissed Lentulus, and took the soldiers under his command. He likewise drew together from the neighbouring provinces as many as he could meet with of Pompey's levies: among the rest, Ulcilles Hirus, who was flying, with six cohorts, from Camerinum, where they had been quartered. Out of all these he formed thirteen cohorts, with which he posted, by great journeys, to Corfinium, where Domitius Ahenobarbus commanded; whom he informed that Cæsar was approaching with two legions. Domitius had already got together, with great expedition, twenty cohorts from Alba, the country of the Marsi, Peligni, and the neighbouring provinces.

XIV. Cæsar having made himself master of Asculum, and obliged Lentulus to retire, ordered the soldiers who had deserted him, to be sought after, and new levies to be made. He remained only one day there, to settle what related to provisions, and then pursued his march to Corfinium. Upon his arrival there, he found five cohorts, whom Domitius had detached from the garrison, employed in breaking down a bridge about three miles distant from the town. But Cæsar's advanced parties attacking them, they quickly abandoned the bridge, and retired to Corfinium. Cæsar having passed with his legions, halted before the town, and encamped under the walls.

XV. Upon this, Domitius engaged by great rewards, persons well acquainted with the country, to carry letters into Apulia to Pompey, wherein he earnestly requested him to come to his aid. He told him, "That it would be easy, in that close country, to shut up Cæsar between two armies, and cut off his provisions: that unless this course was followed, he himself, with above thirty cohorts, and a great number of senators and Roman knights, would be exposed to imminent danger." Meanwhile, having encouraged his men, he disposed engines along the walls, appointed every one his particular post, and, the more to animate them, promised each soldier four acres of land out of his own estate, and, in proportion, to every centurion and volunteer.

XVI. Meantime Cæsar was informed that the people of Sulmona, a town seven miles distant from Corfinium, desired to put themselves under his protection, but were restrained by Q. Lucretius, a senator, and Attius, a Pelignian, who held them in subjection with a garrison, of seven cohorts. He therefore despatched M. Antony thither, with five cohorts of the seventh legion, whose ensigns were no sooner descried from the walls of Sulmona, than the gates were thrown open, and the whole people in a body, both soldiers and townsmen, came out to congratulate Antony on his arrival. Lucretius and Attius endeavoured to escape over the wall: but Attius being taken, and brought to Antony, requested that he might be sent to Cæsar. Antony returned the same day, bringing along with him the cohorts and Attius. Cæsar joined these cohorts to his army, and set Attius at liberty.

XVII. Cæsar resolved to employ the three first days in strongly fortifying his camp, in procuring corn from the neighbouring towns, and waiting the arrival of the rest of his forces. During this space, the eighth legion joined him, with two and twenty cohorts of new levies from Gaul, and about three hundred horse from the king of Noricum. This obliged him to form a second camp on the other side of the town, under the command of Curio. The remaining days were spent in drawing a line with redoubts round the place, which work was nearly completed when the messengers, that had been sent to Pompey, returned.

XVIII. Domitius, perusing the despatches, thought proper to dissemble the contents, and declared, in council, that Pompey would speedily come to their assistance. Meantime he exhorted them to behave with courage, and provide every thing necessary for a vigorous defence. He conferred, however, privately with a few of his most intimate friends, and, in concert with them, determined upon flight. But as his looks and speech were found to disagree; as he behaved not with his usual composure and firmness; and was observed, contrary to custom, to be much in secret conference with his friends; avoiding public appearances, and councils of war : it was not possible for the truth to remain any longer concealed. For Pompey had wrote back, " That he could not put all to hazard for his sake ; that he had neither advised nor consented to his shutting himself up in Corfinium ; that he must therefore endeavour to extricate himself as well as he could, and come and join him with all his forces." But as Cæsar had invested and carried his lines round the place, this retreat was now become impracticable.

XIX. Domitius's design being discovered, the soldiers who were at Corfinium began to assemble in the evening, and, by means of their tribunes, centurions, and other officers, made known their thoughts to one another : " That they were besieged by Cæsar, who had already, in a manner completed his works : that their general, Domitius, in whose promises of assistance they had placed their chief hope, abandoning all concern for their safety, was contriving to escape privately by flight : that it was therefore incumbent upon them to look also to their own preservation." The Marsi at first opposed this resolution, and possessed themselves of the strongest part of the town; nay, the dispute was so warm, that it almost came to be decided by the sword. But

shortly after, being made acquainted with Domitius's intended flight, of which before they had no knowledge; they all, in a body, surrounded Domitius, secured his person, and sent deputies to Cæsar: "That they were ready to open their gates, receive his orders, and deliver Domitius alive."

XX. Though Cæsar was fully sensible of how great importance it was to get possession of the town immediately, and join the garrison to his own army ; lest by largesses, promises of speedy relief, or false reports, any change should be produced ; as in war great revolutions often arise from very trifling causes : yet, fearing that if he introduced his soldiers in the dark, they would take that opportunity to plunder the town, he sent back the deputies, with thanks for their proffer, resolving to have the walls and gates watched with great care. To that end he disposed his men along the works, not at a certain distance, as usual, but in one continued rank, so as to touch each other, and completely invest the town. He ordered the military tribunes, and officers of the cavalry, to patrol about the works, and not only be on their guard against sallies, but even take care to prevent the escape of particular persons. And indeed so alert and vigilant were our soldiers, that not a man closed his eyes that night ; each expecting the event with impatience, and carrying his thoughts from one thing to another ; what would be the fate of the Corfinians, what of Domitius, what of Lentulus, and the other illustrious persons in the place : in fine, what was like to be the issue of so complicated a scene.

XXI. About the fourth watch of the night, Lentulus Spinther called from the wall to the guard, and desired to be conducted to Cæsar. His request being granted, he came out of the town, attended by some of Domitius's soldiers, who never left him till they had conducted him into Cæsar's presence. " He begged him to spare his life, and pardon the injuries he had done him, in consideration of their former friendship. He owned the many obligations he had laid him under, in procuring him an admission into the college of priests, obtaining for him the government of Spain, after the expiration of the pretorship, and supporting him in the demand of the consulship." Cæsar interrupted him by saying : "That he was not come out of the bounds of his province, with an intent to injure any body ; but to repel the

Injuries done him by his enemies; to revenge the wrongs of the tribunes; and to restore to the Roman people, who were oppressed by a small faction of the nobles, their liberties and privileges." Lentulus, encouraged by this speech, asked leave to return into the town, "where, he said, the assurances he had obtained of his own safety, would contribute not a little to the consolation of others, some of whom were so terrified, that they were ready to take desperate resolutions." Leave being granted, he departed for the town.

XXII. As soon as it was light, Cæsar ordered before him all the senators, senators' sons, military tribunes, and Roman knights. There were of senatorian rank, L. Domitius, P. Lentulus Spinther L. Vibullius Rufus, Sextus Quintilius Varus, questor, L. Rutrius; also Domitius's son, and many young men of quality, with a great number of Roman knights, and some decurions, or senators of the neighbouring municipal towns, who had been sent for by Domitius. As soon as they appeared, he gave order to secure them from the insults of the soldiery; and, addressing them in a few words, remonstrated: "That they had made a very ill requital for the many signal services received at his hands." After which, he set them at liberty. He likewise restored to Domitius six millions of sesterces, which that general had brought with him to Corfinium, and deposited in the hands of the two treasurers of the town, who surrendered it to Cæsar. As this was public money, assigned by Pompey to pay the forces with, Cæsar might justly have seized it; but he was willing to show himself generous, as well as merciful. He ordered Domitius's soldiers to take the usual oath to him, decamped that very day; made the ordinary march; and after staying in all seven days before Corfinium, arrived in Apulia, through the territories of the Marrucini, Frentani, and Larinates.

XXIII. Pompey, having intelligence of what passed at Corfinium, retreated from Luceria, to Canusium, and from thence to Brundusium. He ordered all the new levies to join him, armed the shepherds and slaves, furnished them with horses, and formed a body of about three hundred cavalry. Meanwhile the pretor L. Manlius flying from Alba, with six cohorts; and the pretor Rutilus Lupus, from Tarracina, with three; saw Cæsar's cavalry at a distance, commanded by Bivius Cu-

rius; upon which, the soldiers immediately abandoned the two pretors, and joined the troops under the conduct of Curius. Several other parties, flying different ways, fell in, some with the foot, others with the horse. Cn-Magius of Cremona, Pompey's chief engineer, being taken on his way to Brundusium, was brought to Cæsar, who sent him back to Pompey with this message: "That as he had not yet obtained an interview, his design was to come to Brundusium, there to confer with him in relation to the common safety; because they soon would be able to despatch, in a personal treaty, what, if managed by the intervention of others, could not be hindered from running into a tedious negotiation."

XXIV. Having dismissed him with these instructions, he arrived before Brundusium with six legions, three of which were composed of veteran soldiers, and the rest of new levies drawn together upon his march; for as to Domitius's troops, he had sent them directly from Corfinium to Sicily. He found the consuls were gone to Dyrrhachium with great part of the army, and that Pompey remained in Brundusium with twenty cohorts. Nor was it certainly known whether he continued there with design to keep possession of Brundusium, that he might be master of the whole Adriatic Sea, the extreme parts of Italy, and the country of Greece, in order to make war on both sides the gulf; or for want of shipping to transport his men. Fearing, therefore, that it was his intention to keep footing in Italy, he resolved to deprive him of the advantages he might receive from the port of Brundusium. The works he contrived for this purpose were as follows: He carried on a mole on either side the mouth of the haven where the entrance was narrowest, and the water shallow. But as this work could not be carried quite across the port, by reason of the great depth of the sea, he prepared double floats of timber, thirty feet square, which were each secured by four anchors from the four corners, to enable them to resist the fury of the waves. These, extending all the way between the two moles, were covered over with earth and fascines, that the soldiers might pass and repass with ease, and have firm footing to defend them. The front and sides were armed with a parapet of hurdles, and every fourth float had a tower of two stories, the better to guard the work from fire and the shocks of the vessels.

20

XXV. Against these preparations, Pompey made use of several large ships which he found in the port of Brundusium: and having fitted them with towers of three stories, which he filled with a great number of engines and darts, let them loose upon Cæsar's floats, to break through the staccado, and interrupt the works. Thus daily skirmishes happened with darts, arrows, and slings, at a distance. Amidst these hostilities, Cæsar's thoughts were still bent upon peace; and though he could not but wonder that Magius, whom he had sent with proposals to Pompey, was not yet returned with an answer; and even saw his designs and undertakings retarded by his frequent offers of this kind; he nevertheless still persevered in these peaceful resolutions. Accordingly, he despatched Caninius Rebilus, one of his lieutenants, a relation and intimate friend of Scribonius Libo, to confer with him on this subject. He charged him to exhort that nobleman to think seriously of peace, and, if possible, procure an interview between him and Pompey. Could this be effected, he showed there was the greatest ground to believe that peace would soon be concluded on reasonable terms; the honour and reputation of which would in a manner wholly redound to Libo, if, by his mediation, both parties should be prevailed with to lay down their arms. Libo, after conferring with Caninius, waited on Pompey; soon after he returned with this answer; that the consuls were absent, without whom Pompey had no power to treat of an accommodation. Thus Cæsar having often tried in vain to bring about a peace, thought it now time to drop that design, and bend all his thoughts to war.

XXVI. Cæsar having spent nine days about his works, had now half finished the staccado, when the ships employed in the first embarkation, being sent back by the consuls from Dyrrhachium, returned to Brundusium. Pompey, either alarmed at Cæsar's works, or because from the first he had determined to relinquish Italy, no sooner saw the transports arrive, than he prepared to carry over the rest of his forces. And the better to secure himself against Cæsar, and prevent his troops from breaking into the town during the embarkation, he walled up the gates, barricaded the streets, or cut ditches across them, filled with pointed stakes, and covered with hurdles and earth: The two streets which led to the port,

and which he left open for the passage of his men, were fortified with a double palisado of very strong well sharpened stakes. These preparations being made, he ordered the soldiers to embark with great silence, having placed on the walls and towers some select archers and slingers, who were to wait till all the troops had got aboard, and then retire, upon a signal given, to some small ships that waited them at a convenient distance.

XXVII. The people of Brundusium, provoked by the affronts they had received from Pompey, and the insults of his soldiers, wished well to Cæsar's cause; and having notice of Pompey's intended departure while the soldiers were busied with the care of embarking, found means to signify it from the tops of their houses. Cæsar, upon this intelligence, ordered scaling ladders to be prepared, and the soldiers to repair to their arms, that he might not lose any opportunity of acting. Pompey weighed anchor a little before night, and gave the signal for recalling the soldiers that were upon the walls, who repaired with all expedition to the ships prepared for them. Meantime the scaling ladders are applied to the walls, and Cæsar's troops enter the town. But being informed by the Brundusians of the snares and ditches provided for them by the enemy, they were obliged to take a great circuit, which gave Pompey time enough to put to sea. Two transports only, impeded by Cæsar's mole, **were taken** with the **troops on** board.

XXVIII. Though **Cæsar was fully sensible**, that to finish **the war at a blow, he must** pass the sea **immediately, and endeavour to** come up with Pompey, before he could draw his transmarine forces together; yet he dreaded the delay and length of time that such a project might require: because Pompey having carried with him all the ships on the coast, rendered the present execution of the design impracticable. He must therefore wait the arrival of ships from Picenum, Sicily, and the remoter coasts of Gaul, which was a tedious business, and, at that season of the year, subject to great uncertainty. It appeared likewise of dangerous consequence, to suffer a veteran army, and the two Spains, one of which was wholly devoted to Pompey, to strengthen themselves in his rival's interest; to let them grow powerful by levies of horse and foot, and leave Gaul and Italy open to their attacks in his absence. He determined, therefore, to lay aside, for the present, the design of pursuing Pompey, and turn all his thoughts towards Spain. He ordered the magistrates of the municipal towns to assemble all the vessels they could, and send them to Brundusium. He sent Valerius, one of his lieutenants, into Sardinia, with one legion, and the propretor Curio into Sicily with three, ordering him, as soon as he had mastered Sicily, to pass over with his army into Africa.

XXIX. M. Cotta commanded in Sardinia; M. Cato in Sicily; and Africa had fallen by lot to Tubero. The inhabitants of Cagliari, hearing of Valerius's commission, of their own accord, before he had left Italy, drove Cotta out of their city; who terrified by the unanimous opposition he met with from the province, fled into Africa. In Sicily, Cato applied himself with great diligence to the refitting of old ships, and building of new. He sent his lieutenant to raise forces in Lucania, and the country of the Brutians, and ordered the states of Sicily to furnish him with a certain number of horse and foot. When these preparations were almost completed, being informed of Curio's arrival, he called his chief officers together, and complained, " That he was betrayed and abandoned by Pompey, who, without any previous preparation, had involved the commonwealth in an unnecessary war; and upon being questioned by himself and others in the senate, had assured them, that he was abundantly able to sustain it." Having thus declared his mind, he quitted the province, which by this means submitted without trouble to Curio, as Sardinia had before done to Valerius. Tubero arriving in Africa, found Attius Varus in possession of that province, who, after the loss of his cohorts at Auximum, as we have shown above, had fled into these parts, and, with the consent of the natives, taken upon him the command. Here he had found means to levy two legions, by his knowledge of the people and country, where he had been governor some years before, after the expiration of his pretorship. Tubero coming before Utica with his fleet, was forbid the harbour and town; nor could he even obtain leave for his son to land, though he had a fit of sickness upon him, but was obliged to weigh anchor and be gone.

XXX. These affairs despatched, Cæsar, that his troops might enjoy some repose, cantoned them in the nearest towns, and set out himself for Rome. There he assembled the senate, and after complaining of the injuries of his enemies, told them, "That he had never affected extraordinary honours, but waited patiently the time prescribed by the laws, to solicit for a second consulship, to which every Roman citizen had a right to aspire: that the people, with the concurrence of their tribunes, (in spite of the attempts of his enemies, and the vigorous opposition of Cato, who endeavoured, according to custom, to spin out the time in speaking,) had permitted him to stand candidate though absent, and that even in the consulship of Pompey; who, if he disapproved of the decree, why did he let it pass? But if he allowed it, why now oppose the execution? He set before them his moderation, in voluntarily proposing that both parties should lay down their arms, by which he must have been himself divested of his government and command. He displayed the malice of his enemies, who sought to impose terms on him, to which they would not submit themselves; and chose rather to involve the state in a civil war than part with their armies and provinces. He enlarged upon the injury they had done him, in taking away two of his legions, and their cruelty and insolence, in violating the authority of the tribunes. He spoke of his many offers of peace, his frequent desire of an interview, and the continual refusals he had received. For all these reasons, he requested and conjured them to undertake the administration of the republic, jointly with him. But if they declined it through fear, he had no intention to force so great a burden upon them, and would take the whole charge alone. That in the mean time it would be proper to send a deputation to Pompey, to treat of an accommodation: nor was he frighted at the difficulty Pompey had started some time before in the senate; that to send deputies was to acknowledge the superiority of him to whom they were sent, and a sign of timidity in the sender. That this was a little low way of thinking; and that, in the same manner as he had endeavoured at a superiority in action, he would also strive to be superior in justice and equity."

XXXI. The senate liked the proposal of a deputation to Pompey; "but the great difficulty was, to find deputies; every one, out of fear, refusing to charge himself with that commission. For Pompey, at his departure from Rome, had declared in the senate, "That he would esteem those who stayed behind, as no less guilty than those in Cæsar's camp." Thus three days were spent in debates and excuses. The tribune L. Metellus had likewise been suborned by Cæsar's enemies to traverse his design, and hinder whatever he should propose. Which Cæsar coming to understand, and that he only wasted his time to no purpose; he set out from Rome, without effecting what he intended, and arrived in farther Gaul.

XXXII. Here he was informed, that Pompey had sent into Spain Vibullius Rufus, the same who, a few days before, had been made prisoner at Corfinium, and set at liberty by Cæsar; that Domitius was gone to take possession of Marseilles, with seven galleys, which he had fitted out at Igilium and Cosanum, and manned with his slaves, freedmen, and labourers; that the deputies of the above-mentioned state, young men of the first quality, (whom Pompey, at his departure from Rome, had exhorted not to suffer the memory of his past services to their country to be blotted out by those lately received from Cæsar,) had been sent before, to prepare the way for his reception. In consequence of their remonstrances, the inhabitants of Marseilles shut their gates against Cæsar, and summoned to their assistance the Albici, a barbarous people, who had long been under their protection, and inhabited the adjoining mountains. They brought provisions from the neighbouring country and castles, refitted their navy, and repaired their walls and gates.

XXXIII. Cæsar sending for fifteen of the principal men of the city, exhorted them not to be the first to begin the war, but to be swayed rather by the authority of all Italy, than the will of one particular person. He forgot not such other considerations as seemed most likely to bring them to reason. The deputies returning into the town, brought back this answer from the senate: "That they saw the Romans divided into two parties, and it did not belong to them to decide such a quarrel: that at the head of these parties were Pompey and Cæsar, both patrons of their city, the one having added to it the country of the Volcæ Arecomici and Helvians; the other

after the reduction of Gaul, considerably augmented its territories and revenues; that as they were therefore equally indebted to both, it became them not to aid the one against the other; but to remain neuter, and grant neither an admittance into their city nor port."

XXXIV. Whilst these things were in agitation, Domitius arrived at Marseilles with his fleet, and being received into the town, was appointed governor, and charged with the whole administration of the war. By his order, they sent out their fleet to cruise round the coasts; seized and brought in all the merchant vessels they could find, and made use of the nails, rigging, and timber of such as were unfit for service, to repair the rest. They deposited in public granaries all the corn that was to be found in the city, and secured whatever else they thought might be serviceable to them in case of a siege. Cæsar, provoked at these preparations, brought three legions before the town, began to erect towers and galleries, and gave orders for building twelve galleys at Arles, which being finished, launched, and brought to Marseilles, within thirty days from the cutting of the wood they were composed of, he put them under the command of D. Brutus, and having directed the manner of the siege, left the care of it to C. Trebonius, his lieutenant.

XXXV. During these orders and preparations, he sent **C. Fabius** before him **into** Spain, with **three** legions **that had** wintered about Narbonne, charging **him to** secure with all diligence the **passage of the Pyrenean** Mountains, **which was at that time guarded** by a party **of Afranius's army. His** other legions, whose quarters were more remote, had orders to follow as fast as they could. Fabius, according to his instructions, having made great despatch, forced the passes of the Pyrenees, and by long marches came up with Afranius's army.

XXXVI. Pompey had then three lieutenants in Spain, Afranius, Petreius, and Varro. The first of these was at the head of three legions, and governed the nearer Spain. The other two had each two legions, and commanded, the one from the Castilian Forest to the Anas; the other from the Anas, quite through Lusitania, and the territories of the Vettones. These three lieutenants, upon the arrival of Vibullius Rufus, whom Pompey had sent into

Spain, as we have seen above, consulted together, and agreed, that Petreius should join Afranius with his two legions, and that Varro should stay and secure farther Spain. These resolutions being taken, Petreius levied horse and foot in Lusitania, and Afranius in Celtiberia, and the barbarous nations bordering upon the ocean. When the levies were completed, Petreius speedily joined Afranius, through the territories of the Vettones; and both resolved to make Lerida the seat of the war, because the country lay convenient for their purpose.

XXXVII. We have already observed that Afranius had three legions, and Petreius two. Besides these, there were about eighty cohorts, some light, some heavy armed, and five thousand horse, raised in both provinces. Cæsar had sent his legions before him into Spain, with six thousand auxiliary foot, and three thousand horse, who had served under him in all his former wars, and he was furnished with the like number from Gaul, all chosen troops. For hearing that Pompey was coming with his whole force through Mauritania into Spain, he sent circular letters to all the Gallic states, inviting by name those of the most known and approved valour, and in particular a select body of mountaineers from Aquitain, where it borders upon the Roman province. At the same time he borrowed money from the military tribunes and centurions, which he distributed among the soldiers. This policy was attended with two great advantages : it bound the officers to him by the obligation of interest, and the soldiers by the tie of gratitude.

XXXVII. Fabius, by letters and messengers, endeavoured to sound the disposition of the neighbouring states. He had laid two bridges over the Sicoris, four miles distant from each other, for the convenience of foraging, having consumed all the pasture on this side the river. Pompey's generals did the same, with much the like view, which occasioned frequent skirmishes between the horse. Two of Fabius's legions, which was the ordinary guard of the foragers, passing one day according to custom, and the cavalry and carriages following, the bridge broke down on a sudden, by the violence of the winds and floods, and separated them from the rest of the army. Afranius and Petreius perceiving it, by the fascines and hurdles that came down with the stream; detached immediately four legions, with all their cavalry, over the bridge that lay between the town and their camp, and marched to attack Fabius's legions. Upon this L. Plancus, who commanded the escort, finding himself hard pressed, seizing a rising ground, and forming his men into two divisions, posted them back to back, that he might not be surrounded by the enemy's horse. By this disposition, though inferior in number, he was enabled to sustain the furious charge of their legions and cavalry. During the course of the battle, the ensigns of two legions were perceived at a distance, which Fabius had sent by the farther bridge to sustain his party, suspecting what might happen, and that Pompey's generals might seize the opportunity offered them by fortune, to fall upon our men. Their arrival put an end to the engagement, and both parties returned to their respective camps.

XXXIX. Two days after, Cæsar arrived in the camp with nine hundred horse, which he had kept for a body guard. He began by re-establishing in the night the bridge which had been broken down, and was not yet quite repaired. Next day he took a view of the country, and leaving six cohorts to guard the bridge, the camp, and the baggage, marched with all his forces in three lines to Lerida, and stopped near Afranius's camp, where he remained some time under arms, and offered him battle on an even ground. Afranius drew out his troops, and formed them before his camp, half way down the hill. Cæsar, finding that he declined an engagement, resolved to encamp within four hundred paces of the foot of the mountain ; and to hinder his troops from being alarmed or interrupted in their works, by sudden incursions from the enemy, ordered them not to throw up a rampart, which must have appeared and betrayed them at a distance, but to cut a ditch in front, fifteen feet broad. The first and second lines continued in order of battle, as had been resolved from the beginning, and the third carried on the work behind them unperceived. Thus the whole was completed, before Afranius had the least suspicion of his design to encamp there.

XL. In the evening Cæsar retreated with his legions behind the ditch, and passed the whole night under arms. Next day he carried the intrenchment quite round his camp, and because materials for a rampart must have been fetched from a great distance, he con tented himself for the present with a naked ditch, as the day before, allotting a legion to each side of the camp, and keeping the rest of the troops under arms, to cover those that worked. Afranius and Petreius, to alarm our men and disturb the works, advanced with their troops to the foot of the mountain, and threatened to give battle. But Cæsar, trusting to the three legions under arms, and the defence of the ditch, still persisted in his design. At last, after a short stay, and without daring to come forward into the plain, they retreated again to their camp. The third day, Cæsar added a rampart to his camp, and brought into it the six cohorts, with the baggage which he had left in his former camp.

XLI. Between the city of Lerida, and the hill where Petreius and Afranius were encamped, was a plain of about three hundred paces, in the midst of which was a rising ground, which Cæsar wanted to take possession of; because, by that means, he could cut off the enemy's communication with the town and bridge, and render the magazines they had in the town useless. In this hope, he drew out three legions, and having formed them in order of battle, commanded the first ranks of one of them to run before, and gain the place. Afranius perceiving his design, despatched the cohorts that were upon guard before the camp, a nearer way to the same eminence. The contest was sharply maintained on both sides: but Afranius's party, who first got possession of the post, obliged our men to give ground, and being reinforced by fresh supplies, put them at last to rout, and forced them to fly for shelter to the legions.

XLII. The manner of fighting of Afranius's soldiers was, to come forward briskly against an enemy, and boldly take possession of some post, neither taking care to keep their ranks, nor holding it necessary to fight in a close compact body. If they found themselves hard pushed, they thought it no dishonour to retire and quit their posts, following in this the custom of the Lusitanians, and other barbarous nations, as it almost always happens, that soldiers give in to the manners of the country where they have long been used to make war. This manner of fighting, however, as it was new and unexpected, disordered our men, who seeing the enemy come forward, without regard to their ranks, were apprehensive of being surrounded, and yet not think themselves at

liberty to break their ranks, or abandon their ensigns, or quit their post, without some very urgent cause. The first ranks therefore being put into disorder, the legion in that wing gave ground, and retired to a neighbouring hill.

XLIII. Cæsar, contrary to his expectation, finding the consternation like to spread through the whole army, encouraged his men, and led the ninth legion to their assistance. He soon put a stop to the vigorous and insulting pursuit of the enemy, obliged them to turn their backs, and pushed them to the very walls of Lerida. But the soldiers of the ninth legion, elated with success, and eager to repair the loss we had sustained, followed the runaways with so much heat that they were drawn into a place of disadvantage, and found themselves directly under the hill where the town stood, whence when they endeavoured to retire, the enemy again facing about, charged vigorously from the higher ground. The hill was rough, and steep on each side, extending only so far in breadth as was sufficient for drawing up three cohorts; but they could neither be reinforced in flank, nor sustained by the cavalry. The descent from the town was indeed something easier for about four hundred paces, which furnished our men with the means of extricating themselves from the danger into which their rashness had brought them. Here they bravely maintained the fight, though with great disadvantage to themselves, as well on account of the narrowness of the place, as because being posted at the foot of the hill, none of the enemy's darts fell in vain. Still however they supported themselves by their courage and patience, and were not disheartened by the many wounds they received. The enemy's forces increased every moment, fresh cohorts being sent from the camp through the town, who succeeded in the place of those that were fatigued. Cæsar was likewise obliged to despatch small parties to maintain the battle, and bring off such as were wounded.

XLIV. The fight had now lasted five hours without intermission, when our men, oppressed by the multitude of the enemy, and having spent all their darts, attacked the mountain sword in hand, and overthrowing such as opposed them, obliged the rest to betake themselves to flight. The pursuit was continued to the very walls of Lerida, and some out of fear took shelter in the town, which gave our men an opportunity of making good their retreat. At the same time the cavalry, though posted disadvantageously in a bottom, found means by their valour to gain the summit of the mountain, and riding between both armies, hindered the enemy from harassing our rear. Thus the engagement was attended with various turns of fortune. Cæsar lost about seventy men in the first encounter, among whom was Q. Fulginius, first centurion of the Hastati of the fourteenth legion, who had raised himself by his valour to that rank, through all the inferior orders. Upwards of six hundred were wounded. On Afranius's side was slain T. Cæcilius, first centurion of a legion; also four centurions of inferior degree, and above two hundred private men.

XLV. Yet such were the circumstances of this day's action, that both sides laid claim to the victory; the Afranians, because, though allowed to be inferior in number, they had long sustained our attack, kept possession of the eminence which occasioned the dispute, and obliged our men at first to give ground: Cæsar's troops, because they had maintained a fight of five hours, with a handful of men, and in a very disadvantageous post; because they had attacked the mountain sword in hand, because they had driven their adversaries from the higher ground, and compelled them to take shelter in the town. Meantime Afranius fortified the hillock which had been the subject of dispute, with a great number of works, and posted there a large body of troops.

XLVI. Two days after, a very unfortunate accident happened. For so great a storm arose, that the water was never known to be higher in those parts; and the snow came down in such quantities from all the mountains round about, that the river overflowed its banks, and in one day broke down both the bridges Fabius had built over it. Cæsar's army was reduced to great extremities on this occasion. For his camp, as we have before observed, was between the Sicoris and Cinga, two rivers that were neither of them fordable, and necessarily shut him up within the space of no more than thirty miles. By this means, neither could the states that had declared for him supply him with provisions, nor the troops that had been sent beyond the rivers to forage, return, nor the large convoys he expected from Gaul and Italy get to his camp. Add to all this, that it being near the time of harvest, corn was extremely scarce: and the more, as before Cæsar's arrival, Afranius had carried great quantities of it to Lerida; and the rest had been consumed by Cæsar's troops. The cattle, which was the next resource in the present scarcity, had been removed to places of security, on the breaking out of the war. The parties sent out to forage and bring in corn, were perpetually harassed by the Spanish infantry, who being well acquainted with the country, pursued them every where. The rivers themselves did not impede them, because they were accustomed to pass them on blown-up skins, which they always brought with them into the field. Afranius, on the contrary, abounded in all things. He had large magazines of corn already laid up, was continually receiving fresh supplies from the province, and had plenty of forage. The bridge of Lerida furnished all these conveniences without danger, and opened a free communication with the country beyond the river, from which Cæsar was wholly excluded.

XLVII. The waters continued several days. Cæsar endeavoured to re-establish his bridges, but could not get the better of the obstacles occasioned by the swelling of the river, and the enemy's forces stationed on the opposite bank. They found it the easier to prevent his design, as the river was deep and rapid, and they could discharge their darts all along the bank, on that particular spot where our men were at work: whereas it was extremely difficult on our side to struggle with the force of the stream, and, at the same time, guard ourselves against the assaults of the enemy.

XLVIII. Meanwhile Afranius was informed that a large convoy, which was on its way to join Cæsar, had been obliged to halt at the river side. It consisted of archers from Rovergue, Goulish horse, with many carts and much baggage, according to the custom of the Gauls, and about six thousand men of all sorts, with their domestics and slaves; but without discipline or commander, every one following his own choice, and all marching in perfect security, as if they had nothing more to apprehend than in former times. There were likewise many young gentlemen of quality, senators' sons, and Roman knights, with the deputies of the states of Gaul, and some of Cæsar's lieutenants; who were all stopped short by the river. Afranius set out in the night, with three legions, and all his cavalry; and sending the horse before, attacked them when they least expected it. The Gaulish squadrons, forming with great expedition, began the fight. While the contest was upon equal terms, the Gauls, though few in number, bore up against the vast multitude of the enemy; but seeing the legions advance, and having lost some of their men, they retreated to the neighbouring mountains. This delay saved the convoy; for during the skirmish, the rest of the troops gained the higher ground. We lost that day about two hundred archers, a few troopers, and some servants and baggage.

XLIX. All this served to enhance the price of provisions, a calamity inseparable from present scarcity, and the prospect of future want. Corn was already at fifty *denarii* a bushel, the soldiers began to lose their strength, and the evil increased every moment. Nay, so great was the change produced in a few days, and such the alteration of fortune, that while our men were in the utmost want of all kind of necessaries, the enemy had plenty of every thing, and were accounted victorious. Cæsar left nothing untried to remove the present scarcity: he dismissed all the useless mouths, and applied to the states that had declared for him, desiring them to send him cattle where they wanted corn.

L. These things were greatly exaggerated by Afranius, Petreius, and their friends, in the letters they sent, upon this occasion, to Rome. Nor was fame backward in adding to the account; insomuch that the war appeared to be almost at an end. These couriers and letters having reached Rome, there was a great concourse of people at Afranius's house, many congratulations passed, and multitudes of the nobility flocked out of Italy to Pompey; some to carry the first accounts of this grateful news; others, that they might not be so late as to subject them to the reproach of having waited for the event of things.

LI. Affairs being in this extremity, and all the passes guarded by Afranius's parties, without a possibility of repairing the bridges; Cæsar ordered the soldiers to build some light boats, in imitation of those he had formerly seen in Britain, whose keel and ribs were of wood, and the rest of wicker, covered with leather. When he had got a sufficient number, he sent them by night in wagons, twenty-two miles off from his camp. In these he embarked a good number of soldiers, and sent them over the river; took possession unexpectedly of a hill adjoining to the bank on the other side; threw up a fortification before the enemy thought of hindering him; posted a legion in this fortification; and then threw a bridge over the Sicoris in two days. By this means he recovered his foragers, secured the convoy, and opened a passage for future supplies. The same day he detached a great part of his cavalry over the river who, falling unexpectedly upon the enemy's foragers, dispersed up and down, without a suspicion of danger, made a considerable capture of men and horses; and observing some Spanish cohorts on the march to their assistance, skilfully divided themselves into two bodies; one to secure the booty; the other, to receive and return the enemy's charge. One of their cohorts, which had rashly separated from the rest, and advanced too far before the main body, was surrounded and cut to pieces by our men, who returned over the same bridge to the camp, without loss, and enriched with a considerable booty.

LII. Whilst these things passed at Lerida, the people of Marseilles, by the advice of L. Domitius, equipped seventeen galleys, eleven of which were covered. To these they added a multitude of smaller vessels, that they might strike a terror into our fleet by their very number; and manned them with archers, and the mountaineers we have already mentioned, whom they encouraged to perform their part by great rewards and promises. Domitius desired some of these ships, and filled them with the shepherds and labourers he had brought thither with him. Thus furnished and equipped, they sailed with great confidence, in quest of our fleet, which was commanded by Decimus Brutus, and rode at anchor at an island over against Marseilles. Brutus was much inferior to the enemy in number of ships; but Cæsar had manned them with his best soldiers, chosen out of all the legions, and headed by centurions of distinguished bravery, who had petitioned him for this service. These had provided themselves with hooks and grappling-irons, and a great number of darts, javelins, and offensive weapons of all sorts. Thus prepared, upon notice of the enemy's arrival, they stood out to sea, and attacked their fleet. The conflict was sharp and vigorous. For the mountaineers, a hardy race, habituated to arms, and trained up in war, scarce yielded to the Romans in bravery; and, having but just parted from Marseilles, still retained a lively sense of the promises so lately made them. The shepherds too, animated by the hopes of liberty, and fighting under the eye of their master, did wonders to merit his approbation. The townsmen themselves, confiding in the nimbleness of their ships, and the skill of their pilots, eluded the shocks of our vessels, and baffled all their attempts. As they had abundance of sea-room, **they extended their line of battle, in order to** surround **our fleet, or attack our ships singly with a** number of theirs, or in **running along-side,** sweep away a range of **oars. If they were** compelled to come to a **closer engagement,** setting aside the skill and **address of their** pilots, they **relied** wholly on the bravery of their mountaineers. **Our men were** but indifferently provided with rowers and pilots, who had been hastily taken out of some merchant ships, and knew not so much as the names of the tackle. They were incommoded too by the weight and lumpishness of their vessels, which being built in haste, of unseasoned timber, were not so ready at tacking about. But when an opportunity offered of coming to close fight, they would boldly get between two of the enemy's ships; and grappling them with their hooks, charge them on each side, board them, and cut to pieces the mountaineers and shepherds that defend them. In this manner they sunk part of their vessels, **took** some with all the men on board, and **drove the rest** into the haven. In this engagement, **the** enemy had nine galleys sunk or taken.

LIII. **The report of this** battle reaching Lerida, **and Cæsar having** finished his bridge over the Sicoris, **affairs soon** began to put on a new face. **The** enemy dreading the courage of our horse, **durst not** disperse about the country as formerly; but either foraged in the neighbourhood **of the** camp, that they might the sooner make good their retreat; or, by a long circuit, endeavoured to avoid our parties: and upon receiving any check, or even descrying our cavalry at a distance, they would throw down their trusses, and fly. At last, they were reduced to omit foraging several days together, and resolved to pursue it

only by night, contrary to the general custom of war.

LIV. In the mean time the Oscenses and Calagurritani jointly sent deputies to Cæsar, with an offer of their submission and services. The Tarraconenses, Jacitani, and Ausetani, and not many days after, the Illurgavonenses, who inhabit along the banks of the Iberus, followed their example. He only required them to supply him with corn, to which they readily agreed; and having got together a great number of carriage-horses, brought it to his camp. A cohort of the Illurgavonenses, hearing of the resolution taken by their state, deserted from the enemy, and **came over to Cæsar's camp.** The **change was sudden and** great; for, the bridge being finished, provisions secured, this rumour of Pompey's march through Mauritania extinguished, and five considerable states having declared in his favour; a great number of distant provinces renounced their engagements with Afranius, and entered into new ones with Cæsar.

LV. These things having struck a terror into the enemy; that he might not be always obliged to send his cavalry so far about to forage, the bridges lying about seven miles from **his camp, he** bethought himself of draining the **river, by turning some** of its water into canals **thirty feet deep, so as** to make it fordable. **The work** being almost completed, Petreius **and** Afranius grew extremely apprehensive **of being entirely** cut off from their provisions and forage, because Cæsar was very strong in cavalry. They therefore thought proper to quit a post **that** was no longer tenable, and to carry the war into Celtiberia. What contributed still further to confirm them in this resolution was, that of the two contrary parties, concerned in the late war, those who had declared for Sertorius, still trembled at the name of the conqueror, and dreaded his power, though absent; and those who had attached themselves to Pompey, continued to love him for the many services he had done them: but Cæsar's name was hardly **known among these** barbarians. Here they expected **considerable** reinforcements of horse and foot; and doubted not, by taking the advantage of places, to be able to protract the war till winter. In order to execute this plan, they collected all the boats to be found on the Iberus, and ordered them to be brought to Octogesa, a city on that river, about twenty miles from their camp. Here they commanded a bridge of boats to be built; and, having sent two legions over the Sicoris, fortified their camp with a rampart of twelve feet.

LVI. Cæsar, having notice of this by his scouts, laboured day and night at his drains with the utmost diligence; and had already so far diminished the water of the Sicoris, that the cavalry could, with some difficulty, pass over: but it took the infantry as high as the shoulders, who had therefore both the depth of the river and the rapidity of the stream to struggle with. Meanwhile it was known, that the bridge over the Iberus was almost finished, and Cæsar's ford in great forwardness. This was a fresh motive to the enemy to quicken their march: wherefore, leaving two auxiliary cohorts, for a garrison, at Lerida, they crossed the Sicoris with all their forces, and joined the two legions they had sent over before. Cæsar had now no other remedy left but to harass and fatigue them with his cavalry: for if he went with his whole army over his bridge, he lengthened his march prodigiously, and gave Afranius time enough to get to the Iberus. Accordingly the horse having forded the river, came up with Petreius and Afranius's rear, who had decamped about midnight: and making a motion to surround them, began to stop and retard their march.

LVII. At day-break we discovered from the hills near the camp, that the enemy's rear was greatly harassed by our cavalry. Sometimes they obliged them to halt, and disordered their ranks: at other times, the enemy facing about, charged with all their cohorts at once, and forced our men to give ground; who, wheeling again as soon as they began to march, failed not to renew the attack. At this sight, the legionary soldiers, running up and down the camp, complained that the enemy would escape out of their hands, and the war necessarily be prolonged. They addressed themselves to the centurions and military tribunes, and desired them to beg of Cæsar not to spare them; that they feared neither danger nor fatigue, and were ready to pass the river as the horse had done. Cæsar, moved by their alacrity and entreaties, though he saw some danger in exposing his army to the rapidity of a deep river, judged it yet proper to attempt and make trial of the passage. Having therefore withdrawn from every company such as were weak of body, or of less courage than the rest, he left them in the camp with a legion, and all the baggage. The rest of the army happily passed the river, by the assistance of a double line of cavalry, placed above and below them. Some of the infantry were carried away by the violence of the current; but they were picked up and saved by the horse below them; so that no one man was lost. Having passed the river without loss, he drew up his army in order of battle, and began to pursue the enemy in three lines: and such was the ardour of the soldiers, that notwithstanding the army was obliged to make a circuit of six miles, notwithstanding the time necessarily lost in crossing the river, they got up at the ninth hour of the day to the enemy, who had set out at midnight.

LVIII. When Afranius and Petreius perceived them at some distance, being with reason intimidated, they suspended their march, halted on an eminence, and formed in order of battle. Cæsar would not hazard an action with his troops, thus fatigued, and halted likewise in the plain. On this the enemy resumed their march, and he the pursuit; which obliged them to encamp earlier than they designed. Hard by was a range of mountains, and about five miles farther, the ways were difficult and narrow. The enemy retired among these mountains, to avoid the pursuit of the cavalry; and having placed parties in all the passes, to stop Cæsar's army, hoped, by this means, to continue their march to the Iberus, without fear or danger. This was their great affair, and what before all things they should have endeavoured to effect; but, being fatigued by a long march, and their continual skirmishes with Cæsar's cavalry, they deferred it till next day. Cæsar likewise encamped on a hill that lay near him.

LIX. About midnight, the cavalry having surprised some of the enemy, who had adventured a little too far from their camp in quest of water; Cæsar was informed by them, that Pompey's lieutenants were decamping without noise. Immediately he ordered the alarm to be sounded, and gave his army the signal to march. The enemy, finding they should be pursued, kept still; being afraid of a nocturnal flight, wherein they would have had greatly the disadvantage, on account of their heavy baggage which they had with them, and the superiority of Cæsar's cavalry. Next day, Petreius went privately out with a party of horse: take a view of the country. Cæsar likewise detached a squadron for the same purpose, under the command of Decidius Saxa. Both made the like report in their several camps; that for five miles together, the country was level and open, but after that rough and mountainous; and that whoever should first get possession of the defiles, might easily prevent the other army from approaching them.

LX. Upon this, a council of war was held by Petreius and Afranius, to deliberate about the time of beginning their march. The greater number were for setting out by night, in hopes of reaching the defiles before Cæsar could have notice of their departure. Others argued **against** the possibility of decamping privately, **by the** alarm given in Cæsar's **camp the night before:** "That the enemy's **cavalry were continually** patrolling in the night, **and had beset all the** ways and passes: that a nocturnal engagement was to be avoided, because, in a civil war, the soldiers were more apt to listen to their fears, than the obligations of the military oath: that shame and the presence of the centurions and the tribunes, the great instruments of obedience and military duty, could have their proper effect only in the light, which rendered it of infinite importance to wait the approach of day; that in case of a disaster, yet the bulk of the army would escape, and be able to possess themselves of the post in question." This opinion prevailed in the council, and they resolved to set out the next morning by break of day.

LXI. Cæsar having taken a view of the country, decamped as soon as it was light, taking a considerable circuit, and observing no particular route; for the direct way to the Iberus and Octogesa lay in the rear of the enemy's camp. He was therefore obliged to march through valleys and precipices, and over steep rocks, which the soldiers could not climb, out by disencumbering themselves of their arms, and returning them afterwards to one another. But not a man murmured at these difficulties, in hope of seeing a speedy end of all their labours, if they could but gain the Iberus before the enemy, and intercept their provisions. As in this march we pursued at first an opposite course, and seemed to turn our backs upon the enemy, Afranius's soldiers who observed us from their camp, came forth with joyful looks, and insulted us on our supposed flight, imagining the want of provisions

obliged us to return to Lerida. Their generals applauded themselves upon their resolution of not decamping, and were confirmed in the notion of our retreat, as they saw we had neither horses nor carriages; whence they concluded the scarcity must be exceeding great. But when they saw us, after some time, turn to the right, and that our advanced guard had already gained the ground beyond their camp, there was not a man so tardy or indolent, as not to perceive the necessity of decamping and opposing our march. Immediately they ran to arms, and leaving a few cohorts to guard the camp, sallied in a body, pursuing their way directly to the Iberus.

LXII. All depended **upon** despatch, **and** getting the first possession of the defiles and mountains. Our troops were retarded by **the** difficulties of the way, and Afranius's by the continual attacks of Cæsar's cavalry. But such was the situation of the Afranians, that even supposing them to gain the hills first, they could only secure their own retreat, without a possibility of preserving their baggage, and the cohorts left to guard the camp; because Cæsar's army getting between, cut them off from all communication with their own men. Cæsar arrived first at the place in question; and having found a plain beyond the rocks, formed his men in order of battle against the enemy. Afranius, who now saw our army in his front, at the same time that his rear was continually harassed by the cavalry, halted on an eminence, from whence he detached four Spanish cohorts, to take possession of the highest mountain thereabouts; ordering them to make all the despatch they could to seize it, that he might get thither himself with the rest of his forces, and changing his route, march them over the hills to Octogesa. The Spaniards wheeling obliquely, to take possession of the place, were perceived by Cæsar's cavalry; who charged them furiously, broke them at the first onset, surrounded, and cut them in pieces in sight of both armies.

LXIII. Cæsar had now an opportunity of giving the enemy an effectual blow; whose army, in the present consternation it was under, would, he was sensible, make but a faint resistance; more especially as it was surrounded on all sides by the cavalry, and would be obliged to fight on equal ground. He was pressed, on all hands, to give the signal. The lieutenants, centurions, and military tribunes, got round him, urging him not to delay the engagement: "That the soldiers were all eager for a battle; whereas, on the contrary, the Afranians had given many marks of fear: that they had neither dared to support their own detachment, nor offered to descend from the hill, nor been able to withstand the very first charge of our cavalry; that they had brought their ensigns all into one place, where they crowded confusedly round them, without observing ranks or order: that if he was afraid to attack them on the eminence, he would soon have an opportunity of more equal ground, as Afranius would be obliged to remove for want of water."

LXIV. Cæsar was in hopes of terminating the affair without bloodshed, or a battle; because he had intercepted the enemy's provisions. Why therefore, **even** supposing the event to **be** prosperous, should he unnecessarily **lose any of his men?** Why should he **expose to wounds,** soldiers who had so well **deserved** of him? Why, in fine, should **he** tempt fortune? especially as **it** redounded no **less to the** honour of a good general, to gain **the victory** by his conduct, than by the force **of his arms.** He was also touched with compassion for Afranius's soldiers; who, after all, were fellow-citizens, and whom he must have slaughtered, when he could equally succeed without touching their lives. This resolution **was not at** all relished by the army; who, in their discontent, openly declared, that since Cæsar did not lay hold of so favourable an opportunity, nor let them fight when they had a mind, they would not fight when he had a mind. But nothing could shake him. Nay, he even retreated a little, to give Afranius and Petreius liberty to regain their camp, which they did. He then posted troops on the mountains, to guard the defiles, and came and encamped as near the enemy as possible.

LXV. The day after, Pompey's lieutenants, disturbed at finding their provisions cut off, and all the ways to the Iberus intercepted, consulted what was proper to be done. They had it still in their power to return to Lerida, or march to Tarraco. But while they were debating this matter, notice was brought them, that our cavalry had fallen upon their parties sent out in quest of water. Upon this intelligence, they formed several posts of horse and foot intermixed with legionary cohorts; and

began to throw up a rampart from the camp to the place where they watered, that the soldiers might pass and repass under cover, without fear, and without a guard. Afranius and Petreius divided this work between them, and went to give directions about it in person.

LXVI. In their absence, their soldiers found frequent opportunities of conversing with our men, **and sought out every one** his fellow-citizen **and acquaintance.** They began by thanking **them for having spared** them the day before, **owning they were** indebted to them for their lives. **Afterwards they** asked them, if they might trust **to Cæsar's honour;** testifying much grief at being obliged to fight with their countrymen and relations, with **whom** they were united by the strictest ties. **At last** they stipulated even for their generals, whom they would not seem to betray: and promised, if the lives of Petreius and Afranius **were** granted them, to change sides. **At the same** time they sent some of their principal officers to negotiate with Cæsar: and these preliminaries to an accommodation being settled, the soldiers of both armies went into one another's tents, so that the two camps were now in a manner one. A great number of centurions and military tribunes came to pay their court to Cæsar, and beg his protection. The Spanish chiefs, who had been summoned to attend Afranius, and were detained in the camp as hostages, followed their example. Every man sought out his acquaintance and friend, who might recommend and procure him a favourable reception from Cæsar. Things were carried to such a length, that Afranius's son, a young gentleman, treated with Cæsar, by the mediation of Sulpicius, to desire he would give his word for his life, and that of his father. The joy was general; they mutually congratulated each other; the one, in that they had escaped so imminent a danger; and the other, in that they had brought to a happy conclusion so important an enterprise, without striking a blow. Cæsar, in the judgment of all, was upon the point of amply reaping the fruits of his wonted clemency, and every body applauded his late conduct.

LXVII. Afranius, having notice of what passed, quitted the work he was engaged in, and returned to the camp; prepared, as it would seem, to bear with an equal mind whatever should happen. But Petreius was not wanting to himself. He armed his slaves; and joining them to a pretorian cohort of target-bearers, and some Spanish horse, his dependants, whom he always kept about him to guard his person; he instantly flew to the rampart, broke off the conferences of the soldiers, drove our men from the camp, and put all of them he could find to the sword. The rest flocked together; where, alarmed at the danger to which they saw themselves exposed, they wrapped their cloaks round their left arms, drew their swords, and, trusting to the nearness of their camp, defended themselves against the Spanish target-bearers and cavalry, till they had retreated to our advanced guard, who screened them from any further assault.

LXVIII. After this he went through the whole camp, begging his troops, with tears, to have pity on him, and Pompey their general; and that they would not deliver them both up to the cruel vengeance of their enemies. Every one upon this flocks to the head-quarters. There Petreius proposes to the army to bind themselves by a new oath, not to abandon nor betray their commanders, nor to act separately, but all in concert, for the common good. He himself took this oath first, and then exacted it of Afranius, afterwards of the military tribunes and centurions, and lastly of all the companies, man by man. At the same time an order was issued that all who had any of Cæsar's soldiers in their tents should signify it, that they might be put to death in the sight of the whole army. But the majority, detesting this bloody order, carefully hid those who were under their protection, and procured them means to escape in the night. However, the terror they had been thrown into by their generals, the severity shown in punishing, and the new oath they had been obliged to take, defeated, for the present, all hopes of a surrender, changed the soldiers' minds, and reduced the war to its former state.

LXIX. Cæsar ordered diligent search to be made after such of the enemy's soldiers as had come to his camp during the time of conference, and carefully sent them back. Some military tribunes and centurions voluntarily chose to stay with him; whom he afterwards treated with great distinction; promoting the centurions to higher ranks, and honouring the Roman knights with the office of military tribunes.

LXX. The Afranian troops were destitute of forage, and could not water without much difficulty. The legionary soldiers had, indeed, some provisions, because they had been ordered to bring two and twenty days' corn with them from Lerida; but the Spanish infantry and auxiliaries had none; for they neither had opportunities of supplying themselves, nor were their bodies inured to carry heavy burdens. Accordingly, they every day deserted in shoals to Cæsar. In this extremity, of the two expedients proposed, that of returning to Lerida appeared the safest, as they had still some provisions in that city, and might there concert what further measures to pursue. Tarraco was at a greater distance, and they would of course be exposed to more accidents by the way. This resolution being taken they decamped. Cæsar sent the cavalry before, to harass and retard them in their march; and followed himself with the rest of the army. The cavalry gave the enemy no respite, being continually engaged with their rear.

LXXI. The manner of fighting was thus:—Some light-armed cohorts formed the rearguard, which, in a plain, halted from time to time, and made head against our cavalry. When they fell in with an eminence, the very nature of the ground furnished them with the means of defending themselves, because those who were first could cover them behind. But when a valley or descent came in the way, the van could give no assistance to the rear, and our cavalry annoyed them with their darts from the higher ground, which put them in imminent danger. In this case, the legions were obliged to halt, and endeavour to drive back the cavalry a good way, after which they ran down the valley precipitately, until they came to the opposite eminence. For their cavalry, of which they had a considerable number, was so terrified by their ill success in former skirmishes, that, far from being of any service, they were forced to place it in the centre to secure it; and if any of them chanced to straggle from the main body, they were immediately taken by Cæsar's horse.

LXXII. During these continual skirmishes, in which the enemy were often obliged to halt, in order to disengage their rear, it is easy to perceive that their march could not be very expeditious. This was in fact the case; so that after advancing four miles, finding themselves greatly incommoded by the cavalry, they halted on an eminence, and drew a line before them, as it were to encamp, but did not unload their beasts of burden. When they saw that Cæsar had marked out his camp, pitched his tents, and sent his cavalry to forage; suddenly, towards noon, they resumed their march briskly, hoping to be rid of the cavalry which had so much incommoded them. But Cæsar set out immediately with his legions, leaving a few cohorts to guard the baggage, and sent orders to his cavalry to return with all diligence. The cavalry returned accordingly, and having overtaken the enemy before the close of day, attacked their rear so vigorously, that they were almost routed, a great number of soldiers, and even some centurions, being slain. Cæsar's whole army came up, and threatened them with an immediate attack.

LXXIII. As they could then neither choose a proper place for a camp, nor continue their march, they were forced to halt where they were, far from any water, and on very disadvantageous ground. Cæsar did not offer to attack them, for the reasons mentioned before; he would not even permit any tents to be pitched that day, that he might be the readier to pursue with all his forces, should they attempt to escape either by night or by day. The Afranians perceiving the disadvantage of their situation, employed the whole night in throwing up intrenchments, and disposed their camp directly fronting ours. The same they did the following day, from sun-rise till evening. But the farther they extended their camp, and produced their lines, in order to better their position, the farther they went from water, and to avoid one inconvenience, fell into another. The first night nobody went out of the camp for water, and the next day the whole army was obliged to do it in order of battle, so that they could not forage that day. Cæsar wanted to humble them by these misfortunes, and reduce them by want and necessity rather than force. He began, however, to draw lines round the camp, the better to check their sudden sallies and irruptions, to which he foresaw they would be obliged to have recourse at last. Want,

and the desire of marching with less difficulty, soon constrained them to kill all the beasts of burden.

LXXIV. Two days were spent in forming and executing those resolutions; on the third, Cæsar had considerably advanced his works. Afranius and Petreius, sensible of the consequences, drew all their forces out of the camp, and formed them in order of battle. Cæsar previously called in his workmen, assembled his cavalry, and put his army in a condition to receive them, for he was aware of the hurt his reputation might sustain, if, contrary to the opinion of the troops, and the earnest expectations of all, he should still seem to decline an engagement. However, for the reasons already mentioned, he resolved to keep only upon the defensive; and the rather, because the distance between the two camps was so small, that should he even put his adversaries to rout, he could not flatter himself with the hopes of a complete victory. In fact, from camp to camp was not above two thousand feet; the armies were posted on each side of this space, which was left void for the mutual charge and assault of the soldiers. On supposition therefore of a battle, the nearness of their camp furnished an easy retreat to the vanquished. For this reason he resolved to wait the enemy's charge, and not enter the first into action.

LXXV. Afranius's troops were ranged in two lines, consisting of five legions, and the cohorts went to be stationed in the wings formed a body of reserve. Cæsar's army was upon three lines; in the first of which were posted four cohorts, detached out of each of the five legions; in the second three; and in the third the like number, all from their respective legions: the archers and slingers were disposed in the midst, and the cavalry on the two wings. The armies being drawn up in this manner, each general kept firm to his resolution; Cæsar, not to engage, unless forced to it; and Afranius, to prevent the progress of our works. In this posture they continued till sun-set, when both armies returned to their several camps. The next day, Cæsar prepared to finish his lines; and Pompey's lieutenants, as their last resource, endeavoured to find a fordable place in the Sicoris. But Cæsar, penetrating their design, sent his light-armed Germans, with part of his cavalry, over the river, and posted many good bodies of troops along the banks, at a small distance from one another.

LXXVI. At last, having no hope left, and being in want of every thing, wood, water, forage, corn, they demanded an interview, and that it might be, if possible, in some place out of the sight of the soldiers. Cæsar denied the last part of their request, but offered to grant them a public interview; whereupon Afranius, having given his son for a hostage, went to the place appointed by Cæsar, where, in the presence of both armies, he addressed him to this effect: "That it was no just matter of blame, either in him or his soldiers, to have preserved their fidelity to their general, Pompey; but that they had now sufficiently acquitted themselves of their duty, and suffered **enough in** his cause, by the want **of all** kind **of necessaries: that** like wild **beasts caught in a toil, they were** deprived of **the most common enjoyments, having** their bodies oppressed **by want,** and their minds overwhelmed with **ignominy,** that they therefore acknowledged themselves vanquished, and besought and conjured him, not to make a rigorous use of his victory, but to spare the lives of his unhappy countrymen." This speech was delivered with all possible marks of humility and submission.

LXXVII. Cæsar replied, "That he of all mankind, had least reason to complain, or implore compassion: that all the rest had fully done their duty; himself, in forbearing to at**tack** him, with all the advantages of time and place, that the way to an accommodation might be the more open; his army, in returning un**touched,** the men that were in their power, **after** injuries received, **and the massacre of** their comrades: **in fine, even his** own troops, in endeavouring to conclude a peace, whereon they thought their safety depended. Thus all orders had shown an inclination to treat, while Afranius **and Petreius** alone opposed an accommodation, **refusing** both **interview** and truce, and barbarously murdering those whom the faith of a conference had enticed to their camp: that it had therefore happened to them, as frequently happens to men of obstinacy and arrogance, and they were forced to have recourse to those conditions, and earnestly solicit the very same terms, which not long before they had despised. However, he would not take advantage of their present submission, or the favourable circumstances in **which** he found himself, to demand any thing tending to the increase of his own power, but only that they would disband those troops which they had now for so many years kept on foot against him. For with what other view had six legions been sent into Spain; a seventh levied there, so many powerful navies equipped, so many able and experienced officers sent over? These mighty preparations could not be meant against Spain, or to supply the wants of the province, which having enjoyed a long run of peace, had no occasion for such extraordinary forces. Their real **aim was to** pave the way **to his destruction; to effect** which, a new species of power **had been** introduced into the commonwealth, **and the** same man appointed to command in **Italy, at** the gates of Rome, and hold for so many years, though absent, the government of the two most potent provinces of the republic. For this reason the magistrates were stripped of their prerogatives, and not suffered to take possession of their provinces, at the expiration of the pretorship or consulship, as had always been the custom: but particular governors were sent, by the choice and management of a faction. For this reason even the excuse of old age was disallowed; and those who had merited a discharge by their past services, were compelled to take arms again, to complete the number of their troops. In fine, for this reason, he alone had been denied that justice, which was never refused to any general before him; that after having successfully served the commonwealth, he should be allowed to return home, and disband his own army, with some marks of honour, or at least without ignominy. All which, nevertheless, he had hitherto borne, and still resolved to bear with patience; nor was it now his design, to take from them their soldiers, and enlist them, as it would be easy for him to do, but to prevent their employing them against him. Therefore, as he had already intimated, they must resolve to quit Spain, and disband their forces, in which case he would injure no man. This was his final resolution, and the only condition of peace they were to expect."

LXXVIII. These conditions were agreeable to Afranius's soldiers, who, instead of being punished, as they feared, were in some sort rewarded by the discharge procured them. They plainly showed their satisfaction. Fo-while the place and time of their dismission were debating, they signified by their gestures and cries from the rampart, where they stood, that they desired to be disbanded immediately; because no sufficient security could be given for the performance of what was put off till another time. After some discussion of that **article** by Cæsar and Afranius, it was regulated, that those who had houses or possessions in Spain, should be discharged on the spot; and the rest near the Var, a river between Gaul and Italy. Cæsar, on his side, declared that he would hurt nobody, nor force any one to take on in his service.

LXXIX. Cæsar undertook to find them in corn until they got to the Var. He even promised to restore to them all they had lost in the war, that could be known again: himself indemnifying his own soldiers, who hereby lost part of their booty. By **this** conduct he acquired their confidence to such a degree, that he was arbiter of all the disputes they had, either among themselves, or with their commanders. The soldiers being ready to mutiny about their pay, because Petreius and Afranius affirmed it was not yet due, the matter was referred to Cæsar, who determined it to the satisfaction of both parties. About a third of the army was disbanded during the two days they continued here, after which the rest set out for the Var in this order. Two of Cæsar's legions marched at the head, the others in the rear, and the vanquished troops in the middle. Q. Fufius Calenus, one of Cæsar's lieutenants, presided over the march. In this manner they continued their route to the Var, where the remainder of the troops were disbanded.

CÆSAR'S COMMENTARIES

OF

THE CIVIL WAR.

BOOK II.

THE ARGUMENT.

Trebonius continues the siege of Marseilles.—III. Nasidius arrives with a fleet to the relief of the town.—IV. The inhabitants repair their fleet, and join it to that of Nasidius.—V. A sea fight between Brutus and the people of Marseilles.—VI. In which the latter are defeated.—VIII. Trebonius raises a prodigious tower against the town.—IX. Likewise a musculus of uncommon size.—X. By which a tower belonging to the enemy is overthrown.—XI. Upon this the besieged demand a truce.—XIII. Which they afterwards break, and in a sudden sally burn Trebonius's works.—XIV. Trebonius, with wonderful expedition, raises a new and amazing terrace.—XV. Upon which the besieged again treat of a surrender.—XVI. Meanwhile M. Varro, in farther Spain, prepares to oppose Cæsar.—XVII. Cæsar summons a general assembly of the states at Corduba.—XVII. Varro, deserted by his troops, goes over to Cæsar.—XIX. Cæsar having reduced Spain, arrives before Marseilles.—XX. The Marseillians surrender. L. Domitius escapes by sea.—XXI. About the same time, C. Curio sets out for Africa.—XXII. Where, at first, he wars successfully against Varus.—XXIV. But afterwards, Varus having received supplies from king Juba, he rashly ventures a battle, where, after some advantages in the beginning, by means of his cavalry, he is at last cut off with his whole army.

CÆSAR'S COMMENTARIES

OF

THE CIVIL WAR.

BOOK II.

I. WHILE these things passed in Spain, Trebonius, Cæsar's lieutenant, who had been left to carry on the siege of Marseilles, raised terraces for two different attacks, and approached with his towers and galleries. One of the attacks was on the side of the port; the other, towards the mouth of the Rhone, which empties itself into the sea, bordering upon Spain and Gaul. For Marseilles is washed by the sea on three sides, and can be approached by land only on the fourth; of which that part where the citadel stands, being very strong by nature, because of a deep valley that runs before it, requires a long and difficult siege. For the completing of these works, Trebonius drew together, from all parts of the province, a great number of workmen and beasts of carriage; ordered wood and osiers to be brought; and having prepared all things necessary, raised a terrace eighty feet high.

II. But so well was the town provided with all the requisites of war, and so great was the multitude of machines to annoy the besiegers, that no mantles were sufficient to withstand their violence. For they had wooden bars, twelve feet in length, armed at the point with iron, which were shot with such force from their balistæ, that they pierced four rows of hurdles, and entered a considerable way into the ground. To resist the violence of these batteries, the besiegers made use of galleries, whose roofs consisted of pieces of wood of about a foot in thickness, strongly compacted together. Under this cover, the materials necessary for raising the terrace were conveyed: and a tortoise, sixty feet long composed of strong beams, and armed with every thing necessary to defend it against fire and stones, went before, to level the ground. But in spite of all endeavours, the greatness of the works, the height of the wall and towers, and the multitude of machines made use of by the besieged, greatly retarded the approaches. Besides, the mountaineers made frequent sallies, and set fire to the towers and mount: which though our men easily sustained, driving them back with great loss into the town, yet failed not very much to incommode the works.

III. In the mean time L. Nasidius, sent by Pompey to the assistance of Domitius and the Marseillians, with a fleet of sixteen ships, some of which were strengthened with beaks of brass, passed the straits of Sicily unknown to Curio, landed at Messana, and raised so great a terror in the place, that being abandoned by the senate and principal inhabitants, he found means to carry off one of their gallies; and joining it to his own fleet, steered directly for Marseilles, having despatched a frigate before, to apprize Domitius and the inhabitants of his coming, and press them to hazard a second engagement with Brutus, when they should be reinforced by his fleet.

IV. The Marseillians, after their defeat, had drawn as many old ships out of the docks as they had lost in the engagement; and repaired and rigged them with wondrous expedition. They were likewise well provided with rowers and pilots; and had prepared a number of fishing barks, which they filled with archers and engines, and strengthened with roofs, to shelter the rowers from the enemy's darts. The fleet being equipped in this manner, the Marseillians, animated by the prayers and tears of their old men, matrons, and virgins, to exert themselves in defence of their country in so pressing a conjuncture; embarked with **no less confidence and** assurance, than they **had before their late defeat.** For such is the weakness **of the human mind, that** things dark, hidden, and unknown, always produce in us a greater degree of confidence or terror; **as** happened in the present case; for the arrival of Nasidius had filled all men with an uncommon share **of hope and eagerness.** The wind springing up **fair, they set sail,** and rendezvoused at Tauroenta, **a castle** belonging to the town, where Nasidius lay with his fleet. Here they put their ships in order, armed themselves with courage for a second encounter, and entering readily into all the measures proposed by Nasidius, left to him the command of the left wing, and stationed themselves upon the right.

V. Brutus sailed to meet them, with his fleet considerably increased; for besides the ships which Cæsar had caused to be built at Arles, he had also joined to it six more, taken from the Marseillians, which he had refitted and rigged since the late action. Wherefore exhorting his men to despise an enemy, who had not been able to resist them when entire and unvanquished, he advanced against them full of resolution and confidence. It was easy to discern from Trebonius's camp, and the eminences around it, what passed in the town. All the youth that were left, the old men, the women, children, and even the guards upon the walls, extending their hands to heaven, or repairing to the temples, and prostrating themselves at the altars, besought the gods to grant them victory. Nor was there a man among them who did not believe, that their safety depended wholly on the issue of that day's action. For the choice of their youth, and the most considerable men of their city, were all on **board the fleet:** insomuch, that in case of any disaster, they had no resource left; but should they obtain the victory, they were in hopes of preserving their city, either by their own forces, or the reinforcements they expected from without.

VI. Accordingly, in the engagement, they behaved with the **most** determined courage. The remembrance **of** what their wives and children had represented to them at their departure served to exalt their bravery; in a full persuasion, that this was the last opportunity they should have of exerting themselves in defence of their country; and that if they fell in the engagement, their fellow-citizens could not long survive them, as their fate must be the same upon the taking of the town. Our ships being **at** some distance from each other, **both gave the enemy's pilots** an opportunity of showing their **address in** working their vessels, and flying **to the** assistance of their friends, **when** they **were laid hold on by** our grappling hooks. **And indeed, when it** came to a close fight, they seconded **the moun-**taineers with **wonderful resolution, and, in** bravery, seemed to yield but little to our men. At the same time, a great quantity of darts, poured incessantly from their smaller frigates, wounded a great many of our rowers, and such of the soldiers as were without shelter. Two of their galleys fell upon that of Brutus, which was easily distinguished by its flag; but though they attacked him on both sides, he extricated himself with such agility and address, as in a short time to get a little before; which made them run foul of each other so violently, that they were both considerably shattered; one in particular had its beak broken, and was in a manner totally crushed; which being observed by those of our fleet that lay nearest, they suddenly fell upon and sunk them, before they could recover out of their disorder.

VII. In this **encounter, the** ships under Nasidius were of no manner of service to the Marseillians, but quickly **retired out of the** fight. For as they were neither animated by the sight of their country, nor the entreaties of their relations, they were not very forward to expose their lives to hazard, but escaped without hurt from the combat. The Marseillians had five ships sunk, and four taken. **One es-**caped to the coast of hither Spain, with those of Nasidius. Of the rest that remained, one was immediately despatched to Marseilles, to carry thither the news of the defeat. As soon as it drew near the town, all the inhabitants flocked out to know what had passed; and being informed of it, appeared no less dejected than if the city had been taken by storm. However, they still continued their preparations for the defence of the place with as much diligence as ever.

VIII The legionaries, who had the charge

of the works on the right, perceived, that a tower of brick, built at a little distance from the walls, would be of great service to shelter them from the frequent sallies of the enemy. At first they made it very low and small, to guard against sudden incursions. Hither they retired in case of danger: here they defended themselves against the most obstinate attacks of the enemy; nay, even assaulted them in their turn, repulsed, and pursued them. This tower was of a square form, thirty feet every way, allowing for the thickness of the walls, which might be about five feet. Afterwards, (being instructed by experience, which is the best of teachers,) they plainly perceived, that the higher it was carried, the more serviceable it would prove. The manner of effecting it was thus: When the work was raised to the height of one story, they laid a floor over it, the extremities of whose beams were concealed in the thickness of the wall; that they might not, by appearing on the outside, be liable to be set on fire. Thence they continued the wall directly upwards, as far as their galleries and mantles would allow. Here they laid two beams crosswise, whose extremities almost reached the angles of the wall, for supporting the floor, which was to serve as a roof to the whole. Over these beams they laid the joists of the roof, and boarded them with planks. The roof was so contrived as to project a little beyond the wall, in order to suspend from it what might be necessary to shelter the workmen, while employed in completing the story. This floor was paved with tiles and clay, to render it proof against fire, and had besides a covering of strong mattresses, to break the force of stones and darts. At the same time they suspended from the beams of the roof, that projected beyond the wall, curtains made of strong cables, woven to the depth of four feet, and which went round the three sides of the tower that were exposed to the engines of the enemy; having experienced on former occasions, that this kind of cover was impenetrable to any dart or engine whatever. When this part of the tower was finished, roofed, and sheltered from the enemy's blows, they removed their mantles to another, and by means of engines elevated the roof entire from the first story, as far as the curtains would allow. There, secure from all insult, they laboured at the wall, elevating the roof a second time, and thereby enabling

themselves both to continue the work, and lay the interjacent floors. In this manner they proceeded from story to story, mounting them one upon another, till, without danger or wounds, they had completed the number of six, leaving loop-holes in convenient places, for the engines to play through.

IX. When, by means of this tower, they thought they had sufficiently provided for the security of the works around it, they resolved to build a gallery sixty feet long, of wood, two feet in thickness, to extend from the brick tower to the tower of the enemy, and the very walls of the town. The form of the gallery was this:—First, two beams of equal length were laid upon the ground, at the distance of four feet from one another; and in these were fixed little pillars five feet high, joined at the top by beams designed to support the roof of the gallery. Over these were laid rafters, two feet square, fastened strongly with nails and plates of iron. The upper part of the roof was composed of square laths, four inches thick, which were placed at a small distance one from another, to bear the tiles that were to be laid upon them. Thus was the whole finished with a sloping roof, which being partly composed of tiles and mortar, was proof against fire, and had besides a covering of hides, to hinder the mortar from being washed away by spouts of water. Over all we threw strong mattresses, to screen the hides from fire and stones. This work was finished close by the brick tower, under cover of four mantles, and immediately carried forward upon rollers, in the manner ships are launched, till it unexpectedly reached the very tower of the enemy.

X. The Marseillians astonished at so threatening and unlooked-for a machine, pushed forward with levers the largest stones they could find, and tumbled them from the top of the wall upon the gallery. But the strength of the wood resisted the violence of their blows, so that they fell to the ground without doing any hurt. Observing this, they changed their design, and poured down upon us burning barrels of pitch and tallow. But these likewise rolled along the roof without damage, and falling upon the ground, were afterwards thrust away with forks and long poles. Meanwhile our soldiers, under protection of the gallery, were endeavouring with their levers to undermine the enemy's tower. The gal-

2 I

lery itself was defended by the tower of brick, whence our engines played without intermission; insomuch that the enemy, driven from their tower and walls, were at last obliged to abandon their defence. By degrees the tower being undermined, part of it fell down, and the rest was so shaken that it could not stand long.

XI. Upon this the enemy, alarmed at so unexpected a misfortune, discouraged by the downfall of the tower, awed by such a testimony of the wrath of the gods, and dreading the plunder and devastation of their city, came forth in the habit of suppliants, and with outstretched hands, besought the compassion of the army and generals. At this new and unexpected sight, all acts of hostility ceased, and the soldiers, laying aside their ardour for the fight, were eager to hear and get acquainted with the proposals of the enemy, who arriving in presence of the army and generals, threw themselves at their feet, requesting them to suspend all further operations till Cæsar's arrival. They told them: "That as the works were now completed, and the tower destroyed, they were sensible the city could no longer hold out, and therefore meant not to defend it: that in the mean time, no prejudice could arise to the besiegers from this respite, because, if they refused to submit upon Cæsar's coming, he would have it in his power to treat them as he pleased. They added, that if the whole tower should be brought down, it would be impossible to hinder the soldiers from yielding to the desire of plunder, by breaking into and pillaging the town." This, and much more of the same nature, (for the Marseillians are a learned people,) they urged in a very moving and pathetic strain.

XII. The generals, moved by these remonstrances, drew off the soldiers from the works, discontinued the attack, and contented themselves with posting guards in convenient places. Compassion occasioned a kind of truce till Cæsar's arrival; so that on neither side were any acts of hostility committed, but every thing was quiet and secure, as if the siege had been at an end. For Cæsar had earnestly recommended it to Trebonius, by letter, to prevent, if possible, the city's being taken by storm, lest the soldiers, irritated by their revolt, and the resistance they had found, should put all the youth to the sword, as they threatened to do. Nay, they were even then hardly restrained from breaking into the town, and loudly murmured against Trebonius for delaying a conquest which they looked upon as certain.

XIII. But the Marseillians, a nation without faith, aimed at nothing further in all this, than to find a time and opportunity to deceive us, and put in practice the treacherous purpose they had formed. For after some days, our men suspecting no danger, but relying upon the good faith of the enemy, while some were retired to their tents, others laid down to rest in the trenches, overpowered by the long fatigue they had undergone, and all the arms laid up and removed out of sight, suddenly they sallied from the town, and the wind being high, and favourable to their design, set fire to the works. The flame in a moment spread itself on all sides, insomuch that the battery, the mantles, the tortoise, the tower, the machines, and the gallery were entirely destroyed, before it was possible to discover whence the disaster arose. The suddenness of the accident made our men immediately run to their arms, where every one took what came first to hand. Some sallied out upon the enemy, but were checked by the arrows and darts poured upon them from the town; insomuch that the Marseillians, sheltered by their walls, burnt without any difficulty the tower of brick and the gallery. Thus the labour of many months was destroyed in an instant, by the treachery of an enemy, and the violence of the wind. Next day they made the same attempt, favoured by the same wind, and with yet greater assurance, against the tower and terrace of the other attack. They approached them boldly, and threw plenty of fire upon them; but our men, grown wise by their late misfortune, had made all necessary preparations for their defence, so that after losing many men, they were obliged to retreat into the city, without effecting their purpose.

XIV. Trebonius immediately resolved to repair his loss, in which he found himself warmly seconded by the zeal of the soldiers. They saw the works, which had cost so much labour and toil, destroyed by the perfidy of a people, who made no scruple of violating the most sacred engagements: they saw that their credulity had been abused, and that they were become the jest of their enemies, which grieved and provoked them at the same time. But it was still difficult to determine whence they might be supplied with wood, to repair all these works. There was none in the neighbour-hood of Marseilles, the trees having been all cut down for a great way round. They resolved therefore to raise a terrace of a new kind, and such as history no where mentions before that time. They raised two walls of brick, each six feet thick, and distant from one ano-ther, nearly the breadth of the former mount. Over these they laid a floor, and to render it firm, besides its being supported on either side, placed pillars underneath between the walls, to bear it up where it was weakest, or had a greater stress of weight to support. There were moreover cross beams, which rested upon niches in the wall; and to render the several floors proof against fire, hurdles were laid over them, which were afterwards covered with clay. The soldiers, thus sheltered over head by the roof, on the right and left by walls, and before by a breast-work, brought the necessary mate-rials without danger, and by the eagerness with which they laboured, soon completed the whole, leaving overtures in convenient places to sally out upon occasion.

XV. The enemy seeing we had repaired, in so short a time, what they imagined must have cost us the labour of many days; that there was now hope left, either of deceiving us, or sallying out upon us with success; that all the approaches to the city by land, might in like manner be shut up by a wall and towers, so as to render it impossible for them to appear upon their works, our walls over-topping and commanding theirs, that they could neither discharge their javelins, nor make any use of their engines, in which their principal hope lay : and that they were now reduced to the necessity of fighting us upon equal terms, though conscious of their great inferiority in point of valour; they were forced to have recourse again to the same conditions of truce they had so ill observed before.

XVI. M. Varro, in farther Spain, having early notice of what passed in Italy, and be-ginning to distrust the success of Pompey's affairs, spoke in a very friendly manner to Cæsar. He said, "That he was indeed under particular obligations to Pompey, who had made him his lieutenant-general, but at the same time was no less indebted to Cæsar: that he was not ignorant of the duty of a lieu-tenant employed by his general in an office of trust; but that he likewise knew his own strength, and the attachment of the whole

province to Cæsar." After this manner he talked in all companies, nor declared expressly for either side. But when he afterwards under-stood, that Cæsar was detained by the siege of Marseilles; that the armies of Petreius and Afranius had joined, and daily grew stronger by the arrival of new succours; that there was room to hope for every thing; that the hither province had unanimously declared in their favour; that Cæsar himself was reduced to great straits at Lerida, of all which Afranius wrote largely, magnifying his own advantages, he began to alter with fortune. He raised troops over the whole province; added thirty auxiliary cohorts to the two legions he had already under his command; formed great magazines of corn to supply Marseilles, and the armies under Afranius and Petreius; or-dered the Gaditani to furnish him with ten ships of war; caused a considerable number to be built at Hispalis; sent all the money and ornaments he found in the temple of Hercules to Cales; left there a garrison of six cohorts, under the command of Caius Gallonius, a Roman knight, the friend of Damitius, who had sent him hither to look after an in-heritance of his; conveyed all the arms, public and private, to Gallonius's house; spoke every where disadvantageously of Cæsar; declared several times from his tribunal, that Cæsar had been worsted, and that many of his soldiers had gone over to Afranius, as he was well as-sured by undoubted testimonies : by all which, having struck a terror into the Roman citizens of that province, he obliged them to promise him one hundred and ninety thousand sesterees, twenty thousand weight of silver, and one hundred and twenty thousand bushels of wheat. The states well affected to Cæsar he loaded with heavy contributions; confiscated the effects of such as had spoken against the commonwealth; quartered soldiers upon them; harassed them with arbitrary judgments; and in fine, obliged the whole province to take an oath of fidelity to himself and Pompey. Hear-ing of what had passed in hither Spain, he prepared for war. His design was, to shut himself up with his two legions in Cales, where all the provisions and shipping lay, be-cause he very well understood, that the whole province was in Cæsar's interest; for he judged it would be easy in that island, with the ships and provisions he had, to draw out the war into length.

XVII. Cæsar, though called upon by many and necessary affairs to return to Italy, resolved, however, not to leave Spain, till he had entirely quelled the war in that province; for he knew that hither Spain had many obligations to Pompey, and that most of the inhabitants were strongly in his interest. Having therefore detached two legions into farther Spain, under the command of Q. Cassius, tribune of the people, he himself advanced, by great journeys, at the head of six hundred horse. He sent orders before to the magistrates, and the principal men of every state, to meet him by a certain day at Cordova. All obeyed; every state sent his deputies; nor was there a single Roman citizen of any consideration, who did not repair thither on this occasion. The very senate of Cordova, of their own proper motion, shut their gates against Varro, stationed guards and sentinels along the walls, and detained two cohorts, called Colonicæ, which chanced to march that way, that they might serve to protect the town. At the same time those of Carmona, the most considerable state in the province, drove out of their city three cohorts, which Varro had left to garrison the citadel, and shut their gates against them.

XVIII. This determined Varro to make all possible despatch, that he might reach Cales as soon as possible, lest his march should be intercepted; so great and apparent was the affection of the province to Cæsar. When he was advanced a little way, he received letters from Cales, which informed him, "That as soon as Cæsar's edict was known, the principal men of Cales, with the tribunes of the cohorts he had left in garrison, had conspired to drive Gallonius from the city, and preserve the town and island for Cæsar; that this project being formed, they had warned Gallonius to retire of his own accord, while he yet might with safety; threatening, if he did not, to come to some immediate resolution against him: that Gallonius, terrified by so general a revolt, had accordingly left Cales." Upon this intelligence, one of the two legions, known by the name of Vernacula, took up their ensigns in Varro's presence, quitted the camp, and marched directly to Hispalis, where they sat down in the market-place and cloisters, without committing the least act of violence, which so wrought upon the Roman citizens residing in the town, that every one was desirous of accommodating them in their houses. Varro, astonished at these proceedings, turned back with design to reach Italica, but was informed that the gates were shut. At last, finding himself surrounded on all sides, and the ways every where beset, he wrote to Cæsar that he was ready to resign the legion under his command, to whomsoever he should order to receive it. Cæsar sent Sextus Cæsar to take the command; and Varro, having resigned the legion accordingly, came to him at Cordova. After giving him an account of the state of the province, he faithfully resigned all the public money he had in his hands, and informed him of the quantity of corn and shipping he had prepared.

XIX. Cæsar, assembling the states at Cordova, returned thanks severally to all who had declared in his favour: to the Roman citizens, for having made themselves masters of the town in his name; to the Spaniards, for driving out Pompey's garrisons; to the people of Cales, for having frustrated the designs of his enemies, and asserted their own liberty; to the military tribunes and centurions sent thither to guard the place, for having confirmed them in their resolutions by their example. He remitted the tribute imposed by Varro upon the Roman citizens; restored their estates to those who had been deprived of them for speaking their thoughts freely; distributed rewards to a great many, both in public and private, and gave all room to hope for like favours in the issue. After a stay of two days at Cordova, he went to Cales, where he restored to the temple of Hercules all the treasures and ornaments which had been carried off, and lodged in private houses. He committed the government of the province to Q. Cassius, assigned him four legions for that purpose; and embarking for Tarraco on board the fleet which Varro had obliged the Gaditani to furnish, arrived there in a few days. There he found deputies from almost all the states of the province, and having, in like manner as at Cordova, both publicly and privately rewarded some states, he left Tarraco, came by land to Narbonne, and thence to Marseilles. There he was informed of the law touching the dictatorship, and that M. Lepidus the pretor had named him to that office.

XX. The Marseillians, overwhelmed with

a profusion of calamities, reduced to the utmost distress by famine, worsted in two different engagements by sea, weakened by continual sallies, assaulted by a heavy pestilence, occasioned by the length of the siege, and their constant change of diet, (for they were obliged to feed upon old meal and musty barley, which had been long treasured up in their magazines against an accident of this kind,) their tower being overthrown, a great part of their walls undermined, and no prospect of relief from armies or the provinces, which were now all reduced under Cæsar's power, they resolved to surrender in good earnest. But some days before, Domitius, who was apprized of their intentions, having prepared three ships (two of which he assigned to his followers, and embarked in person on board the third,) took occasion during a storm to make his escape. Some of Brutus's galleys, which he had ordered to keep constantly cruising before the port, chancing to get sight of him. prepared to give chase. That in which Domitius was, escaped under favour of the tempest; but the two others, alarmed at seeing our galleys so near them, re-entered the port. Cæsar spared the town, more in regard to its antiquity and reputation, than any real merit it could plead. He obliged the citizens however to deliver up their arms, machines, and ships of war, whether in the port or arsenal; to surrender all the money in their treasury; and to receive a garrison of two legions. Then sending the rest of the army into Italy, he himself set out for Rome.

XXI. About the same time, C. Curio sailed from Sicily into Africa, with two of the four legions which had been put under his command by Cæsar, and five hundred horse; having conceived the highest contempt of the troops headed by P. Attius Varus. After two days and three nights sailing, he landed at a place called Aquilaria. This place is about twenty-two miles distant from Clupea, and has a very convenient harbour for ships in the summer time, sheltered on each side by a promontory. L. Cæsar, the son, waited for him at Clupea, with ten galleys, which P. Attius had taken in the war against the pirates, and repaired at Utica, for the service of the present war. But terrified at the number of ships Curio brought with him, he stood in for the coast; where, running his galley on shore, he left her, and went by land to Adru-

metum. C. Considius Longus commanded in that town, with one legion: and here also the rest of the fleet repaired after Cæsar's flight. M. Rufus the questor pursuing them, with twelve galleys, which Curio had brought with him from Africa, to guard the transports; when he saw Cæsar's own galley upon the strand, he towed her off, and returned with the fleet to Curio.

XXII. Curio ordered him to sail directly for Utica, and followed himself with the land army. After a march of two days, he arrived at the river Bagradas, where he left C. Caninius Rebilus with the legions, and advanced before with the cavalry, to take a view of the Cornelian camp, which was judged to be a situation extremely advantageous. It is a high rock, jutting out into the sea, steep and rough on both sides, but with an easier descent where it fronts Utica. It lies little more than a mile from Utica in a direct line; but as there is a fountain about half way, which runs towards the sea, and overflowing the plain, forms a morass; to avoid this, in marching to Utica, it is necessary to take a compass of six miles. When he had taken a view of this post, he went next and examined Varus's camp, which was under the walls of the town, towards the gate named the Gate of War. The situation of it was extremely advantageous; for on the one side it was covered by the city of Utica itself, and on the other by a kind of theatre, which stood without the walls, the works round which took up so much room, that they rendered the approach to the camp extremely difficult. At the same time he saw all the ways crowded with people, who, out of fear of being pillaged, were carrying their most valuable effects into the city. He detached the cavalry against them to disperse them, and likewise have an opportunity of making some booty. Upon which, Varus ordered six hundred Numidian horse to advance to their assistance, which he further strengthened with four hundred foot, sent by Juba, a few days before, to reinforce the garrison of Utica. This king inherited from his father an affection for Pompey, and besides personally hated Curio; who, during his tribuneship had published a law to deprive him of his kingdom. The Numidian cavalry soon came to blows with ours; but were not able to stand their first charge, retreating to their camp, **with the loss** of a hundred and twenty men.

22

Meantime, upon the arrival of Curio's fleet he ordered proclamation to be made among the merchant ships, which were at Utica, to the number of two hundred, that he would treat them as enemies, if they did not immediately repair to the Cornelian camp. Upon this proclamation, they instantly weighed anchor, and leaving Utica, sailed whither they were ordered; by which means the army was plentifully supplied with every thing they stood in need of.

XXIII. These things despatched, Curio repaired to his camp at Bagrada, where, with the joint acclamations of the whole army, he was saluted by the name of *Imperator*. Next day he led his army towards Utica, and encamped not far from the town. But before he had finished his entrenchments, he was informed by some parties of horse, who were upon the scout, that a powerful body of horse and foot had been sent by the king of Utica: at the same time a great cloud of dust began to appear, and soon after the enemy's van was in view. Curio, astonished at a motion so unexpected, sent the cavalry before to sustain their first charge, and keep them in play: he, meanwhile, drawing off the legions from the works, with all possible expedition, formed them in order of battle. The horse engaged, according to orders; and with such success, that before the legions could be duly drawn up, the whole reinforcement sent by the king, who marched without order or apprehension of danger, falling into confusion, at last betook themselves to flight. The cavalry, wheeling nimbly along the shore, escaped, with little loss, into the town; but great numbers of the infantry were cut to pieces.

XXIV. Next night, two centurions of the nation of the Marsi, with twenty-two private soldiers, deserted from Curio, and went over to Attius Varus. These, either believing the thing themselves, or desirous to carry grateful tidings to Varus, (for we easily believe what we wish, and readily hope that others will fall into our way of thinking,) assured him, that the whole army was extremely averse to Curio, and would infallibly revolt, if he would but advance, and come to a conference with them. Accordingly Varus drew out his legions next day. Curio did the same; and the two armies stood facing one another in order of battle, with a small valley between them.

XXV. Sextus Quintilius Varus, who, as we have related above, had been made prisoner at Corfinium, was now in the enemy's army: for Cæsar having granted him his liberty, he had retired into Africa. Curio had brought over with him from Sicily the very same legions, who had revolted some time before to Cæsar at the siege of Corfinium: so that excepting a few centurions who had been changed, the officers and companies were the same as had formerly served with this very Quintilius. He made use of this handle to debauch the army of Curio; "and began with putting the soldiers in mind of their former oath to Domitius, and to himself, that general's questor; he exhorted them not to carry arms against the old companions of their fortune, who had shared with them in all the hazards of that siege; nor fight in defence of that party, who treated them ignominiously, and as deserters." To these considerations, he added offers of a liberal recompense, if they would follow his fortune and that of Attius. But his speech made no impression upon Curio's troops, so that both armies retired to their respective camps.

XXVI. But an uncommon panic soon spread itself over Curio's camp, which the various discourses of the soldiers served only to increase. For every one had his opinion, and added the suggestions of his own fear to that which he heard from others. These reports spreading from one to many, and receiving additions in every new relation, there appeared to be several authors of the same notions: "That in a civil war it was lawful for every soldier to choose what side he pleased; that the same legion, who a little before had fought on the side of the enemy, might, without scruple, return again to the same cause, since Cæsar's conferring favours upon his enemies, ought not to render them unmindful of prior and greater obligations: that even the municipal towns were divided in their affection, and sided some with one party, some with another." These discourses proceeded not from the Marsi and Peligni alone, but ran like a torrent through the whole camp. However, some of the soldiers blamed their companions for this so great freedom of talk and others, who affected to appear more diligent than the rest, enlarged in their accounts of it to the officers.

XXVII. For these reasons, Curio summoning a council of war, began to deliberate about the proper remedies for this evil. Some were for attacking, at all hazards, the camp of Varus, in order to find employment for the soldiers, whose idleness they considered as the cause of all the present alarms. Besides, it was better, they said to trust to valour, and try the fortune of a battle, than see themselves abandoned by their men, and delivered up to the barbarity of the enemy. Others were for retiring, during the night, to the Cornelian camp, where they would have more time to cure the infatuation of the soldiers: and whence, in case of a disaster, they could, with more safety and ease, make good their retreat into Sicily, by means of the great number of ships they were there provided with. Curio relished neither of these notions: the one, he thought, argued cowardice; the other, a rash boldness: to retreat, would have all the appearance of a shameful flight; to attack, they must resolve to fight in a place of disadvantage. "With what hope," said he, "can we attack a camp fortified by nature and art? And what advantage can we draw from an attempt, whence we shall be obliged to retire with loss? Does not success always secure to a general the affection of his troops, whereas ill fortune is evermore followed with contempt? And what would a decampment imply but an ignominious flight, an absolute despair of all things, and an unavoidable alienation of the whole army? That we ought not to let the modest think we distrust them, nor the insolent that we fear them; because the knowledge of our fear only augments the presumption of the one, and an apprehension of being suspected, abates the zeal of the other. But if what is reported of the discontent of the army be true, which I am yet unwilling to believe, at least to the degree some pretend; we ought, for that reason, rather to hide and dissemble our fears, than by an unreasonable discovery of them, to add strength to the evil; that, as in some cases, it was necessary to conceal the wounds of the body, that the enemy might not conceive hope from our misfortunes; so also ought we to hide the indisposition of an army: that by retreating in the night, as some proposed, they would only furnish a fairer occasion to the ill-affected to execute their purpose: for fear and shame are powerful restraints by day, but night entirely divests them of their force: that he was neither so rash, as to attack a camp without hopes of success;

nor so blinded by fear, as to be at a loss what measures to pursue; that he thought it his duty to examine things to the bottom; and as he had called them together to deliberate upon the present state of affairs, doubted not, with their assistance, to take such measures as would be attended with success."

XXVIII. He then dismissed the council; and assembling the soldiers, put them in mind of what advantage their steadiness and zeal had been to Cæsar at Corfinium, and how serviceable towards the conquest of the greatest part of Italy. "It was you," said he, "that gave the example, and all the municipal towns soon followed: their submission to Cæsar was your work; and therefore it is not without reason, that he is so particularly attached to you, and that Pompey hates you sincerely. It was you that obliged him to quit Italy, without being forced to it by the loss of a battle. Cæsar, who ranks me in the number of his dearest friends, has committed my safety to your care, with Sicily and Africa, without which it would be impossible to defend either Rome or Italy. You are now in the presence of those who exhort you to abandon us: and indeed what could be more desirable to them, than at the same time to ensnare us, and fix upon you the stain of an infinite crime? What worse opinion could an enraged enemy testify of you, than to suppose you capable of betraying those, who own themselves indebted to you for all; and of throwing yourselves into the power of a party, who consider you as the authors of all their misfortunes? Are you strangers to Cæsar's exploits in Spain? Two armies defeated! Two generals overcome! Two provinces brought under subjection! And all this in the space of forty days! Is it likely that those, who, with forces unbroken, could not stand their ground, will be able to resist, now they are vanquished? And will you who followed Cæsar before fortune declared in his favour, now return to the vanquished, when fortune has already decided the quarrel, and you are upon the point of obtaining the reward of your services? They charge you with having abandoned and betrayed them, contrary to the faith of oaths. But is it indeed true, that you abandoned Domitius? Or did he not rather meanly abandon you, at a time when you were ready to suffer every thing for his sake? Did he not, unknown to you, resolve to seek his safety in flight! And were you not, after being thus basely betrayed by him, indebted to Cæsar's goodness for your preservation ? How could your oath bind you to one, who after throwing away the ensigns of his authority, and divesting himself of his office, surrendered himself a private man and a captive into the power of another ? The new engagement you were then brought under alone subsists at present, and ought quite to obliterate that, which the surrender of your general, and his loss of liberty, have made void. But though I doubt not of your being satisfied with Cæsar, you may perhaps have taken offence at me. And, indeed, I have no thought of mentioning any services I may have done you ; which, as yet, come far short of my intentions, and your expectations : but you are not ignorant, that the rewards of military service come not till after the conclusion of the war; and I believe you little doubt what the issue of this will be. Nor need I, on this occasion, decline taking notice of the diligence I have used, the progress already made, and the good fortune that has hitherto attended me. Are you dissatisfied that I have landed my army safe in Africa, without the loss of a single ship? That I dispersed the enemy's fleet at the first onset ? That within the space of two days I have twice defeated their cavalry ? That I forced two hundred of their merchantmen to quit the port of Utica and join me ? And that I have reduced them to a situation where it is impossible for them to receive any supplies either by land or sea ? Can you think of abandoning a cause conducted by such leaders, and attended with such success ; to follow the fortune of those who so ignominiously delivered up Corfinium, relinquished Italy, surrendered Spain, and have already sustained considerable losses in the African war ? I never pretended to more than being a follower of Cæsar : it was you that honoured me with the title of Imperator, which I am ready this moment to resign, if you think me unworthy of the favour. Restore me my former name, that it may not be said I was honoured, to be covered afterwards with the greater ignominy."

XXIX. These remonstrances made such an impression upon the soldiers, that they frequently interrupted him while he was speaking, and appeared deeply touched at his suspecting their fidelity. As he retired, they all gathered round him, exhorting him not to be discouraged, or scruple to hazard a battle, and make trial of their fidelity and bravery. This behaviour of the troops wrought so great a change in the minds of the officers, that Curio with the joint concurrence of them all, resolved to give battle the first opportunity that offered. Accordingly, drawing out his men next day, in the same place he had done for some time past, he ranged them in order of battle. Attius Varus did the same ; that if an opportunity offered, either of corrupting the soldiers, or fighting to advantage, he might be in readiness to lay hold of it.

XXX. Between the two armies lay a valley, as we have observed above, not indeed considerable for its breadth, but steep and difficult of ascent. Both sides waited till the other should pass it, that they might engage to more advantage. Curio observing that all the horse on Varus's right wing, together with the light-armed foot, had ventured down into this valley, detached his cavalry against them, with two cohorts of Marrucinians ; whose first shock the enemy were not able to sustain, but returned full speed to their own men, leaving the light-armed foot behind, who were surrounded and cut to pieces in the sight of Varus's army ; which, fronting that way, was witness to the flight of the one, and the slaughter of the other. Upon this Rebilus, one of Cæsar's lieutenants, whom Curio had brought with him from Sicily, on account of his consummate knowledge in the art of war ; " Why," says he, " do you delay seizing the favourable moment ? You see the enemy struck with terror." Curio made no answer, only desired his soldiers to remember what they had promised the day before, and marching the first, commanded them to follow him. The valley was so steep and difficult, that the first ranks could not ascend, but with the assistance of those that came after. But the Attinian army was so dispirited with fear, and the flight and slaughter of their troops, that they never thought of making resistance, fancying themselves already surrounded by our cavalry ; so that before we could arrive within reach of the dart, the whole army of Varus fled and retreated to their camp.

XXXI. In this flight, one Fabius Pelignus, a centurion of the lowest rank in Curio's army, as he was pursuing the fugitives, called with a loud voice to Varus as if he had been one of his own men, who wanted to admonish him of something. Varus hearing himself named several times, turned and stood still, demanding who he was, and what he wanted. Fabi aimed a blow at his breast with his sword, and would certainly have killed him, had not Varus warded it off with his shield. Fabius himself was soon after surrounded and slain. Meanwhile, the multitude of fugitives so closed up the gates of the camp, and pressed upon one another in such a manner, that more were crowded to death, than fell either in the battle or pursuit. Nay, the camp itself was very near being taken; because great numbers, instead of stopping there to defend it, made directly for the town. But both the nature of the ground, and the fortifications themselves, prevented the assault; and the rather, as Curio's soldiers being armed only for battle, had brought with them none of the necessary tools to force a camp. Curio brought back his army without the loss of a man, Fabius excepted. Of the enemy, about six hundred were killed, and a thousand wounded. After Curio had drawn off his men, all the wounded quitted the camp, and retired into the city, as did a great many others, who, overcome by fear, sheltered themselves there also under the same pretence. Varus observing this, and that a universal dread had seized the army, left only a trumpet in the camp, with a few tents for show, and, about midnight, silently entered the town with all his forces.

XXXII. Next day Curio resolved to besiege Utica, and draw a line of circumvallation round it. There was in the town a multitude of men unfit for the fatigues of war, through a long enjoyment of peace. The inhabitants themselves were strongly attached to Cæsar, for ancient favours received from him. The senate was composed of people greatly differing in their tempers, and the losses already sustained spread terror through all ranks. A surrender was publicly talked of, and all concurred in soliciting Varus not to ruin them by his obstinacy and perverseness. While these things were in agitation, messengers sent by king Juba arrived, who informed them of the approach of his army, and exhorted them to defend the city; which contributed not a little to confirm their wavering minds.

XXXIII. Curio received the same news, but for some time would not believe it, so greatly did he confide in his good fortune. Besides, Cæsar's success in Spain was already known in Africa; whence he concluded it improbable that Juba would attempt any thing against him. But when he was for certain informed

of his being within twenty-five miles of Utica with his whole army, he retired from before the town to the Cornelian camp, laid in great quantities of corn and wood, began to fortify himself, and sent directly to Sicily for the cavalry, and the two legions he had left there. The camp itself was very advantageous for protracting the war, being strong both by nature and art, near the sea, and abounding in water and salt, great quantities of which had been carried thither from the neighbouring salt-pits. Neither ran he any hazard of being straitened for wood and corn, as the country abounded in trees and grain. He resolved, therefore, with the consent of the whole army, to wait here the arrival of the rest of the troops, and make preparation for continuing the war.

XXXIV. This resolution being taken, and meeting with general approbation, some of the townsmen, who had deserted to Curio, informed him, that the war in which Juba was engaged with the Leptitani, having obliged him to return into his own kingdom, he had only sent his lieutenant Sabura, with a small body of forces, to the assistance of the Uticans. Upon this intelligence, to which he too hastily gave credit, he changed his design, and resolved to give battle. The fire of youth, his courage, good success, and self-confidence, contributed greatly to confirm him in this resolution. Urged by these considerations, about the beginning of the night, he sent all his cavalry towards the enemy's camp, which was upon the river Bagradas, and where Sabura, of whom we have spoken before, commanded in chief. But the king followed with all his forces, and was not above six miles behind him. The cavalry which Curio had detached, marched all night, and coming unexpectedly upon the enemy, attacked them before they were ready to receive the charge: for the Numidians, according to the custom of that barbarous country, were encamped without order or rule. Falling upon them therefore, in this confusion, and oppressed with sleep, they slew great numbers, and obliged the rest to fly in the utmost consternation; after which they returned to Curio with the prisoners they had taken.

XXXV. Curio had set out with all his forces about the fourth watch of the night, leaving only five cohorts to guard his camp. After a march of six miles he was met by his cavalry, who informed him of all that had passed. He asked the prisoners, who commanded at Bagradas? They answered, Sabura. Upon this, without making any further inquiries, for fear of being detained too long, he turned to the troops next to him, and said, "Do you not see, fellow-soldiers, that the report of the prisoners corresponds exactly with the intelligence given by the deserters? Juba is not with the army. It must consist of but a few troops, since they were not able to withstand the charge of a small body of horse. Haste, therefore, in the pursuit of glory, booty, and victory." What the cavalry had done was indeed considerable, because they were but few in number in comparison of the Numidians; but as vanity always makes us believe our merit to be greater than it is, they themselves boasted immoderately of the action, and endeavoured to enhance the value of it. They made a mighty parade of the booty. The prisoners too, as well infantry as cavalry, marched in procession before them. And indeed the whole army imagined, that to delay the battle, was no other than to delay the victory; so that the ardour of the troops perfectly seconded Curio's hopes. He therefore hastened his march, ordering the horse to follow, that he might as soon as possible come up with the frighted enemy. But as they were fatigued with their late march, they found themselves unable to keep pace with the army; but stopped, some in one place, some in another; which, however, retarded not Curio's hopes.

XXXVI. Juba having notice from Sabura of the action in the night, detached to his assistance two thousand Spanish and Gallic horse, of his ordinary guard, with that part of the infantry in which he put the greatest confidence. Himself followed leisurely with the rest of the troops, and about forty elephants, suspecting that Curio, who had sent the cavalry before, could not be far off with his army. Sabura drew up his horse and foot, ordering them to give ground upon the enemy's attack, and, as through fear, counterfeit a flight. Meanwhile he told them, that he would give the signal of battle when he saw proper, and direct their motions as the case might require.

XXXVII. Curio, flattered with new hopes, and imagining, by the enemy's motions, that they were preparing for flight, made his troops come down from the mountain into the plain; and advancing still farther, though his army was already very much fatigued,

having marched upwards of sixteen miles, halted at last to give the men breath. That moment Sabura sounded the charge, led on his men in order of battle, and went from rank to rank to animate the troops; but he suffered only the cavalry to come to blows, keeping the infantry at a distance within sight. Curio was not wanting on his side, but exhorted his men to place all their hopes in their valour. And indeed neither the infantry, though fatigued with their march, nor the cavalry, though few in number, and spent with toil, showed any want of valour, or backwardness to fight; though the last in particular did not exceed two hundred, the rest having stopped by the way. These, wherever they attacked the enemy, obliged them to give ground, but they could neither pursue far, nor drive their horses on with impetuosity. On the other hand, the Numidian cavalry began to surround our men, and charge them in the rear. When the cohorts advanced against them, they fell back, and by the quickness of their retreat, eluded the charge, but immediately returning, they got behind our men, and cut them off from the rest of the army. Thus it was equally dangerous for them to maintain their ranks, or advance to battle. The enemy's forces increased continually, by the reinforcements sent from the king; ours, on the contrary, were disabled by fatigue. Neither could our wounded men retire, or be sent to any place of safety, the whole army being invested by the enemy's horse. These despairing of safety, as is usual for men in the last moments of life, either lamented their own fate, or recommended their relations to their fellow-soldiers, if any should be so fortunate as to escape that danger. The whole army was filled with consternation and grief.

XXXVIII. Curio perceiving the general alarm, and that neither his exhortations nor prayers were regarded, ordered the troops to retire with the standards to the nearest mountains, as the only resource in the present exigence. But the cavalry detached by Sabura had already seized them. All hope being now lost, some were slain while endeavouring to fly; others threw themselves upon the ground, partly in despair, partly unable to make any efforts for their own safety. At this moment, Cn. Domitius, who commanded the horse, addressing Curio, entreated him to regain his camp with the few cavalry that remained, promising not to abandon him. "Can I," says Curio, "look Cæsar in the face, after having lost an army he had committed to my charge?" So saying, he continued fighting till he was slain. Very few of the cavalry escaped, those only excepted who had stopped to refresh their horses; for perceiving at a distance the rout of the whole army, they returned to their camp. All the infantry were slain to a man.

XXXIX. When this disaster was known, M. Rufus the questor, whom Curio had left to guard the camp, entreated his men not to lose courage. They begged and requested him to reconduct them into Sicily; which he promised, and ordered the masters of the transports to have their ships in readiness at night along the shore. But fear had so universally seized the minds of the soldiers, that some cried out Juba was arrived with his troops; some that Varus approached with the legions, the dust of whose march they pretended to discern; and others, that the enemy's fleet would be upon them in an instant; though there was not the least ground for these reports. The consternation thus becoming general, each man thought only of his own

safety. Those who were already embarked, sailed immediately, and their flight drew after it that of the transports; so that only a very few small frigates obeyed the summons, and came to the general rendezvous. The disorder was so great upon the shore, every one striving who should first embark, that many boats sunk under the crowd, and others were afraid to come near the land.

XL. Thus only a few soldiers and aged men, who either through interest or compassion were received on board, or had strength enough to swim to the transports, got safe to Sicily. The rest, deputing their centurions to Varus by night, surrendered to him. Juba, coming up next day, claimed them as his property, put the greater number to the sword, and sent a few of the most considerable, whom he had selected for that purpose, into Numidia. Varus complained of this violation of his faith; but durst not make any resistance. The king made his entrance into the city on horseback, followed by a great number of senators, among whom were Servius Sulpicius, and Licinius Damasippus. Here he stayed a few days, to give what orders he thought necessary; and then returned, with all his forces, into his kingdom.

CÆSAR'S COMMENTARIES

OF

THE CIVIL WAR.

BOOK III.

THE ARGUMENT.

CÆSAR'S COMMENTARIES

OF

THE CIVIL WAR.

BOOK III.

I. CÆSAR, as dictator, holding the Comitia, Julius Cæsar, and P. Servilius, were chosen consuls; for this was the year in which he could be elected to that magistracy, consistent with the laws. This affair being despatched, as Cæsar saw public credit at a stand over all Italy, because nobody paid their debts; he ordered that arbiters should be chosen, who should make an estimate of the possessions of all debtors, and should convey them in payment to their creditors, at the price they bore before the war. The regulation he thought best calculated to restore public credit, and prevent the apprehension of a general abolition of debts, which is but too common a consequence of wars and civil dissensions. At the same time, in consequence of an address of the people, he re-established the prætors and tribunes, who had been deprived upon a charge of bribery, at a time when Pompey awed the city by his legions. These decisions were so little conformable to law, that sentence was often pronounced by a party of judges different from those who attended the pleadings. As these had made him an offer of their service in the beginning of the war, he accounted the obligation the same as if he had actually accepted of their friendship; but thought it better their restoration should seem to flow from the people, than appear a mere act of bounty in him, that he might neither be charged with ingratitude to his followers, nor accused of invading the prerogatives of the people.

II. All this business, with the celebration of the Latin festivals, and the holding of the comitia for elections, took him up eleven days,

at the end of which he abdicated the dictatorship, and immediately set out from Rome, in order to reach Brundusium, where he had ordered twelve legions, with all the cavalry, to rendezvous. But he had scarce ships to carry over twenty thousand legionary soldiers, and six hundred horse, which alone hindered him from putting a speedy end to the war. Besides, the legions were considerably weakened by their many losses in the Gallic war, and the long and painful march from Spain; and an unhealthful autumn in Apulia, and about Brundusium, with the change of so fine a climate as that of Gaul and Spain, had brought a general sickness among the troops.

III. Pompey having had a whole year to complete his preparations, undisturbed by wars, and free from the interruption of an enemy, had collected a mighty fleet from Asia, the Cyclades, Corcyra, Athens, Pontus, Bithynia, Syria, Cilicia, Phœnicia, and Egypt, and had given orders for the building of ships in all parts. He had exacted great sums from the people of Asia and Syria; from the kings, tetrarchs, and dynasties of those parts; from the free states of Achaia, and from the corporations of the provinces subject to his command. He had raised nine legions of Roman citizens; five he had brought with him from Italy; one had been sent him from Sicily, consisting wholly of veterans, and called Gemella, because composed of two; another from Crete and Macedonia, of veteran soldiers likewise, who, having been disbanded by former generals, had settled in those parts: and two more from Asia, levied by the care of Len tulus. Besides all these, he had great numbers from Thessaly, Bœotia, Achaia, and Epirus; whom, together with Antony's soldiers, he distributed among the legions by way of recruits. He expected also two legions that Metellus Scipio was to bring out of Syria. He had three thousand archers, drawn together from Crete, Lacedemon, Pontus, Syria, and other provinces; six cohorts of slingers; and two of mercenaries. His cavalry amounted to seven thousand; six hundred of which came from Galatia, under Dejotarus; five hundred from Cappadocia, under Ariobarzanes; and the like number had been sent him out of Thrace, by Cotus, with his son Sadalis at their head. Two hundred were from Macedonia, commanded by Rascipolis, an officer of great distinction; five hundred from Alexandria, consisting of Gauls and Germans, left there by A. Gabinius, to serve as a guard to king Ptolemy; and now brought over by young Pompey in his fleet, together with eight hundred of his own domestics. Tarcundarius Castor and Donilaus furnished three hundred Gallogræcians: the first of these came himself in person; the latter sent his son. Two hundred, most of them archers, were sent from Syria, by Comagenus of Antioch, who lay under the greatest obligations to Pompey. There were likewise a great number of Dardanians and Bessians, partly volunteers, partly mercenaries; with others from Macedonia, Thessaly, and the adjoining states and provinces; who altogether made up the number mentioned above. To subsist this mighty army, he had taken care to amass vast quantities of corn from Thessaly, Asia, Egypt, Crete, Cyrene, and other countries: resolving to quarter his troops, during the winter, at Dyrrhachium, Apollonia, and the other maritime towns, to prevent Cæsar's passing the sea; for which purpose, he ordered his fleet to cruise perpetually about the coasts. Young Pompey commanded the Egyptian squadron; D. Lælius and C. Triarius the Asiatic; C. Cassius the Syrian; C. Marcellus and C. Coponius the Rhodian; Scribonius Libo and M. Octavius the Liburnian, and Achaian; but the chief authority was vested in M. Bibulus, who was admiral of the whole, and gave his orders accordingly.

IV. Cæsar, upon his arrival at Brundusium, harangued his troops, and told them: "That as they were now upon the point of seeing an end of all their toils and dangers, they ought not to scruple at leaving their servants and baggage behind them in Italy, that they might embark with less confusion, and in greater numbers; putting all their hopes in victory, and the generosity of their general." The whole army testified their approbation of what was proposed, and called out that they were ready to submit to his orders. Accordingly having put seven legions on board, as we have before observed, he set sail the fourth of January, and arrived next day at the Ceraunian mountains: where, having found, among the rocks and shelves, with which that coast abounds, a tolerable road; and not daring to go to any port, as he apprehended they were all in the enemy's possession; he landed his troops at a place called Pharsalus, whither he brought his fleet, without the loss of a single ship.

V. Lucretius Vespillo and Minucius Rufus were at Oricum, with eighteen Asiatic ships: and Bibulus had a hundred and ten at Corcyra. But the first durst not hazard an engagement, though Cæsar was escorted by no more than twelve galleys, only four of which had decks; and Bibulus had not time to reassemble his sailors and soldiers, who were dispersed in full security; for no news of Cæsar's approach had reached those parts, till his fleet was seen from the continent.

VI. Cæsar having landed his troops, sent the fleet back the same night to Brundusium, to bring over his other legions and cavalry. Fufius Kalenus, lieutenant-general, had the charge of this expedition, with orders to use the utmost despatch. But setting sail too late, he lost the benefit of the wind, which offered fair all night, and fell in with the enemy. For Bibulus hearing at Corcyra of Cæsar's arrival, forthwith put to sea, in hopes of intercepting some of the transports; and meeting the fleet as it returned empty, took about thirty ships, which he immediately burned, with all that were on board; partly to satisfy his own vengeance for the disappointment he had received; partly to deter the rest of the troops from attempting the passage. He then stationed his fleet along the coast, from Salona to Oricum, guarded all places with extraordinary care, and even lay himself aboard, notwithstanding the rigour of the winter; declining no danger nor fatigue, and solely intent upon intercepting Cæsar's supplies.

VII. After the departure of the Liburnian

galleys, M. Octavius, with the squadron under his command, sailed from Illyricum, and came before Salona. Having spirited up the Dalmatians, and other barbarous nations in those parts, he drew Issa to revolt from Cæsar. But finding that the council of Salona was neither to be moved by promises nor threats, he resolved to invest the town. Salona is built upon a hill, and advantageously situated for defence; but as the fortifications were very inconsiderable, the Roman citizens, residing there, immediately surrounded the place with wooden towers; and finding themselves too few to resist the attacks of the enemy, who soon overwhelmed them with wounds, betook themselves to their last refuge, by granting liberty to all slaves capable of bearing arms, and cutting off the women's hair, to make cords for their engines. Octavius perceiving their obstinacy, formed five different camps round the town, that they might at once suffer all the inconveniences of a siege, and be exposed to frequent attacks. The Salonians, determined to endure any thing, found themselves most pressed for want of corn; and therefore sent deputies to Cæsar to solicit a supply, patiently submitting to all the other hardships they laboured under. When the siege had now continued a considerable time, and the Octavians began to be off their guard, the Salonians, finding the opportunity favourable, about noon, when the enemy were dispersed, disposed their wives and children upon the walls, that every thing might have its wonted appearance; and sallying in a body with their enfranchised slaves, attacked the nearest quarters of Octavius. Having soon forced these, they advanced to the next; thence to a third, a fourth, and so on through the rest; till having driven the enemy from every post, and made great slaughter of their men, they at length compelled them, and Octavius their leader, to betake themselves to their ships. Such was the issue of the siege. As winter now approached, and the loss had been very considerable; Octavius, despairing to reduce the place, retired to Dyrrhachium, and joined Pompey.

VIII. We have seen that L. Vibullius Rufus, Pompey's chief engineer, had fallen twice into Cæsar's hands, and been as often set at liberty; the first time at Corfinium, the next in Spain. Having been therefore twice indebted to him for his life, and being also

much in Pompey's esteem, Cæsar thought him a proper person to negotiate between them. His instructions were: "That it was now time for both to desist from their obstinacy, and lay down their arms, without exposing themselves any more to the precarious events of fortune. That the losses they had already sustained ought to serve as lessons and cautions, and fill them with just apprehensions with regard to the future. That Pompey had been forced to abandon Italy, had lost Sicily and Sardinia, the two Spains, with about a hundred and thirty cohorts of Roman citizens, who had perished in these countries. That himself too had been a considerable sufferer by the death of Curio, the destruction of the African army, and the surrender of his forces at Corcyra. That it was therefore incumbent on them to show some regard to the sinking state of the commonwealth, having sufficiently experienced, by their own misfortunes, how prevalent fortune was in war. That the present moment was the most favourable in this respect; because, not having yet tried one another's strength, and considering them as equals, there would be more likelihood of agreeing on terms: whereas, if one of them once got the superiority, he would exact every thing from the other, and give up nothing. That as hitherto they had been unable to settle the conditions of peace, they ought to refer them to the decision of the senate and people of Rome; and, in the meantime, to obtain a free and unbiassed judgment, both swear to disband their armies in three days' time. That when they were once divested of their national and auxiliary forces, in which their whole confidence lay, they would find themselves under a necessity of submitting to the decree of the senate and people. In fine, that to give Pompey a proof of his readiness to perform these proposals, he would give immediate orders for the discharge of all his forces, both in garrison and in the field.'

IX. Vibullius having received these instructions, thought it necessary to give Pompey speedy notice of Cæsar's arrival, that he might be provided against that event, before he laid open the commission he was charged with. Accordingly, journeying day and night, and frequently changing horses, for the greater expedition, he at length got to Pompey, and informed him that Cæsar was approaching with all his forces. Pompey was at that time in Candavia, from whence he was march-ing through Macedonia, to his winter quarters at Apollonia and Dyrrhachium. Concerned at this unexpected news, he hastened his march to Apollonia, to prevent Cæsar's mak-ing himself master of the sea-coasts. Mean-while Cæsar, having landed his forces, marched the same day to Oricum. Upon his arrival there, L. Torquatus, who commanded in the town for Pompey, with a garrison of Parth-inians, ordered the gates to be shut, and the Greeks to repair to their arms, and man the walls. But they refusing to fight against the authority of the people of Rome, and the in-habitants, of their own accord, endeavouring to admit Cæsar, Torquatus, despairing of re-lief, opened the gates, and surrendered both himself and the town to Cæsar, who readily granted him his life.

X. Cæsar having made himself master of Oricum, marched directly to Apollonia. Upon tho report of his arrival, L. Staberius, who commanded in the place, ordered water to be carried into the castle, fortified it with great care, and demanded hostages of the towns-men. They refused to comply; declaring they would not shut their gates against the consul of the Roman people, nor presume to act in contradiction to the judgment of the senate, and of all Italy. Staberius finding it in vain to resist, privately left the place; upon which, the Apollonians sent deputies to Cæ-sar, and received him into the town. Bulli-denses, Amantiani, with the rest of the neigh-bouring countries, and all Epirus, followed their example; acquainting Cæsar, by their ambassadors, that they were ready to execute his commands.

XI. Meanwhile Pompey, having notice of what passed at Oricum and Apollonia, and being apprehensive for Dyrrhachium, marched day and night to reach the place. At the same time it was reported that Cæsar was not far off; which meeting with the more credit, because of their hasty march, put the whole army into such consternation, that many aban-doning their colours in Epirus and the neigh-bouring states, and others throwing down their arms, every thing had the appearance of a precipitate flight. But upon Pompey's halt-ing near Dyrrhachium, and ordering a camp to be formed; as the army had not even then recovered its fright, Labienus advanced before the rest, and swore never to abandon his gen-

eral, but to share in whatever lot fortune should assign him. The other lieutenants did the same, as likewise the military tribunes and centurions, whose example was followed by the whole army. Cæsar, finding that he was prevented in his design upon Dyrrhachium, pursued his march more leisurely, and en-camped on the river Aspus, in the territories of the Apollonians; that he might protect the possessions of a state, which had so warmly declared in his favour. Here he resolved to pass the winter in tents, and wait the arrival of the rest of his legions out of Italy. Pompey did the like, and having encamped on the other side of the Aspus, assembled there all his legions and auxiliaries.

XII. Kalenus having embarked the legions and cavalry at Brundusium, according to the instructions he had received, put to sea with his whole fleet; but had not sailed very far till he was met by letters from Cæsar, inform-ing him that all the Grecian coasts were guarded by the enemy's fleet. Upon this, he recalled his ships, and returned again into the harbour. Only one continued its route, which carried no soldiers, nor was subject to the or-ders of Kalenus, but belonged to a private commander. This vessel arriving before Oricum, fell into the hands of Bibulus, who, not sparing the very children, put all on board to death, both freemen and slaves. So much did the safety of the whole army depend upon a single moment.

XIII. Bibulus, as we have related above, lay at Oricum, with his fleet; and as he de-prived Cæsar of all supplies by sea, so was he, in like manner, greatly incommoded by Cæsar at land; who, having disposed parties along the coast, hindered him from getting water or wood, or coming near the shore. This was attended with many inconveniences, and threw him into great straits; insomuch that he was obliged to fetch all his other necessaries, as well as wood and water, from the island of Corcyra; and once, when foul weather pre-vented his receiving refreshments from thence, the soldiers were necessitated, for want of water, to collect the dew, which, in the night, fell on the hides that covered their ships. Yet he bore all these difficulties with surprising firmness, and continued resolute in his design of not unguarding the coast. But at last, be-ing reduced to the above-mentioned extremity, and Libo having joined him, they called from on board to M. Acilius and Statius Marcus, two of Cæsar's lieutenants, one of whom guarded the walls of Oricum, and the other the sea-coasts; that they wanted to confer with Cæsar about affairs of the greatest consequence, if they could but have an opportunity. To gain the more credit, they let fall some expressions that seemed to promise accommodation; and in the meanwhile demanded and obtained a truce; for Marcus and Acilius believing their proposals to be serious, knew how extremely grateful they would be to Cæsar, and doubted not but Vibullius had succeeded in his negotiation.

XIV. Cæsar was then at Buthrotum, a town over against Corcyra; whither he was gone, with one legion, to reduce some of the more distant states, and supply himself with corn, which then began to be scarce. Here, receiving letters from Acilius and Marcus, with an account of Libo and Bibulus's demands, he left the legion, and returned to Oricum. Upon his arrival, he invited them to a conference. Libo appeared, and made an apology for Bibulus: " That being naturally hasty, and bearing a personal grudge to Cæsar, contracted during the time of his edileship and questorship, he had, for that reason, declined the interview; to prevent any obstructions from his presence to the success of so desirable and advantageous a design: that Pompey was, and ever had been inclined to lay down his arms, and terminate their difference by an accommodation; but as yet had not sent him sufficient powers to treat; which, however, he doubted not soon to receive, as the council had intrusted him with the whole administration of the war: that if he would therefore make known his demands, they would send them to Pompey, who would soon come to a resolution upon their representations. In the meantime, the truce might continue, and both parties abstain from acts of hostility, till an answer could be obtained." He added something about the justice of their cause, and their forces, both natural and auxiliary; to which Cæsar neither at that time returned any answer, nor do we now think it of importance enough to be transmitted to posterity. Cæsar's demands were: " That he might have leave to send ambassadors to Pompey; and that they would either stipulate for their return, or undertake themselves to convey them in safety: that with regard to the truce; such were the

present circumstances of the war, that their fleet kept back his supplies and transports, and his forces deprived them of water and access to the shore. If they expected any abatement on his side, they must likewise abate in guarding the coast; but if they still persisted in their former vigilance, neither would he yield in what depended on him : that, notwithstanding, the accommodation might go forward without any obstruction from this mutual denial." Libo declined receiving Cæsar's ambassadors, or undertaking for their safe return, and chose to refer the whole matter to Pompey; yet insisted on the truce. Cæsar perceiving that the only aim of the enemy was to extricate themselves out of their present straits and danger; and that it was in vain to entertain any hopes of peace. turned all his thoughts to the vigorous prosecution of the war.

XV. Bibulus having kept at sea for many days, and contracted a dangerous illness by the cold and perpetual fatigue, as he could neither have proper assistance on board, nor would be prevailed upon to quit his post, he at last sunk under the weight of his distemper. After his death, nobody succeeded in the command of the whole fleet; but each squadron was governed, independently of the rest, by its particular commander.

XVI. When the surprise occasioned by Cæsar's sudden arrival was over, Vibullius, in presence of Libo, L. Lucceius, and Theophanes, who were among Pompey's most intimate counsellors, resolved to deliver the commission he had received from Cæsar. But scarce had he begun to speak, when Pompey interrupted him, and ordered him to proceed no further. " What," says he, " is my life or country to me, if I shall seem to be beholden to Cæsar for them? And will it be believed that I am not indebted to him for them, if he, by an accommodation, restores me to Italy?" Cæsar was informed of this speech, after the conclusion of the war, by those who were present when it was delivered : he still continued, however, by other methods, to try to bring about an accommodation.

XVII. As the two camps were only separated by the river Apsus, the soldiers had frequent discourse among themselves; and it was settled by mutual consent, that no act of hostility should pass during the conferences. Cæsar taking advantage of this opportunity, sent P. Vatinius, one of his lieutenants, to for

ward to the utmost an accommodation ; and
to demand frequently with a loud voice,
"Whether it might not be permitted to
citizens, to send deputies to their fellow citizens
about peace : that this had never been denied
even to fugitives and robbers, and could much
less be opposed, when the only design was to
prevent the effusion of civil blood." This and
much more he said, with a submissive air, as
became one employed to treat for his own and
the common safety. He was heard with great
silence by both parties, and received this
answer from the enemy : "That A. Varro
had declared he would next day appear at an
interview, whither the deputies of both parties
might come in perfect security, and mutually
make known their demands." The hour of
meeting was likewise settled ; which being
come, multitudes on both sides flocked to the
place ; the greatest expectations were formed ;
and the minds of all seemed intent upon peace.
T. Labienus, advancing from the crowd, began
in a low voice to confer with Vatinius, as if to
settle the articles of the treaty. But their discourse was soon interrupted by a multitude of
darts that came pouring in on all sides. Vatinius escaped the danger, by means of the soldiers, who protected him with their shields ;
but Cornelius Balbus, M. Plotius, L. Tibur-
tus, centurions, and some private men, were
wounded. Labienus then lifted up his voice,
and cried : "Leave off prating of an accommodation ; for you must not expect peace, till
you bring us Cæsar's head."

XVIII. About the same time, M. Cœlius
Rufus, pretor at Rome for foreign affairs,
having undertaken the cause of the debtors,
on his entrance into his office, ordered his
tribunal to be fixed near that of the city pretor,
C. Trebonius, and promised to receive the
complaints of such as should appeal to him, in
regard to the estimation and payments, made
in consequence of Cæsar's late regulation. But
such was the equity of the decree, and the
humanity of Trebonius, who, in so nice and
critical an affair, thought it necessary to conduct himself with the utmost clemency and
moderation, that no pretence of appeal could
be found. For to plead poverty, personal losses, the hardness of the times, and the difficulty
of bringing their effects to sale, is usual enough
even with reasonable minds : but to own themselves indebted, and yet aim at keeping their
possessions entire, would have argued a total

want both of honesty and shame. Accordingly
not a man was found who had made any such
demand. Cœlius's whole severity, therefore,
was pointed against those, to whom the inheritance of the debtor was adjudged ; and
having once embarked in the affair, that he
might not seem to have engaged himself to no
purpose in an unjustifiable cause, he published
a law, by which he allowed the debtors six
years for the discharge of their debts, which
they were to clear at equal payments, without
interest.

XIX. But the consul Servilius, and the
rest of the magistrates opposing the law, when
he found it had not the effect he expected, he
thought proper to drop that design ; and in
the view of inflaming the people, proposed two
new laws ; the one, to exempt all the tenants
in Rome from paying rents ; the other, for a
general abolition of debts. This bait took
with the multitude, and Cœlius at their head,
came and attacked C. Trebonius on his tribunal, drove him thence, and wounded some
about him. The consul Servilius reported
these things to the senate, who interdicted to
Cœlius the functions of his office. In consequence of this decree, the consul refused him
admittance into the senate, and drove him out
of his tribunal, when he was going to harangue the people. Overwhelmed with shame
and resentment, he openly threatened to carry
his complaints to Cæsar ; but privately gave
notice to Milo, who had been banished for the
murder of Clodius, to come into Italy, and
join him with the remains of the gladiators,
which he had bought formerly to entertain the
people with, in the shows he gave them. With
this view he sent him before to Turinum, to
solicit the shepherds to take arms, and went
himself to Casilinum : where hearing that his
arms and ensigns had been seized at Capua,
his partisans at Naples, and their design of betraying the city discovered ; finding all his
projects defeated, the gates of Capua shut
against him, and the danger increased every
moment, because the citizens had taken arms,
and began to consider him as a public enemy ;
he desisted from the project he had formed,
and thought proper to change his route.

XX. In the meantime Milo, having despatched letters to all the colonies and free
towns, intimating that what he did was in virtue of Pompey's authority, who had sent him
orders by Bibulus, endeavoured to draw over the

debtors to his party. But not succeeding in his design, he contented himself with setting some slaves at liberty, and with them marched to besiege Cosa, in the territory of Turinum. Q. Pædius the prætor, with a garrison of one legion, commanded in the town: and here Milo was slain by a stone from a machine on the walls. Cœlius giving out that he was gone to Cæsar, came to Thurium, where endeavouring to debauch the inhabitants, and corrupt by promises of money the Spanish and Gaulish horse, whom Cæsar had sent thither to garrison the place, they slew him. Thus these dangerous beginnings, that by reason of the multiplicity of affairs wherewith the magistrates were distracted, and the ticklish situation of the times, threatened great revolutions, and alarmed all Italy, were brought to a safe and speedy issue.

XXI. Libo leaving Oricum, with the fleet under his command, consisting of fifty sail, came to Brundusium, and possessed himself of an island directly facing the harbour, judging it of more consequence to secure a post, by which our transports must necessarily pass, than guard all the coasts and havens on the other side. As his arrival was unexpected, he surprised and burned some transports, and carried off a vessel loaded with corn. The consternation was great among our men, insomuch that having landed some foot, with a party of archers, in the night, he defeated our guard of cavalry, and had so far the advantage, by the commodiousness of his post, that he wrote Pompey word, he might draw the rest of the navy on shore, and order them to be careened; for he alone, with his squadron, would undertake to cut off Cæsar's supplies.

XXII. Antony was then at Brundusium, who confiding in the valour of the troops, ordered some boats belonging to the fleet to be armed with hurdles and galleries, and having filled them with chosen troops, disposed them in several places along the shore. At the same time, he sent two three-benched galleys, which he had caused to be built at Brundusium, to the mouth of the harbour, as if with design to exercise the rowers. Libo perceiving them advance boldly, and hoping he might be able to intercept them, detached five quadriremes for that purpose. At their approach, our men rowed towards the harbour, whither the enemy, eager of the pursuit, inconsiderately followed them: for now Antony's armed boats, upon a signal given, came pouring upon them from all parts, and on the very first onset took a quadrireme, with all the soldiers and sailors on board, and forced the rest to an ignominious flight. To add to this disgrace, the cavalry, which Antony had posted all along the coast, hindered the enemy from watering; which reduced them to such straits, that Libo was forced to quit the blockade of Brundusium, and retire with his fleet.

XXIII. Several months had now passed; the winter was almost over; meantime, neither the ships nor legions were yet arrived, which Cæsar expected from Brundusium. He could not help thinking that some opportunities had been lost, as it was certain the wind had many times offered fair, and there was a necessity of trusting to it at last. The longer the delay in sending over the troops, the more vigilant and alert were the enemy in guarding the coast, and the greater their confidence to hinder the passage; nay, Pompey in his letters frequently reproached them, that as they had not prevented the first embarkation, they ought at least to take care that no more of the troops got over; and the season itself was becoming less favourable, by the approach of milder weather, when the enemy's fleet would be able to act and extend itself. For these reasons, Cæsar wrote sharply to his lieutenants at Brundusium, charging them not to omit the first opportunity of sailing, as soon as the wind offered fair, and to steer for the coast of Apollonia, which they could approach with less danger, as it was not so strictly guarded by the enemy, who were afraid of venturing on a coast so ill provided with havens.

XXIV. The lieutenants, roused and emboldened by these letters, and encouraged by the exhortations of the troops themselves, who professed they were ready to face any danger for Cæsar's sake, embarked under the direction of M. Antony and Fufius Kalenus, and setting sail with the wind at south, passed Apollonia and Dyrrhachium next day. Being descried from the continent, C. Coponius, who commanded the Rhodian squadron at Dyrrhachium, put out to sea, and the wind slackening upon our fleet, it was near falling into the hands of the enemy: but a fresh gale springing up at south, saved us from that danger. Coponius however desisted not from the pursuit, hoping by the labour and perseverance of the mariners, to surmount the violence of the tempest; and though we had passed Dyrrhachium with a very hard gale, still continued to follow us. Our men, apprehensive of an attack, should the wind again chance to slacken, seized an advantage fortune threw in their way, and put into the port of Nyphæum, about three miles beyond Lissus. This port is sheltered from the south-west wind, but lies open to the south; but they preferred the hazard they might be exposed to by the tempest, to that of fighting. At that instant, by an unusual piece of good fortune, the wind, which for two days had blown from the south, changed to the south west. This was a sudden and favourable turn; for the fleet so lately in danger from the enemy, was sheltered in a safe commodious port: and that which threatened ours with destruction, was in its turn exposed to the utmost peril. By this unexpected change, the storm, which protected our fleet, beat so furiously on the Rhodian galleys, that they were all, to the number of sixteen, broken to pieces against the shore. Most of the soldiers and mariners perished among the rocks: the rest were taken up by our men, and sent by Cæsar's orders to their several homes.

XXV. Two of our transports, unable to keep up with the rest, were overtaken by the night: and not knowing where the fleet had put in, cast anchor over against Lissus. Otacilius Crassus, who commanded in the place, sent out some boats and small vessels to attack them: at the same time he urged them to surrender, promising quarter to such as would submit. One of these vessels carried two hundred and twenty new-raised soldiers; the other less than two hundred veterans. On this occasion appeared, how great a defence against danger results from firmness of mind. The new levies, frighted at the number of their adversaries, and fatigued with sea-sickness, surrendered on promise of their lives. But when they were brought to Otacilius, regardless of the oath he had taken, he ordered them all to be cruelly slain in his presence. The veterans, on the contrary, though they had both the storm and a leaky vessel to struggle with, abated nothing of their wonted bravery: but having spun out the time till night under pretence of treating, obliged the pilot to run the vessel ashore, where finding an advantageous post, they continued the remainder of the night. At day-break, Otacilius detached against them

about four hundred horse, who guarded that part of the coast, and pursued them sword in hand; but they defended themselves with great bravery, and having slain some of the enemy, rejoined, without loss, the rest of the troops.

XXVI. Upon this the Roman citizens inhabiting Lissus, to whom Cæsar had before made a grant of the town, after fortifying it with great care, opened their gates to Antony, and furnished him with every thing he stood in need of. Otacilius, dreading the consequences of this revolution, quitted the place, and fled to Pompey. Antony having landed his troops, which consisted of three veteran legions, one new raised, and eight hundred horse, sent most of the transports back again to Brundusium, to bring over the rest of the foot and cavalry; retaining, nevertheless, some ships of Gaulish structure, that if Pompey, imagining Italy destitute of troops, should attempt to run thither, as was commonly rumoured, Cæsar might be able to follow him. At the same time he gave Cæsar speedy notice of the number of forces he had brought over with him, and the place where he had landed.

XXVII. This intelligence reached Cæsar and Pompey much about the same time; for both had seen the fleet pass Apollonia and Dyrrhachium, and had in consequence directed their march that way; but neither knew, for some days, into what harbour it had put. On the first news of Antony's landing, the two generals took different resolutions; Cæsar, to join him as soon as possible; Pompey, to oppose his march, and, if possible, draw him into an ambuscade. Both quitted their camps on the Apsus about the same time; Pompey, privately, during the night; Cæsar, publicly, by day. But Cæsar, who had the river to cross, was obliged to fetch a compass, that he might come at a ford. Pompey, on the other hand, having nothing to obstruct his march, advanced by great journeys against Antony; and, understanding that he was not far off, posted his troops on an advantageous ground, ordering them to keep within their camp, and light no fires, that his approach might not be perceived. But Antony, being informed of it by the Greeks, would not stir out of his lines, and sending immediate notice to Cæsar, was joined by him next day. On advice of Cæsar's arrival, Pompey, that he might not be shut up between two armies, quitted the place, and coming with all his forces to Asparagium, a town belonging to the Dyrrhachians, encamped there on an advantageous ground.

XXVIII. About the same time Scipio, notwithstanding some checks he had received near Mount Amanus, assumed the title of emperor, after which he exacted great sums of money from the neighbouring states and princes; obliged the farmers of the revenue to pay the two years' taxes, which lay in their hands, and advance a third by way of loan, and sent orders to the whole province for levying cavalry. Having got a sufficient number together, he quitted the Parthians, his nearest enemies, who not long before had slain M. Crassus, and held Bibulus invested; and marched out of Syria with his legions and cavalry. When he arrived in Asia Minor, he found the whole country filled with terror on account of the Parthian war; and the soldiers themselves declared, that they were ready to march against an enemy, but would never bear arms against a consul, and their fellow-citizens. To stifle these discontents, he made considerable presents to the troops, quartered them in Pergamus and other rich towns, and gave up the whole country to their discretion. Meanwhile the money demanded of the province was levied with great rigour, and various pretences were devised, to serve as a ground to new exactions. Slaves and freemen were subject to a capitation tax. Imports were laid upon pillars and doors of houses. Corn, soldiers, mariners, arms, engines, carriages, in a word, every thing that had a name, furnished a sufficient handle for extorting money. Governors were appointed not only over towns, but over villages and castles; and he that acted with the greatest rigour and cruelty, was accounted the worthiest man and best citizen. The province swarmed with lictors, overseers, and collectors, who, besides the sums imposed by public authority, exacted money likewise on their own account, colouring the iniquitous demands with a pretence that they had been expelled their country and native homes, and were in extreme want of every thing. Add to all these calamities, immoderate usury, an evil almost inseparable from war; for so great sums are then exacted, beyond what a country is able to furnish, they are obliged to apply for a delay, which at any price is still accounted a favour. Thus the debts of the province increased considerably

during these two years. Nor were the Roman citizens the only sufferers on this occasion; for certain sums were demanded of every state and corporation, as a loan upon the senate's decree; and the farmers of the revenue were ordered to advance the next year's tribute, in like manner as when they first entered upon office. Besides all this, Scipio gave orders for seizing the treasures of the temple of Diana at Ephesus, with all the statues of that goddess. But when he came to the temple, attended by many persons of senatorian rank, he received letters from Pompey, desiring him to lay aside all other concerns, and make what haste he could to join him, because Cæsar had passed into Greece with his whole army. In consequence of this order, he sent back the senators who had been summoned to attend him at Ephesus, made preparations for passing into Macedonia, and began his march a few days after. Thus the Ephesian treasures escaped being plundered.

XXIX. Cæsar having joined Antony's army, and recalled the legion he had left at Oricum to guard the sea-coast, judged it necessary to advance farther into the country, and possess himself of the more distant provinces. At the same time deputies arrived from Thessaly and Ætolia with assurances of submission from all the states in those parts, provided he would send troops to defend them. Accordingly he despatched L. Cassius Longinus, with a legion of new levies, called the twenty-seventh, and two hundred horse, into Thessaly; and C. Calvissius Sabinus, with five cohorts, and some cavalry, into Ætolia; charging them in a particular manner, as those provinces lay the nearest to his camp, that they would take care to furnish him with corn. He likewise ordered Cn. Domitius Calvinus, with the eleventh and twelfth legions, and five hundred horse, to march into Macedonia: for Menedemus, the principal man of that country, having come ambassador to Cæsar, had assured him of the affection of the province.

XXX. Calvisius was well received by the Ætolians, and having driven the enemy's garrisons from Calydon and Naupactum, possessed himself of the whole country. Cassius arriving in Thessaly with his legion, found the state divided into two factions. Egesaretus, a man in years, and of established credit, favered Pompey; Petreius, a young nobleman of the first rank, exerted his whole interest in behalf of Cæsar.

XXXI. About the same time Domitius arrived in Macedonia; and while deputies were attending him from all parts, news came that Scipio approached with his legions, which spread a great alarm through the country; as fame, for the most part, magnifies the first appearances of things. Scipio, without stopping any where in Macedonia, advanced by great marches towards Domitius; but being come within twenty miles of him, suddenly changed his route, and turned off to Thessaly, in quest of Cassius Longinus. This was done so expeditiously, that he was actually arrived with his troops, when Cassius received the first notice of his march: for to make the more despatch, he had left M. Favonius at the river Haliacmon, which separates Macedonia from Thessaly, with eight cohorts, to guard the baggage of the legions, and ordered him to erect a fort there. At the same time, king Cotus's cavalry, which had been accustomed to make inroads into Thessaly, came pouring upon Cassius's camp; who, knowing that Scipio was upon his march, and believing the cavalry to be his, retired in a fright to the mountains that begirt Thessaly, and thence directed his course towards Ambracia. Scipio preparing to follow him, received letters from M. Favonius, that Domitius was coming up with his legions, nor would it be possible for him to maintain the post he was in, without his assistance. Scipio, upon his intelligence, changed his resolution, gave over the pursuit of Cassius, and advanced to the relief of Favonius. As he marched day and night without intermission, he arrived so opportunely, that the dust of Domitius's army, and his advanced parties, were descried at the same time. Thus Domitius's care preserved Cassius, and Scipio's diligence Favonius.

XXXII. Scipio continued two days in his camp upon the Haliacmon, which ran between him and the army of Domitius, put his troops in motion on the third, and by day-break forded the river. Early next morning he drew up his troops in order of battle at the head of his camp. Domitius was not averse to an engagement; but as between the two camps there was a plain of six miles, he thought that the fittest place for a field of battle, and drew up his men at some distance from Sci-

pio's camp. Scipio would not stir from his post; yet hardly could Domitius restrain his men from advancing to attack him through a rivulet with steep banks, that ran in the front of the enemy's camp, and opposed their passage. Scipio observing the keenness and alacrity of our troops, and fearing that next day he should either be forced to fight against his will, or ignominiously keep within his camp; after great expectations raised, by too hastily crossing the river, he saw all his projects defeated; and decamping in great silence during the night, returned to his former station, beyond the Haliacmon, and posted himself on a rising ground, near the river. A few days after, he formed an ambuscade, of cavalry, by night, in a place where our men were wont to forage: and when Q. Varus, who commanded the horse under Domitius, came next day, according to custom; suddenly the enemy rose from their lurking holes: but our men bravely sustained the attack, soon recovered their ranks, and in their turn vigorously charged the enemy. About fourscore fell on this occasion; the rest betook themselves to flight; and our men returned to their camp, with the loss of only two of their number.

XXXIII. After his rencounter, Domitius, hoping to draw Scipio to a battle, feigned to decamp for want of provisions: and having made the usual signal for retreating, after a march of three miles, drew up the cavalry and legions in a convenient plain, shrouded from the enemy's view. Scipio, preparing to follow, sent the horse and light-armed infantry before to explore his route, and examine the situation of the country. When they were advanced a little way, and their first squadrons had come within reach of our ambush; beginning to suspect something from the neighing of the horses, they wheeled about, in order to retreat; which the troops that followed observing, suddenly halted. Our men, finding that the ambush was discovered, and knowing it would be in vain to wait for the rest of the army, fell upon the two squadrons that were most advanced. M. Opimius, general of the horse to Domitius, was amongst these, but somehow found means to escape. All the rest were either slain, or made prisoners.

XXXIV. Cæsar having drawn off his garrisons from the sea-coast, as we have related above, left three cohorts at Oricum to defend the town, and committed to their charge the galleys he had brought out of Italy. Acilius, one of his lieutenants, had the command of these troops; who, for the greater security, caused the ships to be drawn up into the harbour behind the town, and made them fast to the shore. He likewise sunk a transport in the mouth of the haven, behind which another rode at anchor, on whose deck a tower was erected, facing the entrance of the port, and filled with troops, to be ready in case of surprise. Young Pompey, who commanded the Egyptian fleet, having notice of this, came to Oricum; weighed up the vessel that had been sunk in the mouth of the harbour; and, after an obstinate resistance, took the other, which had been placed there by Acilius, to guard the haven. He then brought forward his fleet, on which he had raised towers, to fight with the greater advantage; and having surrounded the town on all sides, attacked it by land with scaling ladders, and by sea from the towers, sending fresh men continually in the place of those that were fatigued, and thereby obliged us to yield, through weariness and wounds. At the same time he seized an eminence, on the other side of the town, which seemed a kind of natural mole, and almost formed a peninsula over against Oricum; and by means of this neck of land, carried four small galleys, upon rollers, into the inner part of the haven. Thus the galleys, that were made fast to the land, and destitute of troops, being attacked on all sides, four were carried off, and the rest burned. This affair despatched, he left D. Lælius, whom he had taken from the command of the Asiatic fleet, to prevent the importation of provisions from Biblis and Amantia; and sailing for Lissus, attacked and burned the thirty transports which Antony had left in that haven. He endeavoured likewise to take the town; but the Roman citizens of that district, aided by the garrison Cæsar had left, defended it so well, that at the end of three days, he retired without effecting his purpose, having lost some men in the attempt.

XXXV. Cæsar being informed that Pompey was at Asparagium, marched thither with his army; and having taken the capital of the Parthinians by the way, where Pompey had a garrison; arrived the third day in Macedonia, and encamped at a small distance from the enemy. The next day he drew out all his forces, formed them before his camp, and offered Pompey battle. Finding that he kept within his lines, he led back his troops, and began to think of pursuing other measures. Accordingly, on the morrow, by a long circuit, and through very narrow and difficult ways, he marched, with all his forces, to Dyrrhachium; hoping either to oblige Pompey to follow him thither, or cut off his communication with the town, where he had laid up all his provisions, and magazines of war; which happened accordingly. For Pompey, at first, not penetrating his design, because he counterfeited a route different from what he really intended, imagined he had been obliged to decamp for want of provisions; but being afterwards informed of the truth, by his scouts, he quitted his camp next day, in hopes to prevent him by taking a nearer way. Cæsar, suspecting what might happen, exhorted his soldiers to bear the fatigue patiently; and allowing them to repose during only a small part of the night, arrived next morning at Dyrrhachium, where he immediately formed a camp, just as Pompey's van began to appear at a distance.

XXXVI. Pompey, thus excluded from Dyrrhachium, and unable to execute his first design, came to a resolution of encamping on an eminence, called Petra, where was a tolerable harbour, sheltered from some winds. Here he ordered part of his fleet to attend him, and corn and provisions to be brought him from Asia, and the other provinces subject to his command. Cæsar, apprehending the war would run into length, and despairing of supplies from Italy, because the coasts were so strictly guarded by Pompey's fleet; and his own galleys, built, the winter before, in Sicily, Gaul, and Italy, were not yet arrived, despatched L. Canuléius, one of his lieutenants, to Epirus, for corn. And because that country lay at a great distance from his camp, he built granaries in several places, and wrote to the neighbouring states to carry their corn thither. He likewise ordered search to be made for what corn could be found in Lissus, the country of the Parthinians, and the other principalities in those parts. This amounted to very little; partly occasioned by the soil, which is rough and mountainous, and obliges the inhabitants often to import grain; partly because Pompey, foreseeing Cæsar's wants, had, some days before, ravaged the country of the Parthinians, plundered their houses, and, by means of his cavalry, carried off all their corn.

XXXVII. For these reasons, Cæsar formed a project which the very nature of the country suggested. All round Pompey's camp, at a small distance, were high and steep hills. Cæsar took possession of those hills, and built forts upon them; resolving, as the nature of the ground would allow, to draw lines of communication from one fort to another, and inclose Pompey within his works. His views herein were; first, to facilitate the passage of his convoys, which the enemy's cavalry, which was very strong and fine, would no longer cut off; next, to distress this very cavalry, for want of forage; and lastly, to lessen the great reputation and high idea entertained of Pompey, when it should be reported all over the world, that he had suffered himself to be blockaded, and, as it were, imprisoned by Cæsar's works; and durst not hazard a battle to set himself at liberty.

XXXVIII. Pompey would neither leave the sea and Dyrrhachium, where he had all his magazines and engines of war, and whence he was supplied with provisions by means of his fleet; nor could prevent the progress of Cæsar's works, without fighting, which, at that time, he was determined against. He could do nothing therefore but extend himself, by taking as many hills, and as large a circuit of country as possible, to give his adversary the more trouble, and divide his forces. This he did, by raising twenty-four forts, which took in a circumference of fifteen miles, wherein were arable and pasture lands, to feed his horses and beasts of burden. And as our men had carried their circumvallation quite round, by drawing lines of communication from fort to fort, to prevent the sallies of the enemy, and guard against the attacks in the rear; in like manner, Pompey's men had surrounded themselves with lines, to hinder us from breaking in upon them, and charging them behind. They even perfected their works first, because they had more hands, and a less circuit to inclose. When Cæsar endeavoured to gain any place, Pompey, though determined not to oppose him with all his forces, nor hazard a general action, failed not, however, to detach parties of archers and slingers; who wounded great numbers of our men, and occasioned such a dread of their arrows, that almost all the soldiers furnished themselves with coats of mail, or thick leather, to guard against the danger.

XXXIX. Both parties disputed every post with great obstinacy: Cæsar, that he might inclose Pompey within as narrow a space as possible; and Pompey, that he might have liberty to extend himself; which occasioned many sharp skirmishes. In one of these, Cæsar's ninth legion having possessed themselves of an eminence, which they began to fortify, Pompey seized the opposite mount, with a resolution to hinder their works. As the access on one side was very easy, he sent first some archers and slingers, and afterwards a strong detachment of light-armed foot, plying us, at the same time, with his military engines; which obliged our men to desist; as they found it impossible at once to sustain the enemy's charge, and go forward with their works. Cæsar, perceiving that his men were wounded from all sides, resolved to quit the place and retire. But as the descent, by which he must retreat, was pretty steep, the Pompeians charged him briskly in drawing off, imagining he gave way through fear. Pompey went so far as to say, That he consented to be accounted a general of no merit, if Cæsar's men got off without considerable loss. Cæsar, concerned about the retreat of his men, ordered hurdles to be fixed on the ridge of the hill fronting the enemy; behind which he dug a moderate ditch, and rendered the place as inaccessible as he could, on all sides. When this was done, he began to file off the legionary soldiers, supporting them by some light-armed troops, posted on their flanks, who, with arrows and stones, might repulse the enemy. Pompey's troops failed not to pursue them, with great outcries and fierce menaces, overturned the hurdles, and used them as bridges to get over the ditch. Which Cæsar observing, and fearing some disaster might ensue, should he seem to be driven from a post, which he quitted voluntarily; when his forces were got half down the hill, encouraging them by Antony, who had the command of that legion, he gave the signal to face about, and fall on the enemy. Immediately the soldiers of the ninth legion, forming themselves into close order, launched their darts; and advancing briskly up the hill against the enemy, forced them to give ground, and at last betake themselves to flight; which was not a little incommoded by the hurdles, palisades, and ditch, Cæsar had thrown up to stop their pursuit But our men who sought only to secure their retreat, having killed several of the enemy, and lost only five of their own number, retired without the least disturbance, and inclosing some other hills within their lines, completed the circumvallation.

XL. This method of making war was new and extraordinary; as well in regard to the number of forts, the extent of the circumvallation, the greatness of his works, and the manner of attack and defence, as on other accounts. For whoever undertakes to invest another, is, for the most part, moved thereto, either by some previous defeat he has sustained, the knowledge of his weakness, to take advantage of his distress, to profit by a superiority of forces; or, in fine, to cut off his provisions, which is the most ordinary cause of these attempts. But Cæsar, with an inferior force, besieged Pompey, whose troops were entire, in good order, and abounded in all things. For ships arrived every day, from all parts, with provisions; nor could the wind blow from any quarter, that was not favourable to some of them; whereas Cæsar's army, having consumed all the corn round about, was reduced to the last necessities. Nevertheless the soldiers bore all with singular patience; remembering, that though reduced to the like extremity the year before, in Spain, they had yet, by their assiduity and perseverance, put an end to a very formidable war. They called to mind too their sufferings at Alesia, and their still greater distresses before Avaricum, by which, however, they triumphed over mighty nations. When barley or pulse was given them instead of corn, they took it cheerfully; and thought themselves regaled when they got any cattle, which Epirus furnished them with in great abundance. They discovered in the country a root, called chara, which they pounded and kneaded with milk, so as to make a sort of bread of it. This furnished a plentiful supply; and when their adversaries reproached them with their want, by way of answer to their insults, they threw their loaves at them.

XLI. By this time, the corn began to ripen, and the hopes of a speedy supply supported the soldiers under their present wants. Nay, they were often heard to say one to another, that they would sooner live on the bark of trees, than let Pompey escape. For they were, informed from time to time, by deserters, that

their horses were almost starved, and the rest of their cattle actually dead; that the troops themselves were very sickly; partly occasioned by the narrow space in which they were inclosed, the number and noisome smell of dead carcases, and the daily fatigue to which they were unaccustomed, partly by their extreme want of water. For Cæsar had either turned the course of all the rivers and brooks that ran into the sea, or dammed up their currents. And as the country was mountainous, intermixed with deep valleys, by driving piles into the earth, and covering them with mould, he stopped up the course of the waters. This obliged the enemy to search for low and marshy places, and to dig wells, which added to their daily labour. The wells too, when discovered, lay at a considerable distance from some parts of the army, and were soon dried up by the heat. Cæsar's army, on the contrary, was very healthy, abounded in water, and had plenty of all kinds of provisions, corn excepted, which they hoped to be soon supplied with, as the season was now pretty far advanced, and harvest approached.

XLII. In this method of making war, new stratagems were every day put in practice by both generals. Pompey's soldiers, observing by the fires the place where our cohorts were upon guard, stole thither privately by night, and pouring upon them a flight of arrows, retired instantly to their camp, which obliged our men to have fires in one place, and keep guard in another.

XLIII. Meanwhile P. Sylla, whom Cæsar at his departure had left to command the camp, being informed of what passed, came to the assistance of the cohort, with two legions. His arrival soon put the Pompeians to flight, who could not stand the very sight and shock of his troops; but seeing their first ranks broken, took to their heels, and quitted the place. Sylla checked the ardour of his men, whom he would not suffer to continue the pursuit too far; and it was the general belief, that had he pursued the enemy warmly, that day might have put an end to the war. His conduct, however, cannot be justly censured; for the difference is great between a lieutenant and a general; the one is tied up to act according to instructions; the other, free from restraint, is at liberty to lay hold of all advantages. Sylla, who was left by Cæsar to take care of the camp, was satisfied with having disengaged his own men, and had no intention to hazard a general action, which might have been attended with ill consequences, and would have looked like arrogating the part of a general. The Pompeians found it no easy matter to make good their retreat; for having advanced from a very disadvantageous post to the summit of the hill, they had reason to fear our men would charge them in descending, and the rather, as it was very near sunset, for they had protracted the affair almost till night, in hopes of accomplishing their design. Thus Pompey, compelled by necessity, immediately took possession of an eminence, at such a distance from our fort, as to be secure from darts and military engines. Here he encamped, threw up an intrenchment, and drew his forces together to defend the place.

XLIV. At the same time we were engaged in two other places; for Pompey attacked several castles together to divide our forces, and hinder the forts from mutually succouring one another. In one of these, Volcatius Tullus, with three cohorts, sustained the charge of a **whole** legion, and forced them to retire. In the other, the Germans, sallying out of their intrenchments, slew several of the enemy, and returned again without loss.

XLV. Thus there happened no less than six actions in one day; three near Dyrrhachium, and three about the lines. In computing the number of the slain, it appeared that Pompey lost two thousand men, with several volunteers and centurions, among whom was Valerius Flaccus, the son of Lucius, who had formerly been prætor of Asia. We gained six standards, with the loss of no more than twenty men in all the attacks; but in the fort, not a soldier escaped being wounded; and four centurions belonging to one cohort, lost their eyes. As a proof of the danger they had been exposed to, and the efforts they had sustained, they brought and counted to Cæsar about thirty thousand arrows that had been shot into the fort, and showed him the centurion Scæva's buckler, which was pierced in two hundred and thirty places. Cæsar, as a reward for his services both to himself and the republic, presented him with two hundred thousand asses, and advanced him directly from the eighth rank of captains to the first; it appearing that the preservation of the fort was chiefly owing to his valour. He also distributed military rewards among the other officers and soldiers of that cohort, and assigned them double pay, and a double allowance of corn.

XLVI. Pompey laboured all night at his fortifications, raised redoubts the following days, and having carried his works fifteen feet high, covered that part of his camp with mantelets. Five days after, taking advantage of a very dark night, he walled up the gates of his camp, rendered all the avenues impracticable; and drawing out his troops in great silence about midnight, returned to his former works.

XLVII. Ætolia, Acarnania, and Amphilochis, having been reduced by Cassius Longinus, and Calvisius Sabinus, as we have related above; Cæsar thought it expedient to pursue his conquests, and attempt to gain Achaia. Accordingly he despatched Fufius Kalenus thither, ordering Sabinus and Cassius to join him, with the cohorts under their command. Rutilius Lupus, Pompey's lieutenant in Achaia, hearing of their approach, resolved to fortify the isthmus, and thereby hinder Fufius from entering the province. Delphos, Thebes, and Orchomenus, voluntarily submitted to Kalenus; some states he obtained by force, and sending deputies to the rest endeavoured to make them declare for Cæsar. These negotiations found sufficient employment for Fufius.

XLVIII. Cæsar meanwhile drew up his army every day, offering Pompey battle upon equal ground; **and,** to provoke him to accept it, advanced so near his camp, that his van was within engine-shot **of the** rampart. Pompey, to preserve his reputation, drew out his legions too, but posted them in such a manner, that his third line touched the rampart, and the whole army lay under cover of the weapons discharged from thence.

XLIX. Whilst these things passed in Achaia and at Dyrrhachium, and it was now known that Scipio was arrived in Macedonia, Cæsar still adhering to his former views of peace, despatched Clodius to him, an intimate friend of both, whom he had taken into his service upon Scipio's recommendation. At his departure, he charged him with letters and instructions to this effect: "That he had tried all ways to bring about a peace; but he believed he had hitherto miscarried, through the fault of those to whom his proposals were addressed, because they dreaded presenting them to

Pompey at an improper time: that he knew Scipio's authority to be such, as not only privileged him to advise freely, but even to enforce his counsels, and compel the obstinate to hearken to reason: that he was possessed of an independent command, and had an army at his disposal to give weight to his interposition: that in employing it for so desirable an end, he would gain the indisputable praise of having restored quiet to Italy, peace to the provinces, and saved the empire." Clodius reported this commission to Scipio, and at first met with a favourable reception, but was afterwards denied audience: for Favonius having sharply reprimanded Scipio, as we learned after the conclusion of the war, the negotiation was discontinued, and Clodius returned to Cæsar without success.

L. Cæsar, the more effectually to shut up Pompey's horse at Dyrrhachium, and hinder them from foraging, blocked up the two narrow passes, of which we have spoken, with strong works, and raised forts to defend them. Pompey finding his cavalry rendered by this means unserviceable, conveyed them some days after by sea to his camp again. Forage was so scarce, that they were forced to have recourse to the leaves of trees, and the roots of green reeds, bruised; for the corn sown within their lines was all consumed; nor had they had any supplies but what came a long way about by sea, from Corcyra and Acarnania; and even this was so inconsiderable, that to increase the quantity, they were forced to mix it with barley, and by these contrivances support their horses. At last, all expedients being exhausted, and the horses dying daily, Pompey thought it time to attempt to force the barricade, and set himself at liberty.

LI. Among the cavalry in Cæsar's camp were two brothers, Allobrogians by birth, named Roscillus and Ægus, the sons of Adbucillus, who had long held the chief sway in his own state; men of singular bravery, and who had been of signal service to Cæsar in all his Gallic wars. For these reasons he had raised them to the highest offices in their own country, got them chosen into the senate before they were of age, given them lands in Gaul taken from the enemy, besides pecuniary rewards to a great value, insomuch that from very moderate beginnings they had risen to vast wealth. These men were not only highly honoured by Cæsar on account of their bravery,

but in great esteem with the whole army. But presuming on Cæsar's friendship, and foolishly elated with their prosperity, they used the troopers ill, defrauded them of their pay, and secreted all the plunder to their own use. The Gaulish cavalry, offended at these proceedings, went in a body to Cæsar, and openly complained of the two brothers; adding, among other accusations, that, by giving in false musters, they received pay for more men than they had. Cæsar not thinking it a proper time for animadversion, and regarding them greatly on account of their valour, declined all public notice of the affair, and contented himself with reprimanding them in private, admonishing them to expect every thing from his friendship, and to measure their future hopes by the experience of what he had already done for them. This rebuke, however, disgusted them greatly, and very much lessened their credit with the whole army, which they easily perceived, as well from the raillery they were often forced to bear, as in consequence of the secret reproaches and sense of their own minds. Thus prompted by shame, and perhaps imagining they were not cleared, but reserved to a more favourable opportunity, they resolved to desert, to try their fortunes elsewhere, and search for new friendships. Having imparted their design to a few of their clients, whom they judged fit instruments for so black a treason, they first attempted to murder C. Volusenus, general of the cavalry, (as was afterwards known, when the war was over,) that by so signal a piece of service they might the more effectually recommend themselves to Pompey's favour. But finding that design attended with great hazard, and that no favourable opportunity offered for putting it in execution, they borrowed all the money they could, under pretence of reimbursing the troops, and making restitution; and having bought up a great number of horses, went over to Pompey, with those whom they had made acquainted with their design. As they were persons of noble birth, liberally educated, came with a great train of horses and servants, had been highly honoured by Cæsar, and were universally esteemed on account of their valour, Pompey carried them ostentatiously over all the camp, triumphing in this new and unusual acquisition; for till then, neither horse nor foot-soldier had deserted from Cæsar to Pompey; whereas scarce a day passed without some desertion from Pompey's army, especially among the new levies in Epirus, Ætolia, and those countries that had declared for Cæsar. The brothers being well acquainted with the condition of Cæsar's camp, what was wanting to complete the fortifications, where the foible of the lines lay, the particular times, distance of places, strength and vigilance of the guards, with the temper and character of the officers who commanded in every post, made an exact report of all to Pompey.

LII. Upon this intelligence, having already formed the design of forcing Cæsar's lines, he ordered the soldiers to make coverings of osier for their helmets, and provide themselves with fascines. This done, he embarked by night, in boats and small barks, a great number of light-armed troops and archers, with the fascines for filling up Cæsar's trenches; and having drawn together sixty cohorts from the greater camp and forts, led them about midnight towards that part of the enemy's lines nearest the sea, a good distance from the main camp. Thither likewise he despatched the barks, on board of which were the light-armed troops and fascines, together with all the galleys that lay at Dyrrhachium, giving each their particular instructions. Lentulus Marcellinus the questor, with the ninth legion, had charge of this part of the fortifications: and as his health was but infirm, Cæsar had joined Fulvius Posthumus with him in the command.

LIII. This place was guarded by a ditch, fifteen feet broad, with a rampart towards the enemy, ten feet high, and of equal thickness. Behind this, at the distance of six hundred feet, was another rampart, somewhat lower than the former, and fronting the contrary way. Cæsar, apprehending an attack from the sea, had raised this double rampart, some days before, that he might be able to defend himself against the enemy, should they charge him on both sides at once. But the extent of the circumvallation, and the continued labour of so many days, in inclosing a space of eighteen miles, had not allowed us time to finish the work. Accordingly, the line of communication, which ran along the sea-side, and was to have joined these two ramparts, was not yet completed. This Pompey was informed of by the Allobrogian brothers, which proved of fatal consequence to us. For

while some cohorts of the ninth legion were upon guard, near the sea, suddenly the Pompeians arrived about day-break, and surprised them with their unexpected appearance. At the same time the troops that came by sea launched their darts against the outward rampart and began to fill up the ditch with fascines; while the legionary soldiers, planting their scaling-ladders against the inner works, and plying those that defended them with darts and engines, spread a general terror over that part of the camp, which was still increased by the multitude of archers that came pouring upon them from all sides. The osiers they had bound round their helmets contributed greatly to defend them from the stones thrown down from the rampart, which were the only weapons we had. At last, all things going against us, and our resistance becoming every moment more languid, the enemy discovered the defect before spoken of in our lines; and landing their men between the two ramparts, where the line of communication towards the sea remained unfinished, they attacked our soldiers in the rear, and obliged them to abandon both sides of the works.

LIV. Marcellinus hearing of this disorder, detached some cohorts to sustain the flying troops: but as the rout was becoming general, they could neither persuade them to rally, nor were able to withstand the enemy's charge. The like happened to a second detachment; insomuch that the several supplies sent, by catching the general terror, served only to add to the confusion and danger; for the multitude of runaways rendered the retreat the more difficult. In this action, the eagle-bearer of the ninth legion finding himself dangerously wounded, and that his strength began to fail, called to some troopers who passed by, and said: "I have preserved to the last moment of my life, with the greatest care, this eagle, with which I have been intrusted; and, now I am dying, I return it to Cæsar, with the same fidelity. Carry it to him, I beseech you; nor suffer Cæsar's arms to experience, in losing it, an ignominy, with which they have been hitherto unacquainted." Thus the eagle was preserved; but all the centurions of the first cohort were slain, except the first of the Principes.

LV. And now the Pompeians, having made great slaughter of our men, approached the quarters of Marcellinus, to the no small terror of the rest of the cohorts; when Mark Antony, who commanded in the nearer redoubts, upon notice of what passed, was seen descending from the higher ground, at the head of twelve cohorts. His arrival put a stop to the enemy's progress, and by enabling our men to recover from their extreme terror, restored them to their wonted courage. Soon after Cæsar arrived in person, with some troops, being apprised of the attack by the smoke of the forts, the usual signal on these occasions; and perceiving the loss he had sustained, and that Pompey had forced the lines, being able to **forage, and having an easy** communication **with the sea ; he quitted his** former project, which had proved unsuccessful, and encamped as near Pompey as he could.

LVI. When the intrenchments were finished, Cæsar had notice from his scouts, that a certain number of the enemy's cohorts, which **to them** appeared a complete legion, were retired behind a wood, and seemed to be on their march to the old camp. The situation of the two armies was this : some days before, when Cæsar's ninth legion was sent to oppose a body of Pompey's troops, they thought proper to intrench themselves upon an opposite hill, and form a camp there. This camp bordered upon a wood, and was not above four hundred paces from the sea. But afterwards, for certain reasons, Cæsar removed a little beyond that post; and Pompey, a few days after, took possession of it. But as his design was to place several legions there ; leaving the inner rampart standing, he surrounded it with greater works. Thus the smaller camp, inclosed within one of larger circumference, **served by way** of a castle or citadel. He likewise carried an intrenchment from the left angle of the camp to the river, through a space of about four hundred paces, which enabled him to water freely and without danger. But he too, soon after, changed his mind, for reasons which it is not needful to repeat here ; and abandoned the place, which thereby was left several days without troops, though the fortifications remained entire. Hither the scouts reported they saw the standard of a legion carried which was likewise confirmed by those who were stationed in the higher forts. The place was about five hundred paces distant from Pompey's new camp. Cæsar, desirous to repair the loss he had sus-

tained, and hoping he might be able to surprise this legion, left two cohorts in his intrenchments, to prevent any suspicion of his design ; and with thirty-three more, amongst which number was the ninth legion, which had lost many centurions and soldiers, marched by a different route, as privately as he could, against the legion which Pompey had lodged in the lesser camp. Neither was he deceived in his first conjecture : for he arrived before Pompey could have notice of his design; and though the intrenchments were strong, yet charging the enemy briskly with his left wing, where he himself commanded **in person,** he quickly drove them from the rampart. **But** as the gates were secured by **a** barricade, they still maintained the fight here for some time, our men endeavouring to break in, and the enemy to defend the camp. T. Pulcia, who betrayed the army of C. Antony, as we have related above, gave signal proofs of his valour on this occasion. But our men, at last, prevailed ; and having cut down the barricade, broke first into the greater camp, and afterwards into the fort within it, whither the legion had retired, some of whom were slain, **endeavouring** to defend themselves.

LVII. But fortune, whose influence is very great, as in other things, so particularly in war; often effects mighty changes from the most trifling causes: as happened upon this occasion. For the cohorts of Cæsar's right wing being unacquainted with the situation of the camp, and mistaking the rampart which led to the river for one of its sides, marched on that way in quest of a gate ; but perceiving at length their error, and that nobody defended the intrenchment, they immediately mounted the rampart, and were followed by the whole cavalry. This delay saved **the** enemy for Pompey, having notice of **what** passed, brought up the fifth legion **to** sustain his party ; so that at one and **the same** instant, his cavalry approached ours, and **his** troops were seen advancing in **order of** battle, by those who had taken **possession of the** camp : which quickly changed **the** face of affairs. For Pompey's legion, encouraged by the hope of speedy succours, sallied by the Decuman port, and briskly charged our cohorts. On the other hand, Cæsar's cavalry, who had entered, by a narrow breach in the rampart, foreseeing that a retreat would be extremely difficult, began betimes to think of flying. The right wing, which had no communication with the left, observing the consternation of the cavalry, and fearing they should be overpowered within the camp, retired the same way they had entered. Many, to avoid being engaged in the narrow passes, threw themselves from the rampart, which was ten feet high, into the ditch; where the first ranks being trodden to death, their bodies afforded a safe passage to those that followed. The left wing, who from the rampart whence they had driven the enemy, saw Pompey advancing against them, and their own men flying; fearing to be entangled in the defiles, as they had the enemy upon them, both within and without the camp, retreated the same way they came. Nothing was to be seen but consternation, flying, and disorder: insomuch that all Cæsar's efforts to rally his troops were fruitless. If he seized any by the arm, they struggled till they got away. If he laid hold of the colours, they left them in his hands. Not a man could be prevailed on to face about.

LVIII. In this calamity, what saved the army from entire destruction was, that Pompey, apprehending an ambuscade, (probably because the success was beyond his hopes, as a little before he had seen his men worsted and put to flight,) durst not, for some time, approach the intrenchments: and his cavalry were retarded in the pursuit by Cæsar's troops, who were possessed of all the gates and defiles. Be that as it will, a small matter proved of very great consequence to both parties: for the intrenchment between the camp and the river, stopped the course of Cæsar's victory, when he had already forced Pompey's lines: and the same, by retarding the pursuit of his enemy, saved the army from destruction.

LIX. In these two actions, Cæsar lost nine hundred and sixty private men, thirty officers, and several knights of note, as Flavius Tuticanus Gallus, a senator's son; C. Felginus, of Placentia; A. Gravius, of Puteoli; and M. Sacrativir, of Capua. But the greatest part of these died without wounds, being trodden to death in the ditch, about the works, and on the banks of the river, occasioned by the flight and terror of their own men. He lost also thirty-two colours. Pompey was saluted emperor on this occasion; a title which he bore ever after, and suffered himself to be accosted by: but neither in the letters which he wrote, nor in his consular ensigns, did he think

proper to assume the laurel. The prisoners were delivered up to Labienus at his own request; and this deserter, brutal and cruel as usual, diverted himself with insulting them in their calamity; and asked them sarcastically, if it was usual for veterans to run away; after which, he caused them all to be put to death.

LX. This success gave such confidence and spirit to the Pompeian party, that they now no longer took any concern about the conduct of the war, but began to consider themselves as already victorious. They never reflected on the inconsiderable number of our troops, the disadvantage of the ground, the narrow passes we were engaged in, by their having first possession of the camp, the double danger, both within and without the fortification, and the separation of the two wings of the army, which hindered them from mutually succouring one another. They forgot that the advantage they had gained, was not the effect of a brisk and vigorous attack; and that our men had suffered more by crowding upon one another in the narrow passes, than by the sword of the enemy. In fine, they never called to mind the uncertain chance of war, and upon what minute causes good or bad success often depends; how a groundless suspicion, a panic terror, or a religious scruple, has frequently been productive of the most fatal events; when either by the misconduct of a general, or the terror of a tribune, some false persuasion has been suffered to take root in an army. But as if the victory had been purely the effect of their valour, and no change of fortune was to be apprehended, they every where proclaimed and made public the success of this day.

LXI. Cæsar, seeing all his former projects disconcerted, resolved to submit to fortune, and entirely change the manner of the war. He therefore called in all his forces from the forts, gave up the design of inclosing Pompey, and having assembled his army, addressed them as follows: " That they ought not to be discouraged, or give way to consternation, upon what had lately happened, but oppose their many successful engagements to one slight and inconsiderable check. That fortune had already befriended them greatly, in the reduction of Italy without bloodshed; in the conquest of the two Spains, though defended by warlike troops, under the conduct of skilful and experienced leaders; and in the subjection of the neighbouring provinces, whence they could be plentifully supplied with corn. In fine, they ought to call to mind, how happily they had passed into Greece, through the midst of the enemy's fleets, though possessed of all the coasts and havens. If they were not successful in every thing, they must endeavour, by prudence, to overcome the disappointments of fortune; and attribute their late disaster to the caprice of that goddess rather than to any fault on their side. That he had led them to an advantageous ground, and put them in the possession of the enemy's camp, after driving them from all their works. If either some sudden consternation, the mistaking their way, or any other mishap, had snatched an apparent and almost certain victory out of their hands, they ought to exert their utmost endeavours to repair that disgrace, which would turn their misfortune to a benefit, as happened at Gergovia, where those who at first dreaded to encounter the enemy, demanded earnestly in the end to be led to battle." Having made this speech, he contented himself with stigmatizing, and reducing to private men, some of the standard bearers; for the whole army were so grieved at their loss, and so desirous of expunging the stain their glory had received, that there was no occasion either for the tribunes or the centurions to remind them of their duty; nay, they even undertook to punish themselves by the severest impositions, and demanded with great outcries to be led against the enemy; being seconded by some centurions of the first rank, who, touched with their remonstrances, were for continuing in the post they then possessed, and putting all to the hazard of a battle. But Cæsar did not think it prudent to expose to an action troops that had been just worsted, and in whom might remain too deep impressions of their late fright. He was for allowing them time to recover themselves; and having quitted his works, thought it needful to provide for the security of his convoys.

LXII. Accordingly, after proper care taken of the sick and wounded, and as soon as night approached, he sent all the baggage privately towards Apollonia, under a guard of one legion, with orders not to halt till they had reached the place. This affair despatched, he made two legions remain in the camp, and marching out all the rest about three in

the morning at several gates, ordered them to follow the same route the baggage had taken. Soon after, that this departure might not have the appearance of a flight, and yet be known to the enemy as late as possible, he ordered the usual signal to be given, and setting out with the rest of his forces, lost sight of the camp in a moment. Pompey hearing of his retreat, prepared to follow him without delay, and hoping to surprise the army in its march, whilst encumbered with baggage, and not yet recovered from its consternation, drew out all his troops, and sent out all his cavalry before to retard our rear, which, however, he could not overtake, because Cæsar marching without baggage, had got a great way before him. But when we came to the river Genusus, we found the banks so steep and difficult, that before all the men could get over, Pompey's cavalry came up, and fell upon our hindmost battalions. Cæsar sent his horse to oppose them, intermixed with some light-armed troops; who charged with that vigour and success, as to put them all to rout, and leave a considerable number dead upon the field, and return without loss to the main body of their army.

LXIII. Having completed the intended march of that day, and brought his army over the Genusus, he took up his quarters in his old camp at Asparagium, suffering none of the soldiers to stroll without the rampart, and charging the cavalry, who had been sent out under pretence of foraging, to return immediately to the Decuman port. Pompey likewise having completed that day's march, encamped at his old post at Asparagium, where the troops having nothing to do, because the works were still entire; some made long excursions in quest of wood and forage; others who had come almost without any baggage, by reason the march was undertaken on a sudden, enticed by the nearness of their former camp, laid down their arms in their tents, quitted the intrenchments, and went to fetch what they had left behind them. This rendering them unable to pursue, as Cæsar had foreseen; about noon, he gave the signal for decamping, led forth his troops, and doubling that day's march, gained eight miles upon Pompey, who could not follow him by reason his troops were dispersed.

LXIV. Next day Cæsar decamped again at three in the morning, having sent away his baggage over night, that if he should find himself under a necessity of fighting, he might have his army clear of all encumbrance. The same he did the following days; by which means, though he had very difficult ways to pass, and some great rivers to cross, he suffered no loss during the whole march. For Pompey, after the first day's hinderance, endeavouring in vain by long and forced marches to overtake Cæsar, gave over the pursuit on the fourth, and began to think of taking other measures.

LXV. Cæsar was under a necessity of going to Apollonia, to leave his wounded there, to pay his army, confirm his friends in their duty, and garrison the towns that had submitted. But he took no longer time to these affairs, than the importance of his other engagements would allow. For fearing that Pompey might surprise Domitius Calvinus, he put himself in full march to join him. The scheme he proceeded on was this: that if Pompey took the same route, he must leave the sea, the forces he had at Dyrrhachium, with all his ammunition and provision; which would bring them upon equal terms; if he passed into Italy, Cæsar purposed to join Domitius, and march to its defence by the coast of Illyricum; in fine, should he fall upon Apollonia and Oricum, and endeavour to exclude him from the sea coast; in that case he reckoned to oblige him, by attacking Metellus Scipio, to leave every thing to succour him. Cæsar therefore despatched couriers to Domitius, to acquaint him with his design; and leaving four cohorts at Apollonia, one at Lissus, and three at Oricum, with the sick and wounded, began his march through Epirus and Acarnania. Pompey, on his side, guessing Cæsar's design, made what haste he could to join Scipio, that if Cæsar should march that way, he might prevent his being overpowered; but should he still keep near Corcyra, and the sea, because of the legions and cavalry he expected from Italy; in that case, he purposed to fall upon Domitius with all his forces.

LXVI. For these reasons both generals studied despatch, as well to afford timely succour to their friends, as not to miss an opportunity of distressing their enemies. But Cæsar had turned off to Apollonia; whereas Pompey took the nearest way through Candavia for Macedonia. It happened, too, very unfortunately, that Domitius, who for several days had been encamped near Scipio, quitted that station for the convenience of provisions, and was upon his march to Heraclea Sentica, a city of the Candavians; so that chance seemed to throw him directly in Pompey's way, which Cæsar had not then the least knowledge of. Pompey, too, having sent letters through all the states and provinces, relating to the action at Dyrrhachium, with representations that far exceeded the truth; a rumour began to prevail, that Cæsar had been defeated with the loss of almost all his forces, and was forced to fly before Pompey. These reports raised him many enemies on his march, and induced some states to throw off their allegiance; whence it happened, that the couriers mutually sent by Cæsar and Domitius, were all intercepted. But the Allobrogians in the train of Ægus and Roscillus, who, as we have seen before, had deserted from Cæsar to Pompey, meeting some of Domitius's scouts; either out of ancient custom, because they had served together in the Gallic wars; or from a motive of vain-glory; informed them of all that had passed; of Pompey's victory, and Cæsar's retreat. Advice being given of this to Calvinus, who was not above four hours' march from the enemy, he avoided the danger by a timely retreat, and joined Cæsar near Æginium, a town on the borders of Thessaly.

LXVII. After the junction of the two armies, Cæsar arrived at Gomphi, the first town of Thessaly, as you come from Epirus. A few months before, the inhabitants had of their own accord sent ambassadors to Cæsar, to make an offer of what their country afforded, and petition for a garrison. But the report of the action at Dyrrhachium, with many groundless additions, had by this time reached their ears. And therefore Androsthenes, prætor of Thessaly, choosing rather to be the companion of Pompey's good fortune, than associate with Cæsar in his adversity, ordered all the people, whether slaves or free, to assemble in the town; and having shut the gates against Cæsar, sent letters to Scipio and Pompey to come to his assistance, intimating, "That the town was strong enough to hold out if they used despatch, but by no means in condition to sustain a long siege." Scipio, on advice of the departure of the armies from Dyrrhachium, was come to Larissa with his legions; and Pompey was yet far enough distant from

Thessaly. Cæsar having fortified his camp, ordered mantelets, hurdles, and scaling-ladders to be prepared for a sudden attack; and then exhorting his men, represented, "Of how great consequence it was to render themselves masters of an opulent city, abounding in all things needful for the supply of their wants, and by the terror of whose punishment other states would be awed into submission; and this, he told them, must be done quickly, before any succours could arrive." Accordingly, seizing the opportunity offered by the uncommon ardour of the troops, he attacked the town the same day about three in the afternoon; and having made himself master of it before sunset, gave it up to be plundered. From Gomphi, Cæsar marched directly to Metropolis, and arrived before they were acquainted with the misfortune of their neighbours.

LXVIII. The Metropolitans at first following the example of Gomphi, to which they were moved by the same reports, shut their gates and manned the walls. But no sooner came they to understand the fate of their neighbour city, by some prisoners whom Cæsar had produced for that end, than immediately they admitted him into the town. He suffered no hostilities to be committed, nor any harm to be done them; and so powerful was the example from the different treatment of these two cities, that not a single state in Thessaly refused to submit to Cæsar, and received his orders, except Larissa; which was awed by the numerous army of Metellus Scipio. As the country was good and covered with corn, which was near ripe, Cæsar took up his quarters there, judging it a proper place to wait for Pompey in, and render the theatre of the war.

LXIX. A few days after, Pompey arrived in Thessaly, and joining Metellus Scipio, harangued both armies. He first thanked his own for their late services, and then turning to Scipio's troops, exhorted them to put in for their share of the booty, which the victory already obtained gave them the fairest prospect of. Both armies being received into one camp, he shared all the honours of command with Scipio, ordered a pavilion to be erected for him, and the trumpets to sound before it. This increase of Pompey's forces, by the conjunction of two mighty armies, raised the confidence of his followers, and their assurance of victory to such a degree, that all delays were considered as a hindrance of their return to Italy; insomuch that if Pompey on any occasion acted with slowness and circumspection, they failed not to cry out, "That he industriously protracted an affair, for the despatch of which one day was sufficient, in the view of gratifying his ambition for command, and having consular and pretorian senators amongst the number of his servants." Already they began to dispute about rewards and dignities, and fixed upon the persons who were annually to succeed to the consulship. Others sued for the houses and estates of those who had followed Cæsar's party. A warm debate arose in council in relation to L. Hirrus, whom Pompey had sent against the Parthians, whether, in the next election of pretors, he should be allowed to stand candidate for that office in his absence; his friends imploring Pompey to make good the promise he had made him at his departure, and not suffer him to be deceived by depending on the general's honour; while such as aspired to this office complained publicly, that a promise should be made to any one candidate, when all were embarked in the same cause, and shared the like dangers. Already Domitius, Scipio, and Lentulus Spinther, were openly quarrelling about the high priesthood, which Cæsar was in possession of. They even descended to personal abuse; and pleaded their several pretensions; Lentulus urging the respect due to his age; Domitius, his dignity, and the interest he had in the city; and Scipio his alliance with Pompey. Attius Rufus impeached L. Afranius before Pompey, charging him with having occasioned the loss of the army in Spain. And L. Domitius moved in council, that after the victory, all the senators in Pompey's army and camps, should be appointed judges, and empowered to proceed against those who had stayed in Italy, or who had appeared cool, or shown any indifference to the cause; and that three billets should be given to three judges, one for acquittance, another for condemnation, and a third for a pecuniary fine. In a word, nothing was thought on but honours, or profit, or vengeance; nor did they consider by what methods they were to conquer, but what advantage they should make of victory.

LXX. Cæsar having provided for the subsistence of his troops, who were now no longer fatigued, and had sufficiently recovered from the consternation the different actions at Dyrrhachium had thrown them into; thought it high time to make trial how Pompey stood affected to an engagement. Accordingly he drew out his men, and formed them in order of battle; at first near his own camp, and somewhat distant from the enemy: but perceiving this had no effect upon Pompey, who still maintained his post on the eminences, he each day drew nearer, and by that conduct animated and gave fresh courage to his soldiers. His cavalry being much inferior to the enemy's in number, he followed the method already mentioned; of singling out the strongest and nimblest of his foot-soldiers, and accustoming them to fight intermixed with the horse; in which way of combat they were become very expert by daily practice. This disposition, joined to constant exercise, so emboldened his cavalry, that though but a thousand in number, they would upon occasion sustain the charge of Pompey's seven thousand, even in an open plain, and appear not greatly dismayed at their multitude: nay, they actually got the better in a skirmish that happened between them, and killed Ægus the Allobrogian, one of the two brothers who deserted to Pompey, with several others of his party.

LXXI. Pompey, whose camp was on an eminence, drew up his army at the foot of the mountain, expecting, as may be presumed, that Cæsar would attack him in that advantageous situation. But Cæsar despairing to draw Pompey to battle on equal terms, thought it would be his best course to decamp, and be always on the march; in hopes, that by frequent shifting his ground, he might the better be supplied with provisions; and that as the enemy would not fail following him, in the frequent marches he should make, he might perhaps find an opportunity of attacking them, and forcing them to fight: at least he was sure of harassing Pompey's army, little accustomed to these continued fatigues. Accordingly the order for marching was given, and the tents struck; when Cæsar perceived that Pompey's army, which had quitted their intrenchments, had advanced farther towards the plain than usual, so that he might engage them at a less disadvantage: whereupon, addressing himself to his soldiers, who were just ready to march out of their trenches: "Let us no longer think," says he, "of marching; now is the time for fighting, so long wished for; let us therefore arm ourselves with cour

age, and not miss so favourable an opportunity." This said, he immediately drew out his forces.

LXXII. Pompey likewise, as was afterwards known, had resolved to offer battle, in compliance with the repeated importunities of his friends. He even said in a council of war held some days before, that Cæsar's army would be defeated before his infantry came to engage. And when some expressed their surprise at this speech: "I know," says he, "that what I promise appears almost incredible; but hear the reasons on which I ground my confidence, that you may advance to battle with the greater assurance. I have persuaded the cavalry, and obtained their promise for the performance, that as soon as the armies are formed, they shall fall upon Cæsar's right wing, which they will easily be able to outflank and surround. This must infallibly occasion the immediate rout of that wing, and consequently of the rest of Cæsar's troops, without danger or loss on our side. Nor will the execution be attended with any difficulty, as we are so much superior to them in horse. Be ready therefore for battle; and since the so much desired opportunity of fighting is come, take care not to fall short of the good opinion the world entertains of your valour and experience." Labienus spoke next, highly applauding this scheme of Pompey, and expressing the greatest contempt of Cæsar's army; "Think not," says he, addressing himself to Pompey, "that these are the legions which conquered Gaul and Germany. I was present in all those battles, and can, of my own knowledge, affirm, that but a very small part of that army now remains: great numbers have been killed, as must of necessity happen, in such a variety of conflicts: many perished during the autumnal pestilence in Apulia. many are returned to their own habitations: and not a few were left behind to guard Italy. Have you not heard, that the cohorts in garrison, at Brundusium, are made up of invalids? The forces, which you now behold, are composed of new levies, raised in Lombardy, and the colonies beyond the Po: for the veterans, in whom consisted the main strength of the army, perished all in the two defeats at Dyrrhachium." Having finished this speech, he took an oath, which he proffered to all that were present, never to return to camp otherwise than victorious. Pompey commended his zeal, took the oath himself, and the rest followed his example, without hesitation. After these en gagements, taken publicly in council, they all departed, full of joy and expectation; considering themselves as already victorious, and relying entirely on the ability of their general; who, in an affair of that importance, they were confident would promise nothing without an assurance of success.

LXXIII. When Cæsar approached Pompey's camp, he found his army drawn up in this manner: In the left wing were the two legions delivered by Cæsar, at the beginning of the quarrel, in consequence of a decree of the senate; one of which was called the first, the other the third legion; and here Pompey commanded in person. Scipio was in the centre, with the legions he had brought out of Syria. The Cilician legion, joined to the Spanish cohorts, brought over by Afranius, formed the right wing. These Pompey esteemed his best troops, distributing the less expert between the wings and the main body. He had in all a hundred and ten cohorts, amounting to five and forty thousand; besides two cohorts of volunteers, who had served under him in former wars; and who, out of affection to their old general, though their legal time was expired, flocked to his standard on this occasion, and were dispersed amongst the whole army. His other seven cohorts were left to guard the camp and the adjoining forts. As the Enipeus, a river with very steep banks, covered his right wing, he placed all his horse, slingers, and archers in the left.

LXXIV. Cæsar observing his ancient custom, placed the tenth legion in the right, and the ninth in the left wing. As this last had been considerably weakened by the general actions at Dyrrhachium, he joined the eighth to it in such manner, that they formed as it were but one legion, and had orders mutually to relieve each other. His whole army amounted to fourscore cohorts, making in all twenty-two thousand men; besides two cohorts left to guard the camp. Domitius Calvinus was in the centre, Mark Antony on the left, and P. Sylla on the right. Cæsar took his post opposite to Pompey, at the head of the tenth legion. And as he had observed the disposition of the enemy contrived to outflank his right wing, to obviate that inconvenience, he made a draught of six cohorts from his rear line, formed them into a separate body, and opposed them to Pompey's horse; instructing them in the part they were to act;

and admonishing them, that the success of that day would depend chiefly on their courage. At the same time, he charged the whole army, and in particular the third line, not to advance to battle without orders; which, when he saw it proper, he would give, by making the usual signal.

LXXV. When he was exhorting them to battle, as military custom required, and reminding them of the many favours they had, on all occasions, received at his hands, he chiefly took care to observe, "That they had themselves been witnesses of his earnest endeavours after peace; that he had employed Vatinius to solicit a conference with Labienus, and sent A. Clodius to treat with Scipio; that he had pressed Libo, in the warmest manner, at Oricum, to grant him a safe conduct for his ambassadors; in a word, that he had left nothing unattempted to avoid wasting the blood of his soldiers, and to spare the commonwealth the loss of one of her armies." After this speech, observing his soldiers ardent for the fight, he ordered the trumpets to sound a charge. Among the volunteers in Cæsar's army was one Crastinus, a man of distinguished courage, who the year before, had been first centurion of the tenth legion. This brave officer, as soon as the signal was given, calling to those next him; "Follow me," said he, "you that were formerly under my command, and acquit yourselves of the duty you owe to your general. This one battle more will crown the work, by restoring him to his proper dignity, and us to the enjoyment of our freedom." At the same time, turning to Cæsar: "General," says he, "this day you shall be satisfied with my behaviour, and whether I live or die, I will take care to deserve your commendations." So saying he marched up to the enemy, and began the attack at the head of a hundred and twenty volunteers.

LXXVI. Between the two **armies, there** was an interval sufficient for the onset: but Pompey had given his troops orders to keep their ground, that Cæsar's army might have all that way to run. This he is said to have done by the advice of C. Triarius, that the enemy's ranks might be broken and themselves put out of breath, by having so far to run; of which disorder he hoped to make an advantage. He was besides of opinion, that our javelins would have less effect, by the troops continuing in their post, than if they sprung forward at the very time they were launched and as the soldiers would have twice as far to run as usual, they must be weary and breathless by the time they came up with the first line. But herein Pompey seems to have acted without sufficient reason; because there is a certain alacrity and ardour of mind, naturally planted in every man, which is inflamed by the desire of fighting; and which an able general, far from endeavouring to repress, will, by all methods he can devise, foment and cherish. Nor was it a vain institution of our ancestors, that the trumpets should sound on every side, and the whole army raise a shout, in order to animate the courage of their own men, and strike terror into the enemy. Cæsar's soldiers entirely defeated Pompey's hopes, by their good discipline and experience. For, perceiving the enemy did not stir, they halted, of their own accord, in the midst of their career; and having taken a moment's **breath**, put themselves, a second time, in motion, marched up in good order, flung their javelins, and then betook themselves to their swords. Nor did Pompey's men act with less presence of mind; for they sustained our attack, kept their ranks, bore the discharge of our darts; and having launched their own, immediately had recourse to their swords. At his instant, Pompey's horse, accompanied by the archers and slingers, attacked Cæsar's; and having compelled them to give ground, began to extend themselves to the left, in order to flank the infantry. Whereupon Cæsar gave the appointed signal to the six cohorts, who fell on the enemy's horse with such fury, that they not only drove them from the field of battle, but even compelled them to seek refuge in the highest mountains. The archers and slingers, deprived of their protection, were soon after cut to pieces. Meanwhile the six cohorts, not content with this success, wheeled round upon the enemy's left wing, and began to charge it in the rear: whereupon Cæsar, perceiving the victory so far advanced, to complete it, brought up his third line, which till then had not engaged. Pompey's infantry being thus doubly attacked, in front by fresh troops, and in rear, by the victorious cohorts, could no longer resist, but fled to their camp. Nor was Cæsar mistaken in his conjecture, when, in exhorting his men, he declared that victory would depend chiefly on the six cohorts, which formed the body of reserve, and were stationed to oppose the enemy's

horse; for by them were their cavalry defeated, their archers and slingers cut to pieces, and their left wing surrounded and forced to fly.

LXXVII. Pompey seeing his cavalry routed, and that part of the army on which he chiefly depended put into disorder, despaired of being able to restore the battle, and quitted the field. Repairing immediately to his camp, he said aloud, to the centurions, who guarded the prætorian gate, so as all the soldiers might hear him: "Take care of the camp, and defend it vigorously in case of an attack. I go to visit the other gates, and give orders for their defence." This said, he retired to his tent, despairing of success, yet waiting the event. Cæsar having forced the Pompeians to seek refuge in their camp, and not willing to allow them time to recover from their consternation, exhorted his troops to make the best of their present victory, and vigorously attack the enemy's intrenchments. Though the battle had lasted till noon, the weather being extremely hot; yet, prepared to encounter all difficulties, they cheerfully complied with his orders. The camp was bravely defended, for some time, by the cohorts left to guard it; and particularly by a great number of Thracians, and other barbarians, who made a very stout resistance; for as to such troops as had there sought refuge from the field of battle, they were in too great a consternation to think of any thing more than a safe retreat. It was not, however, possible for the **troops posted** on the rampart, long to stand **the multitude of** darts continually poured upon them; **which, in** the end, obliged them to retire covered with wounds, and under the conduct of their tribunes and centurions, seek shelter in the mountains adjoining to the camp.

LXXVIII. On entering Pompey's camp, we found tables ready-covered, sideboards loaded with plate, and tents adorned with branches of myrtle; that of L. Lentulus, with some others, was shaded with ivy. Every thing gave proofs of the highest luxury, and an assured expectation of victory; whence it was easy to see, that they little dreamed of the issue of that day, since, intent only on voluptuous refinements, they pretended, with troops immersed in luxury, to oppose Cæsar's army accustomed to fatigue, and inured to th want of necessaries.

LXXXI. Pompey finding our men had forced his intrenchments, mounted his horse, quitted his armour for a habit more suitable to his ill fortune, and withdrawing by the Decuman port, rode full speed to Larissa. Nor did he stop there; but continuing his flight day and night, without intermission, he arrived at the sea-side, with thirty horse, and went on board a little bark; often complaining, "That he had been so far deceived in his opinion of his followers, as to see those very men, from whom he expected victory, the first to fly, and in a manner betray him into the hands of his enemies."

LXXX. Cæsar having mastered the enemy's camp, requested his soldiers not to leave the victory imperfect, by busying themselves about the plunder. Finding them ready to obey, he began a line of circumvallation round the mountain. The Pompeians quickly abandoned a post, which, for want of water, was not tenable, and endeavoured to reach the city of Larissa: whereupon Cæsar, dividing his army, left one part in Pompey's camp, sent back another to his own camp, and having, with four legions, taken a nearer road than that by which the enemy passed, he found means to intercept them, and, after six miles march, drew up in order of battle. But the Pompeians once more found protection from a mountain, at the foot of which ran a rivulet. Though Cæsar's troops were greatly fatigued, by fighting the whole day, before night he had flung up some works, sufficient to prevent the enemy from having any communication with the rivulet. As by this step they were cut off from all hopes of relief, or of escaping, they sent deputies to treat about a surrender. Affairs continued in this situation all that night, of which some few senators, who had accompanied them, took the advantage to make their escape. At break of day, they all, by Cæsar's order, came down into the plain, and delivered up their arms; humbly imploring his goodness, and suing for mercy. Cæsar spoke to them with great mildness, and to alleviate their apprehensions, cited various instances of his clemency, which he had, on so many occasions, made evident. In fact, he gave them their lives, and forbade his soldiers to offer them any violence, or to take any thing from them. He then sent for the legions, which had passed the night in camp, to relieve those that had accompanied

him in the pursuit; and being determined to follow Pompey, began his march, and arrived the same day at Larissa.

LXXXI. This battle cost Cæsar no more than two hundred soldiers: but he lost thirty centurions, men of singular courage. Among these latter was Crastinus, whose gallantry and intrepidity, in marching up to battle, has been taken notice of. This brave officer, fighting, regardless of danger, received a wound in the mouth, from a sword. Nor was he deceived in promising himself Cæsar's approbation, who was thoroughly sensible of his merit, and greatly applauded his behaviour in this action. On Pompey's side, there fell about fifteen thousand: but upwards of four and twenty thousand were taken prisoners: for the cohorts that guarded the forts, surrendered to Sylla; though many escaped into the adjacent countries. One hundred and eighty colours were taken, and nine eagles. L. Domitius, flying towards the mountains, and growing faint through the fatigue, was overtaken and killed by some horsemen.

LXXXII. About this time D. Lælius arrived with his fleet at Brundusium, and possessed himself of the island over against the harbour, as Libo had done before. Vatinius who commanded in the place, having equipped several boats, endeavoured to entice some of Lælius's ships within the haven, and took a five-benched galley, with two smaller vessels, that had ventured too far into the port; then disposing his cavalry along the shore, he prevented the enemy from getting fresh water But Lælius having chosen a more convenient season of the year for sailing, brought water in transports from Corcyra and Dyrrhachium; still keeping to his purpose, from which neither the disgrace of losing his ships nor the want of necessaries could divert him, till he received intelligence of the battle of Pharsalia.

LXXXIII. Much about the same time Cassius arrived in Sicily, with the Syrian, Phœnician, and Cilician fleets. And as Cæsar's fleet was divided into two parts, in one of which P. Sulpicius the pretor commanded at Vibo, in the straits; in the other M. Pomponius at Messana; Cassius was arrived at Messana with his fleet before Pomponius had notice of his coming. And finding him unprepared, without guards, order, or discipline, he took the opportunity of a favourable wind, and sent several fire-ships against him, which consumed his whole fleet, thirty-five in number, twenty of which were decked. The terror occasioned by this blow was so great, that though there was an entire legion in garrison at Messana, they durst scarce look the enemy in the face; and would doubtless have delivered up the town, had not the news of Cæsar's victory reached them, by means of the cavalry stationed along the coast. Cassius then sailed for Sulpicius's fleet at Vibo, which finding at anchor near the shore by reason the consternation was become general over the whole island; he put the same stratagem in practice as before. For taking the advantage of a favourable wind, he made forty fire-ships advance against them, and the flame catching hold on both sides, quickly reduced five galleys to ashes. The conflagration continuing to spread, roused the indignation of some veteran soldiers, who had been left to guard the ships. Accordingly **they** went on board, weighed anchor, and, attacking the enemy, took two quinqueremes, in one of which was Cassius himself; but he escaped in a boat. Two three-benched galleys were sunk; and soon after he was informed of the defeat at Pharsalia, by some of Pompey's own followers; for hitherto he had regarded it as a false report, spread about by Cæsar's lieutenants and friends. Upon this intelligence he quitted Sicily, and retired with his fleet.

LXXXIV. Cæsar laying all other thoughts aside, determined to pursue Pompey, whithersoever he should retire, to prevent his drawing together fresh forces, and renewing the war. He marched every day as far as the body of cavalry he had with him could hold out, and was followed, by shorter marches, by a single legion. Pompey had issued a proclamation at Amphipolis, enjoining all the youth of the province, whether Greeks or Romans, to join him in arms. But whether this was with intent to conceal his real design of retreating much farther, or to try to maintain his ground in Macedonia, if nobody pursued him, is hard to determine. Here he lay one night at anchor, sending to what friends he had in the town, and raising all the money he possibly could. But being informed of Cæsar's approach, he departed with all expedition, and came in a few days to Mitylene. Here he was detained two days by the badness of the weather; and having increased his fleet with a few galleys

sailed to Cilicia, and thence to Cyprus. There he was informed, that the Antiochians, and Roman citizens trading hither, had with joint consent seized the castle, and sent deputies to such of his followers as had taken refuge in the neighbouring states, not to come near Antioch at their peril. The same had happened at Rhodes to L. Lentulus, the consul of the foregoing year, to P. Lentulus a consular senator and to some other persons of distinction; who, following Pompey in his flight, and arriving at that island, were refused admittance into the town and harbour, and received an order to withdraw immediately, which they were necessitated to comply with; for the time of Cæsar's approach had now reached the neighbouring states.

LXXXV. Upon this intelligence Pompey laid aside his design of going into Syria, seized all the money he found in the public bank, borrowed as much more as he could of his friends, sent great quantities of brass on board for military uses; and having raised two thousand soldiers, amongst the public officers, merchants, and his own servants, sailed for Pelusium. Here, by accident, was king Ptolemy, a minor, warring with a great army against his sister Cleopatra; whom, some months before, by the assistance of his friends, he had expelled the kingdom, and was then encamped not far distant from her. Pompey sent to demand his protection, and a safe retreat in Alexandria, in consideration of the friendship that had subsisted between him and his father. The messengers, after discharging their commission, began to converse freely with the king's troops, exhorting them to assist Pompey and not despise him in his adverse fortune. Among these troops were many of Pompey's old soldiers, whom Gabinius, having draughted out of the Syrian army, had carried to Alexandria, and, upon the conclusion of the war, left there with the young king's father. The king's ministers, who had the care of the government during his minority, being informed of this, either out of fear, as they afterwards pretended, lest Pompey should debauch the army, and thereby render himself master of Alexandria and Egypt; or despising his low condition,(as friends, in bad fortune, often turn enemies,) spoke favourably to the deputies in public, and invited Pompey to court; but privately despatched Achillas, captain of the king's guards, a man of singular boldness, and

L. Septimius, a military tribune, with orders to murder him. They accosted him with an air of frankness, especially Septimius, who had served under him as a centurion in the war with the pirates; and inviting him into the boat, treacherously slew him. L. Lentulus was likewise seized by the king's command, and put to death in prison.

LXXXVI. When Cæsar arrived in Asia he found that T. Ampius, having formed the design of seizing the treasurer of the Ephesian Diana, and summoned all the senators in the province to bear witness to the sum taken, had quitted that project upon Cæsar's approach and betaken himself to flight. Thus was the temple of Ephesus a second time saved from plunder by Cæsar. It was remarked in the temple of Minerva at Elis, that the very day Cæsar gained the battle of Pharsalia, the image of victory, which before stood fronting the statue of the goddess, turned towards the portal of the temple. The same day, at Antioch, in Syria, such a noise of fighting and trumpets was heard two several times, that the inhabitants ran to arms and manned their walls. The like happened at Ptolemais. At Pergamus, in the inner recesses of the temple, called by the Greeks Adyta, where none but priests are allowed to enter, the sound of cymbals was heard. And in the Temple of Victory, at Trallis, where a statue was consecrated to Cæsar, a palm sprouted between the joining of the stones that arched the roof.

LXXXVII. Cæsar, after a short stay in Asia, hearing that Pompey had been seen at Cyprus, and thence conjecturing that he was for Egypt, because of the interest he had in that kingdom, and the advantages it would afford him, left Rhodes, with a convoy of ten Rhodian galleys and a few others from Asia, having on board two legions, one of which he ordered to follow him from Thessaly, the other detached from Fufius's army in Achaia; and eight hundred horse. In these legions were no more than three thousand two hundred men: the rest, fatigued with the length of the march, or weakened with wounds, had not been able to follow him. But Cæsar depending on the reputation of his former exploits, scrupled not to trust the safety of his person to a feeble escort, believing no place would dare to attempt any thing against him. At Alexandria he was informed of Pompey's death:

and upon landing, was accosted in a clamorous manner by the soldiers, whom Ptolemy had left to garrison the city: and he observed that the mob appeared dissatisfied to see the fasces carried before him, which they interpreted a degradation of the sovereign authority. Though this tumult was appeased, yet each day produced some fresh disturbance, and many of the Roman soldiers were murdered in all parts of the city.

LXXXVIII. For these reasons he sent into Asia for some of the legions which he had raised out of the remains of Pompey's army: being himself necessarily detained by the Etesian winds, which are directly contrary to any passage by sea from Alexandria. Meantime, considering the difference between Ptolemy and his sister, as subject to the cognizance of the Roman people, and of him as consul; and the rather, because the alliance with Ptolemy, the father, had been contracted during his former consulship; he gave the king and Cleopatra to understand, that it was his pleasure they should dismiss their troops, and instead of having recourse to arms, come and plead their cause before him.

LXXXIX. Pothinus the eunuch, governor to the young king, had the chief management of affairs during his minority. This minister complained bitterly to his friends, that the king should be summoned to plead his cause before Cæsar: afterwards finding among those that sided with the king, some who were disposed to enter into his views, he privately sent for the army from Pelusium to Alexandria, and conferred the chief command upon Achillas, the same we have spoken of before: inciting him by letters and promises, both in the king's name and his own, to execute such orders as he should receive from him. Ptolemy, the father, by his will had appointed the eldest of the two sons, and his elder daughter, joint heirs of the kingdom. For the more certain accomplishment of his design, he in the same will implored the protection of the Roman people; adjuring them by all the gods, and the treaties he had made at Rome, to see it put in execution. A copy of this will was sent by ambassadors to Rome, to be deposited in the public treasury; but the domestic troubles preventing it, it was left in the hands of Pompey. The original signed and sealed, was kept at Alexandria.

XC. While this affair was debated before Cæsar, who passionately desired to terminate the matter amicably, and to the satisfaction of both parties, he was informed that the king's army, with all the cavalry, were arrived at Alexandria. Cæsar's forces were by no means sufficient to give them battle without the town; and therefore the only course left was to secure the most convenient posts within the city, till he should get acquainted with Achillas's designs. Meantime he ordered all the soldiers to their arms, and admonished the king, to send some persons of the greatest authority to Achillas, to forbid his approach. Discorides and Serapion, who had both 1 een ambassadors at Rome, and in great credit with Ptolemy, the father, were deputed to this office. But no sooner did they come before Achillas, than without giving them a hearing, or enquiring after the message they brought, he ordered them to be seized and put to death. One was killed upon the spot; and the other, **having received a** dangerous wound, was car- **ried off for dead by** his attendants. Upon **hearing this, Cæsar** took care to secure the king's person, the authority of whose name would authorise his proceedings, and occasion **Achillas and** his associates to be esteemed se- ditious **and** rebellious.

XCI. Achillas's army was far from being contemptible, whether we regard their num- ber, courage, or experience in war. It amounted to twenty thousand effective men, many of whom were originally Romans, brought into the country by Gabinius, when he came to settle Auletes on the throne; and who, having afterwards married and settled in Alexandria, were devoted to the Ptolemean interest. Their were also some brigades raised in Syria and Cilicia, together with a considerable number of renegade slaves, who had deserted their masters, and found protec- tion in Egypt, by entering into the service. If any of these was seized by his master, their companions flocked to his rescue, regarding his safety as a common cause, because they were all embarked in the like guilt. These **would often** take upon them to put to death **the king's** ministers, to plunder the rich, for **the sake of** increasing their pay, to invest the royal palace, to banish some, and send for others home, with other liberties of the like nature, which the Alexandrian army claims by a kind of prescription. Besides these, he had likewise two thousand horse, who, during the **late** troubles, and the wars that ensued, had

had opportunities of inuring themselves to arms. These had restored Ptolemy the father to his kingdom, killed Bibulus's two sons, warred against the Egyptians with success, and acquired a thorough experience in military affairs.

XCII. Achillas trusting to the valour of his troops, and despising the handful of men that followed Cæsar, quickly make himself master of Alexandria, the palace only excepted, where Cæsar thought proper to make his stand, and which he attacked briskly, though without effect. But it was on the side of the harbour that the greatest efforts **were made.** On that, in effect, the victory depended. **Be-** sides two and twenty constant guard-ships, there were in the port fifty galleys, from three to five banks of oars, which the year before had been sent to Pompey's assistance, and were returned since the battle of Pharsalia. Had Achillas been once master of these vessels, he might have cut Cæsar off from all communi- cation with the ocean, and consequently from all hopes of receiving supplies of victuals or forces. Thus the Egyptians, in hopes of a complete victory, and the Romans to avoid a certain ruin, exerted themselves with in- credible vigour. At length Cæsar carried his point, and not only set fire to the vessels above-mentioned, but to all that were in the arsenals, after which he passed some troops into the Isle **of Pharos.**

XCIII. The Pharos is a tower of prodigious height and **wonderful** workmanship, built in an island, **from whence it** takes its name. This island, lying over against Alexandria, makes a haven, and is joined to the continent by a causeway of nine hundred paces, and by a bridge. Here dwell several Egyptians, who have built a town, and live by pillaging the ships that are thrown upon their coast, either by mistake or tempest. As it is situate at the entrance of the port, which is but narrow, it absolutely commands it. Cæsar knowing the importance of this post, whilst the enemy were engaged in the assault, landed some troops there, seized the tower, and put a garrison into it; thereby securing a safe reception for the supplies he had sent for on all sides. In the other quarters of the town, the fight was main- tained with equal advantage, neither party losing ground, because of the narrowness of the passes, which enabled them easily to sup- port themselves. After a few men killed on both sides, Cæsar having secured the most necessary places, fortified them in the night. In this quarter was a small part of the king's palace, where Cæsar was lodged upon his first arrival; and adjoining thereto a theatre, that served instead of a citadel, and had a communication with the port and other arsenals. These works he increased afterwards, that they might serve instead of a rampart, to prevent his being obliged to fight against his will. Meantime Ptolemy's youngest daughter, hoping the throne would be vacant, fled from the palace to Achillas, and joined with him in the prosecution of the war. But they soon disagreed about the command, which increased the largesses to the soldiers, each party endeavouring to gain them by large presents. During these transactions, Pothinus, Ptolemy's governor, and regent of the kingdom, being discovered in a clandestine correspondence with Achillas, whom he encouraged to the vigorous prosecution of his enterprise Cæsar ordered him to be put to death. Su was the commencement of the Alexandrian war

PANSA'S COMMENTARIES

OF

THE ALEXANDRIAN WAR.

THE ARGUMENT.

PANSA'S COMMENTARIES

THE ALEXANDRIAN WAR.

I. The war thus commencing at Alexandria, Cæsar sent to Rhodes, Syria, and Cilicia, for his fleet; to Crete, for archers; and to Malchus, king of the Nabatheans, for cavalry. He likewise ordered military engines to be provided, corn to be brought, and forces despatched to him with all diligence. Meanwhile, he was daily employed in augmenting his works; and such parts of the town as appeared less tenable, were strengthened with tortoises and mantelets. Openings were made in the walls, through which the battering rams might play; and whatever houses were thrown down, or taken by force, were brought within the intrenchments. For Alexandria is in a manner secure from fire, because the inhabitants use no wood in their buildings, the houses being all vaulted, and roofed with tile or pavement. Cæsar's principal aim was, to enclose with works the smallest part of the town, separated from the rest by a morass towards the south. For thus the army would lie closer together, be subject to one command, and could readily despatch relief where it was most wanted. Above all, he by this means made sure of water and forage, which was of so much the more consequence, as he was but ill provided of the one, and wholly destitute of the other. The morass, on the contrary, served abundantly to supply him with both.

II. Nor were the Alexandrians remiss on their side, or less active in the conduct of their affairs. They had sent deputies and commissioners into all parts, where the power and territories of Egypt extend, with orders to levy troops. They had carried vast quantities of darts and engines into the town, and drawn together an innumerable multitude of soldiers. Yet not contented with all these preparations, they established work-shops in every part of the city, for the making of arms, and enlisted all the slaves that were of age, the richer citizens paying and maintaining them. With these they guarded the remoter parts of the town; while the veteran cohorts, exempt from all other service, were quartered in the squares and open places; that on whatever side an attack should be made, they might be at hand to give relief, and march fresh and entire to the charge. All the avenues and passes were shut up by a triple wall, built of square stones, and carried to the height of forty feet. The lower parts of the town were defended by very high towers of ten stories: besides which, they had likewise contrived a kind of moving towers, which consisted of the same number of stories, and being fitted with ropes and wheels, could, by means of horses, as the streets of Alexandria were quite even and level, be conveyed wherever their service was necessary. The city abounding in every thing, and being very rich, furnished ample materials for these several works; and as the people were extremely ingenious, and quick of apprehension, they so well copied what they saw done by us, that our men seemed rather to imitate them. They even invented many things themselves, and at once invested our works and defended their own. Their chiefs every where represented: "That the people of Rome were endeavouring by degrees to steal into the possession of Egypt; that a few years befor

Gabinius had come thither with an army; that Pompey had chosen it for the place of his retreat; that Cæsar was now among them with a considerable body of troops, and notwithstanding his rival's death, made no offers to return; that if they did not therefore find means to expel him, they would soon, from a kingdom, be reduced to a Roman province; that no time was to be lost in this attempt, because the season of the year having put a stop to navigation, he could receive no supplies from beyond sea."

III. Meanwhile, a division arising between Achillas, who commanded the veteran army, and Arsinoe, the youngest daughter of king Ptolemy, as has been demonstrated above; while they mutually endeavoured to supplant one another, each striving to engross the supreme authority; Arsinoe, by the assistance of the eunuch Ganymed, her governor, at length prevailed, and caused Achillas to be slain. After his death, being possessed of the whole power without a rival, she raised Ganymed to the command of the army; who, on his entrance into that high office, augmented the allowance of the troops, and with equal diligence discharged all other parts of his duty.

IV. Alexandria is almost quite hollow underneath, occasioned by the many aqueducts to the Nile, that furnish private houses with water; where being received in cisterns, it settles by degrees, and becomes perfectly clear. This is preserved for the use of the master and his family; for the water of the Nile being extremely thick and muddy, is apt to breed many distempers. The common people, however, are forced to be contented with it, because there is not a single spring in the whole city. The river was in that part of the town where the Alexandrians were masters. Hence Ganymed conceived that a way might be found to deprive the Romans of water; because being distributed into several streets, for the more easy defence of the works, they made use of that which was preserved in the cisterns of private houses. With this view he began a great and difficult work; for having stopped up all the canals by which his own cisterns were supplied, he drew vast quantities of water out of the sea, by the help of wheels and other engines, pouring it continually into the canals of Cæsar's quarter. The cisterns in the nearest houses soon began to taste salter

than ordinary, and occasioned great wonder among the men, who could not think from what cause it proceeded. They were even ready to disbelieve their senses, when those who were quartered a little lower in the town, assured them that they found the water the same as before. This put them upon comparing the cisterns one with another, and by trial they easily perceived the difference. But in a little time the water in the nearest houses became quite unfit for use, and that lower down grew daily more tainted and brackish; upon which such a terror ensued among the troops, that they fancied themselves reduced to the last extremity. Some complained of Cæsar's delay, that he did not order them immediately to repair to their ships. Others dreaded a yet greater misfortune, as it would be impossible to conceal their design of retreating from the Alexandrians, who were so near them; and no less so to embark in the face of a vigorous and pursuing enemy. There were besides a great number of the townsmen in Cæsar's quarter, whom he had not thought proper to force from their houses, because they openly pretended to be in his interest, and to have quitted the party of their fellow-citizens. But to offer here at a defence either of the sincerity or conduct of these Alexandrians, would be only labour in vain, since all who know the genius and temper of the people, must be satisfied that they are the fittest instruments in the world for treason.

V. Cæsar laboured to remove his soldiers' fears, by encouraging and reasoning the case with them, "They might easily," he told them, "find water, by digging wells, as all sea-coasts naturally abounded with fresh springs: that if Egypt was singular in this respect, and differed from every other soil; yet still, as the sea was open, and the enemy without a fleet, there was nothing to hinder their fetching it at pleasure in their ships, either from Parætonium on the left, or Pharos on the right; which two places lying different ways, the wind could neither exclude them from both at the same time; that a retreat was on no account to be thought of, not only by those who had a concern for their honour, but even by such as regarded nothing but life; that it was with the utmost difficulty they could defend themselves behind their works; but if they once quitted that advantage, neither in number nor situation would they be a match for the enemy:

that to embark would require much time, and be attended with great danger, especially where it must be managed by little boats: that the Alexandrians, on the contrary, were nimble and active, and thoroughly acquainted with the streets and buildings: that flushed with so manifest an advantage, they would not fail to run before, seize all the advantageous posts, possess themselves of the tops of the houses, and, by annoying them in their retreat, effectually prevent their getting on board; that they might therefore think no more of retiring, but place all their hopes of safety in victory." Having by this speech re-assured his men, he ordered the centurions to lay aside all other cares, and apply themselves day and night to the digging of wells. The work once begun, they pushed it on so vigorously that the very first night abundance of fresh water was found. Thus with labour on our side, the mighty projects and painful attempts of the Alexandrians were entirely frustrated.

VI. During these transactions, the thirty-seventh legion, composed of Pompey's veterans that had surrendered to Cæsar, embarking by order of Domitius Calvinus, with arms, darts, provisions, and military engines, arrived upon the coast of Africa, a little above Alexandria. An easterly wind, which continued to blow for several days together, hindered their being able to gain the port; but all along that coast it is very safe riding at anchor. Being detained, however, longer than they expected, and pressed with want of water, they gave notice of it to Cæsar by a despatch sloop. Cæsar, that he might himself be able to determine what was best to be done, went on board one of the ships in the harbour, and ordered the whole fleet to follow. He took none of the land forces with him, because he was unwilling to leave the works unguarded during his absence. Being arrived at that part of the coast known by the name of Cherronesus, he sent some mariners on shore to fetch water. Part of these venturing too far into the country for the sake of plunder, were intercepted by the enemy's horse. From them the Egyptians learned that Cæsar himself was on board, without any soldiers. Upon this information, they thought fortune had thrown a fair occasion in their way, of attempting something with success. They therefore manned all the ships that were in condition to sail, and met Cæsar on his return. He declined fighting that day for two reasons; because he had no soldiers on board, and it was past four in the afternoon. The night, he was sensible, must be highly advantageous to his enemies, who were perfectly acquainted with the coast: and he would himself be deprived of the benefit of encouraging his men, which could not be done with any effect in the dark, where courage and cowardice must remain equally unknown. He therefore drew all his ships towards the shore, where he imagined the enemy would not follow him.

VII. There was one Rhodian galley in Cæsar's right wing, considerably distant from the rest. This being observed by the enemy, they came forward with four decked ships, and several open barks, to attack her. Cæsar was obliged to advance to her relief, that he might not suffer the disgrace of seeing one of his galleys sunk before his eyes; though, had he left her to perish, she seemed to deserve it for her rashness. The attack was sustained with great courage by the Rhodians, who though at all times distinguished by their valour and experience in engagements at sea, yet exerted themselves in a particular manner on this occasion, that they might not draw upon themselves the charge of having occasioned a misfortune to the fleet. Accordingly, they obtained a complete victory, took one four-benched galley, sunk another, disabled a third, and slew all that were on board, besides a great number belonging to the other ships. Nay, had not night interposed, Cæsar would have made himself master of their whole fleet. During the consternation that followed upon this occasion, Cæsar finding the contrary winds to abate, took the transports in tow, and advanced with the victorious fleet to Alexandria.

VIII. The Alexandrians, disheartened at this loss, as finding themselves now worsted, not by the superior valour of the soldiers, but by the skill and ability of the mariners, retired to the tops of their houses, and blocked up the entrance of their streets, as fearing our fleet might attack them even by land. But soon after, Ganymed assuring them in council, that he would not only restore the vessels they had lost, but even increase their number; they began to repair their old ships with great expectation and confidence, and resolved to apply more than ever to the putting their fleet in a good condition. And although they had lost above a hundred and ten ships in the port and arsenal, yet did not all this discourage them; because, by making themselves masters at sea, they saw they would have it in their power to hinder Cæsar's receiving any reinforcements or supplies. Besides, being naturally mariners, born upon the sea-coast, and exercised from their infancy in naval affairs, they were desirous to return to that wherein their true and proper strength lay, remembering the advantages they had formerly gained, even with their little ships. They therefore applied themselves with all diligence to the equipping a fleet.

IX. Vessels were stationed at all the mouths of the Nile, for receiving and gathering in the customs. Several old ships were likewise lodged in the king's private arsenals, where they had remained unrigged for many years. These last they refitted, and recalled the former to Alexandria. To supply themselves with oars, they uncovered the porticoes, Academics, and public buildings, and made use of the planks they furnished. Their natural ingenuity, and the abundance of all things to be met with in the city, supplied every want. In fine, they had no long navigation to provide for, and were only solicitous about present exigencies, foreseeing they would have no occasion to fight but in the port. In a few days, therefore, contrary to all expectation, they had fitted out twenty-two quadriremes, and five quinqueremes. To these they added a great number of small open barks; and employing the rowers in the harbour, to practise and exercise themselves, put a sufficient number of soldiers on board, and prepared every thing necessary for an engagement. Cæsar had nine Rhodian galleys (for of the ten which were sent, one was shipwrecked on the coast of Egypt; eight from Pontus, five from Lycia, and twelve out of Asia. Of these ten were quadriremes and five quinqueremes. The rest were of an inferior bulk, and for the most part without decks. Yet trusting to the valour of his soldiers, and knowing the strength of the enemy, he prepared for an engagement.

X. When both sides were come to have sufficient confidence of their own strength, Cæsar sailed round Pharos, and formed in line of battle over against the enemy. The Rhodian galleys were in his right wing, and those of Pontus in his left. Between these he left a space of four hundred paces, to serve for the extending and working the vessels. This disposition being made, he drew up the rest of the fleet as a reserve, giving them the necessary orders, and distributing them in such manner, that every ship followed that to which she was appointed to give succour. The Alexandrians came forth with great confidence, and drew up their fleet, placing their twenty-two quadriremes in front, and disposing the rest behind them in a second line, by way of reserve. They had besides a great number of boats and smaller vessels, that carried fire and combustible weapons, with design to fright us by their number, cries, and flaming darts. Between the two fleets were certain flats, separated by very narrow channels, and which are said to be on the African coast, as being in that division of Alexandria which belongs to Africa. Both sides waited which should first pass these shallows, because whoever entered the narrow channels between them, in case of any misfortune, would find it very difficult either to retreat, or work the ships to advantage.

XI. Euphranor commanded the Rhodian fleet, who for valour and greatness of mind deserved rather to be ranked among the Romans than the Grecians. The Rhodians had raised him to the post of Admiral, on account of his known courage and experience. He perceiving Cæsar's design, addressed him to this effect: "You seem afraid of passing the shallows first, lest you should be thereby forced to come **to an engagement, before** the rest of the fleet can be brought **up. Leave the** matter to us, we will sustain **the fight, and I** hope too without disappointing your expectations, until the whole fleet gets clear of the shallows. It is both dishonourable and afflicting, that they should so long continue in our sight with an air of triumph." Cæsar encouraging him in his design, and bestowing many praises upon him, gave the signal for engaging. Four Rhodian ships having passed the shallows, the Alexandrians gathered round and attacked them. They maintained the fight with great bravery, disengaging themselves by their art and address, and working their ships with so much skill, that notwithstanding the inequality of number, none of the enemy were suffered to run alongside, or break their oars. Meantime the rest of the fleet came up: when, on account of the narrowness of the place, art becoming useless, the success depended wholly, upon valour. The Alexandrians and Romans who were in the town, laying aside all thoughts of attack and defence, mounted the tops of the houses, and all the eminences that could give a view of the fight, addressing the gods by vows and prayers for victory.

XII. The event of the battle was by no means equal. A defeat would have deprived us of all resource either by land or by sea; and even victory itself would not much better our condition. The Alexandrians, on the contrary, by a victory, gained every thing; and if defeated, might yet again have recourse to fortune. It was likewise a matter of the highest concern, to see the safety of all depend upon the bravery of a few, whose want of courage would expose their whole party to destruction. This Cæsar had often represented to his troops during the preceding days, that they might be thereby induced to fight with the more resolution, when they knew the common safety to depend upon their bravery. Every man said the same to his comrade, companion, and friend, requesting him not to disappoint the expectation of those who had chosen him preferably to others for the defence of the common interest. Accordingly they fought with so much resolution, that neither the art nor address of the Egyptians, a maritime and seafaring people, could stand them in any stead, nor the multitude of their ships be of service to them; nor the valour of those selected for this engagement, stand in competition with the determined courage of the Romans. In this action a quinquereme was taken, and a bireme, with all the soldiers and mariners on board, besides three sunk, without any loss on our side. The rest fled towards the town, sheltering themselves under the mole and forts, whither we durst not pursue them.

XIII. To deprive the enemy of this resource for the future, Cæsar thought it by all means necessary, to render himself master of the mole and island; for having already in a great measure completed his works within the town, he was in hopes of being able to defend himself both in the island and city. This resolution being taken, he put into boats and small vessels ten cohorts, a select body of light-armed infantry, and such of the Gallic cavalry as he thought most for his purpose, and sent them against the island; whilst at the same time, to occasion a diversion, he attacked it on the other side with his fleet, promising great rewards to those who should first render themselves masters of it. At first the attack was brisk, and the defence vigorous: for they both annoyed our men from the tops of the houses, and gallantly maintained their ground along the shore; which being steep and craggy, our men could find no way of approach; all the more accessible avenues being skilfully defended by small boats, and five galleys, properly stationed for that purpose. But when, after examining the approaches, and sounding the shallows, a few of our men got upon the shore, and were followed by others, who pushed the islanders, without intermission, the Pharians at last betook themselves to flight. Upon this, abandoning the defence of the port, they quitted their ships, and retired into the town, to provide for the security of their houses. But they could not long maintain their ground there: though to compare small things with great, their buildings resemble those of Alexandria, and their towers were high, and joined together so as to form a kind of wall; and our men had neither ladders, fascines, nor any weapons for assault. But fear often deprives men of counsel and strength, as happened upon this occasion. Those who had ventured to oppose us on even ground, terrified by the loss of a few men, and the general rout, durst not face us from a height of thirty feet; but throwing themselves from the mole, into the sea, endeavoured to gain the town, though above eight hundred paces distant. Many, however, were slain, and about six hundred taken.

XIV. Cæsar giving up the plunder to the soldiers, ordered the houses to be demolished; but fortified the castle at the end of the bridge next the island, and placed a garrison in it. This the Pharians had abandoned; but the other, towards the town, which was considerably stronger, was still held by the Alexandrians. Cæsar attacked it next day; because, by getting possession of these two forts, he would be entirely master of the port, and prevent sudden excursions and piracies. Already he had, by means of his arrows and engines, forced the garrison to abandon the place, and retire towards the town. He had also landed three cohorts, which was all the place would contain; and disposed the rest of his troops abroad to sustain them. He then fortified the bridge on the side of the en emy, built an arch across the entrance of the port, and filled it up, in such a manner, with stones, that not the smallest boat could pass. When the work was almost finished, the Alexandrians sallied, in crowds, from the town, and drew up, in an open place over against the intrenchment we had cast up at the head of the bridge. At the same time, the vessels, which they had been wont to make pass under the bridge, to set fire to our ships of burden, were ranged along the mole. Our men fought from the bridge and the mole; the enemy from the area, over against the bridge, and from their ships, by the side of the mole. While Cæsar, attentive to what passed, was exhorting his troops, a number of rowers and mariners, quitting their ships, threw themselves upon the mole; partly out of curiosity, partly to have a share in the action. At first, with stones and slings, they forced the enemy's ships from the mole; and seemed to do still greater execution with their darts. But when, some time after, a few Alexandrians found means to land and attack them in flank; as they had left their ships without order or discipline, so they soon began to fly with precipitation. The Alexandrians, encouraged by this success, landed in great numbers, and vigorously pushed our men, who were by this time in great confusion. Those that remained in the galleys perceiving this, drew up the ladders, and put off from the shore, to prevent the enemy's boarding them. The three cohorts, who were at the head of the mole, to guard the bridge, astonished at this disorder, the cries they heard behind them, and the general rout of their party; unable, besides, to bear up against the multitude of darts which came pouring upon them, and fearing to be surrounded, and have their retreat cut off, by the departure of their ships, abandoned the defence of the bridge, and ran with all the speed they could, towards the galleys. Some getting on board the nearest vessels, overloaded and sunk them. Part making head against the enemy, and uncertain what course to take, were cut to pieces by the Alexandrians. Others, more fortunate, got to the ships that rode at anchor; and a few, by the help of their bucklers, swam to the nearest vessels. Cæsar endeavouring to re-animate his men, and lead them back to the defence of the works, was exposed to the same danger with the rest: when finding them universally to give ground, he retreated to his own galley; whither such a multitude followed, and crowded after him, that it was impossible either to work or put her off. Foreseeing what must happen, he flung himself into the sea, and swam to a ship that lay at some distance. Hence despatching boats to succour his men, he, by that means, preserved a small number. His own ship, sunk by the multitude that crowded into her, perished with all that were on board. We lost, in this action, about four hundred legionary soldiers, and somewhat above that number of sailors and rowers. The Alexandrians secured the fort by strong works, and a great number of engines; and having cleared away the stones with which Cæsar had blocked up the port, enjoyed henceforward a free and open navigation.

XV. Our men, instead of being disheartened at this loss, seemed rather roused and animated by it. They were making continual sallies upon the enemy, to destroy or check the progress of their works; fell upon them as often as they had an opportunity; and never failed to intercept them, when they ventured to advance beyond their fortifications. In short, the legions were so bent upon fighting, that they even outstripped the orders and exhortations of Cæsar. They were inconsolable for their late disgrace, and impatient to come to blows with the enemy; insomuch that he found it rather necessary to restrain and check their ardour, than incite them to action.

XVI. The Alexandrians, perceiving that success confirmed the Romans, and that adverse fortune only animated them the more; as they knew of no medium between these, on which to ground any further hopes, resolved, either by the advice of the friends of their king who were in Cæsar's quarter, or of their own motion; or, perhaps, on an intimation from the king himself, suggested to him by secret emissaries, to send ambassadors to Cæsar to demand their king. They represented, "That the people, weary of subjection to a woman, of living under a precarious government, and submitting to the cruel laws of the tyrant Ganymed, instead of obeying their own lawful king, desired nothing so much as to have him amongst them: that in granting their request, he would pave the way to an alliance, and extinguish all the fears and objections that had hitherto obstructed it." Though Cæsor know the nation to be false and perfidious, seldom speaking as they really thought, he judged it best, however, to comply with their desire. He even flattered himself, that his condescension in sending back their king at their request, would prevail on them to be faithful; or, as was more agreeable to their character, if they only wanted the king to head their army; at least it would be more for his honour and credit, to have to do with a monarch, than with a band of slaves and fugitives. Accordingly he sent Ptolemy to them, exhorting him " to take the government into his own hands, and consult the welfare of so fair and illustrious a kingdom, defaced by hideous ruins and conflagrations. That he would make his subjects sensible of their duty, preserve them from the destruction that threatened them, and act with fidelity towards himself and the Romans, who put so much confidence in him, as to send him amongst armed enemies." Then taking him by the hand, he told him he was at liberty to depart. But the young prince, thoroughly versed in the art of dissimulation, and no way degenerating from the character of his nation, entreated Cæsar with tears not to send him back: for that his company was to him preferable to a kingdom. Cæsar moved at his concern, dried up his tears; and telling him if these were his real sentiments they would soon meet again, dismissed him. The king, like a wild beast, escaped out of confinement, carried on the war with such acrimony against Cæsar, that the tears he shed at parting, seemed to have been tears of joy. Cæsar's lieutenants, friends, centurions, and soldiers, were not a little pleased at this; because, through his easiness of temper, he had suffered himself to be imposed upon by a child; as if in truth Cæsar's behaviour on this occasion had been the effect of easiness of temper, and not of the most consummate prudence.

XVII. When the Alexandrians found that the restoration of their king had neither rendered their own party stronger, nor the Romans weaker; that the troops despised the youth and weakness of their king; and that their affairs were no way bettered by his presence; they were greatly discouraged: the rather, because a report ran, that a great body of troops was marching by land from Syria and Cilicia to Cæsar's assistance, of which he had not as yet himself received information. This,

however, did not hinder their design of intercepting the convoys that came to him by sea. To this end having equipped some ships, they ordered them to cruise before the Canopic branch of the Nile, by which they thought it most likely our supplies would arrive. Cæsar, who was informed of it, sent likewise his fleet to sea, under the command of Tiberius Nero. The Rhodian galleys made part of this squadron, headed by Euphranor their admiral, without whom he had little hopes of success from any maritime expedition. But fortune, which often reserves the heaviest disasters for those who have been loaded with her highest favours, encountered Euphranor upon this occasion, with an aspect very different from what she had hitherto worn. For when our ships were arrived at Canopus, and the fleets drawn up on each side had begun the engagement, Euphranor, according to custom, having made the first attack, and pierced and sunk one of the enemy's ships; as he pursued the next a considerable way, without being sufficiently sustained by those that followed him, he was surrounded by the Alexandrians. None of the fleet advanced to his relief, either out of fear for their own safety, or because they imagined he would easily be able to extricate himself by his courage and good fortune. Accordingly he alone behaved well in this action, and being abandoned by all the rest, perished with his victorious galley.

XVIII. About the same time Mithridates of Pergamus, a man of illustrious descent, distinguished for his bravery and knowledge in the art of war, and who bore a very high place in the friendship and confidence of Cæsar; having been sent, in the beginning of the Alexandrian war, to raise succours in Syria and Cilicia, arrived by land at the head of a great body of troops, which his diligence, and the affection of these two provinces, had enabled him to draw together in a very short time. He conducted them first to Pelusium, a city which joins Syria to Egypt. Achillas, who was perfectly well acquainted with its importance, had seized and put a strong garrison into it. For Egypt is considered as defended on all sides by strong barriers; towards the sea by the Pharos, and towards Syria by Pelusium, which are accounted the two keys of the kingdom. He attacked it so briskly with a large body of troops, fresh men continually succeeding in the place of those that were fatigued; and urged the assault with so much firmness and perseverance, that he carried it the same day, and placed a garrison in it. Thence he pursued his march to Alexandria, reducing all the provinces through which he passed, and conciliating them to Cæsar, by that authority which always accompanies victory.

XIX. Not far from Alexandria lies Delta, the most celebrated province of Egypt, which borrows its name from the Greek letter so called. For the Nile, dividing the two channels, which gradually run off as they approach the sea, into which they at last discharge themselves, at a considerable distance from one another, leaves an intermediate space in form of a triangle. The king, understanding that Mithridates approached this place, and knowing he must pass the river, sent a great body of troops against him, sufficient, as he thought, if not to overwhelm and crush him, at least to stop his march; for though he earnestly desired to see him defeated, yet he thought it a great point gained, to hinder his junction with Cæsar. The troops that first passed the river, and came up with Mithridates, attacked him immediately, that they might alone have the honour of the victory. Mithridates at first confined himself to the defence of his camp, which he had with great prudence fortified according to the custom of the Romans: but observing that they advanced insolently and without caution, he sallied upon them from all parts, and put a great number of them to the sword; insomuch that but for their knowledge of the places, and the neighbourhood of the vessels in which they had passed the river, they must have been all destroyed. But recovering by degrees from their terror, and joining the troops that followed them, they again prepared to attack Mithridates.

XX. Mithridates sent to inform Cæsar of what had happened. The king was likewise informed on his side. Thus much about the same time, Ptolemy set out to crush Mithridates, and Cæsar to relieve him. The king made use of the more expeditious conveyance of the Nile, where he had a large fleet in readiness. Cæsar declined the navigation of the river, that he might not be obliged to fight the enemy's fleet; and coasting along the African shore, found means to join the victorious troops of Mithridates, before Ptolemy could attack him.

XXI. The king had encamped in a very dangerous place, being an eminence surrounded on all sides by a plain. Three of its sides were secured by various defences: One adjoined to the Nile, the other was steep and inaccessible, and the third was defended by a morass. Between Ptolemy's camp and Cæsar's route lay a narrow river with very high banks, which discharged itself into the Nile. This river was about seven miles from the king's camp; who understanding that Cæsar directed his march that way, sent all his cavalry, with a choice body of light-armed foot, to hinder Cæsar from passing, and maintain an unequal fight from the banks, where courage had no opportunity to exert itself, and cowardice ran no hazard. Our men, both horse and foot, were extremely mortified, that the Alexandrians should so long maintain their ground against them. Wherefore the German cavalry, dispersing in quest of a ford, some found means to swim the river where the banks were lowest; and the legionaries at the same time cutting down several large trees, that reached from one bank to another, and throwing them into the water, by their help got to the other side. The enemy, unable to sustain the first charge, betook themselves to flight; but in vain: for very few returned to the king, being almost all cut to pieces in the pursuit.

XXII. Cæsar, upon this success, judging that his sudden approach must strike great terror into the Alexandrians, advanced towards their camp with his victorious army. But finding it well intrenched, strongly fortified by nature, and the ramparts crowded with armed soldiers, he did not think proper to attack it at that time, as his troops were very much fatigued, both by their march and the late battle; and therefore encamped at a small distance from the enemy. Next day he attacked a fort, in a village not far off, which the king had joined to his camp by a line of communication, with a view of keeping possession of the village. He employed his whole army in this assault; not because it would have been difficult to carry it with a few forces; but with design of falling immediately upon the enemy's camp during the alarm the loss of this fort must give them. Accordingly the Romans, in continuing the pursuit of those that fled from the fort, arrived at last before the Alexandrian camp, where a furious battle ensued. There were two approaches by which it might be attacked: one by the plain, of which we have spoken before; the other by a narrow pass, between their camp and the Nile. The first, which was much the easiest, was defended by a numerous body of their best troops; and the access on the side of the Nile gave the enemy great advantages in distressing and wounding our men; for they were exposed to a double shower of darts: in front from the rampart; behind, from the river; where the enemy had stationed a great number of ships, furnished with archers and slingers, that kept a continual discharge. Cæsar observing that his troops fought with the utmost ardour, and yet made no great progress, on account of the disadvantage of the ground; as he saw they had left the highest part of their camp unguarded, because, being sufficiently fortified by nature, they had all crowded to the other attacks, partly to have a share in the action, partly to be spectators of the issue; he ordered some cohorts to wheel round the camp, and gain that ascent: appointing Carsulenus to command them, a brave officer, and well acquainted with the service. When they had reached the place, where they found but very few to defend it, our men attacked them so briskly, that the Alexandrians, terrified by the cries they heard behind them, and seeing themselves attacked both in front and rear, fled in the utmost consternation on all sides. Our men, animated by the confusion of the enemy, entered the camp in several places at the same time, and running down from the higher ground, put a great number of them to the sword. The Alexandrians, endeavouring to escape, threw themselves in crowds over the rampart next the river. The foremost tumbling into the ditch, where they were crushed to death, furnished an easy passage for those that followed. The king made his escape the same way: but by the crowd that followed him, the ship to which he fled was overloaded and sunk.

XXIII. After this speedy and successful action, Cæsar, in confidence of so great a victory, marched the nearest way by land to Alexandria with his cavalry, and entered triumphant into that part of the town possessed by the enemy. He was not mistaken in thinking, that the Alexandrians, upon hearing of the issue of the battle, would give over all thoughts of war. Accordingly as soon as he was arrived, he reaped the just fruit of his valour and magnanimity. For the Alexandrians, throwing down their arms, abandoning their works, and assuming the habit of suppliants, came forth to surrender themselves to Cæsar, preceded by all those sacred symbols of religion with which they were wont to mollify their offended kings. Cæsar accepting their submission, and encouraging them, advanced through the enemy's works into his own quarter of the town, where he was received with the universal congratulations of his party, who were no less overjoyed at his arrival and presence, than at the happy issue of the war.

XXIV. Cæsar having thus made himself master of Alexandria and Egypt, lodged the government in the hands of those to whom Ptolemy had bequeathed it by will, appointing the people of Rome his executors, and requesting them to confirm his choice. For the eldest of his two sons being dead, he settled the kingdom upon the youngest, in conjunction with his sister Cleopatra, who had always continued faithful to the Romans. The younger Arsinoe, in whose name Ganymed, as we have seen, reigned for some time, he thought proper to banish the kingdom, that she might not raise any new disturbance, before the king's authority should be firmly established. Things thus settled, he carried the sixth legion with him into Syria, leaving the rest to support the authority of the king and queen, who neither stood well in the affections of their subjects, on account of their attachment to Cæsar, nor could be supposed to have given any fixed foundation to their power, in an administration of only a few days' continuance. It was also for the honour and interest of the republic, that if they continued faithful, our forces should protect them; if otherwise, would be in a condition to restrain them. Having thus settled the kingdom, he marched by land into Syria.

XXV. While these things passed in Egypt, king Dejotarus applied to Domitius Calvinus, to whom Cæsar had intrusted the government of Asia and the neighbouring provinces, beseeching him, "Not to suffer Pharnaces to seize and lay waste the Lesser Armenia, which was his kingdom; or Cappadocia, which belonged to Ariobarzanes; because unless they were delivered from these insults, it would be impossible to execute Cæsar's orders, or raise the money they stood engaged to pay.' Domitius, who was not only sensible of the necessity of money to defray the expenses of the war, but likewise thought it dishonourable to the people of Rome and Cæsar, as well as infamous to himself, to suffer the dominions of allies and friends to be usurped by a foreign prince, " That he must withdraw immediately out of Armenia and Cappadocia, and no longer insult the majesty and right of the Roman people, engaged in a civil war." But believing that his deputation would have greater weight, if he was ready to second it himself at the head of an army, he repaired to the legions which were then in Asia, ordering two of them into Egypt, at Cæsar's desire, and carrying the thirty-sixth along with him. To this Dejotarus added two more, which he had trained up for several years, according to our discipline, and a hundred horse. The like number of horse were furnished by Ariobarzanes. At the same time, he sent P. Sextius to C. Plætorius the questor, for the legion which had been lately levied in Pontus; and Quinctius Patisius into Cilicia, to draw thence a body of auxiliary troops. All these forces had orders to rendezvous, as soon as possible at Comana.

XXVI. Meanwhile his ambassadors returned, with Pharnaces' answer: " That he had quitted Cappadocia; but kept possession of the Lesser Armenia, as his own, by right of inheritance: however, he was willing to submit all to the decision of Cæsar, to whose commands he would pay immediate obedience." C. Domitius, sensible that he had quitted Cappadocia, not voluntarily, but out of necessity; because he could more easily defend Armenia, which lay contiguous to his own kingdom, than Cappadocia, which was more remote; and because believing, at first, that Domitius had brought all the three legions along with him, upon hearing that two were gone to Cæsar, he seemed more determined o keep possession; insisted " upon his quitting Armenia likewise, the reason, in both cases, being the same; nor was it just to demand that the matter should be postponed till Cæsar's return, unless things were put in the condition in which they were at first." Having returned his answer, he advanced towards Armenia, with the forces above mentioned, directing his

march along the hills. For from Pontus, by way of Comana, runs a woody ridge of hills, that extends as far as Armenia the Less, dividing it from Cappadocia. The advantages he had in view, by such a march were, that he would thereby effectually prevent all surprises, and be plentifully furnished with provisions from Cappadocia.

XXVII. Meantime Pharnaces was perpetually sending ambassadors to Domitius with presents, and to treat of peace. All these he firmly rejected, telling the deputies; " That nothing was more sacred with him, than the majesty of the Roman people, and the rights of their allies." After a long march, he reached Nicopolis, a city of Armenia the Less, situated in a plain, having mountains, however, on its two sides, at a considerable distance. Here he encamped, about seven miles from the town. Between his camp and Nicopolis, lay a difficult and narrow pass, where Pharnaces placed a chosen body of foot, and all his horse, in ambuscade. He ordered a great number of cattle to be dispersed in the pass, and the townsmen and peasants to show themselves; that if Domitius entered the defile as a friend, he might have no suspicion of an ambuscade when he saw the men and flocks dispersed, without apprehension, in the fields; or if he should come as an enemy, that the soldiers, quitting their **ranks to pillage, might** fall **an** easy prey to his **troops.**

XXVIII. While this design was going forward, he never ceased sending ambassadors to Domitius, with proposals of peace and amity, as fancying by this means, the most easy to insnare him. The expectation of peace kept Domitius in his camp, so that Pharnaces, disappointed of his hopes, and fearing the ambuscade might be discovered, drew off his troops. Next day Domitius approached Nicopolis, and encamped near the town. While our men were working at the trenches, Pharnaces drew up his army in order of battle, forming his front into one line, according to the custom of the country, and securing his wings with a triple body of reserves. Domitius ordering part of the troops to continue under arms before the rampart, completed the fortifications of his camp.

XXIX. Next night, Pharnaces having intercepted the couriers who brought Domitius an account of the posture of affairs at Alexandria, understood that Cæsar was in great dan er, and requested Domitius to send him succours speedily, and came himself to Alexandria by the way of Syria. Pharnaces, upon this intelligence, imagined that protracting the time would be equivalent to a victory; because Domitius, he supposed, must very soon depart. He therefore dug two ditches, four feet deep, at a moderate distance from each other, on that side where lay the easiest access to the town, and our forces might, with most advantage, attack him; resolving not to advance beyond them. Between these, he constantly drew up his army, placing all his cavalry upon the wings without them, which greatly exceeded ours in number, and would otherwise have been useless.

XXX. Domitius, more concerned at Cæsar's danger than his own, and believing he could not retire with safety, should he now desire the conditions he had rejected, or march away without any apparent cause; drew his forces out of the camp, and ranged them in order of battle. He placed the thirty-sixth legion on the right, that of Pontus on the left, and those of Dejotarus in the main body; drawing them up with a very narrow front, and posting the rest of the cohorts to sustain the wings. The armies, thus drawn up on each side, they prepared for battle; and the signal being given at the same time by both parties, the engagement began. The conflict was sharp and various: for the thirty-sixth legion falling upon the king's cavalry, that was drawn up without the ditch, and charged them so successfully, that they drove them to the very walls of the town, passed the ditch, and attacked their infantry behind. But on the other side, the legion of Pontus having given way; the second line, which advanced to sustain them, fetching a compass round the ditch, in order to attack the enemy in flank, was overwhelmed and borne down by a shower of darts, in endeavouring to pass it. The legions of Dejotarus scarce made any resistance; so that the victorious right wing, and main body of the king's army, fell upon the thirty-sixth legion, which yet made a brave stand; and though surrounded by the forces of the enemy, with wonderful presence of mind, cast themselves into an orb, and retired to the foot of a mountain, whither Pharnaces did not think fit to pursue them, because of the disadvantage of the place. Thus the legion of Pontus being almost wholly cut off, with great part of those of Dejotarus, the thirty-sixth legion retreated to an eminence, with the loss of about two hundred and fifty men. Several Roman knights, of illustrious rank, fell in this battle. Domitius, after this defeat, rallied the remains of his broken army, and retreated, by safe ways, through Cappadocia, into Asia.

XXXI. Pharnaces, elated with this success, and hoping that Cæsar would never be able to extricate himself at Alexandria, entered Pontus with all his forces. There acting as conqueror and king, and promising himself a happier destiny than his father, he ravaged their towns, seized the effects of the Roman citizens and natives, inflicted punishments worse than death, upon such as were distinguished by their age or beauty; and having made himself master of all Pontus, as there was no one to oppose his progress, boasted, that he had recovered his father's kingdom.

XXXII. About the same time, we received a considerable check in Illyricum; which province, Q. Cornificius, Cæsar's questor, had defended the preceding months, not only without insult, but even with honour, and a conduct worthy of praise. Cæsar had sent him thither, the summer before, with two legions; and though it was of itself little able to subsist an army, and at that time in particular almost totally ruined by the neighbourhood of so many wars; yet by his prudence, vigilance, and uncommon care, he defended and kept possession of it. For he made himself master of several forts, built on eminences, whose advantageous situation tempted the inhabitants to make descents and inroads upon the country; and gave the plunder of them to his soldiers: which, though but inconsiderable, yet as they were no strangers to the distress and ill condition of the province, did not cease to be grateful; the rather, as it was the fruit of their own valour. And when, after the battle of Pharsalia, Octavius had retreated to that coast with a large fleet; Cornificius, with some vessels of the Judertini, who had always continued faithful to the commonwealth, made himself master of the greatest part of his ships, which joined to those of the Judertini, rendered him capable of sustaining even a naval engagement. And while Cæsar, victorious, was pursuing Pompey to the remotest parts of the earth; upon advice that the enemy had, for the most part, retired into Illyricum, on account of its neighbourhood to Macedonia, and were there uniting into a body, he wrote to Gabinius, "To repair directly thither, with the new-raised legions, and join **Cornificius**, that in case of any danger **to the** province, they might be the better able to protect it; but if less forces sufficed, **to** march into Macedonia, which he **foresaw** would never be free from commotions, **so** long as Pompey lived."

XXXIII. Gabinius, whether he imagined the province better provided than it really was, or depended much upon the auspicious fortune of Cæsar, or confided in his own valour and abilities, having often terminated, with success, difficult and dangerous wars; marched into Illyricum, in the middle of winter, and the most difficult season of the year: where, not finding sufficient subsistence in the province, which was partly ruined, partly ill-affected; and having no supplies by sea, because the season of the year had put a stop to navigation ; he found himself compelled to carry on the war, not according to his own inclination, but as necessity allowed. As he was therefore obliged to lay siege to forts and castles, in a very rude season, he received many checks, and fell under such contempt with the barbarians, that retiring to Salona, a maritime city, inhabited by a set of brave and faithful Romans, he was attacked upon his march; and after the loss of two thousand soldiers, thirty-eight centurions, and four tribunes, got to Salona with the rest; where his wants continually increasing, he died a few days after. His misfortunes and sudden death gave Octavius great hopes of mastering the province. But fortune, whose influence is so great in matters of war, joined to the diligence of Cornificius, and the valour of Vatinius, soon put an end to his triumphs.

XXXIV. For Vatinius, who was then at Brundusium, having intelligence of what passed in Illyricum, by letters from Cornificius, who pressed him to come to the assistance of the province, and informed him, that Octavius had leagued with the barbarians, and, in several places, attacked our garrisons, partly by sea, with his fleet, partly by land, with the troops of the barbarians: Vatinius, I say, upon notice of these things, though extremely weakened by sickness, insomuch that his strength of body no way **answered** his resolu-

tion and greatness of mind ; yet by his valour, surmounted all opposition, the force of his distemper, the rigour of the season, and the difficulties of a sudden preparation. For having himself but a very few galleys, he wrote to Q. Kalenus, in Achaia, to furnish him with a squadron of ships. But these not coming with that despatch which the danger our army was in required, because Octavius pressed hard upon them ; **he fastened beaks to all the** barks and **vessels** that lay in the port, whose number was considerable enough, **though they** were not sufficiently large **for an engagement.** Joining these to **what galleys he** had, and putting the veteran **soldiers** aboard, whereof he had a great number, who had been **left sick at** Brundusium, **when the** army went over to Greece, he sailed for Illyricum ; where having subjected several maritime states that had declared for Octavius ; and neglecting such as continued obstinate in their revolt, because he would suffer nothing to retard his design of meeting the enemy ; he came up with Octavius before Epidaurus; and obliging him to raise the siege, which he was carrying on with great vigour, by sea and land, joined the garrison to his own forces.

XXXV. Octavius, understanding that Vatinius's fleet consisted mostly of small barks, and confiding in the strength of his own, stopped at the Isle of Tauris. Vatinius followed him thither, not imagining he would halt at that place, but because he **was** determined to pursue him **wherever he went.** Vatinius, who had no **suspicion of an enemy, and** whose ships were moreover **dispersed by a** tempest, perceived, **as he approached the isle,** a vessel filled **with soldiers, that advanced towards** him with full **sails.** Upon this, he gave orders for furling the sails, lowering the sail-yards, and arming the soldiers: and hoisting **a** flag, as a signal for battle, intimated to the ships that followed to do the same. Our men prepared themselves in the best manner their sudden surprise would allow, while Octavius advanced, in good order, from the port. The two fleets drew up. Octavius had the advantage as to disposition, and Vatinius in the bravery of his troops.

XXXVI. Vatinius finding himself inferior to the enemy, both in the number and largeness of his ships, resolved to commit the affair to fortune, and, therefore, in his own quinquereme, attacked Octavius in his four-benched galley

This he did with such violence, and the shock was so great, that the beak of Octavius's galley was broke. The battle raged with great fury likewise in other places, but chiefly round the two admirals: for as the ships on each side advanced to sustain those that fought, a close and furious conflict ensued in a very narrow sea, where the nearer the vessels approached, the more had Vatinius's soldiers the advantage. For, with admirable courage, they leaped into the enemy's ships, and forcing them, by this means, to an equal combat, soon mastered them by their superior valour. Octavius's galley was sunk. Many others were taken, or suffered the same fate. The soldiers were partly slain in the ships, partly thrown overboard into the sea. Octavius got into a boat, which sinking under the multitude that crowded after him, he himself, though wounded, swam to his brigantine; where being taken up, and night having put an end to the battle, as the wind blew very strong, he spread all his sails and fled. A few of his ships, that had the good fortune to escape, followed him.

XXXVII. Vatinius, seeing the enemy entirely defeated, sounded a retreat, and entered victorious the port whence Octavius had sailed to fight him, without the loss of a single vessel. He took, in this battle, one quinquereme, two triremes, eight two-benched galleys, and a great number of rowers. The next day was employed in repairing his own fleet, and the ships he had taken from the enemy: after which, he sailed for the island of Issa, imagining Octavius would retire thither after his defeat. In this island was a flourishing city, well affected to Octavius, which, however, surrendered to Vatinius, upon the first summons. Here he understood that Octavius, attended by a few small barks, had sailed, with a fair wind, for Greece, whence he intended to pass on to Sicily, and afterwards to Africa. Vatinius having, in so short a space, successfully terminated the affairs of Illyricum, restored the province, in a peaceable condition, to Cornificius, and driven the enemy's fleet out of those seas, returned victorious to Brundusium, with his army and fleet in good condition.

XXXVIII. While Cæsar besieged Pompey at Dyrrhachium, triumphed at Pharsalia, and carried on the war, with so much danger, at Alexandria, Cassius Longinus, who had been left in Spain as pro-pretor of the farther province; either through his natural disposition, or out of a hatred he had contracted to the province, because of a wound he had treacherously received there, when questor, drew upon himself the general dislike of the people. He discerned this temper among them, partly from a consciousness that he deserved it, partly from the manifest indications they gave of their discontent. To secure himself against their disaffection, he endeavoured to gain the love of the soldiers; and having, for this purpose, assembled them together, promised them a hundred sesterces a man. Soon after, having made himself master of Medobriga, a town in Lusitania, and of Mount Herminius, whither the Medobrigians had retired; and being, upon that occasion, saluted imperator, by the army, he gave them another hundred sesterces each. These, accompanied with other considerable largesses, in great number, seemed, for the present, to increase the good-will of the army, but tended gradually and imperceptibly to the relaxation of military discipline.

XXXIX. Cassius having sent his army into winter-quarters, fixed his residence at Cordova, for the administration of justice. Being greatly in debt, he resolved to pay it by laying heavy impositions upon the province; and, according to the custom of prodigals, made his liberalities a pretence to justify the most exorbitant demands. He taxed the rich at discretion, and compelled them to pay, without the least regard to their remonstrances; frequently improving light and trifling offences, as a handle for all manner of extortions. All methods of gain were pursued, whether great and apparent, or mean and sordid. None that had any thing to lose could escape accusation; insomuch that the plunder of their private fortunes was aggravated by the dangers they were exposed to from pretended crimes.

XL. Thus Longinus, acting the same part when pro-consul which he had done when questor, drew upon himself the like conspiracies against his life. Even his own dependants concurred in the general hatred; who, though the ministers of his rapine, yet hated the man by whose authority they committed those crimes. The odium still increased upon his raising a fifth legion, which added to the expense and burden of the province. The cavalry was augmented to three thousand, with costly ornaments and equipage; nor had the people any respite from his extortions.

XLI. Meanwhile he received orders from Cæsar, to transport his army into Africa, and march through Mauritania, towards Numidia, because king Juba had sent considerable succours to Pompey, and was preparing to send more. These letters filled him with an insolent joy, by the opportunity they offered him of pillaging new provinces and a wealthy kingdom. He therefore hastened into Lusitania, to assemble his legions, and draw together a body of auxiliaries; appointing certain persons to provide corn, ships, and money, that nothing might retard him at his return; which was much sooner than expected; for when interest called, Cassius wanted neither industry nor vigilance.

XLII. Having got his army together, and encamped near Cordova, he made a speech to the soldiers, wherein he acquainted them with the orders he had received from Cæsar, and promised them a hundred sesterces each, when they should arrive in Mauritania. The fifth legion, he told them, was to remain in Spain. Having ended his speech, he returned to Cordova. The same day, about noon, as he went to the hall of justice, one Minutius Silo, a client of L. Racilius, presented him with a paper, in a soldier's habit, as if he had some request to make. Then retiring behind Racilius,(who walked beside Cassius,) as if waiting for an answer, he insensibly drew near; and a favourable opportunity offering, seized Cassius with his left hand, and wounded him twice with a dagger in his right. The noise this occasioned was as a signal to the conspirators, who all rushed upon him in a body. Munatius Plancus killed the lictor, that was next Longinus; and wounded Q. Cassius his lieutenant. T. Vasius, and L. Mergilio, seconded their countryman Plancus; for they were all Italians. L. Licinius Squillus flew upon Longinus himself, and gave him several slight wounds as he lay upon the ground. By this time, his guards came up to his assistance, (for he always had a body of veterans, armed with darts, to attend him,) and surrounded the rest of the conspirators, who were advancing to complete the assassination. Of this number were Calphurnius Salvianus, and Manilius Tusculus. Cassius was carried home; and Minutius Silo, stumbling upon a stone, as he endeavoured to make his escape, was taken

and brought to him. Racilius retired to the neighbouring house of a friend till he should have certain information of the fate of Cassius L. Laterensis not doubting but he was despatched, ran, in a transport of joy, to the camp, to congratulate the second and the new-raised legions upon it, who, he knew, bore a particular hatred to Cassius; and who, immediately upon this intelligence, placed him on the tribunal, and proclaimed him pretor. For there was not a native of the province, nor a soldier of the new-raised legion, nor a person, who by long residence was naturalised to the province, of which kind the second legion consisted, who did not join in the general hatred of Cassius. Meantime Laterensis was informed that Cassius was still alive; at which, being rather grieved than disconcerted, he immediately so far recovered himself as to go and wait upon him. By this time, the thirtieth legion having notice of what had passed, marched to Cordova, to the assistance of their general. The twenty-first and fifth followed their example. As only two legions remained in the camp, the second, fearing they should be left alone, and thereby have their sentiments known, did the same. But the new-raised legion continued firm, nor could be induced by any motives of fear, to stir from its place. Cassius ordered all the accomplices of the conspiracy to be seized, and sent back the fifth legion to the camp, retaining the other three. By the confession of Minutius, he learned, that L. Racilius, L. Laterensis, and Annius Scapula, a man of great authority and credit in the province, and equally in his confidence with Laterensis and Racilius, were concerned in the plot: nor did he long defe. his revenge, but ordered them to be put to death. He delivered Minutius to be racked by his freed-men; likewise Calphurnius Salvianus; who, turning evidence, increased the number of the conspirators; justly, as some think; but others pretend that he was forced. L. Mergilio was likewise put to the torture. Squillus impeached many others, who were all condemned to die, except such as redeemed their lives by a fine; for he pardoned Calphurnius for ten, and Q. Sextius for fifty thousand sesterces; who though deeply guilty yet having, in this manner, escaped death, showed Cassius to be no less covetous than cruel.

XLIII. Some days after, he received let

ters from Cæsar, with an account of Pompey's defeat and flight; which news equally affected him with joy and sorrow. Cæsar's success gave him pleasure; but the conclusion of the war would put an end to his rapines: insomuch that he was uncertain which to wish for, victory, or an unbounded licentiousness. When he was cured of his wounds, he sent to all who were indebted to him, in any sums, and insisted upon immediate payment. Such as were taxed too low, had orders to furnish larger sums. Such Roman citizens as had been levied in the several colonies of the province, and were alarmed at the thoughts of a foreign expedition, obtained their discharge for a certain sum. This brought in a vast revenue, but greatly increased the general hatred. He afterwards reviewed the army, sent the legions and auxiliaries, designed for Africa, towards the straits of Hercules, and went himself to Seville, to examine the condition of the fleet. He stayed there some time, in consequence of an edict he had published, ordering all who had not paid the sums in which they were amerced, to repair to him thither; which created a universal murmuring and discontent.

XLIV. In the mean time, L. Titius, a military tribune of the new-raised legion, sent him notice of a report, that the thirtieth legion, one of those he was carrying with him to Africa, had mutinied at Ilurgis, killed some of the centurions that opposed them, and were gone over to the second legion, who marched another way towards the straits. Upon this intelligence, he set out, by night, with five cohorts of the twenty-first legion, and came up with them in the morning. He stayed there that day, to consult what was proper to be done, and then went to Carmona, where he found the thirtieth and twenty-first legions, with four cohorts of the fifth, and all the cavalry assembled. Here he learned, that the new-raised legion had surprised four cohorts, near Obucula, and forced them along with them to the second legion; where all joining, they had chosen T. Thorius, an Italian, for their general. Having instantly called a council, he sent Marcellus to Cordova, to secure that town, and Q. Cassius, his lieutenant, to Seville. A few days after, news was brought that Cordova had revolted, and that Marcellus, either voluntarily, or through force, (for the reports were various,)

had joined them; as likewise the two cohorts of the fifth legion, that were in garrison there. Cassius, provoked at these mutinies, decamped, and the next day came to Segovia upon the river Xenil. There, summoning an assembly to sound the disposition of the troops, he found that it was not out of regard to him but to Cæsar, though absent, that they continued faithful, and were ready to undergo any danger for the recovery of the province.

XLV. Meantime Thorius marched the veteran legions to Cordova; and that the revolt might not appear to spring from a seditious inclination in him or the soldiers; as likewise to oppose an equal authority to that of Q. Cassius, who was drawing together a great force, in Cæsar's name; he publicly gave out, that his design was to recover the province for Pompey. Nay, perhaps he was really influenced by a love for Pompey, whose name was dear to those legions that had served under Varro. Be this as it will, Thorius at least made it his pretence; and the soldiers were so infatuated with the thought, that they had Pompey's name inscribed upon their bucklers. The citizens of Cordova, men, women, and children, came out to meet the legions; begging they would not enter Cordova as enemies, seeing they joined with them in their aversion to Cassius, and only desired they might not be obliged to act against Cæsar.

XLVI. The soldiers, moved by the prayers and tears of so great a multitude, and seeing they stood in no need of Pompey's name and memory, to spirit up a revolt against Cassius, as he was equally odious to the partisans of both parties; neither being able to prevail with Marcellus, or the people of Cordova, to declare against Cæsar; they erased Pompey's name from their bucklers, chose Marcellus their commander, joined the citizens of Cordova, and encamped near the town. Two days after Cassius encamped on an eminence, on this side the Bætis, about four miles from Cordova, and within view of the town; whence he sent letters to Bogud, in Mauritania, and M. Lepidus, pro-consul of Hither Spain, to come to his assistance as soon as possible, for Cæsar's sake. Meanwhile he ravaged the country, and set fire to the buildings round Cordova.

XLVII. The legions under Marcellus, provoked at this indignity, ran to him, and begged to be led against the enemy, that they might have an opportunity of fighting them before they could have time to destroy, with fire and sword, the rich and noble possessions of the Cordovans. Marcellus, though averse to battle, which, whoever was victorious, must turn to Cæsar's detriment; yet unable to restrain the legions, crossed the Bætis, and drew up his men. Cassius did the same, upon a rising ground: but as he would not quit his advantageous post, Marcellus persuaded his men to return to their camp. He had already begun to retire, when Cassius, knowing himself to be stronger in cavalry, fell upon the legionaries with his horse, and made a considerable slaughter in their rear, upon the banks of the river. This check making Marcellus sensible of the mistake he had committed, in passing the river, he removed his camp to the other side, where both armies frequently drew up, but did not engage, on account of the inequality of the ground.

XLVIII. Marcellus was stronger in foot, for he commanded veteran soldiers, of great experience in war. Cassius depended more on the fidelity than the courage of his troops. The two camps being very near each other, Marcellus seized a spot of ground, where he built a fort, very convenient for depriving the enemy of water. Longinus apprehending he should be besieged, in a country where all were against him, quitted his camp in the night, and, by a quick march, reached Ulla, a town on which he thought he could rely. There he encamped so near the walls, that both by the situation of the place (for Ulla stands on an eminence) and the defences of the town, he was on all sides secure from an attack. Marcellus followed him, and encamped as near the town as possible. Having taken a view of the place, he found himself reduced, by necessity, to do what was most agreeable to his own inclination; and neither engage Cassius, which the ardour of his soldiers would have forced him to, had it been possible; nor suffered him by his exertions, to infest the territories of other states, as he had done those of Cordova. He therefore raised redoubts in proper places, and continued his works quite round the town, enclosing both Ulla and Cassius within his lines. But before they were finished, Cassius sent out all his cavalry: who he imagined might do him great service, by cutting off Marcellus's provisions and forage; and could only be a useless encumbrance upon him, by consuming his provisions, if he was shut up in his camp.

XLIX. A few days after, king Bogud having received Cassius's letters, came and joined him with all his forces, consisting of one legion, and several auxiliary cohorts. For as commonly happens in civil dissensions, some of the states of Spain at that time favoured Cassius, but a yet greater number, Marcellus Bogud came up to the advanced works of Marcellus, where many sharp skirmishes happened with various success; however, Marcellus still kept possession of his works.

L. Meanwhile Lepidus, from the higher province, with thirty-five legionary cohorts, and a great body of horse and auxiliaries, came to Ulla, with design to adjust the differences between Cassius and Marcellus. Marcellus submitted, without hesitation, but Cassius kept within his works, either because he thought his cause the justest, or from an apprehension that his adversary's submission had prepossessed Lepidus in his favour. Lepidus encamped with Marcellus, at Ulla, prevented a battle, invited Cassius into his camp, and engaged his honour to act without prejudice. Cassius hesitated long, but at last desired that the circumvallation should be levelled, and free egress given him. The truce was not only concluded, but the works demolished, and the guards drawn off; when king Bogud attacked one of Marcellus's forts, that lay nearest to his camp, unknown to any, (unless perhaps Longinus, who was not exempt from suspicion on this occasion,) and slew a great number of his men. And had not Lepidus interposed, much mischief would have been done.

LI. A free passage being made for Cassius, Marcellus joined camps with Lepidus; and both together marched for Cordova, while Cassius retired to Carmona. At the same time, Trebonius, the pro-consul, came to take possession of the province. Cassius having notice of his arrival, sent his legions and cavalry into winter quarters, and hastened, with all his effects, to Melaca, where he embarked immediately, though it was the winter season; that he might not, as he pretended, come into the power of Marcellus, Lepidus, and Trebonius: as his friends gave out, to avoid passing through a province, great part of which had revolted from him; but as was more generally believed, to secure the money he had amassed by his numberless extortions. The wind favouring him as far as could be expected at that season of the year, he put into the Iberus, to avoid sailing in the night; and thence continuing his voyage, which he thought he might do with safety, though the wind blew considerably fresher, he was encountered by such a storm, at the mouth of the river, that neither being able to return, because of the stream, nor stem the fury of the waves, the ship, and all that were in her, perished.

LII. Cæsar arriving in Syria from Egypt, and understanding by those who attended him there, from Rome, and the letters he received at the same time, that the government there was upon a very bad footing, and all the affairs of the commonwealth managed indiscreetly: that the contests of the tribunes were producing perpetual seditions, and the remissness of the officers of the legions destroying military discipline; all which required his speedy presence to redress them; thought it yet first incumbent upon him, to settle the state of the provinces through which he passed; that freeing them from domestic conventions, and the fear of a foreign enemy, the laws might have a free course. This he hoped soon to effect in Syria, Cilicia, and Asia, because these provinces were not involved in war. In Bithynia and Pontus indeed he expected more trouble, because he understood Pharnaces still continued in Pontus, and was not likely to quit it easily, being flushed with the victory he had obtained over Domitius Calvinus. He made a short stay in most states of note, distributing rewards both publicly and privately to such as deserved them, determining old controversies, and receiving into his protection the kings, princes, and potentates, as well of the provinces as of the neighbouring countries. And having settled the necessary regulations for the defence of the country, he dismissed them, fully satisfied with himself and the republic.

LIII. After a stay of some days in those parts, he named Sextus Cæsar, his friend and relation, to the command of Syria, and the legions appointed to guard it; and sailed himself for Cilicia, with the fleet he had brought from Egypt. He summoned the states to assemble at Tarsus, the strongest and finest city of the province; where having settled every thing that regarded either it or the neighbouring countries, his warlike ardour would not suffer him to tarry longer; but marching through Cappadocia with the utmost expe-

dition, where he stopped two days at Mazaca, he arrived at Comana, renowned for the ancient and sacred temple of Bellona, where she is worshipped with so much veneration, that her priest is accounted next in power and dignity to the king. He conferred this dignity on Lycomedes of Bithynia, descended of the ancient kings of Cappadocia, who demanded it in right of inheritance; his ancestors having lost it upon occasion of the sceptre's being transferred to another line. As for Ariobarzanes, and his brother Ariarates, who had both deserved well of the commonwealth, he confirmed the first in his kingdom, and put the other under his protection; after which, he pursued his march with the same despatch.

LIV. Upon his approaching Pontus, and the frontiers of Gallo-græcia; Dejotarus, tetrarch of that province, (whose title, however, was disputed by the neighbouring tetrarchs,) and king of the Lesser Armenia, laying aside the regal ornaments, and assuming the habit not only of a private person, but even of a criminal, came in a suppliant manner to Cæsar, " To beg forgiveness, for obeying and assisting Pompey at a time when Cæsar could afford him no protection: urging, that it was his business to obey the governors who were present, without pretending to judge of the disputes of the people of Rome." Cæsar, after putting him in mind " of the many services he had done him, and the decrees he had procured in his favour when consul; that his defection could claim no excuse from want of information, because one of his industry and prudence could not but know who was master of Italy and Rome, where the senate, the people, and the majesty of the republic resided; who in fine was consul after Marcellus and Lentulus; told him, that he would, notwithstanding, forgive his present fault, in consideration of his past services, the former friendship that had subsisted between them, the respect due to his age, and the solicitation o those who interceded in his behalf: adding, that he would refer the controversy relating to the tetrarchate to another time." He restored him the royal habit, and commanded him to join him with all his cavalry, and the legion he had trained up after the Roman manner.

LV. When he was arrived in Pontus, and had drawn all his forces together, which were not very considerable either for their number or discipline, (for except the sixth legion, composed of veteran soldiers, which he had brought with him from Alexandria, and which by its many labours and dangers, the length of its marches and voyages, and the frequent wars in which it had been engaged, was reduced to less than a thousand men; he had only the legion of Dejotarus, and two more that had been in the late battle between Domitius and Pharnaces:) ambassadors arrived from Pharnaces, "To entreat that Cæsar would not look upon him as an enemy, he being ready to submit to all his commands." Particularly they represented: "That Pharnaces had granted no aid to Pompey, as Dejotarus had done, whom he had nevertheless pardoned." Cæsar replied, "That Pharnaces should meet with the utmost justice, if he performed his promises: but at the same time admonished the ambassadors in gentle terms, to forbear mentioning Dejotarus, and not to overrate the having refused aid to Pompey. He told them, he was always ready to forgive the suppliant, but would never look upon private services to himself, as an atonement for public injuries done the province: that Pharnaces's refusal of aiding Pompey had turned chiefly to his own advantage, as he had thereby avoided all share in the disaster of Pharsalia: that he was, however, willing to forgive the injuries done to the Roman citizens in Pontus, because it was now too late to think of redressing them; as he could neither restore life to the dead, nor manhood to those he had deprived of it, by a punishment more intolerable to the Romans than death itself. But that he must quit Pontus immediately, send back the farmers of the revenues, and restore to the Romans and their allies what he unjustly detained from them. These things performed, he might then send the presents which successful generals were wont to receive from their friends:" (for Pharnaces had sent him a golden crown.) With this answer he dismissed the ambassadors.

LVI. Pharnaces promised every thing: but hoping that Cæsar, who was in haste to be gone, would give easy credit to whatever he said, that he might the sooner set out upon more urgent affairs; (for every body knew that his presence was much wanted at Rome,) he performed but slowly, wanted to protract the day of his departure, demanded other conditions, and, in fine, endeavoured to elude his engagements. Cæsar, perceiving his drift,

did now, out of necessity, what he was usually wont to do through inclination, and resolved to decide the affair as soon as possible by a battle.

LVII. Ziela is a town of Pontus, well fortified, though situated in a plain. For a natural eminence, as if raised by art, sustains the walls on all sides. All around are a great number of large mountains, intersected by valleys. The highest of these, famed by the victory of Mithridates, the defeat of Triarius, and the destruction of our army, is not above three miles from Ziela, and has a ridge that almost extends to the town. Here Pharnaces lodged himself, with all his forces, repairing the fortifications of a camp which had proved so fortunate to his father.

LVIII. Cæsar encamped about five miles from the enemy; and observing that the valleys which defended the king's camp would likewise defend his own, at the same distance, if the enemy, who were much nearer, did not seize them before him; he ordered a great quantity of fascines to be brought within the intrenchments. This being quickly performed, next night, at the fourth watch, leaving all the baggage in the camp, he set out with the legions; and arriving at day-break, unsuspected by the enemy, possessed himself of the same post where Mithridates had defeated Triarius. Hither he commanded all the fascines to be brought, employing the servants of the army for that purpose, that the soldiers might not be called off from the works; because the valley, which divided the eminence where he was **intrenching himself from** the enemy, was not above **a mile over.**

LIX. Pharnaces perceiving this next morning, ranged all his troops, in **order of** battle, before his camp. But the approach towards us was so dangerous, that Cæsar concluded it to be no more than a review; or done with design to retard his works, by keeping a great number of his men under arms; or perhaps for ostentation, to show that he trusted no less to his army than the advantage of his post. Therefore keeping only his first line in order of battle, he commanded the rest of the army to go on with the works. But Pharnaces either prompted by the place itself, which had been so fortunate to his father; or induced by favourable omens, as we were afterwards told; or despising the small number of our men that were in arms; for he took all that were employed in carrying materials to the works

le soldiers; or confiding in his veteran army, who valued themselves upon having defeated the twenty-second legion; and at the same time, contemning our troops, whom he had worsted, under Domitius; was determined upon a battle, and to that end began to cross the valley. Cæsar, at first, laughed at his ostentation, in crowding his army in so narrow a place, where no enemy, in his right senses, would have ventured; while, in the mean time, Pharnaces continued his march, and began to ascend the steep hill on which Cæsar was posted

LX. Cæsar, astonished at his incredible rashness and confidence, and finding himself suddenly and unexpectedly attacked, called off his soldiers from the works, ordered them to arms, opposed the legions to the enemy, and ranged his troops in order of battle. The suddenness of the thing occasioned some terror at first; and the chariots, armed with scythes, falling in with our ranks before they were completed, disordered them considerably: however, the multitude of darts discharged against them, soon put a stop to their career. The enemy's army followed them close, and began the battle with a shout. Our advantageous situation, but especially the assistance of the gods, who preside over all the events of war, and more particularly those where human conduct can be of no service, favoured us greatly on this occasion.

LXI. After a sharp and obstinate conflict, victory began to declare for us on the right wing, where the sixth legion was posted. The enemy there was totally overthrown, but in the centre and left the battle was long and doubtful: however, with the assistance of the same gods, we at last prevailed there also, and drove them, with the utmost precipitation, down the hill, which they had so easily ascended before. Great numbers being slain, and many crushed, by the flight of their own troops, such as had the good fortune to escape, were nevertheless obliged to throw away their arms; so that having crossed the valley, and got upon the opposite ascent, they could yet, because unarmed, derive no benefit from the advantage of the ground. Our men, flushed with victory, made no scruple to follow them, and even attack their camp; which they soon

forced, notwithstanding the resistance made by the cohorts left by Pharnaces to guard it. Almost all the whole army was cut to pieces or made prisoners. Pharnaces himself escaped, with a few horse; and had not our soldiers been detained some time, by the assault of the camp, he must certainly have fallen alive into Cæsar's hands.

LXII. Though Cæsar was accustomed to victory, yet the present success gave him no small joy; because he had so speedily put an end to a very great war. The remembrance too of the danger to which he had been exposed, enhanced the pleasure, as he had obtained an easy victory in a very difficult conjuncture. Having thus recovered Pontus, and abandoned the plunder of the enemy's camp to the soldiers, he set out next day, with a guard of light horse. The sixth legion had orders to return to Italy, to receive the honours and rewards they had merited: the auxiliary troops of Dejotarus were sent home: and Cælius Vincinianus was left with two legions to protect the kingdom of Pontus.

LXIII. Through Gallo-græcia and Bithynia he went into Asia, settling all the controversies of the provinces as he passed, and establishing the limits and jurisdictions of the several kings, states, and tetrarchs. Mithridates of Pergamus, who had so speedily and successfully served him in Egypt, as we have related above, a man of royal descent and education, (for Mithridates, king of all Asia, out of regard to his birth, had carried him along with him when very young, and kept him in his camp several years,) was appointed king of Bosphorus, which had belonged to Pharnaces. And thus were the provinces of the Roman people screened from the attempts of barbarous and hostile kings, by the interposition of a prince steadily attached to the interests of the republic. To this was added the tetrarchate of Gallo-græcia, which belonged to him of right, though it had been possessed for some years by Dejotarus. Thus Cæsar, staying no where longer than the necessity of affairs required, and having settled all things relating to the provinces with the utmost success and despatch, returned to Italy much sooner than was expected.

27

2 R

PANSA'S COMMENTARIES

OF THE

AFRICAN WAR

THE ARGUMENT.

PANSA'S COMMENTARIES

OF

THE AFRICAN WAR.

I. CÆSAR setting out from Rome, advanced by moderate journeys towards Sicily; and continuing his march without intermission, arrived on the nineteenth of December at Lilybæum. Designing to embark immediately, though he had only one legion of new levies, and not quite six hundred horse, he ordered his tent to be pitched so near the sea-side, that the waves flowed up to the very foot of it. This he did with a view to take away all hopes of delay, and keep his men in readiness at a day or an hour's warning. The wind at that time proving contrary, he nevertheless suffered none of the soldiers or mariners to come on shore, that he might lose no opportunity of sailing; the rather, because the inhabitants of the province were perpetually talking of the mighty forces of the enemy: a cavalry not to be numbered; four legions headed by Juba, together with a great body of light armed troops; ten legions under the command of Scipio; a hundred and twenty elephants, and fleets in abundance. Yet all these reports alarmed him not, nor aught abated his resolution and confidence. Meantime the number of galleys and transports increased daily; the new levied legions flocked in to him from all parts; among the rest the fifth, a veteran legion, and about two thousand horse.

II. Having got together six legions, and about two thousand horse, he embarked the legions as fast as they arrived, in the galleys, and the cavalry in the transports. Then sending the greatest part of the fleet before, with orders to sail for the island of Aponiana, not far from Lilybæum; he himself continued a little longer in Sicily, to expose to public sale some confiscated estates. Leaving all other affairs to the care of Allienus the pretor, who then commanded in the island; and strictly charging him to use the utmost expedition in embarking the remainder of the troops; he set sail the twenty-seventh of December, and soon came up with the rest of the fleet. As the wind was favourable, and afforded a quick passage, he arrived the fourth day within sight of Africa, attended by a few galleys: for the transports, being mostly dispersed and scattered by the winds, were driven different ways. Passing Clupea and Neapolis with the fleet, he continued for some time to coast along the shore, leaving many towns and castles behind him.

III. When he came before Adrumetum, where the enemy had a garrison, commanded by C. Considius, and where Cn. Piso appeared upon the shore, towards Clupea, with the cavalry of Adrumetum, and about two thousand Moors; having stopped a while, facing the port, till the rest of the fleet should come up, he landed his men, though their number at that time did not exceed three thousand foot, and a hundred and fifty horse. There, encamping before the town, he continued quiet in his intrenchments, without offering any act of hostility, or suffering his men to plunder the country. Meantime the inhabitants manned the walls, and assembled in great numbers before the gates, to defend the town, whose garrison amounted to two legions. Cæsar having taken a view of the place, and thoroughly examined its situation

27*

309

on all sides, returned to his camp. Some blamed his conduct on this occasion, and charged him with a considerable oversight, in not appointing a place of rendezvous to the pilots and captains of the fleet, or at least not delivering them sealed instructions, according to his usual custom; which being opened at a certain time, might have directed them where to assemble. But in this Cæsar acted not without design: for as he knew of no port in Africa that was clear of the enemy's forces, and where the fleet might rendezvous in security, he chose to rely entirely upon fortune, and land where occasion offered.

IV In the mean time, L. Plancus, one of Cæsar's lieutenants, desired leave to treat with Considius, and try, if possible, to bring him to reason. Leave being granted accordingly, he wrote him a letter, and sent it into the town by a messenger. When the messenger arrived, and presented the letter, Considius demanding whence it came, and being told from Cæsar, the Roman general, answered: that he knew no general of the Roman forces but Scipio. Then commanding the messenger to be immediately slain in his presence, he delivered the letter, unopened, to a trusty partisan, with orders to carry it directly to Scipio.

V. Cæsar had now continued a day and a night before the town, without receiving any answer from Considius; the rest of the forces were not yet arrived; his cavalry was very inconsiderable; the troops he had with him were mostly new levies, and not sufficiently numerous to invest the place: neither did he think it advisable, upon his first landing, to expose the army to wounds and fatigue; more especially, as the town was strongly fortified, extremely difficult of access, and the garrison full of spirits, in expectation of a great body of horse, who were said to be upon their march to join them. For all these reasons, he determined not to attempt a siege; lest while he pursued that design, the enemy's cavalry should come behind and surround him. But as he was drawing off his men, the garrison made a sudden sally; and Juba's horse, whom he had sent to receive their pay, happening just then to come up, they jointly took possession of the camp Cæsar had left, and began to harass his rear. This being perceived, the legionaries immediately halted; and the cavalry, though few in number, boldly charged the vast multitude of the enemy. On this occasion it was, that less than thirty Gallic horse, by an incredible and astonishing effort of valour, repulsed two thousand Moors, and drove them quite within the town. Having thus compelled the enemy to retire, and shelter themselves behind their walls, Cæsar resumed his intended march: but observing that they often repeated their sallies, renewing the pursuit from time to time, and again flying when attacked by the horse; he posted some veteran cohorts, with part of the cavalry, in the rear, to cover his retreat, and so proceeded slowly on his march. The farther he advanced from Adrumetum, the less eager were the Numidians to pursue. Meantime, deputies arrived from the several towns and castles on the road, offering to furnish him with corn, and receive his commands. Towards the evening of that day, which was the first of January, he reached Ruspina, and there fixed his camp.

VI. Thence he removed, and came before Leptis, a free city, and governed by its own laws. Here he was also met by deputies from the town, who came, in the name of the inhabitants, to make an offer of their submission and services. Whereupon, placing centurions and a guard before the gates, to prevent the soldiers from entering, or offering violence to any of the inhabitants, he himself encamped towards the shore, not far distant from the town. Hither by accident arrived some of the galleys and transports, by whom he was informed, that the rest of the fleet, uncertain what course to pursue, had been steering for Utica. This obliged him to keep with the army near the sea, and avoid marching into the inland provinces, that he might be at hand to join his troops upon their arrival. He likewise sent the cavalry back to their ships, probably to hinder the country from being plundered, and ordered fresh water to be carried to them on board. Meanwhile the rowers, who were employed in this service, were suddenly and unexpectedly attacked by the Moorish horse, who killed some, and wounded many with their darts. For the manner of these barbarians is to lie in ambush with their horses among the valleys, and suddenly launch upon an enemy; they seldom choosing to engage hand to hand in a plain.

VII. In the mean time, Cæsar despatched letters and messengers into Sardinia and the neighbouring provinces, with orders, as soon as the letters came to hand, to send supplies of men, corn, and warlike stores; and having unloaded part of the fleet, detached it with Rabirius Posthumus, into Sicily, to bring over the second embarkation. At the same time he ordered out ten galleys, to get intelligence of the transports that had missed their way, and maintain the freedom of the sea. C. Sallustius Crispus, the pretor, was likewise sent out at the head of a squadron, to seize Cercina, then in the hands of the enemy, because he heard there was a great store of corn in that island: in giving these orders and instructions, he used all possible endeavours to leave no room for excuse or delay. Meanwhile having informed himself, from the deserters and natives, of the condition of Scipio and his followers; and understanding that they were at the whole charge of maintaining Juba's cavalry; he could not but pity the infatuation of men, who thus rather chose to be tributaries to the king of Numidia, than securely enjoy their fortunes at home with their fellow citizens.

VIII. The third of January he decamped; and leaving six cohorts at Leptis, under the command of Saserna, returned with the rest of the forces to Ruspina, whence he had come the day before. Here he deposited the baggage of the army; and marching out with a light body of troops to forage, ordered the inhabitants to follow with their horses and carriages. Having by this means got together a great quantity of corn, he came back to Ruspina. His design was, as far as I can judge, that by keeping possession of the maritime cities, and providing them with garrisons, he might secure a retreat for his fleet.

IX. Leaving therefore P. Saserna, the brother of him who commanded at Leptis, to take charge of the town, with one legion, and ordering all the wood that could be found to be carried into the place, he set out from Ruspina with seven cohorts, part of the veteran legions who had behaved so well in the fleet under Sulpicius and Vatinius; and marching directly for the port, which lies at about two miles' distance, embarked with them in the evening, without imparting his intentions to the army, who were extremely inquisitive concerning the general's design. His departure occasioned the utmost sadness and consternation among the troops; for being few in number, mostly new levies, and those not all suffered to land; they saw themselves exposed upon a foreign coast, to the mighty forces of a crafty nation, supported by an innumerable cavalry. Nor had they any resource in their present circumstances, or expectation of safety in their own conduct; but derived all their hope from the alacrity, vigour, and wonderful cheerfulness that appeared in the general's countenance: for he was of an intrepid spirit, and behaved with undaunted resolution and confidence. On his conduct, therefore, they entirely relied, and promised themselves to a man, that under so able and experienced a leader, all difficulties would vanish before them.

X. Cæsar having continued the whole night on board, about day-break prepared to set sail: when, all on a sudden, the part of the fleet that had given so much concern, appeared unexpectedly in view. Wherefore, ordering his men to quit their ships immediately, and receive the rest of the troops in arms upon the shore, he made the new fleet enter the port with the utmost diligence; and landing all the forces, horse and foot, returned again to Ruspina. Here he established his camp; and taking with him thirty cohorts, without baggage, advanced into the country to forage. Thus was Cæsar's purpose at length discovered: that he meant, unknown to the enemy, to have sailed to the assistance of the transports that had missed their way, lest they should unexpectedly fall in with the African fleet. Nor would he even impart his design to his own soldiers left behind in garrison; from an apprehension, that when they came to reflect upon their own weakness, and the strength of the enemy, they might too much give way to fear.

XI. Cæsar had not marched above three miles from his camp, when he was informed by his scouts, and some advanced parties of horse, that the enemy's forces were in view. At the same time a great cloud of dust began to appear. Upon this intelligence, Cæsar ordered all his horse, of which he had at that time but a very small number, to advance, as likewise his archers, only a few of whom had followed him from the camp; and the legions to march after him in order of battle, while he went forward at the head of a small party

Soon after, having discovered the enemy at some distance, he commanded the soldiers to repair to their arms, and prepare for battle. Their number in all did not exceed thirty cohorts, with about four hundred horse, and the archers.

XII. Meanwhile the enemy, under the command of Labienus, and the two Pacidii, drew up, with a very large front, consisting mostly of horse, whom they intermixed with light armed Numidians and archers; forming themselves in such close order, that Cæsar's army at a distance mistook them all for infantry; and strengthening their right and left with many squadrons of horse. Cæsar drew up his army in one line, obliged to it by the smallness of his numbers; covering his front with the archers, and placing his cavalry in the two wings, with particular instructions not to suffer themselves to be surrounded by the enemy's numerous horse; for he imagined that he was to have to do only with infantry.

XIII. As both sides stood in expectation of the signal, and Cæsar chose to continue without stirring from his post, as being sensible, that with such few troops, against so great a force, he must depend more on conduct and contrivance than strength; on a sudden, the enemy began to extend themselves, spread out upon the hills, on every side, and prepared to surround our horse, who were hardly able to maintain their ground against them. Meanwhile both the main bodies advancing to engage, the enemy's cavalry, intermixed with some light-armed Numidians, suddenly sprung forward, and attacked the legions with a shower of darts. Our men, preparing to return the charge, their horse retreated a little, while the foot continued to maintain their ground, till the others having rallied, came on again, with fresh vigour, to sustain them.

XIV. Cæsar perceiving that his ranks were in danger of being broken by this new way of fighting, (for our foot, in pursuing the enemy's horse, as they retreated, being forced to advance a considerable way beyond their colours, were flanked by the light-armed Numidians; while, at the same time, they could do but little execution against the cavalry, by reason of the quickness wherewith they retired,) gave express orders, that no soldier should advance above four feet beyond the ensigns. Meanwhile Labienus's cavalry, confiding in their numbers, endeavoured to surround those of

Cæsar; who, being few in number, and overpowered by the multitude of the enemy, were forced to give ground a little, their horses being almost all wounded. The enemy, encouraged by this, pressed on more and more; so that in an instant, the legions being surrounded, on all sides, were obliged to cast themselves into an orb, and fight, as if inclosed with barriers.

XV. Labienus, with his head uncovered, advanced on horseback to the front of the battle, to encourage his men. Sometimes addressing Cæsar's legions: "So ho! you raw soldiers there!" says he, "why so fierce! Has he infatuated you too with his words! Truly he has brought you into a fine condition! I pity you sincerely." Upon this, one of the soldiers: "I am none of your raw warriors, but a veteran of the tenth legion." "Where's your standard?" replied Labienus. "I'll soon make you sensible who I am," answered the soldier. Then pulling off his helmet, to discover himself, he threw a javelin with all his strength at Labienus, which wounding his horse severely in the breast: "Know, Labienus," says he, "that this dart was thrown by a soldier of the tenth legion." However, the whole army was not a little daunted, especially the new levies; and began to cast their eyes upon Cæsar, minding nothing, for the present, but to defend themselves from the enemy's darts.

XVI. Cæsar meanwhile perceiving the enemy's design, endeavoured to extend his order of battle **as much as possible,** directing the cohorts **to face about alternately** to the right and left. **By this means, he** broke the enemy's **circle with his right and** left wings, and attacking one part of **them, thus** separated from the other, with his horse and foot, at last put them to flight. He pursued them but a little way, fearing an ambuscade, and returned again to his own men. The same was done by the other division of Cæsar's horse and foot; so that the enemy being driven back on all sides, he retreated towards his camp, in order of battle.

XVII. Meantime M. Petreius, and Cn. Piso, with eleven hundred select Numidian horse, and a considerable body of foot, arrived to the assistance of the enemy: who recovering from their terror, upon this reinforcement, and again resuming courage, fell upon the rear of the legions, as they retreated, and endeavoured to hinder them from reaching their camp. Cæsar perceiving this, ordered his men to wheel about, and renew the battle. As the enemy still pursued their former plan, and avoided a close engagement, Cæsar, considering that the horses had not yet recovered the fatigue of their late voyage; that they were besides weakened with thirst, weariness, and wounds, and of course unfit for a vigorous and long pursuit, which even the time of the day would not allow, ordered both horse and foot to fall at once briskly upon the enemy, and not slacken the pursuit till they had driven them quite beyond the farthest hills, and taken possession of them themselves. Accordingly, upon a signal given, the enemy fighting in a faint and careless manner, he suddenly charged them with his horse and foot: who in a moment driving them from the field, and over the adjoining hill, kept possession of that post for some time, and then retired slowly, in order of battle, to their camp. The enemy, who, in this last attack, had been very rudely handled, thought proper likewise to do the same.

XVIII. The action being over, a great number of deserters, of all kinds, flocked to Cæsar's camp, besides multitudes of horse and foot, that were made prisoners. By them we learned, that it was the design of the enemy to have astonished our raw troops, with their new and uncommon manner of fighting; and after surrounding them with their cavalry, to have cut them to pieces, as they had done Curio; and that they had marched against us expressly with that intention. Labienus had even said, in the council of war, that he would lead such a numerous body of troops against us, as should fatigue us with the very slaughter, and defeat us even in the bosom of victory; for he relied more on the number than the valour of his troops. He had heard of the mutiny of the veteran legions at Rome, and their refusal to go into Africa; and was likewise well assured of the fidelity of his troops, who had served three years under him in Africa. He had a great number of Numidian cavalry and light-armed troops, besides the Gallic and German horse, whom he had drawn together, out of the remains of Pompey's army, and carried over with him from Brundusium; he had likewise the freedmen raised in the country, and trained to fight on horseback: and the multitude of Juba's for-

ces, his hundred and twenty elephants, his innumerable cavalry and legionaries, amounting to above twelve thousand. Emboldened by the hope such mighty forces raised in him, on the fourth of January, six days after Cæsar's arrival, he came against him, with sixteen hundred Gallic and German horse, nine hundred under Petreius, eight thousand Numidians, four times that number of light-armed foot, with a multitude of archers and slingers. The battle lasted from eleven till sun-set, during which Petreius, receiving a dangerous wound, was obliged to quit the field.

XIX. Meantime Cæsar fortified his camp with much greater care, reinforced the guards, and threw up two intrenchments; one from Ruspina quite to the sea, the other from his camp to the sea likewise; to secure the communication, and receive supplies without danger. He landed a great number of darts and military engines, armed part of the mariners, Gauls, Rhodians, and others, that, after the example of the enemy, he might have a number of light-armed troops, to intermix with his cavalry. He likewise strengthened his army with a great number of Syrian and Iturean archers, whom he drew from the fleet into his camp; for he understood, that within three days Scipio was expected, with all his forces, consisting of eight legions, and four thousand horse. At the same time, he established work-shops, made a great number of darts and arrows, provided himself with leaden bullets and palisades, wrote to Sicily for hurdles and wood to make rams, because he had none in Africa, and likewise gave orders for sending corn; for the harvest, in that country, was like to be inconsiderable, the enemy having taken all the labourers into their service the year before, and stored up the grain in a few fortified towns, after demolishing the rest, forcing the inhabitants into the garrisoned places, and laying waste the whole country.

XX. In this necessity, by soothing the people, he obtained a small supply, and husbanded it with care. Meantime he was very exact in visiting the works, and relieving the guards. Labienus sent his sick and wounded, of which the number was very considerable, in wagons, to Adrumetum. Meanwhile Cæsar's transports, unacquainted with the coast, or where their general had landed, wandered up and down, in great uncertainty; and being attacked, one after another, by the enemy's

2 S

coasters, were, for the most part, either taken or burned. Cæsar being informed of this, stationed his fleet along the coast and islands, for the security of his convoys.

XXI. Meanwhile M. Cato, who commanded in Utica, never ceased urging and exhorting young Pompey, in words to this effect : " Your father, when he was at your age, and observed the commonwealth oppressed by wicked and daring men, and the honest party either slain or driven, by banishment, from their country and relations; incited by the greatness of his mind, and the love of glory, though then very young, and only a private man, had yet the courage to rally the remains of his father's army, and deliver Rome from the yoke of slavery and tyranny under which it groaned. He also recovered Sicily, Africa, Numidia, Mauritania, with amazing despatch; and, by that means, gained an illustrious and extensive reputation among all nations, and triumphed at three-and-twenty, while but a Roman knight. Nor did he enter upon the administration of public affairs, distinguished by the shining exploits of his father, or the fame and reputation of his ancestors, or the honours and dignities of the state. You, on the contrary, possessed of these honours, and the reputation acquired by your father; sufficiently distinguished by your own industry and greatness of mind; will you not bestir yourself, join your father's friends, and vindicate your own liberty, that of the commonwealth, and of every good and honest man?" The youth, roused by the remonstrances of that grave and worthy senator, got together about thirty sail, of all sorts, of which some few were ships of war, and sailing from Utica to Mauritania, invaded the kingdom of Bogud. And leaving his baggage behind him, with an army of two thousand men, partly freemen partly slaves, some armed some not, approached the town of Ascurum, in which the king had a garrison. The inhabitants suffered him to advance to the very walls and gates; when, sallying out, all on a sudden, they drove him quite back to his ships. This ill success determined him to leave that coast, nor did he afterwards land in any place, but steered directly for the Balearean Isles.

XXII. Meantime Scipio, leaving a strong garrison at Utica, began his march, with the forces we have described above, and encamped first at Adrumetum; when after a stay of a few days, setting out in the night, he joined Petreius and Labienus, lodging all the forces in one camp, about three miles distant from Cæsar's. Their cavalry were making continual excursions to our very works, intercepted those who ventured too far in quest of wood or water, and obliged us to keep within our intrenchments. This soon occasioned a great scarcity of provisions among Cæsar's men, because no supplies had yet arrived from Sicily or Sardinia. The season too was dangerous for navigation, and he did not possess above six miles, every way, in Africa, which also greatly straitened him for want of forage. The veteran soldiers and cavalry, who had been engaged in many wars, both by sea and land, and often struggled with wants and misfortunes of this kind, gathering seaweed and washing it in fresh water, by that means subsisted their horses and cattle.

XXIII. While things were in this situation, king Juba, being informed of Cæsar's difficulties, and the few troops he had with him, resolved not to allow him time to remedy his wants, or increase his army. Accordingly he left his kingdom, at the head of a great body of horse and foot, and marched to join his allies. Meantime, P. Sitius, and king Bogud, having intelligence of Juba's march, joined their forces, entered Numidia, and laying siege to Cirta, the most opulent city in the country, carried it in a few days, with two others belonging to the Getulians. They had offered the inhabitants leave to depart in safety, if they would peaceably deliver up the towns; but these conditions being rejected, they were taken by storm, and the citizens all put to the sword. They then fell to ravaging the country, and laying all the cities under contribution : of which Juba having intelligence, though he was upon the point of joining Scipio and the other chiefs, he determined to return to the relief of his own kingdom, rather than run the hazard of being driven from it while he was assisting others, and perhaps, after all, miscarry too in his designs against Cæsar. He therefore retired with his troops, leaving only thirty elephants behind him, and marched to the relief of his own cities and territories.

XXIV. Meanwhile Cæsar, knowing that the province still doubted of his arrival, and imagined that not himself in person, but some of his lieutenants had come over with the forces lately sent, despatched letters to all the several states, to inform them of his presence. Upon this many persons of rank fled to his camp, complaining of the barbarity and cruelty of the enemy. Hitherto he had continued quiet in his post; but touched with their fears, and a sense of their sufferings, he resolved to take the field as soon as the weather would permit, and he could draw his troops together. He immediately despatched letters into Sicily, to Allienus and Rabirius Posthumus the pretors, that without delay or excuse, either of the winter or the winds, they must send over the rest of the troops, to save Africa from utter ruin; because without some speedy remedy, not a single house would be left standing, nor any thing escape the fury and ravages of the enemy. But such was his impatience, and so long did the time appear, that from the day the letters were sent, he complained without ceasing of the delay of the fleet, and had his eyes night and day turned towards the sea. Nor ought we to wonder at his behaviour on this occasion: for he saw the villages burned, the country laid waste, the cattle destroyed, the towns plundered, the principal citizens either slain or put in chains, and their children dragged into servitude under the name of hostages, nor could he, amidst all this scene of misery, afford any relief to those who implored his protection, because of the small number of his forces. He kept the soldiers, however, at work upon the intrenchments, built forts and redoubts, and carried on his line quite to the sea.

XXV. Meanwhile Scipio made use of the following contrivance for training and disciplining his elephants. He drew up two parties in order of battle; one of slingers, who were to act as enemies, and discharge small stones against the elephants; and fronting them, the elephants themselves, in one line, with his whole army behind them in battle-array; that when the enemy, by their discharge of stones, had frightened the elephants, and forced them to turn upon their own men, they might again be made to face the enemy, by the vollies of stones from the army behind them. The work, however, went on but slowly, because these animals, after many years' teaching, are often no less prejudicial to those who bring them into the field, than to the enemy against whom they were intended.

XXVI. Whilst the two generals were thus employed near Ruspina, C. Virgilius Pretor-

ius, who commanded in Thapsus, a maritime city, observing some of Cæsar's transports that had missed their way, uncertain where he had landed or held his camp; and thinking that a fair opportunity offered of destroying them, manned a galley that was in the port with soldiers and archers, and joining with it a few armed barks, began to pursue Cæsar's ships. Though he was repulsed on several occasions, he still pursued his design, and at last fell in with one, on board of which were two young Spaniards, of the name of Titus, who were tribunes of the fifth legion, and whose father had been made a senator by Cæsar. There was with them a centurion of the same legion, T. Salienus by name, who had invested the house of M. Messala, Cæsar's lieutenant, at Messana, and expressed himself in very seditious language; nay even seized the money and ornaments destined for Cæsar's triumph, and for that reason dreaded his resentment. He, conscious of his demerits, persuaded the young men to surrender themselves to Virgilius, by whom they were sent, under a strong guard to Scipio, and three days after put to death. It is said that the elder Titus begged of the centurions who were charged with the execution, that he might be first put to death; which being easily granted, they both suffered according to their sentence.

XXVII. The cavalry that mounted guard in the two camps were continually skirmishing with one another. Sometimes, too, the German and Gallic cavalry of Labienus entered into discourse with those of Cæsar. Meantime Labienus, with a party of horse, endeavoured to surprise the town of Leptis, which Saserna guarded with three cohorts; but was easily repulsed, because the town was strongly fortified, and well provided with warlike engines: but at several times he renewed the attempt. One day, as a strong squadron of the enemy had posted themselves before the gate, their officer being slain by an arrow discharged from a scorpion, the rest were terrified and took flight; by which means the town was delivered from any further attempts.

XXVIII. At the same time Scipio daily drew up his troops in order of battle, about three hundred paces from his camp; and after continuing in arms the greatest part of the day retreated again to his camp in the evening. This he did several times, no one meanwhile offering to stir out of Cæsar's camp, or approach his forces; which forbearance and tranquillity gave such a contempt of Cæsar and his army, that drawing out all his forces, and his thirty elephants, with towers on their backs, and extending his horse and foot as wide as possible, he approached quite up to Cæsar's intrenchments. Upon this Cæsar quietly, and without noise or confusion, recalled to his camp all that were gone out either in quest of forage, wood, or to work upon the fortifications: he likewise ordered the cavalry that were upon guard, not to quit their post until the enemy were within reach of dart; and if they persisted to advance, to retire in good order within the intrenchments. The rest of the cavalry were enjoined to hold themselves in readiness upon the first notice. These orders were not given by himself in person, or after viewing the disposition of the enemy from the rampart; but sitting in his tent, and informing himself of their motions by his scouts, such was his consummate knowledge in the art of war, that he gave all necessary directions by his officers. He very well knew, that, whatever confidence the enemy might have in their numbers, they would yet never dare to attack the camp of a general, who had so often repulsed, terrified, and put them to flight; who had frequently pardoned and granted them their lives; and whose very name had weight and authority enough to intimidate their army. He was besides well-intrenched with a high rampart and deep ditch, the approaches to which were rendered so difficult by the sharp spikes which he had disposed in a very artful manner, that they were even sufficient of themselves to keep off the enemy. He was likewise well provided with military engines, and all sorts of weapons necessary for a vigorous defence, which compensated in some measure for the fewness of his troops, and the inexperience of his new levies. His forbearance therefore did not proceed from fear, or any distrust of the valour of his troops; but because he was unwilling to purchase a bloody victory over the shattered remains of his dispersed enemies, after such a series of great actions, conquests, and triumphs; and therefore resolved to bear their insults and bravadoes, till the arrival of his veteran legions by the second embarkation.

XXIX. Scipio, after a short stay before the intrenchments, as if in contempt of Cæsar, withdrew slowly to his camp; and having called his soldiers together, enlarged upon the terror and despair of the enemy: when encouraging his men, he assured them of a complete victory in a short time. Cæsar made his soldiers again return to their works, and under pretence of fortifying his camp, inured the new levies to labour and fatigue. Meantime the Numidians and Getulians deserted daily from Scipio's camp. Part returned home; part came over to Cæsar, because they understood he was related to C. Marius, from whom their ancestors had received considerable favours. Of these he selected some of distinguished rank, and sent them home, with letters to their countrymen, exhorting them to levy troops for their own defence, and not listen to the suggestions of his enemies.

XXX. While these things pass near Ruspina, deputies from Acilla, and all the neighbouring towns, arrived in Cæsar's camp, with offers of submission, and to supply him with corn and other necessaries, if he would send garrisons to protect them from the enemy. Cæsar readily complied with their demands, and having assigned a garrison, sent C. Messius, who had been edile, to command in Acilla. Upon intelligence of this, Considius Longus, who was at Adrumetum with two legions and seven hundred horse, leaving a garrison in that city, posted to Acilla at the head of eight cohorts: but Messius having accomplished his march with great expedition, arrived first at the place. When Considius therefore approached, and found Cæsar's garrison in possession of the town, not daring to make any attempt, he returned again to Adrumetum. But some days after, Labienus having sent him a reinforcement of horse, he found himself in a condition to renew the siege.

XXXI. Much about the same time, C. Sallustius Crispus, who, as we have seen, had been sent a few days before to Cercina with a fleet, arrived in that island. Upon which C. Decimus, the questor, who, with a strong party of his own domestics, had charge of the magazines erected there, went on board a small vessel and fled. Sallustius meanwhile was well received by the Cercinates, and finding great store of corn in the island, loaded all the ships then in the port, whose number was very considerable, and despatched them to Cæsar's camp. At the same time Allienus, the proconsul, put on board the transports at Lilybæum the thirteenth and fourteenth legions, with eight hundred Gallic horse, and a thousand archers and slingers, and sent them over into Africa. This fleet meeting with a favourable wind, arrived in four days at Ruspina, where Cæsar had his camp. Thus he experienced a double pleasure on this occasion, receiving at one and the same time, both a supply of provisions, and a reinforcement of troops; which animated the soldiers, and delivered them from the apprehensions of want. Having landed the legions and cavalry, he allowed them some time to recover from the fatigue and sickness of their voyage, and then distributed them into the forts, and along the works.

XXXII. Scipio and the other generals were greatly surprised at Cæsar's conduct, and could not conceive how one, who had always been forward and active in war, should all of a sudden change his measures; which they therefore suspected must proceed from some very powerful reasons. Uneasy and disturbed to see him so patient, they made choice of two Getulians, on whose fidelity they thought they could rely; and promising them great rewards, sent them under the name of deserters, to get intelligence of Cæsar's designs. When they were brought before him, they begged they might have leave to speak without offence; which being granted: "It is now a long time, great general," said they, "since many of us Getulians, clients of C. Marius, and almost all Roman citizens of the fourth and sixth legions, have wished for an opportunity to come over to you; but have hitherto been prevented by the guards of Numidian horse. Now we gladly embrace the occasion, being sent by Scipio under the name of deserters, to discover what ditches and traps you have prepared for his elephants, how you intend to oppose those animals, and what dispositions you are making for battle." Cæsar commended them, rewarded them liberally, and sent them to the other deserters. We had soon a proof of the truth of what they had advanced; for next day a great many soldiers of these legions mentioned by the Getulians, deserted to Cæsar's camp.

XXXIII. Whilst affairs were in this posture at Ruspina, M. Cato, who commanded in Utica, was daily enlisting freed men, Africans, slaves, and all that were of age to bear arms, and sending them without intermission to Scipio's camp. Meanwhile deputies from the town of Tisdra came to Cæsar, to inform him, that some Italian merchants had brought three hundred thousand bushels of corn into that city; and to demand a garrison, as well for their own defence as to secure the corn. Cæsar thanked the deputies, promised to send the garrison they desired; and having encouraged them, sent them back to their fellow-citizens. Meantime P. Sitius entered Numidia with his troops, and made himself master of a castle situated on a mountain, where Juba had laid up a great quantity of provisions, and other things necessary for carrying on the war.

XXXIV. Cæsar having increased his forces with two veteran legions, and all the cavalry and light-armed troops that had arrived in the second embarkation, detached six transports to Lilybæum, to bring over the rest of the army. On the twenty-seventh of January, ordering the scouts and lictors to attend him at six in the evening, he drew out all the legions at midnight, and directed his march towards Ruspina, where he had a garrison, and which had first declared in his favour, no one knowing or having the least suspicion of his design. Thence he continued his route, by the left of the camp, along the sea, and passed a little declivity, which opened into a fine plain, extending fifteen miles, and bordered upon a chain of mountains of moderate height, that formed a kind of theatre. In this ridge were some hills that rose higher than the rest, where forts and watch-towers had formerly been erected, and at the farthest of which Scipio's out-guards were posted.

XXXV. Cæsar having gained the ridge, began to raise redoubts upon the several eminences, which he executed in less than half an hour. When he was near the last, which bordered on the enemy's camp, and where, as we have said, Scipio had his out-guard of Numidians, he stopped a moment; and having taken a view of the ground, and posted his cavalry in the most commodious situation, he ordered the legions to throw up an intrenchment along the middle of the ridge, from the place at which he was arrived, to that whence he set out. This being observed by Scipio and Labienus, they drew all their cavalry out of the camp, formed them in order of battle; and advancing about a thousand paces, posted their infantry by way of a second line, somewhat less than half a mile from their camp.

XXXVI. Cæsar, unmoved by the appearance of the enemy's forces, encouraged his men to go on with the work. But when he perceived that they were within fifteen hundred paces of the intrenchment, and that their design was to interrupt and disturb the soldiers, and oblige **him to** draw them off from the **work;** he ordered a squadron of Spanish cavalry, sustained by some light-armed infantry, to attack the Numidian guard upon the nearest eminence, and drive them from that post. They easily possessed themselves of the place, the Numidians being partly killed, and **partly** made prisoners. This **being perceived by** Labienus, that he **might the more effectually** succour the fugitives, **he wheeled off almost the whole** right wing **of the horse. Cæsar waited till he was at a considerable distance** from his own men, and then detached his left wing to intercept his return.

XXXVII. In the plain where this happened was **a** large villa, with four turrets, **which prevented** Labienus from seeing that he was surrounded. He had therefore no apprehension of the approach of Cæsar's horse, till he found himself charged in the rear; which struck such a sudden terror into the Numidian cavalry, that they immediately betook themselves to flight. The Gauls and Germans who stood their ground, being surrounded on all sides, were entirely cut off. This being perceived by Scipio's legions, who were drawn up in order of battle before the **camp,** they fled in the utmost terror and confusion. Scipio and his forces being driven from the plain and the hills, Cæsar sounded a retreat, and ordered all the cavalry to retire behind the works. When the field was cleared, he could not forbear admiring the huge bodies of the Gauls and Germans, who, partly induced by the authority of Labienus, had followed him out of Gaul; partly had been **drawn over by** promises and rewards. Some **being made** prisoners in the battle with Curio, **and, having** their lives granted them, continued faithful, out of gratitude. Their bodies, of surprising shape and largeness, lay scattered all over the plain.

XXXVIII. Next day, Cæsar drew all his forces together, and formed them, in order of battle, upon the plain. Scipio, discouraged **by** so unexpected a check, and the numbers of his wounded and slain, kept within his lines. Cæsar, with his army in battalia, marched along the roots of the hills, and gradually approached his trenches. The legions were, by this time, got within a mile of Uzita, a town possessed by Scipio, whence he had his water, and other conveniences for his army. Resolving therefore to preserve it, at all hazards, he brought **forth** his whole army, and drew them up, **in four lines,** forming the first of cavalry, supported **by elephants, with castles** on their backs. **Cæsar, believing that** Scipio approached with design to give battle, continued where he was posted, not **far from the town.** Scipio meanwhile, having the town **in the** centre of his front, extended his two wings, where were his elephants in full view of our army.

XXXIX. When Cæsar had waited till sun-set, without finding that Scipio stirred from his post; who seemed rather disposed to defend himself by his advantageous situation, than hazard a battle in the open field; he did not think proper to advance farther that day, because the enemy had a strong garrison of Numidians in the town, which besides **covered** the centre of their front; and he foresaw great difficulty in forming, at the same time, an attack upon the town, and opposing their right and left, with the advantage of the ground; especially as the soldiers had continued under arms, and fasted since morning. Having therefore led back his troops to their camp, he resolved next day to extend his lines nearer the town.

XL. Meantime Considius, who besieged eight mercenary cohorts of Numidians and Getulians in Acilla, where C. Messius commanded; after continuing long before the place, and seeing all his works burned and destroyed by the enemy; upon the report of the late battle of the cavalry, set fire to his corn, destroyed his wine, oil, and other stores, and abandoning the siege of Acilla, divided his forces with Scipio, and retired, through the kingdom of Juba, to Adrumetum.

XLI. Meanwhile one of the transports belonging to the second embarkation, in which were Q. Cominius, and L. Ticida, a Roman knight, being separated from the rest of the fleet, in a storm, and driven to Thapsus, was taken by Virgilius, and all the persons on board sent to Scipio. A three-benched galley likewise, belonging to the same fleet, being forced, by the winds, to Ægimurum was intercepted, by the squadron under Varus and M. Octavius. In this vessel were some veteran soldiers, with a centurion, and a few new levies; whom Varus treated respectfully, and sent, under a guard, to Scipio. When they came into his presence, and appeared before his tribunal: "I am satisfied," said he, "it is not by your own inclination, but at the instigation of your wicked general, that you impiously wage war on your fellow-citizens, and on the honestest part of the republic. If, therefore, now that fortune has put you in our power, you will take this opportunity to unite with the good citizens, in the defence of the common-weal, I not only promise you your life, but you may expect to be rewarded. Let me know what you think of the proposal." Scipio having ended his speech, and expecting a thankful return to so gracious an offer, permitted them to reply: when the centurion, who on this occasion was spokesman, thus addressed him: "Scipio," says he, "(for I cannot give you the appellation of general,) I return you my hearty thanks for the good treatment you are willing to show to prisoners of war; and perhaps I might accept of your kindness, were it not to be purchased at the expense of a horrible crime. What! shall I carry arms, and fight against Cæsar, my general, under whom I have served as centurion; and against his victorious army, to whose renown I have so many years endeavoured to contribute by my valour? It is what I will never do; and even advise you not to push the war any further. You know not what troops you have to deal with, nor the difference betwixt them and yours; of which, if you please, I will give you an indisputable instance. Do you pick out the best cohort you have in your army: and give me only ten of my comrades, which are now your prisoners, to engage them. You shall see, by the success, what you are to expect from your soldiers." When the centurion had made this reply, Scipio, incensed at his boldness, and resenting the affront, made a sign to some of his officers to kill him on the spot, which was immediately put in execution. At the same time ordering the other veteran soldiers to be separated from the new levies: "Carry away," said he, "these villains, pampered with the blood of their fellow-citizens." Accordingly they were conducted without the rampart, and cruelly massacred. The new-

raised soldiers were distributed among his legions; and Cominius and Ticida forbid to appear in his presence. Cæsar, concerned for this misfortune, broke, with ignominy, the officers, whose instructions being to secure the coast, and advance to a certain distance into the main sea, to protect and facilitate the approach of the transports, had been negligent on that important station.

XLII. About this time, a most incredible accident befell Cæsar's army. For the Pleiades being set, about nine at night, a terrible storm arose, attended with hail of an uncommon size. But what contributed to render this misfortune the greater, was, that Cæsar had not, like other generals, put his troops into winter quarters; but was every three or four days changing his camp, to gain ground on the enemy; which keeping the soldiers continually employed, they were utterly unprovided of any conveniences to protect them from the inclemency of the weather. Besides, neither officer nor soldier had been permitted to take their equipages or utensils with them, nor so much as a vessel, or a single slave, when they parted from Sicily; and so far had they been from acquiring or providing themselves with any thing in Africa, that by reason of the great scarcity of provisions, they had even consumed their former stores. Impoverished by these accidents, very few of them had tents: the rest had made themselves a kind of covering, either by spreading their clothes, or with mats and rushes. But these being soon penetrated by the storm and hail, the soldiers had no resource left, but wandered up and down the camp, covering their heads with their bucklers, to shelter them from the weather. In a short time the whole camp was under water, the fires extinguished, and all their provisions washed away or spoiled. The same night, the shafts of the javelins belonging to the fifth legion, of their own accord, took fire.

XLIII. In the meantime king Juba, having received advice of the horse-engagement with Scipio, and being earnestly solicited by letters, from that general, to come to his assistance, left Sabura at home, with part of the army, to carry on the war against Sitius; and imagining his name and presence sufficient to free Scipio's troops from the dread they had of Cæsar, began his march, with three legions, eight hundred horse, a body of Numidian cavalry, great numbers of light-armed infantry, and thirty elephants. When he arrived, he lodged himself, with all his forces, in a separate camp, at no great distance from that of Scipio. Cæsar's army had, for some time past, been possessed with no small terror of Juba's forces ; and the report of his approach had increased the inquietude, and produced a general suspense and expectation among the troops. But his arrival, and the appearance of his camp, soon dispelled all these apprehensions, and they as much despised the king of Mauritania, now he was present, as they had feared him, when at a distance. It was easy to be seen, however, that the reinforcement brought by the king, greatly raised the courage and confidence of Scipio. For next day, drawing out all his own and the royal forces, with sixty elephants, he ranged them, in order of battle, with great ostentation, advanced a little beyond his intrenchments, and after a short stay, retreated to his camp.

XLIV. Cæsar, knowing that Scipio had received all the supplies he expected, and judging he would no longer decline coming to an engagement, began to advance along the ridge with his forces, extend his lines, secure them with redoubts, and possess himself of the eminences between him and Scipio. The enemy, confiding in their numbers, seized a neighbouring hill, and thereby prevented the progress of our works. Labienus had formed the design of securing this post, and as it lay nearest his quarters, soon got thither. Cæsar had the same project in view : but before he could reach the place, was necessitated to pass a broad and deep valley, of rugged descent, broken with caves, and beyond which was a thick grove of olives. Labienus perceiving that Cæsar must march this way, and having a perfect knowledge of the country, placed himself in ambush, with the light-armed foot, and part of the cavalry. At the same time, he disposed some horse behind the hills, that when he should fall unexpectedly upon Cæsar's foot, they might suddenly advance from behind the mountain. Thus the enemy, attacked in front and rear, surrounded with danger on all sides, and unable either to retreat or advance, would, he imagined, fall an easy prey to his victorious troops. Cæsar, who had no suspicion of the ambuscade, sent his cavalry before ; and arriving at the place, Labienus's men, either forgetting or neglecting

the orders of their general, or fearing to be trampled to death in the ditch by our cavalry, began to issue in small parties from the rock, and ascend the hill. Cæsar's horse pursuing them, slew some, and took others prisoners : then making towards the hill, drove thence Labienus's detachment, and immediately took possession. Labienus, followed by a small party of horse, escaped with great difficulty.

XLV. The cavalry having thus cleared the mountain, Cæsar resolved to intrench himself there, and distributed the work to the legions. He then ordered two lines of communication to be drawn from the greater camp, across the plain on the side of Uzita, which stood between him and the enemy, and was garrisoned by a detachment of Scipio's army. These lines were so contrived, as to meet at the right and left angles of the town. His design in this work was, that when he approached the town with his troops, and began to attack it, these lines might secure his flanks, and hinder the enemy's horse from surrounding him, and compelling him to abandon the siege. It likewise gave his men more frequent opportunities of conversing with the enemy, and facilitated the means of desertion to such as favoured his cause ; many of whom had already come over, though not **without** great danger to themselves. He wanted also, by drawing nearer the enemy, to see how they stood inclined **to a** battle. Add to **all these** reasons, that **the place** itself being **very low,** he might there **sink some wells ; whereas** before he had **a long and troublesome way** to send for water. **While the legions** were employed in **these works, part of** the army stood ready drawn up before **the** trenches, and had frequent skirmishes **with** the Numidian horse and light-armed foot.

XLVI. In the evening, when Cæsar was drawing off his legions from the works, Juba, Scipio, and Labienus, at the head of all their horse and light-armed foot, fell furiously upon his cavalry : who, overwhelmed by the sudden and general attack of so great a multitude, were forced to give ground a little. But the event was very different from what the enemy expected : for Cæsar, leading back his legions to the assistance of his cavalry, they immediately rallied, turned upon the Numidians, and charging them vigorously whilst they were dispersed and disordered with the pursuit, drove them with great slaughter to the king's camp. And had not night intervened, and the dust raised by the wind obstructed the prospect, Juba and Labienus would both have fallen into Cæsar's hands; and their whole cavalry and light-armed infantry been cut off. Meanwhile Scipio's men, of the fourth and sixth legions, left him in crowds, some deserting to Cæsar's camp, others flying to such places as were most convenient for them. Curio's horse likewise, distrusting Scipio and his troops, followed the same counsel.

XLVII. While these things passed near Uzita, the ninth and tenth legions sailing in transports from Sicily, when they came before Ruspina, observing Cæsar's ships that lay at anchor about Thapsus, and fearing it might be the enemy's fleet stationed there to intercept them, they imprudently stood out to sea; and after being long tossed by the winds, provisions and water failing them, at last arrived at Cæsar's camp.

XLVIII. Soon after they were landed, Cæsar calling to mind their licentious behaviour in Italy, and the rapines of some of their officers, seized the pretence furnished by C. Avienus, a military tribune of the tenth legion, who, when he set out from Sicily, filled a ship entirely with his own equipage and attendants, without taking on board one single soldier. Wherefore, summoning all the military tribunes and centurions to appear before his tribunal next day, he addressed them in these terms: "I could have wished that those, whose insolence and former licentious character have given me cause of complaint, had been capable of amendment, and of making a good use of my mildness, patience, and moderation. But since they know not how to confine themselves within bounds, I intend to make an example of them, according to the law of arms, in order that others may be taught a better conduct. You, C. Avienus, when you was in Italy, instigated the soldiers of the Roman people to revolt from the republic: you have been guilty of rapines and plunders in the municipal towns; and you have never been of any real service, either to the commonwealth, or to your general; lastly, in lieu of soldiers, you have crowded the transports with your slaves and equipage; so that, through your fault, the republic fails in soldiers, who at this time are not only useful, but necessary. For all these causes, I break

you with ignominy, and order you to leave Africa this very day. In like manner, I break you, A. Fonteius, because you have behaved yourself as a seditious officer, and as a bad citizen. You, T. Salienus, M. Tiro, C. Clusinus, have attained the rank of centurions through my indulgence, and not through your own merit; and since you have been invested with that rank, have neither shown bravery in war, nor good conduct in peace. Instead of endeavouring to act according to the rules of modesty and decency, your whole study has been to stir up the soldiers against your general. I therefore think you unworthy of continuing centurions in my army; I break you, and order you to quit Africa as soon as possible." Having concluded this speech, he delivered them over to some centurions, with orders to confine them separately on board a ship, allowing each of them a single slave to wait on them.

XLIX. Meantime the Getulian deserters, whom Cæsar had sent home with letters and instructions, as we have related above, arrived among their countrymen: who, partly swayed by their authority, partly by the name and reputation of Cæsar, revolted from Juba; and speedily and unanimously taking up arms, scrupled not to act in opposition to their king. Juba having thus three wars to sustain, was compelled to detach six cohorts from the army destined to act against Cæsar, and send them to defend the frontiers of his kingdom against the Getulians.

L. Cæsar having finished his lines of communication, and pushed them so near the town, as to be just without reach of dart, intrenched himself there. He caused warlike engines in great numbers to be placed in the front of his works, wherewith he played perpetually against the town; and to increase the enemy's apprehensions, drew five legions out of his other camp. This opportunity gave several persons of rank in both armies a desire to see and converse with their friends, which Cæsar foresaw would turn to his advantage. For the chief officers of the Getulian horse, with other illustrious men of that nation, whose fathers had served under C. Marius, and from his bounty obtained considerable estates in their country, but after Sulla's victory had been made tributaries to King Hiempsal; taking the opportunity of the night, when the fires were lighted, with their horses and servants, to the number of about a thousand, came over to Cæsar's camp near Uzita.

LI. As this accident could not but disturb Scipio and his followers, they perceived, much about the same time, M. Aquinius in discourse with C. Saserna. Scipio sent him word, that he did not do well to correspond with the enemy. Aquinius paid no attention to this reprimand, but pursued his discourse. Soon after one of Juba's guards came to him, and told him in the hearing of Saserna, The king forbids you to continue this conversation. He no sooner received this order than immediately he retired, for fear of offending the king. One cannot wonder enough at this step in a Roman citizen, who had already attained to considerable honours in the commonwealth; that though neither banished his country, nor stripped of his possessions, he should pay a more ready obedience to the orders of a foreign prince, than those of Scipio; and choose rather to behold the destruction of his party, than return into the bosom of his country. Nor was Juba's arrogance confined to M. Aquinius, a new man and an inconsiderable senator; but reached even Scipio himself, a man of illustrious birth, distinguished honours, and high dignity in the state. For as Scipio, before the king's arrival, always wore a purple coat of mail, Juba is reported to have told him, that he ought not to wear the same habit as he did. Accordingly Scipio changed his purple robe for a white one, submitting to the caprice of a haughty barbarian monarch.

LII. Next day they drew out all their forces from both camps; and forming them on an eminence not far from Cæsar's camp, continued thus in order of battle. Cæsar likewise drew out his men, and disposed them in battle array before his lines; not doubting but the enemy, who exceeded him in number of troops, and had been so considerably reinforced by the arrival of king Juba, would advance to attack him. Wherefore, having rode through the ranks, encouraged his men, and given them the signal of battle, he stayed expecting the enemy's charge. For he did not think it advisable to remove far from his lines; because the enemy, having a strong garrison in Uzita, which was opposite to his right wing, he could not advance beyond that place, without exposing his flank to a sally from the town. Besides, the access to Scipio's army was rough and difficult,

and would have disordered his troops before they gave the onset.

LIII. And here it may not be improper to describe the order of battle of both armies. Scipio's troops were drawn up in this manner: he posted his own legions, and those of Juba, in the front; behind them the Numidians, as a body of reserve; but in so very thin ranks, and so far extended in length, that to see them at a distance, you would have taken the main battle for a simple line of legionaries, which was doubled only upon the wings. The elephants were placed at equal distances on the right and left, and sustained by the light-armed troops and auxiliary Numidians. All the bridled cavalry were on the right; for on the left was covered by the town of Uzita, nor had the cavalry room to extend themselves on that side. Accordingly he stationed the Numidian horse, with an incredible multitude of light-armed foot, about a thousand paces from his right, towards the foot of a mountain, considerably removed from his own and the enemy's troops. His design in this was, that during the progress of the battle, the cavalry having room to extend themselves, might wheel round upon Cæsar's left, and disorder it with their darts. Such was Scipio's disposition. Cæsar's order of battle, to describe it from left to right, was as follows: the ninth and seventh legions formed the left wing; the thirteenth, fourteenth, twenty-eighth, and twenty-sixth, the main body; and the thirtieth and twenty-ninth the right. His second line on the right, consisted partly of the cohorts of those legions we have already mentioned, partly of the new levies. His third line was posted to the left, extending as far as the middle legion of the main body, and so disposed, that the left wing formed a triple order of battle. The reason of this disposition was, because his right wing being defended by the works, it behoved him to make his left the stronger, that they might be a match for the numerous cavalry of the enemy; for which reason he had placed all his horse there, intermixed with light-armed foot; and as he could not rely much upon them, had detached the fifth legion to sustain them. The archers were dispersed up and down the field, but principally on the two wings.

LIV. The two armies thus facing one another in order of battle, with a space of no more than three hundred paces between, continued so posted from morning till night without fighting, of which perhaps there never was an instance before. But when Cæsar began to retreat within his lines, suddenly all the Numidian and Getulian horse without bridles, who were posted behind the enemy's army, made a motion to the right, and began to approach Cæsar's camp on the mountain; while the regular cavalry under Labienus continued in their post, to keep our legions in check. Upon this, part of Cæsar's cavalry, with the light-armed foot, advancing hastily, and without orders, against the Getulians, and venturing to pass the morass, found themselves unable to deal with the superior multitude of the enemy; and being abandoned by the light-armed troops, were forced to retreat in great disorder, after the loss of one trooper, twenty-six light-armed foot, and many of their horses wounded. Scipio, overjoyed at this success, returned towards night to his camp. But as fortune's favours are seldom permanent to those engaged in the trade of war, the day after a party of horse, sent by Cæsar to Leptis in quest of provisions, falling in unexpectedly with some Numidian and Getulian stragglers, killed or made prisoners about a hundred of them. Cæsar, meanwhile, omitted not every day to draw out his men, and labour at the works: carrrying a ditch and rampart quite across the plain, to prevent the incursions of the enemy. Nor was Scipio less active in forwarding his works, and securing his communication with the mountain. Thus both generals were busied about their intrenchments, yet seldom a day passed, without some skirmish between the cavalry.

LV. In the meantime, Varus, upon notice that the seventh and eighth legions had sailed from Sicily, speedily equipped the fleet he had brought to winter at Utica; and manning it with Getulian rowers and mariners, went out a cruising, and came before Adrumetum with fifty-five ships. Cæsar, who knew nothing of his arrival, sent L. Cispius, with a squadron of twenty-seven sail, to cruise about Thapsus, for the security of his convoys; and likewise despatched Q. Aquila to Adrumetum, with thirteen galleys, upon the same errand. Cispius soon reached the station appointed to him: but Aquila being attacked by a storm, could not double the cape, which obliged him to put into a creek at some dis-

tance, that afforded convenient shelter. The rest of the fleet anchored before Leptis, where the mariners went on shore, some to refresh themselves, others to buy provisions in the towns, and left their ships quite defenceless. Varus having notice of this from the deserters, and resolving to take advantage of the enemy's negligence, left Adrumetum about nine at night, and arriving early next morning with his whole fleet before Leptis, burned all the transports that were out at sea, and took, without opposition, two five-benched galleys, in which were none to defend them.

LVI. Cæsar had an account brought him of this unlucky accident, as he was inspecting the works of his camp. Whereupon he immediately took horse, went full speed to Leptis, which was but two leagues distant, and going on board a brigantine, ordered all the ships in the port to follow him, and, in this manner, put to sea. He soon came up with Aquila, whom he found dismayed and terrified at the number of ships he had to oppose; and continuing his course, began to pursue the enemy's fleet. Meantime Varus, astonished at Cæsar's boldness and despatch, tacked about with his fleet, and made the best of his way for Adrumetum. But Cæsar, after four miles sail, came up with him, recovered one of his galleys, with the crew and a hundred and thirty men, left to guard her: and took a three-benched galley belonging to the enemy, with all the soldiers and mariners on board. The rest of the fleet doubled the cape, and made the port of Adrumetum. Cæsar could not double the cape with the same wind, but keeping the sea all night, appeared early next morning before Adrumetum. He set fire to all the transports without the haven, took what galleys he found there, or forced them into the harbour; and having waited some time to offer the enemy battle, returned again to his camp. On board the ship he had taken was P. Vestrius, a Roman knight, and P. Ligarius Afranianus, the same who had prosecuted the war against him in Spain, and who, instead of acknowledging the conqueror's generosity, in granting him his liberty, had joined Pompey in Greece; and after the battle of Pharsalia, had gone into Africa to Varus, there to continue in the service of the same cause. Cæsar, to punish his perfidy and breach of oath, gave immediate orders for his execution. But he pardoned P. Vestrius because his brother had paid his ransom at Rome, and he made it appear, that being taken in Nasidius's fleet, and condemned to die, Varus had saved his life, since which, no opportunity had offered of making his escape.

LVII. It is usual for the people of Africa to deposit their corn privately in vaults, under ground, to secure it in time of war, and guard it from the sudden incursions of an enemy. Cæsar, having intelligence of this from a spy, drew out two legions, with a party of cavalry, at midnight, and sent them about ten miles off; whence they returned, loaded with corn, to the camp. Labienus being informed of it, marched about seven miles, through the mountains Cæsar had passed the day before, and there encamped with two legions; where expecting that Cæsar would often come the same way in quest of corn, he daily lay in ambush, with a great body of horse and light-armed foot. Cæsar having notice of this from the deserters, suffered not a day to pass, till the enemy, by repeating the practice often, had abated a little of their circumspection. Then issuing unexpectedly one morning, by the Decuman port, with eight veteran legions, and a party of horse, he ordered the cavalry to march before; who coming suddenly upon the enemy's light-armed foot, that lay in ambush among the valleys, slew about five hundred, and put the rest to flight. Meantime Labienus advanced, with all his cavalry, to support the run-aways, and was on the point of overpowering our small party with his numbers, when suddenly Cæsar appeared with the legions, in order of battle. This sight checked the ardour of Labienus, who thought proper to sound a retreat. The day after, Juba ordered all the Numidians who had deserted their post and fled to their camp to be crucified.

LVIII. Meanwhile Cæsar, being straitened for want of corn, recalled all his forces to the camp; and having left garrisons at Leptis, Ruspina, and Acilla, ordered Cispius and Aquila to cruise with their fleets, the one before Adrumetum, the other before Thapsus, and set fire to his camp at Uzita, he set out, in order of battle, at three in the morning, disposed his baggage in the left, and came to Agar, a town that had been often vigorously attacked by the Getulians, and as valiantly defended by the inhabitants. There encamping in the plain before the town, he went, with part of his army, round the country in quest of provisions; and having found store of barley, oil, wine, and figs, with a small quantity of wheat, after allowing the troops some time to refresh themselves, he returned to his camp. Scipio meanwhile hearing of Cæsar's departure, followed him along the hills, with all his forces, and posted himself about six miles off, in three different camps.

LIX. The town of Zeta lying on Scipio's side of the country, was not above ten miles from his camp; but might be about eighteen from that of Cæsar. Scipio had sent two legions thither to forage; which Cæsar having intelligence of from a deserter, removed his camp from the plain to a hill, for the greater security; and leaving some troops to guard it, marched at three in the morning, with the rest of his forces, passed the enemy's camp, and possessed himself of the town. Scipio's legions were gone farther into the country to forage; against whom setting out immediately, he found the whole army come up to their assistance, which obliged him to give over the pursuit. He took, on this occasion, C. Mutius Reginus, a Roman knight, Scipio's intimate friend, and governor of the town; also P. Atrius, a Roman knight likewise, of the province of Utica, with twenty-two camels, belonging to king Juba. Then leaving a garrison in the place, under the command of Oppius, his lieutenant, he set out upon his return to his own camp.

LX. As he drew near Scipio's camp, by which he was necessitated to pass, Labienus and Afranius who lay in ambuscade among the nearest hills, with all their cavalry and light-armed infantry, started up and attacked his rear. Cæsar, detaching his cavalry to receive their charge, ordered the legions to throw all their baggage into a heap, and face about upon the enemy. No sooner was this order executed, than upon the first charge of the legions, the enemy's horse and light-armed foot began to give way, and were, with incredible ease, driven from the higher ground. But when Cæsar, imagining them sufficiently deterred from any further attempts, began to pursue his march, they again issued from the hills; and the Numidians, with the light-armed infantry, who are wonderfully nimble, and accustom themselves to fight intermixed with the horse, with whom they keep an equal pace, either in advancing or retiring, fell a second time upon our foot. As they repeated this often, pressing upon our rear when we marched, and retiring when we endeavoured to engage, always keeping at a certain distance, and with singular care avoiding a close fight, as holding it enough to wound us with their darts; Cæsar plainly saw that their whole aim was, to oblige him to encamp in that place where no water was to be had; that his soldiers, who had tasted nothing from three in the morning till four in the afternoon, might perish with hunger, and the cattle with thirst. Sun-set now approached; when Cæsar, finding he had not gained a hundred paces complete in four hours, and that, by keeping his cavalry in the rear, he lost many horse, ordered the legions to fall behind, and close the march. Proceeding thus, with a slow and gentle pace, he found the legions fitter to sustain the enemy's charge. Meantime the Numidian horse, wheeling round the hills, to the right and left, threatened to inclose Cæsar's forces with their numbers, while part continued to harass his rear: and if but three or four veteran soldiers faced about, and darted their javelins at the enemy, no less than two thousand of them would take 'to flight; but suddenly rallying, returned to he fight, and charged the legionaries with their darts. Thus Cæsar, one while marching forward, one while halting, and going on but slowly, reached the camp safe, about seven that evening, having only ten men wounded. Labienus too retreated to his camp, after having thoroughly fatigued his troops with the pursuit; in which, besides a great number wounded, his loss amounted to about three hundred men. And Scipio withdrew his legions and elephants, whom, for the greater terror, he had ranged before his camp within view of Cæsar's army.

LXI. Cæsar having such an enemy to deal with, was necessitated to instruct his soldiers, not like a general of a veteran army, which had been victorious in so many battles; but like a fencing-master, training up his gladiators: with what foot they must advance or retire; when they were to oppose and make good their ground, when to counterfeit an attack; at what place, and in what manner, to launch their javelins. For the enemy's light-armed troops gave wonderful trouble and disquiet to our army; because they not only deterred the cavalry from the encounter, by killing their horses with their javelins, but

likewise wearied out the legionary soldiers by their swiftness; for as often as these heavy armed troops advanced to attack them, they evaded the danger by a quick retreat. This gave Cæsar no small trouble; because as often as he engaged with his cavalry, without being sustained by the infantry, he found himself by no means a match for the enemy's horse, supported by their light-armed foot: and as he had no experience of the strength of their legions, he foresaw still greater difficulties when these should be united, as the shock must then be wonderful. The number too, and size of the elephants greatly increased the terror of the soldiers; for which, however, he found a remedy, in causing some of those animals to be brought over from Italy, that his men might be accustomed to the sight of them, know their strength and courage, and in what part of the body they were most likely to be wounded. For as the elephants are covered with trappings and ornaments, it was necessary to inform them what parts of the body remained naked, that they might direct their darts thither. It was likewise needful to familiarize his horses to the cry, smell, and figure of these animals; in all which he succeeded to a wonder; for the soldiers quickly came to touch them with their hands, and to be sensible of their tardiness; and the cavalry attacked them with blunted darts, and by degrees, brought their horses to endure their presence. For these reasons already mentioned, Cæsar was not without his anxieties, and proceeded with more slowness and circumspection than usual, abating considerably of his wonted expedition and celerity. Nor ought we to wonder; for in Gaul his troops had been accustomed to fight in a champaign country, against an open undesigning enemy, who despised artifice, and valued themselves only on their bravery. But now he was to habituate his soldiers to the arts and contrivances of a crafty enemy, and teach them what to pursue, and what to avoid. The sooner, therefore, to instruct them in these matters, he took care not to confine his legions to one place, but, under pretence of foraging, engaged them in frequent marches and countermarches; knowing well that the enemy would take care not to lose sight of him. Three days after, he drew up his forces with great art and marching past Scipio's camp, waited for him in an open plain; but seeing that he still declined a battle, he retreated to his camp in the evening

LXII. Meantime ambassadors arrived from the town of Vacca, bordering upon Zeta, of which we have observed Cæsar had possessed himself. They requested and entreated that he would send them a garrison, promising to furnish **many** of the necessaries of war. At **the same time,** by an uncommon piece of **good** fortune for Cæsar, a deserter informed **him,** that Juba had, by a quick march, reached **the** town, massacred the inhabitants, and abandoned the place itself to the plunder of his soldiers. Thus was Cæsar's garrison prevented from setting out, **and by** that means saved from destruction.

LXIII. Cæsar having reviewed **his** army the eighteenth of February, **advanced** next day, with all his forces, five miles beyond his camp, and remained **a** considerable time in **order** of battle, two miles from Scipio's. When he had waited sufficiently long to invite the enemy **to an** engagement, finding **them** still decline it, he led back his troops. Next **day** he decamped, and directed his march towards Sassura, where Scipio had a garrison of Numidians, and a magazine of corn. Labienus being informed of this motion, fell upon his rear, with the cavalry and light-armed troops: and having made himself master of part of the baggage, was encouraged to attack the legions themselves, believing they would fall an easy prey, under the load and encumbrance of a march. But Cæsar, from a foresight of what might happen, had ordered three hundred men out of each legion, to hold themselves in readiness for action. These being sent against Labienus, he was so terrified at their approach, that he shamefully took to flight, great numbers of his men being killed or wounded. The legionaries returned to their standards, and pursued their **march.** Labienus still followed us at a distance along the summit of the mountains, and kept hovering on **our right.**

LXIV. Cæsar arriving **before Sassure,** took it in presence of the enemy, **who durst** not advance to its relief; and put to the **sword** the **garrison** which had been left there by Scipio, **under the** command of P. Cornelius, who, **after a** vigorous defence, was surrounded and slain. Having given all the corn in the place to the army, he marched next day to Tisdra, where Considius **was** with a strong garrison, and his cohort of gladiators. Cæsar having taken a view of the town, and being deterred from besieging it for want of corn, set out im-

mediately, and, after a march of four miles, encamped near a river. Here he stayed about four days, and retreated to his former camp at Agar. Scipio did the same, and retreated to his old quarters.

LXV. Meantime the Thabenenses, a nation situated in the **extreme** confines of Juba's kingdom, along the sea-coast, and who had been accustomed to live in subjection to that **monarch, having massacred** the **garrison** left there **by the king, sent deputies to Cæsar to** inform him **of what they had** done, and to beg **he would take under** his protection a city which deserved so well of the Roman people. Cæsar, approving their **conduct, sent M.** Crispus, the tribune, with a cohort, **a party of** archers, and **a** great number of **warlike** engines, to charge himself with the defence of Thabena.

LXVI. At the **same time the** legionary soldiers, who, either on account of sickness, or for other reasons, had not been able to come over into Africa with the rest, to the number **of four** thousand foot, four hundred horse, and **a** thousand archers and slingers, **now** arrived all together. With these, and his **former** troops, he advanced into a plain eight miles distant from his own camp, and four from that of Scipio, where he waited the enemy in order of battle.

LXVII. The town of Tegea was **below** Scipio's camp, where he had a garrison of four hundred horse. These he drew up on the right and left of the town; and bringing forth his legions, formed them in order of battle, upon a hill somewhat lower than his camp, and which was about a thousand paces distant from it. After he had continued a considerable time in this posture, without offering to make any attempt, Cæsar sent some squadrons of horse, supported by his light-armed infantry, archers, and slingers, to charge the enemy's cavalry, who were posted before the town. Our men advancing upon the spur, Placidius began to extend his front, that he might at once surround and give us a warm reception. Upon this Cæsar detached three hundred legionaries to our assistance, while at the same time Labienus was continually sending fresh reinforcements, to replace those that were wounded or fatigued. Our cavalry, who were only four hundred in number, not being able to sustain the charge of four thousand, and being besides greatly incommoded by the light-armed Numidians, began at last o give ground; which Cæsar observing, detached the other wing to their assistance; who joining those that were like to be overpowered, they fell in a body upon the enemy, put them to flight, slew or wounded great numbers, pursued them three miles quite to the mountains, and then returned to their own men. Cæsar continued in order of battle till four in the afternoon, and then retreated to his camp without the loss of a man. In this action Placidius received a dangerous wound in the head, and had many of his best officers either killed or wounded.

LXVIII. When he found that the enemy were by no means to be prevailed with to fight him upon equal terms, and that he could not encamp nearer them for want of water, in consideration of which alone, not from any confidence in their numbers, the Africans had dared to despise him; he decamped the fourteenth of April at midnight, marched sixteen miles beyond Agar to Thapsus, where Vergilius commanded with a strong garrison, and there fixed his camp. The very first day he began the circumvallation, and raised redoubts in proper places, as well for his own security, as to prevent any succours from entering the town. This step reduced Scipio to the necessity of fighting, to avoid the disgrace of abandoning Vergilius and the Thapsitani, who had all along remained firm to his party; and therefore following Cæsar without delay, he posted himself in two camps, eight miles from Thapsus.

LXIX. Between a morass and the sea was a narrow pass of about fifteen hundred paces, by which Scipio hoped to throw succours into the place. But Cæsar, from a foresight of what might happen, had the day before raised a very strong fort at the entrance of it, where he left a triple garrison; and encamping with the rest of his troops in form of a half moon, carried his works round the town. Scipio, disappointed of his design, passed the day and night following a little above the morass; but early next morning advanced within a small distance of our fort, where he began to intrench himself about fifteen hundred paces from the sea. Cæsar being informed of this, drew off his men from the works; and leaving Asprenas the proconsul, with two legions, to guard the camp and the baggage, marched all the rest of his forces with the utmost expedition to the place where the enemy were

posted. He left part of the fleet before Thapsus, and ordered the rest to make as near the shore as possible towards the enemy's rear, observing the signal he should give them, upon which they were to raise a sudden shout, that the enemy, alarmed and disturbed by the noise behind them, might be forced to face about.

LXX. When Cæsar came to the place, he found Scipio's army in order of battle before the intrenchments, the elephants posted in the two wings, and part of the soldiers employed in fortifying the camp. Upon sight of this disposition, he drew up his army in three lines, placed the second and tenth legions on the right wing, the eighth and ninth in the left, five legions in the centre, covered his flanks with five cohorts posted over against the elephants, disposed the archers and slingers in the two wings, and intermingled the light-armed troops with his cavalry. He himself on foot went from rank to rank, to rouse the courage of the veterans, putting them in mind of their former bravery, and animating them by his soothing address. He exhorted the new levies to emulate the bravery of the veterans, and endeavour by a victory to attain the same degree of glory and renown.

LXXI. As he ran from rank to rank, he observed the enemy very uneasy, hurrying from place to place, one while retiring behind the rampart, another coming out again in great tumult and confusion. As the same was observed by many others in the army, his lieutenants and volunteers begged him to give the sign of battle, as the immortal gods promised him a certain victory. While he hesitated with himself, and strove to repress their eagerness and desires, as being unwilling to yield to the importunity of men, whose duty it was to wait his orders; on a sudden a trumpet, in the right wing, without his leave, and compelled by the soldiers, sounded a charge. Upon this all the cohorts ran to battle, in spite of the endeavours of the centurions, who strove to restrain them by force, but to no purpose. Cæsar perceiving that the ardour of his soldiers would admit of no restraint, giving good-fortune for the word, spurred on his horse, and charged the enemy's front. On the right wing the archers and slingers poured their javelins without intermission upon the elephants, and by the noise of their slings and stones, so terrified these unruly animals, that turning upon their own men, they trode them down in heaps, and rushed through the gates of the camp, that were but half finished. At the same time the Mauritanian horse, who were in the same wing with the elephants, seeing themselves deprived of their assistance, betook themselves to flight. Whereupon the legions, wheeling round the elephants, soon mastered the enemy's intrenchments. Some few that made resistance were slain: the rest fled with all expedition to the camp they had quitted the day before.

LXXII. And here we must not omit taking notice of the bravery of a veteran soldier of the fifth legion. For when an elephant, which had been wounded in the left wing, and roused to fury by the pain, ran against an unarmed sutler, threw him under his feet, and leaning on him with his whole weight, brandishing his trunk, and raising hideous cries, crushed him to death; the soldier could not refrain from attacking the animal. The elephant, seeing him advance with his javelin in his hand, quitted the dead body of the sutler, and seizing him with his trunk, wheeled him round in the air. But the soldier, amidst all the danger, losing nothing of his courage, ceased not with his sword to strike at the elephant's trunk, who at last overcome with the pain, quitted the prey, and fled to the rest with hideous cries.

LXXIII. Meanwhile the garrison of Thapsus, either designing to assist their friends, or abandon the town, sallied by the gate next the sea, and wading navel deep in the water, endeavoured to reach the land. But the servants and followers of the camp, attacking them with darts and stones, obliged them to return again to the town. Scipio's camp meanwhile being forced, and his men flying on all sides, the legions instantly began the pursuit, that they might have no time to rally. When they arrived at their former camp, by means of which they hoped to defend themselves, they began to think of choosing a commander, to whose authority and orders they might submit; but finding none on whom they could rely, they threw down their arms and fled to Juba's quarters. This being likewise possessed by our men, they retired to a hill; where despairing of safety, they endeavoured to soften their enemies, saluting them by the name of brethren. But

this stood them in little stead : for the veterans, transported with rage and anger, were not only deaf to the cries of their enemies, but even killed or wounded several citizens of distinction in their own army, whom they upbraided as authors of the war. Of this number was Tullius Rufus the questor, whom a soldier knowingly ran through with a javelin ; and Pompeius Rufus, who was wounded with a sword in the arm, and would doubtless have been slain, had he not speedily fled to Cæsar for protection. This made several Roman knights and senators retire from the battle, lest the soldiers, who after so signal a victory assumed an unbounded license, should be induced by the hopes of impunity to wreak their fury on them likewise. In short, all Scipio's soldiers, though they implored the protection of Cæsar, were yet in the very sight of that general, and amidst his entreaties to his men to spare them, universally, and without exception, put to the sword.

LXXIV. Cæsar having made himself master of the enemy's three camps, killed ten thousand of them, and put the rest to flight, retreated to his own quarters, with the loss of no more than fifty men, and a few wounded. In this way he appeared before Thapsus, and ranged all the elephants he had taken in the battle, amounting to sixty-four, with their ornaments, trappings, and castles, in full view of the place. He was in hopes by this evidence of his success to induce Vergilius to surrender. He even called and invited him to submit, reminding him of his clemency and mildness ; but no answer being given, he retired from before the town. Next day, after returning thanks to the gods, he assembled his army before Thapsus, praised his soldiers in presence of the inhabitants, rewarded the victorious, and from his tribunal extended his bounty to every one, according to their merit and services. Setting out thence immediately, he left the proconsul C. Rebellius, with three legions, to continue the siege, and sent Cn. Domitius with two, to invest Tisdra, where Considius commanded. Then ordering M. Messala to go before with the cavalry, he began his march to Utica.

LXXV. Scipio's cavalry, who had escaped out of the battle, taking the road of Utica, arrived at Parada ; but being refused admittance by the inhabitants, who heard of Cæsar's victory, they forced the gates, lighted a great fire in the middle of the forum, and threw all the inhabitants into it, without distinction of age or sex, with their effects; avenging in this manner, by an unheard of cruelty, the affront they had received. Thence they marched directly to Utica. M. Cato, some time before, distrusting the inhabitants of that city, because of the privileges granted them by the Julian law, had disarmed and expelled the populace, obliging them to dwell without the warlike gate, in a small camp environed with a slight intrenchment, round which he had planted guards, while at the same time he held the senators under confinement. The cavalry attacked their camp, as knowing them to be well-wishers to Cæsar, and to avenge, by their destruction, the shame of their own defeat. But the people, animated by Cæsar's victory, repulsed them with stones and clubs. They therefore threw themselves into the town, killed many of the inhabitants, and pillaged their houses. Cato, unable to prevail with them to abstain from rapine and slaughter, and undertake the defence of the town, as he was not ignorant what they aimed at, gave each a hundred sesterces to make them quiet. Sylla Faustus did the same out of his own money; and marching with them from Utica, advanced into the kingdom of Juba.

LXXVI. A great many others that had escaped out of the battle, fled to Utica. These Cato assembled, with three hundred more who had furnished Scipio with money for carrying on the war, and exhorted them to set their slaves free, and, in conjunction with them, defend the town. But finding that though part assembled, the rest were terrified and determined to fly, he gave over the attempt, and furnished them with ships to facilitate their escape. He himself, having settled all his affairs with the utmost care, and commended his children to L. Cæsar, his questor, without the least indication which might give cause of suspicion, or any change in his countenance and behaviour, privately carried his sword into his chamber when he went to sleep, and stabbed himself with it. But the wound not proving mortal, and the noise of his fall creating a suspicion, a physician, with some friends, broke into his chamber, and endeavoured to bind up the wound; which he no sooner was sensible of, than tearing it open with his own hands, he expired, with undaunted resolution and presence of mind. The Uticans,

though they hated his party, yet in consideration of his singular integrity, his behaviour so different from that of the other chiefs, and the wonderful fortifications he had directed to defend their town, interred him honourably. L. Cæsar, that he might procure some advantages by his death, assembled the people, and after haranguing them, exhorted them to open their gates, and throw themselves upon Cæsar's clemency, from which they had the greatest reason to hope the best. This advice being followed, he came forth to meet Cæsar. Messala having reached Utica, according to his orders, placed guards at the gates.

LXXVII. Meanwhile Cæsar leaving Thapsus, came to Usceta, where Scipio had laid up great store of corn, arms, darts, and other warlike provisions, under a small guard. He soon made himself master of the place, and marched directly to Adrumetum, which he entered without opposition. He took an account of the arms, provisions, and money in the town; pardoned Q. Ligarius, and C. Considius; and leaving Livineius Regulus there, with one legion, set out the same day for Utica. L. Cæsar meeting him by the way, threw himself at his feet, and only begged for his life. Cæsar, according to his wonted clemency, easily pardoned him: as he did likewise Cæcina, C. Ateius, P. Atrius, L. Colla, father and son, M. Eppius, M. Aquinius, Cato's son, and the children of Damasippus. He arrived at Utica in the evening by torchlight, and continued all that night without the town.

LXXVIII. Next morning early he entered the place, summoned an assembly of the people, and thanked them for the affection they had shown to his cause. At the same time, he censured severely, and enlarged upon the crime of the Roman citizens and merchants, and the rest of the three hundred, who had furnished Scipio and Varus with money; but concluded with telling them that they might show themselves without fear, as he was determined to grant them their lives, and content himself with exposing their effects to sale; yet so, that he would give them notice when their goods were to be sold, and the liberty of redeeming them upon payment of a certain fine. The merchants, half dead with fear, and conscious that they merited death, hearing upon what terms life was offered them, greedily accepted the condition, and entreated Cæsar that he would impose a certain sum in gross upon all the three hundred. Accordingly he amerced them in two hundred thousand sesterces, to be paid to the republic, at six equal payments, within the space of three years. They all accepted the condition, and considering that day as a second nativity, joyfully returned thanks to Cæsar.

LXXIX. Meanwhile king Juba, who had escaped from the battle with Petreius, hiding himself all day in the villages, and travelling only by night, arrived at last in Numidia. When he came to Zama, his ordinary place of residence, where were his wives and children, with all his treasures and whatever he held most valuable, and which he had strongly fortified at the beginning of the war; the inhabitants, having heard of Cæsar's victory, refused him entrance, because upon declaring **war** against the Romans, he had raised a mighty pile of wood in the middle of the forum, designing, if unsuccessful, to massacre all the citizens, fling their bodies and effects upon the pile, then setting fire to the mass, and throwing himself upon it, destroy all without exception, wives, children, citizens, and treasures, in one general conflagration. After continuing a considerable time before the gates, finding that neither threats nor entreaties would avail, he at last desired them to deliver him his wives and children, that he **might** carry them along with him. But re**ceiving** no answer, and seeing them deter**mined to** grant him nothing, he quitted the **place, and** retired to one of his country seats **with Petreius and a few horse.**

LXXX. **Meantime the Zamians sent am**bassadors to **Cæsar at Utica,** to inform him what they had done, **and to request his** assistance against Juba, who **was drawing his** forces together to attack them. **They assured** him of their submission, and **resolution to** defend the town for him. Cæsar **commended** the ambassadors, and sent them **back to acquaint** their fellow-citizens, that he was coming him**self to their** relief. Accordingly setting out the next **day from** Utica, with his cavalry, he directed his **march** towards Numidia. **Many** of the **king's** generals met him on the way, and sued **for** pardon: to all whom, having given a favourable hearing, they attended him to Zama. The report of his clemency and mildness spreading into **all** parts, the whole

Numidian cavalry flocked to him at Zama, and were there delivered of their fears.

LXXXI. During these transactions, Considius, who commanded at Tisdra, with his own retinue, a garrison of Getulians, and a company of gladiators, hearing of the defeat of his party, and terrified at the arrival of Domitius and his legions, abandoned the town; and privately withdrawing, with a few of the barbarians, and all his money, took his way **towards Numidia.** The Getulians, to render themselves masters of his treasures, murdered him by the way, and fled every man where he could. **Meantime** C. Vergilius, seeing himself shut up by sea and land, without power of making a defence; his followers all slain or put to flight; M. Cato dead by his own hands at Utica; Juba despised and deserted by his own subjects; Sabura and his forces defeated by Sitius; Cæsar received without opposition at Utica: and that of so vast an army, nothing remained capable of screening him or his children; thought it his most prudent course to surrender himself and the city to the proconsul Caninius, by whom he was besieged.

LXXXII. At the same time king Juba, seeing himself excluded from all the cities of his kingdom, and that there remained no hopes of safety; having supped with Petreius, proposed an engagement, sword in hand, that they might die honourably. Juba, as being the **stronger, easily** got the better of his adversary, and laid him dead at his feet; but endeavouring afterwards to run himself through the body, **and wanting** strength to accomplish it, he was **obliged to have recourse** to one of his slaves, and, by his entreaties, prevailed upon him **to perform that** mournful office.

LXXXIII. In the meantime, P. Sitius, having **defeated the** army of Sabura, Juba's lieutenant, and slain the general, and marching with a few troops through Mauritania, to join Cæsar, chanced to fall in with Faustus and Afranius, who were at the head of the party that had plundered Utica, amounting in all to about fifteen hundred men, and designing to make the best of their way to Spain. Having expeditiously placed himself in ambuscade during the night, and attacking them by day-break, he either killed or made them all prisoners, except a few that escaped from the **van.** Afranius and Faustus were taken among the rest, with their wives and children. but some few days after, a mutiny arising among the soldiers, Faustus and Afranius were slain. Cæsar pardoned Pompeia, the wife of Faustus, with her children, and permitted her the free enjoyment of all her effects.

LXXXIV. Meanwhile Scipio, with Damasippus, and Torquatus, and Plætorius Rustianus, having embarked on board some galleys, with a design to make for the coast of Spain; and being long and severely tossed by contrary winds, were at last obliged to put into the port of Hippo, where the fleet commanded by P. Sitius chanced at that time to be. Scipio's vessels, which were but small and few in number, were easily surrounded and sunk, by the larger and more numerous ships of Sitius; on which occasion Scipio, and all those whom we have mentioned above, as having embarked with him, perished.

LXXXV. Meanwhile Cæsar, having exposed the king's effects to public sale at Zama, and confiscated the estates of those, who, though Roman citizens, had borne arms against the republic; after conferring rewards upon such of the Zamans as had been concerned in the design of excluding the king, he abolished all the royal tribunes, converted the kingdom into a province; and appointing Crispus Sallustius to take charge of it, with the title of proconsul, returned again to Utica. There he sold the estates of the officers that had served under Juba and Petreius, fined the people of Thapsus twenty thousand sesterces, and the company of Roman merchants there thirty thousand; fined likewise the inhabitants of Adrumetum in thirty thousand, and their company in fifty thousand; but preserved the cities and their territories from insult and plunder. Those of Leptis, whom Juba had pillaged some time before, and who, upon complaint made to the senate by their deputies, had obtained arbitrators and restitution, were enjoined to pay yearly three hundred thousand pounds of oil; because, from the beginning of the war, in consequence of a dissension among their chiefs, they had made an alliance with the king of Numidia, and supplied him with arms, soldiers, and money. The people of Tisdra, because of their extreme poverty, were only condemned to pay annually a certain quantity of corn.

LXXXVI. These things settled, he embarked at Utica on the thirteenth of June, and three days after arrived at Carales, in Sardinia. Here he condemned the Sulcitani in a fine of one hundred thousand sesterces, for receiving and aiding Nasidius's fleet; and instead of a tenth, which was their former assessment, ordered them now to pay an eighth to the public treasury. He likewise confiscated the estates of some who had been more active than the rest, and weighing from Carales on the twenty-ninth of June, coasted along the shore, and, after a voyage of twenty-eight days, during which he was several times obliged to put into port, by contrary winds, arrived safe at Rome.

PANSA'S COMMENTARIES

OF THE

SPANISH WAR

THE ARGUMENT.

The commencement of the Spanish war.—II. Cæsar marches to attack Cordova.—III. At the same time throws succours into Ulia, besieged by Pompey.—IV. The attempt upon Cordova obliges Pompey to raise the siege of Ulia.—V. Pompey advancing to the relief of Cordova, Cæsar attacks Ategua, whither he is followed by Pompey.—VII. Both intrench themselves in mountainous places, of difficult access.—IX. Pompey attacking a fort belonging to Cæsar, is repulsed.—X. Cæsar continues the siege of Ategua.—XI. Repulses a sally from the town.—XIII. Various skirmishes between the two armies.—XV. Cruelty of the townsmen.—XVI. Cæsar repulses them in a second sally.—XVII. Tullius treats with Cæsar about a surrender.—XVIII. Continuation of the siege.—XIX. The town surrenders.—XX. Pompey removes his camp towards Ucubis.—XXII. Behaviour of the Bursavolenses.—XXIII. Cæsar and Pompey both encamp near Ucubis, where some skirmishes happen.—XXV. Single combat of Turpis and Niger.—XXVI. Great numbers of the enemy desert to Cæsar. Some of Pompey's letters intercepted.—XXVII. Both parties encamp in the plain of Munda.—XXVIII. A great battle ensues.—XXXI. In which Pompey is totally defeated.—XXXII. Cæsar besieges the runaways in Munda.—XXXIII. Attacks and makes himself master of Cordova.—XXXV. Likewise of Hispalis; whence he is expelled, and again recovers it. The Mundanses, under the pretence of a surrender, preparing to attack our men, are themselves put to the sword.—XXXVII. Carteia surrenders to Cæsar. Pompey makes his escape.—XXXIX. Pompey is slain.—XL. Some of Cæsar's ships burned.—XLI. Cæsar's troops take possession of Munda, and afterwards invest Urano.—XLII. Cæsar's speech to the people of Hispalis.

PANSA'S COMMENTARIES

OF

THE SPANISH WAR.

I. Pharnaces being vanquished, and Africa reduced, those who escaped fled into Spain, to young Cn. Pompey; who having got possession of the farther province, whilst Cæsar was employed in distributing rewards in Italy, endeavoured to strengthen himself by engaging the several states to join him: and partly by entreaty, partly by force, soon drew together a considerable army, with which he began to lay waste the country. In this situation of things, some states voluntarily sent him supplies, others shut the gates of their towns against him; of which, if any chanced to fall into his hands by assault, how well soever a citizen might have deserved of his father, yet if he was known to be rich, some ground of complaint was never wanting, under pretence of which to destroy him, that his estate might fall a prey to the soldiers. Thus the enemy, encouraged by the spoils of the vanquished, increased daily, in number and strength; insomuch that the states in Cæsar's interest were continually sending messengers into Italy, to press his immediate march to their relief.

II. Cæsar, now a third time dictator, and nominated also a fourth time to the same dignity, hastening, with all diligence, into Spain, to put an end to the war, was met upon the way by the ambassadors of Cordova, who had deserted from the camp of Cn. Pompey. They informed him that it would be an easy matter to make himself master of the town by night, because the enemy as yet knew nothing of his arrival in the province, the scouts sent out by Cn. Pompey to inform him of Cæsar' ap-

proach having been all made prisoners. They alleged besides many more other very probable reasons; all which so far wrought upon him, that he sent immediate advice of his arrival to Q. Pedius, and Q. Fabius Maximus, his lieutenants, to whom he had left the command of the troops in the province, ordering them to send him all the cavalry they had been able to raise. He came up with them much sooner than they expected, and was joined by the cavalry, according to his desire.

III. Sextus Pompey, the brother of Cnicus, commanded at this time at Cordova, which was accounted the capital of the province. Young Cnicus Pompey himself was employed in the siege of Ulia, which had now lasted some months. The besieged having notice of Cæsar's arrival, sent deputies to him, who passed unobserved through Pompey's camp, and requested with great earnestness, that he would come speedily to their relief. Cæsar, who was no stranger to the merit of that people, and their constant attachment to the Romans, detached about nine at night eleven cohorts, with a like number of horse, under the command of L. Julius Paciecus, a good officer, well known in the province, and who was besides perfectly acquainted with the country. When he arrived at Pompey's quarters, a dreadful tempest arising, attended with a violent wind, so great a darkness ensued, that it was difficult to distinguish even the person next you. This accident proved of great advantage to Paciecus; for being arrived at Pompey's camp, he ordered the

335

the cavalry to advance two by two, and march directly through the enemy's quarters to the town. Some of their guards calling to know who passed, one of our troopers bid them be silent, for they were just then endeavouring by stealth to approach the wall, in order to get possession of the town ; and partly by this answer, partly by favour of the tempest, which hindered the sentinels from examining things diligently, they were suffered to pass without disturbance. When they reached the gates, upon a signal given, they were admitted ; and both horse and foot raising a mighty shout, after leaving some troops to guard the town, sallied in a body upon the enemy's camp ; who having no apprehension of such an attack, were almost all like to have been made prisoners.

IV. Ulia being relieved, Cæsar, to draw Pompey from the siege, marched towards Cordova ; sending the cavalry before, with a select body of heavy-armed foot ; who as soon as they came within sight of the place, got up behind the troopers, without being perceived by those of Cordova. Upon their approach to the walls, the enemy sallied in great numbers, to attack our cavalry ; when the infantry leaping down, fell upon them with such fury, that out of an almost infinite multitude of men, very few returned to the town. This so alarmed Sextus Pompey, that he immediately sent letters to his brother, requesting him to come speedily to his relief, lest Cæsar should make himself master of Cordova before his arrival. Thus Cn. Pompey, moved by his brother's letters, quitted the siege of Ulia, which was upon the point of surrendering, and began his march towards Cordova.

V. Cæsar arriving at the river Bætis, which he found too deep to be forded, sunk several baskets of stones in it ; and raising a bridge upon them, supported by double beams, carried over his forces in three bodies. Pompey arriving soon after with his troops, encamped directly over against him. Cæsar, to cut off his provisions and communication with the town, ran a line from his camp to the bridge. Pompey did the same ; insomuch that a struggle arose between the two generals, which should first get possession of the bridge ; and this daily brought on small skirmishes, in which sometimes the one, sometimes the other party had the better. At last the dispute becoming more general, they came to a close fight,

though upon very disadvantageous ground. for both sides striving earnestly to obtain the bridge, they found themselves as they approached straitened for want of room, and extending themselves towards the river side, many fell headlong from the banks. Thus the loss was pretty equal ; for on either side lay heaps of slain : and Cæsar, for many days, used all possible endeavours to bring the enemy to an engagement on equal terms, that he might bring the war to a conclusion as soon as possible.

VI. But finding that they carefully avoided a battle, with a view to which chiefly he had quitted the route of Ulia ; he caused great fires to be lighted in the night, repassed the river with all his forces, and marched towards Ategua, one of their strongest garrisons. Pompey having notice of this from the deserters, retreated the same day to Cordova, by a very narrow and difficult road, with a great number of carriages and machines of war. Cæsar began his attack upon Ategua, and carried lines quite round the town ; of which Pompey having intelligence, set out upon his march the same day. But Cæsar had taken care beforehand to secure all the advantageous posts, and possess himself of the forts : partly to shelter his cavalry, partly to post guards of infantry for the defence of his camp. The morning of Pompey's arrival was so foggy, that he found means, with some cohorts and troops of cavalry, to hem in a party of Cæsar's horse, and fell upon them in such a manner, that very few escaped slaughter.

VII. The following night Pompey set fire to his camp, passed the river Salsus, and marching through the valleys, encamped on a rising ground, between the towns of Ategua and Ucubis. Cæsar meanwhile continued his approaches, cast up a mount, and brought forward his machines. The country all around is mountainous, and seems formed for war. The river Salsus runs through the plains, and divides them from the mountains, which all lie upon the side of Ategua, at about two miles distance from the river. Pompey's camp was upon these mountains, within view of both the towns, but nearer to Ategua ; to which he could however send no relief, though his army consisted of thirteen legions. Of these he chiefly relied on four : two Spanish ones, which had deserted from Trebonius ; one formed out of the Roman colonies in those parts, and a fourth, which he had brought with him from Africa. The rest were for the most part made up of fugitives and deserters. As to light-armed foot and cavalry, we far exceeded him both in the number and goodness of the troops.

VIII. But what proved principally serviceable to Pompey's design of drawing out the war into length, was the nature of the country, full of mountains, and extremely well adapted to encampments. For almost the whole province of Farther Spain, though of an extremely fertile soil, and abounding in springs, is nevertheless very difficult of access. Here too, on account of the frequent incursions of the natives, all the places remote from great towns, are fortified with towers and castles, covered, as in Africa, not with tiles, but with earth. On these they place sentinels, whose high situation commands an extensive view of the country on all sides. Nay, the greatest part of the towns of this province are built on mountains, and places exceedingly strong by nature, the approaches to which are extremely difficult. Thus sieges are rare and hazardous in Spain, it not being easy to reduce their towns by force, as happened in the present war. For Pompey, having established his camp between Ategua and Ucubis, as related above, and within view of both towns, Cæsar found means to possess himself of an eminence very conveniently situated, and only about four miles from his own camp, on which he built a fortress.

IX. Pompey, who, from the nature of the ground, was covered by the same eminence, and besides at a sufficient distance from Cæsar's quarters, soon became sensible of the importance of this post: and as Cæsar was separated from it by the river Salsus, he imagined that the difficulty of sending relief would prevent his attempting any thing of that kind in its defence. Relying on this persuasion, he set out about midnight, and attacked the fort, which had been very troublesome to the besieged. The enemy upon their approach, setting up a shout, discharged the javelins, in great numbers, and wounded multitudes of our men: but those in the fort making a vigorous resistance, and despatching messengers to the greater camp to inform Cæsar of what had happened, he hastened to their relief, with three legions. His approach struck the enemy with terror: many were slain, and a

great number made prisoners; nay, multitudes in their flight threw away their arms; insomuch that above four-score shields were found which they had left behind them.

X. The day after Arguetius arrived from Italy, with the cavalry, and five standards taken from the Saguntines: but was forced to quit his post by Asprenas, who likewise brought a reinforcement from Italy to Cæsar. The same night Pompey set fire to his camp, and drew towards Cordova. A king named Indus, who was bringing some troops to Cæsar, with a party of cavalry, following the pursuit of the enemy too briskly, was made prisoner, and slain by the Spanish legionaries. Next day our cavalry pursued those who were employed in carrying provisions from the town to Pompey's camp, almost to the very walls of Cordova, and took fifty prisoners, besides horses. The same day, Q. Marcius, a military tribune in Pompey's army, deserted to us. At midnight, the besieged fell furiously upon our works, and by all the methods they could devise, threw fire and combustible matter into the trenches. When the attack was ended, C. Fundanius, a Roman knight, quitted the enemy, and came over to us.

XI. Next day, two Spanish legionaries, who pretended they were slaves, were made prisoners by a party of our horse; but being brought to the camp, they were known by the soldiers, who had formerly served under Fabius and Pedius, and deserted from Trebonius, who would grant no quarter, but massacred them immediately. At the same time, some couriers, sent from Cordova to Pompey, entering our camp by mistake, were seized, had their hands cut off, and then were dismissed. About nine at night, the besieged, according to custom, spent a considerable time in casting fire and darts upon our soldiers, and wounded a great number of men. At day-break they sallied upon the sixth legion, who were busy at the works, and began a sharp contest, in which, however, our men got the better, though the besieged had the advantage of the higher ground: and fifty of their horse, who had begun the attack, being vigorously opposed on our side, notwithstanding all the inconveniences we fought under, were obliged to retire into the town, with many wounds.

XII. Next day Pompey began a line from the camp to the river Salsus; and a small party of our horse, being attacked by a much

2 X

greater body of the enemy, were driven from their post, with the loss of three of their number. The same day, A. Valgius, the son of a senator, whose brother was in Pompey's camp, mounted his horse and went over to the enemy, leaving all his baggage behind him. A spy, belonging to Pompey's second legion, was taken and slain. At the same time, a bullet was shot into the town, with this inscription: That notice should be given by the signal of a buckler, when Cæsar advanced to storm the town. This encouraging some to hope that they might scale the walls, and possess themselves of the town without danger, they fell the next day to sapping them, and threw down a considerable part of the outward wall. They then endeavoured to mount the breach, but were made prisoners, and afterwards employed by the garrison to make an offer of surrendering the town to Cæsar, on condition that he would suffer them to march out with their baggage. The answer was, that it had been always his custom to give, not accept of conditions: which being reported to the garrison, they set up a shout, and began to pour their darts upon our men from the whole circuit of the wall; which gave reason to believe that the garrison intended that day to make a vigorous sally. Wherefore surrounding the town with our troops, the conflict was for some time maintained with great violence, and one of our batteries threw down a tower belonging to the enemy, in which were five of their men and a boy, whose office it was to observe the battery.

XIII. After this, Pompey erected a fort on the other side of the Salsus, in which he met with no interruption from our men, and gloried not a little in the imagination of having possessed himself of a post so near us. Also the following day, extending himself in like manner still farther, he came up with our out-guard of cavalry; and charging them briskly, obliged several squadrons, and the light-armed foot, to give ground; many of whom, by reason of the smallness of their numbers, incapable of any vigorous opposition, were trodden down by the enemy's horse. This passed within view of both camps, and not a little animated the Pompeians, to see our men pushed so far; but being afterwards reinforced by a party from our camp, they faced about with design to renew the fight.

XIV. In all battles of the horse this is found to hold; that when the troopers dismount with design to charge the infantry, the match evermore proves unequal, as happened on the present occasion. For a select body of the enemy's light-armed foot, coming unexpectedly upon our horse, they alighted to sustain the charge. Thus in a very little time, from a horse it became a foot skirmish, and again from a foot, changed to a horse encounter, in which our men were driven back to their very lines; but being there reinforced, about a hundred and twenty-three of the enemy were slain, several forced to throw down their arms, many wounded, and the rest pursued quite to their camp. On our side, a hundred and eleven men were slain, besides twelve foot soldiers and five troopers wounded.

XV. Towards the evening of the same day, the fight, as usual, was renewed before the walls; and the enemy having thrown many darts, and a great quantity of fire from the battlements, proceeded afterwards to an action of unexampled cruelty and barbarity: for in the very sight of our troops they fell to murdering the citizens, and tumbling them headlong from the walls; an instance of inhumanity of which no parallel is to be found in the history of the most savage nations.

XVI. When night came on, Pompey sent a messenger, unknown to us, to exhort the garrison to make a vigorous sally about midnight, and set fire to our towers and mount. Accordingly having poured upon us a great quantity of darts and fire, and destroyed a considerable part of the rampart, they opened the gate which lay over against, and within view of Pompey's camp, sallied out with all their forces, carrying with them fascines to fill up the ditch; hooks and fire to destroy and reduce to ashes the barracks, which the soldiers had built mostly of reeds to defend them from the winter; and some silver and rich apparel to scatter among the tents, that while our men should be employed in securing the plunder, they might fight their way through, and escape to Pompey; who, in expectation that they would be able to effect their design, had crossed the Salsus with his army, where he continued all night in order of battle, to favour their retreat. But though our men had no apprehension of this design, their valour enabled them to frustrate the attempt, and repulse the enemy, with many wounds. They even made themselves masters of the spoil their arms, and some prisoners, who were put to death next day. At the same time a deserter from the town informed us, that Junius, who was employed in the mine when the citizens were massacred, exclaimed against it as a cruel and barbarous action, which ill suited the kind treatment they had received, and was a direct violation of the laws of hospitality. He added many things besides, which made such an impression upon the garrison, that they desisted from the massacre.

XVII. The next day Tullius, a lieutenant-general, accompanied by C. Antonius of Lusitania, came to Cæsar, and addressed him to this effect: "Would to heaven I had rather been one of your soldiers, than a follower of C. Pompey, and given those proofs of valour and constancy in obtaining victories for you, rather than in suffering for him. The only advantage we reap from following his banners are doleful applauses; being reduced to the condition of indigent citizens, and by the melancholy fate of our country ranked among its enemies; who having never shared with Pompey in his good fortune, find ourselves yet involved in his disgrace; and after sustaining the attack of so many armed legions, employing ourselves day and night in works of defence, exposed to the darts and swords of our fellow-citizens: vanquished, deserted by Pompey, and compelled to give way to the superior valour of your troops, find ourselves at last obliged to have recourse to your clemency, and implore that you will not show yourselves less placable to fellow-citizens, than you have so often been to foreign nations." "I am ready," returned Cæsar, "to show the same favour to citizens which vanquished nations have always received at my hands."

XVIII. The ambassadors being dismissed, when they arrived at the gate of the town, Tiberius Tullius observing that C. Antony did not follow him, returned to the gate and laid hold of him, upon which drawing a poniard from his breast, he wounded him in the hand, and in this condition they both fled to Cæsar. At the same time the standard-bearer of the first legion came over to our camp, and reported that the day when the skirmish happened between the horse, no less than thirty-five of his company fell; but it was not allowed to mention it in Pompey's camp, or so much as own the loss of one man. A slave, whose master was in Cæsar's camp, and who had left his wife and son in the city, cut his master's throat, and deceiving the guards, escaped privately to Pompey's camp; whence, by means of a bullet, on which he inscribed his intelligence, he gave us notice of the preparations made for the defence of the place. When we had read the inscription, those who were employed to throw the bullet returning to the city, two Lusitanian brothers deserted, and informed us, that Pompey in a speech made to his soldiers had said: That as he found it impossible to relieve the town, he was resolved to withdraw privately in the night, and retire towards the the sea; to which one made answer, that it was better to hazard a battle, than take refuge in flight; for which he was immediately killed. At the same time some of his couriers were intercepted, who were endeavouring to get into the town. Cæsar sent the letters to the inhabitants, and one of the messengers begging his life, he granted it, with promise of further reward, if he would set fire to the enemy's wooden turret. The enterprise was not without difficulty: he undertook it, however, but was slain in the attempt. The same night a deserter informed us that Pompey and Labienus were greatly offended at the massacre of the citizens.

XIX. About nine at night, one of our wooden towers, which had been severely battered by the enemy's engines, gave way as far as the third story. At the same time a sharp action happened near the walls, and the besieged, assisted by a favourable wind, burned the remaining part of that tower and another. Next morning a matron threw herself from the wall, and came over to our camp, reporting, that the rest of her family had intended the same, but were apprehended and put to death: likewise a letter was thrown over, in which was written; "Minutius to Cæsar: Pompey has abandoned me; if you will grant me my life, I promise to serve you with the same fidelity and attachment I have hitherto manifested towards him." At the same time the deputies who had been sent before to Cæsar by the garrison, now waited on him a second time, offering to deliver up the town next day, upon a bare grant of their lives; to which he replied that he was Cæsar, and would perform his word. Thus having made himself master of the place the nineteenth of February, .. was saluted emperor by the army.

XX. Pompey, being informed by some deserters that the town had surrendered, removed his camp towards Ucubis, where he began to build redoubts, and secure himself with lines. Cæsar also decamped and drew near him. At the same time a Spanish legionary soldier deserting to our camp, informed us, that Pompey had assembled the people of Ucubis, and given it them in charge to inquire diligently who favoured his party, who that of the enemy. Some time after, the slave, who, as we have related above, had murdered his master, was taken in a mine and burnt alive. About the same time eight Spanish centurions came over to Cæsar; and in a skirmish between our cavalry and that of the enemy, we were repulsed, and some of our light-armed foot wounded. The same night we took four of the enemy's spies. One, as being a legionary soldier, was beheaded, but the other three, who were slaves, were crucified.

XXI. The day following, some of the enemy's cavalry and light-armed infantry deserted to us; and about eleven of their horse falling upon a party of our men that were sent to fetch water, killed some, and took others prisoners; amongst which last were eight troopers. Next day Pompey beheaded seventy-four persons as favourers of Cæsar's cause, ordering the rest, who lay under the same suspicion, to be carried back to the town, of whom a hundred and twenty escaped to Cæsar.

XXII. Some time after, the deputies of Bursavola, whom Cæsar had taken prisoners in Ategua, and sent along with his own ambassadors to their city, to inform them of the massacre of the Ateguans, and what they had to apprehend from Pompey, who suffered his soldiers to murder their hosts, and commit all manner of crimes, with impunity, arriving in the town, none of our deputies, except such as were natives of the place, durst enter the city, though they were all Roman knights and senators. But after many messages backward and forward, when the deputies were upon their return, the garrison pursued and put them all to the sword, except two, who escaped to Cæsar, and informed him of what had happened. Some time after, the Bursavolenses sending spies to Ategua, to know the truth of what had happened, and finding the report of our deputies confirmed, were for stoning to death

him who had been the cause of the murder of the deputies, and were with difficulty restrained from laying violent hands upon him, which in the end proved the occasion of their own destruction. For having obtained leave of the inhabitants to go in person to Cæsar and justify himself, he privately drew together some troops; and when he thought himself strong enough, returned in the night, and was treacherously admitted into the town; where he made a dreadful massacre of the inhabitants, slew all the leaders of the opposite party, and reduced the place under his obedience. Soon after, some slaves who had deserted informed us, that he had sold all the goods of the citizens, and that Pompey suffered none of his soldiers to quit the camp but unarmed, because since the taking of Ategua, many despairing of success, fled into Bæthuria, having given over all expectation of victory; and that if any deserted from our camp, they were put among the light-armed infantry, whose pay was only sixteen asses a day.

XXIII. The day following Cæsar removed his camp nearer to Pompey's, and began to draw a line to the river Salsus. Here, while our men were employed in the work, some of the enemy fell upon us from the higher ground, and as we were in no condition to make resistance, wounded great numbers, obliging us, contrary to custom, to retreat. This being perceived, two centurions of the fifth legion passed the river, and restored the battle; when urging the enemy with astonishing bravery, one of them fell overwhelmed by the multitude of darts discharged from above. The other continued the combat for some time; but seeing himself in danger of being surrounded, as he was endeavouring to make good his retreat, he stumbled and fell. His death being known, the enemy flocked together in still greater numbers, upon which our cavalry passed the river, and drove them quite back to their intrenchments; but pursuing them with too much heat, were surrounded by their cavalry and light-armed foot: where, but for the most astonishing efforts of bravery, they must all unavoidably have been made prisoners; for they were so hemmed in by the enemy's lines, that they wanted room to defend themselves. Many were wounded on our side in these two encounters, and among the rest Clodius Aquitius; but as the fight was carried on mostly at a distance, only the two centurions, of whom mention has been already made, and whom the desire of glory rendered regardless of their own safety, were killed.

XXIV. Next day both parties withdrawing from Soricaria, we continued our works. But Pompey, observing that our fort had cut off his communication with Aspavia, which is about five miles distant from Ucubis, judged it necessary to come to a battle. Yet he did not offer it upon equal terms, but chose to draw up his men upon a hill, that he might have the advantage of the higher ground. Meanwhile both sides endeavouring to possess themselves of an eminence that lay extremely convenient, we at last got the better of the Pompeians, and drove them from the plain. The slaughter was very great, and would have been still greater, had they not been protected by the mountain rather than their valour. Night came on very opportunely to favour their escape; without which our men, though few in number, would have entirely cut off their retreat. Pompey lost on this occasion three hundred and twenty-four light-armed foot, and about a hundred and thirty-eight legionary soldiers, besides those whose armour and spoils we carried off. Thus the death of the two centurions, which happened the day before, was fully revenged.

XXV. The day after, Pompey's horse advanced according to their usual custom to our lines; for only the cavalry durst venture to draw up on equal ground. They therefore began to skirmish with our men who were at work, the legionaries calling out to us at the same time to choose our field of battle, with design to make us believe that they desired nothing so much as to come to blows. Upon this invitation our men quitted the eminence where they were encamped, and advanced a great way into the plain, desiring no advantage of ground. But none of the enemy had the boldness to present themselves, Antistius Turpio excepted; who, presuming on his strength, and fancying no one on our side a match for him, offered us defiance. Upon this ensued a combat not unlike that recorded of Memnon and Achilles. For Q. Pompeius Niger, a Roman knight, born in Italy, quitting his rank, advanced to the encounter. The fierce air of Antistius having engaged the attention of all, the two armies drew up to be spectators of the issue of this challenge, and

expressed no less impatience than if the whole fortune of the war had depended upon it; and the wishes on both sides for success were equal to the anxiety and concern each felt for his own combatant. They advanced into the plain with great courage, having each a resplendent buckler of curious workmanship. And doubtless the combat would have been soon decided, had not some light-armed foot, drawn up near the lines, to serve as a guard to the camp, because of the approach of the enemy's horse * * * Our horse in retreating to the camp, being warmly pursued by the enemy, suddenly faced about with great cries; which so terrified the Pompeians, that they immediately betook themselves to flight, and retreated to their camp with the loss of many of their men.

XXVI. Cæsar, to reward the valour of the Cassian troops, presented them with thirteen thousand sesterces, distributed ten thousand more among the light-armed foot, and gave Cassius himself two golden chains. The same day, A. Bebius, C. Flavius, and A. Trebellius, Roman knights of Asti, with their horses richly caparisoned and adorned with silver, came over to Cæsar, and informed him, that all the rest of the Roman knights in Pompey's camp had, like them, conspired to come and join him, but that a discovery being made of their design, by a slave, they had been all seized, themselves excepted, who during the confusion found means to escape. The same day letters were intercepted, sent by Pompey to Ursao, importing: "That hitherto he had all the success against the enemy he could desire, and would have ended the war much sooner than was expected, could he have brought them to fight him upon equal terms: that he did not think it advisable to venture new-levied troops on a plain: that the enemy defending themselves with their lines, seemed inclinable to draw out the war to length, investing city after city, and thence supplying themselves with provisions; that he would therefore endeavour to protect the towns of his party, and bring the war to as speedy an issue as possible: that he would send them a reinforcement of some cohorts, and made no doubt of forcing Cæsar in a short time to an engagement, by cutting off his provisions."

XXVII. Some time after, as our men were carelessly dispersed about the works, a few horse were killed, who had gone to a forest of olives to fetch wood. Several slaves deserted at this time, and informed us, that ever since the action at Soritia on the seventh of March, the enemy had been under continual alarms, and appointed Attius Varus to guard the lines. The same day Pompey decamped, and posted himself in an olive-wood over against Hispalis. Cæsar, before he removed, waited till midnight, when the moon began to appear. At his departure he ordered fire to be set to the fort of Ucubis, which the enemy had abandoned, and that the whole army should rendezvous in the greater camp. He afterwards laid siege to Ventisponte, which surrendered; and marching to Carruca, encamped over against Pompey, who had burned the city, because the garrison refused to open the gates to him. A soldier who had murdered his brother in the camp, being intercepted by our men, was scourged and put to death. Cæsar, still pursuing his march, arrived in the plains of Munda, and pitched his camp opposite to that of Pompey.

XXVIII. Next day as Cæsar was preparing to set out with the army, notice was sent him by his spies, that Pompey had been in order of battle ever since midnight. Upon this intelligence he ordered the standard to be erected. Pompey had taken this resolution in consequence of his letter to the inhabitants of Ursao, who were his firm adherents, in which he told them that Cæsar refused to come down into the plain, because his army consisted mostly of new-levied troops. This had greatly confirmed the city in its allegiance, which therefore serving as a sure resource behind him, he thought he might hazard a battle without danger; and the rather, as he was very advantageously encamped: for, as we observed before, this country is full of hills, which run in a continued chain, without any considerable breaks or hollows.

XXIX. But we must by no means omit an accident which fell out about this time. The two camps were divided from one another by a plain about five miles in extent, insomuch that Pompey by his situation enjoyed a double defence. On one side, the town seated on an eminence; on the other, the nature of the ground where the camp stood: for across this valley ran a rivulet, which rendered the approach of the mountain extremely difficult, because it formed a deep morass on the right.

Cæsar made no doubt but the enemy would descend into the plain and come to a battle, and his whole army were of the same mind; the rather because the plain would give their cavalry full room to act, and the day was so serene and clear, that the gods seemed to have sent it on purpose to bring on an engagement. Our men rejoiced at the favourable opportunity: some, however, were not altogether exempt from fear, when they considered that their all was at stake, and the uncertainty of what might be their fate an hour after. He advanced, however, to the field of battle, fully persuaded that the enemy would do the same; but they durst not venture above a mile from the town, being determined to shelter themselves under its walls. Our men still continued before them in order of battle; but although the equality of the ground sometimes tempted them to come and dispute the victory, they nevertheless still kept their post on the mountain, in the neighbourhood of the town. We doubled our speed to reach the rivulet, without their stirring from the place where they stood.

XXX. Their army consisted of thirteen legions: the cavalry was drawn up on the wings, with six thousand light-armed infantry, and about the same number of auxiliaries. We had only eighty heavy armed cohorts, and eight thousand horse. When we came to the extremity of the plain, as the ground was very disadvantageous, it would have been dangerous for us to advance farther, because the enemy were ready to charge us from the eminences: and therefore, that we might not rashly entangle ourselves, Cæsar had taken care to mark beforehand how far we might advance with safety. The army when commanded to halt, murmured greatly, as if they had been kept back from a certain victory. The delay, however, served to enliven the enemy, who fancied that our troops were afraid of coming to blows. They therefore had the boldness to advance a little way, yet without quitting the advantage of their post, the approach to which was extremely dangerous. The tenth legion, as usual, was on the right; the third and fifth on the left, with the auxiliary troops and cavalry. At length the battle began with a shout.

XXXI. But though our men were superior to the enemy in courage, they nevertheless defended themselves so well by the advantage of the higher ground, the shouts were so loud, and the discharge of darts on both sides so great, that we almost began to despair of victory. For the first onset and clamour, with which an enemy is most apt to be dismayed, were pretty equal in the present encounter. All fought with equal valour; the place was covered with arrows and darts, and great numbers of the enemy fell. We have already observed that the tenth legion was on the right, which, though not considerable for the number of men, was nevertheless formidable on account of its courage; and so pressed the enemy on that side, that they were obliged to draw a legion from the right wing to reinforce the left, and prevent its being taken in flank. Upon this motion, our cavalry on the left fell upon Pompey's right wing, weakened by the departure of the legion: but they defended themselves with so much bravery and resolution, as to stand in need of no new troops to support them. Meanwhile the clashing of armour, mingled with the shouts of the combatants, and the groans of the dying and wounded, terrified the new-raised soldiers; for, as Ennius says, they fought hand to hand, foot to foot, and shield to shield. But though the enemy fought with the utmost vigour, they were obliged to give ground, and retire towards the town. The battle was fought on the feast of Bacchus, and the Pompeians were entirely routed and put to flight; insomuch that not a man could have escaped, had they not sheltered themselves in the place whence they advanced to the charge. The enemy lost on this occasion upwards of thirty thousand men, and among the rest Labienus and Attius Varus, whose funeral obsequies were performed upon the field of battle. They had likewise three thousand Roman knights killed, partly of Italy, partly of the province. About a thousand were slain on our side, partly foot, partly horse; and five hundred wounded. We gained thirteen eagles and standards, and made seventeen officers prisoners. Such was the issue of this action.

XXII. The remains of Pompey's army retreating to Munda, with design to defend themselves in that town, it became necessary to invest it. The dead bodies of the enemy, heaped together, served instead of a rampart, and their javelins and darts were fixed up as palisades. Upon these we hung their bucklers to supply the place of a breast-work, and fixing the heads of the deceased upon swords and lances, planted them all around the work, to strike the greater terror into the besieged, and keep awake in them a sense of our bravery. Amidst these mournful objects did they find themselves shut in, when our men began the attack, which was managed chiefly by the Gauls. Young Valerius, who had escaped to Cordova with some horse, informed Sextus Pompey of what had happened; who, upon receipt of the mournful news, distributing what money he had about him to the troopers, left the town about nine at night, under pretence of going to find out Cæsar, to treat of an accommodation. On the other side Cn. Pompey, attended by a few horse and foot, took the road of Carteia, where his fleet lay, and which was about a hundred and seventy miles distant from Cordova. When he was arrived within eight miles of the place, he sent P. Calvitius, his camp-marshal, before, to fetch a litter to carry him to the town, because he found himself out of order. The litter came, and when he entered the town, those of his party waited on him privately, to receive his orders about the management of the war. As they assembled round the place in great crowds, Pompey, quitting his litter, put himself under their protection.

XXXIII. Cæsar, after the battle, seeing the circumvallation of Munda completed, marched to Cordova. Those of the enemy who had escaped the slaughter, possessing themselves of a bridge upon the approach of our men, called out to them with an air of derision, What! we are no more than a handful of men escaped from the battle, and shall we be allowed no place of retreat? Immediately they prepared to defend the bridge. Cæsar passed the river, and encamped on the other side. Scapula, who had stirred up the freedmen to a revolt, escaping after the battle to Cordova, when he found himself besieged, assembled all his followers, ordered a funeral pile to be erected, and a magnificent supper served up; when, putting on his richest dress, he distributed his plate and ready money among his domestics, supped cheerfully, anointed himself once and again, and last of all, ordered one of his freedmen to despatch him, and another to set fire to the pile.

XXXIV. Cæsar had no sooner encamped before the place, than a division arose among the inhabitants, between those who favoured

Cæsar, and those who were in the interest of Pompey, attended with so rude a clamour, that it reached our camp. During the contest, some legions, composed partly of fugitives, partly of slaves manumitted by Pompey, came and surrendered themselves to Cæsar. But the thirteenth legion prepared to defend the place, and with that view possessed themselves of the walls and some towers, in spite of all the opposition they met with; which obliged the other party to send deputies to Cæsar for aid. Upon this, those who escaped out of the battle set fire to the place, and our men entering at the same time, slew about twenty-two thousand of them, besides those who were slain without the walls; and thus became masters of the town. Whilst Cæsar was employed in this siege, those who were blocked up at Munda made a sally, but were driven back into the town with considerable loss.

XXXV. Thence Cæsar marched to Hispalis, which sent deputies to sue for pardon, and obtained it. Though the citizens assured him that they were able to defend the town with their own forces, he nevertheless thought it proper to send Caninius, his lieutenant, thither with some troops, and encamped himself before the place. There was in the town a strong party of Pompeians, who, displeased to see Cæsar's troops received within the walls, deputed secretly one Philo, a zealous partisan of Pompey, and well known in Lusitania, to beg assistance of Cecilius Niger, surnamed The Barbarous, who lay encamped near Lenius, with a strong army of Lusitanians. These approached the town towards night, got over the walls, surprised the sentinels and garrison, shut the gates, and began to defend the place.

XXXVI. During these transactions, deputies arrived from Carteia, with accounts of their having secured Pompey; hoping by this service to atone for their former fault of shutting the gates against Cæsar. Meantime the Lusitanians in Hispalis still continued pillaging the town, which, though known to Cæsar, did not yet determine him to press it too hard, lest they should in despair set fire to the town, and destroy the walls. It was resolved in council to suffer the Lusitanians to escape in the night by a sally, yet so that the thing might not appear designed. In this sally, they set fire to the ships that were in the river Bætis, and while our men were employed in extinguishing the flames, endeavoured to get off; but being overtaken by the cavalry, were mostly cut to pieces. Thence he marched to Asta, which submitted. Munda having been now a long while besieged, many of those who had escaped out of the battle, despairing of safety, surrendered to us; and being formed into a legion, conspired among themselves, that, upon a signal given, the garrison should sally out in the night, while they at the same time should begin a massacre in the camp. But the plot being discovered, they were next night, at the changing of the third watch, all put to death without the rampart.

XXXVII. The Carteians, while Cæsar was employed in reducing the other towns upon his route, fell into a dissension about young Pompey. There were two parties in the town, one that had sent the deputies to Cæsar, and another in the Pompeian interest. These last prevailing, seized the gates, and made a dreadful slaughter of their adversaries. Pompey himself was wounded in the fray, but escaping to his ships, fled with about thirty galleys. Didius, who was at Cadiz, with Cæsar's fleet, hearing of what had happened, immediately sailed in pursuit of them, stationing at the same time some cavalry and infantry along the coast, to prevent his getting off by land. Pompey had departed with so much precipitation from Cartæia, that he took no time to furnish himself with water, which obliging him to stop by the way, Didius came up with him after four days' sailing, took some of his ships, and burned the rest.

XXXVIII. Pompey, with a few followers, escaped to a place strongly fortified by nature; of which the troops sent in pursuit of him having certain intelligence by their scouts, followed day and night. He was wounded in the shoulder and left leg, and had besides strained his ancle, all which greatly retarded his flight, and obliged him to make use of a litter. A Lusitanian having discovered the place of his retreat, he was quickly surrounded by our cavalry and cohorts. Seeing himself betrayed, he took refuge in a post naturally strong, and which could easily be defended by a few men, because the approach to it was extremely difficult. We attempted to storm it, but were repulsed, and vigorously pursued by the enemy; and meeting with no better success, after several trials, we at length resolved to lay siege to the place, it seeming too hazardous to force it. Accordingly a ter-face was raised, and lines drawn round the place; which the enemy perceiving, thought proper to betake themselves to flight.

XXXIX. Pompey, as we have observed above, being lame and wounded, was in no condition to make a speedy retreat; and the rather, because the place was such, that he could use neither horse nor litter. He saw his people driven from the fort, massacred on all sides, and himself left without resource. In this extremity he fled to a cave, where he could not easily be discovered, unless he was betrayed by the prisoners. Here he was slain, and his head brought to Cæsar, the twelfth of April, just as he was setting out for Hispalis, and afterwards exposed to the view of the people.

XL. After the death of young Pompey, Didius, proud of his success, hauled some of his vessels ashore to be refitted, and retired himself to a neighbouring fort. The Lusitanians who had escaped from the battle of Munda, rallying in great bodies, found themselves strong enough to make head against him. Though the preservation of the fleet was what principally engaged his attention, he was yet necessitated to make frequent sallies, to check the insolence of the enemy. These daily skirmishes gave an opportunity of projecting an ambuscade; for which purpose they divided their troops into three bodies. Didius sallied according to custom; when, upon a signal given, one of the parties advanced to set fire to the fleet, and another counterfeiting a retreat, drew him insensibly into the ambuscade, where he was surrounded and slain with most of his followers, fighting valiantly. Some escaped in boats which they found on the coast; others made for the galleys by swimming, and weighing anchor, stood out to sea. A great many saved themselves in this manner, but the Lusitanians got all the baggage. Cæsar meanwhile returned from Cales to Hispalis.

XLI. Fabius Maximus, whom he had left to continue the siege of Munda, carried on the approaches with great success; insomuch that the enemy seeing themselves shut up on all sides, resolved to attempt a sally; but were repulsed with great loss. Our men seized this opportunity to get possession of the town, and made all the rest prisoners. Thence they drew towards Urso, a town exceedingly strong both by nature and art, and capable of resisting an enemy. For there is not so much as a

rivulet within eight miles of the place, nor any spring, but that which supplies the town. Add to all this, that the wood necessary for building towers and other machines, was to be fetched from a distance of six miles; because young Pompey, to render the siege more difficult, had cut down all the wood round the place; which obliged our men to bring all the materials for carrying on the siege from Munda.

XLII. During these transactions at Munda and Urso, Cæsar, who was returned from Cales to Hispalis, assembled the citizens, and made the following speech: "That when he was advanced to the questorship, he had chosen their province preferably to all others, and during his continuance in that office, done them every service in his power: that during his pretorship, he had obtained for them of the senate the abolition of the taxes imposed by Metullus, declared himself their patron, procured their deputies a hearing at Rome, and made himself many enemies, by undertaking the defence both of their private and public rights. In fine, that when he was consul, he had, though absent, rendered the province all the services in his power; that instead of making a suitable return for so many favours, they had always discovered the utmost ingratitude, both towards him and the people of Rome; as well in the last war as the preceding. You," says he, "though no strangers to the law of nations, and the rights of Roman citizens, have yet, like barbarians, often violated the sacred persons of Roman magistrates. You attempted in open day, in the public square, to assassinate Cassius. You have been always such enemies to peace, that the senate could never suffer the province to be without legions. You take favours for offences, and insults for benefits, are insolent and restless in peace, **and** cowardly and effeminate in war. Young Pompey, though only a private citizen, nay a fugitive, was received among you, and suffered to assume the ensigns of **magistracy**. After putting many citizens **to death, you** still furnished him with **forces, and even urged** him to lay waste the country and province. Against whom do you hope to be victorious? Can you be ignorant, that upon the supposition of my overthrow, the people of Rome have still ten legions capable not only of making head against you, but of bringing the whole earth under subjection?"

• • • • • • • • • • • • • • • • • • • •

30*

2 Y

AN

INDEX

OF

ANCIENT AND MODERN GEOGRAPHY

TO

CÆSAR'S COMMENTARIES.

☞ The words in Roman Letters denote the ancient names, and those in *Italic*, the modern.

A

ACARNANIA, a region of Epirus, *Carnia*.

Achaia, sometimes taken for all Greece; but most commonly for a part of it only, in Peloponnesus, *Romania Alta*.

Acilla, or Acholla, a city of Africa, unknown.

Actium, a promontory of Epirus, now called the *Cape of Tigalo*, famous for a naval victory gained near it, by Augustus, over M. Antony.

Addua, the *Adda*, a river that rises in the Alps, and parting the duchy of Milan from the state of Venice, falls into the Po, above Cremona.

Adduasdubis, a river of Burgundy, the *Doux*.

Adriatic Sea, the *Gulf of Venice*, at the bottom of which that city is situate.

Adrumetum, a town in Africa, *Mahometta*.

Ædui, the *Autunois*, a people of Gaul, near *Autun*, in the country now called *Lower Burgundy*.

Ægean Sea, the *Archipelago*, a part of the Mediterranean, which lies between Greece, Asia Minor, and the Isle of Crete.

Ægimurus, an island in the African Sea, *Galetta*.

Æginium, a town of Thessaly.

Ægyptus, *Egypt*, one of the most ancient, fertile, and celebrated kingdoms in Africa.

Æmilia Via, a Roman road in Italy, from Rimini to Aquileia, and from Pisa to Dertona.

Ætolia, a country of Greece, *Despotato*.

Africa, one of the four great continents into which the earth is divided.

Agar, a town in Africa, unknown.

Agendicum, a city of the Senones, *Sens*.

Alba, a town of Latium in Italy, *Albano*.

Albici, a people of Gaul unknown: some make them the same with the *Vivarais*.

Albis, the *Elbe*, a large and noble river in Germany, which has its source in the Giant's mountains, in Silesia, on the confines of Bohemia, and passing through Bohemia, upper and lower Saxony, falls into the North Sea at Ritzabuttel, about sixty miles below Hamburgh.

Alemanni, a people of ancient Germany, who inhabited between the Maine, the Rhine, and the Danube, and from whom the French still give this name to all the Germans.

Alemannia, the country inhabited by the Alemanni.

Alesia, or Alexia, a town of the Mandubians, *Alise*.

Alexandria, a city of Egypt, *Scanderia*. It was built by Alexander the Great, 333 years before Christ.

Aliso, by some supposed to be the town now called *Leilburg*; or, according to Junius, *Wesel*, in the dutchy of Cleves; but more probably *Eleen*.

Allobroges, an ancient people of Gallia Transalpina who inhabited that country which is now called *Dauphiny, Savoy* and *Piedmont*.

Alps, a ridge of high mountains, which separate France and Germany from Italy. That part of them which separates Dauphiny from Piedmont, had the name of the Cottian Alps.

Alsatia, a province of Germany, in the upper circle of the Rhine. *Alsace.*

Amagetobria, a city of Gaul, unknown.

Amantia, a town in Macedonia, *Porto Raguseo*.

Amanus, a mountain of Syria, *Scanderona*.

Amani Pylæ, or Amanicæ Portæ, *Straits of Scanderona*.

Ambarri, a people of Gaul, uncertain.

Ambialites, a people of Gaul, of *Lambelle* in *Bretagne*. Others take the word to be only a different name for the Ambiani.

Ambiani, or Ambianenses, the people of *Amiens*.

Ambianum, a city of Belgium, *Amiens*.

Ambibari, a people of Gaul, those of *Ambie* in Normandy.

Ambivareti, a people of Gaul, the *Vivarais*.

Ambivariti, an ancient people of *Brabant*, between the Rhine and the Maese.

Ambracia, a city of Epirus, *Arta*.

Ambrones, an ancient people, who lived in the country which is now called the *Canton of Berne*, in Switzerland.

Amphilochia, a region of Epirus, *Anfilocha*.

Amphipolis, a city of Macedonia, *Cristopoli* or *Emboli*.

Anartes, a people of Germany, *Walluchians, Servians,* or *Bulgarians.*

Anas, a **river of Spain,** the *Guadiana* or *Rio Roydera*.

Ancalites, a people of Britain, of the Hundred of *Henley*, in Oxfordshire.

Anchialos, a city of Thrace, near the Euxine Sea, now called *Kinkis*.

Ancona, a city of Italy, *Ancona*.

Andes, *Angers*, in France, the capital of the dutchy of Anjou.

Batavia, or Batavorum Insula, *Holland*, a part of which still retains the name of *Betuwe*.

Belgæ, the inhabitants of Gallia Belgica. The original Belgæ were supposed to be of German extraction; but passing the Rhine, settled themselves in Gaul.

Belgia, Belgium, or Gallia Belgica, the *Low Countries*, or *Netherlands*.

Bellocassi, or Velocasses, a people of Gaul, inhabiting the country of *Bayeux* in Normandy.

Bellovaci, an ancient renowned people among the Belgæ, inhabiting the country now called *Beauvais* in France.

Bergoa, a city of Macedonia, now called *Veria*.

Bessi, a people of Thrace, *Bessarabia*.

Bethuria, a region of Hispania Lusitanica, *Estremadura*.

Betones, or Barones, a people of Hispania Tarraconensis, *Birones*.

Bibracte, a town of Burgundy, now called *Autun*, the capital of the *Ædui*.

Bibrax, a town of Rheims, *Brains*, or *Breme*.

Bibroci, a people of Britain; according to Camden, *the Hundred of Bray*, in Berkshire.

Bigerriones, a people of Gaul, inhabiting the country now called *Bigorre*, in Gascony.

Bithynia, a country of Asia Minor, adjoining to Troas, over against Thrace, *Becangial*.

Biturigos, a people of Guienne, in France, of the country of *Berry*.

Bœotia, a country in Greece; parted from Attica by Mount Citheron. It had formerly several other names, and was famous for its capital, Thebes; but is now called *Stramulipa*.

Boii, an ancient people of Germany, who, passing the Rhine, settled in Gaul, the *Bourbonnois*.

Boraui, an ancient people of Germany, supposed by some to be the same as the Burii.

Bosphorani, a people bordering upon the Euxine Sea, *the Tartars*.

Bosphorus, two straits of the sea so called; one *Bosphorus Thracius*, now the *Straits of Constantinople*; the other Bosphorus Cimmerius, now the *Straits of Caffa*.

Brannovices, the people of *Morienne*, in France.

Bratuspantium, a city of Gaul, belonging to the Bellovaci, *Beauvais*.

Britannia, *Britain*, an island containing *England*, *Scotland*, and *Wales*.

Bructeri, an ancient people of the Netherlands, in East Friesland, afterwards called *Broeckmarelsnd*.

Brundusium, a city of Italy, *Brindisi*.

Brutii, a people of Italy, *the Calabrians*.

Bucinobantes, an ancient people of Germany, who lived opposite to *Mentz*.

Bulgaria, a part of the Lower Mœsia, between Mount Hæmus and the Danube.

Bullis, a town in Macedonia, unknown.

Burii, an ancient people of Germany, who inhabited the island of *Bornholm*.

Burserobunses, a people of Hispania Bætica, thought to be the same with the Ursaoneuses.

Buthrotum, a city of Epirus, *Butrinto* or *Botrento*.

Byzantium, an ancient city of Thrace, called at several times Ligos, Nova Roma, and now *Constantinople*.

Byzaryus, a city and province of Africa, within the kingdom of Tunis.

C

Cabillonum, a city of ancient Gaul, *Chalons sur Saone*.

Cadetes, a people of Gaul, unknown.

Cadurci, a people of Gaul, inhabiting the country of *Quercy*.

Cæcinus, a river of Locris, in ancient Greece.

Cæresii, a people of Belgic Gaul, inhabiting the country round Namur.

Cæsarea, the chief city of Cappadocia.

Cassia Silva, the *Cassian Forest*, supposed to be a part of the Hercynian Forest; about the dutchy of Cleves and Westphalia.

Calagurritani, a people of Hispania Tarraconensis, inhabiting the province of *Calahorra*.

Caletes, an ancient people of Belgic Gaul, inhabiting the country called *Le Pais de Caulx*, in Normandy, betwixt the Seine and the Sea.

Caletum, the town of *Calais*, in **Picardy**, over against Dover.

Calydon, a city of Ætolia, *Aylon*.

Camerinum, a city of Umbria, in Italy, *Camarino*.

Campania, the pleasantest part of Italy, in the kingdom of Naples, now called *Terra di Lavori*.

Campi Canini, a place in the Milanese, in Italy, not far from Bolinona.

Campi Catalaunici, supposed to be the large plain, which begins about two miles from Chalons sur Marne.

Candavia, a country of Macedonia, *Cucuria*.

Caninefates, an ancient people of the lower part of Germany, near Batavia, about where Gorckum, on the Maese, in South Holland, now is.

Cannæ, a poor village in Apulia, famous only for a great overthrow of the Romans there by Hannibal.

Canopus, *Bechir*, a famous city of Egypt, whence the Canopic branch of the Nile derived its name.

Cantabria, an ancient warlike people of Spain, properly of the provinces of *Guipuscoa*, and *Biscay*.

Cantium, a part of England, *the county of Kent*.

Canusium, a city of Apulia in Italy, *Canosa*.

Capitol, one of the seven hills in ancient Rome, on which the Romans had a famous fortress, founded by Tarquinius Priscus, and perfected by Tarquinius Superbus.

Cappadocia, a large country in Asia Minor, upon the Euxine Sea.

Capreæ, Caprea, an island on the coast of Campania.

Capua, Capoa, a city **in** the kingdom of Naples, in the province of Lavoro.

Carales, a city of Sardinia, *Cagliari*.

Caralitani, the people of *Cagliari*, in Sardinia.

Carbilis, a city of Spain, near Cordura.

Carcaso, a city of Gaul, *Carcassone*.

Carmona, a town of Hispania Bætica, *Carmone*.

Carni, an ancient people, who inhabited a part of Noricum, whose country is yet called *Carnioli*.

Carnutes, an ancient people of France, inhabiting the territory yet called *Chartrain*.

Carpi, an ancient people near the Danube.

Cartucca, a town in Spain, uncertain.

Carteia, a town of Spain, *Algeziva*, or *Tarifa*.

Carthage, once the most famous city of Africa, the rival of Rome, built by Queen Dido, about 70 years after Rome, according to some: but Justin will have it built before Rome; Appian before the destruction of Troy; and Velleius before Tyre itself.

Carthago Nova: *Carthagena*, a city of Murcia, in Spain, built by Asdrubal, general of the Carthaginians.

Casilloum, a town in Italy, *Castelluzzo*.

Caspian Sea, a vast lake between Persia, great Tartary, Muscovy, and Georgia, said to be six hundred miles long, and near as broad.

Cassandrea, a city of Macedonia, *Cassandria*.

Cassi, a people of ancient Britain, *the Hundred of Caishow, in Hertfordshire*.

Castellom Menapiorum, *Kessel*, a town in Brabant, on the river Neerse, not far from the Maese.

Castra Posthumiana, a town in Hispania Bætica, *Castro el Rio*.

Castra Vetera, **an** ancient city in Lower Germany, in **the** dutchy **of** Cleves; some say where *Santon*, others **where** *Bytthen* now is.

Castulonensis Saltus, a city of Hispania Tarraconensis, *Castona la Vieja*.

Catti, an ancient people of Germany, who inhabited part of the country now called *Hesse*, and *Thuringia*; from the mountains of Hartz, to the Weser and the Rhine.

Catuaci, corrupted probably **from Atuatici**. Some make them the same with the **people of** *Douay*, in France.

Caturiges, an ancient people of Gaul, inhabiting the country of *Embrun*, or *Ambrun*, alias *Charges*.

Cebenna Mons, the mountains of the *Cevennes*, in Gaul, separating the Helvians from Auvergne.

Celeja, a city of Noricum Mediterraneum, now *Cilley*.

Celtæ, a people of Thrace, about the mountains of Rhodope and Hæmus.

Celtæ, an ancient people of Gaul, in that part called Gallia Comata, between the Garumna and Sequana, from whom that country was likewise called Gallia Celtica.

Celtiberi, an ancient people of Spain, descended from the **Celtæ**, who settled about the river Iberus, or *Ebro*, from whom the country was called Celtiberia, now *Arragon*.

Cenimagni, or Iceni, an ancient people of Britain, inhabiting the counties of *Suffolk, Norfolk, Cambridgeshire*, and *Huntingdonshire*.

Cenla Mons, that part of the Alps which separates Savoy from Piedmont.

Cenni, an ancient people of Celtic extraction.

Cenomani, a people of Gallia Celtica, in the country now called *Le Manceau*, next adjoining to that of the Insubres

Centrones, an ancient people of Flanders, about the **ci** of *Courtray*, dependent on the Nervians.

Centrones, an ancient people of Gaul, inhabiting the **country** of Tarantaise.

Ceraunl Montes, mountains of Epirus, *Monti di Chimeru*

Cercina, **an** island on the coast of Africa, *Chercara, Cercare*.

Chersonesus, a peninsula **of** Africa, near Alexandria.

Chersonesus Cimbrica, **a** peninsula on the Baltic, now *Jutland*, part of *Holstein, Dilmarsh*, and *Sleswic*.

Cherusci, a great and warlike people of ancient Germany, between the Elbe and **the** Weser, about the country now called *Mansfield*, part of the Dutchy of *Brunswick*, and the diocess of *Hildesheim* and *Halberstadt*.

Chiavenna, the capital of a country of that name, on the river Meir, with a strong castle, in Switzerland.

Chrysopolis, a city of Bithynia, now called *Scutari*, opposite to Constantinople.

Cimbri, *the Jutlanders*, a very ancient northern people, who inhabited Chersonesus Cimbrica.

Cimmerii, an ancient people near the Euxine Sea, whence the Bosphorus Cimmerius, *Tartars*.

Cinga, a river of Spain, *Cinca* or *Senga*.

Cingulum, **a town** of Picenum in Italy, *Cingoli*.

Cirta, a town in Africa, *Constantina*, or *Constantina*, al. *Tadel*.

Clupea, a maritime city of Africa, *Quipeo*.

Cocamsea, a people of Gaul; according to some the *Hainault*.

Colmbra, an ancient city of Portugal, once destroyed, but not rebuilt, on the river *Mondego*.

Colchis, a country in Asia, near Pontus, including the present *Mingrelia*, and *Georgia*.

Comana Pontica, a city of Asia Minor *Com* or *Tobuchzon*.

Comana **of Cappadocia**, *Arminacha*.

Compsa, **a city of** Italy, *Conza*, or *Cossa*.

Concordia, **an ancient city of the province of Friuli,** in Italy, now in **ruins**.

Condrusi, **or** *Condrusnes*, an ancient people of Belgium, dependent on the Treviri, whose country is yet called *Condrats*, between Liege and Namur.

Confluens Mosl et Rheni, *Coblentz*.

Corcyra, an island of Epirus, *Corfu*.

Corduba, a city of Hispania Bætica, *Cordova*.

Corfinium, a town belonging to the Peligni in Italy, *St. Pelino*, al. *Pentima*.

Corinthus, a famous and rich city of Achaia in Italy, in the middle of the isthmus going into Peloponnesus.

Cornelia Castra, a city of Africa, between Carthage and Utica.

Corsica, a considerable island in the Mediterranean Sea, near Sardinia, which still retains its name, and at present belongs to France.

Cosanum, a city of Calabria, in Italy, *Cassano*.

Cremona, an ancient city of Gallia Cisalpina, which retains its name to this day, and is the metropolis of the *Cremonese*, in Italy.

Creta, one of the noblest islands in the Mediterranean Sea, now called *Candia*.

Ctesiphon, a town of Assyria, over against Seleucia.

Coriosolites, a people of Gaul, inhabiting *Cornouails* in Bretagne.

Cyclades, islands in the Ægean Sea, *L'Isole dell' Archipelago*.

Cyprus, an island in the Mediterranean Sea, between Syria and Cilicia, *Cipro*.

Cyrene, an ancient and once a fine city of Africa, situate over against Maiapan, the most southern cape of Morea, *Cairoan*.

Cyzicus, Chizico, formerly one of the largest cities of Asia Minor, in an island of the same name, on the White Sea.

D

Dacia, an ancient country of Scythia, beyond the Danube, containing part of *Hungary, Transylvania, Wallachia*, and *Moldavia*.

Dalmatia, a part of Illyricum, now called *Sclavonia*, lying between Croatia, Bosnia, Servia, and the Adriatic Gulf.

Danube, the largest river in Europe, which has its rise in Suabia, and after flowing through that country, Bavaria, Austria, Hungary, Servia, Bulgaria, Moldavia, Bessarabia, and part of Tartary, taking in its course a great number of noted rivers, some say sixty, falls into the Black or Euxine Sea, in two arms.

Dardania, the ancient name of a country in upper Mœsia, which became afterwards a part of Dacia, *Rascia*, and part of *Servia*.

Decetia, a town in Gaul, *Decize*, on the Loire.

Delphi, a city of Achaia, *Delpho*, al. *Salona*.

Delta, a very considerable province of Egypt, at the mouth of the Nile. **Errif.**

Dualbintea, an ancient people of Gaul, inhabiting the country called *Le Perche*; al. *Dixblores* in Bretagne; al. *Löwen* of Brabant; al. *Lendout*, over against Britain.

Dubis, a river of Burgundy, *Le Doux*.

Duratium, commonly supposed to be a city of Gaul, in the province of Poitou; but in fact Cæsar uses Duratius for the name of a nobleman of considerable rank.

Durocortorum, a city of Gaul, *Rheims*.

Dyrrhachium, a city of Macedonia, *Durazzo, Dratri*.

E

Eburones, an ancient people of Germany, inhabiting part of the country, now the bishopric of *Liege*, and the country of *Namur*.

Eburovices, a people of Gaul, inhabiting the country of *Evreux*, in Normandy.

Egypt, one of the most ancient, fertile, and celebrated kingdoms in Africa.

Elaver, a river of Gaul, the *Allier*.

Eleutheri, a people of Celtic Gaul, *la Rouergue*.

Elis, a city of Peloponnesus, *Belvidera*.

Elusates, an ancient people of Gaul, inhabiting the country of *Euse*, in Gascony.

Ephesus, an ancient and celebrated city of Asia Minor, *Efeso*.

Epidaurus, a maritime city of Dalmatia, *Ragusa*.

Epirus, a country in Greece, between Macedonia, Achaia, and the Ionian Sea, by some now called *Albania Inferior*.

Esui, a people of Gaul, those of *Sees*; but ...e word seems rather a corruption from *Ædui*.

Esubii, corrupted from *Unelli*, or *Lexovii*, properly the people of *Lisieux*, in Normandy.

F

Fanum, a city of Umbria, in Italy, *Fano*.

Fesole, an ancient city of Italy, in the Dutchy of Florence, anciently one of the twelve considerable cities of Hetruria.

Fini, an ancient people of Prussia.

Fixeum, anciently reckoned the eastern mouth of the Rhine, now called the *Ulie*, and is a passage out of the Zuyder Sea into the North Sea.

Forum Flaminii, a city of Umbria, three miles from Fulginium, yet called *Fossomine*.

Forum Julium, *Frejus*, an ancient town on the coast of Provence in France.

Fossa Mariana, a canal made by C. Marius, near Marseilles, for the conveyance of ships from the sea, into the Rhone.

Fossæ Marinæ, a city of Gallia Narbonensis, now called *Aigues Mortes*.

Frentani, an ancient people of Italy, *Abruzzo Capitanata*.

Frisii, the ancient inhabitants of *Friesland*.

G

Gabali, an ancient people of Gaul, inhabiting the country of *Givaudan*.

Gades, *Cadiz*, an ancient and considerable city of Spain.

Gaditani, the people of Gades, or *Cadiz* in Spain.

Galatia, a country of Asia Minor, lying between Cappadocia, Pontus, and Paphlagonia; now called *Chiangare*.

Galli, the people of ancient Gaul, now the *French*.

Gallia, the ancient and renowned country of Gaul, a *France*. It was divided by the Romans into,

Gallia Cisalpina, Togaea, or Togata, now *Lombardy*, between the Alps and the river Rubicon; and

Gallia Transalpina, or Comata, comprehending *France, Holland, the Netherlands*; and farther subdivided into,

Gallia Belgica, now a part of *Lower Germany* and the *Netherlands*; with *Picardy*; divided by Augustus, into Belgica and Germania; and the latter into prima and secunda.

Gallia Celtica, now *France*, properly so called, divided by Augustus into Lugdunensis and Rothomagensis.

Gallia Aquitanica, now *Gascony*; divided by Augustus into prima, secunda, and tertia; and

Gallia Narbonensis, or Braccata, now *Languedoc, Dauphiny*, and *Provence*.

Gallicia, a province of Spain, of a large extent, once a kingdom, and comprehending *old Castile*, but now a part of the kingdom of *Leon*.

Gallo-græcia, a country of Asia Minor, the same as *Galatia*.

Garites, a people of Gaul, inhabiting the country now called *Gavre, Gavaraon*.

Garoceli, or Graioceli, an ancient people of Gaul, about *Mount Cenis*, or *Mount Genevre*: others place them in the *Val de Morienne*.

Garumna, the *Garonne*, one of the largest cities of France, which rising in the Pyrenees, flows through Guienne, forms the vast bay of Garonne, and falls by two mouths, into the British Seas.

Garumni, an ancient people of Gaul, in the neighbourhood of the *Garonne*.

Gebenna Mons, the mountains of the *Cevennes*, which separated the Helvians from the Arverni.

Geldura, a fortress of the Ubii, on the Rhine, not improbably the present village of *Gelb*, on that river, eleven German miles from Neus.

Genabum, *Orleans*, an ancient town in Gaul, famous for the massacre of the Roman citizens committed there by the Carnutes.

Geneva, a city of Savoy, now a free republic, upon the borders of Helvetia, at the going out of the Rhone from the Lake Lemanus, anciently a city of the Allobroges.

Genusus, a river of Macedonia, uncertain.

Gepidæ, or Gepidi, an ancient northern people, supposed to have dwelt about the mouth of the Vistula.

Gergovia, the name of two cities in ancient Gaul, the one belonging to the Boii, the other to the Arverni. Their situation is not certainly known.

Germania, *Germany*, one of the largest countries of Europe, and the mother of those nations, which, in the fall of the Roman empire, conquered all the rest.

Gesatæ, a kind of militia among the ancient Germans.

Getæ, an ancient people of Scythia, who inhabited betwixt Mœsia and Dacia, on each side of the Danube. Some think their country the same with the present *Wallachia*, or *Moldavia*.

Getulia, a province in the kingdom of Morocco, in Barbary.

Gomphi, a town in Thessaly, *Gonfi*.

Gorduni, a people of Belgium, the ancient inhabitants of *Ghent*; according to others, of *Courtray*.

Gotini, an ancient people of Germany, who were driven out of their country by Marobuduus.

Græcia, *Greece*, a large part of Europe, called by the Turks *Romelia*, containing many countries provinces, and islands, once the nursery of arts, learning and sciences.

Levaci, a people of Brabant, not far from Louvain, whose chief town is now called *Leue*.

Letri, a people of Gallia Belgica, where now Lorrain, will skilled in darting. Their chief city is now called *Foul*.

Lexovii, an ancient people of Gaul, *Lisieux* in Normandy.

Liburni, an ancient people of Illyricum, inhabiting part of the present *Croatia*.

Ligeris, the Loire, one of the greatest and most celebrated rivers of France, said to take one hundred and twelve rivers in its course: it rises in Valey, and falls into the Atlantic 40 miles below Nantes.

Heruli, an ancient northern people, who came first out of the Bay of Aquitain, below Nantz.

Liguria, a part of ancient Italy, extending from the Apennines to the Tuscan Sea, containing *Ferrara*, and the territories of *Genoa*.

Lilybeum, the most western promontory of the island of Sicily, where stood a city of the same name, now *Capo Boco*.

Limo, or Limonum, a city of ancient Gaul, *Poictiers*.

Lingones, a people of Gallia Belgica, inhabiting in and about *Langres*, in Champagne.

Lissus, an ancient city of Macedonia, *Alessio*.

Lucani, an ancient people of Italy, inhabiting the country now called *Balisveute*.

Luceri, an ancient city of Italy, *Lucera*.

Lusitania, *Portugal*, a kingdom on the west of Spain, formerly a part of it.

Lutetia, *Paris*, an ancient and famous city, the capital of all France, on the river *Seine*.

Lydia, an inland country of Asia Minor, formerly governed by the famous Croesus, who was the last king of it, *Carania*.

Lygii, an ancient people of upper Germany, who inhabited the country now called *Silesia*, and on the borders of *Poland*.

M

Macedonia, a large country, of great antiquity and fame, in Greece, containing several provinces, now under the Turks.

Maeotis Palus, a vast lake in the north part of Scythia, now called *Marbianco*, or *Mare della Tana*. It is about six hundred miles in compass, and the river Tanais disembogues itself into it.

Magetobria, or Amagetobria, a city of Gaul, uncertain.

Malaca, a city of Hispania Baetica, *Malaga*.

Mandubii, an ancient people of Gaul, *l'Ansois*, in Burgundy.

Marcomanni, a nation of the Suevi, whom Cluverius places between the Rhine, the Danube, and the Neckar; who settled, however, under Marobodus, in *Bohemia* and *Moravia*.

Marrucini, an ancient people of Italy, inhabiting the country now called *Abruzzo*.

Marsi, an ancient people of Italy, inhabiting the country now called *Ducado de Marsi*.

Massilia, *Marseilles*, a large and flourishing city of Provence, in France, on the Mediterranean; said to be very ancient, and, according to some, built by the Phoenicians; but as Justin will have it by the Phocians, in the time of Tarquinius, king of Rome.

Matisco, an ancient city of Gaul, *Mascon*.

Matrona, a river in Gaul, the *Marne*.

Mauritania, *Barbary*, an ancient large region of Africa, divided into Caesariensis, Tingitana, and Sitifensis.

Mazaca, a city of Cappadocia, *Tivaria*.

31

Mediomatrices, a people of Lorrain, on the Moselle, about the city of *Metz*.

Mediterranean sea, the first discovered sea in the world, still very famous, and much frequented, which breaks in, from the Atlantic Ocean, between Spain and Africa, by the Straits of Gibraltar, or Hercules' Pillar, the *ne plus ultra* of the ancients.

Medobrega, a city of Lusitania, *Armenna*.

Meldae, according to some, the people of the *Meaux*, but more properly corrupted from *Belgae*.

Melodunum, an ancient city of Gaul, upon the Seine, above Paris, *Melun*.

Menapii, an ancient people of Gallia Belgica, who inhabited on both sides of the Rhine. Some take them for the inhabitants of *Cleves*; and others of *Antwerp*, *Ghent*, &c.

Mesopotamia, a large country in the middle of Asia, between the Tigris and the Euphrates, *Diarbeck*.

Messana, an ancient and celebrated city of Sicily, still known by the name of *Messina*.

Metaurus, a river of Umbria, now called *Metoro*, in the Dutchy of Urbino.

Metiosedum, an ancient city of Gaul, on the Seine below Paris, *Corbeil*.

Metropolis, a city of Thessaly, between Pharsalus and Gomphi.

Mitylene, a city of Lesbos, *Metelin*.

Moesia, a country of Europe, and a province of the ancient Illyricum, bordering on Panonia, divided into the Upper, containing *Bosnia* and *Servia*, and the Lower, called *Bulgaria*.

Mona, in Caesar, the Isle of *Man*; in Ptolemy, *Anglesey*.

Morini, an ancient people of the Low Countries, who probably inhabited on the present coast of *Boulogne*, on the confines of *Picardy* and *Artois*, because Caesar observes that from their country was the nearest passage to Britain.

Mosa, the *Maese* or *Meuse*, a large river of Gallia Belgica, which falls into the German Ocean below the Briel.

Mosella, the *Moselle*, a river which, running through Lorrain, passes by Triers and falls into the Rhine at Coblentz, famous for the vines growing in the neighbourhood of it.

Munda, an ancient city of Spain, *Monda*; al *Ronda la Veja*.

Mursa, a town and castle in Sclavonia, at the conflux of the Draw and Danube, now called *Esseek*, famous for a bridge three miles over.

Mysia, a country of Asia Minor, not far from the Hellespont, divided into Major and Minor.

N

Nabathaei, an ancient people of Arabia, uncertain.

Nannetes, an ancient people of Gaul, inhabiting about *Nantes*.

Nantuates, an ancient people of the north part of Savoy, whose country is now called *Le Chablais*.

Narbo, *Narbonne*, an ancient Roman city, in Languedoc, in France, said to be built a hundred and thirty-eight years before the birth of Christ.

Narisci, the ancient people of the country now called *Nortgoe*, in Germany, the capital of which is the famous city of Nuremberg.

Naupactus, an ancient and considerable city of Aetolia, now called *Lepanto*.

Neapolis, a city of Italy, which still retains the name of *Naples*.

Provincia Romana, or Romanorum, one of the southern provinces of France, the first the Romans conquered and brought into the form of a province, whence it obtained its name, which it still in some degree retains, being called at this day *Provence*.

Prusa or *Prusæ*, *Buron*, a city of Bithynia, at the foot of Olympus, built by Hannibal.

Ptolemais, an ancient city of Africa, *St.Jean D'Acre*.

Pyrenæi Montes, the *Pyrenees*, or *Pyrenean Mountains*, one of the largest chains of mountains in Europe, which divided Spain from France, running from east to west eighty-five leagues in length.

R

Ravenna, a very ancient city of Italy, near the coast of the Adriatic Gulf, which still retains its ancient name. In the decline of the Roman empire, it was some time the seat of the emperors of the West; as it was likewise of the Visi-Gothic kingdom.

Rauraci, a people of ancient Germany, near the Helvetii, who inhabited near where *Basil* in Switzerland now is.

Rhedones, an ancient people of Gaul, inhabiting about *Rennes*, in Bretagne.

Rhætia, the country of the *Grisons*, on the Alps, near the Hercynian Forest.

Rhemi, the people of *Rheims*, a very ancient, fine, and populous city of France, in the province of Champagne, on the river Vesle.

Rhenus, the *Rhine*, a great and famous river in Germany, which formerly divided it from Gaul. It springs out of the Rhætian Alps, in the western borders of Switzerland, and the northern of the Grisons, from two springs which unite near Coire, and falls into the Maese and the German Ocean, by two mouths, whence Virgil calls it Rhenus bicornis.

Rhodanus, the *Rhone*, one of the most celebrated rivers of France, which rises from a double spring in Mont de la Fourche, a part of the Alps, on the borders of Switzerland, near the springs of the Rhine, and after a vast circuit through France, falls into the Mediterranean, by five mouths.

Rhodope, a famous mountain of Thrace, now called *Valiza*.

Rhodus, *Rhodes*, a celebrated island in the Mediterranean, upon the coast of Asia Minor, over against Caria.

Rhyndacus, a river of Mysia, in Asia, which falls into the Propontis.

Roma, *Rome*, once the seat of the Roman empire, and the capital of the then known world, now the immediate capital of Campagna di Roma only, on the river Tiber, and the papal seat; generally supposed to have been built by Romulus, in the first year of the seventh Olympiad.

Roxolani, a people of Scythia Europæa, bordering upon the Alani: their country, anciently called Roxolania, is now *Red Russia*, belonging to the crown of Poland.

Ruspina, an ancient maritime city of Africa, *Sousa*.

Rutheni, an ancient people of Gaul, *la Rouergue*.

S

Sabis, the *Sambre*, a river of the Low Countries, which rises in Picardy, and falls into the Maese at Namur.

Saguntini, the people of Saguntum, a noble city of ancient Spain, the memory of which is recorded with honour, for the fidelity shewn to its allies the Romans, *Morvedre*.

Salassi, an ancient city of Piedmont, whose chief town was where now *Aosta* is situate.

Salluvii, *Salyes*, a people of Gallia Narbonensis, about where *Aix* now is.

Salona, an ancient city of Dalmatia, and a Roman colony; the place where Dioclesian was born, and whither he retreated, after he had resigned the imperial dignity.

Salsum, a river of Hispania Bætica, *Rio Salado*, or *Guadajos*.

Samarobriva, *Amiens*, an ancient city of Gallia Belgica, enlarged and beautified by the emperor Antoninus Pius, now the chief city of Picardy, on the river Somme.

Santones, the ancient inhabitants of *Guienne* or *Xaintoigne*.

Sardinia, a great island in the Mediterranean, which in the time of the Romans had forty-two cities, now belonging to the Duke of Savoy, with the title of king.

Sarmatia, a very large northern country, divided into Sarmatia Asiatica, containing *Tartary*, *Petigora*, *Circassia*, and the country of the *Morduits*; and Sarmatia Europæa, containing *Russia*, part of *Poland*, *Prussia*, and *Lithuania*.

Sarsora, a town in Africa, unknown.

Savus, the *Save*, a large river, which rises in upper Carniola, and falls into the Danube at Belgrade.

Scaldis, the *Scheldt*, a noted river in the Low Countries, which rises in Picardy, and washing several of the principal cities of Flanders and Brabant, in its course, falls into the German Ocean by two mouths, one retaining its own name, and the other called the *Honte*.

Scandavia, anciently a vast northern peninsula, containing what is yet called *Schonen*, anciently Scania, belonging to *Denmark*; and part of *Sweden*, *Norway*, and *Lapland*.

Scythia, a large country, properly Crim-Tartary, but in history and geography greatly extended, and particularly divided into Scythia Asiatica, on either side of Mount Imaus; and Scythia Europæa, about the Euxine Sea; and the Mæotic Lake.

Seduni, an ancient people of Switzerland, *Sion*.

Sedusii, an ancient people of Germany, on the borders of Suabia.

Segni, an ancient German nation, neighbours of the Condrusi, *Zulpich*.

Segontiaci, a people of ancient Britain, inhabiting about *Holshot* in Hampshire.

Segovia, a city of Hispania Bætica, *Segovia la menor*.

Segusiana, a people of Gallia Celtica, about where now *Lionois Forest* is situate.

Senones, an ancient nation of the Celtæ, inhabiting about the *Senonois*, in Gaul.

Sequana, the *Seine*, one of the principal rivers of France, arising in the dutchy of Burgundy, not far from a town of the same name, and running through Paris, and by Roan, forms at Candebec a great arm of the sea.

Sequani, an ancient people of Gallia Belgica, inhabiting the country now called the *Franche Comte*, or the *Upper Burgundy*.

Sesuvii, an ancient people of Gaul, inhabiting about *Sees*.

Sibuzates, an ancient people of Gaul, inhabiting the country of *Buch*.

Sicilia, *Sicily*, a large island in the Tyrrhene Sea, at the south-west point of Italy, formerly called the store-house of the Roman empire, and the first province the Romans possessed out of Italy

Sicoris, a river in Catalonia, the *Segre*.

Sigambri, or Sicambri, an ancient people of Lower Germany, between the Maese and the Rhine, where *Guelderland* is; though by some placed on the banks of the Maine.

Silicensis, a river of Hispania Bœtica, *Rio de las Algamitas*. Others think it a corruption from *Singuli*.

Sinuessa, a city of Campania, not far from the Savo, an ancient Roman colony, now in a ruinous condition; *Rocca di Mondragone*.

Soricaria, a city of ancient Spain, unknown.

Soritia, an ancient town in Spain, unknown.

Sotiates, or Santiates, an ancient people of Gaul, inhabiting the country about *Aire*.

Sparta, a city of Peloponnesus, now called *Misithra*, said to be so ancient as the days of the Patriarch Jacob.

Spoletum, *Spoleto*, a city of great antiquity, of Umbria, in Italy, the capital of a dutchy of the same name, on the river Tesino, where are yet some stately ruins of ancient Roman and Gothic edifices.

Suessiones, an ancient people of Gaul, *le Soissonnois*.

Suevi, an ancient, great and warlike people of Germany, who possessed the greatest part of it, from the Rhine to the Elbe, but afterwards removed from the northern parts, and settled about the Danube, and some marched into Spain, where they established a kingdom.

Sulchitani, an ancient people of Sardinia, unknown.

Sulmo, an ancient city of Italy, *Sulmona*.

Sunici, an ancient people of the dutchy of *Limburg*, where there is yet a place called *Sunich*, a name probably borrowed from them.

Syracusæ, *Saragusa*, once one of the noblest cities of Sicily, said to be built by Archias, a Corinthian, above seven hundred years before Christ. The Romans besieged and took it during the second Punic war, on which occasion the great Archimedes was killed. It has been so entirely destroyed, that it has no remains to show of its antiquity.

Syria, a large country of Asia, containing several provinces, now called *Souristan*.

Syrtes, *the Deserts of Barbary*; also two dangerous sandy gulfs, in the Mediterranean, upon the coast of Barbary, in Africa, called the one Syrtis magna, now the *Gulf of Sidra*; the other Syrtis parva, now the *Gulf of Capes*.

T

Tamesis, the *Thames*, a celebrated and well known river of Great Britain.

Tanais, the *Don*, a very large river in Scythia, dividing Asia from Europe. It rises in the province of Resan, in Muscovy, and flowing through the Crim-Tartary, runs into the Mæotic Lake, near a city of the same name, now in ruins, and in the hands of the Turks.

Tarbelli, a people of ancient Gaul, near the Pyrenees, inhabiting about *Ayx*, and *Bayonne*, in the country of *Labourd*.

Tarracina, an ancient city of Italy, which still retains the same name.

Tarraco, *Tarragona*, a city of Spain, which, in ancient time, gave name to that part of it called Hispania Tarraconensis; by some said to be built by the Scipios, though others say before the Roman conquest, and that only enlarged it. It stands on the mouth of the river Tulcis, now *el Francoli*, with a small haven on the Mediterranean.

Tarsus, *Tarso*, the metropolis of Cilicia, famous for being the birth-place of St. Paul.

Tarusates, an ancient people of Gaul, uncertain according to some, *le Toursan*.

Taurus, an island in the Adriatic Sea, unknown.

Taurois, the name of a castle near Marseilles.

Tauros Mons, the greatest mountain in all Asia, extending from the Indian to the Ægean Sea, called by different names in different countries, viz. Imaus, Caucasus, Caspius, Ceraunius, and in Scripture, Ararat. Herbert says it is fifty English miles over, and fifteen hundred long.

Tectosages, *see* Volcæ.

Tegea, a city of Africa, unknown.

Tenchtheri, a people of ancient Germany bordering on the Rhine, near *Overyssel*.

Tergestini, an ancient people inhabiting about *Arieste*, in the confines of Istria and the Carni.

Terni, an ancient Roman colony, on the river Nare, twelve miles from Spoletum.

Tentones, or *Teutoni*, an ancient people bordering on the Cimbri, the common ancient name for all the Germans, whence they yet call themselves *Teutsche*, and their country *Teutschland*.

Thabena, a city of Africa, unknown.

Thapsus, a maritime city of Africa, uncertain.

Thebæ, a city of Bœotia, in Greece, said to have been built by Cadmus, destroyed by Alexander the Great, but rebuilt, and now known by the name of *Stives*.

Thermopylæ, a famous pass on the great mountain Oeta, leading into Phocis, in Achaia, now called *Bocca di Lupo*.

Thessaly, a country of Greece, formerly a great part of Macedonia, now called *Janna*.

Thessalonica, the chief city of Macedonia, now called *Salonichi*.

Thracia, a large country of Europe, eastward from Macedonia, commonly called *Romania*, bounded by the Euxine and Ægean Seas.

Thurii, or Turii, an ancient people of Italy, *terra Trologneto*.

Tigurinus Pagus, a nation of the Helvetians, the ancient inhabitants of the canton of *Zurich*, in Switzerland.

Tisdra, or *Tisdrus*, an ancient city of Africa, *Cairoan*.

Tolosa, *Thoulouse*, a city of Aquitain, of great antiquity, the capital of Languedoc, on the Garonne.

Toxandri, an ancient people of the Low Countries, about *Treda* and *Gertruydenburg*; but, according to some, of the diocese of *Liege*.

Tralles, an ancient people of Lydia, in Asia Minor, *Chara*.

Treviri, the people of *Treves*, or *Triere*, a very ancient city of Lower Germany, on the Moselle, said to have been built by Trebetas, the brother of Ninus. It was made a Roman colony in the time of Augustus, and became afterwards the most famous city of Gallia Belgica. It was for some time the seat of the western empire, but it is now only the seat of the Ecclesiastical Elector named from it.

Triboci, or Triboces, a people of ancient Germany, inhabiting the country of *Alsace*.

Trinobantes, a people of ancient Britain, inhabitants of the counties of *Middlesex* and *Hertfordshire*.

Troja, *Troy*, a city of Phrygia, in Asia Minor, near Mount Ida, destroyed by the Greeks after a ten years siege.

Tubantes, an ancient people of Germany, about *Westphalia*.

Tugium, a city and canton of Helvetia, or Switzerland, now called *Zug*.

Tulingi, an ancient people of Germany, who inhabited about where *Stulingen* in Switzerland is.

Tungri, an ancient people inhabiting about where Tongres, in Liege, now is.

Turones, an ancient people of Gaul, inhabiting about *Tours.*

Tuscia, *Tuscany,* a very large and considerable region of Italy, anciently called Tyrrhenia, and Etruria.

Tyber, one of the most noted, though not largest rivers of Italy, which rises in one of the Apennines, and among other places, passing through Rome, falls into the Tyrrhenian Sea at *Ostia.*

Tygris, a rapid river of Asia, which, in its course, unites with the Euphrates.

Tyrus, *Tyre,* an ancient city of Phœnicia, upon the Mediterranean, famous for its traffic and riches.

V

Vacca, a town in Africa, unknown.

Vahalis, *the Waal,* the middle branch of the Rhine, which, passing by Nimeguen, falls into the Maase, above Gorcum.

Valencia, a city of Spain, which gives name to a whole kingdom, about a mile from the Mediterranean, supposed to be built by Junius Brutus.

Valencia, *Valence,* a city of Gallia Narbonensis, now in Dauphiny, on the rivers Rhone and Isere.

Vangiones, an ancient people of Germany, about the city of *Worms.*

Varus, the *Var,* a river in Gaul, that flows into the Ligurian Sea.

Ubii, an ancient people of Lower Germany, who inhabited about where *Cologne* and the dutchy of *Juliers* now are.

Ucubia, a town in Hispania Bætica, *Lucubi.*

Velauni, an ancient people of Gaul, inhabiting about *Velal.*

Vellaunodunum, a town in Gaul, about which geographers are much divided; some making it *Auxerre,* others *Chasteau Landon,* others *Villeneuve* in Lorrain, others *Veron.*

Velocasses, an ancient people of Normandy, about *Rouen.*

Veneti: this name was anciently given as well to the *Venetians,* as to the people of *Vannes,* in Bretagne, in Gaul, for which last it stands in Cæsar.

Venetia, *Venice,* a noble city of Italy, built upon sixty islands, joined together by five hundred bridges, at **the** top of the Adriatic Gulf, the capital of a powerful commonwealth.

Ventisponte, a town of Spain, unknown.

Veragri, a people of Gallia Lugdunensis, whose chief town was Aguanum, now *St. Maurice.*

Verbigenus, or Urbigenus Pagus, a nation or canton of the Helvetians, inhabiting the country in the neighbourhood of *Orbe.*

Vercelli Campi, the *Plains of Vercellæ,* famous for a victory the Romans obtained there over the Cimbri. The city of that name is in Piedmont, on the river Sesia, on the borders of the dutchy of Milan.

31 *

Veromandui, a people of Gallia Belgica, whose country, now a part of Picardy, is still called *Vermondois.*

Verona, a city of Lombardy, the capital of a province of the same name, on the river Adige, said to be built by the Gauls two hundred and eighty-two years before Christ. It has yet several remains of antiquity.

Vesontio, *Besançon,* the capital of the Sequani, now the chief city of Burgundy.

Vettones, a people of Spain, inhabiting the province of *Estremadura.*

Vibo, a town in Italy, not far from the Sicilian Straits, *Bibona.*

Vienna, a city of Narbonese Gaul, *Vienne* in Dauphiny.

Vindelici, an ancient people of Germany, inhabitants of the country of Vindelicia, otherwise called Rætia Secunda.

Vistula, the *Weichsel,* a famous river of Poland, which rises in the Carpathian mountains, in upper Silesia, and falls into the Baltic, not far from **Dantzic,** by three months.

Visurgis, the *Weser,* a river of Lower Germany, which rises in Franconia, and, among other places of note, passing by Bremen, falls into the German Ocean, not far from the mouth of the Elbe, between that and the Ems.

Uila, or Ulia, a town in Hispania Bætica, in regard to whose situation geographers are not agreed; some making it *Monte major,* others *Vaena,* others *Villa.*

Umbria, a large country of Italy, on both sides of the Apennines.

Unelii, an ancient people of Gaul, uncertain.

Vocates, a people of Gaul, on the confines of the La pordenses.

Vocontii, an ancient people of Gaul, inhabiting about *Die,* in Dauphiny, and *Vaison* in the county of Venisse.

Vogesus Mons, the mountain of *Vauge,* in Lorrain, or, according to others, *de Foucilles.*

Volcæ Arecomici, and Tectosages, an ancient people of Gaul, inhabiting the *Upper* and *Lower Languedoc.*

Ursao, a town of Hispania Bætica, *Osuna.*

Usæa, a town of Africa, whose situation is not certainly known.

Usipetes, an ancient people of Germany, who frequently changed their habitation.

Utica, a city of Africa, famous for the death of Cato; *Biserte.*

Uxellodunum, a town in Gaul, whose situation is not known; according to some *Useoldun.*

Uzita, a town unknown.

X

Xantones, the same with the Santones, or people of *Xantonge.*

Z

Zama, a town in Africa, famous for the defeat of Hannibal there by Scipio, now called *Zamora.*

Zeta, a maritime city of Africa, now *Zerbi.*

Ziela, or Zela, a city of Pontus, *Arzila.*

Zingitana, a part of ancient Africa, now included in the kingdom of *Algiers.*

AN
INDEX
OF
PERSONS AND THINGS.

The Numerals refer to the Book, the Figures to the Section. G. stands for the Wars in Gaul ; C. for the Civil Wars ; Al. for the Alexandrian ; Af. for the African ; Sp. for the Spanish War.

A

Acco, prince of the Senones, his conduct on Cæsar's approach, G. vi. 3. Condemned in a council of the Gauls, ibid. 44.

Achillas, captain of Ptolemy guards, sent to kill Pompey, C. iii. 85. Appointed by Pothinus commander of all the Egyptians' forces, ibid. 89. Heads an army of twenty thousand veteran troops, ibid. 91. Variance between him and Arsinoe, Ptolemy's sister, Al. 3.

Acilla, demands a garrison from Cæsar, Af. 30. Besieged in vain by Considius, 30, 40.

Adiatomus, sallies upon Crassus at the head of a chosen body of troops, G. iii. 22.

Adrumetum, held by Considius Longus with a garrison of one legion, C. ii. 23. Cæsar makes himself master of it, Af. 77.

Æduans, complain to Cæsar of the ravages committed in their territories by the Helvetians, G. i. 9. Join in a petition against Ariovistus, ibid. 23. At the head of one of the two leading factions of Gaul, G. vi. 12. Cæsar quiets an intestine commotion among them, G. vii. 30. And prevents their revolting from the Romans, ibid. 33. Which nevertheless comes to pass soon after, ibid. 52.

Æginurus, a trireme belonging to Cæsar, taken there by Varus and Octavius, Af. 41.

Æginium, Domitius joins Cæsar near that place, C. iii. 56.

Ægus and Roscillus, their perfidious behaviour towards Cæsar, C. iii. 21.

Ætolia, recovered from Pompey by the partizans of Cæsar, C. iii. 30.

Afranius, Pompey's lieutenant, his exploits in conjunction with Petreius, C. i. 38. Carries the war into Celtiberia, ibid. 55. Surrenders to Cæsar, ibid 76. Prevails with one of his slaves to despatch him, Af. 81.

Africans, a crafty warlike people, Af. 9. Their manner of concealing their corn, ibid. 57.

Agar, defended with great bravery against the Gætulians, Af. 68.

Agendicum, Cæsar quarters four legions there, G. vi. 40. Labienus leaves his baggage in it under a guard of new levies, and sets out for Lutetia, G. vii. 54.

Alba, Domitius levies troops in that neighbourhood, C. i. 13.

Albici, a kind of mountaineers taken into the service of the Marseillians, C. i. 34.

Alces, a species of animals resembling in some respects a goat, to be found in the Hercynian forest, G. vi. 25.

Alesia, Cæsar shuts up Vercingetorix there, G. vii. 68. Surrounds it with lines of circumvallation and contravallation, ibid. 69. Obliges it to surrender, ibid. 82.

Alexandria, Cæsar pursues Pompey thither, C. iii. 87. Is unexpectedly entangled in a war at that place, ibid. 88. Difficulties Cæsar had to encounter there for want of water, Al. 4. Cæsar enters the town with his victorious army, and receives it into his protection, ibid. 23.

Alexandrians, an acute and ingenious people, Al. 2. But treacherous and without faith, ibid 4. They petition Cæsar to send them their king, ibid. 16.

Allier, Cæsar eludes the vigilance of Vercingetorix, and by an artifice passes that river, G. vii. 33.

Allobroges, supposed to be not well affected to the Romans, G. i. 5. Complain to Cæsar of the ravages of the Helvetians, ibid. 9.

Alps, Cæsar crosses them with five legions, G. i. 8. Sends Galba to open a free passage over them to the Roman merchants, G. iii. 1.

Amagetobria, famous for a defeat of the Gauls there by Ariovistus, G. i. 23.

Amantia submits to Cæsar, and sends ambassadors to know his pleasure, C. iii. 10.

Amanus, a mountain in Asia near which Scipio sustains some losses, C. iii. 28.

Ambarri, complain to Cæsar of the ravages committed in their territories by the Helvetians, G. i. 9.

Ambialites, join in a confederacy with the Veneti against Cæsar, G. iii. 9.

Ambiani furnish ten thousand men, to the general confederacy of the Belgians against Cæsar, G. ii. 4. Join with the Veneti in their revolt from the Romans, G. iii. 9. Sue for peace, and submit themselves to Cæsar's pleasure, G. ii. 15.

Ambiorix, his artful speech to Sabinus and Cotta, G. v. 23. Cæsar marches against him, G. vi. 27. Ravages and lays waste his territories, ibid. 31. Endeavours in vain to get him into his hands, ibid 43.

Ambivareti, ordered to furnish their contingent for raising the siege of Alesia, G. vii. 69.

Ambivariti, the German cavalry sent to forage among them, G. iv. 6.

Ambracia, Cassius directs his march towards that place, C. iii. 31.

Amphilochi, reduced by Cassius Longinus, C. iii. 47.

358

THE END.

THE

HISTORY

OF

THE CONSPIRACY OF CATILINE

AND

THE JUGURTHINE WAR

BY C. CRISPUS SALLUSTIUS

TRANSLATED

BY WILLIAM ROSE, A. M.

———————

NEW YORK:

H. W. DERBY, 625 BROADWAY.

.1801.

PREFACE.

As the usefulness of translations of the classics is universally allowed, so the difficulty of succeeding in them will be readily granted by all who have ever attempted it. To translate a modern author of genius, into a modern language, is no easy task, though so many of the modern languages resemble one another; it must therefore be extremely difficult to translate any of the classical writers of Greece or Rome into such a language as ours, the idioms and structure of which are so very different from those of the Greek and Latin languages. But this is not all; the translator must not only find proper phrases to convey the images of his author, but he must animate his images with the same spirit; for it is with translations as with painting; if the air and spirit of the original are wanting, there can be no true resemblance.

The translator of Sallust was very sensible of the difficulty of his undertaking, and hopes the candid reader will make fair and equitable allowances for the defects that attend the execution of it. His great aim has been to preserve a due medium between a verbal, and too bold and free a translation; having made it his first care to preserve the sentiment of his author; and his next, to adhere to his words, as far as he was able to express them in an easy and natural manner. By this method he flatters himself that he has, in some measure, answered both the ends he proposed in translating Sallust; the first of which was, to furnish such young gentlemen as have made a tolerable progress in the Latin tongue, with such a version of him, as, at the same time that it had all the advantages of a literal translation, should be free from that flatness which is inseparable from such, and read with tolerable ease and fluency. His other view was to present such as are not capable of reading Sallust himself, and yet are desirous of being acquainted with the memorable transactions of which he gives an account, with such a translation of him as should have somewhat of the air of an original.

But here the reader will be apt to say: What occasion for a new translation of Sallust? Are there not several very good ones already?—The translator would be far from derogating from the merit of any former translations of his author; and in answer to this question, all he has to say is, that if his has but equal merit with any of them, as he humbly apprehends it has, there will still be this additional recommendation of it; that besides the neatness of the impression, it may be purchased at an easier price than the others : a circumstance which, he imagines, will plead strongly in his favour with the generality of readers.

He has nothing farther to add, but that if this his first essay meets with a favourable reception from the public, it will be a powerful inducement to him to continue his labours in the same way ; by which means it will be in the power of almost every parent to furnish his child with useful translations of the school classics in a neat and elegant form, and at a very easy rate.

CAIUS CRISPUS SALLUSTIUS was born at Amiternum, in the country of the Sabines, in the year of Rome six hundred and sixty-eight, during the third consulship of L. Cornelius Cinna, and the first of Cn. Papirius Carbo. He was descended from a Plebeian family, as appears from his having been one of the tribunes of the people, and from the many invectives against the nobility that are scattered up and down his works. In his early years his inclination led him to the study of learning, to which he applied with the greatest diligence, and made uncommon progress under the care of Atteius Prætextatus, called Philologus, one of the ablest grammarians of the age.

It appears that he had turned his thoughts, in his younger days, to the writing of history, for which he had, unquestionably, great talents ; but, as he himself intimates in his preface to the History of Catiline's Conspiracy, he was diverted from this pursuit by the workings of ambition. It were to be wished, for the sake of his character, that he had kept close to his original design, and not meddled with the management of public affairs : his reputation would then have been free from many of those stains with which it is now blemished. The Roman manners, in the age wherein he lived, were extremely licentious and depraved ; corruption prevailed in the state, and the most barefaced venality in all the courts of justice ; the worthiest patriots, the best friends to liberty, suffered, while the basest parricides were exalted ; the Patricians and Plebeians were engaged in the most violent struggles ; and as the one or the other happened to prevail, they oppressed the opposite party with wanton rage and fury : so that, considering the degeneracy of the times, it is the less to be wondered at, if he caught the infection, and was borne away by such a torrent of corruption.

If we may credit the ancient declaimer, who, under the name of Cicero, has inveighed against Sallust, his youth was stained with the foulest acts of lewdness ; and indeed the gross enormities of his more advanced years render it highly probable. We are told by M. Varro, an author worthy of credit, that he was caught in adultery with Fausta, the daughter of Sylla, and severely whipped by her husband Milo, who likewise obliged him to pay a considerable sum of money. There are other charges against him, believed chiefly upon the authority of the above-mentioned declaimer ; but we shall not detain the reader by enumerating them.

5

From his being quæstor, which was probably in the year of Rome six hundred and ninety-three, he bore no public office till the year seven hundred and one, at which time he was made tribune of the people. In this office he improved the opportunity that was put into his hands of revenging himself upon Milo, the murderer of Clodius, for the treatment he had received from him on the score of Fausta. Having gained over to his interest two other tribunes, Q Pompeius Rufus, and Munacius Plancus Bursa, he employed all the arts of party and faction to keep up the ill humour of the populace against him; haranguing continually, and terrifying the city with forged stories of magazines of arms prepared by Milo, for massacring his enemies, and burning the city. Nor was he less active in raising a clamour against Cicero, whom he threatened with trials and prosecutions, in order to deter him from pleading Milo's cause; giving out upon all occasions, that Clodius was indeed killed by Milo, but by the advice and contrivance of a greater man.

In the year seven hundred and three, he was expelled the Senate by the then censors, Appius Claudius and Calpurnius Piso, on account of his lewd and profligate life. The year following, however, he was restored to the dignity of senator by Julius Cæsar, and likewise made quæstor; in which office he is charged with great corruption, with making sale of every thing he could, and using it only as an occasion of plunder. During Cæsar's second dictatorship he was made prætor, an honour which had like to have proved fatal to him. For endeavouring in vain to quiet a sedition which arose among Cæsar's troops in Campania, that were designed for Africa, he went to Rome to give Cæsar an account of it; and was pursued by a considerable body of them, who would certainly have put him to death, if they had overtaken him. Cæsar, upon his arrival, calmed the commotion, and passed over into Africa, with part of his army, taking Sallust along with him; whom, a few days after his landing, he sent with part of his fleet into the island of Cercina, at that time in the possession of the enemy, being informed that there was a great quantity of corn in it, of which he stood very much in need. C. Decimus, the quæstor, who had been left with a strong party to secure the corn, upon the prætor's approach embarked in a small vessel, and made his escape. Sallust met with a favourable reception from the natives, found great plenty of corn, loaded his ships, and returned to Cæsar. What other services he performed during the course of the war, does not appear; but it is certain he was closely attached to Cæsar's party and interest.

When the war in Africa was ended, Cæsar bestowed upon him the government of Numidia, which he plundered in the most inhuman manner. No one indeed could be more rapacious than he was, during the course of his administration in this province; a reproach which falls the more heavily upon him, as he had inveighed so keenly against corruption and corrupt magistrates, and bestowed so high encomiums on virtue and equitable government. With the spoils of his infamous magistracy he purchased a country-house at Tivoli, and one of the noblest dwellings in Rome on the Quirinal mount, with beautiful gardens, which to this day is called the gardens of Sallust. In what manner he spent the remainder of his days, we have no account; he died in the year of Rome seven hundred and nineteen.

Though Sallust's character as a man has been held in just abhorrence and detestation, as an historian he has been ever highly admired by the best judges. His talents for history were certainly very great; and where he pursues the thread of it, he does it in the most perspicuous, agreeable, and instructive manner: his style is clear and nervous; his narration natural; his descriptions beautiful; his reflections curious and solid; his speeches animated and persuasive; **and his** characters **just and** striking. After all, he is not without his faults, and those very great ones. He is very apt to start from his subject, in order to display his own abilities, and to run into digressions, which, however ingenious and entertaining, have an air of affectation and self-sufficiency. His vanity appears clearly in his prefaces, which are full of compliments to himself; and instead of being pertinent introductions to his history, seem rather designed to represent the importance of his own character and studies. They abound indeed with virtuous sentiments, and bitter invectives against corrupt governors; though these, by the way, seem rather to proceed from private pique and resentment, than from a genuine abhorrence of corruption, or a truly patriot zeal for the public good.

His history of the war with Jugurtha **is a** masterly performance; but his partiality to Cæsar, and his treatment of Cicero, are unpardonable faults in the account of Catiline's conspiracy. When he draws the characters of Cato and Cæsar, he considers them only as two great subjects in the service of a free state, and acquiring fame by different ways and qualities; without once mentioning the most material difference between them—that the one laboured earnestly, through the whole **course** of his life, to preserve and reform the state, whilst the other did all in his **power to** corrupt and destroy it. Did we know nothing more of Cæsar than what Sallust says of him, we should certainly take his character for a great and amiable **one.** But he has only given us **the** fair side of it, if it may be properly said that it had one, without representing him in his true colours; as the friend and patron of the abandoned, the depraved, and desperate; as the promoter of public abuse and corruption; as one who took pleasure in embroiling and debauching the state; and as a monster **of ambition.** He put on, indeed, the guise of clemency, for which he has been highly celebrated by his flatterers, as if **it** had been a real, and not an assumed quality in him. But surely no one, who is acquainted with his character, will assert, that he, who was guilty of the greatest cruelty in making war upon and enslaving his country, would have relinquished his mad schemes of ambition, if gentle methods had failed him, rather than have recourse to acts of blood and vengeance. After having seen how Marius and Sylla were hated for their personal cruelties, no wonder that he should put on the appearance of this, as well as of other virtues. But that clemency was not his natural character, we have the express testimony of his friend Curio, who well knew him : Cælius too, one of his partisans, freely says of him, in a letter to Cicero, that he meditated nothing but what was violent and tragical, nor even spoke in any other strain.

As partiality has made Sallust bestow false colours upon the character of Cæsar, so prejudice has kept him from placing that of Cicero in a clear and full light. He represents him indeed as an active, sensible, and diligent magistrate, allows him the character of an excellent consul, but bestows no greater degree of praise upon him, than what could not well be dissembled by an historian ; and even what he says of him does not seem to come directly from the heart. But was no more than this scanty measure of praise due to the immortal Cicero ? No greater tribute due from an impartial historian to the saviour of his country ? Was this doing full justice to the superior abilities, the undaunted courage, the unwearied diligence, and uncommon sagacity, whereby Cicero baffled so desperate a conspiracy, and saved Rome .rom one of the greatest dangers that had ever threatened her ? Is it not the duty of an historian to throw distinguished lustre on distinguished merit, and to brighten the character of a national deliverer ? If so, then surely Sallust has fallen far short of his, in the account he has given of Catiline's conspiracy, which for this reason is a very defective performance.

Had Cæsar done what Cicero did, his conduct had been related in very different strains, his praises copiously set before the reader, and his character represented in the fullest light. We should then have seen that masterly address, wherewith both senate and people were managed ; that dexterity and artful management, whereby orders of men, the most averse to each other, were united in the common interest of their country ; and that vigilance, wherewith the secret machinations of the conspirators were watched in silence, and a sufficient force prepared to resist them, before their black schemes were laid before the senate, amply displayed, and finely illustrated, together with a full account of the extraordinary honours which were the rewards of such distinguished services.

CONSPIRACY OF CATILINE.

MEN who would act up to the dignity of their nature, ought not to pass their lives in obscurity, like the beasts of the field, formed with bodies prone to the earth, and under necessary subjection to their appetites.

Now our faculties are twofold; those of the soul, and those of the body; the soul was designed for sovereign command, the body for subjection; the former we enjoy in common with the gods, the latter with the brute creation. So that to me it appears more agreeable to nature, to pursue glory by the abilities of the mind, than those of the body; and as our lives are but of short duration, it should be our study to render our memory immortal. For the splendour derived from riches and beauty is short-lived and frail; virtue alone confers immortality.

It has, however, been a great and long debate, whether success in war is most owing to bodily strength or mental abilities; for, as counsel is necessary before we enter upon action; after measures are duly concerted, speedy execution is equally necessary; so that neither of these being sufficient singly, they prevail only by the assistance of each other. Accordingly, kings of old (for this was the first title of authority among men) applied themselves differently, some, to strengthen their bodies by exercise; others, to improve their minds. Then, indeed, ambition had no share in influencing the conduct of men, every one was satisfied with his own. But after Cyrus began in Asia, and the Lacedæmonians and Athenians in Greece, to conquer cities and nations, when the lust of power was thought a sufficient reason for commencing a war, and glory was measured by the extent of dominions, then it was discovered by experience, that genius conduces most to success. And if kings and rulers would exert their abilities in peace, as they do in war, the condition of human affairs would be much more steady and uniform; nor should we see so frequent revolutions and convulsions in states, and such universal confusion. For the same arts, by which dominion was at first acquired, will serve to secure it. But when, instead of industry, moderation, and equity, sloth, licentiousness, and pride prevail, the fortune of a state changes with its manners. And thus power always passes from him who has least merit, to him who has most.

It is to the powers of the mind we owe the invention and advantages of agriculture, navigation, and architecture, and indeed all the other arts of life. Yet many there are in the world, who, abandoned to sloth and sensuality, without learning or politeness, pass their lives much like travellers; and who, in opposition to the design of nature, place their whole happiness in animal pleasure, looking upon their minds as a heavy burden. The life and death of such as these, are to me of equal value, since there is no notice taken of either. He only seems to me to be truly alive, and to enjoy his rational nature, who, by engaging in an active course of life, pursues the glory that is derived from noble actions, or the exercise of some honourable employment. Now, amidst a great variety of occupations, nature has directed men to different pursuits.

To act well for the state is glorious, and to

1

write well for it, is not without its merit. A man may become illustrious in peace or in war; many have been applauded for performing heroic actions, many for relating them. And though the **character of the** historian is not reckoned **so** glorious as that of the hero; yet, to me it appears a very arduous task to write history well; since the style must be suited to the subject. Besides, many look upon the censure of faults, as the effect of malice and envy; and when the glorious achievements of brave and worthy men are related, every reader will be easily inclined to believe what he thinks he could have performed himself, but will treat what exceeds that measure, as false and fabulous.

As for me, like most others, I had, in my younger days, a strong desire for a share in the administration; but found many obstructions in my way: for, instead of modesty, justice, and virtue, licentiousness, corruption, and avarice flourished; which, though my soul, as yet untainted with evil habits, utterly abhorred; yet amidst such general depravity, my tender years were caught by ambition; and although I avoided, in the general tenor of my conduct, the corrupt practices of the age, yet, being fired with the same ardour for preferment that others were, I was thence exposed to envy and reproach, as well as they.

As soon, however, as my mind was delivered from the many crosses and dangers attending this pursuit, and I had determined to retire, during the remainder of my life, from the administration, it was not my intention to waste **such** valuable time in sloth and indolence, nor **to** pass my days in agriculture, hunting, or the like servile **occupations**; but resuming my former design, from which the cursed spirit of ambition had diverted me, **I resolved to employ** myself in writing such parts of **the Roman history**, as appeared to me to **be most deserving of** being transmitted to posterity; **and this I chose** the rather, because my mind was neither influenced by hope or fear, nor attached **to any** party in the state: accordingly, I shall **here**, with the utmost veracity, give a short account of Catiline's conspiracy; a memorable attempt, both for the enormous wickedness of it, and the danger it threatened. But before I enter directly upon the story, I shall give a short character of the man.

LUCIUS CATILINE was descended of an illustrious family: he was a man of great vigour both of body and mind; but of a disposition extremely profligate and depraved. From his youth he took pleasure in civil wars, massacres, depredations, and intestine broils: and in these he employed his younger days. His body was formed for enduring cold, hunger, and want of rest, **to** a degree indeed incredible: his spirit was daring, subtle, and changeable; he was expert in all the arts of simulation and dissimulation; covetous of what belonged to others, lavish of his **own**; violent **in** his passions; he had eloquence **enough, but a** small share of wisdom. His boundless **soul** was constantly engaged in extravagant **and** romantic projects, too high to be attempted.

Such was **the** character of Catiline; who, after Sylla's usurpation, was fired with a violent desire of seizing the government; and, provided he could but carry his point, he was not at all solicitous by what means. His spirit, naturally violent, was daily more and more hurried to the execution of his designs, by his poverty and the consciousness of his crimes; both which evils he had heightened by the practices above mentioned. He was encouraged to it by the wickedness of the state, thoroughly debauched by luxury and avarice; vices equally fatal, though of contrary natures.

Now that I have occasion to mention the Roman manners, I am naturally led to look back a little to past ages, and to give a short account of the institutions of our ancestors, both in war and peace; how they governed the state, and in what grandeur they left it; and how, by a gradual declension, it has fallen from the highest degree of virtue and glory, to the lowest pitch of vice and depravity.

The Trojans, as far as I can learn, who were forced to fly from their native country, and wandered up and down, without any fixed abode, under the conduct of Æneas, were the founders of Rome, together with the Aborigines, a barbarous race, subject to no laws, and restrained by no authority, but altogether independent and unaccountable. It is incredible how easily these two nations, after they came to inhabit the same city, formed into one people, though differing in original, language, and manners. Afterwards, when wholesome institutions, an increase of territory and inhabitants, had rendered their state sufficiently flourishing and glorious; their opulence, such as the hard fate of almost all human affairs, became the object of envy; neighbouring princes and nations fell upon them in war, and but few of their friends came to their assistance; the rest, struck with terror, kept at a distance from the danger.

The Romans, however, fearless and undaunted, equally upon their guard both within and without the walls, acted with spirit and resolution; concerted their measures; encouraged one another; boldly faced the enemy; and by their arms protected their liberty, their country, and their families: then, after having repelled their own dangers, they carried assistance to their confederates, and procured themselves alliances, more by conferring than receiving favours.

The form of their goverment was monarchical; but monarchy circumscribed by laws: a select number of men, whose bodies were indeed enfeebled with years, but their minds in full vigour, formed a council for the direction of public affairs; they were called FATHERS, either on account of their age, or a similitude of concern. Afterwards when the regal government, which was established for maintaining liberty and aggrandizing the state, degenerated into pride and tyranny, they abolished it, and created two magistrates with annual power; this they thought would be the most effectual method to prevent that insolence, which a long continuance of power generally inspires.

This change in the form of their government produced a great alteration in their manners; every one now exerted the utmost of his capacity in the service of his country, and was ready to display his talents upon all occasions. For under tyrants, the worthy are more exposed to jealousy than the worthless, and great abilities are always dreaded by them. It is incredible to relate, how much the city increased in a short time, after the recovery of its liberty, so great was the ardour of its citizens for glory. The youth, as soon as they were able to bear arms, betook themselves to the camp, where they were trained up to war by labour and practice; and they took greater pleasure in fine armour and war horses, than in lewdness and banqueting. To such men no toils were unusual, no situation grievous, no enemies formidable; their resolution surmounted all difficulties. But their chief contest for glory was with one another; every one laboured to signalize himself in the view of his fellow-soldiers, by striving to be the first in wounding the enemy, and scaling the walls. This they reckoned riches, this glory, and high rank. They were

fond of applause, but liberal of money; they desired only a competent share of riches, but boundless glory. I could relate upon what occasions a handful of Romans has defeated mighty armies; and what cities, strongly fortified by nature, they have taken by assault; but this would carry me too far from my undertaking.

Yet surely fortune bears sovereign influence over every thing; it is she that brightens or obscures all things more from caprice and humour, than a regard to truth and justice. The actions of the Athenians were, I am ready to grant, sufficiently great and noble; though not to such a degree as fame has represented them; but as they had writers of great genius, their achievements are celebrated throughout the world as the greatest that ever were: and the bravery of those who performed them, is reckoned just as great as the abilities of these illustrious authors in extolling them. But the Roman people wanted this advantage, because their ablest men were the most employed in the service of the state. None cultivated their minds without bodily application. The worthiest men preferred doing to speaking; and chose rather that others should commend their virtuous actions, than they relate those of others.

Good morals, therefore, were cultivated both at home and abroad. A spirit of perfect harmony and disinterestedness every where prevailed. Laws had no greater influence in determining them to the practice of justice and equity, than natural disposition. The only quarrels, dissensions, and disputes they exercised, were against the public enemy: all the contests that subsisted among the citizens, were in virtuous deeds. They were magnificent in their offerings to the gods; frugal in their families; and faithful to their friends. Bravery in war, and equity and moderation in peace, were the only means by which they supported themselves and the public affairs: and, as the clearest evidence of these virtues, I find, that, in time of war, such as engaged the enemy contrary to orders, or continued in the field after a retreat was sounded, were more frequently punished, than those who abandoned their standards, or quitted their posts; and in peace, they conducted the administration more by the force of favours than of terror; and, if they received an injury, chose rather to forgive than revenge it.

But when by probity and industry the state was become powerful; when mighty princes were conquered in war; barbarous nations and potent states reduces. to obedience; when Carthage, that vied with Rome for the empire of the world, was utterly demolished, and sea and land lay every where open to her power; then fortune began to exert her malice, and throw every thing into confusion. Ease and riches, the grand objects of the pursuit of others, depressed and ruined those, who had, without regret, undergone toils and hardships, distresses and dangers. First a love of money possessed their minds; then a passion for power; and these were the seeds of all the evils that followed. For avarice rooted out faith, probity, and every worthy principle; and, in their stead, substituted insolence, inhumanity, contempt of the gods, and a mercenary spirit. Ambition obliged many to be deceitful, to belie with their tongues the sentiments of their hearts; to value friendship and enmity not according to their real worth, but as they conduced to interest; and to have a specious countenance, rather than an honest heart. These corruptions at first grew by degrees, and were sometimes checked by correction. At last, the infection spreading like a plague, the state was entirely changed, and the government, from being the most righteous and equitable, became cruel and insupportable.

At first, indeed, the minds of men were more influenced by avarice than ambition, a vice which has some affinity to virtue; for the desire of glory, power, and preferment, is common to the worthy and the worthless; with this difference, that the one pursues them by direct means; the other, being void of merit, has recourse to fraud and subtlety; avarice has money for its object, which no wise man ever coveted. This vice, as if impregnated with deadly poison, enervates both soul and body; is always boundless and insatiable; nor are its cravings lessened by plenty or want. But when Sylla had, by force of arms, made himself master of the state, and, from fair beginnings, brought matters to a bloody issue, his victorious troops gave themselves up to rapine and violence: one coveted a house, another lands: they observed neither measure nor moderation, but exercised the most enormous and inhuman outrages upon the citizens. Besides, Sylla, to gain the affections of the army which he had commanded in Asia, had, contrary to the rules of our ancestors, allowed them too great latitude, and indulged them in luxury: the warlike tempers of the soldiers, who were now without employment, became easily enervated, by their delicious quarters, and a life of pleasure. There the Roman troops first habituated themselves to lewdness and drinking; to admire statues, pictures, and sculpture; to make spoil of them both publicly and privately; to plunder the temples of the gods, and to ravage every thing both sacred and profane. An army thus disposed, and victorious too, was sure to leave nothing to the conquered. For success unhinges the minds of wise men; how then should they who were so depraved, use their victory with moderation?

When riches began to be held in high esteem, and attended with glory, honour, and power; virtue languished, poverty was deemed a reproach, and innocence passed for ill-nature. And thus luxury, avarice, and pride, all springing from riches, enslaved the Roman youth; they wantoned in rapine and prodigality; undervalued their own, and coveted what belonged to others; trampled upon modesty, friendship, and continence; confounded things divine and human, and threw off all manner of consideration and restraint.

To see the difference between modern and ancient manners, one needs but take a view of the houses of particular citizens, both in town and country, all resembling, in magnificence, so many cities; and then behold the temples of the gods, built by our ancestors, the most religious of all men. But they thought of no other ornament for their temples, than devotion; nor for their houses, but glory: neither did they take any thing from the conquered, but the power of doing hurt. Whereas their descendants, the most effeminate of all men, have plundered from their allies, by the most flagrant injustice, whatever their brave ancestors left to their conquered enemies; as if the only use of power was to do wrong.

It is needless to recount other things, which none but those who saw them will believe; as the levelling of mountains by private citizens, and even covering the sea itself with fine edifices. These men appear to me to have sported with their riches, since they lavished them in the most shameful manner, instead of enjoying them with honour. Nor were they less addicted to lewdness, and all manner of extravagant gratifications: men prostituted themselves like women; women laid aside all regard to chastity. To procure dainties for their tables, sea and land were ransacked. They indulged to sleep, before nature craved it; the returns of hunger and thirst were anticipated with luxury and cold and fatigue were never so much as felt. The Roman youth, after they had spent their fortunes, were prompted by such depravations to commit all manner of enormities; for their minds, impregnated with evil habits, and unable to resist their craving appetites, were violently bent upon all manner of extravagances, and all the means of supplying them.

In so great and debauched a city, Catiline had always about him, what was no difficult matter to find in Rome, bands of profligate and flagitious wretches, like guards to his person. For all those who were abandoned to gluttony and voluptuousness, and had exhausted their fortunes by gaming, feasting, and lewdness; all who were overwhelmed by debts, contracted to purchase pardon for their crimes; add to this, parricides and sacrilegious persons from all quarters; such as were convicted for crimes, or feared conviction; nay farther, all who lived by perjury and shedding the blood of citizens; lastly, all whom wickedness, indigence, or a guilty conscience, disquieted, were united to Catiline in the firmest bonds of friendship and intimacy. Or if any person of an unblameable character became familiar with him; by daily conversation, and the snares that were laid to debauch him, he too soon resembled, and even equalled, the rest. But what he chiefly courted was the intimacy of young men: their minds being soft and pliable, were easily ensnared. Some of these he provided with harlots; bought horses and dogs for others, gratifying the favourite passion of each: in a word he spared no expense, nor even his own honour, to engage them heartily in his interests. Some there were, I know, who thought that the youth who frequented Catiline's house were guilty of unnatural lewdness; but this rumour, I apprehend, was more owing to other reasons, than that there was any clear evidence of the fact.

As for Catiline himself; he had, when very young, been guilty of many abominable acts of lewdness; debauched a Vestal, and a young lady of quality, with several other atrocious crimes, in open contempt of all law and order; afterwards he conceived a passion for Aurelia Orestilla, one who had nothing but her beauty to recommend her; and because she scrupled to marry him, on account of his having a son who was arrived at years of maturity, it is believed as a certain fact, that he destroyed that son, and made his house desolate, to open a way to this so infamous an alliance. And this indeed appears to me to have been the principal cause that pushed him on to the execution of the conspiracy. For his guilty soul, at enmity with gods and men, could find no rest; so violently was his mind torn and distracted by a consciousness of guilt. Accordingly his countenance was pale, his eyes ghastly, his pace, one while quick, another slow; and indeed in all his looks there was an air of distraction.

As for the youth whom he had seduced in the manner above related, they were trained up to wickedness by various methods: he taught them to be false witnesses, to forge deeds, to throw off all regard to truth, to squander their fortunes, and slight dangers: and after he had stripped them of all reputation and shame, he pushed them on to crimes still more heinous; and, even when no provocation was given, it was their practice to ensnare and murder those who had never injured them, as well as those who had. For he chose to be cruel and mischievous without any cause, rather than the hands and spirits of his associates should lose their vigour for want of employment.

Catiline, confiding in these friends and accomplices, formed a design to seize the government: he found an additional encouragement from the number of those who were oppressed with debts throughout the state, and the disposition of Sylla's soldiers, who, having squandered away what they had lately acquired, and calling to remembrance their former conquests and depredations, longed for a civil war. Besides, there was no army in Italy: Pompey was carrying on a war in the remotest parts of the earth: he himself was in great hopes of obtaining the consulship: the senate seemed careless of the public; and all things were quiet: a conjuncture of circumstances extremely favourable to his designs.

Accordingly, about the first of June, in the consulship of L. Caesar and C. Figulus, he first applied himself to his accomplices: some he encouraged, others he sounded; acquainted them how strongly he was supported; how few forces the government had to oppose him; and laid before them the great advantage that would attend the conspiracy. Having sufficiently sifted them, he called all those together who were most necessitous and daring.

In this assembly were found of senatorial rank, P. Lentulus Sura, P. Autronius, I. Cassius Longinus, C. Cethegus, P. Sylla and S. Sylla, the sons of Servius; L. Vargunteius, Q.

Annius, M. Porcius Læcca, L. Bestia, and Q. Curtius : of the equestrian order, M. Fulvius Nobilior, L. Statilius, P. Gabinius Capito, and C. Cornelius, to whom were joined many from the colonies and municipal towns, all men of figure in their several countries. There were likewise several noblemen engaged in this conspiracy, though not so openly ; men excited not by want, or any pressing consideration, but by the hopes of lawless power. Besides these, almost all the youth, especially the youth of quality, favoured Catiline's undertaking: even those who had it in their power to live at their ease, nay, splendidly and luxuriously, preferring uncertainties to certainties, and discord to peace. Some there were at that time too, who believed that M. Licinius Crassus was privy to the design ; because he hated Pompey, who was at the head of a great army ; to reduce whose power, he would willingly have promoted any interest whatever: besides, he hoped, if the conspiracy succeeded, that he should find it easy to make himself head of the conspirators.

Some time before this, a like conspiracy had been formed by a few, among whom was Catiline, of which I shall give the best account I am able.

In the consulship of L. Tullus and M. Lepidus, P. Autronius and P. Sylla, who were chosen to succeed them, had been prosecuted for bribery at elections, and punished. Not long after, Catiline was likewise convicted of bribery, and hindered from suing for the consulship, because he could not declare himself a candidate within the limited time. At this time too, Cn. Piso, a young nobleman, extremely bold, indigent, and factious, was instigated by his poverty and depraved morals to raise commotions in the state. Catiline, Autronius, and he, entering into a combination about the fifth of December, determined to murder the consuls L. Torquatus and L. Cotta in the capitol, on the first of January: upon which Catiline and Autronius were to seize the consulship, and send Piso with an army to take possession of both the Spains. But their design being discovered, they put off the assassination-plot to the fifth of February ; at which time they proposed not only to murder the consuls, but likewise most of the senators. And if Catiline had not been too forward in giving the signal to his associates, before the senate-house, there had been that day the most bloody massacre Rome had ever seen. But as no great number of the conspirators had yet got together, the scheme was frustrated.

Notwithstanding this, Piso, though he had only the office of quæstor, was afterwards sent into Nether-Spain, in quality of proprætor, by the interest of Crassus ; because he knew him to be an irreconcileable enemy to Pompey. Nor was the senate indeed averse to his having the province, for they were desirous to have so turbulent a citizen at a great distance from them ; besides, a great many, who wished well to the interests of the state, looked upon him as a defence to it, now the power of Pompey was become formidable. But Piso, in his march to his province, was murdered by some Spanish horse he had in his army. Some there are who ascribe his death to his haughty, arbitrary, and tyrannical behaviour in his command, which the Barbarians could not bear. Others allege, that these soldiers assassinated Piso by Pompey's order, whose old followers they were, and devoted to his interest: that the Spaniards had never attempted any such thing before, but had often submitted patiently to the merciless orders of their commanders. As for me, I shall leave the matter undetermined ; and have now said enough of the first conspiracy.

When Catiline saw those, whose names we have already given, assembled together ; though he had often conferred with them singly, yet, judging it proper to address and encourage them in a body, he withdrew with them into a private part of the house, where none could hear him but the conspirators, and there spoke to them in the following manner :—

" If your bravery and fidelity were not well known to me, the present opportunity had occurred to no purpose; vain would all our great hopes have been ; the power of seizing the government had dropped into our hands in vain ; nor should I, depending upon dastardly and irresolute associates, have hazarded certainties for uncertainties. But as I have upon many important occasions proved your bravery and attachment to me, I have dared to engage in an enterprise of the highest consequence and the greatest glory. It is an additional encouragement to me, when I consider the harmony of our desires and aversions, which is the firmest bond of friendship.

" Now the nature of my undertaking you have already heard severally ; and my ardour to put it in execution increases daily, when I consider what must be our future lot, unless we recover our liberty. For since the government came under the power and management of a few, kings and princes have been tributary to them, and nations have paid them taxes; whilst all the rest of us citizens, however worthy or brave, noble or plebeian, have remained as a sorry mob, without interest or authority, slaves to those to whom we should be a terror, were the state but in its due vigour. All away, preferment, interest, and riches, are now in their hands, or those of their favourites; to us they have left nothing but dangers, repulses from public dignities, the terror of tribunals, and the **buffetings of poverty.** Which indignities, how long will ye tamely submit to, ye bravest of **men? Is it not better** to die in a brave attempt, **than to drag a** wretched and infamous life, and **to lose it at last shamefully,** after having been the sport of other men's insolence? But I take **gods and men to witness, that success is in our hands:** our bodies and minds are in full vigour; **on the other** hand, they are on the decline in every respect, oppressed with years and riches. All that is necessary, is only to make the attempt; when once the undertaking is set on foot, every thing else will follow in course. For who, that has the spirit of a man, can bear with patience, that they should have such a superfluity of riches as to lavish them in raising mighty edifices on the deep, and levelling mountains, whilst we have not so much as the necessaries of life; that they should be multiplying their seats, whilst we have no fixed habitation; that though they are constantly buying pictures, statues, and vessels of curious workmanship, pulling down new houses, and building others; in short, though they waste and dissipate their wealth by every extravagant method; yet, by all the efforts of profusion, they are unable to exhaust it. As for us, we have poverty at home, and debts abroad: our condition is bad, our expectation much worse: finally, what have we left but **a wretched life?** Rouse then to action! Behold the **object you** have often wished for, behold liberty! **and in** her train, riches, glory, and honour, all full in your view! all these rewards fortune has prepared for the conquerors. But let the present conjuncture and opportunity; let your dangers, your poverty, and the glorious spoils of war, animate you more powerfully than any words of mine. As for me, use me as you please, either as a leader or as a private soldier. I shall always be with you, both in council and execution. But I hope

to act as consul with you in this enterprise; if, after all, I am not deceived in my opinion of you, and you prefer not slavery to empire."

Upon hearing this harangue, his associates, who were all extremely wretched, destitute of every thing, and even void of every honest hope; though they were pleased with the thought of embroiling the state, and even looked upon that as a great recompense; yet most of them desired, that he would declare to them upon what terms they were to engage in the war, and what were to be their rewards; what strength they had to depend upon, **and what** hopes of success. Then Catiline **promised** them an abolition of their debts, the proscription of the rich; dignities, sacred and civil; plunder, and every other advantage **that** the uncontrolled pleasures of conquerors include. Besides, he told them that Piso and P. Sitius Nucerinus were both privy to his design; the former with an army in Spain, the other at the head of one in Mauritania. That C. Antonius was candidate for the consulship, whom he hoped to have for his colleague; one who was his intimate, and embarrassed with all manner of difficulties; and that in conjunction with him he would begin the execution of his design, as soon as they should enter upon their office. After this he proceeded to inveigh bitterly against all men of worth; commended his own accomplices, and calling to every one **by** his name, some he put in mind of their poverty, others of their amours, several of their dangers and disgraces, and many of the booty they had got in consequence of Sylla's victory. Then, perceiving all their spirits elevated, he pressed them to take care of his interest at the next election, and dismissed the assembly.

Some there were at that time, who said, that Catiline, when he had ended his **speech,** and proceeded to administer an oath to his associates, presented them all round with a bowl of human blood mixed with wine; that, when they had all tasted **and sworn, as** is usual in solemn sacrifices, he disclosed his design to them; and that he did this in order to engage them more strictly to mutual faith, as each was privy to the guilt of another in so horrible a fact. But some believe that this, and much more, was invented by those, who thought to allay the odium which fell upon Cicero for putting the conspirators to death, by aggravating their crimes. But I could never meet with clear evidence for so extraordinary a fact.

In this conspiracy was Q. Curius, a man of no mean family, but loaded with crimes, and, as a mark of disgrace, expelled the senate by the censors. This man had an equal share of levity and audaciousness; whatever he heard, he disclosed; nor could he even conceal his own crimes: in a word, he neither considered what he said or did. There had been, for a long time, a criminal correspondence between him and Fulvia, a lady of quality; but finding himself less agreeable to her than formerly, because his poverty would not suffer him to be so liberal; all on a sudden he began to tempt her with great promises, boasting of seas and mountains of wealth; sometimes he threatened to kill her, if she would not be obsequious: in a word, he behaved more haughtily than he had ever done before. When Fulvia learned the ground of this insolent behaviour, she did not conceal what threatened so much danger to the state; but, without mentioning her author, discovered to many all that she had heard of Catiline's conspiracy. This discovery made the people zealous to confer the consulship on M. T. Cicero: for before this, most of the nobility stormed through envy, and thought that the consular dignity was in a manner profaned, if a new man, however deserving, should be raised to it. But when danger threatened, pride and envy were dropped.

Accordingly, when the assembly for elections was held, M. Tullius and C. Antonius were declared consuls, which was a heavy blow to the conspirators. Catiline's fury, however, was not in the least abated; he exerted himself every day more and more; provided magazines of arms in all the most convenient places of Italy; borrowed money, either on his own credit or that of his friends, and conveyed it to Fæsulæ, to one Manlius, who first began the war. At this juncture, he is said to have engaged in his interest great numbers of all ranks; and some women too, who had once been able to support a vast expense by prostitution; but when age had lessened their gain, though not their luxury, had contracted great debts. By their means, he expected to bring over to his party the city slaves to set fire to the city, and either engage their husbands, or, in case of refusal, have them slain.

Among these was Sempronia, a woman of a masculine spirit, and who had often been engaged in many daring and hardy enterprises. In her person and family, in her husband and children, she was abundantly happy; well acquainted with the Greek and Roman languages, and had more charms in music and dancing than became a virtuous woman, with many other accomplishments subservient to luxury. Indeed, there was nothing she less valued than honour and chastity; and it is hard to say, whether she spared her money or her reputation least. So raging and violent was her lust, that she made advances to men more frequently than they did to her. She had often forfeited her faith, perjured herself to avoid paying her debts, been privy to murders; in a word, her extravagance and indigence had carried her to the utmost excesses of wickedness. Notwithstanding all this, she had a great deal of wit, could compose verses, was very facetious in conversation, could talk modestly, tenderly, or satirically: in short, she excelled in humour and pleasantry.

Having taken these measures, Catiline, notwithstanding his late repulse, declared himself a candidate for the consulship against the ensuing year; in hopes, if he should be chosen, of using Anthony as he pleased. Nor was he inactive in the meantime, but contriving endless machinations for the destruction of Cicero, who was not wanting in dexterity and subtilty to defeat them. For, from the beginning of his consulship, he had successfully employed Fulvia, to engage, by force of promises, Q. Curius, whom we have already mentioned, to discover all Catiline's designs; and by promising a province to his colleague, he had prevailed upon him not to act against the state. Besides, he had always about him a number of his friends and clients to guard his person. When the day of election came, Catiline, finding that neither his suit for the consulship, nor his plots to cut off Cicero in the field of Mars, had succeeded, determined upon open war, and to try the utmost extremities, since his secret attempts had ended in disappointment and infamy.

Accordingly, he despatched C. Manlius to Fæsulæ and the adjacent part of Etruria, one Septimius of Camertes to the territory of Picenum, and C. Julius into Apulia; others too he sent to different places, just as he thought it subservient to his purpose. Meanwhile he was making several efforts at Rome at once; laying fresh snares against the life of the consul; contriving to set fire to the city; placing armed men in convenient posts: he himself was constantly armed, and ordered his followers to be so too; was ever pressing them to be upon their guard, and prepared for action; day and night he was in a hurry; lived without sleep; and was nevertheless indefatigable under all his toils. At last, perceiving that his numerous efforts were unsuccessful, he employed M. Porcius Læcca to summon together the principal conspirators once more in the dead of night; and after having complained grievously of their inactivity, he informed them that he had sent Manlius to command a body of men, which he had prepared to take up arms; that he had likewise despatched others to different places to begin the **war**; and that he himself longed earnestly to go to the army, if he could but first destroy Cicero, for that he greatly obstructed all his measures.

Now, when all the rest remained fearful and irresolute, C. Cornelius, a Roman knight, and **L. Vargunteius, a senator**, offered their service; **they** agreed to go that very night to Cicero's house, with a few armed men, under pretence of making him a visit, and to assassinate him by surprise. Curius, as soon as he learned what danger threatened the consul, despatched Fulvia to acquaint him with the plot; so that when they came, entrance was denied them, and their black attempt frustrated.

Meanwhile Manlius was exciting the people in Etruria to take arms; who, both from their poverty and their resentment of the injuries done them under Sylla's usurpation, when they were deprived of their lands and all they had, were of themselves desirous of innovations. **He** likewise engaged robbers of all kinds, who **were** very numerous in that country, with **some** of Sylla's old soldiers too, who by their debauchery and extravagance had squandered away **all** their former acquisitions.

Cicero, upon hearing of these transactions, was struck with so threatening an evil; and not being able any longer to defend the city against the plots of the conspirators by his own private management, nor being apprised of the strength or views of Manlius's army, laid the matter before the senate, which already had been the subject of public conversation. Whereupon the senate, as was usual in cases of extreme danger, passed a decree that the consuls should take care the state suffered no detriment; by which they were empowered (such is the policy of the Roman government) to raise forces, make war, exercise an unlimited jurisdiction over the citizens and allies, and to bear sovereign command both in the city and in the field; none of which things fall under their authority, without a special ordinance of the people.

A few days after, L. Lœnius, a senator, read a letter in the senate, which he said was brought him from Fæsulæ; acquainting him that C. Manlius had taken arms about the latter end of October, with a numerous body of men. To this, some added, as is usual on such occasions, accounts of omens and prodigies; others related that unusual cabals were held, arms carried to different places, and that the slaves were arming in Capua and Apulia. Whereupon, by a decree of the senate, Q. Marcius Rex was sent to Fæsulæ, and Q. Metellus Creticus to Apulia and the adjacent parts: both these officers had been commanders of armies, and were waiting without the city for the honour of a triumph, which was refused them by the malice of a few, whose custom it was, to make sale of every thing honourable and infamous. The prætors too, Q. Pompeius Rufus and Q. Metellus Celer, were sent, the one to Capua, the other to Picenum; and power was given them to raise forces, according to the exigency of the times and the degree of danger. Besides, the senate decreed, that if any one would make any discovery concerning the conspiracy against the state, he should have, if a slave, his liberty and a hundred thousand sesterces; if a freeman, his pardon and two hundred thousand. It was likewise decreed, that bands of gladiators should be sent to Capua and the other municipal towns, according to the strength of each; and that guards should be posted at Rome, in every quarter, under the command of the inferior magistrates.

With all these things the city was deeply affected, and assumed a new face; from the highest jollity and riot, such as spring from a lasting peace, sorrow of a sudden appeared upon every countenance. There was nothing but universal hurry and confusion; no place was thought secure; no person fit to be trusted; they neither enjoyed peace, nor were at war; every one measured the public danger by their private fears. The women, too, full of apprehensions of war, which the great power of the state had formerly secured them against, gave themselves up to sorrow and lamentation; raised their suppliant hands to heaven; bewailed their tender children; were eager for news; frighted at every thing; and laying aside their pride and pleasures, became anxious for them selves and their country. Yet the cruel spirit of Catiline persisted in the same desperate pursuit, notwithstanding the preparations that were made to defeat his measures, and though he himself stood arraigned by L. Paulus, upon the Plautian law; nay, he even came to the senate-house, the better to dissemble his design; as if, provoked by injurious representations, he only came to clear his character. As soon as he appeared, the consul Cicero, either fearing some bad effects from his presence, or fired with indignation, made that flaming speech, so useful to the state, which he afterwards published. As soon as he had sat down, Catiline, resolved to deny every article, with downcast looks and suppliant voice, begged of the fathers not to believe too hastily what was alleged against him; that such was his birth, and such had been his conduct from his youth, that he had reason to hope for a very favourable impression from the public; and it was not to be imagined, that one of the patrician order, whose ancestors, as well as himself, had done so many services to the Roman people, should want to overturn the government; while Cicero, a stranger, and late inhabitant of Rome, was so zealous to defend it. As he was going on with his invectives against the consul, the senate, raising a general outcry, called him traitor and parricide. Upon which, abandoning himself to fury and despair, ‘Since,’ says he, ‘I am circumvented and driven headlong by my enemies, I will quench the flame raised about me, by the common ruin.’

Upon this, he rushed out of the assembly, and went home; where reflecting much with himself, and considering that his designs against the consul had proved unsuccessful, and that it was impossible to set fire to the city, by reason of the guards that were placed every where; he judged it most advisable to reinforce his army, and to make all necessary preparations for war, before the legions were raised; and accordingly set out in the dead of night for Manlius's camp, with a few attendants. Before his departure, however, he gave instructions to Lentulus and Cethegus, and those of his associates whom he knew to be most daring and resolute, to strengthen the party by all possible means; to despatch the consul as soon as they could; to have every thing in readiness for the intended massacre, the firing of the city, and the other feats of war; promising, that he himself would, in a short time, come to the city at the head of a great army.

During these transactions at Rome, C. Manlius sent deputies to Q. Marcius Rex, with orders to accost him in the following manner:—

We call gods and men to witness, O general, that we have neither taken up arms against our country, nor with a view to hurt any particular person, but to defend ourselves from injuries, wretched and needy as we are, through the violence and cruelty of usurers; most of us deprived of our habitations, and all of our reputation and fortunes; none of us allowed the protection of the laws, as our forefathers were, nor so much as the liberty of our persons, when nothing else is left us; such has been the cruelty of the usurers and prætors. Your ancestors, out of compassion to the people of Rome, have often relieved their wants by their decrees; and but lately, in our own times, on account of the great pressure of debts, they have obliged the creditors to compound, and that with the approbation of every worthy man. The people have often taken arms, and separated from the senate, prompted either by a passion for power, or the insolence of their magistrates; as for us, we neither desire power nor riches, which are the sources of all the wars and contests among men; liberty is our aim, that liberty which no brave man will lose but together with his life. Wherefore we conjure you and the senate, to espouse the interests of your wretched fellow-citizens, to restore to us the protection of the laws, torn from us by the iniquity of the prætors; and not reduce us to the fatal necessity of studying to perish in such a manner, as amply to revenge our own blood on those who have oppressed us.

To this, Q. Marcius replied, ‘That if they had any petition to present to the senate, they must forthwith quit their arms, and repair to Rome as suppliants; that such had been the clemency and compassion of the senate and people of Rome on all occasions, that no one had ever applied to them in vain for relief.’

Now Catiline, in his way to the camp, sent letters to several persons of consular dignity, and indeed to every one of distinguished merit; representing, ‘That being beset with false accusations, and unable to resist the faction of his enemies, he submitted to his fortune, and was going a voluntary exile to Marseilles; not that he was conscious of the horrid treason he was charged with, but out of regard to the tranquillity of the state, and to prevent any disturbances that might arise from his opposition.'

But a letter of a quite different kind was read in the senate by Q. Catulus, which he declared he had received from Catiline; a copy of which here follows:

L. Catiline to Q. Catulus, health.

Your great friendship to me, which I have so often proved when in my greatest dangers, inspires me with confidence to apply to you upon this occasion. Wherefore, I shall not offer you any defence of my present measures; as I am conscious of no guilt, I shall only make a declaration of my innocence, for the truth of which I appeal to the gods.

Being provoked by injuries and false accusations; deprived of the rewards of my services; and disappointed of the dignity I sued for; I have, according to my usual practice, undertaken the cause of the oppressed; not that I am urged to this by my debts, for my estate is sufficient to discharge what I owe on my own account; and Orestilla would (such is her generosity) clear all my engagements on account of others, out of her own fortune and that of her daughters. But seeing men of no merit raised to the highest honours of the state, and myself set aside upon groundless jealousies, I have, upon this account, taken such measures for preserving the small remains of my dignity, as my present situation will sufficiently justify. I should have said more to you; but I am just now informed that violent measures are taken against me; I therefore conclude with recommending Orestilla to your protection; beseeching you, by the regard you have for your own children, to defend her from injuries. Adieu.

Having staid a few days with C. Flaminius in the territory of Reate till he had furnished that neighbourhood, which had before been gained over to his party, with arms, he proceeded with the fasces, and the other ensigns of consular authority, to Manlius's camp. When this was known at Rome, the senate declared Catiline and Manlius enemies to the state; with pardon to such of their followers as should quit their arms by a certain day, those only excepted who were under sentence for capital crimes. They likewise decreed, that the consuls should levy forces; that C.

Antonius should pursue Catiline with all expedition, and Cicero stay to defend the city. The Roman state, at this juncture, appears to me to have been in a condition extremely deplorable; since, though all nations, from the rising to the setting sun, were reduced to its obedience; though peace and prosperity, the greatest blessings of life, in the estimation of men, reigned at home; there were yet some of her citizens desperately bent on their own ruin and that of the commonwealth. For, notwithstanding the two decrees of the senate, not a man was found, amongst the numerous followers of Catiline, to accept the reward, and discover the conspiracy; not a single person to desert his camp. So strong a spirit of disaffection had, like a pestilence, taken possession of their minds.

Nor were the conspirators and their accomplices the only disaffected persons; the whole body of the populace, from their passion for a revolution, approved Catiline's designs; nor in this did they act contrary to their usual character. For in all states, those that are poor envy the possessions of the great; extol the extravagant; hate what they have been long accustomed to; long for changes; and from a dislike to their own condition, endeavour to throw every thing into confusion: in times of public disorder and discord, they find their subsistence without any trouble; since poverty is always attended with this advantage, that it has nothing to lose. But the Roman populace were become extremely degenerate, from several causes; chiefly, because all who were remarkable for wickedness and violence; such as had squandered their fortunes in riot and extravagance; in a word, all they who were forced from their native country for their crimes, flocked to Rome from all quarters, as into a common sink. Many again were continually reflecting upon Sylla's success; whence they had seen some common soldiers raised to the dignity of senators, and others so enriched, that in pomp and splendour they lived like kings; and every one hoped, in case of a civil war, to gain the victory, and the same advantages from it. Besides, the young men in the country, who were accustomed to earn a scanty subsistence by their labour, being drawn to Rome by the allurements of public and private largesses, preferred the ease of the city to their hard labour in the fields: these, with all others of the like character, found their support in

3 D

the calamities of the state. So that it is not to be wondered at, that such men as these, oppressed with poverty, of dissolute lives, and extravagant views, should consult the interests of the state, just as far as they were subservient **to their own.** They too, whose parents had **been** proscribed, whose estates had been confiscated, and who had been deprived of the privileges of citizens, under the tyranny of Sylla, had the same expectations from a war **as** the others had. Moreover, all they who were of any party different from that of the senate, wished rather to see the state embroiled, than themselves without power; a mighty evil! which, after having lain dormant for many years, had again revived in the city.

For, after the tribunitian authority was restored, under the consulship of Pompey and Crassus, certain young men, whose age and spirits were full of fire, having acquired that high dignity, began by inveighing against the senate, to inflame the populace; then by largesses and great promises to heighten their rage; and thus gained great credit and power to themselves.

The greatest part of the nobility exerted their utmost efforts in opposition to them; in appearance, to support the grandeur of the senate, but in reality, their own. For, to declare the truth in few words, all who raised commotions in the state in those days, made use of specious pretences; some to assert the rights of the people; others to advance the authority of the senate; all to promote the public good; whilst every one only endeavoured to gain power to himself. Their contests were carried on without any bounds or **moderation; and** whatever party prevailed, made a cruel use **of the victory.**

But when Pompey **was sent against the** pirates and Mithridates, **the power of the people** declined, and the **whole sway was in the** hands of a few. These engrossed **all public** offices, the government of the **provinces, and** every thing else; lived unaccountable themselves, in great ease and security; **overawed** the popular magistrates with impeachments, and thus prevented them from spiriting up the people. But as soon as there was any hope of a change in the state, the old contest fired the minds of the populace. And if Catiline had conquered in the first engagement, or come off but with equal loss, great distress and calamity must certainly have overwhelmed the state: nor would the conquerors have long enjoyed their victory; but, when they were weakened and exhausted, whoever had most power would have seized the government, and subverted liberty.

Some there were, however, who, though not concerned in the conspiracy, yet immediately joined Catiline. Amongst these was A. Fulvius, the son of a senator; who was taken upon the road, brought back to the city, and put to death by his father's orders. At the same time Lentulus, in obedience to Catiline's orders, was endeavouring to gain over, by himself or others, all such as from their characters or circumstances he thought proper to be employed in bringing about a revolution; not only citizens of Rome, but all that could bear arms.

Accordingly he employed one P. Umbrenus to apply to the deputies of the Allobroges, and engage them, if possible, to join in the war: for he imagined that, as they were oppressed both with public and private debts, and the whole nation of the Gauls was naturally warlike, it would be no difficult matter to persuade them to enter into such a design. Umbrenus, having traded in Gaul, was known to most of the principal men in it, and acquainted with their characters. Accordingly, without any delay, as soon as he saw the deputies in the Forum, after putting a few questions to them concerning the state of their nation, and affecting a deep concern for their grievances, he proceeded to ask, what issue they hoped for to their calamities? then, perceiving that they complained of the covetousness of our magistrates; that they inveighed against the senate for yielding them no protection; and that they expected from death alone a remedy to their miseries; he replied, " If you will only act like men, I will put you upon a method to get rid of all your pressures." The Allobroges, upon hearing this, conceived mighty hopes, and besought Umbrenus to take pity upon them; for that there was no enterprise so difficult or dangerous, wherein they would not with the utmost readiness engage, provided it would free their state from so vast a load of debt. He then carried them to the house of D. Brutus, which joined to the Forum, and was a very proper place for such a consultation, Sempronia being an accomplice, and Brutus then from Rome. To give the greater weight to what he had to say, he sent for Gabinius too, before whom he laid open to them the conspiracy, named all who were engaged in it, and also many innocent persons, of every rank, to give them the greater courage, and then dismissed them, after they had promised their assistance.

The Allobroges, however, were long in suspense what course to take. On one side were pressing debt, a passion for war, and the prospect of great advantages from victory : on the other superior power, safe measures, and instead of uncertain hopes, a certain recompense. While they were thus balancing, the fortune of Rome prevailed. Accordingly they discovered all they knew of the conspiracy to Q. Fabius Sanga, upon whose patronage their nation chiefly depended. Cicero, apprised of the matter by Sanga, ordered the deputies to feign a mighty zeal for the conspiracy, to go to the rest of the accomplices, to promise largely, and endeavour to bring them under as clear conviction as possible.

Much about the same time, there were commotions in Hither and Further Gaul, in the territory of Picenum, in Brutium and Apulia. For those whom Catiline had sent thither, acted like madmen, pushing inconsiderately all their measures at once ; and by their consultations in the night-time, their carrying arms to and fro, their eager haste, and precipitate proceedings, caused more alarm than danger. Many of these, Q. Metellus Celer the prætor committed to prison, agreeably to the decree of the senate ; as did C. Muræna in Hither Gaul, where he was deputy governor.

At Rome, in the mean time, Lentulus, with the other heads of the conspiracy, presuming upon a sufficient force, resolved that, as soon as Catiline arrived with his army in the territory of Fæsulæ, L. Bestia, the tribune, should assemble the people, inveigh against Cicero's conduct, and lay the blame of so distressful a war upon the best of consuls ; that, upon this signal, the whole body of the conspirators should, on the ensuing night, betake themselves to the discharge of their respective parts, which were said to be assigned them in the following manner : Statilius and Gabinius, with a considerable party, were to set fire at once to twelve of the most convenient places in the city, that in the general hurry they might the more easily reach the consul, and all those whom they designed to assassinate. Cethegus was to force Cicero's house, and put him to death ; whilst

others were employed elsewhere in the like manner : young men too there were, living as yet with their parents, (mostly indeed from amongst the nobility,) who were to kill their fathers ; and when they had spread their consternation and horror every where by flames and massacre, they were to march out and meet Catiline.

While they were thus resolving and form'ng their measures, Cethegus was constantly complaining of want of spirit in his associates ; that by their irresolution and delay, they abused the fairest opportunities ; that in so dangerous an enterprise, action was more necessary than deliberation ; that for himself, would a few only but support him, he would, notwithstanding the cowardice of others, attack the senate-house. As he was naturally of a daring resolute spirit, and brave in his person, he thought the success depended upon expedition.

Now the Allobroges, according to Cicero's instructions, procured a meeting, by means of Gabinius, with the rest of the conspirators ; and demanded from Lentulus, Cethegus, Statilius, and likewise from Cassius, an oath signed severally by them, to carry to their countrymen, who otherwise would not be easily prevailed upon to engage in an affair of so great importance. The rest, suspecting nothing, readily granted it ; but Cassius promised that he would be in their country in a short time, and accordingly left Rome a little before the deputies. In company with these, Lentulus sent one Volturcius of Crotona, that, before they went home, they might ratify the league with Catiline by mutual ties. He likewise gave Volturcius a letter for Catiline in the following words:

"Who I am, you will learn from him whom I have sent to you. Consider your great danger, and remember you are a man : recollect what your situation requires : seek assistance from all, even the lowest."

Besides, he gave him verbal instructions to expostulate with Catiline, "how he could reject the assistance of the slaves, when he was declared a public enemy by the senate :" to acquaint him likewise, that all preparations were made in Rome, according to his directions ; and that he himself must not delay to advance.

Upon this, Cicero, on the night fixed for the departure of the deputies, from whom he had learned all, ordered the prætor V. Flaccus, and C. Pomptinus, to lie in wait for the Allobroges at the Milvian bridge and to secure them. H acquainted them at the same time with the reason of thus employing them, and left them to act as they should see occasion. According to orders, they posted their guards quietly, and silently beset the bridge. When the deputies and Volturcius arrived, a shout was set up on both sides, and the Gauls soon understanding their design, immediately surrendered themselves to the prætors. Volturcius at first, encouraging his companions, defended himself with his sword against the numbers who surrounded him; but seeing himself forsaken by the deputies, he began earnestly to beseech Pomptinus as his acquaintance, to spare his life; at last, full of dread and despair, he surrendered himself to the prætors, as if they had been foreign enemies.

Immediately upon this, messengers were despatched with an account of it to Cicero, who was seized at once with great joy and anxiety. He was glad to see the state rescued from ruin, by a full discovery of the conspiracy; but what perplexed him, was the difficulty of knowing how to proceed against citizens of such eminence, convicted of such horrid treason. To punish them, he thought, would create him many enemies, and to let them pass unpunished, would ruin the state; wherefore, arming his mind with resolution, he ordered Lentulus, Cethegus, Statilius, and Gabinius to be summoned before him, as likewise Cæparius of Terracina, who was upon the point of marching to Apulia to raise the slaves. The others came immediately; but Cæparius, having gone from home a little before, and learned that all was discovered, had fled from the city. The consul took Lentulus, who was then prætor, by the hand, and conducted him to the senate, which he had assembled in the temple of Concord, whither he ordered the rest to be brought under guard. Volturcius and the deputies were introduced into a very full house, and Flaccus was ordered to bring the packet of letters which he had received from them.

Volturcius being questioned about his journey, the packet of letters, and, lastly, what his design was, and from what motives he acted; made, at first, ridiculous pretences, affecting to know nothing of the conspiracy. But being promised his pardon, upon the security of the public faith, he discovered every thing; and told them, that a few days before Gabinius and Cæparius had drawn him in for an associate;

that he knew no more than the deputies did; only he used to hear Gabinius say, that P. Autronius, Ser. Sulla, L. Vargunteius, with many more, were engaged in the conspiracy. The Gauls gave the same account; they likewise convicted Lentulus (who pretended ignorance of the whole matter) not only by his letters, but by his common discourse, "that, according to the Sibylline oracles, three of the Cornelian family should be sovereigns of Rome: that Sylla and Cinna had been so already; and he himself was now the third, appointed by the Fates to be master of the city; besides, that the present was the twentieth year from the burning of the capitol, which the augurs, from several prodigies, had often foretold would produce a civil war and much bloodshed." Upon this, the letters were read, and the criminals having acknowledged their signets, the senate decreed, that Lentulus should lay down his office, and, together with the rest, be kept in custody. Accordingly, Lentulus was delivered to P. Lentulus Spinther, who was then ædile; Cethegus to Q. Cornificius; Statilius to C. Cæsar; Gabinius to M. Crassus; and Cæparius (who was taken in flight, and brought back immediately before) to Cn. Terentius, a senator.

Meanwhile the populace, which at first, from their passion for a revolution, were too fond of a civil war, upon discovery of the conspiracy, changed their sentiments; cursed the designs of Catiline; extolled Cicero to the skies; and, like people rescued from bondage, gave themselves up to mirth and jollity. For though they expected more advantage than loss, by the ordinary events of the war; yet they looked upon the firing of the city as an inhuman, barbarous attempt and extremely distressful to themselves; whose whole substance consisted in what supported them from day to day, and what they daily wore.

The day after, was brought before the senate one L. Tarquinius, who was going to join Catiline, as was reported, and apprehended by the way. This man offering to give a particular account of the conspiracy, upon the security of the public faith for his pardon, was ordered by the consul to declare what he knew. He then gave the senate almost the same account Volturcius had done, of the design to fire the city of the intended massacre of the best citizens, and of the march of the army to Rome; adding, that he was sent by Crassus to tell Catiline not to be disheartened by the apprehending of Lentulus, Cethegus, and others of the conspirators, but to make the greater haste to the city, to rescue them from danger, and revive the spirit of the rest.

When Tarquinius named Crassus, a man of high quality, great riches, and vast credit in the state; they all called out, that he was a false witness, and desired that it might be debated. Some thought it quite incredible; others, though they believed the charge to be true, yet thought that a person of so great influence ought at such a juncture rather to be courted than exasperated: besides, most of the senators were under private obligations to Crassus. Accordingly, it was agreed in a full senate, at the motion of Cicero, that Tarquinius's evidence appeared to be false; that he should be ordered to prison, and confined till he discovered by whose advice he had framed so impudent a falsehood. Some there were at that time, who thought that this evidence was a contrivance of P. Autronius, that Crassus, by being involved in the same danger with the rest of the conspirators, might protect them by his power. Others said, that Tarquinius was put upon it by Cicero, to prevent Crassus from embroiling the state, by undertaking to protect villains, as was his custom. I heard Crassus indeed himself affirm, that this contumely was fixed upon him by Cicero.

Yet, at the same time, Q. Catulus and C. Piso were not able to prevail upon Cicero, either by interest, importunity, or any offers whatever, to have C. Cæsar falsely accused by the Allobroges, or any other evidence. For both these gentlemen were inveterate enemies to him; Piso, because Cæsar had obtained judgment against him for bribery, in sentencing to death a man beyond the Po, unjustly; Catulus was fired with resentment, because Cæsar, though but a young man, in their competition for the office of high-priest, had carried it against him in his old age, after having enjoyed the highest honours of the state. Now this they thought was a favourable opportunity to bring him under suspicion: for by his great liberality to private persons, and great largesses to the people, he had contracted vast debts. But not being able to persuade the consul to so black a crime, they themselves, by going about from man to man, and charging Cæsar with many instances of guilt, which they pretended to have heard from Volturcius and the Allobroges, brought great odium upon him, insomuch that certain Roman knights, who were posted about the temple of Concord, as a guard to the senate, whether struck with the greatness of the danger, or animated by a nobler principle, to testify their zeal for the public, threatened him as he came out of the house with their drawn swords.

Whilst these things were transacting in the senate, and rewards decreeing to the deputies of the Allobroges and Volturcius, whose discoveries were approved; the freedmen, and a few of the dependants of Lentulus, went into different parts of the city, some endeavouring to prevail upon the slaves and workmen in the streets, to rescue him by force; others searching after the ringleaders of the mob, who used for hire to raise commotions in the state. Cethegus, too, sent messengers to his domestic slaves and freedmen, fellows trained up to audacious enterprises, begging of them to form themselves into an armed body, and come to his deliverance. The consul, as soon as he received information of these proceedings, placed guards as the time and exigency required; and assembling the senate, desired to know, what they would please to determine, concerning those who were now in custody? A full senate had indeed but lately declared them public traitors. Then D. Junius Silanus, who was first asked his opinion, as being consul elect, voted for capital punishment to be inflicted, not upon the prisoners only, but likewise upon L. Cassius, P. Furius, P. Umbrenus, and Q. Annius, if they should be apprehended: but afterwards yielding to the strength of Cæsar's arguments, he declared himself of the same sentiments with Tiberius Nero, who had proposed that the guards should be strengthened, and the debate adjourned. Cæsar, when asked by the consul in his turn, spoke as follows:

"It is the duty of all men, conscript fathers, in their deliberations upon subjects of difficult determination, to divest themselves of hatred and affection, of revenge and pity. The mind, when clouded with such passions, cannot easily discern the truth; nor has any man ever gratified his own headstrong inclination, and at the same time answered any valuable purpose. When we exercise our judgment only, it has sufficient force; but when passion possesses us, it bears sovereign sway, and reason is of no avail. I could produce a great many instances of kings and states pursuing wrong measures when influenced by resentment or compassion.

But I had rather set before you the example of our forefathers, and show how they acted, in opposition to the impulses of passion, but agreeably to wisdom and sound policy. In the war which we carried on with Perses king of Macedonia, Rhodes, a mighty and flourishing city, which owed all its grandeur too to the Roman aid, proved faithless, and became our enemy. But when the war was ended, and the conduct of the Rhodians came to be taken into consideration, our ancestors pardoned them, that none might say the war had been undertaken more on account of their **riches** than of injuries. In all the Punic wars too, though the Carthaginians, both in time of peace and even during a truce, had often **insulted** us in the most outrageous manner, **yet, our** ancestors never improved any opportunity of retaliating; considering more what was worthy of themselves, **than what** might in justice be done against **them.**

" In like manner, conscript fathers, ought **you to** take care, that the wickedness of **Lentulus, and** the rest of the conspirators, **weigh not** more with you, than a regard to your own honour; and that, while you gratify your resentment, you do not forfeit your reputation. If a punishment, indeed, can be invented adequate to their crimes, I approve the extraordinary proposal made; but if the enormity of their guilt is such, that human invention cannot find out a chastisement proportioned to it, my opinion is, that we ought to be contented with such as the law has provided.

" Most of those who have spoke before me, **have, in a** pompous and affecting manner, lamented the **situation of the** state; they have **enumerated all the calamities** of war, and the many distresses **of** the conquered; virgins ravished; youths unnaturally abused; children torn from the embraces of their **parents;** matrons forced to bear the brutal **insults** of victorious soldiers; temples and **private houses** plundered; all places filled with flames and slaughter: finally, nothing but arms, carcasses, blood, and lamentations to be seen.

" But, for the sake of the immortal gods, to what purpose were such affecting strains? Was it to raise in your minds an abhorrence of the conspiracy? as if he, whom so daring and threatening a danger cannot move, could be inflamed by the breath of eloquence. No, this is not the way; nor do injuries appear **light** to any one that suffers them; many

stretch them beyond their due size. But, conscript fathers, different allowances are made to different persons, when such as live in obscurity are transported by passion to the commission of any offences, there are few who know it; their reputation and fortune being upon a level: but those who are invested with great power, are placed upon an eminence, and their actions viewed by all; and thus the least allowance is made to the highest dignity. There must be no partiality, no hatred, far less any resentment or animosity, in such a station. What goes by the name of passion only in others, when seen in men of **power,** is called pride and cruelty.

" As for me, conscript fathers, I look upon all tortures as far short of what these criminals deserve. But most men remember best what happened last; and forgetting the guilt of wicked men, talk only of their punishment, if more severe than ordinary. I am convinced, what D. Silanus, that brave and worthy man, said, was from his zeal to the state, and that he was neither biassed by partiality nor enmity; such is his integrity and moderation, as I well know. But his proposal appears to me not indeed cruel, (for against such men what can be cruel !) but contrary to the genius of our government. Surely, Silanus, you were urged by fear, or the enormity of the treason, to propose a punishment quite new. How groundless **such fear is,** it is needless **to show;** especially **when, by the diligence of so able a** consul, such **powerful forces are provided for** our security; **and as to the punishment, we** may say, what **indeed is the truth, that to those** who live in sorrow **and misery,** death is but a release from trouble; that it is death which puts an end to all the calamities of men, beyond which there is no room for care and joy. But why, in the name of the gods, did not you add to your proposal, that they should be punished with stripes? Was it, because the Porcian law forbids it? But there are other laws too which forbid the putting to death a condemned Roman, and allow him the privilege of banishment. Or was it because whipping is a more severe punishment than death? Can any thing be reckoned too cruel or severe against men convicted of such treason? But if stripes are a lighter punishment, how is it consistent to observe the law in a matter of small concern and disregard it in one that is of greater?

" But you will say, Who will find fault with

any punishment decreed against traitors to the state? I answer, time may, so may sudden conjunctures; and fortune, too, that governs the world at pleasure. Whatever punishment is inflicted on these parricides, will be justly inflicted. But take care, conscript fathers, how your present decrees may affect posterity. All bad precedents spring from good beginnings; but when the administration is in the hands of wicked or ignorant men, these precedents, at first just, are transferred from proper and deserving objects, to such as are not so.

"The Lacedemonians, when they had conquered the Athenians, placed thirty governors over them; who began their power by putting to death, without any trial, such as were remarkably wicked, and universally hated. The people were highly pleased at this, and applauded the justice of such executions. But when they had by degrees established their lawless authority, they wantonly butchered both good and bad without distinction; and thus kept the state in awe. Such was the severe punishment which the people, oppressed with slavery, suffered for their foolish joy.

"In our own times, when Sylla, after his success, ordered Damasippus and others of the like character, who raised themselves upon the misfortunes of the state, to be put to death, who did not commend him for it? all agreed that such wicked and factious instruments, who were constantly embroiling the commonwealth, were justly put to death. Yet this was an introduction to a bloody massacre. For whoever coveted his fellow-citizen's house, either in town or country, nay oven any curious piece of plate, or fine raiment, took care to have the possessor of it put upon the list of the proscribed.

"Thus they, who had rejoiced at the punishment of Damasippus, were soon after dragged to death themselves; nor was an end put to this butchery, till Sylla had glutted all his followers with riches. I do not indeed apprehend any such proceedings from M. Cicero, nor from these times. But in so great a city as ours, there are various characters and dispositions. At another time, and under another consul, who may have an army too at his command, any falsehood may pass for facts; and when, upon this precedent, the consul shall, by a decree of the senate, draw the sword, who is to set bounds to it? who to moderate its fury?

"Our ancestors, conscrip fathers, never

wanted conduct nor courage; nor did they think it unworthy of them, to imitate the customs of other nations, if they were useful and praiseworthy. From the Samnites they learned the exercise of arms, and borrowed from them their weapons of war; and most of their ensigns of magistracy from the Tuscans; in a word, they were very careful to practise whatever appeared useful to them, whether amongst their allies or their enemies; choosing rather to imitate than envy what was excellent.

"Now in those days, in imitation of the custom of Greece, they inflicted stripes on guilty citizens, and capital punishment on such as were condemned. But when the commonwealth became great and powerful, and the vast number of citizens gave rise to factions; when the innocent began to be circumvented, and other such inconveniences to take place; then the Porcian and other laws were made, which provided no higher punishment than banishment for the greatest crimes. These considerations, conscript fathers, appear to me of the greatest weight against our pursuing any new resolution on this occasion. For surely, their virtue and wisdom, who, from so small beginnings, raised so mighty an empire, far exceed ours, who are scarce able to preserve what they acquired so gloriously. What, shall we discharge the conspirators, you'll say, to reinforce Catiline's army? By no means: but my opinion is this; that their estates be confiscated; their persons closely confined in the most powerful cities of Italy; and that no one move the senate or the people for any favour towards them, under the penalty of being declared by the senate an enemy to the state, and the welfare of its members."

When Cæsar had made an end of speaking, and the rest of the senators, either by words or signs, approved or disapproved of the several proposals made; Cato, being asked his opinion, delivered it in the following speech:

"I am very differently affected, conscript fathers, when I view our present situation, and the danger we are in; and then consider with myself the proposals made by some senators who have spoken before me. They appear to me to have reasoned only about the punishment of those, who have entered into a combination to make war upon their country, upon their parents, upon religion and private property; whereas our present circumstances warn us rather to guard against them, than to consider in what manner we shall punish them. You may take vengeance for other crimes after they are committed; but if you do not prevent the commission of this, when it is once accomplished, in vain will you have recourse to the tribunals. When the city is once taken, no resource remains to the conquered citizens.

"Now I conjure you by the immortal gods, you who have always valued your fine houses in town and country, your pictures, your statues, more than the welfare of the state; if you are desirous to preserve these things, which, whatever their real value be, you are so fond of; if you would have leisure for pursuing your pleasures; rouse for once out of your lethargy, and take upon you the defence of the state. The debate is not about the public revenues, nor the oppression of our allies: no; our liberties, our lives are in danger.

"Often, conscript fathers, have I spoken in this house; often have I complained of the luxury and avarice of our fellow-citizens; upon which account I bear the enmity of many: I, who never indulged myself in any vice, nor even cherished the thoughts of any, could not easily pardon the crimes of others. And though you little regarded my remonstrances, yet the commonwealth remained firm; her native strength supported her, even under the negligence of her governors. But the present debate is not about the goodness or depravity of our morals; nor about the greatness or prosperity of the Roman empire: no, it is whether this empire, such as it is, shall continue our own, or, together with ourselves, fall a prey to the enemy.

"And, in such a case, will any one talk of gentleness or mercy? We have long since lost the true names of things. To give away what belongs to others, is called generosity; to attempt what is criminal, fortitude; and thence the state is reduced to the brink of ruin. Let them, since such is the fashion of the times, be generous from the spoils of our allies; merciful to the plunderers of the treasury; but let them not be prodigal of our blood, and by sparing a few bad citizens, destroy all the good.

"C. Cæsar has just now spoke, with great strength and accuracy, concerning life and death, taking for fictions, I doubt not, the vulgar notions of an infernal world; where the bad, separated from the good, are confined to dark, frightful, and melancholy abodes. Accordingly, his proposal is, that their estates be confiscated, and their persons confined in the corporate towns; from an apprehension, I imagine, that, if they were kept at Rome, they might be rescued by force, either by their fellow-conspirators, or a mercenary mob: as if wicked, and profligate persons were only to be found in this city, and not all over Italy: or, as if there were not more encouragement to the attempts of the desperate, where there is least strength to resist them.

"This then is an empty proposal, if he fears any danger from them; but if, amidst this so great and universal consternation, he alone is void of fear; so much the more does it concern me, to be afraid, both for myself and you.

"Wherefore, in determining the fate of Lentulus and the other prisoners, be assured, that you likewise determine that of Catiline's army, and all the conspirators. The more vigour and resolution you exert, so much the less spirit and courage will they have; but if they observe the least remissness in your proceedings, they will presently fall upon you with fury.

"Do not think it was by arms our ancestors raised the state, from so small beginnings, to such grandeur: if so, we should have it in its highest lustre; as having a greater number of allies and citizens, of arms and horses, than they had. But there were other things from which they derived their greatness, such as we are entirely without. They were industrious at home, and exercised an equitable government abroad; their minds were free in council, neither swayed by crimes nor passion. Instead of these virtues, we have luxury and avarice; poverty in the state, and great wealth in the members of it; we admire riches, and abandon ourselves to idleness; we make no distinction between the virtuous and the wicked; and all the rewards of virtue are possessed by ambition. Nor is it at all strange, whilst each of you pursues his separate interest; whilst you abandon yourselves to pleasure at home, and here in the senate are slaves to money or favour; that attacks are made upon the state when thus forsaken. But no more of this.

"Romans of the highest quality have conspired to destroy their country, and are endeavouring to engage the Gauls, the sworn enemies of the Roman name, to join them. The commander of the enemy is hovering over us with an army, and yet at this very juncture you delay and hesitate how to proceed against such of the conspirators as are seized within your walls. Would you extend your compassion to wards them ? be it so; they are young men only, and have offended through ambition; send them away armed too: what would be the consequence of this gentleness and mercy ? why this, when they got arms in their hands, it would prove your utter ruin.

"Our situation is indeed dangerous; but you are not afraid: yes, you are very much; only from effeminacy and want of spirit you are in suspense, waiting every one the motions of another: trusting perhaps to the immortal gods, who have often saved this commonwealth in the greatest dangers. But assistance is not obtained from the gods by idle vows, and supplications like those of women; it is by vigilance, activity, and wise counsels, that all undertakings succeed; if you resign yourselves to sloth and idleness, it will be in vain to implore the assistance of the gods; you will only provoke them to anger, and they will make you feel it.

"In the days of our ancestors, A. Manlius Torquatus, in a war with the Gauls, ordered his son to be put to death, for having engaged the enemy without orders; and thus a young man of great hopes was punished for too much bravery. And do you demur about the doom of the most barbarous parricides?

"Their present offence, perhaps, is unsuitable to their former character: show a tender regard then for the dignity of Lentulus, if you find that he himself ever showed any for his own chastity, for his honour, for gods or men; pardon Cethegus, in consideration of his youth, if this is not the second time of his making war upon his country. For what need I mention Gabinius, Statilius, Cæparius? who, if they had possessed the least degree of reflection, would never have embarked in such wicked designs against the state.

"Finally, conscript fathers, were there any room for a wrong step on this occasion, I should suffer you to be corrected by the consequences, since you disregard my reasonings. But we are surrounded on all sides: Catiline is hovering over our heads with an army; we have enemies within the walls, and in the very heart of the city. No preparations can be made, no measures taken, without their knowledge: hence the greater reason for despatch.

"My opinion then is this, that since by a detestable combination of profligate citizens the state is brought into the greatest danger; since they are convicted by the evidence of Volturcius, and the deputies of the Allobroges, and their own confession, to have entered into a conspiracy for destroying their fellow-citizens and native country, by slaughter, conflagration, and other unheard-of cruelties; they be put to death, according to the ancient usage, as being condemned by their own mouths."

When Cato had done speaking, all of consular dignity, and the greatest part of the senate, indeed, applauded his opinion; extolled his resolution to the skies; and reproached one another with pusillanimity. Cato was looked upon as a great and illustrious patriot; and a decree passed conformable to his proposal.

Now, as I have read and heard much of the glorious achievements of the Roman people, in war and peace, both by sea and land; I was very desirous to discover the cause to which they were principally owing. I knew that they had often, with a handful of men, engaged mighty armies: I was not ignorant, that with small forces they had carried on war against powerful princes; that they had often supported themselves under the severe buffetings of adverse fortune; that the Greeks surpassed them in eloquence, and the Gauls in military glory. And having duly weighed every cause, I was convinced, that all was owing to the great virtue of some particular persons; hence it was that poverty triumphed over riches, and a handful of men prevailed over great numbers. Nay, after Rome became depraved by luxury and sloth, the commonwealth still supported herself by her native strength, under the miscarriages of her magistrates and generals; even when, like a mother past bearing, she did not produce, for a long time, any citizen of distinguished merit.

Two, however, I myself remember, Cato and Cæsar, both men of great abilities, but different characters; whom, as so fair an opportunity presents itself, I would not omit taking notice of; but shall endeavour, in the best manner I am able, to display the temper and manners of each.

As to their extraction, years, and eloquence, they were pretty nigh equal. Both of them had the same greatness of mind, both the same degree of glory, but in different ways: Cæsar was celebrated for his great bounty and generosity; Cato, for his unsullied integrity: the former became renowned by his humanity and compassion; an austere severity heightened the dignity of the latter. Cæsar acquired glory by a liberal, compassionate, and forgiving temper; as did Cato, by never bestowing any thing. In the one, the miserable found a sanctuary; in the other, the guilty met with certain destruction. Cæsar was admired for an easy yielding temper; Cato, for his immoveable firmness. Cæsar, in a word, had formed himself for a laborious, active life; was intent upon promoting the interest of his friends, to the neglect of his own; and refused to grant nothing that was worth accepting; what he desired for himself, was to have sovereign command, to be at the head of armies, and engaged in new wars, in order to display his military talents. As for Cato, his only study was moderation, regular conduct, and above all, rigorous severity. He did not vie with the rich in riches, nor in faction with the factions; but, taking a nobler aim, he contended in bravery with the brave; in modesty with the modest; in integrity with the upright; and was more desirous to be virtuous, than appear so: so that the less he courted fame, the more it followed him.

When the senate had agreed to Cato's proposal, as I have already related, the consul thought it most expedient to put the sentence in execution immediately, lest any new attempt should be made in the night, which was just at hand; and accordingly ordered the triumvirs to get every thing in readiness for it. He himself, after posting the guards, conducted Lentulus to prison, as the prætors did the rest.

There is a place in the prison, after a small descent to the left, called Tullus's dungeon, sunk about twelve feet under ground, secured on all sides with strong walls, and above with an arch of stone; a dark, noisome solitude, frightful to behold. Lentulus, being thrust down into this place, was presently strangled by the executioners, appointed for that purpose. Such was the death of this noble patrician, who had borne the office of consul, and was descended from the most illustrious family of the Cornelii: a death due to his life and crimes. Cethegus, Statilius, Gabinius, and Cæparius, were executed in the same manner.

During these transactions at Rome, Catiline, out of all the forces which he had carried with him, and those under the command of Manlius, formed two legions; filled up the several cohorts, according to the number of his men: then distributing equally amongst them all the volunteers, with those who were sent him by his associates, he soon saw his legions complete; though he had at first but two thousand men. But of these a fourth part only were completely armed; the rest were furnished with whatever chance threw in their way,—some had darts, some spears, and others sharp stakes.

As soon as Antony approached with his army, Catiline betook himself to the mountains; one while advancing towards Rome, another towards Gaul; and by this means deprived the enemy of an opportunity of fighting him. He was indeed in daily hopes of receiving great reinforcements, if his accomplices executed their designs at Rome. In the mean time he refused to take the slaves into his service, who flocked to him in great numbers from the very beginning; trusting to the strength of the conspiracy, and likewise conceiving that it would be bad policy, to appear to blend the cause of freemen with that of fugitive slaves.

But when news reached the camp that the conspiracy was discovered at Rome; that Lentulus, Cethegus, and the rest above mentioned were put to death; most of those, who were tempted to take arms by the hopes of spoil, or a passion for changes, presently left him. The rest he led by long marches over steep mountains into the territory of Pistorium, with a design to escape into Cisalpine Gaul by obscure roads.

Q. Metellus Celer, who at that time commanded three legions in the territory of Picenum, judged that Catiline, in his present difficulties, would take this very course. Accordingly, having learned from his deserters what route he had taken, he immediately decamped, and posted himself at the foot of the mountains, just where Catiline was obliged to pass in his way to Gaul. Nor was Antony far behind, who pursued the flying rebels through ways more level, at the head of a great army. When Catiline saw himself enclosed by the mountains and the enemies' troops; that his designs had miscarried in the city; that there was neither hope of escaping nor receiving any succour; he thought his best way, in such a situation, was to try the fortune of a battle, and determined to engage Antony as soon as possible. Accordingly, assembling his troops, he spoke to them in the following manner:

"I have learned by experience, fellow-soldiers, that words cannot inspire courage, nor a general's speech render a spiritless and timorous army, brave and intrepid. Every man displays in battle, just so much courage as nature or habit has given him, and no more. It is to no purpose to exhort him, whom neither glory nor danger can animate; his fear deprives him of his hearing. I have assembled you, fellow-soldiers, to instruct you in a few particulars, and to lay before you the grounds of my final resolution.

"You all know what a dreadful calamity Lentulus by his slow and spiritless conduct has brought upon himself and us; and how I have been prevented from marching into Gaul, by waiting for reinforcements from Rome. In what posture our affairs now are, you all see as well as I. Two armies, one from Rome, another from Gaul, obstruct our motions. Want of provisions and other necessaries will not allow us to make any longer stay here, were we ever so desirous of doing it. To what place soever you think of marching, you must open yourselves a passage with your swords. I conjure you, then, to summon up all your courage; to act like men resolute and undaunted; to remember when you engage, that you carry in your hands riches, honour, and glory; nay, even your liberty and your country. If we overcome, all will be safe; we shall have plenty of provisions; the corporate towns and colonies will be all ready to receive us. But if we flinch through fear, the very reverse will be our fate; nor will any place or friend protect those, whom arms could not. Let me add to this, my fellow-soldiers, that we have different motives to animate us, from what the opposite army has. We fight for our country, for our liberty, for our lives; they, for no interest of their own, but only to support the power of a few. Let this consideration, then, engage you to fall upon them the more courageously, remembering your former bravery.

"We might, indeed, have passed our days, with the utmost infamy, in banishment: some of you too might have lived at Rome, depending for your subsistence upon others, after having lost your own estates. But such a condition appearing infamous and intolerable to men of spirit, you resolved upon the present course; which if you desire to leave, you must exert your courage: none but a conqueror hath ever exchanged war for peace. For to hope for security from flight, when you have turned from the enemy the arms which serve to defend you, is the height of madness. In battle, the most timorous are always in the most danger: courage is a wall of defence. When I consider your characters, fellow-soldiers, and reflect upon your past achievements, I have great hopes of victory: your spirit, your age, your virtue, encourage me: and our necessity too, which even inspires cowards with bravery. For the straitness of our situation will prevent the enemies' numbers from surrounding us. But should fortune envy your bravery, be sure you fall not, without taking due vengeance upon the enemy; suffer not yourselves to be taken and butchered like cattle; but fight rather like men, and leave the enemy a bloody and mournful victory."

Pausing a little after this speech, he ordered to sound to battle; and led down his forces in their ranks to the plain. Then, sending away all the horses, in order to encourage his men the more, by making the danger of all equal; he himself, on foot, drew up his army in order of battle, according to its number and the nature of the place. For as there lay a plain on his left, bounded by the mountains, and a steep rock on his right, he placed eight cohorts in his front, and the rest he posted in closer order to support them.

From amongst these, he drew out the choicest centurions, the honorary veterans, and the bravest and best armed of the common soldiers, and placed them in the front. He appointed C. Manlius to command the right, and a native of Fæsulæ the left; he himself with his freedmen, and such troops as he had raised in the colonies, stood by the eagle; the same which C. Marius was said to have had in his army in the Cimbrian war.

On the other side, C. Antony, being hindered by the gout from being present at the engagement, gave the command to M. Petreius his lieutenant-general.

He posted the veteran cohorts, which he had raised on this occasion, in the front; and the rest of his army behind them, as a body of reserve. He himself rode from rank to rank, and addressing himself to his men by their names, entreated and conjured them " to remember that they were now to engage against unarmed robbers, in defence of their gods, their country, their children, and their property.' As he was an old soldier, having served in th army upwards of thirty years, as tribune, pre fect, lieutenant-general, or prætor, and that with distinguished renown; he knew most of the soldiers and their gallant actions; and by calling these to remembrance, he roused their courage.

Petreius having taken all his measures with the utmost precaution, sounded to battle, and ordered his cohorts to advance slowly: the enemy did the same. But when they were come near enough for the light-armed soldiers to begin the fight, they set up a mighty shout, rushed with great fury into a close engagement, and, laying aside their darts, made use of their swords only. The veterans, mindful of their former bravery, pressed vigorously upon the rebels, who made a bold resistance; so that the fight was maintained with great obstinacy. Catiline was all the while in the first line, at the head of a light-armed body; sustaining such as were severely pressed; putting fresh men in the room of those that were wounded; providing for every exigence, often charging the enemy in person, and performing at once the duty of a brave soldier and a great commander.

Petreius, when he found that Catiline, contrary to his expectations, exerted himself with great vigour, brought up the Prætorian cohort against his main body, broke their ranks, and made great slaughter of them, as he did likewise of the others who maintained their ground elsewhere. Then he fell upon both the wings at once. Manlius and the other officer from Fæsulæ were both killed, fighting in the fore-most rank. Catiline, when he saw his forces routed, and himself left with a few only; mindful of his birth and former dignity, rushed headlong into the thickest of the foe, where he fell, covered with wounds, and fighting to the last.

When the engagement was ended, it evidently appeared with what undaunted spirit and resolution Catiline's army was fired. For the body of every one was found upon that very spot, which, during the battle, he had fought from; those only excepted who were forced from their posts by the Prætorian cohort; and even they, though they fell a little out of their ranks, were all wounded before. Catiline himself was found, far from his own men, amidst the dead bodies of the enemy, breathing a little, with an air of that fierceness still in his face which he had when alive. Finally, in all his army there was not so much as one free citizen taken prisoner, either in the engagement or in the flight; for they spared their own lives as little as those of the enemy. The army of the republic obtained the victory, indeed, but it was neither a cheap nor a joyful one; for their bravest men were either slain in battle or dangerously wounded. As there were many, too, who went to view the field, either out of curiosity or a desire of plunder, in turning over the dead bodies, some found a friend, some a relation, and some a guest; others there were likewise who discovered their enemies; so that through the whole army there appeared a mixture of gladness and sorrow, joy and mourning

WAR AGAINST JUGURTHA

It is an unjust complaint that mankind have made of their nature, as being frail and of short duration, and governed more by chance than by virtue. For, on the contrary, you will find nothing, upon reflection, greater or more excellent; and that men want industry more than time or abilities.

The director and governor of human life is the soul; which, when it pursues glory in the paths of virtue, is abundantly prevalent, nay, even crowned with renown, and stands in no need of the aids of fortune, which can neither bestow nor take away probity, industry, or any worthy quality. But when the soul becomes enslaved to ignoble passions, and abandoning itself to indolence and sensual pleasure, has, by a course of debauchery, lost in sloth its vigour, time, and abilities, the frailty of nature is blamed. For it is usual with men to blame the course of things for the evils they bring upon themselves. Whereas, would they but engage in virtuous pursuits with the same ardour and spirit as they do in such as are uninteresting, nay, and dangerous too, they would no more be governed by fortune, than fortune by them; they would even arrive at such sublime heights of grandeur, as, from being mortals to become immortal through glory.

For as man is compounded of soul and body, so all our actions and all our pursuits partake of the one or the other. Accordingly, beauty, great wealth, strength of body, and other things of the like nature, are of short duration; but the noble productions of the soul are, like itself, immortal. Moreover, the good things of the body, and of fortune, as they have a beginning, so they have a period; and all things indeed that rise and increase fall and decay. But the soul is incorruptible and immortal; the governor of human kind; which animates and comprehends all things, but is comprehended by nothing itself. So that the depravity of those is the more surprising, who, sunk in sensuality, spend their lives in luxury and idleness; and suffer their minds, the noblest and most refined part of their frame, to lie uncultivated, and languish in indolence; especially, since there are so many and such various accomplishments by which the mind may acquire the highest renown.

Magistracy and high command, though among the number of such pursuits, yet do not appear to me to be at all desirable at this conjuncture, nor indeed any share in the administration; since honours are neither bestowed on the virtuous, nor are they who obtain authority by infamous means, the more secure, or the more honourable, for enjoying it. For to govern your country and kindred by force, though you may have it in your power, and may even rectify abuses, is, however, a dangerous situation; especially since all innovations in a state threaten slaughter, banishment, and all the miseries of war. To strive for power to no purpose, and to reap nothing by continual fatigue but public odium, is extreme madness; unless we imagine any one to be possessed of so base and pernicious a spirit, as to sacrifice his honour and liberty to the power of a few.

Among the different ways of employing men's abilities, that of writing history is of eminent use; but I shall say nothing of its excellence, because many have already shown it; and lest I should be charged with vanity for extolling what I am myself engaged in. There are some, however, I doubt not, who, because I have resolved to pass my days at a distance from any share in the management of public affairs, **will be** ready to call this my **undertaking,** however great and useful in itself, **an indolent amusement:** this, at least, will be **the language of** such, who think the **task** of **saluting the** people by their names, and courting their favour by feasts, the greatest of all.

But if these men will only consider at what **times I** was promoted in the state; the dignity **of** those who were then unsuccessful in their pursuit of employment; and **what** sort of men have since got into the **senate, they will** certainly allow that I altered **my sentiments** upon just grounds, and not from **indolence; and that** the state will reap more benefit by my retiring from business, than by the caballings of others. For I have often heard that Q. Maximus and P. Scipio, with other great men of our state, were wont to say, that, upon beholding the images of their ancestors, their minds were powerfully animated to virtue. Not that the wax, or the figure, made so strong an impression upon their minds; it was only the recollection of the glorious achievements of their forefathers, **that** excited that generous flame in the breasts **of** those brave men, which they could never extinguish, till they had attained the like degree of glory and reputation.

How different are the manners of the present age; in which there is not a man to be found who vies with his ancestors in probity and industry, but in riches only and extravagance. Nay, even persons of obscure birth, who were formerly wont to anticipate nobility by their virtuous deeds, aspire now after places of honour and power by secret contrivances; and money got by injustice and violence, rather than by worthy accomplishments. As if the prætorship, consulship, and all the other dignities, conferred glory and renown of themselves, and did not owe their estimation to the good behaviour of such as are vested with them. But I have been carried too far, and taken too much freedom, from my concern for the depravity of the state. Now I come to my purpose.

I am going to write the history of a war which the Roman people carried on with Jugurtha, king of the Numidians; a subject which I have made choice of, because, in the first place, the war was a terrible and obstinate one, and the

success long uncertain; and likewise because a check was then given, for the first time, to the exorbitant pride of the nobility: a contention which confounded all things, divine and human; and was carried to such a height of madness and fury, that it ended in a civil war, and the desolation of Italy. But, before I enter upon this task, I shall trace a few things backwards, that what follows may appear in a clearer and stronger **light.**

During **the** second Punic war, wherein Hannibal, **the** Carthaginian general, reduced the power of Italy more than **had ever been** done since the Roman **name became formidable,** Masinissa, **king of the Numidians,** being received into **the Roman friendship, by P.** Scipio, afterwards surnamed **Africanus, on account** of his gallant achievements, performed many and glorious exploits: in consideration of which, when the Carthaginians were overcome, and Syphax taken, who had an extensive and powerful kingdom in Africa, all the cities and lands that had been taken from him were given to Masinissa by the Roman people. This prince continued a faithful and useful ally to us, till death put an end to his reign: upon which, his son Micipsa succeeded alone to the kingdom, his brothers Manastabal and Gulussa dying some time before. Micipsa had two sons, Atherbal and Hiempsal; but kept at his court, and educated with the same care as his own children, the son of his brother Manastabal, called Jugurtha, whom Masinissa had left in a private condition, because he was born of a concubine.

This youth, **when he grew up, with** all the advantages **of strength of** body, a graceful person, and, above all, a fine genius did not suffer himself to be carried away with luxury and idleness; but agreeably to the manners of the nation, accustomed himself to ride, to throw the dart, to contend with his companions in running; and though he surpassed all in glory, he was still beloved by all. Besides, he spent a good deal of time in the chase; and was always the first, or amongst the first, in wounding the lion, and other wild beasts; and though he performed a great many brave deeds, he never boasted of himself. Micipsa was at first highly pleased with this, thinking that the bravery of Jugurtha would reflect glory upon his reign: but when he considered that he himself was now grown old, that his children were very young, and that Jugurtha was in the prime of life, and growing daily in reputation, he was deeply affected, and his mind distracted with perplexing thoughts. The consideration of the ambitious nature of man, and his impetuosity in gratifying his desires, alarmed him; and likewise the favourable opportunity arising from his own age and that of his children, which was a temptation strong enough to transport even men of moderate views; add to all this, the great affection of the Numidians for Jugurtha, which made him apprehensive, lest, should he destroy him by artifice, it might occasion a sedition, or a civil war.

Being thus beset with difficulties, and finding that it was not possible for him to destroy so popular a man, either by force or fraud, he resolved to expose him to the dangers of war, as he was of a daring disposition, and fond of military glory, and thus try what fortune would do. Accordingly, Micipsa, being to despatch auxiliaries of horse and foot to the Romans, who were then laying siege to Numantia, sent him to Spain, as their commander; in hopes that he would be cut off, either from an ostentation of his courage or the efforts of the enemy. But that matter fell out quite contrary to his expectation. For as soon as Jugurtha, who had great vivacity and penetration, became acquainted with the temper of P. Scipio the Roman general, and the character of the enemy, he in a short time acquired so high renown, by his great labour and application, his submissive obedience to orders, and exposing himself often to dangers, that he was extremely beloved by our men, and dreaded by the Numantians. He was, indeed, both brave in action, and wise in council; qualities very seldom united in the same person: precaution being generally accompanied with fear, and courage with rashness.

Accordingly, Scipio employed Jugurtha to put all his most difficult enterprises in execution, took him into the number of his intimate friends, and grew fonder of him daily, as one who succeeded in all his schemes and undertakings. To these advantages were added great generosity and address; by which means he had contracted an intimate friendship with many of the Romans.

There were many at that time in our army, some of high rank, others newly raised, who preferred riches to virtue and honour; men of factions dispositions, of great power at Rome, and more distinguished among our allies by their figure than their honesty. These inflamed the mind of Jugurtha, (of itself ambitious enough,) by assuring him, "that when Micipsa died, he alone would have the kingdom of Numidia; as he was a person of such distinguished merit, and all things venal at Rome."

Upon the destruction of Numantia, when Scipio had determined to dismiss the auxiliaries, and return home himself, having bestowed great presents and high encomiums upon Jugurtha, in presence of the whole army, he brought him into his tent; and there advised him in private, "to court the friendship of the Roman people in a public rather than private way, and not to bestow bribes on any: that it was dangerous to purchase from a few, what belonged to all. If he would but continue in his virtuous practices, that glory and sovereignty would fall to him of course; but if he hurried on precipitately, his money would prove his ruin."

After having given him this advice, he dismissed him with the following letter to Micipsa. "Your nephew Jugurtha has highly distinguished himself, during the siege of Numantia; which, I am sure, will give you great joy. His great merit has made him dear to me; and I shall use my endeavours that he be so to the senate and people of Rome. I congratulate you, indeed, on this occasion, as my friend: for in him you have a man worthy of you, and his grandfather Masinissa."

The king, finding that what he had learned from common fame was confirmed by Scipio's letter, was so touched with the merit and interest of the man, that he altered his purposes, and endeavoured to gain him by favours. Accordingly he immediately adopted him, and, by his will, made him joint-heir with his sons to the kingdom. A few years after, being worn out with age and infirmities, and, finding that the period of his life was approaching, he is said to have addressed himself to Jugurtha, in the presence of his friends and relations, as also of Atherbal and Hiempsal, to this purpose:

"I took thee, Jugurtha, when a fatherless infant, and without hopes or fortune, under my own care; as I promised myself, that my favour would render me as dear to thee as if I had been thy father. Nor have I indeed been disappointed; for, not to mention thy other great and noble achievements, thy late behaviour at Numantia reflects honour upon me and my kingdom. By thy gallant behaviour thou hast united us to the Romans in closer ties of friendship than before, and revived the honour of our family in Spain. In a word, (what is the most difficult thing among men,) that hast even overcome envy itself by thy glory. Now, as nature is putting a period to my days, I beseech and adjure thee, by this right hand and the honour of a prince, to embrace with a tender and affectionate regard these my sons, thy near relations by birth, thy brethren by my generosity; and not to prefer the friendship of strangers, to that of persons united to thee by blood.

"It is not troops, or treasures, that are the support of a kingdom, but friends; whom you can neither acquire by force, nor purchase with money: they are only to be procured by good offices and fidelity. Now, who should be more closely united in friendship than brothers? or what stranger will be found faithful to him who is an enemy to his own relations? I leave you a kingdom, strong indeed, if you are virtuous and agree; but weak, if you are wicked and at variance with one another. For by union small states flourish, whilst the greatest are destroyed by divisions.

"Now, it is more incumbent upon thee, Jugurtha, as surpassing thy brethren in age and wisdom, to take care that no dissensions arise; for in all contests, the most powerful, even though he receive an injury, is still thought to have done it, because he is most able. As for you, Atherbal and Hiempsal, observe and reverence this worthy man: imitate his bravery; and let it never be said, that Micipsa was happier in his adopted children than in his own."

Jugurtha, though he was very sensible of the king's insincerity, and had himself quite different views from what he pretended, yet made a very dutiful reply, suitable to the occasion. Micipsa died a few days after; and after his funeral was celebrated with royal magnificence by the young princes, they met together to regulate their affairs.

Hiempsal, the youngest of them, who was naturally violent, and had been accustomed to treat Jugurtha with contempt, on account of his mean birth by his mother, seated himself at Atherbal's right hand, to prevent Jugurtha's sitting in the middle, the most honourable place among the Numidians; and though he was prevailed upon by the importunity of his brother to yield to superior age, and go to the

farther side, yet it was with reluctance. At this interview, after much reasoning about the administration of affairs, Jugurtha proposed, among other things, to repeal all the ordinances and regulations of Micipsa for the last five years of his life; as he was worn out with age, and the vigour of his faculties lost. Hiempsal replied, "that he was entirely of the same opinion; since Jugurtha had been made partner of the kingdom by adoption, only within three years."

This expression sunk deeper in Jugurtha's mind, than any one imagined; insomuch that, from that very time, being distracted with rage and fear, he was eagerly bent upon the destruction of Hiempsal, and continually meditating by what secret means to effect it. But these operating too slowly for the violence of his resentment, which was not in the least abated, he determined to execute his design at any rate. At the first meeting of the princes, already mentioned, it was agreed, that, to prevent mutual disputes, the public treasure should be divided, and the kingdom too, with the portion of each marked out by distinct boundaries; and certain times were appointed for both these purposes, but first for the distribution of the money.

In the meantime, the young princes retired to different places adjacent to where the treasure lay: Hiempsal, particularly, to Thermida, where he happened to lodge in the house of one who was Jugurtha's principal lictor, and had always been his favourite and confidant. Fortune presenting Jugurtha with so fit an instrument, he loaded him with promises, and prevailed upon him to go, under pretence of seeing his house, and provide himself with false keys to the gates; for the true ones were always carried to Hiempsal; assuring him, that when matters were ready he himself would come with a considerable body of men.

The Numidian soon executed his orders, and introduced Jugurtha's soldiers by night, agreeably to his instructions; who, as soon as they entered the house, went different ways in quest of the prince; put to death all they found asleep, and all such as they met; searched every private apartment; broke open such as were shut; and filled the whole house with confusion and horror. Meanwhile Hiempsal was discovered, concealing himself in a mean apartment belonging to a servant maid, whither he had fled, full of dread, upon the first alarm, being unacquainted with the house. The Numidians, according to their instructions, carried his head to Jugurtha.

The news of so horrible a murder soon flew over all Africa. Atherbal, and all of those who had been subject to Micipsa, were seized with terror: the Numidians divided into two parties; the greater number declared for Atherbal, but the best soldiers for Jugurtha; who immediately raised as great an army as possible, reduced several cities by force under his obedience, got others to submit to him, and pushed for nothing less than to be master of all Numidia. Atherbal, though he had despatched ambassadors to Rome, to inform the senate of the murder of his brother, and his own distressful situation, yet depending upon the number of his men, he resolved to hazard a battle; but being defeated upon the first onset, he fled to our province, and from thence went to Rome.

Jugurtha having thus executed his designs, and made himself master of all Numidia; when he came to reflect at his leisure upon his enormous crimes, began to dread the Roman people, and had no hopes of security against their resentment, but in the avarice of the nobility, and in his money. He therefore sent ambassadors to Rome, in a few days, with great store of gold and silver; and ordered them first of all to load his old friends with presents, then to make new ones: in a word, to spare no money for bringing over to his interest as many as possible.

When the ambassadors were arrived at Rome, and, according to the king's instructions, had sent large presents to his friends and others of great interest in the senate; so great a change happened, that Jugurtha, who was before held in detestation, grew all on a sudden into mighty favour with the nobility; many of whom being gained over by bribes, and others hoping to be bribed, used all their interest with every senator, to prevent any rigorous resolution against him. When the ambassadors thought their cause was safe, a day was fixed for the senate to give audience to both parties. Upon which occasion, it is said that Atherbal spoke in the following manner:

"My father's orders to me, conscript fathers, in his dying moments, were, that I should look upon myself as having the administration of the kingdom of Numidia only, the right and sovereignty being yours; and likewise to endeavour to be as serviceable to the Roman people as possible, both in war and peace; to esteem you as my kindred and relations; adding, if I did so, I should find in your friendship, forces, riches, with every necessary support to my kingdom. When I was going to pursue these orders of my dying father, Jugurtha, the most wicked wretch on earth, in open contempt of your authority, stripped me, the grandson of Masinissa, the hereditary friend and ally of the Roman people, of my kingdom and my all.

"Since I was to be reduced to so wretched a condition, conscript fathers, I wish I could have implored your aid, rather on account of my own services, than those of my ancestors; above all, that I could have had a title to such aid, without standing in need of it, or, if I did, have received it as my due. But as innocence of itself is but a weak defence; and as it was not in my power to form the heart of Jugurtha, I have fled to you for protection, conscript fathers, to whom I am forced to be a burden before I have done any service, which is my greatest misfortune. Other kings have been either conquered by you, and then received into your alliance, or in their distress have implored your friendship: our family commenced allies to the Roman people during their war with Carthage, at a time when the Roman honour was more to be regarded than their fortune.

"Do not suffer me, conscript fathers, who am descended from that family, and the grandson of Masinissa, to implore your aid in vain. If I had nothing to plead in order to obtain it but my wretched condition, that I, who was but lately a prince, of high descent, of signal renown, and great power, am now reduced by complicated misery, destitute and forlorn, and dependent upon others for succour; it would still become the dignity of the Roman people to protect me from oppression, and not to suffer any man to enlarge his territories by iniquity. But I have been forced from those very possessions which the Roman people gave my ancestors, and from whence my father and grandfather, in conjunction with you, drove Syphax and the Carthaginians. It is your bounty, conscript fathers, that is torn from me; and in the injuries done me you are insulted.

"Alas! miserable man that I am! Are these the fruits of thy generosity, O my father! that he whom thou didst adopt, he whom thou hast left joint-heir to thy kingdom with thy own sons, should, of all others, be the instrument to extirpate thy race! shall our family never find quiet? must ours be ever a bloody lot? must the devouring sword and banishment be always our portion?

"Whilst the Carthaginians continued in power, no wonder we were exposed to all manner of calamities. Our enemies were at our doors, you our friends were afar off; and all our hopes in our arms. When Africa was freed from that plague, we enjoyed the sweets of peace, as having no enemies, unless you commanded us to treat any as such; when, on a sudden, Jugurtha, with insupportable audaciousness, glorying in his pride and cruelty, murders my brother, his near relation, and seizes his kingdom as the reward of his crime: then, finding that he could not destroy me by the same wicked snares, he fell upon me with open force, at a time when, trusting to your power, I expected neither war nor violence, drove me from my country and my home, and reduced me to that wretched condition wherein I now appear before you, destitute of every thing, and so oppressed with misery, that I am safer any where than in my own kingdom.

"I have often, conscript fathers, heard my father say, and I was myself of the same opinion, that whoever set themselves carefully to cultivate friendship with you, were engaged indeed in an arduous undertaking, but were of all others the most secure. Our family has done all that was in their power for you; they have assisted you in all your wars; it is in your power, conscript fathers, now that you enjoy peace, to place us in a state of security. My father left behind him us two brothers, and by adopting Jugurtha for a third, thought to engage him in the closest union with us. One of the three is already murdered; and it was with difficulty I escaped from the bloody hands of the other.

"What shall I do? or whither had I best go, miserable man that I am! all the supports of my family are cut off. My father through age yielded to the lot of human nature; Jugurtha, trampling upon every tie of nature and gratitude, imbued his wicked hands in the blood of my brother. My other friends and relations, wherever he took them, he has destroyed by a variety of cruel deaths: some he has crucified; others he has thrown to wild beasts; those few, whose lives he has spared, are imprisoned in gloomy dungeons, there to lead a life more insupportable than death, in sorrow and anguish.

"Were I still in possession of all that I have lost; were my circumstances, which are now so wretched, as flourishing as formerly, and those persons who are now my enemies, my friends as before; I should yet apply to you, conscript fathers, for succour in case of any sudden calamity befalling me; to you, whom it becomes, on account of your great power and dominion, to maintain equity and prevent injustice every where. But now that I am banished from my country, from my home, forsaken by all, destitute of every thing suitable to my rank, to whom shall I go, to whom shall I apply for aid? Shall I apply to such nations and princes as are all the avowed enemies of our family, on account of our friendship with you? have I any place to go to, where there are not monuments of hostilities committed by my ancestors upon your account? or can any one who has ever been your enemy have compassion upon me?

"We were, moreover, taught by Masinissa, never to cultivate friendship with any but the Roman people; to enter into no other engagements; to make no other alliances; that in your friendship we should find abundant security; and if your empire should fall by a change of fortune, we too must be involved in the same ruin. By your own bravery and the favour of the gods, you are still great and mighty; all your undertakings are crowned with success, and every thing yields to your power; so that you can the more easily redress the grievances of your allies. One thing only I am afraid of; lest the favour of some persons here for Jugurtha, whom they little know, should give a wrong bias to their minds; such, I hear, are making their utmost efforts in his behalf; and importuning particular senators not to come to any resolution against him, in his absence, without hearing his defence; alleging that my grievances are all pretended, and that I was under no necessity of flying, but might have continued with safety in my own kingdom.

"O that I could but see him, by whose enormous cruelty I am reduced to this degree of wretchedness, practising such simulation! and that either you or the immortal gods would, for once, take human affairs under your care; that he who now boasts and triumphs in his crimes, may atone by extreme tortures for his monstrous ingratitude to my father, the murder of my brother, and the evils he has made me suffer.

"And now, O my dearest brother! though thou wert cut off in the flower of thy days, by the hands of one who of all men should have been the last to have done it; yet I think thy fate rather matter of joy than of grief; for by thy fall thou didst not so much lose thy kingdom, as escape the hardships of flight, banishment, poverty, and all the calamities which oppress me. But I, wretched and forlorn, driven from the throne of my ancestors into an abyss of misery, afford a rueful spectacle of the uncertainty of human affairs; know not what course to take, whether I shall revenge thy wrongs, whilst I myself stand in need of assistance; or whether I shall attempt the recovery of my kingdom, when my death or life depends on the power of others. I could wish it were honourable to put an end to my misery by a voluntary death; to prevent that infamy which must necessarily fall upon me, if, sinking under the weight of my afflictions, I should tamely submit to injustice. Now, as I have no inclination to live, and yet cannot die but with dishonour, I adjure you, conscript fathers, by yourselves, by your children and parents, by the majesty of the Roman people, succour me in my distress, curb haughty oppression, and suffer not the kingdom of Numidia, which is your own, to fall a prey to a usurper, and to be stained with the blood of our family."

When the king had made an end of speaking, the deputies from Jugurtha, trusting more to their money than the justice of their cause, made a short reply, that Hiempsal had been put to death by the Numidians for his cruelty; that Atherbal, after he had made war without any provocation, and was defeated, complained that he could not execute his schemes of oppression; that Jugurtha begged of the senate, not to believe him changed from what they had known him at Numantia, nor to regard the words of an enemy more than his own actions. Then both parties withdrew, and the affair was immediately debated.

The patrons of the deputies, and a great many more, corrupted by their influence, disregarded what Atherbal had said; highly extolled Jugurtha's bravery; and by their interest, their pleadings, and indeed every other possible method, endeavoured as strenuously to defend the crimes and infamy of another, as if it had been in support of their own reputation. On the other hand, there were a few who, preferring justice and equity to money, gave it as their opinion, that Atherbal should be assisted, and ample vengeance taken for Hiempsal's death.

He who distinguished himself most in support of this opinion, was Æmilius Scaurus, a man of high rank, active, factious, passionate, for power, honour, and riches, but one who concealed his vices very artfully. This man perceiving that Jugurtha's money was distributed in a shameless and notorious manner, and fearing lest such barefaced bribery should, as is usual on the like occasions, raise public odium, restrained his passion for money.

That party, however, prevailed in the senate, which preferred money and favour to truth and equity; and it was decreed that ten commissioners should divide the kingdom, which Micipsa had possessed, between Jugurtha and Atherbal. The principal person in the commission was L. Opimius, a man of eminence and great authority in the senate, because, when consul, he had put to death C. Gracchus and M. Fulvius, and avenged the nobility upon the commons with great fury. Jugurtha, though he knew this senator was his friend at Rome, yet received him with the most solicitous respect; and, by great presents and ample promises, brought him to sacrifice honour, reputation, and in a word, every thing else, to his interest. He applied to the other commissioners in the same manner, and succeeded with most of them: some few indeed there were who set a higher value upon their honour than money. In the division of the kingdom, that part of Numidia which borders upon Mauritania, and is the most fertile and populous, was assigned to Jugurtha. Atherbal had the other; which was indeed better furnished with ports and fine buildings, but of greater beauty than importance.

My subject here seems to require of me a short account of the situation of Africa, and of those nations with whom we have had war or alliance. As for those other countries, which excessive heats, the difficulty of travelling, and vast deserts, have made less frequented, I shall say nothing at all; it being very difficult to meet with any certain information concerning them. My account of the rest I shall despatch with all possible brevity.

In the division of the globe, most authors reckon Africa a third part of the whole: there being but few who divide it into Asia and Europe, and include Africa in Europe. It is bounded on the west, by the straits which join our sea to the ocean; on the east, by spacious sloping plains, by the natives called Catabathmos. The sea of Africa is tempestu ous, and without harbours; the soil is fruitful in grain and good for pasture, but produces few trees; here it seldom rains, and there are but few springs of water. The natives have hale bodies, are remarkable for their agility, and can endure much fatigue: most of them die of old age, except such as are destroyed by the sword or wild beasts; for few of them are cut off by diseases: noxious animals they have in great numbers.

Concerning the original inhabitants of Africa, and such as settled in it afterwards, with the manner of their uniting together, I shall here give a short account, different indeed from the common one, but such as was interpreted to me out of the Carthaginian books, said to be those of king Hiempsal, and agreeable to the opinion of the natives themselves; but for the truth of the relation, let the authors be accountable.

Africa was at first possessed by the Getulians and Libyans, a savage and unpolished people, who lived upon the flesh of wild beasts, or fed upon the herbs of the field, like cattle; subject to no laws, discipline, or government; without any fixed habitation; wandering from place to place, and taking up their abode wherever night overtook them. But when Hercules died in Spain, as the Africans think he did, his army, made up of diverse nations, having lost their general, and many competitors arising for the command, dispersed in a short time. Those that were Medes, Persians, and Armenians, sailed over into Africa, and took possession of those places that lie upon our sea. But the Persians settled nearer the ocean; and they made houses to themselves of their ships turned upside down, because there was no timber in the country, nor had they an opportunity of importing it from Spain, having no commerce with that nation, on account of its great distance from them by sea, and their language, which was not understood there. These by degrees mixed with the Getulians by intermarriages; and because they were constantly shifting from place to place, trying the goodness of the soil, they called themselves Numidians. The houses of the Numidian peasants, which they call mapalia, are still like the hulls of ships, of an oblong form, with coverings rising in the middle, and bending at each end.

The Libyans, who lived near the African sea, mingled with the Medes and Armenians:

for the Getulians lay more to the sun, almost under the equinoctial line. The Libyans built cities very soon; for being separated from Spain only by the straits, they exchanged commodities with that country. By degrees they corrupted the name of the Medes, calling them, in their barbarous language, Moors. Now the Persians soon became a powerful people, and multiplied so greatly, that the youth, leaving their parents, on account of their vast numbers, and retaining their new name of Numidians, took possession of the country bordering upon Carthage, which is still called Numidia. Afterwards assisting each other, they reduced their neighbours, either by the terror or force of their arms, under their dominion, and thus acquired great glory and reputation, especially those who advanced farthest along our sea coast; because the Libyans were less warlike than the Getulians. At last almost all lower Africa was possessed by the Numidians; and the conquered nations, forming but one people with the conquerors, went by the same name.

Afterwards the Phoenicians came; some of whom left their homes to ease their country, which was overstocked with inhabitants; others were prompted by ambition and engaged the populace, and such as were fond of novelty, to follow them. They built Hippo, Adrumetum, Leptis, and other cities on the sea coast; which growing powerful in a short time, proved, some of them a defence, others an honour to their mother cities. For, as to Carthage, I think it is better to be altogether silent than to say but little; besides, it is time to return to my subject.

From the plains of Catabathmos, then, which separate Egypt from Africa, as we go along the sea coast, the first city is Cyrene, a colony from Thera. Next to this are the two Syrtes, with Leptis between them; then the altars of the Phileni, which bound the Carthaginian empire on the side of Egypt; and afterwards other Punic cities. The rest of Africa, as far as Mauritania, is possessed by the Numidians: the Moors are nearer to Spain. Above Numidia, as I have been informed, are the Getuli, who live, some of them in huts, while others wander about without any fixed abode. Beyond them are the Ethiopians; and then countries scorched by the heat of the sun. In the war with Jugurtha, the Romans had governors of their own in most of the Punic cities, and those places which had been lately subject to Carthage. Great part of the Getulians were under Jugurtha; and the Numidians too, as far as the river Mulucha. The Moors were all subject to Bocchus, who knew nothing of the Romans but the name; nor was he known to them before, either in war or peace. I have now said enough of Africa and its inhabitants for my purpose.

After Numidia was divided by the Roman commissioners, and they returned home; when Jugurtha, contrary to his fears, saw himself rewarded for his crimes, he was fully persuaded of the truth of what he had heard from his friends at Numantia, that all things were to be bought at Rome; and being encouraged too by the promises of those whom he had loaded with presents, he resolved to seize Atherbal's kingdom. He was himself, indeed, of a daring disposition, and an excellent soldier; but he whose destruction he aimed at was quiet, spiritless, of a meek temper, obnoxious to insults, and more apt to be terrified than to inspire terror. Accordingly, on a sudden he invades his territories with a powerful body, takes many prisoners, cattle, and other booty, sets fire to his cities; and, flying about with his cavalry from place to place, ravaged his country. He then returned into his own kingdom with all his forces, thinking that Atherbal would have recourse to arms for redress, and thus furnish him with a pretext for war. But he, not looking upon himself as a match for Jugurtha at arms, and relying more upon the Roman friendship than his own subjects, sent ambassadors to complain to Jugurtha of such outrages; and though they returned with an insulting answer, yet he determined to suffer any thing, rather than enter into a war in which he had succeeded so badly before. This did not, however, allay the insatiable ambition of Jugurtha, who had already, in his mind, taken possession of Atherbal's kingdom. Therefore he began now to make war, not as before, at the head of a band of plunderers, but with a great army, and openly aimed at the sovereignty of all Numidia: wherever he marched, he took cities, laid waste the country, committed universal depredation, and did every thing to inspire his men with courage, and strike terror into the enemy.

Atherbal, finding that he must either quit his kingdom or defend it by arms, submitted to necessity, and raising forces, marched against

Jugurtha: so that both armies encamped near the city Cirta, not far from the sea; but as the evening approached, they did not engage. When night was almost past, and day began to dawn, Jugurtha's men, upon a signal given, broke into the enemy's camp, and falling upon them, whilst some were scarce awake and others just taking their arms, put them to flight. Atherbal, with a few horse, made his escape to Cirta; and was so closely pursued, that if the Italians in great numbers had not repulsed the Numidians from the walls, the war between the two kings had been begun and ended in the same day. Jugurtha upon this laid close siege to the town, and by towers, moving galleries, and engines of all sorts, strove to take it; being desirous to be master of it, before the ambassadors, who he heard were sent to Rome before the battle, should arrive there. But as soon as the senate had notice of the war, they despatched three ambassadors, all young men, with orders to go to each of the kings, and acquaint them, that it was the pleasure and appointment of the senate and people of Rome they should quit their arms, and decide their differences by law rather than the sword; that thus they would act as the dignity of Rome and their own interests required.

The ambassadors arrived quickly in Africa, making the greater despatch, because, whilst they were preparing to depart, a report both of the engagement and siege of Cirta reached Rome; but this report was but little credited. Jugurtha, upon hearing their commission, replied, "that nothing was more sacred, nothing dearer to him, than the authority of the senate; that from his youth he had endeavoured to merit the approbation of every person of eminent worth; that he had gained the friendship of Scipio, that excellent man, by his virtuous conduct, not by infamous arts: that Micipsa had in consideration of his good qualities, and not for want of children, adopted him joint-heir with his own sons to the kingdom. But the braver and more deserving his conduct had been, the less could his spirit bear with insults. That Atherbal had laid snares for his life, which, when he discovered, he endeavoured to defeat: that the Roman people would neither set a just nor a wise part, if they denied him the common right of nations: finally, that he would quickly send deputies to Rome, to satisfy them concerning all his proceedings."

With this answer the ambassadors departed

35*

without being allowed access to Atherbal. Jugurtha, when he thought they had left Africa, perceiving it impossible to take Cirta by assault, on account of its natural strength, begirt it with a trench and rampart, raised towers, and filled them with armed men. He likewise tried day and night all possible methods both of force and stratagem; one while tempting the besieged with promises, another endeavouring to terrify them by threats; constantly animating his men and pushing every necessary measure with the utmost diligence. Atherbal, finding his affairs in extreme danger, his enemy determined on his ruin, no hopes of succour, and that the war could not be continued long for want of provisions, chose two of the most active and resolute of those who fled with him to Cirta, and prevailed upon them, by great promises and an affecting representation of his distress, to venture in the night time through the enemy's lines, to the next shore, and from thence to Rome. The Numidians in a few days executed their orders. Atherbal's letter was read in the senate; and was to this effect:

"It is not my fault, conscript fathers, that I make such frequent application to you; it is the violence of Jugurtha that forces me to it, who is so resolutely determined upon my destruction, that he pursues it without regarding your resentment or that of the immortal gods themselves. He prefers my blood to every other consideration; insomuch that I, though a friend and ally of the Roman people, have been besieged by him almost five months; nor **does** the generosity of my father Micipsa to him, nor the authority of your decrees, avail any thing towards my relief. Whether famine or the sword presses hardest upon me, I am unable to say. My wretched situation discourages me from writing at greater length concerning Jugurtha; having learned by experience how little credit is given to the miserable: this, however, I will venture to add, that I am sensible he aims at something beyond my ruin, and that he can never expect to enjoy my kingdom and your friendship; which of these he prefers to the other, can be a secret to none. For first he murdered my brother Hiempsal, then he drove me from my father's kingdom. Let these, however, be considered as injuries done to our family, and no ways affecting you; **yet** now he keeps by force a kingdom that is yours, and besieges me, who was appointed by

you king of the Numidians. How much he regarded the orders you sent him by your deputies, my dangers abundantly show. What remains, then, but that you have recourse to force, which alone can move him? As for me I could wish, that what I write at present, and what I formerly complained of before the senate, was altogether groundless, rather than it should be verified by my sufferings. But since I was born to **be a spectacle of Jugurtha's** cruelty, I do not **beg to be rescued from death** or distress, but only **from** falling into his hands, and from the tortures that are prepared for me. Dispose of the kingdom of Numidia, which is your own, as you may judge most proper; but I conjure you by the majesty of the Roman empire, and by the faith of friendship and alliance, deliver me from the impious hands of Jugurtha, if you have any regard for the memory of my grandfather Masinissa."

Upon reading this letter, there were some senators who proposed that an army should be sent into Africa, and succours despatched to Atherbal with all expedition; and that Jugurtha's disobedience to their orders should be forthwith taken into consideration. But the king's advocates strenuously opposed such measures; and thus the public good, as is generally the case, was sacrificed to private interest. Ambassadors were chosen, however, to be sent into Africa; men of age and dignity, who had borne the highest offices of the state; amongst whom was M. Scaurus, whom we have already mentioned, a man of consular dignity, and at that time prince of the senate. These, observing that the public odium was great against Jugurtha, and being pressed by the Numidians to make all possible haste, embarked in three days; and arriving soon at Utica, wrote to Jugurtha, to come directly into the Roman province; for that they had orders to him from the senate.

When he found that men of such eminence and authority at Rome were come to oppose his designs, he was distracted between fear and ambition. On the one hand, he dreaded the resentment of the senate if he did not obey their deputies; on the other, his eager passion for power hurried him on to the execution of his wicked undertaking. At last ambition prevailed; and surrounding Cirta with all his army, he made a general assault, labouring with all his might to break into it; as he hoped, by dividing the enemy's forces, to have a chance for victory, either by force or artifice. But this attempt miscarrying, and finding that his great aim, of getting Atherbal into his possession, before he met the deputies, could not be effected, he came with a few horse into the Roman province, that he might not, by longer delay, incense Scaurus, of whom he stood in great awe. Upon his arrival, though the deputies, in the name of the senate, denounced grievous threatenings against him for continuing the siege, yet after a long debate they departed without success.

When an account of this was brought to Cirta, the Italians, by whose bravery the town was defended, persuading themselves that their persons would not be violated after a surrender, in consideration of the Roman power, advised Atherbal to deliver himself and the town to Jugurtha, without insisting on any conditions, but that of having his own life, as the senate would take care of every thing else. Atherbal, though he was very sensible that nothing was less to be depended upon than Jugurtha's word, yet considering that it was in the power of those who advised him to force him to a compliance in case of refusal, yielded to the proposal of the Italians, and surrendered. Upon which Jugurtha put Atherbal to death immediately upon the rack, and then slaughtered all the Numidian youth and foreign merchants without distinction.

When this was known at Rome, and began to be debated in the senate, the king's former advocates, by their intrigues, by their interest with particular senators, and often by protracting the time in long speeches, endeavoured to qualify the horror of his crimes; and had not C. Memmius, tribune of the people elect, a man of spirit, and a declared enemy to the power of the nobility, informed the Roman people, that the design of all this was to procure impunity to Jugurtha for his crimes by means of a faction, the public indignation against him would undoubtedly have vanished by their studied delays; so powerfully did favour and the king's money operate. But the senate, through a consciousness of the injustice of their proceedings, began to dread the resentment of the people, and complying with the Sempronian law, decreed Numidia and Italy the provinces of the next consuls, who were declared to be P. Scipio Nasica, and L. Bestia Calpurnius. To the former of these Italy fell, and to the latter Numidia. Then an army was raised to be sent into Africa; and a decree was made for the payment of it, and for every thing necessary to carry on the war.

When Jugurtha heard this news, so contrary to his hopes, as he had a strong persuasion that every thing was to be had at Rome for money, he sent his son and two of his intimate friends on an embassy to the senate, and ordered them, as he had formerly done those he sent after having murdered Hiempsal, to bribe all sorts of men. Upon their approach to Rome, Bestia consulted the senate, "whether the deputies of Jugurtha should be admitted within the walls;" and it was decreed, "that unless they came to surrender Jugurtha and his kingdom, they must depart out of Italy within ten days." This the consul, by the senate's orders, signified to the Numidians; and thus they returned without doing any thing.

Calpurnius, in the meantime, having raised an army, chose for his lieutenant-generals persons of quality and intrigue, whose authority he hoped would support him in whatever he might do amiss; amongst whom was Scaurus, of whose temper and character we have already given an account. The consul himself had indeed many excellent endowments both of body and mind, but avarice rendered them all useless: he was hardy, of great penetration and foresight, well skilled in war, and not to be moved by dangers or surprise. The legions marched through Italy to Rhegium, where they embarked for Sicily, and from thence were transported to Africa; so that Calpurnius, who had early provided himself with all necessaries, entered Numidia with great vigour, took a great number of prisoners, and several cities by storm. But when Jugurtha began by his deputies to tempt him with money, and to lay before him the difficulties of the war in which he was engaged, his soul, sick with avarice, was easily softened. He took Scaurus, however, as his partner and adviser in all his schemes; who, though he had at first vigorously opposed the king, even when most of his party were already corrupted, was nevertheless prevailed upon by a vast sum of money, to desert the cause of honour and equity, for that oppression and injustice.

Jugurtha at first only purchased a suspension of the war, flattering himself that in the meantime he should succeed at Rome, either by favour or money; but hearing that Scaurus was engaged in his interest, he con ceived high hopes of obtaining peace, and determined to treat with him in person concerning the terms of it. In the meantime, to remove any apprehensions of danger from his coming, the consul sent Sextius the quæstor to Vacca, where Jugurtha was; but under pretence of receiving corn, which Calpurnius had publicly ordered the deputies to provide, since a truce was granted, till a surrender should be made. Jugurtha, at last, came into the camp, as he had determined; and after a short speech to the council of officers, to lessen the odium of his crimes, he proposed to deliver himself up. The terms he afterwards settled privately with Bestia and Scaurus; and was, the day after, admitted to a surrender, as if the matter had been concluded in due form by majority of voices. Accordingly thirty elephants, some cattle, with a great number of horses, and a small sum of money, were, agreeably to the order of the council, delivered to the quæstor. Calpurnius goes to Rome, to assist at the election of magistrates; all being quiet in Numidia and in our army there.

When the transactions in Africa, and the manner of proceeding there, came to be known at Rome, the behaviour of the consul was the subject of conversation in all companies; the people were filled with indignation, and the senate with perplexity; not knowing whether they should ratify so dishonourable a treaty, or make void the ordinance of the consul. The authority of Scaurus, who was said to be the adviser and associate of Bestia, was what principally diverted them from acting a just and honourable part. While the senate was thus in suspense, C. Memmius, whose freedom of spirit and sworn enmity to the power of the nobility we have already mentioned, stirred up the people in their assemblies to revenge their own wrongs: warned them not to desert the interests of the public and their own liberty; laid before them many instances of the haughty and tyrannical behaviour of the nobility, and used every possible method to inflame the minds of the populace against them.

Now, as the eloquence of Memmius was at that time in great reputation and of great influence at Rome, I have thought proper to transcribe one of his speeches, out of many; and above all others, that which he made to an assembly of the people, after the return of Bestia, in the following strain:

" If my zeal for the public good did not bear down every other consideration, Romans, there are many motives to dissuade me from adhering to your interests; motives great and powerful—the strength of the opposite party; your tameness of spirit; the universal prevalence of injustice; and above all, innocence rather exposed to danger, than crowned with honour. For it really gives me pain to relate with what insolent scorn you have been treated by a few great men, for these fifteen years; how basely your great champions have been suffered to perish unrevenged; how your former spirit is sunk through indolence and effeminacy, who, even now, when your enemies are at your mercy, do not stir against them; and are, even now, afraid of those to whom you should be a terror! But notwithstanding all this, my spirit obliges me to oppose the power of the faction; nor will I fail to use that liberty which is transmitted to me by my father; but whether with or without success depends entirely upon you, O Romans. Not that I advise you to redress your wrongs by arms, as your ancestors have often done; there is no need of violence, none of leaving the city; since they must certainly ruin themselves by their own proceedings. After the murder of Tiberius Gracchus who was charged by them with having aimed at the sovereignty, the severest cruelties were exercised towards the Roman people. After C. Gracchus and M. Fulvius were put to death, many of your body perished in prison; nor was it law, but their own good pleasure, that put an end to both these massacres. But let restoring the people their rights pass for aiming at the sovereignty; let it be deemed lawful to remedy what could not otherwise be remedied than by shedding the blood of Roman citizens! You have, for several years, with secret indignation beheld the treasury robbed; beheld kings and free nations pay tribute to a few of the nobles; and those few adorned with public honours, and possessed of immense wealth. Nay, looking upon the commission of such enormities with impunity as but a small matter, they have at last betrayed your laws, your majesty, every thing divine and human, into the hands of your enemies. Nor for all this are they touched with remorse or shame; no, they appear in public with great pomp, displaying their sacerdotal dignities, their consulships, their triumphs; as if these dignities possessed by them were really honourable, and not marks of their usurpation. Slaves bought with money do not submit to the unjust commands of their masters; and can you, Romans, who are born to command, tamely submit to slavery?

" But who are they who have seized upon the commonwealth? The most profligate of all men; their hands dyed with the blood of their fellow-citizens; men of boundless avarice, of enormous guilt, and matchless pride; men who turn honour, faith, public spirit, and, in short, whatever is just or unjust, into gain. Some of them owe their security to their having murdered your tribunes, others to lawless prosecutions, and most of them to their having shed your blood: so that they who have done you the greatest wrong are in the greatest safety; and instead of being afraid of punishment at your hands for their numerous crimes, from your cowardice they make you afraid of them. As their desires, their aversions, their fears are the same, they are closely united together: now such a conformity of inclinations among good men is friendship, but faction when found among the wicked.

" But were you as much concerned for the preservation of your liberty as they are for establishing their tyranny, the commonwealth would not be torn in pieces as it now is; and your favours, instead of being conferred on the most audacious, would be bestowed on the most deserving. Your ancestors twice withdrew from the city, to mount Aventine, in arms, in order to assert their rights and establish their dignity: and will not you labour with all your might to maintain the liberty they have transmitted to you? nay, will not you labour with the greater zeal, as it is more dishonourable to lose what has been acquired, than not to have acquired it at all?

" Here some will ask me, What then would you have done? I answer, I would have those punished who have betrayed the commonwealth to an enemy; not by force or violence, a method of punishment which though they deserve, yet does not become your dignity to inflict; but by a legal prosecution, and the evidence of Jugurtha himself; who, if he has really surrendered himself, will obey your commands; but if he despises them, you may then judge what kind of peace or surrender it is, from whence Jugurtha derives impunity for his crimes,—a few great men immense wealth, and the state nothing but loss and infamy. But perhaps you are not as yet satiated with the tyranny of these men, and are best pleased with those times, when kingdoms, provinces, law, the administration of justice, war and peace, in a word, every thing divine and human, were at the disposal of a few, while you, the Roman people, always invincible, and lords of the world, were humbly content to be allowed to live. For was there a man of you, who had spirit to refuse the yoke? As for me, though I look upon it as very dishonourable to a man tamely to bear ill usage: yet I should patiently see you pardon the most guilty criminals, because they are your fellow-citizens, were it not that your compassion would prove your own certain ruin.

" Such, indeed, is the mischievous spirit of these men, that to pardon their past crimes will signify little to you, if you do not deprive them of power to repeat them; and nothing will remain to you but continual anxiety, when you find that you must either be slaves, or preserve your liberty by force. For what hope is there of mutual faith and concord between them and you? They desire to be lords, you to be free: they to oppress you, you to defend yourselves: in a word, they use your allies like enemies, your enemies like allies. Can peace or friendship possibly subsist between persons of such opposite dispositions?

" Wherefore I advise and exhort you, not to suffer such enormous villany to go unpunished. It is not the robbing of the treasury, nor extorting money from your allies, that now come under your consideration,—crimes which, however heinous, yet are become so common that they pass for nothing. It is the authority of the senate, it is your own mighty power, that is betrayed to a very terrible enemy, and the commonwealth exposed to sale both at home and abroad. Which crimes, unless you prosecute, and take vengeance upon the guilty, what remains but to live the slaves of those who committed them!—for to do with impunity what one pleases, is being a king.

" I do not hereby mean, O Romans, to encourage you to wish that these your fellow citizens may be found to have acted basely rather than honourably; but only warn you, not to ruin the good and deserving by pardoning the wicked. Besides, it is much wiser in any government to forget services rather than wrongs: for a good man by being neglected becomes only more indolent; whereas a bad man grows still worse. Let me add, if injuries are prevented, you will seldom stand in need of assistance."

By this and the like speeches, C. Memmius persuaded the Roman people to send L. Cassius, who was then prætor, to Jugurtha, and bring him to Rome upon the public faith; that, by his evidence, Scaurus and the rest, who were charged with betraying their trust for money, might be clearly convicted. Whilst these measures were pursuing at Rome, the officers whom Bestia had left with the command of the army at Numidia, in imitation of their general's conduct, committed many and infamous crimes. Some, for a sum of money, restored Jugurtha his elephants; others sold him his deserters; and some plundered the provinces at peace with the Romans; such was the violence of avarice, which, like a plague, had taken possession of their minds.

The prætor Cassius, in consequence of this ordinance of the people, procured by Memmius, to the great surprise of the nobility, went to Jugurtha, and persuaded him, though sore afraid, and from a consciousness of his guilt diffident of his cause, " that since he had already delivered himself up to the Roman people, he should try their mercy rather than their power." He likewise engaged to him his own faith, which Jugurtha reckoned as strong a security as that of the public. Such at that time was the reputation of Cassius.

Jugurtha accordingly came to Rome with Cassius; yet without any regal pomp, and dressed in such a manner as to excite pity. But though he was himself of an intrepid spirit, and was moreover encouraged by assurances from those, in reliance upon whose power and villany he had committed the above-mentioned crimes; yet, by a vast sum of money he secured the assistance of C. Bæbius, tribune of the people, one who had impudence enough to protect him against all law and all manner of injuries.

When an assembly of the people was called by Memmius, though they were so highly exasperated against Jugurtha, that some of them were for putting him in irons, others for putting him to death like a public enemy, according to the ancient usage, unless he discovered his associates; yet Memmius, more concerned for their dignity than the gratification of their fury, endeavoured to calm the tumult and soften their minds, and declared that he would take care that the public faith should not be violated. At last, having obtained silence, and ordered Jugurtha to be brought before the assembly, he proceeded in

his speech, recounted all his wicked actions both in Rome and Numidia; laid open his unnatural behaviour to his fathers and brothers; adding, that the Roman people, though they were not ignorant by whom he had been aided and supported, still desired full information of the whole from himself. If he declared the truth, he had much to hope from the faith and clemency of the Roman people; but if he concealed it, he would not save his friends by so doing, but ruin himself and his hopes for ever.

When Memmius had made an end of speaking, and Jugurtha was ordered to reply, the tribune Bæbius, who had been secured by a sum of money, as we have already mentioned, desired him to be silent: and though the people there assembled were highly incensed and endeavoured to frighten him with their cries, with angry looks, nay and often with violence, and every other method which indignation inspires, yet his impudence triumphed over it all. The people departed, after being thus mocked; Jugurtha, Bestia, and the rest, who were at first terribly afraid of this prosecution, assumed greater courage.

There was at this juncture a certain Numidian at Rome, called Massiva, the son of Gulussa, and grandson of Masinissa; who, having taken part against Jugurtha in the war between the three kings, had fled out of Africa upon the surrender of Cirta and the murder of Atherbal. Sp. Albinus, who with Q. Minucius Rufus succeeded Bestia in the consulship, persuaded this man to apply to the senate for the kingdom of Numidia; as he was descended from Masinissa, and Jugurtha the object of public abhorrence on account of his crimes, and alarmed with daily fears of the punishment he deserved. The consul, who was very fond of having the management of the war, was more desirous that the public disturbances should be continued than composed. The province of Numidia had fallen to him, and Macedonia to his colleague. When Massiva began to prosecute his claim, Jugurtha, finding that he could not rely upon the assistance of his friends, some of whom were seized with remorse, others restrained by the bad opinion the public had of them, and by their fears, ordered Bomilcar, who was his faithful friend and confidant, " to engage persons to murder Massiva for money, by which he had accomplished many things; and to do it by privat means, if possible; but if those were ineffectual, by any means whatever."

Bomilcar quickly executed the king's orders, and by employing proper instruments, discovered his places of resort, his set times, and all his motions; and when matters were ripe, laid a scheme for the assassination. One of those who were to put the murder in execution, attacked Massiva and slew him, but so imprudently, that he was himself apprehended; and being urged by many, especially by the consul Albinus, confessed all. Bomilcar was arraigned, more agreeably to reason and justice than to the law of nations; for he accompanied Jugurtha, who came to Rome upon the public faith. Jugurtha, though clearly guilty of so foul a crime, did not however give over endeavouring to bear down the force of truth, till he perceived that the horror of his guilt was such as to baffle all the power of favour or money. Upon which, though he had upon the prosecution of Bomilcar given fifty of his friends as sureties for his standing his trial, he sent him privately to Numidia; being more concerned for his kingdom than his friends: for he was afraid, were this favourite to be punished, lest the rest of his subjects should be discouraged from obeying him. In a few days he himself followed, being ordered by the senate to depart out of Italy. When he left Rome, it is reported that, having frequently looked back to it without saying any thing, he at last broke out into these words: "A venal city, and ripe for destruction, when a purchaser can be found."

The war being now revived, Albinus made haste to transport into Africa, money, provisions, and every thing necessary for the use of the army; and soon after followed himself, that he might put an end to the war, either by defeating the enemy, by obliging Jugurtha to surrender, or by any other means, before the time for election of magistrates, which was near at hand. Jugurtha, on the contrary, endeavoured to protract time, and was continually finding fresh pretences for delay: one while he promised to surrender; another he feigned distrust; when the enemy pressed him, he gave way; and soon after, lest his men should be discouraged, he attacked them in his turn. Thus did he baffle the consul by an alternate course of hostilities and proposals of peace. Some there were at that time who imagined that Albinus was not ignorant of the king's designs,

and who could not believe that the protracting of the war, after such vigorous preparations, was so much owing to inactivity as to fraud.

The time being elapsed, and the elections at hand, Albinus went to Rome, leaving his brother Aulus to command in the camp as prætor. The commonwealth was at this time terribly agitated by the contentions of the tribunes of the people. Two of these, P. Lucullus and L. Annius, endeavoured to continue in their office, notwithstanding the opposition of all their colleagues; which contest kept off the election for a whole year. Upon this delay, Aulus, who was left proprætor in the camp, as we have already related, conceiving hopes of either terminating the war, or, by the terror of his army, obliging the king to give him a sum of money, drew his men out of their winter-quarters in the month of January, and by long marches, under the rigours of the season, reached Suthul, where the king's treasure lay. The sharpness of the weather, and the situation of this place, rendered it impossible to take or even to besiege it; for besides its being built upon a steep rock and strongly walled, the plains that surrounded it were turned into a perfect marsh by the winter rains. Notwithstanding all this, Aulus, either as a feint to frighten the king, or blinded by avarice, to make himself master of the town on account of the treasure, framed moving galleries, threw up trenches, and made all necessary preparations for a siege.

Jugurtha, perceiving the proprætor's ignorance and vanity, made use of several arts to increase his madness and presumption; frequently sent deputies to him with humble messages, whilst he himself, affecting fear, led his army through forests and narrow passes. At last Aulus, in hopes that the king would surrender upon conditions, was tempted to quit Suthul and pursue him. Jugurtha, appearing to fly before him, by this means drew him into countries utterly unknown to him, the better to execute his own designs. In the meantime he employed cunning instruments day and night to debauch our army; bribing the centurions and officers of horse, some to desert to him, and others upon a signal given to quit their posts. Having thus far pursued his schemes successfully, on a sudden, in the dead of night, he surrounded Aulus's camp with a great body of Numidians. The Roman soldiers being struck with this alarm, some took their arms

THE WAR .

some hid themselves, and others encouraged those that were afraid. There was every where the greatest consternation: the number of the enemy was great, the night was dark and cloudy, and danger on every side: in a word, it was impossible to determine whether it was safest to maintain their ground or fly. Meanwhile, a cohort of Ligurians, two troops of Thracian horse, with a few common men, deserted to Jugurtha, by whom they had been corrupted, as we have already related; and a centurion of the first rank, belonging to the third legion, opened a passage to the enemy into the camp, at which all the Numidians poured in, by delivering up a strong post, the defence of which was assigned him. Our men shamefully fled, and the most of them throwing away their arms, took possession of a neighbouring hill.

Night and the plunder of the camp hindered the enemy from improving the victory. Next day, Jugurtha, at a conference with Aulus, told him, that though both he and his troops were at his mercy, being hemmed in on all sides with sword and famine, yet, mindful of the inconstancy of human affairs, if he would conclude a treaty with him, he would dismiss them all unhurt; only making them pass under the yoke, and obliging them to quit Numidia in ten days. The conditions, though very rigorous and extremely dishonourable, were yet submitted to, as they were thereby all delivered from the fear of death; and a peace was concluded upon the king's terms.

When this was known at Rome, fear and sorrow seized all the city. Some were deeply concerned for the glory of the empire; others, unacquainted with war, trembled for their liberty; all were filled with indignation against Aulus, those especially who had distinguished themselves often by their bravery in war, that with arms in his hands he should consult his safety rather by submitting shamefully than defending himself gallantly. The consul Albinus, dreading the public odium, and thereby great danger, on account of his brother's infamous conduct, consulted the senate upon the treaty; yet in the mean time raised recruits for the army, sent for auxiliaries from the Latins and allies, and made all necessary preparations with the utmost diligence. The senate, as was fit they should, decreed, that without their authority and that of the people, no treaty could be concluded. The consul not being allowed

by the tribunes of the people to transport into Africa what forces he had raised, went thither himself in a few days without them: for the whole army, according to agreement, had quitted Numidia, and wintered in our province. Upon his arrival, though he had an eager desire to march against Jugurtha, and thereby lessen the public odium under which his brother had fallen, yet when he found that the courage of the soldiers was sunk by their late flight, and not only so, but that they were without discipline, extremely licentious and debauched, he resolved, after mature deliberation, to attempt nothing.

At Rome, in the meantime, C. Mamilius Limetanus, one of the tribunes, proposed to the people to pass an ordinance, for arraigning those by whose encouragement Jugurtha had disobeyed the decrees of the senate; those who had received money from him, when sent as deputies to him, or trusted with the management of the war against him; those who had restored him his elephants and deserters; and likewise those who had taken upon them to enter into any engagements with the enemy relating to peace or war. Such as were aimed at by this ordinance, not daring openly to oppose it, some through their consciousness of deserving it, others through fear of falling a sacrifice to the heat of party, professed to be pleased with it and the like proceedings; yet secretly endeavoured to prevent its passing by means of their friends, especially the Latins and the other Italian allies. But it is almost incredible how zealous the people were upon this occasion, and with what eagerness they voted, authorized, and passed the ordinance; more indeed out of hatred to the nobility, against whom it was levelled, than out of any regard to the welfare of the state; so violent was the fury of party.

Whilst the rest were seized by fear, M. Scaurus, who had been lieutenant-general to Bestia, as above related, during the rejoicings of the people, the flight of those of his party, and the distraction of the city, got himself named one of the three commissioners, who were appointed by the ordinance of Mamilius to put it in execution. The prosecution followed, and was managed with great severity and violence, to gratify the mad humour and clamour of the people, who upon this occasion used their superiority with great insolence, as the nobility had often done.

The distinction of the people and senate into opposite parties, with all the mischievous practices consequent upon it, took its rise at Rome a few years before, and sprung from profound quiet, and the abundance of those things which men set the highest value upon. For before the destruction of Carthage, the people and senate jointly governed the state with great moderation and harmony; the citizens had no contests with one another on account of power and influence; fear of their enemies kept the state in good order: but when this fear was removed, pride and debauchery, **the** usual attendants of prosperity, poured in **upon them.** So that peace, which they so ardently **wished** for in the time of war and danger, **when they** obtained it, proved more fatal **to them than either;** for the nobility began to **convert** their dignity into tyranny; the people, **their** liberty into licentiousness, and all, indeed, centering their views in themselves only, laboured to get as much power and property as they possibly could. Thus, whilst each party strove to have all power in its hands, the commonwealth, which lay between both, was miserably rent. The faction of the nobility, however, prevailed; for the authority of the people, being loose, and divided among a multitude, had less force; so that all affairs, both at home and abroad, were managed by a few. They disposed of the treasury, provinces, magistracies, public dignities, and triumphs. The populace were oppressed by poverty and military service, while the generals, with a few great ones, engrossed all the spoils of victory: and even the parents and children of the soldiers were driven from their estates, if they happened to border upon any of the grandees. Thus did avarice, in conjunction with power, **without** moderation or restraint, invade, pollute, and lay waste every thing, disregarding what was **just** or sacred, till it rushed headlong to **its own** ruin. For as soon as there arose any **from among the** nobility **who** preferred real glory **to unjust** power, the state was in an uproar; and such civil broils ensued, as if the universe had **been** dissolving.

For after Tiberius and Caius Gracchus, whose ancestors had done signal service to the state; both in the Carthaginian and other wars, began to attempt the recovery of the people's rights, and to lay open the wickedness of a few great men; the nobility, being conscious of their guilt and under terrible apprehensions,

endeavoured to defeat their designs, sometimes by means of our Italian allies and the Latin state, and sometimes by means of the Roman knights, whom the hopes of being admitted to a partnership in power with the nobility had drawn off from the interests of the people. First they murdered Tiberius, whilst tribune of the people, and, in a few years after, Caius, who was pursuing his brother's measures, together with M. Fulvius Flaccus, both invested with the triumviral authority of planting colonies. And indeed the Gracchi, through an eager desire of carrying their point, did not act with moderation; for it is better to yield, than to conquer opposition by unlawful means.

The nobility, using the advantage they had gained according to their own wanton humour, put many citizens to death, banished others, and rendered themselves more terrible for the future, rather than more powerful; a method of proceeding which has ruined many flourishing states; whilst parties have endeavoured to conquer each other, and to treat the conquered with the utmost cruelty. But were I to enter into a minute detail of the views and animosities of our parties, with the conduct of our citizens, and to treat so copious a subject in its full extent, time would fail me sooner than matter. I return then to my design.

After the treaty of Aulus and the shameful flight of our army, Metellus and Silanus, consuls elect, shared the provinces between them; and Numidia fell to Metellus, a man of spirit untainted reputation, and equally esteemed by both parties, though he opposed that of **the** people. As soon as he entered upon his office, considering that his colleague had an equal share of all the other duties of the consulship, he employed his thoughts wholly upon the war which he was to conduct. Accordingly, having little dependence upon the old army, he made new levies; sent for auxiliaries from all parts; provided arms, horses, and all other warlike implements, with great plenty of provisions; and, in a word, every thing necessary in a war, which required various management and many things to conduct it properly. In making these preparations, he was vigorously assisted by the senate, our allies, and those of the Latin state; foreign princes of their own accord sent him auxiliaries; and, in short, the whole city supported him with the greatest zeal. When all things were furnished and regulated according to his wishes, he passed over into Numidia.

leaving his fellow-citizens full of great hopes; not only on account of his many excellent qualities, but chiefly because he had a soul never to be subdued by money. For it was the avarice of our commanders that, till this time, had ruined our affairs in Numidia, and rendered the enemy successful.

Upon his arrival in Africa, the army of the proconsul, Spurius Albinus, was delivered to him: but an army spiritless and unwarlike; incapable of sustaining danger or fatigue; readier to talk than to act; without any order or discipline; and accustomed to plunder our allies, whilst itself was the spoil of the enemy: so that the depravity of the soldiers occasioned the general more anxiety, than their numbers gave him either support or confidence. But though Metellus saw the summer far advanced, from the elections being put off, and considered that his fellow-citizens were impatient for the issue; yet he determined not to enter upon action, till, by restoring the ancient discipline, he had enabled the soldiers to endure fatigue. For Albinus, struck with the disgrace of his brother Aulus and the overthrow of his troops, having resolved not to stir out of the province during so much of the summer as he commanded, kept the soldiers for the most part in the same camp, till stench or want of forage obliged them to remove. Besides, contrary to all the rules of war, no watch was kept in the camp; the men left their ensigns at pleasure, and the leaders, together with the soldiers, wandered abroad day and night, robbing the farms, pillaging the fields, and striving to exceed one another in carrying off cattle and captives, which they exchanged with the merchants for wine and other such things; nay, they sold the corn that was allowed them by the state, and bought their bread from day to day. In a word, all the excesses of idleness and luxury that can either be expressed or imagined, prevailed in that army.

Metellus appears to me to have approved himself as able and wise a man, by the manner in which he cured these great disorders, as by his conduct against the enemy; so just a medium did he observe between a servile desire to gain the affections of the soldiers, and a severity in punishing them. For by his first edict he removed every thing that could administer to idleness, ordering, " that none should sell bread or any dressed victuals in the camp: that no sutlers should follow the army: and that no common soldier should have a servant, or any

beast of burden, either in the camp or on a march." He made other regulations too with great judgment. Besides, he decamped daily, marching his army through cross and difficult places; fortified his camp with a ditch and palisade, as if an enemy had been at hand; set guards, and changed them often; and went frequently round them all himself, attended by his lieutenant-generals. On a march too he was equally vigilant, appearing one while in the front, another in the rear, and often in the main body; to see that none quitted their ranks, that all kept close by their standards, and carried their own arms and **provisions.** Thus, in a short time, he restored discipline and vigour to his troops, rather by preventing abuses than punishing them.

Jugurtha, in the meantime, having learned from his emissaries what measures were taken by Metellus, whose integrity he had been convinced of when at Rome, began to despair of success, and thought of surrendering himself in good earnest. Accordingly he sent ambassadors to the consul, with power to deliver up all to the Romans, only stipulating for his own life and that of his children. But Metellus, who had learned by experience that the Numidians were a faithless people, fickle and fond of change, applied to each of the ambassadors apart; and when, by sifting them, he found they were proper instruments for his purpose, he engaged them by great promises to deliver **up** Jugurtha to him alive, if possible; if not, to bring him his head: and his answer to their embassy he gave them in **public.** In a few days after, he went into Numidia **at the head of a resolute** army, where he found none of the symptoms of war, but the **country-houses full** of inhabitants, flocks and herds feeding in the fields, and the husbandmen all at work. **The** king's officers came from the towns and cottages to meet him, offering to furnish him with carriages and provisions, and, in a word, to do whatever he should order them. Metellus, notwithstanding all this, was still upon his guard; marched with his ranks, as if the enemy had been at hand; and sent scouts to view the country a great way round, looking upon these marks of submission as contrived for show only, and to draw him into an ambush. Wherefore he himself marched always in the front, with some light-armed cohorts, and a select body of slingers and archers: leaving his lieutenant-general, C. Marius, at the head of the cavalry to bring up the rear.

The auxiliary horse he placed on each wing, and gave the command of them to the tribunes of the legions and the præfects of the cohorts, mixing with them the light-armed foot, that the enemy's cavalry might be repulsed, on what side soever they made their attack. For Jugurtha had so much subtlety, so perfect a knowledge of the country, and such abilities in war, that it was uncertain whether he was more mischievous when at a distance or near, when making proposals for peace or openly engaged in war.

Not far from Metellus's route there was a city called Vacca, the most famous for commerce in all Numidia, very much frequented by Italians, who came to it for traffic, and many of whom had settled in it. The consul put a garrison into this place, either to try whether Jugurtha would bear with it, or because he was pleased with its situation; and likewise ordered corn and other necessaries to be brought him; supposing, as was very natural for him to do, that his army would be abundantly supplied, from such a concourse of traders and such plenty of provisions; and that the place itself would be very convenient for executing the designs he had already formed. In the meantime Jugurtha renewed his applications to the consul with greater earnestness, still sending ambassadors to implore peace, and offering to deliver up all he had, without stipulating for any thing but his own life and that of his children. The consul having engaged these ambassadors, as he had the first, to betray their master, sent them back without either promising or denying the peace; waiting, in the meantime, the execution of what they had undertaken.

When Jugurtha compared the words of Metellus with his actions, and found that his own arts were practised upon him, that whilst he was amused with the hopes of peace, he was warmly pursued with war; when he saw that he had lost one of his strongest cities, that the enemy was well acquainted with his territories, and his subjects solicited to revolt; being forced by his desperate situation, he determined to hazard a battle. Accordingly, having got intelligence of the enemy's route, and conceiving hopes of victory from the advantages which the country gave him, he raised a force as great as he could, and by private ways got before the army of Metellus.

In that part of Numidia which, upon the division of it, fell to the share of Atherbal, was a river called Muthul, flowing from the south: parallel to which, at the distance of about twenty miles, there was a mountain of equal length, desert and uncultivated. Between this mountain and the river, almost at an equal distance from each, rose a hill of prodigious height, covered with olives, myrtles, and other trees, such as grow in a dry and sandy soil; the intermediate plain was all desert for want of water, those parts only excepted which bordered upon the river, in which were many groves, and abundance of cattle and inhabitants. Jugurtha took possession of this hill, which flanked the Romans in their march to the river, extending his front as far as possible; and giving the command of the elephants and part of the foot to Bomilcar, with orders how to act, he posted himself with all the horse and the choicest of the foot nearer the mountain. Then he rode round the several squadrons and battalions, conjuring them "to summon up their former bravery, and, mindful of their late victory, to defend themselves and their country from the Roman avarice. They were to engage with those whom they had already vanquished, and forced to pass under the yoke; and who had only changed their general, but not their spirit. As for himself, he had done all that was incumbent upon a general to do; had secured to them the advantages of the ground, which they were well acquainted with, and the enemy a stranger to; and had taken care not to expose them to an unequal engagement with an enemy superior in number or skill: they should, therefore, when the signal was given, fall vigorously upon the Romans; this day would either crown their former toils and victories, or be a prelude to the most grievous calamities." Besides, addressing himself singly to such as he rewarded with honours or money for their gallant behaviour, he put them in mind of his favours, and proposed them to others as patterns for their imitation. In a word, he applied to all, in a manner suited to the disposition of each, and by promises, threatenings, and entreaties, roused their courage.

In the meantime, Metellus descending from the mountain with his army, without knowing any thing of the enemy's motions, discovered them upon the hill. At first he did not know what to think of so strange an appearance; for the Numidian horse and foot were posted among the bushes, by reason of the lowness of which they were neither altogether covered nor yet entirely discerned; the obscurity of the place, and their own artificial posture, preventing them from being clearly seen: but soon finding that it was an ambush, he made his army halt a little; and altering the disposition of it, he made the flank next the enemy thrice as strong as before, distributed the slingers and archers among the infantry, placed all the cavalry in the wings; and animating them by a short speech suitable to the occasion, advanced, in this order, towards the plain.

But observing the Numidians to keep their ground, without offering to stir from the hill, and fearing lest, from the heat of the season and the scarcity of water, his army would be distressed by thirst, he ordered his lieutenant-general Rutilius, with the light-armed cohorts and a detachment of horse, to march before him to the river, and secure a place to encamp on; judging that the enemy would, by frequent skirmishes, and attacks upon his flank, endeavour to retard his march, and to harass his men by thirst and continual fatigue, as they had no hopes of success in battle. He then advanced gently, as his circumstances and situation allowed him, in the same order as he had descended from the mountain; posted Marius in the centre, and marching himself in the left wing, at the head of the cavalry, which was now become the front.

Jugurtha, when he saw that the Roman rear had got beyond his first rank, detached two thousand foot to take possession of that part of the mountain from whence Metellus had descended, that it might not serve the enemy for a place of security if they were routed; and then, giving the signal, fell upon them. Some of his men made great slaughter in our rear, whilst others charged us on the right and left; they advanced furiously, fought vigorously, and every where broke our ranks. Even those of our men who opposed them with the greatest firmness and resolution, were baffled by their disorderly manner of fighting; being wounded at a distance, and unable to return blow for blow, or come to a close engagement: for the Numidian cavalry, according to the instructions they had received from Jugurtha, when any of the Roman troops advanced against them, immediately fled, not in close order, or in a body, but dispersed as wide as possible. As they could not, however, by this means discourage us from pursuing them, yet, being superior in

number, they charged us either in flank or rear; and when the hill seemed more convenient to fly to than the plain, their horses, being accustomed to it, made their way more easily through the thickets; whilst ours, not being used to such rough and difficult places, could not follow them.

The whole transaction, indeed, afforded a spectacle various and perplexed, dismal and shocking; some flying, others pursuing: all separated from their fellows; no standard kept to; no ranks observed; every one standing upon his defence, and repulsing his adversary, wherever he was attacked; arms and darts, horses and men, enemies and fellow-citizens, blended together in wild confusion; nothing acted by counsel, nothing by authority, but chance over-ruling every thing: so that though the day was far spent, the event was still uncertain. At last, both sides being fatigued with fighting and the heat of the day, Metellus, perceiving the Numidian vigour abated, rallied his men by degrees, restored their ranks, and posted four legionary cohorts against the enemy's foot, a great part of which had, through weariness, retired to the rising grounds for repose. At the same time he entreated and exhorted his men not to lose their courage, nor suffer a flying enemy to be victorious; adding, that they had no camp nor castles to fly to, but that all their hopes were in their arms. Nor was Jugurtha, indeed, in the meantime inactive, but rode about, animated his men, renewed the fight, and at the head of a select body, made all possible efforts; supported his men, where they were pressed; charged the enemy vigorously, where they wavered; and where they stood firm, annoyed them with darts at a distance.

Thus did these two generals contend; both excellent officers and equally matched, but unequally supported. Metellus had brave men, but a bad situation; Jugurtha had every other advantage but that of soldiers. At last the Romans, considering that no place of refuge was left them; that the enemy avoided every opportunity of engaging, and that night approached; advanced up the hill, according to orders, and made themselves masters of it. The Numidians, having lost this post, were routed and put to flight, but few of them slain: their own swiftness, and our being unacquainted with the country, saved most of them.

In the meantime, Bomilcar, to whom Ju

gurtha, as we have already related, had given the command of the elephants and part of the foot, when he saw that Rutilius had passed him, drew down his men gently into the plain; where, without being interrupted, he drew them up in order of battle, as the exigency required, whilst the lieutenant-general was marching with great haste to the river, whither the consul had sent him; nor did he neglect to inform himself of what the Romans were doing on every side. As soon as he had learned that Rutilius was encamped, and free from all apprehensions of danger; and perceiving that the noise of the battle, wherein Jugurtha was engaged, grew greater; fearing lest the lieutenant-general, upon discovering the matter, should return to the relief of our men in distress, in order to obstruct his passage, he extended his front, which before, distrusting the bravery of his troops, he had formed close and compact; and in this order advanced to the camp of Rutilius.

The Romans on a sudden perceived a great cloud of dust, which at first they supposed was raised by the wind driving the dry soil; for the country being covered with bushes hindered their view of the Numidians: but observing it to continue constant, and approach nearer and nearer as the army moved, they perceived what the cause of it was; and flying to their arms, drew up before the camp, according to orders. When the enemy was come up, they encountered on both sides with terrible shouts. The Numidians maintained the fight as long as they thought their elephants could be of any service to them; but when they saw them entangled among the branches of the trees, and surrounded by our men, they betook themselves to flight, and throwing away their arms, escaped most of them unhurt, partly by the advantage of the hill and partly by that of the night.

Four elephants were taken; the rest, forty in number were all slain. The Romans, however, though fatigued with their march, with fortifying their camp, and fighting; and though all highly pleased with their success, yet, as Metellus tarried beyond their expectation, they advanced resolutely in order of battle to meet him: for such was the Numidian subtilty, as to leave no room for inactivity or remissness. When they were at a small distance from one another, as the night was dark, the noise on both sides greatly alarmed each with the apprehensions of an approaching enemy; and

this mistake had like to have produced the most fatal consequences, if some horsemen, despatched by both parties, had not discovered the true cause of it. Whereupon their fear was quickly changed into gladness; the soldiers joyfully called to one another by name: mutually recounted their late exploits: and every one extolling his own gallant behaviour to the skies. For such is the nature of human affairs; upon a victory, even cowards may boast; whilst a defeat casts reproach even on the brave.

Metellus continued four days in the same camp; took proper care of the wounded; conferred the usual military rewards on such as had distinguished themselves in the late engagements; commended the whole army, which he assembled with that view; returned them his public thanks; then exhorted them "to act with equal courage in what farther remained, which was but little. They had already fought sufficiently for victory; their future labours would be only to enrich themselves with plunder." In the meantime, however, he despatched away deserters, and other proper persons, to discover where Jugurtha was; what he was doing; whether he was at the head of an army, or attended only with a few; and how he brooked his defeat. The king, he found, had retired into woods and places fortified by nature, and raised an army more numerous than the former, but weak and spiritless; better acquainted with tilling and pasture, than with war: the reason of which was, that, upon a defeat, none of the Numidians follow their king, excepting his horseguards; the rest go wherever they please. Nor is this reckoned any reproach, it being the custom of the nation.

Metellus, when he saw that the king's spirit was still undaunted, that the war was to be renewed, which could not be carried on but just as Jugurtha pleased; and moreover considered, upon what unequal terms he engaged the enemy, who suffered less by a defeat, than he did in defeating them; he resolved to pursue the war, not regularly by pitched battles, but in a different manner. Accordingly, he marches into the richest parts of Numidia; ravages the country; takes many towns and castles, that were either slightly fortified or without garrisons, and burns them; orders the youth to be put to the sword, and gives every thing else to the soldiers for spoil. This man-

ner of proceeding struck such terror, that many
hostages were given him; corn, and other necessaries plentifully supplied; and garrisons
suffered to be placed wherever he judged convenient. These measures alarmed the king
more than the loss of the late battle; for he,
who had no hopes but in flying before us, was
now forced to follow us; and though he could
not defend his own territories, he was obliged
to wage war in those possessed by the Romans.
Under this difficulty, however, he pursued such
measures as seemed most advisable. He ordered the greatest part of his army to continue together, whilst he himself, with a select
body of cavalry, pursued Metellus; and by
marching in the night-time through by-roads,
he surprised such of our men as were rambling
over the country; most of whom being unarmed
were slain, many were taken prisoners, and none
escaped without being wounded. For before
any assistance could be sent them from the
camp, the Numidians had, according to orders,
retired to the neighbouring hills.

In the meantime, there was great joy at
Rome when they heard of the management of
Metellus; "how he had conducted himself
and his army according to the ancient discipline; had, by his bravery, come off victorious,
though under the disadvantage of situation;
had made himself master of the enemy's country; and forced Jugurtha, whom the infamous
conduct of Aulus had lately rendered so insolent, to place all his hopes of safety in flight and
deserts." The senate, therefore, appointed
public thanksgivings and oblations to the immortal gods for the success of their arms. The
city, before full of anxiety for the event of the
war, was now full of joy, and nothing was to
be heard but the praises of Metellus; which
made him exert more vigorous efforts to obtain
a complete victory: with which view he pushed
all his measures with the utmost diligence,
still guarding, however, against any surprise
from the enemy; and remembering, that after
glory comes envy. Thus the more renowned
he was, the more vigilant he became; nor since
the late unexpected attack from Jugurtha,
would he suffer his men to spread themselves
over the country in quest of plunder. When
he stood in need of corn or forage, he detached
all the cavalry, with some bands of foot, to
guard it. One part of the army he commanded
himself, and Marius the other; the country was
laid waste more by fire than depredations.

The two bodies of the army encamped separately, but at a small distance from each other;
and when there was occasion for it, they
united; but in order to spread terror and
desolation the farther, they acted apart. Jugurtha all this time followed them upon the
mountains, watching some favourable opportunity or situation to attack them; and whenever he heard which way they intended to
march, he destroyed the forage and the springs,
of which there was great scarcity. One
while he presented himself to Metellus, another
to Marius; sometimes he fell upon their rear,
and then presently drew off to the hills; by
and by he attacked them again, now in one
quarter, now in another; neither venturing a
battle, nor suffering them to be quiet; but only
endeavouring to hinder the execution of their
designs.

When the Roman general perceived that he
was harassed by the artful management of the
enemy, who avoided all occasions of giving
him battle, he determined to lay siege to Zama, a very considerable city, and the bulwark
of the kingdom on that side; supposing that
Jugurtha would not fail to advance to the relief
of his subjects in that distress, and that an engagement would thereupon ensue. But Jugurtha, having got intelligence of this design
from the deserters, reached Zama by great
marches before Metellus; encouraged the inhabitants to defend their walls, and reinforced
them with a body of deserters, who were the
most desperate of all his forces, as they durst
not betray him. He promised besides, that he
would return in due time to their assistance at
the head of an army. Having thus regulated
his affairs, he withdrew into the most solitary
parts of the country; and soon after being informed that Marius, with a few cohorts, was
sent from the army as it marched, to bring
provisions from Sicca, which was the first town
that revolted from him after his defeat, he
went thither by night, with a select body of
horse, and attacked the Romans just as they
were returning through the gate. At the
same time he called aloud to the inhabitants,
"to fall upon the cohorts in the rear; that
fortune presented them with an opportunity of
performing a noble achievement; which if
they did, that he should for the future enjoy
his kingdom, and they their liberties in safety."
And had not Marius advanced the standards,
and got speedily out of the town, the greatest

part of the inhabitants, if not all, would certainly have changed sides; such is the inconstancy of the Numidians. But Jugurtha's troops, who, being animated by him, had for a short time maintained the fight, finding themselves pressed by the Romans with superior vigour, fled with the loss of a few of their men, and Marius arrived before Zama.

This town was built on a plain; better fortified by art than nature; well furnished with every thing necessary; and abounding with men and arms. Metellus, having regulated every thing as the occasion and undertaking required, surrounded it with his army; assigned his lieutenants their several posts of command; and then, upon a signal given, a great shout was raised at once from all quarters. This, however, did not terrify the Numidians, who waited the attack without any disorder, full of ardour and resolution. Accordingly the encounter began; our men fought each according to his inclination; some at a distance, with stones and slings; some withdrew after they had attacked, and others came in their place; one while they undermined the walls, another they endeavoured to scale them; all eager to engage the enemy in close fight. The townsmen, on the other hand, rolled down stones on those who came nearest the walls; and discharged darts, stakes, and burning torches of pitch and sulphur upon them. Nor were such of our men as kept at a distance through fear, the more secure for it; most of them being wounded by weapons thrown by engines, or by force of arm. So that the cowards were exposed to equal danger with the brave, without sharing their glory.

During this contest at Zama, Jugurtha, at the head of a great body of troops, surprised the Roman camp, and by reason of the negligence of the guard, who apprehended nothing less than an attack, broke in at one of the gates. Our men, struck with sudden consternation, consulted their safety, each according to his character: some fled, others had recourse to their arms, and many of them were wounded or slain. Of all the number, there were only forty who acted like Romans: they, forming themselves into a body, took possession of a rising ground, which they maintained against the most vigorous efforts of the enemy to dispossess them; and even returned the darts that were thrown at them, which did the more exe-

cution, as they were few against many. If the Numidians ventured nearer them, then they exerted their utmost bravery; slaying, routing, and putting them to flight.

In the meantime, whilst Metellus was carrying on the siege of Zama with great vigour, he heard a noise and shouting behind him, like that of an enemy; and turning his horse, observed men flying towards him, a certain proof that they were his own. Wherefore he immediately sent the whole cavalry to the camp, and soon after C. Marius with the auxiliary cohorts, conjuring him with tears, " by their mutual friendship, by his regard to the public welfare, not to suffer such a stain to rest upon a victorious army, nor the enemy to escape without taking ample vengeance upon them." Marius quickly executed his orders.

Jugurtha now found himself and his men embarrassed in our intrenchments: some threw themselves over the rampart; the rest, striving to get through the gates, which were too narrow, obstructed one another; so that after the loss of a great many men, he betook himself to his strong holds. Metellus, not succeeding in his attempt upon the town, returned in the evening with his army to the camp.

The next day, before he returned to renew the assault, he posted all his horse without the camp, with orders to guard that side on which he expected Jugurtha would appear; and having distributed the guard of the gates and the adjoining posts amongst the tribunes, he advanced to the town, and made an assault upon the walls as he had done the day before. Jugurtha in the meantime, leaving his covert, fell suddenly upon our men. Those of the advanced guard being somewhat terrified, were put into disorder, but quickly relieved by the rest; so that the Numidians could not have maintained their ground any longer, if their foot, mixing with their horse, had not done great execution among us; for the horse, trusting to the assistance of the foot, did not charge as formerly, advancing and retiring by turns, but pressed forward with great vigour, grappled with our men and broke them; then delivered them up, when nigh conquered, to be despatched by their light-armed foot.

During this very time there was a sharp conflict at Zama: the lieutenants and tribunes made prodigious efforts in their several posts; all placing their hopes of victory in their own bravery, rather than in the assistance of others. The townsmen, too, made a vigorous resistance, boldly repulsing our men, and defending themselves resolutely in every quarter. They were more eager, indeed, on both sides, to wound the enemy than to protect themselves. A confused noise of exhortations, shouts of joy, and groans, arose continually; the din of arms reached the skies, and darts flew thick on every side. Those who defended the walls, when they found the fury of the besiegers ever so little abated, viewed the engagement of the cavalry with great earnestness: and according as Jugurtha prevailed or not, you might have observed their joy or concern: nay, as if they could have been heard or seen by their friends, some advised them, others encouraged them, making signs with their hands, and moving their bodies this way and that, as if they had been avoiding darts or throwing them. When Marius, who commanded in that quarter, observed this, he purposely slackened his attack, as if he had lost all hopes of success, and suffered them to view the engagement at the camp without interruption. Then, whilst their attention was closely engaged, he made a sudden and vigorous assault upon the walls; and the soldiers had almost gained the top of them with their scaling ladders, when the townsmen flying to their defence, poured down upon the besiegers stones, fire, and all sorts of weapons. Our men sustained all this for a while; but some of the ladders breaking down, and those who stood upon them tumbling headlong, the rest retreated each as he could, the greatest part of them covered with wounds, few escaping unhurt. At last, night put an end to the combat.

Metellus, finding that his attempt upon the town was unsuccessful; that Jugurtha was determined not to engage, unless by surprise, or where he had the advantage of the ground, and that the summer was already over, left Zama, and placed garrisons in those cities which had revolted to him, and were strong by nature or well fortified; then put his army into winter quarters in those parts of our province where it borders upon Numidia. Nor did he spend his time there, as others had done, in luxury and inaction; but finding what small progress he made in the war by fighting, he formed a design to defeat the king by employing the treachery of his friends against him instead of arms. Accordingly he applies to Bomilcar, who had been at Rome with Jugurtha, and being ar-

raigned for the murder of Massiva, had fled from thence to evade his trial, abandoning his sureties. This man, who had the best opportunity of betraying the king upon account of his great intimacy with him, Metellus prevailed upon, by the force of promises, to come, first to a private conference with him; then, pledging his honour, "that if he would deliver to him Jugurtha dead or alive, he would procure him his pardon from the senate, with the enjoyment of his whole fortune;" he easily persuaded the Numidian, who was naturally faithless, and likewise afraid lest, if a peace was concluded with the Romans, he should, by the articles of it, be delivered up to punishment.

Bomilcar, as soon as he found an opportunity, accosted Jugurtha, when full of anxiety, and lamenting his lot; and with tears in his eyes pressed and conjured him, "to consult at last his own safety, that of his children, and the Numidians, who had been so zealously devoted to his service. He begged of him to consider, that he had been defeated in every engagement; that his country was laid waste; many of his subjects taken; many of them slain; the strength of his kingdom exhausted; that he had already sufficiently tried the bravery of his troops and the inclination of fortune, and ought now to take care lest the Numidians, whilst he thus delayed, should provide for their own safety." By these and the like arguments he prevailed upon the king to surrender. Accordingly ambassadors were sent to Metellus, to let him know that Jugurtha was ready to submit to whatever he should desire, and to deliver himself and his kingdom absolutely to his disposal. Metellus forthwith ordered all those of senatorial rank to be summoned from their winter quarters, and advised with them, and others whom he thought proper to consult upon the occasion; acting herein according to ancient usage. Then, agreeably to an order of the council, he sent deputies to Jugurtha, commanding him, "to deliver up to the Romans two hundred thousand pounds of silver, all his elephants, with some horses and arms." This being immediately complied with, he ordered "all our deserters to be brought him in chains." A great part of them were brought accordingly; the rest, who were but few in number, had fled for refuge to Bocchus king of Mauritania, upon the first appearance of a surrender. When Jugurtha, thus stripped of his arms, men, and money, was himself summoned to Tisidium;

surrender to the consul, he began again to change his mind, and to dread the punishment which he was conscious to himself was due to his crimes. Many days were spent by him in irresolution: one while he preferred any terms whatever to war, being tired with calamities; another, he considered what a terrible fall it was from a throne to servitude: but at last he determined to renew the war, after he had needlessly divested himself of so considerable a part of his strength. The senate at Rome, too, having met to consult about the distribution of provinces, had, during this juncture, decreed Numidia to Metellus.

About the same time, as C. Marius, who happened to be at Utica, was sacrificing to the gods, he was told by a diviner, "that great and wonderful things were presaged to him; he should therefore pursue whatever designs he had formed, and trust the gods for their success; he might try fortune as much as he pleased, all his undertakings would succeed." Now Marius had been long seized with an ardent desire of the consulship, and had indeed every qualification for obtaining it, except that of a noble descent: he had industry, probity, vast knowledge in war, great spirit in battle, uncommon sobriety, a soul that disdained to be enslaved to riches or pleasure, and which only thirsted after glory. He was born at Arpinum, where he passed his childhood; and as soon as he was of age to bear arms, he did not give himself up to the study of Grecian eloquence, nor to the delicacies of Rome, but to the life of a soldier; and thus, in a short time, did this excellent genius, by a proper course of discipline, acquire a masterly knowledge in war: so that when he made his first suit to the people for the military tribuneship, though the greatest part of them did not know his face, his character was so well known, that he obtained it by the voices of all the tribes. After that, he mounted still higher; and in every office which he bore behaved so well, that he was always thought to deserve a greater. Yet Marius, with all his merit, till this time (for ambition afterwards hurried him into strange excesses) had not dared to stand for the consulship. For though the people at that time conferred all the other offices, that of consul the nobility engrossed to themselves: every new man, however renowned or distinguished by his merit, was reckoned by them unworthy of that supreme magistracy, and, as it were, a profane person.

When Marius perceived that the answer from the diviner was agreeable to his own inclinations, he petitioned Metellus for leave to go to Rome to stand for the consulship. Metellus, though he had a great deal of virtue and honour, and other desirable qualities, yet possessed a haughty and disdainful spirit, the common failing of the nobility; he was, therefore, at first struck with so extraordinary a request, expressed his great surprise at his designs, and advised him, as in friendship, — not to entertain such unreasonable views, nor suffer his mind to be exalted above his station; it did not become every man to aspire after every thing; he ought to be contented with his present condition; in a word, he ought to take care not to demand that of the Roman people which they might justly refuse him." When, after these and the like remonstrances, he still found Marius steady to his purpose, he promised to grant his request, as soon as the condition of public affairs would allow him. After this, as he still continued to urge his petition, Metellus is reported to have told him; "that he had no need to be in such a hurry, for that it would be time enough for him to stand for the consulship, when his son was of age to join with him." This youth was then about twenty years of age, and serving under his father, but had no command.

This fired Marius with a more ardent desire of obtaining the consulship, and highly incensed him against Metellus; so that he blindly followed the dictates of ambition and resentment, the worst of counsellors. He did and said every thing that could promote his views: he gave greater liberty to the soldiers under his command in their winter quarters than formerly; he inveighed severely to our traders, then in great numbers at Utica, against Metellus's manner of conducting the war, and boasted greatly of himself; "that were but half the army under his command, he would in a few days have Jugurtha in chains: that the consul prolonged the war on purpose, being a vain man, possessed of kingly pride, and fond of command." All which was the more readily believed by those traders, as they had suffered in their fortunes by the long continuance of the war; and to an impatient spirit, no measures appear expeditious enough.

There was, besides, in our army a Numidian named Gauda, the son of Manastabal, and grandson of Masinissa, whom Micipsa had appointed next heir to his immediate successors; one whose bodily disorders had impaired the faculties of his mind. This man had applied to Metellus for a seat next him, and afterwards for a troop of Roman horse for his guard, and was denied both: the seat, because it was conferred on none but those whom the Roman people distinguished with the title of kings; the troop, because it would be an affront to the Roman horse to be body guards to a Numidian. This double refusal filled his mind with discontent, in the height of which Marius accosted him, and prompted him to seek revenge for the affronts put upon him by the general, promising him his assistance. By soothing speeches he filled the imagination of the man, whose faculties were weakened by diseases, with a high conceit of his own dignity, extolling him "as a prince, a person of great importance, the grandson of Masinissa; one who would forthwith get the kingdom of Numidia, were Jugurtha once taken or slain, which would presently happen, if he himself was made consul, and had the management of the war."

By these means, not only Gauda, but the Roman knights, soldiers, and traders, were all engaged, some by Marius, most of them by their hopes of a speedy peace, to write to their friends at Rome concerning the war, with severe invectives against Metellus, and to desire Marius might be made general. Thus the consulship was solicited for him by great numbers of men, in a manner highly honourable to him. The people, too, at this juncture having given a deep wound to the power of the nobility by the Mamilian law, were proceeding to raise plebeians to the chief magistracies; so that every thing favoured the views of Marius.

Jugurtha, in the meantime, having dropped his purpose of surrendering, and begun the war afresh, made preparations for it with the utmost diligence and despatch. He raised an army; endeavoured by threats or promises, to recover the cities which had revolted from him; fortified what places he still held; made or bought arms and warlike stores, in the room of those which he had parted with in hopes of peace; solicited the Roman slaves to join him; tempted those who were in the garrisons with his money; in a word, he left nothing unattempted; raised commotions every where, and pushed every possible measure. In consequence of these efforts, the principal inhabitants of Vacca, where Metellus had placed a garrison upon the first proposals made by Jugurtha for a peace, being wearied out with the king's importunities, and indeed not alienated from him in their affections, entered into a conspiracy for betraying the city. For the populace were, what they generally are every where, more especially in Numidia, inconstant, seditious, fond of disturbances and innovations, and enemies to tranquillity and repose. Having concerted their scheme, they pitched upon the third day following for the execution of it; because that being a festival, to be celebrated throughout all Africa, was thought a more proper season to inspire mirth and jollity, than fear and distrust. When the day came, the conspirators invited the centurions, the military tribunes, and T. Turpilius Silanus, governor of the city, to their several houses, and butchered them all amidst the feast, except Turpilius; after which they fell upon the soldiers, who, as it was a day of rejoicing, were dispersed over the town, without their arms, and under no command. The populace joined them, part of them being instructed beforehand by the nobility, and others pushed on by their passion for such proceedings, being highly pleased with the commotion and the novelty of the thing, though they neither knew what was transacting, nor the reason of it.

The Roman soldiers, struck with this sudden alarm, and not knowing whence it arose, nor what course to take, fled in great confusion to the castle, where their standards and shields lay; but found it shut and guarded by the enemy. The city gates too were shut, to prevent their escape; and to heighten their calamity, the women and children with great fury poured down upon them, from the tops of the houses, stones and whatever else came to their hands. Being thus beset with danger in various shapes, without being able to guard against it, and the bravest men incapable of resisting the weakest hands; the worthless and the worthy, the daring and the cowardly, perished all alike unrevenged. During so direful a massacre, whilst the Numidians exercised the utmost rage and cruelty, and the city was shut on all sides, Turpilius the governor escaped unhurt, the only Italian who did so: but whether this was owing to the kindness of his host, to private compact, or chance, does not clearly appear; which way so ever it was, he must be considered as worthless and infamous wretch, since in so great a calamity to the state, he preferred an inglorious life to unsullied honour.

Metellus, when he heard of what had passed at Vacca, was so deeply afflicted, that he did not appear in public for some time; but indignation mixing with his grief, he made all possible haste to revenge the injury. Accordingly he drew out the legion which wintered with him, with as many light Numidian horse as he could get together, and marching about sunset at the head of this detachment, he arrived next morning, about the third hour, in a certain place enclosed on all sides with small eminences. There, the soldiers being fatigued with the length of their march, and refusing to obey any further orders, he informed them that the town of Vacca was not above a mile off; and that it became them patiently to endure the small remaining fatigue, since it was to take vengeance for the death of their fellow-citizens, the bravest of men, and miserably massacred. He likewise generously offered them the whole plunder; and having thus roused their courage, he placed the cavalry in the front, ordering them to extend themselves as wide as possible, and the foot to march in close array, concealing their standards.

The inhabitants of Vacca observing an army march towards them, judged rightly at first, that it was Metellus, and accordingly shut their gates; but when they saw that the lands were not ravaged, and that those in the front were Numidian horse, they next imagined it was Jugurtha, and went out with great joy to meet him. Our horse and foot, upon a sudden signal given, immediately fell upon them; some cut off the rabble that poured out of the city in great numbers; others hastened to secure the gates; and part seized upon the towers: their thirst of vengeance, and hopes of plunder, making them forget their weariness. Thus the people of Vacca triumphed only for two days in their treachery; and their city, which was great and opulent, was delivered up wholly to the fury of our soldiers, eager for vengeance and rapine. Turpilius, the governor of the city, who, as we have already related, was the only one that made his escape, was summoned before Metellus, to answer for his conduct; but not clearing himself, he was condemned, sentenced to be scourged, and then put to death: a punishment inflicted upon him as a native of Latium.

About this time, Bomilcar, at whose instigation Jugurtha had offered to surrender, though he was prevented by fear from doing it, was very desirous of bringing about a revolution, for the king and he were filled with distrust of each other. Accordingly he was contriving plots for Jugurtha's destruction both day and night; and, after revolving a variety of schemes in his mind, he took Nabdalsa for his associate, a nobleman of great riches and highly beloved by his countrymen, who used to command an army apart from the king, and manage all such affairs as Jugurtha, when fatigued with others, or engaged in those of greater moment, could not despatch himself; by which means he acquired great glory and wealth.

A day was agreed upon by those two for the execution of the plot, and all other measures were left to be regulated as occasion should require: upon which Nabdalsa went to the army, which, agreeably to the king's orders, he kept in the neighbourhood of our winter quarters, in order to prevent the ravaging the country with impunity. But being afterwards struck with the enormity of the enterprise, and prevented by fear from coming at the time appointed, Bomilcar, who was impatient to accomplish his design, and greatly concerned lest his associate should depart from his late engagements, and consult his own safety by a discovery, sent a letter to him by such as he could confide in, wherein he upbraided him with effeminacy and want of spirit; called the gods, by whom he had sworn, to witness; and warned him, " not to turn the rewards offered by Metellus to his own destruction; Jugurtha's ruin was at hand; the only thing to be considered was whether it was to be effected by their bravery or that of Metellus; he ought therefore to think with himself which he would make choice of, a great recompense, or a cruel death."

It happened, that Nabdalsa received this letter at a time when, being much fatigued after a great deal of exercise, he was reposing himself on his bed: upon reading it, he was at first filled with great anxiety; then, as is usual to minds burdened with cares, sleep seized him. He had in his service a certain Numidian of approved fidelity, who was highly in favour, and acquainted with all his designs except this last: this man, when he heard that a letter was brought, supposing that there would be occasion, as usual, for his service or counsel, went into his master's tent, and finding him asleep took the letter, which lay negligently behind his head on the pillow, and read it; and having discovered the plot, went with all possible haste to the king. Nabdalsa, who waked soon after, missing his letter, and being informed by deserters of all that had passed, endeavoured at first to have his accuser intercepted; but failing in that, he went directly to the king, to try to appease him. He affirmed that he was prevented from making the discovery himself, by the treachery of his servant; and with tears in his eyes conjured him, "by their mutual friendship, by his faithful past services, not to suspect him of so foul a crime." To this the king returned a gracious answer, very different from what he thought; and putting Bomilcar to death, with others whom he knew to be accomplices in the plot, he suppressed his resentment, lest, by making any more sacrifices to his vengeance, he should occasion an insurrection.

From this time Jugurtha enjoyed no tranquillity of mind day or night; judged himself insecure in every place, with every person, and upon every occasion; equally distrusted his subjects and his enemies; was constantly upon his guard; affrighted at every noise; passed his nights one while here, another there, often in places very unsuitable to royal dignity; sometimes started out of his sleep in the dead of night, and snatching his arms, raised an alarm. Thus did his fears, like a phrenzy, continually tear and transport him.

Metellus, when he received intelligence by deserters of the fate of Bomilcar and the discovery of the plot, made preparations afresh with the utmost vigour, as if the war had been but just beginning. And as Marius was constantly importuning him for leave to be gone, he now dismissed him, thinking it improper to trust him, as he served with reluctance, and bore him personal enmity. At Rome too, the populace, when they learned the contents of the letters which were sent from Africa concerning Metellus and Marius, were well pleased with the accounts of both. The high quality of the general, which had hitherto been a motive for honouring him, exposed him now to the odium of the people; whilst the obscurity of his lieutenant's birth recommended him to their favour: but still the different parties were more influenced by their partiality, than the good or bad qualities of either. Besides, the factious magistrates inflamed the multitude, by charging Metellus with capital crimes, in all

their harangues, and highly celebrating the merit of Marius. At length the people were so fired, that the mechanics and boors, whose whole substance and credit were derived from their daily labour, quitting their several employments, crowded from all quarters to attend upon Marius; and were more concerned for his advancement, than for procuring the necessaries of life to themselves. The nobility being thus depressed, the consulship was bestowed upon a new man, which had not happened for many years before. After this, when the people were asked by Manlius Mantinus, tribune of the people, to whom they would commit the management of the war against Jugurtha, they in a full assembly assigned it to Marius, which rendered abortive the decree of the senate, that a little before had decreed Numidia to Metellus.

In the meantime Jugurtha, finding himself bereft of his confidants, most of whom indeed had been put to death by him, and the rest apprehending the like fate had fled, some to the Romans, others to king Bocchus, was agitated with great perplexity of mind, and knew not what to do. He saw it was impossible to carry on the war without ministers, and thought it dangerous to risk the fidelity of new ones, after having met with so much treachery in the old: no scheme, no advice, no person could please him; he shifted his marches, and changed his officers every day; one while he moved towards the enemy, another towards the deserts; oftentimes he placed all his security in flight, presently after in arms; nor could he determine whether the fidelity or courage of his subjects was least to be confided in: thus, which way soever he turned his thoughts, he found nothing but vexation and discouragement.

During this irresolution, Metellus on a sudden appeared with his army. Jugurtha improved what little time he had to draw up his men in order of battle; after which the combat began, and which was maintained for some time where the king fought in person, but the rest of the army was routed and put to flight upon the first encounter. The Romans took all their standards and arms, with a small number of prisoners. The swiftness of the Numidians, indeed, in all their engagements with the Romans, was more serviceable to them than their arms.

After this defeat, Jugurtha, having less hopes of success than ever, retired with some deserters and part of his cavalry to the deserts and from thence to Thala, a great and wealthy town, where his treasure was chiefly kept, and his children educated in a very princely manner. When Metellus was informed of this, though he knew that between the adjoining river and the city he had to march through a wilderness of fifty miles' extent, yet, hoping to put an end to the war by the reduction of that city, he determined to bid defiance to all difficulties, and attempted even to triumph over nature herself. He therefore gave orders that the usual burdens should be taken from the beasts of carriage, and that they should be laden only with corn for ten days, together with leathern bottles, and other utensils proper for carrying of water. Besides, he got together all the beasts of burden he could find in the neighbouring country, and loaded them with vessels of every kind, but mostly of wood, procured from the cottages of the Numidians. He moreover commanded the natives of the neighbourhood, who had surrendered themselves to him after the defeat of the king, to furnish themselves with as much water as they could carry, and bring it to a certain place, which he appointed, fixing the time for doing it. For a supply to himself, he loaded his beasts from the river, which, as we have already related, was the nighest water to the town: and thus provided he advanced towards Thala.

When he was arrived at the place where he had ordered the Numidians to meet him, and had pitched and fortified his camp, such a flood of rain is said to have fallen as would alone have been more than sufficient for the whole army. Provisions, too, were brought him in greater plenty than he expected; for the Numidians, as is usual with those who have submitted to new masters, had even brought more than was demanded of them. The soldiers, from a principle of superstition, chose chiefly the water which fell from the heavens; for they imagined they were the objects of the particular care of the immortal gods, and this greatly heightened their courage. The next day, contrary to Jugurtha's expectation, they arrived before Thala. The inhabitants, who imagined themselves sufficiently secured by their situation, were struck with astonishment at so strange an event; but nevertheless made vigorous preparations for defending themselves, as did our men for attacking them.

The king, thinking now that nothing was too hard for Metellus, who had by his vigour triumphed over arms, places, seasons, nay, even over nature herself, which forces every thing else to submit to her, fled out of the town in the night-time, with his children and great part of his treasure. Nor did he ever after tarry above a day or night in one place; pretending that it was business which thus hurried him, though in reality he was apprehensive of treasonable practices, which he hoped to prevent by his expedition; being persuaded that such designs were only formed by leisure and opportunity.

Metellus, finding that the inhabitants were determined to fight in their own defence, and that the city was strong both by art and nature, surrounded it with a trench and rampart; then ordered his men to roll the moving machines to all convenient places, to raise mounds upon them, and towers upon the mounds, in order to defend the work and those who conducted it. The besieged did not fail to make other preparations against these, and acted with great spirit and vigour; nothing indeed was left unattempted on either side. The Romans at length, spent with much toil and many sharp conflicts, made themselves masters of the bare city, after a forty days' siege; the whole spoil being destroyed by the deserters. For they, as soon as they found the walls beaten by the battering rams, and their own case desperate, carried away the gold and silver, with whatever else was esteemed valuable, to the royal palace; and there, after glutting themselves with wine and feasting, they committed all to the flames, the wealth, the palace, and their own lives; inflicting voluntarily upon themselves the severest punishment they could have apprehended from the enemy, had they fallen into their hands.

Just when Thala was taken, deputies came to Metellus from Leptis, to beg of him that he would send them a garrison and a governor; for that one Hamilcar, a factious nobleman, whom neither the power of the magistrates nor the authority of the laws was able to restrain, was labouring to bring about a revolution; and that unless he sent them present assistance, they, the allies of Rome, would be in the utmost danger. The people of Leptis had indeed, at the beginning of the war with Jugurtha, sent first to the consul Bestia, and afterwards to Rome, desiring to be admitted to friendship and alliance with us. From that time, their request being granted, they continued our good and faithful allies, and readily complied with all the orders they received from Bestia, Albinus, and Metellus. Wherefore they easily obtained from the general what they requested of him. Four cohorts of Ligurians were sent thither, and C. Annius as governor.

The city of Leptis was founded by the Sidonians, who, we are told, quitted their country on account of their civil broils, and came by sea into those parts: it is situated between the two Syrtes, places so called from their quality. They are two bays almost in the extremity of Africa, of unequal bigness, but naturally alike; near the shores of which the sea is very deep; elsewhere it is sometimes deep, sometimes shallow, just as the wind happens to blow. For when the sea begins to swell, and to be agitated by the winds, the waves roll along with them slime, sand, and stones of a prodigious size; so that as the wind shifts, the bed of the waters changes; and from this quality of dragging their channel they derive their name of Syrtes.

The inhabitants of this city have by their intermarriages with the Numidians changed their native language, but still retained the greatest part of the laws and customs of the Sidonians, which they have done the more easily, because of their being at so great a distance from the Numidian court: for between them and such parts of Numidia as are well peopled are vast deserts.

Now that the affairs of Leptis have led me to discourse of this country, it seems not improper to give an account of a famed and surprising adventure of two Carthaginians:—the place puts me in mind of it.

Whilst the Carthaginians were masters of the greatest part of Africa, the Cyrenians too were a powerful and wealthy people. Between them there lay a vast sandy plain, altogether uniform, without river or mountain to ascertain the boundaries of their several territories; which proved the occasion of long and bloody wars. After their fleets and armies had been often routed and put to flight on both sides, and they had considerably weakened one another, apprehending lest some common enemy should fall upon the conquerors or conquered, both equally exhausted, they came first to a cessation of arms, then to an agreement, that each city should send out deputies at a stated time, and that the place where they met should be the common boundary of their dominions. Two brothers having the same name, that of

Philænus, were sent from Carthage, and travelled with great expedition. The Cyrenians advanced more slowly, whether from laziness or chance I have not been able to learn. This much is certain, that those parts are sometimes impassable, being equally liable to be agitated with tempests as the sea itself. For when the wind blows hard in these vast and naked plains, the sand being hurled from the earth, and driven with a mighty force, fills the mouths and eyes of travellers; and thus depriving them of their sight, hinders them from proceeding. The Cyrenians, finding themselves surpassed in expedition, and apprehending a severe punishment at home, for having occasioned so great a loss to their country, charged the Carthaginians with setting out before the limited time, made a mighty bustle, and declared they would do any thing rather than yield. Now when the Carthaginians desired any other method of deciding the matter that was but fair, the Cyrenians gave them their choice, "either of being buried alive in that place, where they were for fixing the boundary of their dominions, or of suffering them to proceed as far as they thought proper upon the same terms." The Philæni, accepting the condition, sacrified their persons and lives to the good of their country, and were buried alive in that very spot. There the Carthaginians erected altars sacred to them, and instituted other solemnities in Carthage itself, to immortalize their fame. I now return to my subject.

Jugurtha, **after the loss of** Thala, thinking nothing a sufficient security against Metellus, fled with a few **attendants through vast deserts,** into the country of the Getulians, a brutal unpolished race, and then unacquainted with the Roman name. Of these he got together a great number, and accustomed them by degrees to move in ranks, to follow their standards, to obey orders, and to perform all military exercises. Moreover, by great presents and greater promises, he gained over to his interest the greatest favourites of king Bocchus; and, applying to the king by their means, prevailed upon him to undertake a war against the Romans. This was the more easily effected, because Bocchus was filled with resentment against the Romans, for having refused to admit him into their friendship and alliance, which he had sent ambassadors to Rome to desire in the beginning of our war with Jugurtha; an alliance, extremely advantageous on such an occasion, but obstructed by a few noblemen, who, blinded with avarice, made it their custom to turn every thing into sale, whether honourable or infamous. Besides, Bocchus had, some time before, married a daughter of Jugurtha; though such an alliance is little regarded among the Numidians and Moors; for all have a plurality of wives, some ten, others more, according to their abilities to maintain them; and their kings consequently more than any. Amidst such a variety of women, the heart of man is distracted; so that none of them are looked upon as his companion, but all equally treated with contempt.

Accordingly the kings met with their armies at a place agreed on by both, where, after pledging their faith to one another, Jugurtha set himself to inflame the spirit of Bocchus, by representing to him " that the Romans were oppressive, insatiably covetous, and the common enemies of mankind; that they had the same cause for making war upon Bocchus as upon himself, and so many other nations, namely, their lust of dominion, which made them look upon all independent states as their enemies; that at present they pursued him as an enemy, as they had, a little before, king Perses and the Carthaginians; and that, for the future, whatever prince appeared considerable for his power, would be treated by them as an enemy."

After having said this and much more to the same purpose, they resolved upon marching to Cirta, because Metellus had there lodged his booty, prisoners, and baggage; whence Jugurtha thought that he should find his account abundantly, either in taking the city, or engaging the Romans if they came to its relief. Such was the subtlety of the Numidian, who, **by this** impatience for action, wanted only to prevent Bocchus from entertaining any thoughts of peace; lest, by delays, he might choose something very different from war.

Metellus, when he received intelligence of the confederacy of the kings, was more circumspect than when he had only to do with Jugurtha, whom he had so often defeated. He was not forward, as formerly, to engage the enemy upon all occasions, but, fortifying his camp, waited for the kings not far from Cirta; thinking it better, as the Moors were a new enemy, not to fight till he was acquainted with their character, that so he might do it with the more advantage. In the meantime he was informed from Rome that the province of Nu-

midia was assigned to Marius, for of his being advanced to the consulship he had heard before. This news mortified him extremely, and transported him beyond all the rules of decency or dignity; insomuch that he could neither refrain from tears, nor moderate his tongue. For, though he was a man otherwise eminently distinguished for every noble quality, he wanted strength of mind to bear up under vexation and grief. Some imputed this weakness to pride; others, to a worthy spirit provoked by bad usage: many to a deep concern, that the victory, already gained, should be snatched out of his hands. As for me, I have the greatest reason to believe that the advancement of Marius gave him more uneasiness than his own wrongs, and that he would have quitted his province with less regret, if it had been bestowed upon any other than Marius.

Not concerning himself therefore any further in the war through indignation, and thinking it folly to take care of the interest of another at his own hazard, he despatched deputies to king Bocchus, to admonish him, " not to become an enemy to the Roman people without any provocation: that he had now a fine opportunity of entering into friendship and alliance with them, which ought greatly to be preferred by him to war. What confidence soever he placed in his own strength, that still he ought not to exchange certainties for uncertainties; that it was an easy matter to begin a war, but extremely difficult to conclude it: that it was not in the power of the same person to undertake and to terminate it: that the conqueror could only drop it, though even a coward might stir it up: that he should therefore consult his own interest and that of his kingdom, and not blend his own flourishing circumstances with the desperate fortune of Jugurtha." To this the king replied courteously, " that he too desired peace, but pitied Jugurtha; if he were to be included in it, they should soon agree." Again the Roman general sent deputies with an answer to the demands of Bocchus, who was satisfied with some particulars, and rejected others. Thus, by sending and returning deputies, the time was spun out, and the war protracted, agreeably to Metellus's desire, without any hostilities.

Marius, who had been created consul by the people with all the proofs of the warmest zeal for his interest, as we have above related, when he was likewise made governor of Numidia by them, behaved towards the nobility

against whom he was before highly exasperated, with more fury and insolence than ever;
sometimes he insulted particular persons, sometimes the whole body. He was continually
boasting that he had wrested the consulship
from them like spoils from a vanquished enemy, with many things of the like nature, all
to extol himself and mortify them. In the
meantime, his principal care was to provide
every thing necessary for the war; he demanded recruits for the legions; and sent for auxiliaries from foreign states, kings, and allies.
He, moreover, summoned from Latium all the
bravest men, most of whom he himself knew
by their having served with him, so that there
were but few whose characters he had learned
from common fame; and even, by the force of
persuasion, prevailed upon the discharged veterans to go along with him. Nor durst the
senate, though his avowed enemies, deny him
any thing, nay they even cheerfully decreed
him recruits; because they imagined the populace would be averse to enlist, and so Marius
would either not be able to pursue the war, or
lose the affections of the people. But herein
they were disappointed; so eager a desire of
going with Marius had seized most of them.
Every man flattered himself to return crowned
with victory, and enriched with spoil, with the
like pleasing thoughts. Marius indeed had,
by a speech of his, not a little contributed to
raise their expectations; for, after all he desired
had been granted him, resolving to raise
recruits, he called an assembly of the people,
both to encourage them to follow him, and to
inveigh against the nobility, as he was wont:
he then harangued them in the following manner :—

"I know, Romans, that most of those who
apply to you for preferment in the state, assume
a different conduct from what they observe after they have obtained it. When they are
candidates, they are active, condescending, and
modest; when magistrates, haughty and indolent; but to me the contrary conduct appears
reasonable. For in proportion as the good of
the state is of more importance than the consulship or prætorship, the greater care and
attention is requisite to govern the commonwealth, than to court its dignities. I am very
sensible what an arduous task is imposed upon
me by your generous choice of me; to make
preparations for the war, and yet to be sparing
of the treasury; to oblige those to serve, whom

you would not willingly offend; to attend to
every thing both at home and abroad; and to
perform all this amidst a confederacy of envi-
ous men, eternally obstructing your measures,
and caballing against you, is, O Romans, a
more difficult undertaking than can easily be
imagined. Moreover, if others fail in the discharge of their duty, the ancient lustre of
their family, the heroic actions of their ancestors, the credit of their **kindred and** friends,
and their numerous **dependants**, afford them
protection. As for me, I have no hopes but in
myself; my firmness and integrity alone must
protect me, every other support would be of
little avail. I am well aware too, Romans,
that the eyes of all are upon me; that all honest, all candid men, pleased with my successful
endeavours to serve the state, wish well to
me; but that the nobility watch for an opportunity to ruin me. Whence I must labour the
more strenuously that you be not ensnared by
them; and that they be disappointed. From
my childhood to the present time, my manner
of life has been such, that toils and dangers
are now habitual to me. The course I pursued, Romans, merely from a disinterested principle, before you conferred any favours upon
me, I shall be far from discontinuing now you
have bestowed so noble a recompense. Those
who put on the deceitful guise and semblance
of virtue, to obtain power, must, when possessed of it, find it difficult to act with moderation; but to me, whose whole life has been an
uninterrupted series of laudable pursuits, virtue, through the **force of** habit, is become natural.

"You **have ordained that** I should have the
management **of the war** against Jugurtha; an
ordinance highly displeasing to the nobility.
Now, pray consider with yourselves, whether
you had not better alter your choice, and employ upon this, or any other like occasion, one
of the tribe of the nobility, a man of an ancient
family, surrounded with the images of his ancestors, and who has never been in the ser
vice: see how, upon such an important occasion, he will hurry and be confounded, and,
ignorant of the whole of his duty, apply to
some plebeian to instruct him in it. And thus
it commonly happens, that he, whom you
have appointed your general, is obliged to find
another from whom to receive his orders. I
myself, Romans, know some who, after they
were made consuls, began to read the history

of our ancestors, and the military precepts of the Greeks. Preposterous method! For though, in the order of time, the election to offices precedes the exercise of men, yet, in the order of things, qualifications and experience should precede election.

" Compare me now, Romans, who am but a new man, with these haughty nobles. What they only read or heard of, I have seen performed, or performed myself: what they have gathered from books, I have learned in the service. Now do you yourselves judge, whether practice or speculation are of greatest value. They despise me for the meanness of my descent; I them, for their indolence: I am upbraided with my fortune, they with their crimes. I am of opinion that nature is always the same, and common to all; and that those who have most virtue, have most nobility. Suppose it were possible to put the question to the fathers of Albinus or Bestia, whether they would rather have chosen me for their descendent, or them? What answer do you think they would make, but that they should have desired to have had the most deserving men for their sons? but if they have reason to despise me, they have the same to despise their ancestors, whose nobility, like mine, took its rise from their military virtue. They envy my advancement, let them likewise envy my toils, my integrity, my dangers; for by these I gained it. These men, in truth, blinded with pride, live in such manner as if they slighted the honours you have to bestow, and yet sue for them as if they had deserved them. Deluded men! to aspire at once after two things so opposite in their natures; the enjoyment of the pleasures of effeminacy, and the fruits of a laborious virtue. When they harangue too before you, or in the senate, they employ the greatest part of their eloquence in celebrating their ancestors, and vainly imagine that their exploits reflect a lustre on themselves: whereas it is quite the reverse; for the more illustrious their lives were, the more scandalous is the spiritless and unmanly behaviour of these their descendents. The truth of the matter is plainly this; the glory acquired by ancestors, is like a light diffused over the actions of their posterity, which neither suffers their good nor bad qualities to be concealed. This light, Romans, is what I want; but, what is much more noble, I can relate my own achievements.

" See only how unreasonable they are! What they arrogantly claim to themselves for the ex-

ploits of others, that they deny me for my own; and what reason do they give for it? why truly this, because I have no images of my ancestors to show, and my nobility is no older than myself, which certainly it is more honourable for one to acquire himself, than to debase that which he derives from his ancestors.

" I am very sensible, that if they had a mind to reply to what I now advance, they would do it with great eloquence and accuracy. Yet, as they have given a loose to their calumniating tongues upon every occasion, not only against me, but likewise against you, ever since you have conferred this dignity upon me, I was resolved to speak, lest some should impute my silence to a consciousness of my own guilt,

" Though I am abundantly satisfied, that no speech whatever can hurt me; since, if what is said be true it must be to my honour; if false, my life and conduct will confute it; but because your determination is blamed, in bestowing upon me the highest dignity of the state, and trusting me with the conduct of affairs of such importance; consider again and again, whether you had not better alter your choice. I cannot, indeed, boast of the images, triumphs, or consulships of my ancestors, to raise your confidence in me; but, if it is necessary, I can show you spears, standards, collars, and other military presents in great plenty, besides scars of wounds all received before. These are my statues; these the proofs of my nobility, not derived from ancestors, as theirs are, but such as I have myself acquired by many toils and dangers.

" My language too is unpolished; but that gives me small concern: virtue shows itself with sufficient clearness. They stand in need of the artful colourings of eloquence, to hide the infamy of their actions. Nor have I been instructed in the Grecian literature: why truly I had little inclination to that kind of instruction, which did not improve the authors of it in the least degree of virtue. But I have learned other things far more useful to the state: to wound the enemy; to watch; to dread nothing but infamy, equally to undergo cold and heat; to lie upon the bare ground; and endure at the same time hunger and fatigue. These lessons shall animate my troops; nor shall I ever be rigorous to them, and indulgent to myself; or borrow my glory from their toils. This is the manner of commanding that is useful to the state; this is what suits the equality of citizens. For to treat the army with severity, whilst you indulge yourself in ease and pleasure, is to act the tyrant, not the general. By a conduct like this, your ancestors gained immortal honour both to themselves and the republic; which our nobility, though so unlike them in their character, relying upon, despise us who imitate them; and demand of you all public honours, not on account of their personal merit, but as due to their high rank: arrogant men! but widely mistaken. Their ancestors left them everything in their power to leave them; their wealth, their images, their high renown; but their virtue they did not leave them, nor indeed could they; for it can neither be given, nor received as a gift.

"They call me an unpolished ill-bred fellow, because I cannot entertain elegantly, have no buffoon, and pay no higher wages to my cook than to my steward; every part of which charge, Romans, I readily own. For I have learned from my father and other venerable persons, that delicacy belongs to women, labour to men; that a virtuous man ought to have a larger share of glory than riches; and that arms are more ornamental than splendid furniture.

"But let them still pursue what is so dear and delightful to them; let them indulge in wine and women; let them spend their old age, as they did their youth, in banqueting and the lowest sensual gratifications; let them leave sweat and dust, and other such things, to us, to whom they are more agreeable than the most elegant entertainments. But even this they will not do; for after having debased themselves by the practice of the foulest and most infamous vices, these most detestable of all men endeavour to deprive the brave of the rewards that are due to them. Thus, by the greatest injustice, luxury and idleness, the most mischievous vices, are no ways prejudicial to those who are guilty of them; at the same time that they threaten the innocent commonwealth with ruin.

"Now since I have answered these men, as far as my own character was concerned, though not so fully as their infamous behaviour deserved, I shall add a few words concerning the state of public affairs. And first of all, Romans, be of good courage as to Numidia; since you have now removed all that hitherto secured Jugurtha, namely, the covetousness, incapacity, and haughtiness of our commanders. There is an army there likewise, well

acquainted with the country; but indeed more brave than fortunate; for a great part of it has been destroyed by the rapaciousness and rashness of its commanders. Do you, therefore, who are of age to bear arms, join your efforts to mine, and assume the defence of the commonwealth; nor let the fate of others, or the haughtiness of the late commanders, discourage any of you: when you march, when you engage, I will always be with you, to direct you how to act, and to share every danger with you. In a word, I shall desire you to act no otherwise in any instance, than as you see me do. Moreover, all things are now ripe for us,—victory, spoil, and glory; and though they were uncertain, or at a distance, it would still be the duty of every good citizen to assist the state. For no man ever became immortal by inactivity; nor did ever any father wish his children might never die, but rather that they might live like useful and worthy men. I should add more to what I have already said, if words could inspire cowards with bravery; for to the valiant I think I have said enough."

Marius, upon delivering the speech, finding the minds of the people animated, ordered provisions, money, and other necessaries for the war, to be embarked with all expedition; and sent his lieutenant A. Manlius along with them. In the meantime he himself was employed in levying troops, accepting all who were inclined to go, without observing the ancient method of enrolling those of certain classes only. The greatest part of them consisted of such as were, upon account of their poverty, exempted from bearing arms: which conduct of his some imputed to the scarcity of better men, others to a design of making his court to the rabble, to whom he first owed his reputation, and then his advancement. Add to this, that to one who aims at power, the most needy are the properest assistants; since they have no property to be solicitous about, and think every thing honourable that is gainful. Marius, setting sail for Africa, with a number of troops somewhat greater than had been decreed him, in a few days arrived at Utica. There the army was delivered up to him by P. Rutilius, lieutenant-general to Metellus; for Metellus avoided the sight of Marius, that he might not behold what he never could bear to hear.

The consul, having completed his legions and auxiliary cohorts, marched into a fertile country, abounding in plunder: where, whatever he took, he bestowed upon the soldiers. Then he assailed such fortresses and towns as were not very strong by nature, nor well garrisoned; and had frequent skirmishes in different places. In the meantime the new-raised soldiers learned to join in an encounter without fear; they saw that such as fled were either taken or slain; that the bravest were the most secure; that by arms, our liberty, our country, **our** parents, and every thing else were protected, and glory and riches acquired. Thus **in a** short time the new men matched the veterans, and the bravery of both became equal.

The two kings, as soon as they had notice of the arrival of Marius, retired each into places of difficult access. This was the contrivance of Jugurtha, who by this means hoped that the **enemy** would disperse, and so afford him an opportunity of falling upon them; supposing that the Romans would, like most others, become more remiss and licentious when their fears were removed.

Metellus in the meantime, upon his return to Rome, was received, contrary to his expectations, with the greatest demonstrations of joy and affection; being equally dear to the commons and senate, now that the popular odium had subsided. As for Marius, he showed great activity and prudence in observing the enemy's measures and pursuing his own; in considering what might tend to promote or obstruct either; informing himself of the separate marches of the two kings; and preventing all their machinations. He suffered no remissness in his own army, nor rest nor security in those of the kings; insomuch that, having frequently attacked both the Getulians and Jugurtha, as they were carrying off the plunder of our allies, he always routed them; and even forced the king himself, not far from Cirta, to cast away his arms and fly. But when he considered **that all** this was only matter of empty show and applause, without producing any thing decisive; he resolved to invest all the cities that by the strength of their garrisons, or situation, gave the enemy the greatest advantage against us; as Jugurtha would thus be stripped of all his strong holds, if he suffered them to be taken, or to be brought to an engagement. For Bocchus had frequently sent deputies to him, to signify his desire of the Roman friendship, and that no hostilities were to be apprehended from him. But whether this was only pretence, that he might fall upon us unawares with the greater success; or whether it proceeded from the inconstancy of his temper, one while prompting him to war, another to peace; I have not been able to discover.

The consul, in pursuance of his design, advanced against the strong towns and forts, some of which he took by assault, and others he gained over to him by threats or promises. At first, indeed, he attempted only small towns, thinking that Jugurtha, in order to protect his subjects, would come to a battle: but finding that he kept at a distance, and was employed in other affairs, he thought it was time to enter upon greater and more difficult enterprises.

There stood, in the midst of vast deserts, a large and strong city called Capsa, said to have been founded by the Libyan Hercules. The citizens, by reason of the many immunities they enjoyed under Jugurtha, who exercised a gentle government over them, were thought to be faithfully devoted to him. They were secured against their enemies not only by good fortifications, numbers of men and magazines of arms, but much more by the difficulty of approaching them: for the whole country round, except the fields adjoining to the town, was barren and uncultivated, without water, and infested with serpents, whose rage, like that of other wild beasts, is heightened by famine, and who, though naturally mischievous, are still more so when they are inflamed by thirst. Marius had an ardent desire to master this place, not only on account of its importance for the purposes of war, but because of the difficulty of the undertaking: as an additional motive, too, Metellus had acquired great glory by taking Thala, a town that much resembled it in strength and situation, except that at Thala there were several springs not far from the town; whereas the inhabitants of Capsa had only one, and that within the city, without any other supply of water but from the heavens. This people, as well as the other inhabitants of Africa who lived at a distance from the sea, and in a rustic manner, the more easily supported this scarcity of water, because the Numidians live mostly upon milk and venison, without the use of salt, or, indeed, any other incentive to appetite: the sole purpose of eating and drinking among them is to satisfy the necessary demands of nature, and not to gratify luxury and intemperance.

The consul took all possible precautions in this undertaking; but relied, I am apt to think, upon the gods for success ; as human prudence could not sufficiently provide against so great difficulties. To his other discouragements was added scarcity of corn, the Numidians applying themselves more to grazing than tillage : besides, what grain there was, had been carried off, by the king's orders, into fortified places ; and as it was the end of summer, the ground was parched and produced nothing. He acted, however, considering his condition, with great prudence and foresight. The cattle he had taken some days before, he committed to the auxiliary cavalry to conduct ; and ordered his lieutenant A. Manlius to march with the light cohorts to the city Laris, where he had placed his provisions and military chest ; telling him, that he was going in pursuit of plunder, and would join him in a few days. Thus concealing his design, he marched directly to the river Tana.

In his march, he every day distributed cattle among the companies of foot and troops of horse in equal proportion, and took care to have bottles made of their hides : thus he at once made the want of corn less sensibly felt, and provided such utensils as were soon to become necessary, whilst all were ignorant of his intentions. After six days' march they arrived at the river, and had already made a great number of bottles. Having pitched his camp there, and fortified it slightly, he ordered his men to refresh themselves, that they might be ready to march at sun-set ; and likewise to lay aside all their baggage, and load themselves and their beasts of burden only with water. At the time appointed he decamped, and marching the whole night, encamped again in the morning. The same he did the next night ; and the third, long before dawn, he came to a place full of small hills, about two miles from Capsa, where he passed the remaining part of the night, concealing his forces with the greatest possible care. But as soon as day appeared, and the Numidians, being under no apprehensions of an enemy, had many of them left the town, he instantly ordered all his horse, with the nimblest of his foot, to fly to Capsa and secure the gates. He himself followed with great despatch, not suffering any of his men to stray for plunder. When the inhabitants found this, the great consternation wherewith they were seized, the unexpected calamity that befell them, and the consideration that many of their fellow-citizens were without the

walls in the hands of the enemy, forced them to surrender. Their city, however, was burnt ; the youth put to the sword ; all the rest sold ; and the plunder given to the soldiers. This severe course, contrary to the laws of war, was not occasioned by the avarice or cruelty of the consul ; but was taken, because the place was very advantageous to Jugurtha, and of difficult access to us ; the citizens, an inconstant perfidious race, not to be curbed by favours or terrors.

After Marius had executed so bold an enterprise without any detriment to his men, his name, which was indeed great and renowned before, became now much more so. All his actions, even those that were too forward, were looked upon as the effects of superior abilities ; the soldiers, being under a gentle command, and withal enriched by him, extolled him to the skies ; the Numidians dreaded him as more than mortal : in short, both allies and enemies believed he had either the spirit of a deity, or that the gods assisted him in all things.

After this success, the consul advanced against other towns ; in taking some of which he met with opposition from the Numidians ; but most of them were deserted by their inhabitants, who dreaded the tragical fate of Capsa ; and these he burned to the ground. Thus all parts were filled with lamentations and slaughter. At last, having made himself master of many places, and most of them without loss of blood, he engaged in another enterprise, not so hazardous as that of Capsa, but equally difficult.

Not far from the river of Mulucha, which separated the kingdoms of Jugurtha and Bocchus, there stood, in the midst of a plain, a small fort, upon a rock of considerable breadth at top, and prodigiously high ; naturally as steep on every side as art or labour could have made it, except one part very strait. As the king's treasure was kept in this place, Marius exerted his utmost efforts to take it ; and succeeded more by chance than prudent management : for the castle was abundantly provided with men, arms, provisions, and a spring of water ; its situation rendered it impossible to make use of mounds and turrets, and all the machinery of a siege ; the way to it was very narrow, with a precipice on each side ; the moving galleries were pushed against it with great danger, and to no purpose ; for when they advanced but ever so little, they were destroyed by fire or great stones. The soldiers could neither stand firmly to advance their works, for the steepness of the rock; nor make use of their batteries, without exposing themselves to great danger. The bravest of them were either slain or wounded, and the rest greatly discouraged.

Now Marius having thus spent many toilsome days, debated with himself, whether he should abandon his enterprise, as it proved unsuccessful, or wait the interposition of fortune, which had been so often favourable to him. Whilst he was under this sore perplexity for several days and nights together, a Ligurian, a common soldier of the auxiliary cohorts, going out of the camp in search of water, happened to observe, not far from the side of the castle opposite to that where the attack was made, some snails crawling among the rocks; of which gathering one, then another, and still climbing to procure more, he was got insensibly almost to the top of the mountain: where, perceiving every thing quiet, the natural desire of seeing unknown objects prompted him to proceed. It happened that there grew, in that very place, a great oak out of the side of the rock, which bending downward a little near the root, then taking a turn, mounted upward, as all trees naturally do.

The Ligurian, one while laying hold of the branches of this tree, another of the prominences of the rock, got so high at last as to be able to survey the whole plan of the castle, without being disturbed by the Numidians, who were all engaged on that side where the attack was made. After he had carefully examined whatever he thought would be of use to him in the execution of his design, he returned the same way, not hastily, as he went up, but pausing at every step, and observing every thing with the utmost care. He then hastened to Marius, informed him of what he had done, pressed him to make an attempt upon the castle on that side where he himself had mounted, and promised that he would lead the way, and be the first to face the danger. Marius sent some of those who attended him along with the Ligurian to examine into the proposal; who according to their different judgments reported that the undertaking was easy or difficult. The consul, however, took courage upon it, and determined to make the attempt the next day; appointing for that purpose a guard of four centurions with their companies, and five trumpeters, the nimblest he could find, ordering them all

to follow the directions of the Ligurian, who, when the time was come, and every thing provided and put in order, advanced to the place.

The centurions, according to the instructions which they had received from their guide, had changed their arms and dress, and marched with their head and feet bare, that they might have the freer prospect, and climb more easily. They had their swords over their shoulders, and their bucklers too, which were of the Numidian kind, and made of leather, both for lightness, and that they might not sound if they happened to dash against the rock. The Ligurian, leading the way, tied cords about the stones, and such old roots of trees as appeared here and there, to assist the soldiers in climbing; lending his hand, from time to time, to such as were discouraged at so rugged a march. When the ascent was steeper than ordinary, he sent them up before him unarmed, and then followed himself with their arms. What appeared extremely difficult and threatening even to their best endeavours, he tried; and by ascending and descending several times, encouraged the rest to follow him, and then retired to make way for them. At length after much tedious labour, they gained the castle, which was quite naked on that side, the enemy being all engaged, as at other times, in the opposite quarter. When Marius was informed of the success of the Ligurian, though he had kept the Numidians employed all day long by a continued attack, yet now encouraging the soldiers, he sallied out of his galleries, and drawing up his men into the form of a shell, advanced against the castle. At the same time too, in order to terrify the enemy, he plied them hard with engines, archers, and slingers, at a distance. The Numidians, who had often before broke to pieces and even burnt the Roman galleries, did not now defend themselves within their battlements, but spent whole days and nights without their walls, railing at the Romans, and charging Marius with madness. They threatened our men with being made slaves to Jugurtha, and were, indeed, extremely insolent on account of their success.

While both sides were warmly engaged in a vigorous struggle for glory and empire on the one hand, and life and liberty on the other, the trumpets on a sudden sounded in the enemy's rear. Upon which the women and children, who had come out to see the engagement, fled; after them such as were next the walls; and at last all, armed and unarmed. The Romans upon this pressed onward with greater vigour, overthrowing the enemy, and only wounding most of them; then going over the heaps of slain, they flew to the walls, all thirsting for glory, and striving each to get before the other, not one person stopping for plunder. Thus accidental success justified the rashness of Marius, and even his imprudence contributed to heighten his glory.

During this transaction, L. Sylla the quæstor arrived in the camp with a great body of horse, having been left at Rome by Marius, to raise them in Latium and among our allies. And here, as this circumstance has led me to make mention of so extraordinary a man, I thought it would not be improper to give some account of his genius and character; especially as I do not design to speak of him elsewhere, and as L. Sisena, the best and most accurate of all those who have given us his history, appears to me not to have spoken of him with so much freedom as he should have done.

Sylla was descended from an eminent patrician family; but its lustre was almost quite obscured by the degeneracy of his late ancestors. He was perfect master of the learning both of Greece and Rome; of a great spirit; fond of pleasures, but fonder of glory; when business did not call him, he indulged to luxury, but never suffered his business to be hindered by it, unless in the case of his divorce, in which he ought to have acted in a more honourable manner. He was eloquent, artful, easy, and obliging in his friendships; of vast reach in disguising his designs; liberal of every thing, especially of his money. He was, indeed, the happiest of all men, before his success in the civil wars; yet his fortune never surpassed his merit; so that many have made it a question, whether he were more brave or more fortunate. As to his behaviour after the civil war, I know not how it is to be recounted, whether with greater shame or horror.

When Sylla, as we have already related, was come into Africa, and had joined Marius in his camp, though he was before raw and ignorant in the art of war, yet in a short time he became a very able warrior. He was, moreover, very affable to the soldiers; granted favours to many upon their asking them, and to many without asking; was backward to receive benefits himself, but more forward to repay them than if they had been a debt of money; would never have any returns for what favours he bestowed, but rather aimed at bringing as many as possible under obligations to him. He often entered into conversation with the common men, talking sometimes jocosely, sometimes seriously; was with them upon every occasion, in their marches, in their works, and in their watchings; nor did he, in the meantime, wound the character of the consul, or any other worthy person, according to the base practice of those who are actuated by ambition; striving assiduously to suffer none to surpass him in counsel or action, in both which he almost excelled all others. By this conduct and these qualifications, he was in a short time greatly beloved by Marius and the whole army.

Now Jugurtha, after he had lost Capsa and other strong and important places, with a great deal of money besides, sent messengers to Bocchus, to press him to hasten his march into Numidia; for that this was a proper time to give the enemy battle. But finding him irresolute, and weighing the motives for peace and those for war, he gained over his confidants by money, as he had formerly done; nay, and promised the Moor himself the third part of Numidia, upon condition that the Romans were either driven out of Africa, or he recovered his whole dominions by a treaty of peace. Bocchus, tempted with such an offer, marched immediately to Jugurtha. When both armies were joined, they fell upon Marius, as he was going into winter-quarters, towards the close of the evening: persuading themselves, that, in case of a defeat, the **night** would secure them, and if they proved victorious, it would be no disadvantage to **them, since they were so** well acquainted with the **country; whereas the** darkness must distress the Romans, whatever were the event.

The enemy was already in full view, just as the consul was receiving manifold information of their approach; and before the army could be formed or the baggage drawn together, nay, before the signal or any orders could be given, the Moorish and Getulian horse poured upon them; not in due order, or any regular method of engaging, but in scattered parties, just as chance huddled them together. Our men, though alarmed with so unexpected an onset, yet mindful of their former bravery, boldly grasped their arms, all ready to encounter the enemy, or defend those that were yet unarmed. Some of them mounted their horses, and advanced against the foe. The whole action had more the resemblance of a fray of robbers, than of a regular battle; horse and foot were jumbled together, without standards or ranks; some were cut to pieces, others were mangled; many, whilst they were engaging the foe vigorously in front, were themselves attacked in rear; neither courage nor arms were a sufficient security; for the enemy, being far more numerous, surrounded us on all sides. At last, our men, in whatever place they happened to meet in parties, both the veterans and new-raised soldiers (for they too had learned war by practice and example) threw themselves into circular bodies; and thus, having a front every way, they sustained the shock of the enemy.

In this distressful situation Marius was not in the least daunted, nor his courage more sunk than on former occasions; but with his own troop, which he had filled up with men of the greatest bravery, without any regard to personal friendship in the choice of them, flew about to every quarter, one while succouring his own men in distress, another charging the thickest of the enemy in person; and by using his sword did all the service he could to his troops, since it was impossible for him to act the part of a general amidst so great confusion. By this time the day was quite spent, without the barbarians abating any thing of their fury; nay, agreeably to the orders of the kings, who thought the darkness an advantage to them, they charged with greater ardour than before. Whereupon Marius, as the best measure his circumstances would admit of, in order to secure a place of refuge for his army, resolved to take possession of two hills near each other: in one of which, though not large enough to encamp on, there was a plentiful spring of water: the other was very proper for a camp, because it was very high and steep, and required but little fortification. He ordered Sylla to pass the night by the spring, with his cavalry: he himself having by degrees drawn together his scattered troops, the enemy being still in no less confusion, went straight with them to the other hill. The kings, being thus discouraged by the difficulty of the ascent from making any further attack, did not, however, suffer their forces to retire, but besetting both hills, pitched all round them with their disorderly multitudes. Then the barbarians, kindling many fires, passed most of the night in mirth and jollity, bounded to and fro, and

shouted terribly after their usual manner. Their leaders, too, were highly elated, and behaved like conquerors, because they had not been obliged to fly. All this was easily perceived by the Romans in the dark, being situated upon the upper ground, and gave them no small encouragement. Marius's confidence being increased by the unskilful conduct of the enemy, he ordered a profound silence to be kept, not even suffering the trumpets to sound as usual, when the guard was changed. As soon as day appeared, when the enemy were now weary and just fallen asleep, he directed all the trumpets, both of horse and foot, throughout the army, to sound at once, and the soldiers to pour down upon the enemy with a terrible shout.

The Moors and Getulians, being suddenly roused by so horrid and unusual a noise, could neither fly nor take arms, and were utterly incapable to act or contrive any thing for their own security, to such a degree, that being stunned with the noise and frightful shouts, severely pressed by our men, without receiving any assistance from their own leaders, they sunk like men stupified under this tumult, terror, and amazement. In short, they received a total overthrow, most of their arms and military standards were taken, and more were killed in that battle than all the former: for sleep and extraordinary surprise had prevented their flight.

Marius now pursued his march into his winter-quarters, which he determined to fix in the maritime towns, for the sake of provisions. In the meantime his late victory made him neither remiss nor imperious; but, as if the enemy had been in view, he marched with his army in form of a square. Sylla commanded the cavalry on the right; A. Manlius, with the slingers and archers, as also the Ligurian cohorts, on the left: in the front and rear he posted the tribunes with the light-armed foot. The deserters, being of small account, were employed to observe the motions of the enemy, as they were perfectly well acquainted with the country. Besides, the consul, as if he had committed no share of the command to any other, carefully attended to every thing himself, went to every quarter, extolling some, reprimanding others, just as they deserved it; and as he was constantly armed and ready for action himself, he obliged the soldiers to be so too. Nor was he less cautious in fortifying his camp, than he was in his march. He committed the guard of the gates to the cohorts of the legions, and that without the gates to the auxiliary horse, placing others upon the lines and ramparts, and visiting them all round in person: not so much from any distrust that his orders would not be performed, as to animate his men to undergo their fatigues with the greater cheerfulness, when they saw their general take an equal share. And indeed Marius, both now and all the time he was employed in the war against Jugurtha, maintained good order in the army more by the shame of offending, than the fear of punishment: which some imputed to his passion for popularity; others alleged that, being inured to hardships from childhood, he took pleasure in what others reckon the greatest misery. This much, however, is certain; the affairs of the state were managed with as much success and dignity as if his command had been ever so rigorous.

At last, on the fourth day, when they were not far from Cirta, the scouts appeared on all sides, advancing with great haste; whence it was concluded that the enemy were not far off: but as they returned from different quarters, yet all with the same account, the consul not knowing how to draw up his army, resolved not to alter its disposition, but waited the coming of the enemy, in the same order and the same place. This disconcerted Jugurtha, who had divided his troops into four parts, flattering himself that some of them must certainly attack the Romans in the rear with advantage. In the meantime Sylla, upon whom the enemy first fell, encouraging his men, charged the Moors at the head of some troops in as close order as possible; the rest, without moving from their ground, defended themselves from the darts thrown at a distance, and cut to pieces all who ventured to come up to them.

During this engagement of the horse, Bocchus attacked our rear with a body of foot brought by his son Volux, but which had not marched expeditiously enough to be present at the former battle. Marius was then in the front, making head against Jugurtha, who fought there with a numerous force. But the Numidian prince, when he heard of the arrival of Bocchus, wheeled about with a few attendants to our foot, and cried with a loud voice in Latin, which he learned at the siege of Numantia, "that they fought to no purpose, for that he had slain Marius a little before with his own hand;" and at the same time showed them his sword dyed with the blood of one of our foot, slain by him in the encounter with great

bravery. Our men hearing this were more struck with so shocking a report that was consistent with the opinion they had of the veracity of the author of it: on the contrary, the barbarians were inspired with fresh courage, and with greater fury than ever, pushed the Romans, who were disheartened, and upon the point of betaking themselves to flight, when Sylla, having routed those he was engaged with, fell upon the Moors in their flank; whereupon Bocchus immediately fled. Jugurtha, whilst he endeavoured to sustain his men, and maintain a victory which he had almost gained, was enclosed both on the right and left by our horse; and, having slain all about him, broke singly through the enemy, and got off amidst a shower of darts. By this time, too, Marius, who had routed the cavalry, came to the relief of his men who he heard had given ground. And now the enemy was entirely defeated in every quarter.

Then it was that a tragical spectacle presented itself all over the widely extended plain; some flying, others pursuing; some killed, others taken; horses and men prostrate in the agonies of death. Many wounded, and though impatient to fly, unable to do it; one while striving to rise, and instantly dropping down again. In a word, the ground was covered, as far as the eye could reach, with arms and carcases, and the intermediate spaces stained with blood and gore.

The consul, now undoubtedly conqueror, pursued his march to Cirta, as at first he intended. Here, five days after the defeat of the barbarians, deputies came to him from Bocchus, requesting of him, in his name, to send two persons, whom he could entirely confide in, to the king, that he might treat with them upon matters that concerned his own interest, and likewise that of the Roman people. The consul immediately sent L. Sylla and A. Manlius, who, though they went at the king's request, yet thought proper to accost him with a speech, in order to dispose him to peace, if he still seemed averse to it: or if he desired it, to strengthen that disposition. Accordingly Sylla, to whom Manlius gave precedence, in consideration of his eloquence, and not of his seniority, thus briefly addressed himself to Bocchus:—

" It is a great pleasure to us, king Bocchus, that the gods have disposed a prince of your merit to prefer peace to war, and no longer to stain your own distinguished character by uniting with Jugurtha, the most detestable of all men; since you have thus delivered us from the disagreeable necessity of pursuing you both with the like vengeance; you, for your mistake in assisting him; and him, for his enormous crimes. The Roman people, even in the infancy of their state, when their territory was but small, always reckoned it better policy to procure friends than subjects; thinking it safer to rule over such as yielded a willing obedience, than those who openly obeyed through compulsion. Nor can any alliance be more advantageous to you than ours: one great reason is, that we are at a great distance from you, so that you cannot be apprehensive of receiving any injuries from us, and yet we are ready to be as serviceable to you as if we were your neighbours. As another inducement, we have already as many subjects as we wish for, and only want to increase the number of our friends, of whom neither we, nor any other state, can ever have enough. I wish, indeed, you had at first taken the present course; in that case, you would certainly before now have received more benefits from the Roman people, than you have suffered calamities from their arms. But since it is the determination of fortune, which over-rules the greatest part of human affairs, that you should make trial of the force of our enmity, as well as of our friendship, embrace quickly the occasion she now offers, and accomplish speedily what you have now begun. You have many opportunities, and many things in your power, for retrieving your past mistakes by future services. To conclude, be firmly persuaded of this, that the Romans are never to be overcome in generosity. Their power in war, you yourself have already proved."

To all this Bocchus returned a very courteous answer, making at the same time a brief apology for his misconduct; alleging, "that he had recourse to arms from no hostile intention, but purely to defend his own territories; that he could not bear to see Marius lay waste that part of Numidia which was his own by the right of war, as having conquered it from Jugurtha; that he had formerly sent ambassadors to Rome desiring to be admitted to an alliance, and was rejected; but that he was willing to omit mentioning old things, and to send deputies again to the senate, if Marius consented to it." This being granted him, the mind of the barbarian was again changed by such of his confidants as were corrupted by presents from 'ugurtha; who, when he heard that Sylla and Manlius had been sent to Bocchus, apprehended what was really contriving against him.

Marius in the meantime, having settled his army in winter-quarters, marched into the deserts, with a detachment of light-armed cohorts and part of his cavalry, to besiege a tower of Jugurtha's, where he had placed all the Roman deserters for a garrison. Now again Bocchus, either reflecting upon his two late defeats, or wrought upon by some others of his confidants, whom Jugurtha had not corrupted, resumed his former sentiments, and chose from amongst his friends five ambassadors, of proved integrity and eminent abilities: these he ordered to go to Marius, and afterwards, if he should think proper, to Rome; giving them full powers to negotiate affairs, and end the war upon any terms. The ambassadors departed speedily for the winter-quarters of the Romans; but being beset on the road, and stripped of all they had, by Getulian robbers, they pursued their march to Sylla, whom the consul, when he began his expedition, had left propraetor. Sylla received them, not as such faithless enemies deserved, but in a respectful and generous manner: the barbarians were so pleased with this, that they gave no credit to the report of the Roman avarice, and concluded Sylla to be their friend, from his munificence towards them. For there were many ignorant, even in those days, that bounties were ever given from interested views; every generous man being then thought benevolent, and all presents to proceed from kindness. Before him, therefore, they laid their orders from Bocchus, beseeching him at the same time to assist them with his advice and good offices. They likewise spoke in high terms of the wealth, honour, and power of their king, forgetting nothing which they thought would be subservient to their design, or tend to gain the favour of the quaestor. When Sylla had promised all they desired, and instructed them in what manner to address Marius, and afterwards the senate, they still waited there about forty days.

Marius not succeeding in his enterprise, returned to Cirta; and being informed of the arrival of the ambassadors, ordered both Sylla and them to come to him. He likewise summoned L. Bellienus the praetor from Utica, and all those of senatorian rank who were to be found in the country. He examined, together with them, Bocchus's instructions to his ambassadors, whereby they had power given them to go to Rome, and to apply to the consul for a cessation of arms till they should return. Sylla and the greatest part of the council approved of this. But there were a few, who, unacquainted with the nature of human affairs, which are never fixed, but always changing, and constantly for the worse, proposed more violent measures.

The Moors, having obtained all they desired, three of them proceeded to Rome, with C. Octavius Rufo, who had come into Africa as quæstor, with money for the army; two returned to the king, who heard with pleasure the account they gave him of all that had passed, and especially the kindness of Sylla, and the many demonstrations of friendship they had received from him. His deputies at Rome, having implored pardon of the senate for the misconduct of the king, into which, they said he had fallen through the artifices of Jugurtha, and desired to be admitted into friendship and alliance, received the following answer :—

" The senate and people of Rome are always mindful both of favours and injuries. They pardon Bocchus, however, because he repents of his transgression, and will admit him into friendship and alliance when he deserves it."

As soon as Bocchus had notice of this, he wrote to Marius to send Sylla to him, that by his counsel matters might be adjusted between them. Sylla was sent accordingly, with a guard of horse and foot, Balearian slingers, a certain number of archers, and a cohort from Pelignum with light arms for the sake of expedition ; which however secured them, as well as any other, against the enemy's darts, which were but slight. On the fifth day of their march, Volux, the son of Bocchus, appeared on a sudden in the open plains at the head of a thousand horse, who advancing hastily and without any order, seemed more numerous than they really were, and made Sylla and those that were with him suspect they were enemies. Whereupon every one made ready, adjusted their arms, and put themselves in a posture of defence; they were not, indeed, without their fears; but their hopes were greater, as being victorious, and to engage with those they had often conquered. In the meantime, the horsemen, who were sent to reconnoitre them, returned with tidings that removed all their apprehensions.

As soon as Volux arrived, he addressed himself to the quæstor, acquainting him that he was come by his father's orders to receive and to guard him. Accordingly they continued their march together for that and the following day without any alarm; but in the evening, when they had already pitched their camp, the Moorish prince ran to Sylla with an air of consternation, and told him, trembling, that he was informed by his scouts, " that Jugurtha was near at hand;" at the same time asking and entreating the quæstor " to fly away with him privately in the night." To which Sylla resolutely replied, " that he was not afraid of the Numidian, whom he had so often defeated ; that he did not distrust the courage of his troops ; and that, were he sure of meeting certain destruction, he would stand his ground, rather than fly infamously, and betray those whom he commanded, merely to save a life, at best but of precarious tenure, and which might perhaps in a short time be cut off by some distemper."

Volux, however, proposing to him to march in the night-time, he approved of his advice ; and immediately ordered his men to make a great number of fires in the camp, after they had supped, and then to march silently, at the first watch of the night. Next morning about sun-rise, when they were all thoroughly tired with their march, as Sylla was encamping, the Moorish horsemen acquainted him, that Jugurtha had pitched his camp about two miles further. Upon hearing this, our men were seized with great consternation, as believing themselves betrayed and led into an ambush by Volux ; and some even proposed putting him to death, for that so vile a traitor oughtnot to go unpunished.

But Sylla, though he entertained the same suspicion as the rest, would not suffer his men to offer him any violence. He exhorted them " to be of good courage; that a few brave troops had often prevailed against a numerous army ; that the less they spared themselves in battle, the more secure they would be; that none, who had arms in their hands, should seek assistance from their heels which were unarmed, nor in the midst of danger turn their backs, which were blind and defenceless, towards the enemy." Then invoking almighty Jove to bear testimony to the guilt and treachery of Bocchus, he ordered Volux to depart his camp, as one who had hostile intentions. He, with tears in his eyes, entreated him " not to entertain any such suspicion of him; that nothing of this had happened by any treachery in him, but rather through the subtility of Jugurtha, who, being constantly in quest of intelligence, had discovered his route. How

ever, as he had no great force with him, and
depended entirely upon Bocchus for strength
and support, he did not imagine that he would
dare to make any open attempt, where the son
of Bocchus must be witness to it; so that he
thought his best course would be to march
boldly through the middle of his camp. That
as for himself, he would either send his Moors
before, or leave them there, and accompany
Sylla singly." In such an extremity this proposal was approved of. Accordingly they immediately advanced, and passed without molestation; Jugurtha being surprised at their
unexpected coming, and not having time to
take any resolution. In a few days after, they
got to the end of their journey.

There was at that time a certain Numidian
called Aspar, in the court of Bocchus, with
whom he enjoyed great freedom and familiarity, having been despatched thither by Jugurtha, as soon as he had notice that Sylla had
been sent for, in order to take care of his interest, and to pry narrowly into all the designs
of Bocchus. There was likewise one Dabar
in his court, the son of Massugrada, and descended from Masinissa, but not of equal quality, by his grandmother, for his father was born
of a concubine. Bocchus, whose favour and
confidence he had gained by his many excellent accomplishments, having found him upon
many former occasions a true friend to the Romans, despatched him forthwith to Sylla, to
acquaint him, "that he was ready to do whatever the Romans required; that Sylla himself
might appoint the day, the place, and even the
hour of conference; that he had reserved every
thing to be adjusted by himself and Sylla; that
an ambassador there from Jugurtha ought not
to give him umbrage, since he was admitted to
the negociation with the sole view of facilitating
it, as it was impossible by any other means to
defeat the dark measures of that prince."

But I find that Bocchus acted more like a perfidious African, than agreeably to what he professed, amusing both the Romans and Jugurtha
with hopes of peace; and that he frequently
debated with himself, whether he should deliver up Jugurtha to the Romans, or Sylla
to Jugurtha; his inclinations leading him to
be against us, and his fears for us.

Sylla replied, "that he should say but little
before Aspar, reserving what he had to add, to
be communicated in secret to the king alone, or
at least in the presence of very few;" instruct-

ing Dabar at the same time as to the answer
which he expected to receive from Bocchus,
in the presence of others. When the time appointed for the conference arrived, Sylla declared, "that he came by order of the consul to
know his final resolution as to peace or war."

The king, agreeably to his instructions, desired Sylla to return about ten days after, at
which time he should have a full answer, for
that as yet he had come to no determination.
Upon this they both departed to their respective camps. But when the night was far advanced, Bocchus sent privately for Sylla;
none were admitted on either side but trusty
interpreters, except Dabar, a man of strict
honour, who mediated between them, and was
sworn by mutual consent, to make faithful representations to both. Upon which the king
began thus:—

"I never imagined, that I, the most powerful prince in this part of the world, and the
richest of all the princes I know, should ever
be under obligations to a private person. And
indeed, Sylla, before I knew you, I have often
assisted great numbers at their own request,
and many of my own accord, but never stood
in need of the assistance of any myself. The
case is now altered; an alteration for which
others usually mourn, but I rejoice. I shall
always glory once to have had occasion for
your friendship, which I value above every
thing. And as a proof of my sincerity, accept
of my forces, my arms, my money, and whatever else you desire; use them as your own;
and after all, never think, as long as you live,
that I have made you a sufficient requital for
your favours. My gratitude shall still continue the same; nor shall you ever desire any
thing in vain that is in my power to do for you,
if I only know it. For in my opinion it is more
dishonourable for a prince to be outdone in
generosity, than vanquished in arms.

"As to the affairs of your commonwealth,
whose interests you are come hither to take
care of, hear what I have briefly to say. I
never made war upon the Roman people; nor
so much as intended it: I only defended my
own dominions against an armed force that
came to invade them; and now, since it is
your pleasure, I shall desist. Carry on the
war with Jugurtha just as you think proper. I
shall never pass the river Mulucha, the boundary betwixt me and Micipsa, nor suffer Jugurtha to come over to my side. If you have any

thing further to ask worthy of Boechus and your republic, it shall be granted you."

Sylla returned a brief and modest reply to all that related to himself; but as to the peace and negociation, he spoke at great length. He told the king, " that what he proposed, would be looked upon by the Romans as no kindness at all, since their arms had been successful. He must do something that should appear more for their benefit than for his own; an easy task, as he had Jugurtha in his power, whom if he delivered up to the Romans, they would then be greatly indebted to him, and admit him freely to their friendship and alliance, with a grant of that part of Numidia which he claimed."

The king at first refused this condition, urging " the ties of blood, those of affinity, and solemn leagues; alleging too, that he was apprehensive lest, by acting so treacherously, he should lose the affections of his subjects, who loved Jugurtha, and abhorred the Romans." But yielding at last to the importunity of Sylla, he promised to do whatever he desired of him. They then concerted measures for conducting the mock treaty of peace, which Jugurtha, now quite weary of the war, passionately desired. And having thus laid their plot, they departed.

Boechus the next day sent for Aspar, Jugurtha's minister, and acquainted him, that Dabar had told him from Sylla, the war might be concluded upon conditions: he should therefore go and discover the sentiments of his master. Aspar went with great joy to Jugurtha's camp; and having received ample instructions, returned with great expedition to Boechus in eight days, and told him, " that Jugurtha was disposed to comply with whatever was required of him, only he could not trust Marius, having often made treaties of peace before with the Roman generals, which were never ratified at Rome. If Boechus would consult not only Jugurtha's interest but his own, and have a sure peace, he should procure a meeting of all the parties, under pretence of conferring about the terms of it, and then deliver up Sylla to him. If he had in possession a person of such importance, a treaty of peace would then be concluded by order of the senate and people of Rome, who would never suffer one of his quality to continue in the hands of the enemy, into which

he had fallen, not through any ill conduct, but for performing his duty to the state."

The Moor, after having long reflected upon this proposal, at last consented to it; but whether with a fraudulent design or sincerity, is not clear. The inclinations of princes indeed, as they are generally violent, so they are unsteady, and often inconsistent. Time and place being now appointed for a treaty, Boechus one while talked with Sylla, another with Jugurtha's minister; caressed each, and made the same promises to both, who were thereupon equally pleased, and conceived equal hopes. But the night before the day fixed for the treaty, the Moor, calling his friends together, then suddenly changing sentiments, and dismissing them, is reported to have had many violent struggles with himself; insomuch that his frequent changes of countenance, and external agitations, clearly discovered, notwithstanding his silence, the various emotions of his mind. At last, however, he sent for Sylla, and, in concert with him, laid a plot for the Numidian.

When the day came, and Boechus was informed that Jugurtha was near at hand, he, with a few of his courtiers, and our quæstor, went out, under pretence of doing him honour, to meet him, as far as a little eminence, in full view of those who were placed in ambush. Thither, according to agreement, the Numidian prince came unarmed with many friends: and immediately, upon a signal given, those who lay in wait to seize him rushed upon him all at once. They who accompanied him were put to the sword. He himself was delivered in chains to Sylla, who conducted him to Marius.

About this time, our general Q. Cæpio and M. Manlius had an unfortunate battle with the Gauls, which spread consternation over all Italy. The Romans had always been strongly of opinion, and now no less so, that all other nations must yield to their bravery; but that, when they fought with the Gauls, they were only to aim at the preservation of their state, and not at glory. Now as soon as it was known at Rome that the war in Numidia was at an end, and that Jugurtha was coming in chains; Marius, though absent, was chosen consul, and Gaul decreed him for his province. On the first of January he triumphed with great glory. At this juncture, indeed, the hopes and security of Rome rested upon him.

THE END.

www.ingramcontent.com/pod-product-compliance
Lightning Source LLC
Chambersburg PA
CBHW021330080925
32270CB00048B/2258